INSTRUCTOR'S MANUAL AND TEST-ITEM FILE

# A History of Western Music

SEVENTH EDITION

**INSTRUCTOR'S MANUAL AND TEST-ITEM FILE**

*J. Peter Burkholder, Donald J. Grout, and Claude V. Palisca*

# A History of Western Music

SEVENTH EDITION

*Amy Edmonds*

CHIEF, MUSIC DIVISION
THE DISTRICT OF COLUMBIA PUBLIC LIBRARY
WASHINGTON, D.C.

*Roger Hickman*

PROFESSOR OF MUSICOLOGY
CALIFORNIA STATE UNIVERSITY
LONG BEACH, CALIFORNIA

W • W • NORTON & COMPANY • NEW YORK • LONDON

Printed in the United States of America

Composition and layout by Roberta Flechner Graphics
Manufacturing by Victor Graphics

**ISBN 0-393-92684-2 (pbk.)**

W. W. Norton & Company, Inc., 500 Fifth Avenue, New York, NY 10110
www.wwnorton.com
W. W. Norton & Company Ltd., Castle House, 75/76 Wells Street, London W1T 3QT

1 2 3 4 5 6 7 8 9 0

# CONTENTS

## Part V The Nineteenth Century



## Part VI The Twentieth Century and After

# ABBREVIATIONS

| | |
|---|---|
| *EMH* | Sarah Fuller, ed., *European Musical Heritage, 800–1750* (New York: McGraw-Hill, 1987). |
| *HAM* | Archibald T. Davison and Willi Apel, eds., *Historical Anthology of Music* (Cambridge: Harvard University Press, 1946–50). |
| *HAMW* | James R. Briscoe, ed., *Historical Anthology of Music by Women* (Bloomington: Indiana University Press, 1987). |
| *HWM* | J. Peter Burkholder, Donald Jay Grout, and Claude V. Palisca, *A History of Western Music,* 7th ed. (New York: W. W. Norton, 2006). |
| *LU* | *The Liber Usualis with Introduction and Rubrics in English* (New York: Desclée Co., 1961, and other editions). |
| *NAWM* | J. Peter Burkholder and Claude V. Palisca, eds., *Norton Anthology of Western Music,* 2 vols. 5th ed. (New York: W. W. Norton, 2006). |

# INTRODUCTION

*A History of Western Music* (*HWM*) by J. Peter Burkholder, Donald Jay Grout, and Claude V. Palisca is the leading college textbook for music history in the United States. The flexibility of conception and structure allows the text to be used in a variety of music history courses that encompass different class sizes, instructor approaches, and student levels and backgrounds. This manual is designed to help instructors adapt *HWM* to meet the needs of their students and of their individual approaches to teaching music history.

Among the many features of this manual are two new chapters: **Planning Your Syllabus**, a step-by-step guide to building a successful syllabus that includes several possible course outlines, and **Where Is It Now? HWM6 to HWM7**, a concordance correlating topics and page numbers in the sixth edition with the seventh.

For each chapter of *HWM*, this manual presents an outline of the chapter, a set of twenty objective questions, several essay questions, a list of important names and terms, and suggestions for supplementary activities. The outlines provide overviews of the material in each chapter of *HWM*, incorporating material from the composer boxes as well as from the commentaries in the *Norton Anthology of Western Music* (*NAWM*). Hence, the outlines can be used as a starting point for creating lectures and PowerPoint displays.

The objective questions are compatible with most computerized grading systems. Essay questions ask students to summarize or compare the main points of each chapter. Terms for identification are drawn from the textbook and include musical terms, place and event names, and names of influential people or groups. Many of these terms do not appear in the textbook's glossary. The terms are listed in the order in which they appear in the textbook, so that distributing these lists at the beginning of each unit can help students take more useful notes in lectures.

Among the suggestions for supplemental reading/listening/activities are opportunities for group study and performance. This section also includes recommendations for audio and video recordings of works discussed in the textbook but not included in *NAWM*. When there is no strong pedagogical purpose for suggesting a particular recording, we have opted for recent ones, which are more likely to be available in libraries or for purchase. Several of the operas discussed in the textbook are available on DVD.

Some of the supplemental suggestions can help instructors wishing to expand their discussions of American music, women in music, African-American music, and Latin American music beyond the material included in *HWM*. To this end, several chapters in this manual suggest recordings, anthologies, and readings that can further develop these topics.

Supplemental readings include citations for books of interest that were published after *HWM* went to press as well as source readings drawn from anthologies still in print. A few of these cite the full reading from which an excerpt in *HWM* was drawn; others demonstrate points instructors may want to develop in their lectures.

# PLANNING YOUR SYLLABUS

The syllabus is an essential document for all college-level courses. It serves as a guide for students, a contract between teacher and students, and a record of your course that may be reviewed by your department, college, or university. Typically, a syllabus contains the following information:

Course title and description
Faculty information
Course objectives
Required and recommended texts
Grading policies
Exams and written projects
Academic integrity
Student expectations
Course outline

Since most instructors have extensive experience in creating a syllabus, this guide will begin with the course outline, the section that will need the most attention. If this is your first syllabus, you may want to review the other sections first and return to the outline at a later time.

## COURSE OUTLINE

### OVERVIEW

The seventh edition of *A History of Western Music* features shorter chapters for ease of reading and greater flexibility in structuring courses. These chapters are divided into six Parts:

Part I: The Ancient and Medieval Worlds (Chapters 1–6)
Part II: The Renaissance (Chapters 7–12)
Part III: The Seventeenth Century (Chapters 13–17)
Part IV: The Eighteenth Century (Chapters 18–22)
Part V: The Nineteenth Century (Chapters 23–29)
Part VI: The Twentieth Century and After (Chapters 30–35)

The distribution of this material into semester courses is governed by several considerations. For two-semester courses, the division should coincide with the volumes of the *Norton Anthology of Western Music* (*NAWM*), which break between the Baroque and Classic eras. Hence, Semester I would include Chapters 1–19, and Semester II would cover Chapters 20–35. A viable alternative would be to divide the material after Chapter 22, which would allow more time for the music of the nineteenth and twentieth centuries.

Three-semester courses could follow the text divisions, with each semester treating two Parts. The principal question would be the placement of Beethoven, the subject of Chapter 23. Since Beethoven appears as the opening chapter in Part V, some instructors may place him in the third semester. Others may consider him at the end of the second semester, along with Haydn and Mozart.

The following division is recommended for a four-semester course: Semester 1 (Parts I and II), Semester 2 (Parts III and IV), Semester 3 (Part IV, beginning with Beethoven in Chapter 23), and Semester 4 (Part VI).

### STANDARD OUTLINE

The following standard outline is designed for a thirty-week course. The division of material is based on the general formula of five weeks for each era. Instructors teaching three- or four-semester courses should expand areas that need more time. Some alternatives to this standard outline will be suggested in the next section. In the outline below, full titles of the works from *NAWM* are added so that you can more readily see what material is covered in these chapters. For the student syllabus, you may want to identify these works by their *NAWM* numbers only.

**Week 1**

Topics: The Earliest Music, Music in Greece and Rome, Music in the Early Christian Church
Reading: Chapter 1 (2–23) and Chapter 2 (24–49)
Listening: NAWM 1–2
*Epitaph of Seikilos,* song (epigram)
Euripides: *Orestes,* Greek tragedy, excerpt: Stasimon chorus

**Week 2**

Topics: Roman Liturgy and Chant
Reading: Chapter 3 (50–70)
Listening: NAWM 3–7
Mass for Christmas Day, Gregorian chant Mass
Chants from Vespers for Christmas Day, Gregorian chant Office
Ascribed to Wipo of Burgundy: *Victimae paschali laudes,* sequence
Tropes on *Puer natus: Quem queritis in presepe* and Melisma
Hildegard of Bingen: *Ordo virtutum,* sacred music drama: Chorus, *In principio omnes*

**Week 3**

Topics: Secular Music, Early Polyphony
Reading: Chapter 4 (71–86) and Chapter 5 (87–94)
Listening: NAWM 8–16
Bernart de Ventadorn: *Can vei la lauzeta mover,* canso (troubadour song)
Comtessa de Dia: *A chantar,* canso (troubadour song)
Adam de la Halle: *Jeu de Robin et de Marion*: Rondeau, *Robins m'aime*
Walther von der Vogelweide: *Palästinalied* (*Nu alrest lebe ich mir werde*), Minnelied
Cantiga 159: *Non sofre Santa María,* from *Cantigas de Santa María*
*La quarte estampie royal,* from *Le manuscrit du roi*
Organa from *Musica enchiriadis*
*Alleluia Justus ut palma,* free organum, from *Ad organum faciendum*
*Jubilemus, exultemus,* versus in Aquitanian polyphony

**Week 4**

Topics: Notre Dame Polyphony, Motets, English Polyphony, Ars Nova
Reading: Chapter 5 (94–115) and Chapter 6 (116–126)
Listening: NAWM 17–24
Léonin: *Viderunt omnes,* organum duplum
Clausulae on *Dominus* from *Viderunt omnes*
Pérotin: *Viderunt omnes,* organum quadruplum
*Ave virgo virginum,* conductus
Motets on tenor *Dominus*
Adam de la Halle: *De ma dame vient/Dieus, comment porroie/Omnes,* motet
*Sumer is icumen in,* rota
Philippe de Vitry: *In arboris/Tuba sacre fidei/Virgo sum,* motet

**Week 5**

Topics: Machaut, Trecento, **Midterm Exam**
Reading: Chapter 6 (126–145)
Listening: NAWM 25–30
Guillaume de Machaut: *La Messe de Nostre Dame,* mass: Kyrie
Guillaume de Machaut: *Rose, liz, printemps, verdure,* rondeau
Johannes Ciconia: *Sus une fontayne,* virelai
Jacopo da Bologna: *Fenice fù,* madrigal
Gherardello da Firenze: *Tosto che l'alba,* caccia
Francesco Landini: *Non avrà ma' pietà,* ballata

**Week 6**

Topics: Renaissance Introduction, English and Burgundian Music, Ockeghem
Reading: Chapter 7 (146–166), Chapter 8 (167–189), and Chapter 9 (190–198)
Listening: NAWM 31–37
*Alleluia, A newë work,* carol
John Dunstable: *Quam pulchra es,* motet or cantilena
Binchois (Gilles de Bin): *De plus en plus,* rondeau
Guillaume Du Fay: *Resvellies vous,* ballade
Guillaume Du Fay: *Conditor alme siderum,* hymn in fauxbourdon style
Guillaume Du Fay: *Se la face ay pale,* ballade, and *Missa Se la face ay pale*, cantus-firmus mass: Gloria
Jean de Ockeghem: *Missa De plus en plus,* mass: Agnus Dei

**Week 7**

Topics: Generation of Josquin des Prez, The Reformation, Palestrina
Reading: Chapter 9 (198–209) and Chapter 10 (210–232)
Listening: NAWM 38–45
Henricus Isaac: *Innsbruck, ich muss dich lassen,* Lied
Josquin des Prez: *Ave Maria . . . virgo serena,* motet
Josquin des Prez: *Missa Pange lingua,* mass: Kyrie and part of Credo
Josquin des Prez: *Mille regretz,* chanson

Martin Luther: *Nun komm, der Heiden Heiland* and *Ein' feste Burg,* chorales
Loys Bourgeois: Psalm 134, *Or sus, serviteurs du Seigneur,* metrical psalm
William Byrd: *Sing joyfully unto God,* full anthem
Giovanni Pierluigi da Palestrina: *Pope Marcellus Mass:* Credo and Agnus Dei I

**Week 8**

Topics: Spain, Germany, Italian Madrigal
Reading: Chapter 10 (233–239) and Chapter 11 (240–255)
Listening: NAWM 46–53
Tomás Luis de Victoria: *O magnum mysterium,* motet, and *Missa O magnum mysterium,* mass: Kyrie
Orlando di Lasso: *Tristis est anima mea,* motet
Juan del Encina: *Oy comamos y bebamos,* villancico
Marco Cara: *Io non compro più speranza,* frottola
Jacques Arcadelt: *Il bianco e dolce cigno,* madrigal
Cipriano de Rore: *Da le belle contrade d'oriente,* madrigal
Luca Marenzio: *Solo e pensoso,* madrigal
Carlo Gesualdo: *"Io parto" e non più dissi,* madrigal

**Week 9**

Topics: Secular Music in France and England, Instrumental Music, Venice
Reading: Chapter 11 (255–263) and Chapter 12 (264–285)
Listening: NAWM 54–62
Claudin de Sermisy: *Tant que vivray,* chanson
Claude le Jeune: *Revecy venir du printans,* chanson
Thomas Morley: *My bonny lass she smileth,* ballett
Thomas Weelkes: *As Vesta was,* madrigal
John Dowland: *Flow, my tears,* air or lute song
Pierre Attaingnant (publisher): Basse danse and Branle gay, from *Danseries a 4 parties, second livre*
Luis de Narváez: From *Los seys libros del Delphín,* works for vihuela
William Byrd: *Pavana Lachrymae,* pavane variations
Giovanni Gabrieli: *Canzon septimi toni a 8,* from *Sacrae symphoniae,* ensemble canzona

**Week 10**

Topics: **Midterm Exam**, Baroque Introduction, Early Opera
Reading: Chapter 13 (286–306) and Chapter 14 (307–318)
Listening: NAWM 63–66
Claudio Monteverdi: *Cruda Amarilli,* madrigal
Giulio Caccini: *Vedrò 'l mio sol,* continuo madrigal
Jacopo Peri: *Le musiche sopra l'Euridice,* opera, excerpt
Claudio Monteverdi: *L'Orfeo,* opera, excerpt from Act II

**Week 11**

Topics: Monteverdi, Spread of Italian Opera, Vocal Chamber Music, Sacred Music
Reading: Chapter 14 (318–327) and Chapter 15 (328–343)
Listening: NAWM 67–73
Claudio Monteverdi: *L'incoronazione di Poppea,* opera, Act I, scene 3
Antonio Cesti: *Orontea,* opera, excerpt from Act II
Barbara Strozzi: *Lagrime mie,* cantata
Alessandro Grandi: *O quam tu pulchra es,* solo motet
Giacomo Carissimi: *Historia di Jephte,* oratorio, excerpt
Heinrich Schütz: *O lieber Herre Gott,* SWV 287, from *Kleine geistliche Konzerte I,* sacred concerto
Heinrich Schütz: *Saul, was verfolgst du mich,* SWV 415, from *Symphoniae sacrae III,* sacred concerto

**Week 12**

Topics: Instrumental Music, Music of France, England, Spain, and America
Reading: Chapter 15 (344–352) and Chapter 16 (353–383)
Listening: NAWM 74–81
Girolamo Frescobaldi: Toccata No. 3
Girolamo Frescobaldi: Ricercare after the Credo, from Mass for the Madonna, in *Fiori musicali*
Biagio Marini: *Sonata IV per il violino per sonar con due corde,* from Op. 8
Jean-Baptiste Lully: *Armide,* tragédie lyrique, excerpts
Elisabeth-Claude Jacquet de la Guerre: Suite in A Minor, from *Pièces de clavecin,* Book I
Henry Purcell: *Dido and Aeneas,* opera, conclusion
Tomás de Torrejón y Velasco, *La púrpura de la rosa,* opera, excerpt
Juan de Araujo: *Los coflades de la estleya,* villancico

**Week 13**

Topics: Late Seventeenth-Century Italy and Germany, Vivaldi

Reading: Chapter 17 (384–413) and Chapter 18 (414–429)

Listening: NAWM 82–85

Alessandro Scarlatti: *Clori vezzosa, e bella,* conclusion, cantata

Arcangelo Corelli: Trio Sonata, Op. 3, No. 2

Dieterich Buxtehude: Praeludium in E Major, BuxWV 141

Antonio Vivaldi: Concerto for Violin and Orchestra in A Minor, Op. 3, No. 6, from *L'estro armonico*

**Week 14**

Topics: Music in France, Bach Instrumental Music

Reading: Chapter 18 (429–437) and Chapter 19 (438–450)

Listening: NAWM 86–89

François Couperin: *Vingt-cinquième ordre,* excerpt, keyboard suite

Jean-Philippe Rameau: *Hippolyte et Aricie,* opera, conclusion of Act IV

Johann Sebastian Bach: Prelude and Fugue in A Minor, BWV 543

Johann Sebastian Bach: Chorale Prelude on *Durch Adams Fall,* BWV 637

**Week 15**

Topics: Bach Sacred Music, Handel

Reading: Chapter 19 (450–471)

Listening: NAWM 90–92

Johann Sebastian Bach: *Nun komm, der Heiden Heiland,* BWV 62, cantata

George Frideric Handel: *Giulio Cesare,* opera, excerpt: Act II, scenes 1–2

George Frideric Handel: *Saul,* oratorio, Act II, scene 10

**Week 16**

Topics: Opera, Song, and Church Music in the Early Classic Era

Reading: Chapter 20 (472–505)

Listening: NAWM 93–97

Giovanni Battista Pergolesi: *La serva padrona,* intermezzo, excerpt

Johann Adolf Hasse: *Cleofide,* opera, excerpt: Act II, scene 9, *Digli ch'io son fedele*

John Gay: *The Beggar's Opera,* ballad opera, excerpt from scene 13

Christoph Willibald Gluck: *Orfeo ed Euridice,* opera, excerpt from Act II, scene 1

William Billings: *Creation,* fuging tune

**Week 17**

Topics: Instrumental Music in the Early Classic Era, Haydn

Reading: Chapter 21 (506–524) and Chapter 22 (525–536)

Listening: NAWM 98–103

Domenico Scarlatti: Sonata in D Major, K. 119

Carl Philipp Emanuel Bach: Sonata in A Major, H. 186, Wq. 55/4, second movement

Giovanni Battista Sammartini: Symphony in F Major, No. 32, first movement

Johann Stamitz: Sinfonia No. 8 in E-flat Major

Johann Christian Bach: Concerto for Harpsichord or Piano and Strings in E-flat Major, Op. 7, No. 5, first movement

Franz Joseph Haydn: String Quartet in E-flat Major, Op. 33, No. 2 (*The Joke*), fourth movement

**Week 18**

Topics: Haydn Symphonies and String Quartets, Mozart Instrumental Works

Reading: Chapter 22 (536–560)

Listening: NAWM 104–106

Franz Joseph Haydn: Symphony No. 92 in G Major (*Oxford*)

Wolfgang Amadeus Mozart: Piano Sonata in F Major, K. 332, first movement

Wolfgang Amadeus Mozart: Piano Concerto in A Major, K. 488, first movement

**Week 19**

Topics: Mozart Operas, Revolution, Beethoven Early and Middle Periods

Reading: Chapter 22 (560–565) and Chapter 23 (566–586)

Listening: NAWM 107–109

Wolfgang Amadeus Mozart: *Don Giovanni,* opera, excerpt: Act I, scenes 1–2

Ludwig van Beethoven: Piano Sonata in C Minor, Op. 13 (*Pathétique*), third movement

Ludwig van Beethoven: Symphony No. 3 in E-flat Major, Op. 55 (*Eroica*), first movement

**Week 20**

Beethoven Late Period, **Midterm Exam**, Schubert Lieder

Reading: Chapter 23 (586–594) and Chapter 24 (595–611)

Listening: NAWM 110–112

Ludwig van Beethoven: String Quartet in C-sharp Minor, Op. 131, first and second movements

Franz Schubert: *Gretchen am Spinnrade,* Lied

Franz Schubert: *Winterreise,* song cycle, excerpt: *Der Lindenbaum*

**Week 21**

Topics: Romantic Song and Piano Music
Reading: Chapter 24 (611–630)
Listening: NAWM 113–120
Robert Schumann: *Dichterliebe,* song cycle, excerpt: *Im wunderschönen Monat Mai*
Henry R. Bishop: *Home! Sweet Home!,* theatrical song and drawing-room ballad
Stephen Foster: *Jeanie with the Light Brown Hair,* parlor song
Robert Schumann: *Fantasiestücke,* Op. 12, excerpts
Fryderyk Chopin: Mazurka in B-flat Major, Op. 7, No. 1
Fryderyk Chopin: Nocturne in D-flat Major, Op. 27, No. 2
Franz Liszt: *Trois études de concert,* No. 3: *Un sospiro*
Louis Moreau Gottschalk: *Souvenir de Porto Rico (Marche des Gibaros)*

**Week 22**

Topics: Romantic Orchestral, Chamber, and Choral Music
Reading: Chapter 25 (631–658)
Listening: NAWM 121–124
Hector Berlioz: *Symphonie fantastique,* fifth movement: "Dream of a Witches' Sabbath"
Felix Mendelssohn: Concerto for Violin and Orchestra in E Minor, Op. 64, third movement: Allegretto non troppo—Allegro molto vivace
Clara Schumann: Piano Trio in G Minor, Op. 17, third movement: Andante
Felix Mendelssohn: *Elijah,* oratorio, excerpt: No. 42, Chorus: *And then shall your light break forth*

**Week 23**

Topics: Romantic Opera, Verdi, Wagner
Reading: Chapter 26 (659–678) and Chapter 27 (679–698)
Listening: NAWM 125–128
Gioachino Rossini: *Il barbiere di Siviglia,* Act II, scene 5: Cavatina, *Una voce poco fa*
Carl Maria von Weber: *Der Freischütz,* Act II, finale: Wolf's Glen scene
Giuseppe Verdi: *La traviata,* Act III, scena and duet
Richard Wagner: *Tristan und Isolde,* excerpt from Act I, scene 5

**Week 24**

Topics: Opera in France, Russia, and Other Nations, Brahms, Wagnerians
Reading: Chapter 27 (698–713) and Chapter 28 (714–736)
Listening: NAWM 129–133
Georges Bizet: *Carmen,* excerpt: Act I, No. 10, seguidilla and duet
Modest Musorgsky: *Boris Godunov,* Coronation scene
Arthur Sullivan: *The Pirates of Penzance,* operetta, excerpt: *When the foeman bares his steel*
Johannes Brahms: Symphony No. 4 in E Minor, finale
Richard Strauss: *Don Quixote,* excerpts: theme and variations 1 and 2

**Week 25**

Topics: Diverging Traditions, **Midterm Exam**
Reading: Chapter 29 (737–755)
Listening: NAWM 134–135
Amy Marcy Beach: Quintet for Piano and Strings in F-sharp Minor, Op. 67, third movement
John Philip Sousa: *The Stars and Stripes Forever,* march

**Week 26**

Topics: Vernacular Traditions, Modern Music, The Avant-Garde
Reading: Chapter 30 (758–800)
Listening: NAWM 136–140
Scott Joplin: *Maple Leaf Rag,* piano rag
Gustav Mahler: *Kindertotenlieder,* orchestral song cycle: No. 1, *Nun will die Sonn' so hell aufgeh'n*
Claude Debussy: *Nuages,* from *Trois Nocturnes*
Sergei Rachmaninov: Prelude in G Minor, Op. 23, No. 5
Alexander Scriabin: *Vers la flamme,* poem for piano

**Week 27**

Topics: Schoenberg, Berg, Webern, Stravinsky, Bartók, Ives
Reading: Chapter 31 (801–843)
Listening: NAWM 141–148
Arnold Schoenberg: *Pierrot lunaire,* Op. 21, excerpts
Arnold Schoenberg: Piano Suite, Op. 25, excerpts
Alban Berg: *Wozzeck,* opera, excerpt: Act III, scene 3
Anton Webern: Symphony, Op. 21, first movement
Igor Stravinsky: *The Rite of Spring,* excerpts
Igor Stravinsky: *Symphony of Psalms,* first movement
Béla Bartók: *Music for Strings, Percussion and Celesta,* third movement
Charles Ives: *General William Booth Enters into Heaven,* song

**Week 28**

- Topics: Between the Wars: Jazz, Popular Music, and the Classical Tradition
- Reading: Chapter 32 (844–864) and Chapter 33 (865–892)
- Listening: NAWM 149–158
  - Bessie Smith: *Back Water Blues,* song
  - King Oliver: *West End Blues*
  - George Gershwin: *I Got Rhythm,* from *Girl Crazy*
  - Duke Ellington: *Cotton Tail*
  - Paul Hindemith: *Un cygne,* from *Six Chansons,* for a cappella chorus
  - Dmitri Shostakovich: Symphony No. 5, Op. 47, second movement
  - Silvestre Revueltas: *Sensemayá,* for orchestra
  - Ruth Crawford Seeger: String Quartet 1931, fourth movement
  - Aaron Copland: *Appalachian Spring,* excerpt
  - William Grant Still: *Afro-American Symphony,* first movement

**Week 29**

- Topics: Postwar Popular Music, Serialism
- Reading: Chapter 34 (893–931)
- Listening: NAWM 159–165
  - Dizzy Gillespie: *Anthropology*
  - Olivier Messiaen: *Quartet for the End of Time,* first movement
  - Benjamin Britten: *Peter Grimes,* opera, excerpt: end of Act III
  - Samuel Barber: *Hermit Songs,* No. 8: *The Monk and His Cat*
  - George Crumb: *Black Angels, Thirteen Images from the Dark Land,* excerpts
  - Milton Babbitt: *Philomel,* section I
  - Krzysztof Penderecki: *Threnody for the Victims of Hiroshima*

**Week 30**

- Topics: The Avant-Garde, Music for Band, End of the Millennium
- Reading: Chapter 34 (931–940) and Chapter 35 (941–965)
- Listening: NAWM 166–172
  - John Cage: *Music of Changes I,* for piano
  - Karel Husa: *Music for Prague 1968*, for concert band, first movement: Introduction and fanfare: Adagio
  - John Adams: *Phrygian Gates*
  - Ellen Taaffe Zwilich: Symphony No. 1, first movement
  - Arvo Pärt: Magnificat antiphons
  - Sofia Gubaidulina: *Rejoice!* Sonata for Violin and Violoncello, fifth movement
  - Bright Sheng: *Seven Tunes Heard in China,* for solo cello, No. 1: *Seasons*

## ALTERNATIVE ORGANIZATIONS

The seventh edition of *A History of Western Music* maintains a more consistent chronological structure than earlier versions. Within the sub-periods, the material is generally organized by composer, region, or genre, depending on the characteristics of a given era. The instructor may choose to follow the order of the text or to define topics that involve readings from several chapters. The seventh edition's shorter chapters and sub-headings are designed to facilitate a variety of approaches to presenting the material. The following outline presents some alternate ways of organizing the content of the text and the corresponding page numbers in the seventh edition.

**Renaissance Era: organized by genre**

- The Mass
  - Du Fay 184–189
  - Ockeghem 194–198
  - Josquin des Prez 206–207
  - Palestrina, Victoria 229–235
- The Motet
  - Du Fay 183–184
  - Josquin des Prez 205–206
  - Gombert 224–226
  - Lasso 235–238
- Secular Vocal Music
  - Burgundian chanson 178–183
  - Ockeghem, Busnoys 192–194
  - Isaac Lieder 201–202
  - Josquin des Prez 207
  - Sixteenth century 240–263
    - Villancico, Frotolla 242–244
    - Italian madrigal 244–255
    - Chanson 255–258
    - English madrigal 259–261
    - English lute air 261–262

**Baroque Era: organized by genre**

- Opera
  - Invention of opera 307–327
  - Lully 359–365
  - England 373–376
  - Spain 379–380
  - Late seventeenth-century Italy 386
  - Germany 403
  - Rameau 435–436
  - Handel 460–464
- Secular Vocal Music
  - Early seventeenth century 328–332
  - French Baroque 365–366
  - Spain 380–381
  - Late seventeenth-century Italy 387–389
  - Germany 403
- Sacred Vocal Music
  - Early seventeenth century 332–342

| | |
|---|---|
| French Baroque | 366 |
| Spain | 381 |
| Late seventeenth-century Italy | 390–391 |
| Germany | 404–405 |
| J. S. Bach | 450–456 |
| Handel oratorio | 464–468 |
| Instrumental Music | |
| Early seventeenth century | 344–351 |
| French Baroque | 366–372 |
| England | 377–378 |
| Spain | 382 |
| Late seventeenth-century Italy | 391–400 |
| German organ | 405–410 |
| Other German | 410–412 |
| Vivaldi | 423–429 |
| Couperin | 430–431 |
| Bach organ | 445–447 |
| Bach harpsichord | 447–449 |
| Bach orchestral | 449–450 |
| Handel | 469 |
| **Romantic Era: organized by genre** | |
| Song | |
| Schubert, Robert & Clara Schumann | 605–613 |
| British and American | 613–615 |
| Brahms | 723–724 |
| Wolf | 732–733 |
| Faure | 739–741 |
| Piano Music | |
| Early nineteenth century | 615–629 |
| Brahms | 723 |
| Liszt | 728–729 |
| Franck | 739 |
| Orchestra Music | |
| Early nineteenth century | 632–645 |
| Brahms | 718–722 |
| Liszt | 728 |
| Bruckner | 730–731 |
| Richard Strauss | 733–735 |
| Tchaikovsky | 741–742 |
| Other composers | 742–747 |
| Mahler | 772–776 |
| Chamber Music | |
| Early nineteenth century | 645–649 |
| Brahms | 722–723 |
| Franck | 739 |
| Choral Music | |
| Early nineteenth century | 650–657 |
| Brahms | 725 |
| Liszt | 729 |
| Bruckner | 731–732 |
| Italian Opera | |
| Early nineteenth century | 660–668 |
| Verdi | 683–688 |
| Verismo, Puccini | 688–689 |
| French Opera | |
| Early nineteenth century | 668–672 |
| Later nineteenth century | 698–701 |
| German Opera | |
| Weber | 673–675 |
| Wagner | 690–698 |
| Opera in Other Countries | |
| United States | 675–678 |
| Russia | 701–709 |
| Other regions | 709–712 |
| Ballet | |
| Early nineteenth century | 672 |
| **Twentieth Century and Beyond: organized by tradition** | |
| Vernacular Tradition | |
| Early twentieth century | 765–770 |
| Between the wars | 844–864 |
| Postwar | 896–908 |
| End of the millennium | 950–952 |
| Classical Tradition | |
| Early twentieth century | 770–795 |
| Modernism | 801–843 |
| Between the wars | 864–892 |
| Postwar | 908–931, 936–940 |
| End of the millennium | 952–965 |
| Avant-Garde | |
| Early twentieth century | 795–799 |
| Postwar | 931–936 |

## OTHER SECTIONS OF THE SYLLABUS

The following information may help you if you are preparing a syllabus for the first time. If you would like to view a model, you are invited to look at the syllabus for Music M401: History and Literature of Music I: Antiquity to 1750 at the Indiana University School of Music taught by J. Peter Burkholder: www.music.indiana.edu/som/courses/m401. You will want to note the date of his posted syllabus, since it may still contain references to the sixth edition.

### COURSE TITLE AND DESCRIPTION

The title and description of the course should be based on those from your school bulletin or course catalog. There may also be a good description in departmental files under "standard course syllabus." Descriptions can vary in length, but a brief note might read as follows:

> Music 433 surveys the history of Western music from antiquity to 1750. This course is intended for music majors who have taken two semesters of music theory and is part of a two-semester sequence that is followed by Music 467.

## FACULTY INFORMATION

In a quick and easy-to-read format, you should include your office number, phone number, e-mail address, and contact hours. If you have teaching assistants, similar information should be added for them as well.

## COURSE OBJECTIVES

Course objectives are usually listed as a series of goals telling the students what they will learn in the class. The following are some examples:

- To understand the development of musical styles, genres, and compositional procedures, and their relevance to other eras and repertories
- To develop score reading and analytical skills
- To become familiar with the masterworks of Western music history
- To recognize performance issues and to research historical performance practices
- To improve writing skills about music and musical styles

## REQUIRED AND RECOMMENDED TEXTS

Under this heading you should include the texts that students need to purchase as well as suggested resources that might assist them in their studies. Here is a sampling:

Required Course Materials

- J. Peter Burkholder, Donald Jay Grout, and Claude V. Palisca, *A History of Western Music,* 7th ed. (New York: W. W. Norton, 2006)
- *Norton Anthology of Western Music,* vol. 1: Ancient to Baroque, 5th ed., J. Peter Burkholder and Claude V. Palisca, eds. (New York: W. W. Norton, 2006).
- *Norton Recorded Anthology of Western Music,* vol. 1: Ancient to Baroque, 5th ed., J. Peter Burkholder and Claude V. Palisca, eds.

Suggested Course Materials

- Piero Weiss and Richard Taruskin, eds., *Music in the Western World: A History in Documents* (New York: Schirmer, 1984)
- J. Peter Burkholder and Jennifer L. King, *Study and Listening Guide for A History of Western Music,* 7th ed., and *Norton Anthology of Western Music,* 5th ed. (New York: W. W. Norton, 2006)
- Kate L. Turabian, *A Manual for Writers,* 6th ed. (Chicago: U. of Chicago, 1996) or any other writing manual of your choice

## GRADING POLICIES

In this section, you will need to tell the students how they will be graded, and the weight of each required activity in determining their final grade. You should include your make-up policy. In most institutions you cannot simply say that there are no make-ups for missed work or exams. You should consult the wording of the standard policy at your college or university.

## EXAMS AND WRITTEN PROJECTS

Students should be informed as to the nature of the exams and written projects. You should include the number of quizzes or exams, their nature (essay, multiple choice), and when they occur. Written projects should be part of your course, and details about topics, writing style, and research methods can be included here.

## ACADEMIC INTEGRITY

In a brief statement, students should be warned about cheating and plagiarism. You should refer them to the official code of your college or university, remind them that there are severe penalties, and tell them that they are responsible for knowing these regulations. Ignorance of the policy is not excusable.

## STUDENT EXPECTATIONS

In this section, inform the students of what you expect from them, both in class and outside. If you have an attendance or class participation requirement, this is a good place to describe it. Work outside of class should include reading, listening, and writing. You may want to include Internet sources that they can use for help, including the Naxos music library and the Norton companion Web site (www.wwnorton.com/musichistory).

# WHERE IS IT NOW? HWM6 TO HWM7

| HWM6 Topics and Pages | HWM7 Chapter and Pages | |
|---|---|---|
| Chapter 1 | | |
| Greek and Roman Music, 1–17 | Chapter 1 | 4–23 |
| Early Christian Church, 17–29 | Chapter 2 | 24–34 |
| Chapter 2 | | |
| Roman Chant and Liturgy, 31–46 | Chapter 3 | 50–65 |
| Plainchant Notation, 36–38 | Chapter 2 | 34–41 |
| Later Developments of Chant, 46–50 | Chapter 3 | 65–70 |
| Medieval Music Theory, 50–57 | Chapter 2 | 41–49 |
| Secular Song and Dance, 57–66 | Chapter 4 | 71–86 |
| Chapter 3 | | |
| Development of Polyphony, 70–95 | Chapter 5 | 87–111 |
| Hocket, 89 | Chapter 6 | 125 |
| Chapter 4 | | |
| Ars Nova, 96–105 | Chapter 6 | 116–132 |
| Trecento, 106–111 | Chapter 6 | 135–141 |
| Late Fourteenth-Century France, 111–113 | Chapter 6 | 132–135 |
| Musica Ficta, 113–118 | Chapter 6 | 142–144 |
| Instruments, 118–120 | Chapter 6 | 141–142 |
| Chapter 5 | | |
| English Music, 123–129 | Chapter 8 | 167–175 |
| Burgundian Music, 129–132 | Chapter 8 | 175–178 |
| Du Fay, 132–141 | Chapter 8 | 180–189 |
| Binchois, 135 | Chapter 8 | 178–180 |

| HWM6 Topics and Pages | HWM7 Chapter and Pages | |
|---|---|---|
| **Chapter 6** | | |
| Age of Renaissance, 144–154 | Chapter 7 | 148–166 |
| Ockeghem, 154–161 | Chapter 9 | 192–198 |
| Next Generation, 161–163 | Chapter 9 | 198–202 |
| Busnoys, 165 | Chapter 9 | 192–193 |
| Josquin des Prez, 164–169 | Chapter 9 | 202–209 |
| Isaac, 170–172 | Chapter 9 | 201 |
| **Chapter 7** | | |
| Generation of 1520–1550, 177–183 | Chapter 10 | 224–226 |
| Italian Madrigal, 183–194 | Chapter 11 | 240–255 |
| Secular Music Outside of Italy, 194–205 | Chapter 11 | 255–263 |
| Spain, 198–199 | Chapter 11 | 242–243 |
| Instrumental Music, 205–219 | Chapter 12 | 264–285 |
| **Chapter 8** | | |
| Reformation, 224–233 | Chapter 10 | 210–224 |
| Counter-Reformation, 234–246 | Chapter 10 | 226–238 |
| William Byrd, 246–247 | Chapter 10 | 222–224 |
| **Chapter 9** | | |
| Age of Baroque, 251–260 | Chapter 13 | 288–306 |
| Early Opera, 260–273 | Chapter 14 | 307–318 |
| Spread of Italian Opera, 273–276 | Chapter 14 | 319–321 |
| Late Monteverdi, 277 | Chapter 14 | 318–319 |
| Venice, 276–278 | Chapter 14 | 321–327 |
| Vocal Chamber Music, 278–285 | Chapter 15 | 329–332 |
| Venetian Polychoral Music, 285–287 | Chapter 12 | 282–284 |
| Catholic and Lutheran Sacred Music, 287–294 | Chapter 15 | 332–342 |
| Instrumental Music, 294–302 | Chapter 15 | 344–352 |
| French Lute and Keyboard Music, 302–304 | Chapter 16 | 366–372 |
| **Chapter 10** | | |
| Later Italian Opera, 309–314 | Chapter 17 | 384–386 |
| Later French Opera, 315–320 | Chapter 16 | 353–365 |
| England Music for Theater, 320–323 | Chapter 16 | 372–375 |
| German Opera, 323–324 | Chapter 18 | 403 |
| Later Italian Cantata, 324–326 | Chapter 17 | 387–389 |
| Song in Other Countries, 326–327 | Chapter 16 | 365–366, 403 |
| Later Italian Sacred, 327–330 | Chapter 17 | 390–391 |
| German Sacred Music, 330–332, 334–341 | Chapter 17 | 404–405 |
| French Sacred Music, 332–333 | Chapter 16 | 366 |
| English Sacred Music, 333–334 | Chapter 16 | 366–372 |
| **Chapter 11** | | |
| Baroque Organ, 345–351 | Chapter 17 | 405–410 |
| Harpsichord Music, 351–352 | Chapter 17 | 410 |
| François Couperin, 352–354 | Chapter 18 | 430–431 |
| Keyboard Sonata, 354–356 | Chapter 17 | 412 |
| Ensemble Music in Italy, 356–364 | Chapter 17 | 391–397 |
| Orchestra Suite, 364–366 | Chapter 17 | 410–411 |
| Concerto, 366–369 | Chapter 17 | 397–400 |

| HWM6 Topics and Pages | HWM7 Chapter and Pages | |
|---|---|---|
| Chapter 12 | | |
| Vivaldi, 373–380 | Chapter 18 | 423–429 |
| Rameau, 381–386 | Chapter 18 | 432–437 |
| J. S. Bach, 386–405 | Chapter 19 | 441–457 |
| Handel, 405–416 | Chapter 19 | 457–470 |
| Chapter 13 | | |
| Enlightenment, Classic Era, 420–432 | Chapter 20 | 472–485 |
| Early Italian Opera, 432–440 | Chapter 20 | 485–493 |
| Later Comic Opera, 440–442 | Chapter 20 | 489–490 |
| Other Languages, Opera Reform, 442–447 | Chapter 20 | 494–500 |
| Song and Church Music, 447–450 | Chapter 20 | 500–505 |
| Early Classic Instrumental Music, 450–460 | Chapter 21 | 506–524 |
| Chapter 14 | | |
| Haydn, 465–488 | Chapter 22 | 526–546 |
| Mozart, 488–509 | Chapter 22 | 546–565 |
| Chapter 15 | | |
| Beethoven, 513–539 | Chapter 23 | 571–594 |
| Chapter 16 | | |
| Romanticism, 542–545 | Chapter 24 | 595–605 |
| Orchestra Music, 545–554 | Chapter 25 | 631–645 |
| Liszt Orchestra Music, 555–557 | Chapter 28 | 728–730 |
| Brahms Orchestra Music, 558–561 | Chapter 28 | 718–722 |
| Bruckner Orchestra Music, 561–563 | Chapter 28 | 730–732 |
| Tchaikovsky Orchestra Music, 563–565 | Chapter 29 | 741–742 |
| Dvořák Orchestra Music, 565 | Chapter 29 | 744 |
| Chapter 17 | | |
| Music for Piano, 571–586 | Chapter 24 | 615–629 |
| Gottschalk, 572 | Chapter 24 | 629 |
| Brahms Piano Music, 586 | Chapter 28 | 723 |
| Fanny Hensel and Clara Schumann, 587 | Chapter 24 | 618–619 |
| Chamber Music, 587–590 | Chapter 25 | 645–649 |
| Brahms Chamber Music, 590–593 | Chapter 28 | 722–723 |
| Franck, 593 | Chapter 29 | 739 |
| The Lied, 593–597 | Chapter 24 | 605–613 |
| Brahms Lieder, 597–598 | Chapter 28 | 723–724 |
| Choral Music, 598–601 | Chapter 25 | 650–657 |
| Liszt Choral Music, 601 | Chapter 28 | 729 |
| Bruckner Choral Music, 601–602 | Chapter 28 | 731–732 |
| Brahms Choral Music, 602 | Chapter 28 | 725 |
| Chapter 18 | | |
| Early Italian Opera, 603–608 | Chapter 26 | 660–668 |
| Early French Opera, 608–611 | Chapter 26 | 668–672 |
| Later French Opera, 612–613 | Chapter 27 | 698–701 |
| Verdi, 614–617 | Chapter 27 | 683–688 |
| Early German Opera, 618–621 | Chapter 26 | 673–675 |
| Wagner, 621–628 | Chapter 27 | 690–698 |

| HWM6 Topics and Pages | HWM7 Chapter and Pages | |
|---|---|---|
| Chapter 19 | | |
| Wolf, 631–632 | Chapter 28 | 732–733 |
| Mahler, 632–638 | Chapter 30 | 772–776 |
| Richard Strauss Instrumental, 638–641 | Chapter 28 | 733–735 |
| Richard Strauss Operas, 641–643 | Chapter 30 | 776–780 |
| Bohemia Instrumental Music, 644–646 | Chapter 29 | 744 |
| Glinka, 646–647 | Chapter 27 | 701–702 |
| Tchaikovsky Opera, 647 | Chapter 27 | 702–703 |
| Mighty Handful Opera, 647–651 | Chapter 27 | 703–709 |
| Mighty Handful Instrumental Music, 647–651 | Chapter 29 | 742–744 |
| Rachmaninov, Scriabin, 651–654 | Chapter 30 | 790–795 |
| Bohemia Opera, 654 | Chapter 27 | 709–711 |
| Janáček, 654–655 | Chapter 30 | 788–789 |
| Grieg, 655 | Chapter 29 | 745–746 |
| Sibelius, 656–659 | Chapter 30 | 789–790 |
| Elgar, 659 | Chapter 29 | 746–747 |
| Spain, 659–660 | Chapter 30 | 786 |
| French Traditions, Fauré, 660–663 | Chapter 29 | 739–741 |
| Debussy, 663–667 | Chapter 30 | 780–785 |
| Satie, 667–668 | Chapter 30 | 796–797 |
| Ravel, 669–670 | Chapter 30 | 785–786 |
| Verismo, Puccini, 670–671 | Chapter 27 | 688–689 |
| Chapter 20 | | |
| Twentieth Century Introduction, 676–679 | Chapter 30 | 758–764 |
| Bartók, 680–684 | Chapter 31 | 829–836 |
| Soviet Union, 684–688 | Chapter 33 | 876–880 |
| Gubaidulina, 688–689 | Chapter 35 | 962–963 |
| Vaughn Williams and Holst, 689–691 | Chapter 30 | 787–788 |
| Britten, 691–692 | Chapter 34 | 912–914 |
| Tippett, 692 | Chapter 34 | 916–917 |
| Davies, 692–693 | Chapter 34 | 937 |
| Germany, 693–699 | Chapter 33 | 870–876 |
| Villa-Lobos and Chávez, 699 | Chapter 33 | 880–883 |
| Ginastera, 699 | Chapter 34 | 915 |
| Les Six, 699–701 | Chapter 33 | 868–870 |
| Stravinsky, 702–709 | Chapter 31 | 819–829 |
| Chapter 21 | | |
| Schoenberg, Berg, Webern, 713–725 | Chapter 31 | 802–819 |
| Total Serialism, 725–726 | Chapter 34 | 917–918 |
| Boulez, 726 | Chapter 34 | 918–920 |
| Messiaen, 726–729 | Chapter 34 | 909–912 |
| Xenakis, 729 | Chapter 34 | 928 |
| Electronic Music, 729–731 | Chapter 34 | 925–928 |
| Penderecki and Ligeti, 732–733 | Chapter 34 | 928–931 |
| Indeterminacy, 734–735 | Chapter 34 | 932–935 |
| Stockhausen, 735–737 | Chapter 34 | 926, 937 |
| Lutosławski, 737 | Chapter 34 | 935–936 |

| HWM6 Topics and Pages | HWM7 Chapter and Pages | |
|---|---|---|
| Chapter 22 | | |
| Music in the Colonies, 740–743 | Chapter 20 | 503–505 |
| German Immigration, 743–744 | Chapter 29 | 747–748 |
| Lowell Mason, Shape-Note Singing, 744 | Chapter 25 | 655–656 |
| Spirituals, 746 | Chapter 29 | 753–755 |
| Amy Beach, 746–747 | Chapter 29 | 749 |
| Stephen Foster, 747 | Chapter 24 | 614 |
| Bands, 747–748 | Chapter 29 | 749–752 |
| Ragtime, 748 | Chapter 30 | 768–769 |
| Blues, 749–750 | Chapter 32 | 851–853 |
| Jazz in the 1920s, Big Bands, 750–751 | Chapter 32 | 854–857 |
| Bebop, 751–752 | Chapter 34 | 906–908 |
| Country Music, 752 | Chapter 34 | 897–898 |
| Rhythm-and-Blues; Rock and Roll, 752–753 | Chapter 34 | 898–902 |
| Musical Comedy, 753–754 | Chapter 32 | 849–850 |
| | Chapter 34 | 902–903 |
| Ives, 754–757 | Chapter 31 | 836–843 |
| Cowell, 758 | Chapter 33 | 884–885 |
| Ruth Crawford Seeger, 758–759 | Chapter 33 | 885–886 |
| Varèse, 759–760 | Chapter 33 | 883–884 |
| Copland, 760–761 | Chapter 33 | 887–889 |
| Virgil Thomson, 761–762 | Chapter 33 | 890 |
| Grant Still, 762–763 | Chapter 33 | 889–890 |
| Hanson and Piston, 764 | Chapter 34 | 925–928 |
| Sessions, 764–765 | Chapter 34 | 928–931 |
| Carter, 765–766 | Chapter 34 | 921–922 |
| University as Patron, 767–769 | Chapter 34 | 909 |
| Babbitt, 769–770 | Chapter 34 | 918 |
| Partch, 771 | Chapter 34 | 923 |
| Crumb, 772–773 | Chapter 34 | 923–924 |
| Electronic Music, 773–774 | Chapter 34 | 927–928 |
| Gershwin, 775 | Chapter 32 | 857–858 |
| Duke Ellington, 775 | Chapter 32 | 859–862 |
| Schuller, 775 | Chapter 34 | 916 |
| John Cage, 776–777 | Chapter 34 | 923, 932–935 |
| Minimalism, 777–780 | Chapter 35 | 952–956 |
| Barber, 780 | Chapter 34 | 914 |
| Tower, 781 | Chapter 35 | 963 |
| Zwilich, 781 | Chapter 35 | 957 |
| Rochberg, 782 | Chapter 34 | 937, 961 |
| Foss, 782 | Chapter 34 | 937 |
| Berio, 782–783 | Chapter 34 | 920–921, 937–938 |
| Del Tredici, 783–784 | Chapter 35 | 961–962 |

| NAWM4, Vol. 1 | NAWM5, Vol. 1 |
|---|---|
| 1 | 1 |
| 2 | 2 |
| 3 | 3 |
| 4 | 4 |
| 5 | 5 |
| 6 | 7 |
| 7 | 6 |
| 8 | 10 |
| 9 | 8 |
| 10 | 9 |
| 13 | 15 |
| 14 | 16 |
| 17 | 20 |
| 19 | 24 |
| 20 | 26 |
| 22 | 28 |
| 23 | 30 |
| 25 | 32 |
| 27 | 34 |
| 28 | 35 |
| 29 | 36 |
| 31b | 37 |
| 32 | 40 |
| 34 | 38 |
| 35 | 49 |
| 36 | 50 |
| 38 | 51 |
| 39 | 52 |
| 40 | 53 |
| 41 | 54 |

| NAWM4, Vol. 1 | NAWM5, Vol. 1 |
|---|---|
| 42 | 55 |
| 44 | 58 |
| 45 | 59 |
| 46 | 61 |
| 47 | 45 |
| 48 | 46 |
| 49 | 47 |
| 50 | 44 |
| 51 | 64 |
| 52 | 65 |
| 53 | 63 |
| 54 | 66 |
| 55 | 67 |
| 56 | 68 |
| 57 | 69 |
| 60 | 70 |
| 61 | 71 |
| 62 | 73 |
| 65 | 74 |
| 68 | 77 |
| 69 | 79 |
| 71 | 84 |
| 73a & d | 86 |
| 75 | 83 |
| 78 | 87 |
| 79 | 88 |
| 80 | 89 |
| 83 | 91 |
| 84 | 92 |

| NAWM4, Vol. 2 | NAWM5, Vol. 2 |
|---|---|
| 85 | 93 |
| 86 | 94 |
| 87 | 95 |
| 88 | 96 |
| 89 | 98 |
| 90 | 100 |
| 91 | 99 |
| 92 | 101 |
| 93 | 102 |
| 95 | 103b |
| 97 | 104 |
| 99 | 106 |
| 101 | 108 |
| 103 | 109 |
| 104 | 110 |
| 110 | 119 |
| 111 | 111 |
| 112 | 112 |
| 113a | 113 |
| 117 | 125 |
| 119 | 127 |
| 120 | 126 |
| 121 | 128 |
| 124 | 133 |
| 126 | 140 |
| 128 | 138 |
| 130 | 147 |
| 132 | 171 |
| 133 | 161 |
| 134 | 145a |
| 135 | 141 |
| 137 | 143 |
| 138 | 144 |
| 140 | 134 |
| 143 | 157 |
| 146a & b | 163 |
| 147 | 164 |
| 149 | 168 |

**INSTRUCTOR'S MANUAL AND TEST-ITEM FILE**

# A History of Western Music

SEVENTH EDITION

# CHAPTER 1 Music in Antiquity

I. Music in Antiquity
   A. Only historical traces of the music from past eras survive.
      1. Physical objects, such as musical instruments
      2. Visual images of musicians and instruments
      3. Writings about music and musicians
      4. Music as preserved in notation
   B. Ancient Greek music influenced Western music.
      1. The ancient Greeks left more surviving evidence than other ancient cultures.
      2. Western music has its roots in antiquity, especially in ancient Greek theoretical writings.

II. Prehistoric Music-Making
   A. Before 36,000 B.C.E.: Whistles and flutes made from animal bones survive from the Stone Age in Europe (**HWM Figure 1.1**).
   B. Sixth millennium B.C.E.: Images in Turkish cave paintings show drummers accompanying dancers and driving out game.
   C. Fourth millennium B.C.E.
      1. Surviving Bronze Age metal instruments include bells, cymbals, rattles, and horns.
      2. Stone carvings show plucked stringed instruments.

III. Ancient Mesopotamia (see map, **HWM Figure 1.2**)
   A. Home to several cultures, the first true cities, and the first known forms of writing (cuneiform)
   B. Some clay tablets written in cuneiform mention music.
   C. Pictures show music-making with instruments.
   D. Surviving instruments include lyres and harps.
      1. Lyres (see **HWM Figures 1.3** and **1.4**)
         a. Strings run parallel to the resonating soundboard.
         b. A crossbar supported by two arms secures the strings.
         c. The number of strings varies.
      2. Harps
         a. Strings are perpendicular to the soundboard.
         b. A neck attached to the soundbox secures the strings.
   E. Other instruments from the period include lutes, pipes, drums, bells, and other percussion instruments.
   F. The ruling class left the most evidence because they could buy instruments and hire scribes.
   G. Most uses of music in ancient Mesopotamia were similar to those of today.
      1. For rituals, including weddings and funerals
      2. In daily life, including nursery songs, work songs, and dance music
      3. For entertainment at feasts
      4. For religious ceremonies and processions
      5. Epics sung with instrumental accompaniment
   H. Written documentation from Mesopotamia
      1. Word lists from ca. 2500 B.C.E. include terms for instruments, tuning procedures, performers, techniques, and genres (types of musical composition).
      2. The earliest known composer is Enheduanna (fl. ca. 2300 B.C.E.).
         a. She was a high priestess at Ur.
         b. She composed hymns (songs to a god) to the god and goddess of the moon.
         c. Only the texts of her hymns survive.
      3. Babylonian musicians began writing about music ca. 1800 B.C.E.
         a. Instructions for tuning a string instrument

using a seven-note diatonic scale (playable on the white keys of a piano)

b. Interval theory, with names of intervals used to create the earliest known notation (see **HWM Figure 1.5**)
   (1) **HWM Figure 1.5** dates from ca. 1400–1250 B.C.E.
   (2) Not enough is known about the notation to transcribe it.
   (3) The poem seems to be a hymn to the wife of the moon god, but the language (Hurrian) cannot be translated entirely.

c. Although Babylonians had a form of notation, musicians most likely performed from memory, improvised, or used notation as a recipe for reconstructing a melody.

d. Babylonian music theory seems to have influenced later Greek theory.

IV. Other Civilizations

A. Instruments, images, and writings about East Asian musical cultures survive, but they seem not to have influenced Greek or European music.

B. Egyptian sources include artifacts, paintings, and hieroglyphic writings in tombs, but scholars have not been able to determine whether there is any notated music.

C. The Bible describes ancient musical practices in Israel (which in turn influenced Christian music), but ancient copies of the Bible may not have any notation.

V. Ancient Greece (see **HWM Figure 1.6**) comprised a wide area and left us enough evidence to construct a well-rounded view of its musical culture.

VI. Instruments and Their Uses

A. Evidence of Greek instruments survives in writings, archaeological remains, and hundreds of images on pots.

B. Aulos (see **HWM Figure 1.7**)
   1. A reed instrument
   2. The body consisted of two pipes with fingerholes.
   3. Pitch could be changed by position in the mouth, air pressure, and fingering.
   4. Images show the two pipes being fingered the same, but they could produce octaves, parallel fifths or fourths, drones, and unisons.
   5. The aulos was used in the worship of Dionysus.
      a. Dionysus was the god of fertility and wine, hence the drinking scene in **HWM Figure 1.7.**
      b. The aulos accompanied or alternated with choruses in the great tragedies of Aeschylus, Sophocles, and Euripides that were written for Dionysian festivals.

C. The lyre (see **HWM Figure 1.8**)
   1. There were several types, but they usually had seven strings and would be strummed with a plectrum, or pick.
   2. The player held the instrument in front, supporting it on the hip and from a strap around the left wrist.
   3. Both hands were free to touch the strings.
      a. The right hand strummed the strings.
      b. The fingers of the left hand touched the strings, perhaps to dampen them or to create harmonics.
   4. The lyre was associated with Apollo, god of light, prophecy, learning, and the arts (especially music and poetry).
      a. Both men and women played the lyre.
      b. Learning to play the lyre was a core element of education in Athens.
      c. The lyre was used to accompany dancing, singing, weddings, and the recitation of epic poetry such as Homer's *Iliad* and *Odyssey.*
      d. The lyre was also played for recreation.
   5. The kithara was a large lyre.
      a. Used in processions, sacred ceremonies, and in the theater
      b. Played standing up (see **HWM Figure 1.9**)

D. Rise of virtuosity
   1. By the sixth century B.C.E. or earlier, the aulos and kithara were played as solo instruments.
   2. Contests and music festivals became popular after the fifth century B.C.E.
      a. An account of a musical competition in 582 B.C.E. describes a performance for aulos.
      b. **HWM Figure 1.9** comes from a jar (amphora) awarded as a prize in a contest.
   3. Famous artists performed for large crowds, gave concert tours, and demanded high fees from wealthy patrons.
   4. Women were excluded from competition but could perform recitals, often to critical acclaim.
   5. Other than the virtuoso soloists, the majority of professional performers were slaves or servants.

VII. Greek Musical Thought

A. We know about Greek musical thought through two kinds of writings:
   1. Philosophical doctrines that describe music's place in the cosmos, its effects, and its proper uses in society

2. Systematic descriptions of the materials of music (music theory)

B. Music in Greek mythology
   1. Gods and demigods were musical practitioners.
   2. The word *music* (from *mousiké*) comes from the Muses.

C. Performance of music
   1. Music as a performing art was called melos (the root of the word *melody*).
   2. Music was monophonic, consisting of one melodic line.
   3. There was no concept of harmony or counterpoint.
   4. Instruments embellished the melody while a soloist or chorus sang the original version, creating heterophony.
   5. Music and poetry were nearly synonymous.
      a. There was no word for artful speech without music.
      b. Many Greek words for poetic types are musical terms—e.g., *hymn.*

D. Music and number
   1. Pythagoras and his followers recognized the numerical relationships that underlay musical intervals—e.g., 2:1 results in an octave, 3:2 a fifth, and 4:3 a fourth.
   2. *Harmonia* was the concept of an orderly whole divisible by parts.
      a. The term applied to the order of the universe.
      b. Music was allied to astronomy through the notion of harmonia.
      c. Mathematical laws were the underpinnings of musical intervals and the movements of heavenly bodies alike.
      d. From Plato's time until the beginning of modern astronomy, philosophers believed in a "harmony of the spheres," unheard music created by the movement of planets and other heavenly bodies.

E. Music and ethos
   1. Greek writers believed that music could affect ethos, one's ethical character.
      a. Music's mathematical laws permeated the visible and invisible world, including the human soul.
      b. The parts of the human soul could be restored to a healthy balance (harmony) by the correct type of music.
   2. Aristotle's *Politics* sets out a theory of how music affects behavior (see **HWM Source Reading,** page 16).
      a. The Mixolydian, Dorian, and Phrygian melodies (combinations of mode, melodic turns, and general style) each had specific effects on the listener.
      b. Aristotle argued that music should be part of education because of its power to influence a person's soul.
      c. The theory of imitation holds that a person will imitate the ethos of the music they hear.
      d. Aristotle admits that music is enjoyable (see last sentence of **HWM Source Reading,** page 16) and enjoyment is acceptable when part of education and ethos.
      e. He discourages high-born citizens from training to become professionals or entering in competitions because performing for pleasure alone is menial and vulgar.
   3. Plato's *Republic* urges balance between gymnastics and music, and only certain types of music, in education.
      a. The Dorian and Phrygian *harmoniai* fostered the virtues of temperance and courage.
      b. Music should not have complex scales or mixed genres, rhythms or instruments.
      c. Changes in musical conventions could lead to lawlessness in art and anarchy in society.
      d. Plato's uses for music are more restrictive than Aristotle's.

VIII. Greek Music Theory

A. Aristoxenus, *Harmonic Elements and Rhythmic Elements* (ca. 330 B.C.E.)
   1. Distinguishes between continuous movement of voice and diastematic (intervallic) movement
   2. Defines note, interval, and scale
   3. Intervals defined abstractly (versus Babylonian definition based on specific strings of the lyre or harp)

B. Tetrachord theory
   1. Tetrachord: four notes bounded by a perfect fourth
   2. Three genera (classes) of tetrachord, defined by the second and third pitches, descending (see **HWM Example 1.1**)
      a. Diatonic: tone - semitone - tone
      b. Chromatic: minor third - semitone - semitone
      c. Enharmonic: major third - quartertone - semitone
      d. Intervals varied in size, creating "shades" within each genus.

3. The genera were an attempt to explain actual musical practices.
4. Aristoxenus said the diatonic was the oldest genera; the enharmonic, the most difficult to hear.

C. Greater Perfect System (see **HWM Example 1.2**)
1. Tetrachords put together to form a two-octave range
   a. Tetrachords with common outer notes are conjunct
   b. Tetrachords with a tone between them are disjunct
2. One added note at the bottom (Proslambanomenos)
3. The middle note was called *mese.*
4. Each of the four tetrachords was named.
   a. Meson: the tetrachord beginning with mese and descending
   b. Diezeugmenon (disjunct): beginning a tone above mese and ascending
   c. Hypaton (conjunct): the tetrachord below Meson
   d. Hyperbolaion (conjunct): the tetrachord above Diezeugmenon
5. Although the pitches had names, there was no absolute fixed pitch.

D. Species (the ways that perfect consonances could be divided)
1. Cleonides noted that the perfect fourth, fifth, and octave could be subdivided in a limited number of ways in the diatonic genus.
2. The perfect fourth could be divided three ways (see **HWM Example 1.3a**).
   a. S - T - T (semitone - tone - tone)
   b. T - T - S
   c. T - S - T
3. The perfect fifth has four species (see **HWM Example 1.3b**).
4. The octave has seven species (see **HWM Example 1.3c**).
   a. Octave species result from combinations of species of fourth and fifth.
   b. Cleonides used names the "ancients" supposedly used:
      (1) B-b: Mixolydian
      (2) c-c': Lydian
      (3) d-d': Phrygian
      (4) e-e': Dorian
      (5) f-f': Hypolydian
      (6) g-g': Hypophrygian
      (7) a-a': Hypodorian
   c. The Babylonians recognized the same diatonic tunings.
   d. Medieval theorists used the same names for their modes but they do not match Cleonides' species.

E. Other meanings for the names used by Cleonides
1. Styles of music practiced in different regions of the Greek world (see map, **HWM Figure 1.6**)
2. Harmoniai
   a. Scale types or melodic styles
   b. Plato and Aristotle used the ethnic names with and without prefixes
3. Tonoi (singular: tonos)
   a. Scale or set of pitches within a specific range
   b. Associated with character and mood, the higher tonoi being more energetic.

IX. Ancient Greek Music

A. Surviving pieces and fragments
1. About forty-five survive.
2. Most are from relatively late periods, i.e., from the fifth century B.C.E. to the fourth.
3. All employ a notation that places letters above the text to indicate notes and durations.
4. The earliest fragments are choruses from plays by Euripides (ca. 485–406 B.C.E.).
5. Later works include hymns and an epitaph on a tombstone.
6. The musical style is consistent with music theory of the time.

B. **NAWM 1** Epitaph of Seikilos (see **HWM Figure 1.10** and **Example 1.4**)
1. **HWM Example 1.4** shows the Greek notation above the transcription.
   a. Alphabetical signs indicate the notes.
   b. Marks indicating doubling or tripling of the basic rhythmic unit are above the alphabetical signs.
2. Melody
   a. Diatonic
   b. The range is an octave.
   c. The octave species is Phrygian.
   d. The tonos is Iastian, a transposed version of **HWM Example 1.2.**
   e. The melody balances rising and falling gestures with each line.
3. Text
   a. In keeping with the Iastian tonos, the text suggests moderation.
   b. The epitaph urges readers to be light-hearted while also acknowledging death.

C. **NAWM 2** Fragment from Euripides' *Orestes*
1. Survives on a scrap of papyrus from ca. 200 B.C.E. (see **HWM Figure 1.11**)
2. Only the middle portion of its seven lines of text survives.
3. The style is consistent with descriptions of Euripides' music.
   a. Combines diatonic with either chromatic or enharmonic genus

b. Instrumental notes are interspersed with vocal.
4. The text is a chorus for women.
5. The meter of the text uses dochmaic foot, used for passages of intense agitation and grief.
6. Chromatic or enharmonic notes reinforce the ethos of the poetry.

X. Music in Ancient Rome
A. Less evidence survives for music of ancient Rome than for ancient Greece.
1. No settings of texts survive.
2. Images, written descriptions, and some instruments are all that remain.
B. Romans took much of their musical culture from Greece.
1. Lyric poetry was often sung.
2. Cicero, Quintilian, and others believed cultured people should be educated in music.
3. In the first and second centuries C.E., when other aspects of Greek culture were imported, virtuosity, choruses, and competitions became popular.
C. Roman instruments
1. The tibia, an instrument similar to the aulos, was used for ceremonies and theater.
2. Other instruments included the tuba, a long straight trumpet.
3. The most characteristic instruments were the cornu and buccina, circular horns.
4. **HWM Figure 1.12** shows tibias and cornus used in a funeral procession.
D. Production of music declined when the Roman economy declined.
E. Roman music seems not to have influenced later musical developments in Europe.

XI. The Greek Heritage
A. Many characteristics of Greek music continued in later Western music.
1. Music remained essentially melodic until the eleventh century.
2. The meter and rhythm of the text influenced the music.
3. Memory and musical conventions played an important part in many later traditions.
B. Greek musical thought influenced later generations.
1. Plato's idea that music can influence character persists today.
2. Medieval music theory and church music used Greek concepts.
3. Opera composers looked to the Greek tragedies for models of how to combine music and drama.
4. In the twentieth century, composers looked to the Greeks for inspiration.

## SUGGESTIONS FOR FURTHER READING/LISTENING/ACTIVITIES

*Musique de la Grèce antique* (Harmonia Mundi France, HMA 1901016) contains recordings of most of the known fragments of ancient Greek music. The realizations are inventive and make a good starting point for discussion of the relationship between notation and performance.

Selections from Plato's *The Republic* and Aristotle's *The Politics* can be found in Thomas J. Mathiesen, ed., *Source Readings in Music History,* rev. ed., Vol. 1: *Greek Views of Music* (New York: W. W. Norton, 1998).

For full-length translations of Greek musical treatises, see Andrew Barker, ed., *Greek Musical Writings,* 2 vols. (New York: Cambridge University Press, 1984–1989).

Using a monochord or another stringed instrument, demonstrate the ratios of intervals by playing harmonics and dividing the string length.

Bring a simple harp to class and have students help tune each genera of the tetrachords and the Greater Perfect System.

## OBJECTIVE QUESTIONS

1. Prehistoric European cultures left behind what instruments?
a. lyres
b. harps
c. instruments made from bones
d. drums
e. There are no surviving instruments from European prehistory.

Answer: c

2. The earliest known Mesopotamian composer is __________.
a. Lyricus, whose poetry became synonymous with all poetry
b. Ur, a king who ruled from ca. 1400–1350 B.C.E.
c. Aristoxenus, a theorist who composed hymns and psalms
d. Cleonides, who composed music for plays
e. Enheduanna, a high priestess who composed hymns

Answer: e

3. Which statement is true of Babylonian music?
   a. Although Babylonians had a form of notation, musicians most likely performed from memory, improvised, or used notation as a recipe for reconstructing a melody.
   b. Babylonian musicians relied on a complex system of notation, and several untranscribable fragments that survive indicate notation for many aspects of performance.
   c. The Babylonians had no system of notation, and only brief references to music-making survive.
   d. Babylonian musicians improvised, and several instructional manuals for how to improvise have survived, but translation is difficult because of the technical language.
   e. No evidence survives to tell us anything about Babylonian music.

   Answer: a

4. The most popular ancient Greek wind instrument was the __________.
   a. aulos
   b. bone flute
   c. lyre
   d. kithara
   e. tuba

   Answer: a

5. The lyre was associated with which Greek god?
   a. Dionysus
   b. Hercules
   c. Xena
   d. Apollo
   e. Pythagoras

   Answer: d

6. Which of these statements is true?
   a. Women performed in all spheres of Greek musical performance.
   b. Women could perform virtuosic recitals but could not compete.
   c. Women could perform only at temples devoted to goddesses.
   d. Women performed only within the home.
   e. Women were excluded from any type of musical performance in Ancient Greece.

   Answer: b

7. Heterophony refers to __________.
   a. all performers singing or playing one melody in unison
   b. one person singing or playing a melody with embellishment while others sing or play the original
   c. a complex set of principles based on the relationship between intervals and the movement of celestial bodies
   d. a scale of four notes
   e. playing a two-bored reed instrument frequently portrayed on clay pots

   Answer: b

8. The rhythm of ancient Greek music was intimately tied to __________.
   a. poetic meter
   b. religious beliefs
   c. dance rhythms
   d. the mode of the melody
   e. its ceremonial function

   Answer: a

9. Ancient Greek musical writings included __________.
   a. descriptions of musical practices of the time
   b. doctrines on the nature of music
   c. doctrines on the proper uses of music in society
   d. all of the above
   e. none of the above

   Answer: d

10. The Doctrine of Ethos is the theory that music __________.
    a. can influence a person's morality
    b. creates a sound in the heavens
    c. should be performed ethically
    d. has eight tonoi
    e. is a sacred gift from God

    Answer: a

11. Which of the following statements describes the sources for notated music of ancient Greece?
    a. There are few surviving examples.
    b. There are hundreds of surviving examples.
    c. The only surviving examples are those composed for plays.
    d. There are no surviving examples.
    e. The surviving examples do not notate rhythm.

    Answer: a

12. Which of the following statements is true of ancient Greek music education?
    a. Music was used to teach numbers and number theory.
    b. Music was considered one of the fine arts and was taught alongside drama.

c. Only women were encouraged to cultivate music, because they could not become warriors.
d. When Plato and Aristotle wrote about education they ignored music.
e. Young boys were sent to conservatories to learn to sing epics.

Answer: c

13. The theory of imitation holds that __________.
a. music is capable of imitating sounds and ideas from the external world
b. students should learn musical skills by emulating a master teacher
c. the poor can rise in station by imitating the music of the elite
d. a person will imitate the ethos of the music they hear
e. the planets make an inaudible music that influences life on Earth

Answer: d

14. Ancient Greek music theory included the concepts of __________.
a. counterpoint, semitones, and intervals
b. intervals, scales, and tetrachords
c. major and minor intervals, and a system of twelve modes
d. dissonant intervals and interval inversion
e. major and minor keys and triads

Answer: b

15. The Greater Perfect System consists of ________.
a. rules for making music in Plato's idealized republic
b. a series of tetrachords linked to form a two-octave range of usable pitches
c. Cleonides' system of octave species
d. the Roman system of music, which they believed was an improvement over the Greek system
e. a four-note extension of the Lesser Perfect System

Answer: b

16. The names for the modes came from ________.
a. Babylonian mode names
b. composers noted for composing in those modes
c. the first lines of famous songs in those modes
d. ethnic groups of ancient Greece
e. the names of famous music theorists

Answer: d

17. The three genera of tetrachords in the Greek system of music theory are __________.
a. major, minor, and harmonic
b. Dorian, Phrygian, and Lydian
c. diatonic, chromatic, and enharmonic
d. Platonic, Aristotelian, and Boethian
e. sacred, secular, and mixed

Answer: c

18. Which of the following statements is true of art music in ancient Rome?
a. There is no written documentation of art music in ancient Rome.
b. Images, written descriptions, and some instruments are all that remain.
c. Several examples in untranscribable notation survive, along with dozens of texts.
d. Gregorian chant was sung in ancient Rome and survives in Catholic church books.
e. Numerous examples of music and text survive.

Answer: b

19. Instruments similar to trumpets and horns were used in ________.
a. ancient Europe
b. Mesopotamia
c. Babylon
d. ancient Greece
e. ancient Rome

Answer: e

20. The person who first recognized the numerical relationships that underlay musical intervals was ________.
a. Pythagoras
b. Plato
c. Aristotle
d. Aristoxenus
e. Cleonides

Answer: a

## SHORT-ESSAY QUESTIONS

1. What kinds of evidence exists about music-making in the eras before written music?
2. Describe the main theoretical components of music as described by ancient Greek theorists.
3. Discuss the types of instruments used in ancient cultures and their roles.
4. Define the theory of imitation. Which philosophers discussed it? What was its role in education?

## TERMS FOR IDENTIFICATION

lyre
harp
genre
hymn
Muse
melos
monophonic
heterophony
Plato
Aristotle
harmonia
harmony of the spheres
ethos
theory of imitation
tetrachord
Greater Perfect System
Cleonides
diatonic
enharmonic
chromatic
genera
harmoniai
tonoi (tonos)
tibia
tuba
cornu

# CHAPTER 2 The Christian Church in the First Millennium

I. The Diffusion of Christianity
   A. Though Jesus of Nazareth (Christ) was a Jew, he charged his disciples to "make disciples of all nations" (Matthew 28:19).
   B. St. Paul (ca. 20–ca. 67 C.E.) and other apostles brought Christianity to the Near East, Greece, and Italy.
   C. By 313 Christianity was established in most cities of the Roman Empire, despite persecution.
   D. In 313, Emperor Constantine I (r. 310–37) issued the Edict of Milan, legalizing Christianity.
   E. In 392, Emperor Theodosius I (r. 374–95) made Christianity the official religion of the Roman Empire and suppressed all others, except for Judaism.
   F. By 600, virtually the entire area once controlled by Rome was Christian and organized by the principles of the empire (see **HWM Figure 2.1**).
      1. Territories were called dioceses.
      2. A hierarchy headed by patriarchs in Rome and other cities included local churches, bishops, and archbishops.

II. The Judaic Heritage
   A. Some elements of Christian observances derive from Jewish traditions.
      1. Chanting of Scripture
      2. Singing of psalms (poems of praise from the Hebrew Book of Psalms)
   B. Temple sacrifice at the Second Temple of Jerusalem (destroyed by Romans in 70 C.E.)
      1. Ritualistic sacrifice of an animal (usually a lamb) was an integral part of worship services.
      2. During the sacrifice, a choir of Levites (members of the priestly class) sang psalms.
      3. Trumpets and cymbals were also used.
      4. Priests and sometimes worshipers ate some of the offering, depending on the occasion.
   C. Synagogues
      1. Synagogues were centers for readings and homilies rather than worship.
      2. Scripture was chanted to a system of melodic formulas based on phrase divisions of the text (*cantillation*).
      3. Readings were assigned to particular days or festivals.
   D. Christian parallels with Jewish practices
      1. Much of the Mass (see **HWM Chapter 3**) includes rituals similar to Jewish practice.
      2. Jesus' Last Supper, commemorated in the Mass, is a symbolic sacrifice and related to the Passover meal, which is accompanied by psalm-singing.
      3. Singing psalms is a central element of all Christian observances.
      4. Melodic formulae used for singing psalms may have derived from Jewish cantillation.

III. Music in the Early Church
   A. Biblical references to musical activity
      1. Matthew 26:30 and Mark 14:26 refer to Jesus and his followers singing hymns.
      2. In Ephesians 5:19 and Colossians 3:16, Paul exhorts Christians to sing "psalms and hymns and spiritual songs."
   B. Historical references to Christian music
      1. Pliny the Younger, governor of a Roman province, reported Christians singing "a song to Christ as if to a god" in about 112 C.E.
      2. In the fourth century, official acceptance led to

public meetings in large buildings called basilicas (see **HWM Figure 2.2**).
3. Egeria, a Spanish nun on a pilgrimage to Jerusalem, described services there ca. 400 C.E. (see **HWM Source Reading,** page 27).
    a. She describes the Sunday morning Vigil, which would later be called Matins.
    b. Priests sang psalms followed by a response from the congregation.
    c. Prayers followed each of the three psalms.
    d. After the psalms, the basilica was filled with incense and the bishop read from the Gospel (the section of the New Testament that relates the history of Christ's life).
    e. After the reading, the bishop exited to the accompaniment of hymns.
    f. After the bishop's exit, there was another psalm and prayer.

C. Early church leaders (known today as "the church fathers") encouraged music for sacred purposes only.
1. St. Augustine (354–430) feared music's ability to arouse strong feelings (see **HWM Source Reading,** page 28).
    a. In his *Confessions,* he describes shedding tears at the psalms.
    b. He believed that feeling inspired by a musical performance was a good thing if the inspiration came from the meaning of the words.
    c. When he was "moved more by the song than by what [was] sung," it was sinful.
2. Other church fathers prohibited instrumental music.
    a. Instrumental music, lacking words, could not convey Christian teachings.
    b. They feared evoking pagan practices, such as spectacles involving dancing.
3. The eternal welfare of the soul was of paramount importance, above earthly enjoyment.

IV. Divisions in the Church and Dialects of Chant

A. The division of the Roman Empire into two parts in 395 was the most significant division of the early Church.
1. The Western Empire
    a. Ruled by Rome or Milan
    b. Subject to invasions by Germanic tribes
    c. Collapsed in 476
2. The Eastern Empire
    a. Centered at Constantinople (formerly Byzantium, now Istanbul)
    b. Survived until Constantinople fell to the Turks in 1453.
3. The western church (Roman Catholic)
    a. Ruled by the bishop of Rome, known as the pope (Italian *papa*)
    b. After the third century, Latin, the language of the Roman Empire, was the official language of the western church.
4. The eastern church (Byzantine)
    a. Greek was the official language of the eastern church.
    b. The Byzantine Church is the ancestor of today's Orthodox churches.

B. Christian rites
1. Although each branch of the Church had a different rite, all rites had the same components.
    a. A church calendar including special events and times of year
    b. A liturgy (body of texts and ritual actions assigned to each service)
    c. A repertory of *plainchant* or *chant* (unison song for prescribed texts)
2. Chant dialects
    a. Gregorian chant was the most important for the history of Western music.
    b. Other dialects included Byzantine, Ambrosian, and Old Roman.

C. Byzantine chant
1. Scriptural readings were chanted with formulas that reflected the phrasing of the text.
2. Psalms and especially hymns were sung to fully developed melodies.
3. There were eight modes, or *echoi,* to classify chants.
4. Many chant melodies were created from standard formulas through a process called centonization.
5. Byzantine melodies were the basis for other Orthodox traditions (e.g., Russian), but over time the traditions diverged.

D. Western dialects
1. Several European areas had their own rites, with their own liturgy and body of chant.
2. Milan: Ambrosian chant
    a. Named for St. Ambrose, bishop of Milan from 374–97.
    b. Whether the chants survive from Ambrose's time is a mystery.
    c. Despite efforts to suppress it, Ambrosian chant survives in Milan today.
3. Rome was successful in suppressing the chant traditions in other areas.
4. Gregorian chant is the result of the collaboration of Roman leaders and Frankish (French) kings to codify chant.

V. The Creation of Gregorian Chant
   A. The Schola Cantorum (School of Singers)
      1. The choir that sang for observances officiated by the pope
      2. Founded in the late seventh century
      3. Helped to standardize chant melodies in the early eighth century
   B. Chant in the Frankish Kingdom
      1. Between 752 and 754, Pope Stephen II traveled through the Frankish kingdom with the Schola Cantorum.
      2. Pepin the Short (r. 751–68), king of the Franks
         a. Ordered the Roman liturgy and chant to be performed in his domain, replacing the native Gallican rite
         b. Codification of chant helped Pepin consolidate the kingdom.
      3. Charlemagne (Charles the Great, r. 768–814)
         a. Pepin's son
         b. Expanded the kingdom to include present-day western Germany, Switzerland, and northern Italy
         c. Brought singers from Rome to the north to teach the chant.
         d. On Christmas Day in 800, Pope Leo III crowned Charlemagne emperor, initiating the Holy Roman Empire (see **HWM Figures 2.3 and 2.4**).
   C. Gregorian chant as we know it results from a collaboration between Frankish and Roman singers.
      1. Some melodies survived unchanged.
      2. Franks may have altered some chants.
      3. Some melodies came from Gallican (regional Frankish) chant.
      4. Some melodies were developed in the Frankish kingdom north after the eighth century.
   D. The Legend of St. Gregory
      1. St. Gregory the Great (Pope Gregory I, r. 590–604)
      2. Attribution of chant to Gregory I may be due to confusion with Pope Gregory II, r. 715–731.
      3. The legend claims that the Holy Spirit, in the form of a dove, dictated the chant melodies to Gregory I (see **HWM Figure 2.5**).
      4. The English may have originated the legend.
         a. They adopted Roman chant earlier than the Franks.
         b. They revered Pope Gregory I as the founder of their church.
   E. After the Franks adopted Gregorian chant it spread throughout western Europe.
   F. Chant in Rome: Old Roman chant
      1. Manuscripts from the eleventh and twelfth centuries show a different chant being used in Rome.
      2. Texts are the same as Gregorian.
      3. Melodies are more elaborate.
      4. Scholars still dispute whether this tradition represents the original, more elaborate, chant from which Gregorian derived, or a later embellishment to a Gregorian tradition.

VI. The Development of Notation
   A. Oral transmission
      1. After ancient Greek notation had been forgotten, chant was transmitted from memory.
      2. Writer Isadore of Seville (ca. 560–636) wrote that "Unless sounds are remembered by man, they perish, for they cannot be written down."
      3. Simple melodies may have been memorized.
      4. Complex melodies may have been improvised within strict conventions, like Jewish cantillation and Byzantine centonization.
         a. Other oral traditions use formulas to re-create melodies, e.g., Balkan epic singers.
         b. Some chants seem to have been composed in this way (see **HWM Example 2.1**).
            (1) Although each verse is different, they all have the same outline.
            (2) The same cadential formula closes each verse.
         c. When melodies were written down, formulaic structures remained intact.
   B. The earliest chant notation
      1. The attempt to standardize chant depended on reliable transmission from person to person.
      2. Notation, a way to write down music, may have been in use by Charlemagne's time.
      3. The earliest surviving books of chant with music notation date from the ninth century.
      4. Signs called *neumes* (Latin *neuma,* meaning "gestures") were placed above words (see **HWM Figure 2.6**).
         a. Neumes may have derived from signs for inflection and accent, similar to accent marks in modern French.
         b. Neumes designated melodic direction, not specific notes.
         c. Melodies were still learned by ear, but the neumes served as reminders.
         d. In the tenth and eleventh centuries, scribes (see **HWM Music in Context,** page 40) placed heighted or diastemic neumes at varying heights to indicate relative sizes of intervals (see **HWM Figure 2.7**).

5. Lines to indicate specific pitches
    a. A horizontal line scratched in the parchment in diastematic notation helped orient the neumes around a specific note.
    b. In some manuscripts the line represented the location of the semitone in the chant, i.e., either F or C, and would be labeled with these letters (the origin of our clefs).
6. Guido of Arezzo, a monk in the eleventh century, developed a system with additional lines (see **HWM Figure 2.8**).
    a. Red ink for F, with the letter written in the left margin
    b. Yellow ink for C, with the letter written in the left margin
    c. Between each line would be one note.
    d. This system evolved to a four-line staff, the precursor of the five-line staff still in use today.
    e. Although specific notes were indicated, there was still no sense of absolute pitch.

C. Solesmes chant notation
1. In 1903, Pope Pius X proclaimed modern editions created by the monks of Solesmes as the official Vatican editions.
2. **HWM Examples 2.2** and **2.3** show the same chant, the gradual, *Viderunt omnes,* in Solesmes notation and in transcription.
    a. **Example 2.2** begins with an indication of the type of chant (Grad. for gradual), the mode (5), and the first letter of the chant in large typeface (V for Viderunt).
    b. **Example 2.3** uses the modern conventions for chant transcriptions—stemless notes, with slurs to indicate notes grouped as neumes in the original.
3. Features of Solesmes notation
    a. Four-line staff
    b. Either C or F clef (but pitch is relative)
4. Each note or notegroup is called a neume.
    a. A neume may not have more than one syllable of text.
    b. Composite neumes (notegroups) are read left to right. (E.g., ter- of *terrae,* which notates c'–a'–c')
    c. Repeated single-note neumes are sung as if tied or slightly pulsed. (E.g., -te of *Jubilate*)
    d. Diamond-shaped notes in descending groups are the equivalent of square notes. (E.g., o- of *omnes* and the final three notes)
    e. Small notes indicate voiced consonants sung with a partially closed mouth. (E.g., -tum of *Notum* and con- of *conspectum*)
    f. The quilisma, a wavy neume, may have indicated a vocal ornament in original sources.
5. Flat and natural (but not sharp) could be notated.
    a. Accidentals are valid until the beginning of the next word or vertical division line.
    b. On *omnis* both occurrences of B are flatted.
    c. In the following word, *terra,* a natural sign is not needed because the flat sign from *omnis* does not carry to a new word.
6. Solesmes editions were intended for use in church, not scholarship, and therefore have additional signs not in their source manuscripts.
    a. Dots after notes double their value.
    b. Horizontal dashes (present in some medieval sources) indicate a slight lengthening (e.g., the first note of -es of *fines*).
    c. Vertical lines mark divisions of a melody.
    d. Asterisks show where the chorus takes over from the soloist.
    e. *ij* and *iij* indicate repetitions of the preceding phrase, twice and three times respectively (see **HWM Example 3.5**).

VII. Music Theory and Practice

A. Two writers transmitted the legacy of Greek music theory: Martianus Capella and Boethius.

B. Martianus Capella's treatise *The Marriage of Mercury and Philology* (early fifth century)
1. Describes the seven liberal arts
    a. The trivium of the verbal arts: grammar, dialectic, rhetoric
    b. The quadrivium of the mathematical disciplines: geometry, arithmetic, astronomy, and harmonics (music)
2. The section on music is a modified translation of Aristides Quintalianus's *On Music.*

C. Boethius (ca. 480–ca. 524) was the most revered authority on music in the Middle Ages.
1. Born into a wealthy Roman family
2. Consul and minister to Theodric, ruler of Italy
3. He wrote *De institutione musica* (The Fundamentals of Music) when he was a young man.
4. His main sources are a long treatise by Nichomachus and Ptolemy's *Harmonics.*
5. Concepts in *De institutione musica*
    a. The three types of music
        (1) *musica mundana* (the music of the universe): numerical relations governing the movement of stars, planets, seasons, and the elements

(2) *musica humana* (human music): unification of body, soul, and their parts
(3) *musica instrumentalis* (instrumental music): audible music produced by voices or instruments

b. Music's power to influence character made it important in educating the young.
c. The study of music through reason was a higher pursuit than the performance of music; therefore, a philosopher of music was the true musician, not a singer or instrumentalist.

D. Practical theory
1. In contrast to Boethius's philosophical approach, many treatises from the ninth century through the later Middle Ages were oriented toward practical concerns.
2. *Musica enchiriadis* (Music Handbook) and *Scolica enchiriadis* (Excerpts from Handbooks)
a. Anonymous ninth-century treatise with examples
b. Directed at students who aspired to religious posts
c. Introduces a system for notating chant
d. Describes eight modes
e. Provides exercises for locating semitones in chant
f. Explains consonances and their use in polyphony (see **HWM Chapter 5**)
3. Guido of Arezzo's *Micrologus* (ca. 1025–28)
a. A practical guide for singers, commissioned by the bishop of Arezzo
b. Covers notes, intervals, scales, modes, composition, and improvisation

VIII. The Church Modes
A. By the eleventh century, the system had achieved its complete form.
B. Modes can be described as species with different arrangements of whole and half steps in relationship to a final, the main note of the mode and usually the last note in the melody.
C. Each of the four finals have two associated modes (see **HWM Example 2.4a**).
1. Authentic modes range from a step below the final to an octave above it.
2. Plagal modes range from a fourth or fifth below the final to a fifth or sixth above it.
3. To medieval singers, each of the eight modes had a distinctive character, even though the two modes on the same final might sound similar to modern ears.

D. The only chromatic pitch was B-flat, which frequently appears in melodies in modes 1, 2, 4, 5, and 6.
E. Although the pitch arrangements of the modes seem like octave species (as suggested by **HWM Example 2.4b**), melodies often exceeded an octave range.
F. The tenor or reciting tone is the most frequent or prominent note in a chant.
1. In authentic modes the tenor is a fifth above the final.
2. In plagal modes the tenor is a third below the corresponding tenor of the authentic mode with the same final.
3. When the tenor would be a B, it is moved upward to C.
G. Modes were used to classify chants and arrange them in books for liturgical use.
1. Many chants fit the theory well (e.g., *Viderunt omnes,* **HWM Example 2.3**).
a. It begins on its final, F.
b. It rises to its tenor, C, which predominates in most phrases.
c. It rises to the octave above its final.
d. The classification of mode 5 fits this chant well.
2. The theory doesn't fit chants composed before the eleventh century.
H. Greek names were given to the church modes in the tenth century, based on a misreading of Boethius (see **HWM Example 2.4b**).
1. Authentic modes received the ethnic names.
a. Dorian (with a final of D)
b. Phrygian (with a final of E)
c. Lydian (with a final of F)
d. Mixolydian (with a final of G)
2. Plagal modes were prefixed with *hypo*
a. Hypodorian (with a final of D)
b. Hypophrygian (with a final of E)
c. Hypolydian (with a final of F)
d. Hypomixolydian (with a final of G)
3. The attempt to explain their own music theory in Greek terms shows how important it was for medieval scholars to ground their work in Greek tradition.

IX. Solmization
A. Guido of Arezzo devised a set of syllables for students to use in sight-singing.
B. The syllables correspond to the first syllables of each phrase of the hymn *Ut queant laxis* (see **HWM Example 2.5**).
C. The syllables ut–re–mi–fa–sol–la correspond to C–D–E–F–G–A.

D. Guido's system did not include a syllable for B, which is now designated as *ti*.

E. Hexachords
   1. There are three pairs of semitones in chant: E–F, A–B-flat, B–C
   2. Guido's six-note pattern (a hexachord) contained only one semitone, between E and F.
   3. By transposing the syllables to F or G, a singer could learn chants with other semitone combinations (see **HWM Example 2.6**).
   4. Each hexachord has a name.
      a. A hexachord with no B (C–A) is called "natural."
      b. A hexachord with a B-flat (F–D) is "soft."
      c. A hexachord with a B-natural (G–E) is "hard."
      d. The half-step always occurs between the syllables *mi* and *fa*.
   5. The lowest hexachord began with a G.
      a. It was *ut* in the hexachord system.
      b. It was also named with the Greek letter *gamma*, Γ.
      c. The resulting name was *gamma-ut*, from which the word gamut derives.
   6. A singer would use mutation to change among the three hexachords when learning a new chant (see **HWM Example 2.7**).

F. Followers of Guido created a pedagogical aid called the "Guidonian Hand" (see **HWM Figure 2.12**).
   1. Each joint of the hand stood for one of the twenty notes of the system.
   2. Other notes were considered "outside the hand."
   3. Teachers pointed to the different joints of the finger to teach their students intervals.

G. Thanks to Guido's innovations, a teacher could "produce a perfect singer" in one to two years, instead of the ten years required when teaching by rote.

X. Echoes of History

A. Although we do not have information about ancient Jewish or early Christian music, many of their traditions were passed to the medieval church, which in turn influenced future eras of European music.

B. Developments of the Middle Ages, such as notation on staff lines, solmization, and clef signs, continue to this day and make our knowledge of a thousand years of music history possible.

## SUGGESTIONS FOR SUPPLEMENTAL READING/LISTENING/ACTIVITIES

For a discussion of musical terms used in the Bible, read or assign passages from James McKinnon, ed., *Music in Early Christian Literature* (New York: Cambridge University Press, 1987).

For a fuller discussion of topics covered in this chapter, see David Hiley, *Western Plainchant: A Handbook* (New York: Oxford University Press, 1993). Of particular interest are transcriptions of several examples of early chant notation (406–441), an explanation of Guido's teaching method (466–69), a discussion of regional chant repertoires (524–560), and a brief but detailed history of the codification of the Gregorian chant repertoire under Charlemagne (514–523).

*The New Oxford Companion to Music* (New York: Oxford University Press, 1983), 1248–9, shows St. Gall neumes, modern plainchant notation (square-note) equivalents, and round-note transcriptions.

*The Graduale Triplex,* published by the Monks of Solesmes (1979), reproduces unheighted neumes above or below modern square-note notation when early sources are available. On pages 47–8 *Puer Natus est* (**NAWM 3a**) and its psalm offer excellent examples of the relationship between ancient and modern neume shapes.

Bring volumes of the *Paleographie Musicale* or *Monumenta Palaeografica Gregoriana* facsimile editions to class to show students what chant notation and liturgical books looked like during different stages in the development of notation.

Have the students transcribe **NAWM 3a,** *Puer natus est,* or another example from chantbook notation to modern notation using **NAWM 6** as a model. Show them the same chant in the *Graduale Triplex,* published by the Monks of Solesmes. This book reproduces the neumes from two early sources above and below the modern chant notation. *Puer natus est* is on page 47.

For excerpts from Guido's *Epistola de ignoto cantu* ("Letter on singing unheard songs," ca. 1030), see *Music in the Western World: A History in Documents,* ed. Weiss and Taruskin (New York: Schirmer, 1984), pages 51–54.

Have students learn and sing the hymn *Ut queant laxis* (LU 1342) as a demonstration of Guido's solfege system.

Have students sing **HWM Example 2.7,** the beginning of *Viderunt omnes,* using solmization syllables, then work out the rest of the chant using Guido's hexachord system. After they feel comfortable with the system, have them try to sight-sing an example from **NAWM 3.**

## OBJECTIVE QUESTIONS

1. The eight church modes are defined primarily by their __________.
   a. intonation, tenor, mediant, and termination
   b. neumes and plagals
   c. solmization and ambitus
   d. range, final, and reciting tone
   e. none of the above

   Answer: d

2. The chant tradition centered in the city of Milan is known as __________.
   a. Ambrosian chant
   b. Old Roman chant
   c. Mozarabic chant
   d. Milanese chant
   e. none of the above

   Answer: a

3. Charlemagne is credited with __________.
   a. attempting to bring chant practices in the Frankish kingdom into line with Roman chant practice
   b. suppressing Ambrosian chant
   c. developing the theory of eight Byzantine modes
   d. introducing psalm-singing into Christian worship
   e. inventing a system of sight-singing

   Answer: a

4. Which of these subjects was not part of the quadrivium according to Martianus Capella?
   a. arithmetic
   b. astronomy
   c. geometry
   d. music
   e. rhetoric

   Answer: e

5. The Schola Cantorum was __________.
   a. a group of singers under Charlemagne's direction
   b. the choir that sang for observances officiated by the pope
   c. a university in Paris that specialized in music theory
   d. a group of composers who revitalized Gregorian chant
   e. the heavenly choir of angels

   Answer: b

6. Early in the first century C.E., Jewish music __________.
   a. was performed by professional singers in synagogue
   b. was performed by a choir of Levites at the Temple of Jerusalem
   c. was considered evil and something religion should fight
   d. was performed only in the privacy of one's home
   e. was performed only by the cantor

   Answer: b

7. The church fathers believed __________.
   a. that music was evil and should be banished from religion
   b. that music was good and should be performed often
   c. that music could be good or evil and that only the right kinds of music should be sung in worship
   d. that instrumental music was good, but vocal music was evil
   e. that vocal music was good, but only if accompanied

   Answer: c

8. The sixth-century writer who compiled a compendium of Greek music theory based on Nichomachus and Ptolemy was __________.
   a. Boethius
   b. St. Augustine
   c. Plato
   d. Isadore of Seville
   e. St. Ambrose

   Answer: a

9. Which of the following Christian practices does not come from Jewish worship?
   a. Reading of Scripture
   b. The use of melodic formulas for singing psalms
   c. Symbolic meal (Jesus' Last Supper)
   d. Eight modes for singing chants
   e. Assigning specific readings to specific days

   Answer: d

10. Early church leaders believed that instrumental music __________.
    a. could inspire Christian devotion
    b. added pageantry to celebrations
    c. could evoke pagan practices, and therefore should be suppressed
    d. was irrelevant to considerations of the place of music in Christian worship
    e. should use Jewish instruments to remind listeners of Christianity's Jewish roots

    Answer: c

11. Egeria's description of a fourth-century worship service describes __________.
    a. priests singing elaborate melodies as the congregation listened passively
    b. priests singing psalms and the congregation singing responses
    c. priests and the congregation singing together
    d. the congregation singing all the parts of the service as the priests conducted the ceremony
    e. no singing throughout the entire ceremony

    Answer: b

12. The style of chant known as "Gregorian" originated as __________.
    a. a body of chant composed by Pope Gregory I
    b. a synthesis of Roman and Frankish chant styles
    c. a synthesis of Ambrosian and Old Roman chant styles
    d. Byzantine chant
    e. an attempt to return to Jewish practices

    Answer: b

13. The earliest notated chantbooks date from __________.
    a. the second century
    b. the fourth century
    c. the seventh century
    d. the ninth century
    e. the tenth century

    Answer: d

14. The first use of a line to indicate pitch level helped the singer to locate __________.
    a. the final of the chant
    b. the tenor of the chant
    c. the location of the semitone
    d. the proper hexachord
    e. the lowest pitch of the chant

    Answer: c

15. Which of the following is *not* an innovation by Guido of Arezzo?
    a. solmization
    b. staff lines
    c. letter names for the lines of the staff
    d. hexachord theory
    e. modal theory

    Answer: e

16. Solesmes notation was created for __________.
    a. singers of the Schola Cantorum
    b. Charlemagne's music teachers
    c. Byzantine basilicas
    d. readers of the *Musica Enchiriadis*
    e. official chant books in the twentieth century

    Answer: e

17. Hexachords can begin on which pitches?
    a. C, F, G
    b. C, D, E, F
    c. D, E, F, G
    d. only C
    e. A, B, C

    Answer: a

18. *Musica humana* was defined as __________.
    a. secular music
    b. music made by human beings rather than the spheres
    c. unheard harmony of the human body
    d. songs sung by God to His followers
    e. psalms, hymns, and recitations

    Answer: c

19. The definition of *authentic* in modal theory is __________.
    a. modes derived from Greek modes
    b. modes in which the melody ranges from a note below the final to approximately an octave above it
    c. modes in which the melody ranges from a fifth below the final to approximately a fourth or a fifth above it
    d. modes that can be sung on a single hexachord
    e. modes used by the Schola Cantorum

    Answer: b

20. The use of Greek names for church modes comes from __________.
    a. reorganization of the modal system based on research on the Greek modes

b. a misreading of Greek modal theory
c. the church modes' origins in Ancient Greek musical practice
d. the use of Greek as the language of learning in the Middle Ages
e. an attempt to make church music appealing to pagans in northern Europe

Answer: b

## SHORT-ESSAY QUESTIONS

1. Discuss the theoretical foundations of the eight church modes.
2. Trace the development of notation, citing sources of innovation and approximate dates.
3. Describe the relationship of Gregorian chant to other chant traditions.
4. Discuss the ways in which Greek music theory influenced medieval music theory.

## TERMS FOR IDENTIFICATION

psalms
cantillation
rite
church calendar
Ambrosian chant
Schola Cantorum
Gregorian chant
Old Roman chant
oral tradition
notation
neume
diastematic
heighted
Guido
clef
staff
Solesmes notation
liturgy
centonitization
quadrivium
trivium
musica mundana
musica humana
musica instrumentalis
church modes
final
authentic
plagal
tenor
reciting tone
hexachord
*gamma-ut*
gamut
solmization
mutation
Guidonian hand

# CHAPTER 3 Roman Liturgy and Chant

I. The Roman Liturgy
   A. Purpose
      1. Educate new converts
      2. Reinforce lessons
      3. The church's teachings were the path to salvation.
      4. Music carried the words.
   B. Church calendar
      1. Stories from Christ's life cycle through the year.
      2. Feast days celebrate important events.
         a. Christmas (December 25) marks Christ's birth.
         b. Easter, the Sunday after the first full moon of spring, celebrates Christ's resurrection.
         c. Commemoration of saints (exemplary Christians considered models of faith)
      3. Preparatory seasons
         a. Advent begins four Sundays before Christmas.
         b. Lent starts on Ash Wednesday, forty-six days before Easter.

II. Mass
   A. The Mass is the most important service in the Roman church (see **HWM Figure 3.2**).
      1. The central ritual is a symbolic reenactment of Christ's Last Supper with his disciples (see **HWM Figure 3.1**).
      2. Other ritual actions include Bible readings, prayers, and psalm-singing.
      3. In monasteries, convents, and major churches, Mass is performed daily.
      4. In all churches, Mass occurs on Sunday.
   B. In the first millennium, congregants were supposed to feel awe in Mass.
      1. Church buildings were often the tallest buildings in a town.
      2. Artwork such as sculptures, tapestries, and paintings depicted Christian teachings.
      3. Priests dressed in colorful clothing.
      4. Bibles, crosses, and ritual chalices were decorated with gold and jewels.
   C. Texts of the Mass (see **HWM Figure 3.2**)
      1. Proper
         a. Parts of the Mass whose words vary depending on the day in the church calendar are called "proper."
         b. The musical parts are known by their function: Introit, Gradual, Alleluia, Offertory, Communion.
      2. Ordinary
         a. Parts of the Mass with invariable words (but many possible melodies) are called "ordinary."
         b. The musical parts are known by their first words: Kyrie, Gloria, Credo, Sanctus, Agnus Dei.
         c. Most musical settings of the Mass after the fourteenth century set only the Ordinary texts.
   D. Parts of the Mass (see **HWM Figure 3.2** and **NAWM 3)**
      1. Introductory section
         a. Introit: an entrance with music
         b. Kyrie, a threefold musical invocation of the Greek words *Kyrie eleison* and *Christe eleison* (Lord have mercy, Christ have mercy), derived from Byzantine practices.
         c. Gloria (Greater Doxology) is a formula of praise to God and plea for mercy.

2. Liturgy of the Word
   a. Bible readings and church teachings
   b. Florid chants, based on psalm texts, follow the readings.
   c. The Gradual
      (1) From *gradus*, stair-step, where it was sung
      (2) Replaced by another Alleluia on some days during the Easter season
   d. Alleluia
      (1) From the Hebrew word *Halleluja* ("praise God")
      (2) Replaced by the tract, a more somber chant, during Lent
   e. Sequence sung by the choir after the Alleluia on major feast days
   f. An optional sermon closes the Liturgy of the Word on most days.
   g. On Sundays and feast days, the Credo, a statement of beliefs, comes after the sermon.
3. Liturgy of the Eucharist (Reenactment of the Last Supper)
   a. The Offertory
      (1) Sung by the choir as the priest prepares bread and wine for communion
      (2) A florid chant on a psalm text
      (3) Followed by spoken prayers and the Secret, a prayer read in silence by the priest
   b. The Sanctus (Holy, Holy, Holy)
      (1) Preceded by the Preface, a dialogue between the priest and choir
      (2) The text begins with the angelic chorus of praise from Isaiah 6:3.
      (3) The priest then speaks the Canon, which includes the consecration of the bread and wine.
      (4) The priest sings the Lord's Prayer.
   c. The Agnus Dei (Lamb of God)
      (1) Sung by the choir
      (2) Adapted from a litany
      (3) The priest takes communion on behalf of all assembled (instead of sharing it, as was the custom earlier and again today).
   d. The Communion
      (1) Sung by the choir after the priest takes communion
      (2) The text is based on a psalm.
      (3) The priest intones the Postcommunion prayer.
   e. Ite, missa est (dismissal)
      (1) The priest chants the dismissal.
      (2) The choir responds.
      (3) The name for the service comes from *missa* ("Mass" in English).
4. St. Basil (ca. 330–378) commented on the power of music to help listeners receive the message of the text (see **HWM Figure 3.2**).

III. The Office
   A. A series of eight services celebrated daily (see **HWM Figure 3.3**)
   B. Members of monasteries and convents observe both the Office and the Mass.
   C. The *Rule of St. Benedict* (ca. 530) codified practices for monastic life.
   D. The musical elements of the Office
      1. Several psalms
         a. A chant (antiphon) would be sung before and after the psalm.
         b. Over the course of a normal week, all 150 psalms would be sung at least once.
      2. Bible readings with musical responses called responsories
      3. Hymns
      4. Canticles (poems from the Bible, but not part of the Book of Psalms)
   E. Egeria (**HWM Source Reading,** page 27) described Matins.

IV. Liturgical Books
   A. Books were copied by hand in the Middle Ages.
   B. Books for the Mass
      1. Texts are in the *Missal*
      2. Chants are in the *Gradual*
   C. Books for the Office
      1. Texts are in the *Breviary*
      2. Chants are in the *Antiphoner*
   D. Modern books
      1. In the nineteenth century, the monks of Solesmes edited the official chant books, including the *Gradual* and *Antiphoner.*
      2. The *Liber Usualis* (Book of Common Use)
         a. The most frequently used chants were collected into the *Liber Usualis* by Solesmes monks.
         b. The chants of **NAWM 3** and **4** come from the *Liber Usualis.*

V. Characteristics of Chant
   A. Manner of performance
      1. Responsorial: soloist alternates with the choir or congregation
      2. Antiphonal: two halves of the choir alternate singing
      3. Direct: no alternation
      4. Some chant genres descend from these practices though their structure has changed.

a. Introit and Communion were originally antiphonal psalms.
b. The Gradual and Alleluia were originally responsorial.
c. By the late Middle Ages, all four were performed responsorially.

B. Text-setting
1. Syllabic: chants in which almost every syllable has one note
2. Neumatic (from *neume*): chants in which each syllable has from one to six notes
3. Melismatic: chants that include melismas (long melodic passages on a single syllable)
4. Some chants have different text-setting styles within the same chant.

C. Recitation formulas
1. Formulas that can be used with many different texts
2. Even fully composed melodies sometimes reflect an underlying formula.

D. Melody and declamation
1. In large medieval churches, sung words were heard more easily than spoken words.
2. Chants were not composed to depict emotions or images.
3. Accentuation of Latin sometimes influenced composition.
a. Often a melodic phrase had an arch shape that reflected Latin speech.
b. High notes sometimes brought out accented syllables.
c. A change of text-setting style sometimes highlighted important words (e.g., a change from syllabic to melismatic or vice-versa).

VI. Genres and Forms of Chant

A. Recitation formulas: simple formulas for declaiming prayers and Bible passages
1. The priest or an assistant sings the formulas, sometimes with a response from the choir or congregation.
2. The formulas are simple.
a. Most words are chanted on a single pitch (usually A or C).
b. Motives mark the ends of phrases and sentences.
3. The formulas pre-date modal theory and are not assigned to any mode.

B. Psalm tones (see **HWM Example 3.1** and **NAWM 4a**)
1. Slightly more complex than recitation formulas
2. Used for singing psalms in the Office
3. One for each of the eight church modes plus one extra formula (Tonus peregrinus, which has two reciting tones)
4. The structure can be adapted to any of the psalms.
a. Psalms have two-part verses.
b. Intonation: a rising motive for the beginning of the first verse of the psalm
c. Tenor: reciting pitch, used for the majority of the syllables
d. Mediant: cadence formula for the mid-point of a psalm verse
e. Termination: final cadence formula for the end of each psalm verse (variable)
f. Lesser Doxology (Gloria Patri)
(1) Text praising the Trinity (Father, Son, and Holy Spirit)
(2) Added to the end of the psalm and sung with the same formula
(3) This text adds a Christian context for the psalm, which is from Hebrew Scriptures.
g. The termination formula
(1) Used for the final phrase of each verse
(2) This is indicated in chant books, in **HWM Example 3.2,** and in **NAWM** with the letters EUOUAE, the vowels of the end of the Lesser Doxology ("et in secular sa*eculorum*, *amen*").
h. Canticles are sung to slightly more elaborate versions of the psalm tones.

C. Office antiphons
1. Added to psalms to reflect the church calendar
2. Texts
a. Biblical
b. Original
c. Refer to the event or person being commemorated that day
3. Relationship to psalm (see **HWM Example 3.2** or **NAWM 4a**)
a. The mode of the antiphon determined which psalm tone would be used for the psalm.
b. The opening motive of the antiphon determined which of the several possible terminations would be used (designated by the letters EUOUAE).
4. Performance
a. The cantor (the leader of the choir) sings the opening words of the antiphon (to the asterisk in modern chant books).
b. The choir sings the rest of the antiphon.
c. The two half-choirs alternate singing the psalm verses or half-verses.
d. The whole choir sings the reprise of the antiphon.

5. Style
    a. Mostly syllabic
    b. Melodies are simple yet fully composed and independent.
    c. The structure and accentuation of the text are clearly delineated.
    d. The alternation of antiphon and psalm contrasts the final (prominent in the antiphon) with the tenor (prominent in the psalm).

D. Office hymns (see **HWM Example 3.3** or **NAWM 4b**)
1. The choir sings a hymn in every Office.
2. Strophic text-setting: all stanzas sung to the same music
3. Melodies
    a. Move by seconds and thirds
    b. Arch-shaped contour, with a peak toward the middle

VI. Antiphonal Psalmody

A. In the Mass
1. In the early Mass, psalms with antiphons accompanied actions—e.g., the entrance (introit) and communion.
2. From the later Middle Ages to today, the Introit and Communion are performed responsorially instead.
    a. The cantor begins the antiphon.
    b. The choir completes the antiphon.
    c. Soloist(s) and choir alternate the psalm verse and Lesser Doxology.
    d. The choir sings the reprise of the antiphon.
3. Mass antiphons are more elaborate than Office antiphons (see **NAWM 3j**).

B. Responsorial psalmody in Office and Mass
1. Responsorial psalmody of the Office and Mass derive from early Christian practice.
    a. A soloist sang each psalm verse.
    b. The choir or congregation sang the response.
2. Because a soloist sang the verses, these chants are more melismatic and elaborate.
3. Office responsories
    a. Common elements include a respond, a verse, and full or partial repetition of the respond.
    b. Matins includes nine Bible readings, each followed by a Great Responsory in neumatic to melismatic style.
    c. Other Office services pair Bible readings with a Short Responsory in neumatic style.

C. Graduals (e.g., **HWM Example 2.2** and **NAWM 3d**, *Viderunt omnes*)
1. More melismatic than responsories
2. Very long melismas
3. The cantor begins the respond, which is completed by the choir.
4. One or more soloists sing the verse.
5. The choir joins on the last phrase.
6. The respond is not repeated.

D. Alleluia (see **HWM Example 3.5** or **NAWM 3e**)
1. The word "alleluia" is the respond.
2. Between the two repetitions of the "alleluia" is a psalm verse.
3. A long melisma, called a *jubilus*, extends the end of the final syllable of the last "alleluia."
4. Sometimes the end of the verse repeats all or part of the respond melody.
5. Performance
    a. Soloist sings the first part of the respond (to the asterisk).
    b. The choir repeats the respond (as indicated by *ij*).
    c. The choir sings the jubilus.
    d. The soloist sings the verse.
    e. The choir joins the soloist at the end of the verse (indicated by an asterisk).
    f. The soloist sings the first part of the respond.
    g. The choir joins in at the jubilus.
6. Despite its elaborate construction, the Alleluia is similar in style to other chants.
    a. Motion primarily by steps and thirds
    b. Gently arching contours
    c. Prominent pitches reinforce the sense of mode, in this case Mode 2.

E. Offertories (see **NAWM 3g**)
1. Today, offertories have been shortened to include only the respond.
2. In the Middle Ages, they were performed during the offering of bread and wine.
    a. Choral respond
    b. Two or three psalm verses set to ornate music and sung by a soloist
    c. Reiteration of the second half of the respond after each psalm verse

F. Tract (see **HWM Example 2.1**)
1. Several psalm verses with no responses (direct solo psalmody)
2. Each verse combines recitation with florid melismas.
3. Many melodic passages are common to different Tracts, indicating a tradition of oral composition based on formulas.

VIII. Chants of the Mass Ordinary
  A. Development
    1. Originally sung by the congregation to simple syllabic melodies
    2. The choir took over the singing of these chants after the congregation's participation was reduced.
    3. Starting in the ninth century, church musicians composed elaborate melodies for the church's trained singers to sing.
  B. Credo (**NAWM 3f**)
    1. Always set in syllabic style because of its long text
    2. Because it is a statement of faith, it was the last of the Ordinary chants to be assigned to the choir instead of the congregation.
    3. The priest begins the Credo and the choir completes it.
  C. Gloria (**NAWM 3c**)
    1. Most settings are neumatic.
    2. The priest begins the Gloria and the choir completes it.
  D. Sanctus (**NAWM 3h**)
    1. Repetitions in the text are often reflected in the music.
    2. The text begins with the word *sanctus* ("holy"), repeated three times.
    3. The second and third sections of the text end with "Hosanna in excelsis" ("Hosanna in the highest").
      a. When the music for the second and third sections are similar, the chant's form is ABB'.
      b. When only the music for the Hosanna is repeated, the chant's form is A BC DC.
    4. The text setting is usually neumatic.
  E. Agnus Dei (**NAWM 3i**)
    1. Like the Sanctus, the text setting is usually neumatic, and repetitions of text often inspire music composed to reflect repetitions.
    2. The text of the Agnus Dei sets a prayer three times, with the final repetition a slight variant.
    3. Possible settings of music: AAA, ABA, AB CB DB
  F. Kyrie (**NAWM 3b**)
    1. With few words and symmetrical construction, the text lends itself to many forms.
      a. Three statements each of "Kyrie eleison," "Christe eleison," and "Kyrie eleison."
      b. AAA BBB CCC' (as in **NAWM3b**)
      c. AAA BBB AAA'
      d. ABA CBC EFE'
    2. Usually performed antiphonally, between two half-choirs that alternate statements.
    3. The final "Kyrie" is often extended by adding a phrase and sung by both half-choirs together.

IX. Additions to the Authorized Chants
  A. Musicians continued to add to the repertoire even after standardization in the eighth and ninth centuries.
    1. When new feast days were added to the calendar, musicians created new chants or adapted old ones.
    2. New genres: tropes, sequences, and liturgical dramas
  B. Trope
    1. Expansion on an existing chant in order to increase its solemnity
    2. Adding new words and music before the chant and often between phrases
      a. The most common type of trope
      b. Added to Introits and Glorias
      c. The new words often explained or expanded on the original text (e.g., **NAWM 3a** and **NAWM 5**).
    3. Adding melody by extending a melisma or creating new ones
    4. Adding text (called *prosula* or "prose") to existing melismas
    5. Style was usually neumatic, sometimes borrowing motives from the original chant.
    6. Soloists usually sang the tropes.
    7. Trope composition flourished in the tenth and eleventh centuries, declined during the twelfth, and was banned in the sixteenth century by the Council of Trent (see **HWM Chapter 10**).
  C. Sequence (**NAWM 6,** *Victimae pascali laudes*)
    1. Development began in the ninth century.
    2. The name derives from an earlier practice called *sequentia,* meaning something that follows.
    3. Connection to the Alleluia
      a. Melodies may have originated as melismas that replaced the jubilus of the Alleluia, and some sequences draw melodic material from the Alleluia.
      b. One form of sequence was an extended melisma on "Alleluia."
      c. Scholars used to believe that the sequence originated as texts added to Alleluia melodies, but now they believe only previous sequence melodies received new texts.
    4. Notker Balbulus ("The Stammerer," ca. 840–914) is the most famous early writer of sequence texts (see **HWM Source Reading,** page 67).

5. Form
   a. Series of paired verses, except for the first and last, which are single
   b. Each new pair has a new syllable count and musical stanza.
   c. There is no standard number of stanzas.
   d. The resulting form is A BB CC . . . N
   e. By the twelfth century, many sequences (such as those by Adam of St. Victor, d. 1146) lacked the unpaired first and last phrases and stanza lengths were more even.
6. The mode is usually clear, with most phrases ending on the final.
7. The Council of Trent banned all but four sequences. Those not banned include *Victimae pascale laudes* (for Easter) and *Dies irae* (for the Requiem, or Mass for the Dead).

D. Liturgical drama
1. Although not part of the liturgy, plays that were linked to the liturgy are called liturgical dramas.
2. Tropes in dialogue form introduced important feast days.
   a. *Quem queritis in sepulchro* ("Whom do you seek in the tomb"), which precedes the Easter Introit, portrays an angel and the three Marys who went to Jesus' tomb.
   b. *Quem queritis in presepe* ("Whom do you seek in the manger") (**NAWM 6**) precedes the Christmas Introit and is in the same mode.
   c. Liturgical dramas preceding Introits may have been performed outside the church (see commentary to **NAWM 6**).
3. Other plays depict Biblical events, such as *The Slaughter of the Innocents.*
4. All parts were usually sung by male clergy, even the women's roles.

X. Hildegard of Bingen (1098–1179)

A. Women were excluded from religious music-making everywhere but in convents.

B. Convent life
1. As in monasteries, convent life revolved around the eight daily Office services and Mass.
2. Women could perform all duties of their convent except officiating at Mass.
3. Unlike women in other spheres of society, nuns had access to intellectual pursuits, including reading Latin and composing music.

C. Hildegard's accomplishments (see **HWM Figure 3.6** and **biography,** page 69)
1. She was prioress and abbess of her own convent (near Bingen).
2. She had visions and became famous for her prophecies.
3. She preached throughout Germany.
4. She wrote prose works on science and healing.
5. *Scivias* ("Know the Ways," 1141–51), is a book about her visions.

D. Hildegard's music
1. By the 1140s, she had begun to set her poems to music.
2. Two manuscripts, organized in a liturgical cycle, preserve her songs.
3. The style varies from syllabic hymns and sequences to highly melismatic responsories.
4. Her style includes wide ranges, exceeding an octave by a fourth or fifth.
5. A few distinctive melodic figures appear in many of her works.
   a. A rising fifth followed by a stepwise descent
   b. Circling around a cadential note
   c. Successive leaps spanning an octave or more
6. Some words or syllables received special treatment to bring out the meaning (e.g., **NAWM 6,** "oculus tuus" and "ad Patrem").
7. She claimed that her songs were divinely inspired, a claim that buttressed her credibility in a time when nuns were restricted to activities within their convent.
8. Her writings were published in the nineteenth century.
9. Her music was rediscovered in the late twentieth century.
10. She is now the best-known and most recorded composer of sacred monophony.

E. *Ordo virtutum* (The Virtues, ca. 1151)
1. Hildegard's most extended musical work
2. A sacred music drama comprising eighty-two songs
3. The text is a morality play, with allegorical and human characters.
   a. Three souls: Happy, Unhappy, and Penitent
   b. Prophets
   c. Virtues
   d. The Devil (the only spoken part)
4. The final chorus of the Virtues (**NAWM 7**)
   a. Functions as an epilogue
   b. Incorporates Hildegard's characteristic melodic motives, such as a rising fifth from e–b'
   c. The play ends with a prose speech by Christ followed by a short prayer.

XI. The continuing presence of chant
  A. From the ninth through the thirteenth centuries, polyphonic music was based on chant.
  B. Chant was reformed twice: once in the late sixteenth and early seventeenth centuries, and again in the late nineteenth and early twentieth centuries.
  C. Until the Second Vatican Council (1962–65) chant continued to be the basis of Catholic worship.
  D. After the Second Vatican Council, chant was performed only in monasteries and concert halls.
  E. The Benedictine monks of Santo Domingo de Silos in Spain released a CD called "Chant," which was a best-selling CD in Europe and the United States in 1994.

## SUGGESTIONS FOR SUPPLEMENTARY READINGS/LISTENING/ACTIVITIES

There are many good sources for additional recorded examples of chant. One that indicates the mode for each track is "Gregorian Sampler," sung by The Monastic Choir of the Abbey of St. Peter, Solesmes (Paraclete Press, S.829, 1988). The complete proper chants of the Mass for the Easter season may be found on "The Chants of Easter," sung by the Gloriæ Dei Cantores (Paraclete Press, GDCD 015, 1994). For examples of chant devoted to saints, or for chants sung by women, The Choir of the Benedictine Nuns at the Abbey of Regina Laudis in Bethlehem, Connecticut, has released "Women in Chant" (Sounds True STA M004D, 1997). The first track of this CD demonstrates a call to worship using monastic bells. The first antiphon is paired with Psalm 109 *Dixit Dominus,* **NAWM 4a,** sung to a different psalm tone than the *NAWM* version.

Divide the class in half and sing **NAWM 4a** antiphonally, reading first from modern notation and then from chantbook notation. After the students have memorized the formula, have them sing a different psalm to the same formula.

Students may enjoy excerpts from "The Feast of Fools," the New Year's liturgy in which the lowest-ranked members of the church assume the principal roles in the singing of chant. The recording by the New London Consort (Editions de L'Oiseau-Lyre, 433 194-2) contains both serious and playful selections, such as the Gambler's Prayer and hymns to Bacchus.

Sequences by Notker Balbulus can be found on the Ensemble Gilles Binchois recording, "Musique et Poésie à Saint Gall: Séquences et tropes du IXe siècle" (Harmonia Mundi HMC 905239, 1997). The cover illustration for this CD shows Notker with a pen in one hand and a scraper (the medieval equivalent of an eraser) in the other.

Hildegard's *O Ecclesia* is an excellent example of her style of compositional technique as described in Chapter 3 of *HWM.* Sequentia's recording on "Voice of the Blood" (Deutsche Harmonia Mundi, 05472 77346 2, 1995) pits soloist against choir, making the double versicle structure easy to hear.

The complete *Ordo Virtutum* is available on CD, performed by Sequentia (Deutsche Harmonia Mundi, 05472 77394 2, 1998) and by Gothic Voices on "A Feather on the Breath of God" (Hyperion CDA 66039, 1984).

## OBJECTIVE QUESTIONS

1. The prescribed texts and rites that collectively constitute the religious services of the church are known as the __________.
   a. Eucharist
   b. Rule of St. Benedict
   c. liturgy
   d. Divine Office
   e. Mass

   Answer: c

2. Psalms are typically preceded and followed by chants called __________.
   a. Alleulias
   b. antiphons
   c. responsories
   d. psalm tones
   e. doxologies

   Answer: b

3. A(n) __________ chant is sung by a soloist in alternation with a choir.
   a. antiphonal
   b. direct
   c. responsorial
   d. melismatic
   e. proper

   Answer: c

4. The main sung parts of the Ordinary portion of the Mass are __________.
   a. Kyrie, Gloria, Alleluia, Credo, Greater Doxology
   b. Kyrie, Gloria, Credo, Sanctus, Agnus Dei

c. Kyrie, Alleluia, Gradual, Responsory
d. Kyrie, Gloria, Credo, Sanctus, Divine Office
e. Kyrie, Psalm Tone, Matins, Alleluia, Ite missa est

Answer: b

5. Which of these chants has a text that can be set as an ABA form?
   a. Credo
   b. Gloria
   c. Antiphon
   d. Kyrie
   e. Ite missa est

   Answer: d

6. Notker Balbulus is known for __________.
   a. codifying the sung parts of the Mass
   b. writing the rules that governed life in monasteries and convents
   c. writing dramas based on biblical events
   d. composing sequences
   e. instigating chant reform in the twentieth century

   Answer: d

7. Chants that have sections with many notes per syllable are called __________.
   a. melismatic
   b. modal
   c. syllabic
   d. neumatic
   e. tropes

   Answer: a

8. Psalm tones consist of __________.
   a. D, E, F, and G
   b. the pitches of the gamut
   c. chants for the Office
   d. antiphons and the Lesser Doxology
   e. intonation, tenor, mediant, and termination

   Answer: e

9. The Divine Office is __________.
   a. the headquarters for Gregorian chant regulation
   b. a system for notating chant
   c. a series of psalms and chants performed eight times per day
   d. the prescribed readings, chants and rituals for the entire church year
   e. the room of the Cathedral where the bishop prepares the bread and wine for communion

   Answer: c

10. The performance of most chants begins with __________.
    a. a prayer asking for just intonation
    b. an introduction on the organ
    c. all singers beginning at the beginning
    d. half the choir singing the first few words, followed by the other half on the next few words
    e. the priest or cantor singing the first few words

    Answer: e

11. Which of the following statements is true of the Proper of the Mass?
    a. The texts and music change according to the church calendar.
    b. The texts stay the same from day to day but the music differs.
    c. It had a stricter code of behavior than other parts of the liturgy.
    d. It is performed eight times per day.
    e. It can be performed only by men.

    Answer: a

12. In chantbooks, the letters EUOUAE indicate __________.
    a. instructions for instrumental performance
    b. the last vowels in the Lesser Doxology
    c. the method for singing the Greater Doxology
    d. the psalm tone to be used
    e. that the chant has been approved by the Council of Trent

    Answer: b

13. When sung, the sequence typically follows the __________.
    a. Alleluia
    b. Kyrie
    c. Divine Office
    d. Rule of St. Benedict
    e. psalm tone

    Answer: a

14. The definition of trope is __________.
    a. the vestment worn by the cantor
    b. the portion of chant sung by the cantor
    c. an addition of words, music, or both to an established chant
    d. the formula used by the cantor or priest for reciting the Bible readings for the day
    e. a passage that was probably descended from an oral tradition of improvising music according to set guidelines

    Answer: c

15. The *Rule of St. Benedict* was __________.
    a. the period during which St. Benedict was pope and codified chant
    b. the earliest staff line
    c. the prescribed practices for all Catholic worship
    d. the prescribed practices for Catholics in monasteries
    e. the law forbidding the use of the tritone

    Answer: d

16. Hymns were sung as part of __________.
    a. the Mass
    b. tropes
    c. the Divine Office
    d. the Liturgy of the Eucharist
    e. all worship services

    Answer: c

17. Which of these statements is true?
    a. Nuns were prohibited from singing or speaking during services.
    b. Nuns were permitted to speak but not to sing during services.
    c. Nuns were permitted to sing, but only during Mass.
    d. Nuns never heard or sang any music because they believed it could hurt their character.
    e. Nuns were required to sing the same music as monks in monasteries.

    Answer: e

18. The Council of Trent outlawed all but four __________.
    a. chant books
    b. psalm tones
    c. sequences
    d. terminations
    e. Tracts

    Answer: c

19. Some liturgical dramas originated as __________.
    a. nonliturgical dramas
    b. Greek musical theater
    c. psalm verses sung antiphonally
    d. sequences
    e. dialogues preceding introits

    Answer: e

20. Hildegard of Bingen is known for __________.
    a. composing both the words and music for chants and a liturgical drama
    b. writing a treatise on the Divine Office
    c. being put to death for her outlandish singing style
    d. creating a system of notation for use in convents
    e. teaching Notker Balbulus how to sing

    Answer: a

## SHORT-ESSAY QUESTIONS

1. Discuss the following chant [select an example from **NAWM 3** or use *Speciosus forma,* LU 400], explaining its mode, style of performance, melodic characteristics, and text-setting style.
2. Compare and contrast the Mass and the Divine Office, citing differences in performance and composition as appropriate. Use examples from *NAWM* to illustrate your points.
3. Discuss the methods for singing psalms, and the role that psalms played in the liturgy in both the Mass and the Office. Use examples from *NAWM* to illustrate your points.
4. Describe the ways in which composers expanded on the standard chant repertoire from the ninth century onward.

## TERMS FOR IDENTIFICATION

liturgy
Mass
Ordinary
Proper
Liturgy of the Word
Liturgy of the Eucharist
Divine Office
*Rule of St. Benedict*
Matins
Lauds
Vespers
neume
*Liber usualis*
responsorial
antiphonal
cantor
syllabic
neumatic
melismatic/melisma
recitation
psalm tone
intonation
tenor
mediant
termination
EUOUAE
Lesser Doxology
canticle
antiphon
responsory
hymn
psalmody
Introit
Kyrie
Gloria
Collect
Alleluia
Gradual
Sanctus
Communion
Agnus Dei
Ite, missa est
Tract
jubilus
trope
sequence
liturgical drama

# CHAPTER 4 Song and Dance Music in the Middle Ages

I. European Society, 800–1300
  A. Secular vs. sacred traditions
    1. Outside the church, few people could read music.
    2. Secular music was rarely written down.
  B. Successors to the Roman Empire
    1. The Byzantine Empire comprised Asia Minor and southeastern Europe.
    2. The Arab world was the strongest.
      a. Began to expand after the founding of Islam (around 610)
      b. Occupied a vast territory, from modern-day Pakistan to North Africa, and Spain.
    3. Western Europe, the weakest of the three, was influenced by the others.
      a. Charlemagne's coronation as emperor marked an assertion of continuity with the Roman past, but after the death of his son, Louis the Pious (r. 814–43), his kingdom was divided, and the only centralized kingdom in western Europe was in England.
      b. Western Europe learned about ancient Greek writing thanks to Byzantine copies.
    4. Arab contributions to western Europe's culture
      a. Transmitted knowledge of Greek philosophy and science, technology, and mathematics
      b. Arab rulers were patrons of the arts and education, inspiring Charlemagne to support intellectual and cultural life.
  C. Society in western Europe
    1. The economy was largely agricultural.
    2. Most people lived in rural areas.
    3. There were three broad classes (see **HWM Figure 4.2**).
      a. Nobility, including knights, controlled the land and fought wars.
      b. Clergy, including priests, monks, and nuns, were devoted to a religious life.
      c. Peasants, the majority of the population, worked the land and served the nobles.
    4. The growth of cities
      a. By 1300, several cities had populations over 100,000 (small by today's standards).
        (1) Paris had about 200,000 residents.
        (2) Venice, Milan, and Florence had about 100,000 each.
        (3) London had a population of about 70,000.
      b. Artisans in cities organized themselves into groups called *guilds* to regulate their crafts and protect their interests.
      c. Doctors, lawyers, merchants, and artisans formed the new middle class.
    5. Learning and the arts thrived.
      a. Schools
        (1) Cathedral schools were established throughout Europe from 1050–1300.
        (2) After 1200, independent schools for laymen spread as well.
        (3) Universities were founded in Bologna, Paris, Oxford, and other cities.
      b. Achievements
        (1) Works of Aristotle and other writers were translated from Greek and Arabic into Latin (the language of scholarship).
        (2) Developments in science and philosophy

(3) Poems in Latin and vernacular languages, many of which were sung, diverged from ancient models.

II. Latin and Vernacular Song
   A. Songs in Latin
      1. Versus (pl. *versus*)
         a. Sacred song, sometimes attached to the liturgy
         b. Rhymed poetry, usually with a regular pattern of accents
         c. Monophonic versus appeared in Aquitaine in southwestern France in the eleventh century.
         d. The music was newly composed, not adapted from chant.
      2. Conductus (pl. *conductus*)
         a. Similar to versus, with original music and rhymed, rhythmical texts in Latin
         b. Originated in the twelfth century
         c. Original function was to "conduct" a celebrant or a liturgical book from one location to another during the liturgy
         d. The term was later used for any serious Latin song with a rhymed, rhythmical text regardless of the subject.
      3. Goliard songs
         a. Composed in the late tenth through thirteenth centuries by wandering students and clerics
         b. Texts are in Latin.
         c. Topics include religious themes, satire, and celebration of earthly pleasures such as eating and drinking.
   B. Songs in vernacular languages (i.e., languages other than Latin in Europe)
      1. There are almost no descriptions or examples of the music of the peasants.
      2. Only a few street cries and folk songs have been preserved, through their quotation in music intended for educated audiences.
      3. Epic poems in vernacular languages have been written down, but not the music.
         a. *Chanson de geste* ("song of deeds")
            (1) Epics in northern French vernacular
            (2) Topics celebrated deeds of national heroes
            (3) The most famous chanson de geste is *Song of Roland* (ca. 1100), about a battle between Charlemagne's army and Muslims in Spain.
         b. Epics from other countries include England's *Beowulf* (eighth century), the Norse eddas (ca. 800–1200), and the German *Song of the Nibelungs* (thirteenth century).
   C. Professional musicians
      1. Few records survivc to document the professional musicians of the Middle Ages.
      2. Bards in Celtic lands sang epics at banquets, accompanying themselves on harp or fiddle.
      3. Jongleurs (see **HWM Figure 4.3**)
         a. Traveling entertainers who told stories and performed tricks in addition to performing music
         b. The word *jongleur* comes from the same root as the English word "juggler."
      4. Minstrel (from the Latin *minister*, "servant")
         a. By the thirteenth century, the term meant any specialized musician.
         b. Many were highly paid, unlike the jongleurs.
         c. They were on the payrolls of courts and cities.
         d. They came from many economic backgrounds.

III. Troubadour and Trouvère Song
   A. French aristocrats cultivated courtly song by poet-composers who composed in two vernacular languages (see **HWM Figure 4.4**).
      1. In the southern region, the language was Occitan and the poet-composers were called troubadours.
      2. In the northern region, the language was Old French and the poet-composers were called trouvères.
      3. The two languages were also named for their words for "yes."
         a. Occitan was *langue d'oc*, the language of "oc" for yes.
         b. Old French was *langue d'oïl*, in which "yes" was oïl (pronounced like present-day oui).
      4. The root words *trobar* and *trover* meant "to compose a song," and later "to invent" or "to find."
      5. Female troubadours were called *trobairitz*
   B. Troubadours and trouvères came from many backgrounds.
      1. Their biographies, called *vidas,* were written down, and many vidas survive.
      2. Some were members of the nobility, e.g., Guillaume IX, duke of Aquitaine (1071–1126) and the Countess of Dia (fl. late twelfth and early thirteenth centuries).
      3. Some were born to servants at court, e.g., Bernart de Ventadorn (ca. 1130–ca. 1200), shown in **HWM Figure 4.5.**

4. Others were accepted into aristocratic circles because of their accomplishments and demeanor, despite their middle-class roots.
5. Some performed their own music; others entrusted their music to a jongleur or minstrel.

C. Surviving songs
1. The songs were preserved in *chansonniers* (songbooks).
2. Troubadour songs
   a. About 2,600 survive.
   b. Only one-tenth survive with melodies.
3. Trouvère songs
   a. About 2,100 survive.
   b. Two-thirds survive with melodies.
4. When songs were copied into more than one chansonnier, there are differences, indicating oral transmission before the songs were written down.

D. The central theme was *fin' amors* (Occitan) or *fine amour (*French)
1. Translated as "courtly love" or, more precisely, "refined love"
2. Idealized love that refined the lover
3. Love from a distance, with respect and humility
4. The object was a real woman, usually another man's wife.
5. The woman was unattainable, making unrewarded yearning a major theme (e.g., **NAWM 8,** *Can vei la lauzeta mover* by Bernart de Ventadorn).
6. When women wrote poetry, they focused on the woman's point of view (e.g., **HWM Example 4.1** and **NAWM 9,** *A chantar* by the Countess of Dia).
7. The artistry of the poems demonstrates the poets' refinement and eloquence.

E. Melodies
1. Strophic, with every stanza being set to the same melody
2. Text-setting is syllabic with occasional groups of notes, especially on a line's penultimate syllable.
3. Range is narrow, within a ninth.
4. Modal theory was not part of the composers' thinking, yet most melodies fit the theory, with the first and seventh modes being most common.
5. Melodies move primarily stepwise.
6. Form
   a. Most troubadour melodies have new music for each phrase.
   b. AAB form is common in trouvère melodies and was used by some troubadours as well (e.g., *A chantar*).
7. The form of *A chantar* incorporates musical rhyme.
   a. Seven-line stanzas
   b. The form is AAB, with each section ending with the same melody (a musical rhyme).
   c. At the level of the phrase, the form is ab ab cdb, with "b" being the musical rhyme.
8. Rhythm is usually not notated.
   a. Some scholars believe melodies were sung with each syllable receiving the same duration.
   b. Other scholars believe the songs were sung with a meter corresponding to the meter of the poetry.
   c. Dance songs were most likely sung metrically, and elevated love songs may have been sung more freely, but modern editions will vary because of competing views.

F. Musical plays
1. Musical plays were built around narrative pastoral songs.
2. The most famous was *Jeu de Robin et de Marion* (The Play of Robin and Marion, ca. 1284) by Adam de la Halle (**NAWM 10**).
3. Adam de la Halle (ca. 1240–1288)
   a. The last great trouvère
   b. Depicted in **HWM Figure 4.6**
   c. His complete works were collected into a manuscript, which indicates he was held in high esteem.
4. *Robin m'aime* (**NAWM 10**) is a rondeau.
   a. Dance song with a refrain
   b. Form is AbaabAB.
      (1) Capital letters indicate the refrain (same music, same text).
      (2) Lower case letters indicate new text for A or B.
   c. Another setting is polyphonic and notated in precise durations, indicating a metrical rhythm.

G. Rise and fall of troubadour tradition
1. Its origins include three possible genres.
   a. Arabic songs
   b. Versus
   c. Secular Latin songs
2. Albigensian Crusade, declared by Pope Innocent III in 1208, destroyed the culture and courts of southern France.
3. Troubadours dispersed, spreading their influence to neighboring lands.

IV. Song in Other Lands
  A. England
    1. French was the language of kings and nobility in England because of the Norman Conquest of 1066.
    2. The lower classes spoke Middle English.
    3. A few songs in Middle English survive with melodies.
    4. Most surviving poems in Middle English were probably meant to be sung.
  B. Minnesinger
    1. Knightly poet-musicians who wrote in Middle High German
    2. They were modeled on the troubadours.
    3. Flourished between the twelfth and fourteenth centuries
    4. They sang Minnelieder (love songs) emphasizing faithfulness, duty, and service in the knightly tradition.
    5. The songs are strophic, with the bar form (AAB) the most common.
      a. A
        (1) Called *Stollen*
        (2) Each has the same poetic meter, rhyme scheme, and melody.
      b. B
        (1) Called *Abgesang*
        (2) Usually longer than the *Stollen*
        (3) The ending may quote part or all of the ending of the *Stollen.*
    6. Crusade songs were a new genre with the Minnesingers.
      a. Songs about experiences of crusaders who renounced worldly comforts to travel on Crusades.
      b. Example: **NAWM 11,** by Walther von der Vogelweide (ca. 1170–1230), depicted in **HWM Figure 4.7**.
  C. Cantigas de Santa Maria
    1. Over four hundred songs in Gallican-Portuguese in honor of the Virgin Mary
    2. King Alfonso el Sabio (The Wise) of Castile and Léon in northwest Spain directed the compilation of these songs in about 1270–1290.
    3. Four beautifully illuminated manuscripts preserve these songs.
    4. Most songs described miracles performed by the Virgin.
      a. Mary had been venerated since the twelfth century.
      b. **NAWM 12** describes how Mary caused a piece of stolen meat to jump about, revealing where it was hidden.
    5. The songs all have refrains.
      a. In performance, a group singing the refrains could have alternated with a soloist singing the verses.
      b. Songs with refrains were often associated with dancing, as shown in some of the illustrations in the Cantigas manuscripts.

V. Medieval Instruments
  A. Illustrated manuscripts often depicted instruments, although the notated music's single melodic line did not offer any indication of instrumental participation.
  B. Europeans adapted instruments brought from the Byzantine Empire or from the Arabs in North Africa and Spain.
  C. String instruments as depicted in **HWM Figure 4.8** (left to right)
    1. Vielle (fiddle)
      a. The principle medieval bowed instrument
      b. Predecessor of the Renaissance viol and modern violin
      c. Five strings tuned in fourths and fifths, with one or more used as a drone
    2. Hurdy-gurdy
      a. Three-stringed vielle played mechanically with a hand-crank
      b. The player depresses levers to change pitches on the melody string.
      c. The other two strings are drones.
    3. Harp in the English style
    4. Psaltery
      a. The remote ancestor of the harpsichord and piano
      b. Strings are attached to a frame over a wooden sounding board.
      c. The player plucks the strings.
  D. Wind and percussion instruments
    1. Flute (depicted in **HWM Figure 4.9**)
      a. Transverse flute, similar to the modern flute
      b. Made from wood or ivory
      c. No keys, only holes
    2. Shawm, a double-reed instrument similar to the oboe
    3. Medieval trumpet
      a. Straight
      b. No valves, so it could play only pitches of the harmonic series
    4. Bagpipe
      a. The universal folk instrument
      b. The pipes and chanter are reed instruments.
      c. The player inflates a bag, which forces air through the chanter and drone pipes.

5. Bells were used in church and as signals.

E. Organs
1. Monastic churches had started installing organs by ca. 1100.
2. Organs were common in cathedrals by 1300.
3. Portative organ
   a. Small enough to be carried with a strap around the neck
   b. One set of pipes
   c. The right hand played the keys while the left worked the bellows.
4. Positive organ
   a. Placed (*positum*) on a table
   b. An assistant pumped the bellows as the musician played.

VI. Dance Music

A. Songs for dancing
1. Only about two dozen melodies survive.
2. The carole (see **HWM Source Reading,** page 85)
   a. The most popular dance in France from the twelfth through the fourteenth centuries
   b. One or more of the dancers sang the song as the others danced in a circle.
   c. Instrumentalists also participated.

B. Instrumental music for dancing
1. About fifty dance tunes survive from the thirteenth and fourteenth centuries.
   a. Most are notated as monophonic pieces, but several players could participate.
   b. Some are set in polyphony for performance on a keyboard instrument.
   c. These tunes are the earliest surviving notated instrumental music.
   d. Features include steady beat, clear meter, repeated sections, and predictable phrasing.
2. Estampie
   a. The most common medieval instrumental dance
   b. Several sections, each played twice but with different endings
      (1) The first ending was open (*ouvert*), or incomplete
      (2) The second ending was closed (*clos*), or complete.
      (3) The same open and closed endings were usually used for all the sections.
   c. Triple meter
   d. Estampies from *Le Manuscrit du roi* (The Manuscript of the King)
      (1) This chansonnier includes eight "royal estampies."
      (2) The fourth of these is **NAWM 13.**
3. Istampita
   a. The fourteenth-century Italian relative of the estampie
   b. The same form, with repeating sections, but the sections are longer
   c. Meter is duple or compound.

## SUGGESTIONS FOR FURTHER READING/LISTENING/ACTIVITIES

Students may already know the story of Abelard, who was castrated as punishment for his affair with a student. Some of his songs survive, including some planctus (laments) that have been issued on "Monastic Song: Twelfth-Century Monophonic Chant," performed by Theatre of Voices (Harmonia Mundi France, HMU 907209, 1998).

Recordings of monophonic versus and conductus can be found on "Nova Cantica: Latin Songs of the High Middle Ages" (Harmonia Mundi, D-7800, 1990).

For lyrics by the goliards, see *Love Lyrics from the Carmina Burana,* edited and translated by P.G. Walsh (Chapel Hill: University of North Carolina Press, 1993). Many of the songs have been recorded on "Carmina Burana," by The Boston Camerata (Erato 0630-14987-2, 1996), including *O Fortuna*, the lyrics of which are well known from Carl Orff's setting.

Bring a published facsimile of a chansonnier to class and point out the similarity of notation for chant and secular song. Note that all of the sources for secular song were written long after most of the composers were dead, and there are numerous variations among these handwritten sources. Depending on the manuscript, you may also be able to note places where the music was never written in, places where the manuscript was damaged, the names of composers written in margins, and so on, showing how uneven and incomplete the transmission of this repertoire has been.

Additional examples of secular song from France can be found in *Songs of the Troubadours and Trouvères,* edited by Samuel Rosenberg, Margaret Switten, and Gérard Le Vot (New York: Garland, 1998) and the accompanying compact disc. Pages 98–9 of the anthology give the complete texts for all the stanzas of Beatriz de Dia's *A chantar* (**NAWM 9**), and page 99 shows a photographic facsimile of the source manuscript.

**NAWM 8,** *Can vei la lauzeta mover*, and **NAWM 9,** *A chantar*, are two of the most frequently performed songs of the troubadour repertoire. Have students listen to two performances and compare the interpretations of the performers. Note differences in instrumentation, rhythm, and expression. "Montségur: La tragédie cathare" by La Nef (Dorian D116252, 1996) and "Troubadours" by the Clemencic Consort (Harmonia Mundi S.A. HMC 90396) contain both songs.

For additional information on the music of the troubadours, including performance practice, see Elizabeth Aubrey, *Music of the Troubadours (*Bloomington: Indiana University Press, 1996).

Many recordings of this repertoire feature several instruments accompanying the voice. Examples of trouvère songs sung to the accompaniment of a single instrument can be found on "Chansons de Trouvères" (Harmonia Mundi France 907184, 1996).

Sequentia's "Trouvères" (Deutsche Harmonia Mundi 77155-2-RC, 1984) contains three-voice songs by Adam de la Halle; *Belle Doette,* a well-known *chanson de toile;* works by Petrus de Cruce (see **HWM Chapter 5**); and several estampies. For other rondeaux by Adam de la Halle, see "La Chambre des Dames: Chansons et Polyphonies de Trouvères" (Diabolus in Musica D2604, 1997).

The complete *Jeu de Robin et Marion* has been recorded by the Schola Cantorum Basiliensis (Focus 913, 1993).

Some songs in English do survive, though most are sacred. Students may already be familiar with *Ther is no rose of swych vertu,* recorded by Anonymous 4 on "On Yoolis Night" (Harmonia Mundi HMU 907099, 1993). Other songs are available on "Sumer is icumen in: Chants Médiévaux anglais" (Harmonia Mundi France HMC 901154, 1985), sung by the Hilliard Ensemble, and "Miri it is" (Chandos 9396, 1995), performed by the Dufay Collective.

For additional information on Minnesang, see James V. McMahon, *The Music of Early Minnesang* (Columbia, South Carolina: Camden House, 1990). Recorded examples of songs by Oswald von Wolkenstein can be found on "Lieder," sung by Sequentia (Deutsche Harmonia Mundi 05472-77302-2, 1993).

Bring a map of the routes used by crusaders and pilgrims to show how musical styles could be transmitted across large geographical areas.

Medieval Spain was home to a confluence of Jewish, Islamic, and Christian cultures, giving rise to a theory that secular music in Christian Europe is the descendent of Arabic traditions passed on via Crusades and pilgrimages. The two-CD set "Iberian Garden," performed by Altramar (Dorian DIS 80151, 1997 and DIS-80158, 1998) juxtaposes examples of cantigas against Hebrew and Arabic music from the Middle Ages. Philip Pickett's New London Consort places the cantigas within the context of the pilgrimage to Santiago on "The Pilgrimage to Santiago" (Editions de L'Oiseau-Lyre 433 148-2, 1991).

For recorded demonstrations of musical instruments and an interesting interpretation of *Kalenda maya* (available in HAM), play excerpts from "The Instruments of the Middle Ages and Renaissance" (Vanguard Classics, OVC 8093, OVC 8094, 1997).

Ensemble Alcatraz's recording "Danse Royale" (Elektra Nonesuch 9 79240-2, 1990) contains many lively performances of estampies.

## OBJECTIVE QUESTIONS

1. The aristocratic composer-poets of northern France were the __________.
   a. troubadours
   b. trouvères
   c. Meistersinger
   d. Minnesinger
   e. jongleurs

   Answer: b

2. The term *conductus* refers to __________.
   a. any serious Latin song with a rhymed, rhythmical text regardless of the subject
   b. a French song about an unattainable woman and the lengths a man will go to meet her
   c. a musical instrument used by the leader in circular dances
   d. the standards of behavior expected of noble men when approaching women
   e. instrumental music having paired stanzas with open and closed endings

   Answer: a

3. Love was a main topic of secular song among all but the __________.
   a. troubadours
   b. trouvères
   c. goliards
   d. Minnesinger
   e. all of the above sang about love

   Answer: e

4. Which of the following statements is true of the notation of secular song?
   a. It was never written down.
   b. Only pitch was notated precisely.
   c. Pitch and rhythm were notated precisely.
   d. Pitch, rhythm, and vocal inflections were notated precisely.
   e. Pitch, rhythm, and instrumentation were notated precisely.

   Answer: b

5. Secular song in Germany __________.
   a. was written in French, the language of the nobility because of the Norman Conquest
   b. was influenced by the music of the troubadours but was written in German
   c. was outlawed by the German bishop
   d. was written in Latin only
   e. was never written down

   Answer: b

6. The estampie and istampita were __________.
   a. stringed instruments
   b. wind instruments
   c. Spanish devotional songs
   d. dance forms
   e. types of organs

   Answer: d

7. "Courtly love" as expressed in song usually described __________.
   a. lovers who were indescribably happy with each other
   b. a man who loves an unattainable or unavailable woman
   c. a man and woman who played tennis
   d. a man who has filed suit against a woman
   e. none of the above

   Answer: b

8. The vielle was which type of string instrument?
   a. a five-stringed instrument played with a bow
   b. a three-stringed instrument played with a crank
   c. a harp in the English style
   d. a keyboard instrument that was the ancestor of the harpsichord
   e. a one-stringed instrument used for teaching the intervals

   Answer: a

9. The shawm was similar to what modern-day instrument?
   a. flute
   b. trumpet
   c. oboe
   d. violin
   e. accordian

   Answer: c

10. Which of these statements is true of percussion instruments in the Middle Ages?
    a. Percussion instruments were outlawed as vestiges of paganism.
    b. Bells and drums are commonly depicted in medieval art.
    c. There were no percussion instruments other than drums.
    d. There were no percussion instruments other than bells.
    e. Songbooks of the Middle Ages specified large groups of percussion instruments for many songs.

    Answer: b

11. Portative and positive refer to two types of __________.
    a. dance forms
    b. string instruments
    c. trumpets
    d. organs
    e. love lyrics

    Answer: d

12. *Chanson de Roland* is an example of a(n) __________.
    a. estampie
    b. troubadour song
    c. chanson de geste
    d. vida
    e. chansonnier

    Answer: c

13. The troubadours wrote and sang songs in which language?
    a. Latin
    b. Occitan (langue d'oc)
    c. Old French (langue d'oïl)
    d. Spanish
    e. Gallego-Portuguese

    Answer: b

14. The Cantigas de Santa Maria were written in which language?
    a. Latin
    b. Occitan (langue d'oc)
    c. Old French (langue d'oïl)
    d. Spanish
    e. Gallego-Portuguese

    Answer: e

15. Jongleurs were __________.
    a. traveling entertainers who juggled as well as sang
    b. vielle players hired for their virtuoso skills
    c. troubadours from noble backgrounds
    d. female troubadours
    e. students who sang secular songs in Latin

    Answer: a

16. Goliards were __________.
    a. traveling entertainers who juggled as well as sang
    b. vielle players hired for their virtuoso skills
    c. troubadours from noble backgrounds
    d. female troubadours
    e. students who sang secular songs in Latin

    Answer: e

17. Which statement is true of surviving examples of secular song?
    a. Only a few fragments survive.
    b. They were meticulously preserved by the kings of Spain, France, and Germany.
    c. A few dozen survive in a manuscript dedicated to the king of France.
    d. A few thousand texts survive, but only some have music.
    e. Thousands of texts survive, all with music.

    Answer: d

18. Bar form can be expressed as __________.
    a. AAB
    b. ABCDA
    c. AABCA
    d. AaABabA
    e. AbaabAB

    Answer: a

19. A chansonnier was __________.
    a. a singer who traveled from castle to castle
    b. an entertainer who juggled as well as sang
    c. a songwriter who specialized in love songs
    d. the northern French equivalent of a trobairitz
    e. a book of songs

    Answer: e

20. Adam de la Halle's *Jeu de Robin et Marion* is an example of a(n) __________.
    a. troubadour song
    b. crusade song
    c. carole
    d. musical play
    e. chanson de geste

    Answer: d

## SHORT-ESSAY QUESTIONS

1. Discuss the role of instruments in secular music in the tenth through the thirteen centuries. Discuss instruments, genres, and performance practices using examples you have studied in class.
2. Compare and contrast the troubadours, trouvères, and Minnesinger, citing examples in *NAWM.* Discuss the social, religious, and political factors that affected music as well as aspects of the music and poetry.
3. Trace the influences of the Church and religion on secular music from the tenth through the thirteenth centuries. In what ways did secular music borrow from religious music? In what ways did musicians' musical training impact secular music-making?
4. Describe the varied roles of women in secular music of the tenth through the thirteenth centuries, as composers, audience, and topic of song.

## TERMS FOR IDENTIFICATION

versus
conductus
goliard
vernacular
epic
chanson de geste
bard
jongleur
minstrel
troubadour
trouvère
chansonnier
Minnesinger
cantiga
vielle
hurdy-gurdy
transverse flute
shawm
portative organ
positive organ
carole
estampie
istampita
trobairitz

# CHAPTER 5 Polyphony through the Thirteenth Century

I. The church prospered during this period of economic growth for Europe.
   A. Popes strengthened their control.
   B. Donors funded new monasteries and convents.
   C. New religious orders were founded by St. Francis (Franciscans), St. Dominic (Dominicans), St. Clare, and others.
   D. Large church buildings were erected.
      1. Romanesque style in the eleventh and early twelfth centuries
         a. Round arches in the style of the Roman basilica
         b. Frescoes and sculptures decorated the buildings.
      2. Gothic style from the mid-twelfth century onward
         a. Tall, spacious buildings with soaring vaults
         b. Slender columns
         c. Large stained-glass windows
   E. Scholasticism sought to reconcile classical (Greek) philosophy with Christian doctrine.
      1. St. Anselm
      2. St. Thomas Aquinas
   F. Polyphony, in which voices sing together in independent parts, flourished.
      1. At first, polyphony merely decorated chant in performance, much as medieval art decorated manuscripts and cathedrals.
      2. Polyphonic pieces added extra grandeur to chants.
      3. Its function as commentary on a chant resembled the process of troping.
      4. Advances in notation made more elaborate genres possible.
      5. Precepts of later Western music were established with medieval polyphony.
         a. Counterpoint, the combination of multiple independent lines
         b. Harmony, the regulation of simultaneous sounds
         c. Notation
         d. Composition, distinct from performance

II. Early Organum
   A. Origins in performance
      1. Drone
         a. Singing or playing a melody against a sustained pitch
         b. The drone pitch may have been the modal final, and sometimes the fifth above as well, as they have been in European folk traditions.
      2. Doubling in parallel consonant intervals was probably common before it was explained in anonymous ninth-century treatises.
   B. Ninth-century organum (see **HWM Example 5.1** and **NAWM 14a–b**)
      1. Described in *Musica enchiriadis* and *Scolica enchiriadis*
      2. The term *organum*
         a. Two or more voices singing different notes in agreeable combinations
         b. Used for several styles of polyphony from the ninth through the thirteenth centuries
      3. Parallel organum
         a. Duplication of a chant melody (principal voice)
         b. An organal voice duplicates the chant melody in parallel motion a fifth below.

c. In medieval thought, fifths were considered perfect and beautiful consonances.
d. Either voice could be doubled at the octave (e.g., **HWM Example 5.1b**).
4. Mixed parallel and oblique organum
a. Adjustments were necessary to avoid tritones.
b. When the chant includes e, the organal voice may not move below c.
c. When the chant includes b, the organal voice may not move below g.
d. The organal voice instead remains on one note while the chant voice moves (oblique motion).
e. **HWM Example 5.2** and **NAWM 14c** combine oblique and parallel motion.
f. Cadences converge on the unison.
g. These adjustments to parallelism opened the door for more independent polyphony.

C. Eleventh-century polyphony
1. Guido of Arezzo described a range of choices in his *Micrologus* (ca. 1025–28), some of which could be written down instead of improvised.
2. The Winchester Troper (early eleventh century)
a. A manuscript from Winchester Cathedral in England
b. Wulfstan of Winchester (fl. 992–996), cantor at the cathedral, was the likely composer.
c. 174 organal voices for chant, composed rather than improvised
3. Free Organum (late eleventh century), **HWM Example 5.3, NAWM 15**
a. *Ad organum faciendum* (On Making Organum) is a set of instructions with examples.
b. Organal voice is now usually above the chant rather than below.
c. The two voices may cross.
d. Parallel, oblique, and contrary motion are allowed.
e. Consonances remain the unison, fourth, fifth, and octave.
f. Cadences
(1) Cadences on the unison (sometimes preceded by a third)
(a) e.g., **NAWM 15,** system 4 on c-e
(b) B-flat–G to A unison
(c) F–D to E unison
(2) Cadences on the octave (sometimes preceded by a sixth)
(a) C–E to unison D on *florebit*
(b) C–E to unison D at final cadence
g. Motion is note-against-note (one organal note for each chant note).
h. Sung by soloists in solo portions of the Mass and Office
i. Also sung in troped sections of the Mass Ordinary

III. Aquitainian Polyphony: The Early Twelfth Century
A. The main sources
1. Three manuscripts once held in the Abbey of St. Martial in Limoges, in Aquitaine, and copied in Aquitainian notation.
2. The Codex Calixtinus, prepared in central France and brought to the Cathedral of Santiago de Compostela in northwest Spain in 1173 (see **HWM Figure 5.2**).
3. The style is known as Aquitainian and sometimes St. Martial polyphony.
B. The repertoire
1. Settings of chant, including sequences, Benedicamus Domino melodies, and solo portions of responsorial chant
2. Most of the works are versus (see **HWM Chapter 4**).
C. Two styles coexisted (e.g., **NAWM 16** and **HWM Example 5.4**).
1. Discant
a. Both parts move at about the same rate.
b. One to three notes in the upper part for each note in the lower voice
2. Florid organum
a. The lower voice moves more slowly than the upper voice.
b. For each note in the lower voice the upper voice sings note groups of varying lengths.
c. The lower voice is now called *tenor* (from the Latin *tenere*, "to hold") because it "holds" the principal melody.
3. Both styles could be used in the same work
a. **HWM Example 5.4** Verse 2 is in florid organum.
(1) Melismas of three to fifteen notes in the upper part
(2) The penultimate syllable typically has a longer melisma.
b. **HWM Example 5.4** Verse 4 is in discant.
4. Notation
a. In score format (**HWM Figure 5.2**)
b. Both voices are written above the text.
c. Alignment of the voices suggests both voices sang the words.
5. Durations are not indicated, leaving many possibilities open.
a. The tenor proceeds at a steady pace, with

compare their texts and rhythmic features, and determine whether the motetus voice appears in more than one motet. Hendrik van der Werf's *Integrated Directory of Organa, Clausulae, and Motets of the Thirteenth Century* (Rochester, NY: self-published, 1989) lists clausulae by their source chant. For transcriptions of clausulae, see Rebecca A. Baltzer, ed., *Le Magnus Liber Organi de Notre-Dame de Paris, Vol. V, Les Clausules a Deux Voix du Manuscrit de Florence, Biblioteca Medicea-Laurenziana, Pluteus 29.1* (Monaco: Éditions de L'Oiseau-Lyre, 1994). The introductory essay (in English) discusses substitution on page xlvi.

*Ars cantus mensurabilis* is translated in James McKinnon, ed., *Source Readings in Music History, rev. ed., Vol. 1: The Early Christian Period and the Latin Middle Ages* (New York: W. W. Norton, 1998).

Additional examples of secular motets from the thirteenth century can be found on: Gothic Voices, "The Marriage of Heaven and Hell: Motets and Songs from Thirteenth-Century France" (Hyperion, CDA 66423, 1991); Anonymous 4, "Love's Illusions: Music from the Montpellier Codex" (Harmonia Mundi, HMU 907109, 1994); and Camerata Nova, "Codex Bamberg" (Stradivarius STR 33476, 1999). The latter includes examples of hockets, a genre made possible by Franconian notation but not discussed here. Instrumentalists may find the hocket *In seculum viellatoris* of interest because the title suggests it was composed for vielle or in the style of vielle music. For a modern transcription of this repertoire, see Gordon Anderson, *Compositions of the Bamberg Manuscript: Bamberg, Staatsbibliothek, Lit. 115 (olim Ed.IV, 6)* (Rome: American Institute of Musicology, 1977).

*Beata viscera* (not to be confused with the monophonic conductus of the same title by Pérotin) is one of the most frequently recorded of the Worcester Fragments pieces. It demonstrates the English qualities of parallel harmony and major tonality very clearly and will prepare students to hear the "Englishness" of later composers. It is also a good example of a conductus with caudae. It is available on "Worcester Fragments," sung by the Orlando Consort (Amon Ra CD-SAR 59, 1993) and "An English Ladymass," by Anonymous 4 (Harmonia Mundi HMU 907080, 1992). For a transcription, see *Polyphonic Music of the Fourteenth Century,* Volume 14 (Monaco: Editions de L'Oiseau-Lyre, 1956–1958) or *The Oxford Anthology of Music: Medieval Music,* edited by Thomas Marrocco and Nicholas Sandon (New York: Oxford University Press, 1977).

## OBJECTIVE QUESTIONS

1. The first description of polyphonic music is contained in _________.
   a. The Winchester Troper
   b. *Ad organum faciendum*
   c. *Musica enchiriadis*
   d. *Magnus Liber Organi*
   e. *Ars cantus mensurabilis*

   Answer: c

2. Which composer composed quadruplum, or organa for four voices?
   a. Léonin
   b. Pérotin
   c. Franco of Cologne
   d. Anonymous IV
   e. Petrus de Cruce

   Answer: b

3. The medieval motet began as an elaboration or troping of which genre?
   a. substitute clausulae
   b. florid organum
   c. sequence
   d. conductus
   e. Alleluia

   Answer: a

4. A new system of rhythmic notation based on relationships among the shapes of individual notes and their duration was described in the thirteenth century by _______.
   a. Guido of Arezzo
   b. Pérotin
   c. Franco of Cologne
   d. Johannes de Garlandia
   e. Anonymous IV

   Answer: c

5. The voice that holds the chant melody is called the _________.
   a. tenor
   b. cauda
   c. organal voice
   d. original voice
   e. trope

   Answer: a

6. Discant is the style of composition used to set the __________.
   a. troped sections of chant
   b. melismatic sections of solo portions of chant
   c. syllabic sections of solo portions of chant
   d. melismatic sections of choral portions of chant
   e. syllabic sections of choral portions of chant

   Answer: b

7. Which of the following is not a feature of the polyphonic conductus?
   a. The tenor voice came from Gregorian chant.
   b. The text was rhymed metrical poetry.
   c. A melisma called a cauda sometimes preceded or followed phrases.
   d. The tenor voice had the same rhythmic speed as the upper voices.
   e. It died out ca. 1250.

   Answer: a

8. The six rhythmic modes were indicated by __________.
   a. the rhythm of the syllables
   b. different note shapes for different durations
   c. meter signs at the beginnings of lines
   d. vertical lines between measures
   e. patterns of ligatures

   Answer: e

9. In a thirteenth-century motet, the second voice from the bottom is called the __________.
   a. duplum
   b. triplum
   c. alto
   d. countertenor
   e. tenor

   Answer: a

10. Organum in which all the voices sing in measured rhythm is called __________.
    a. copula
    b. organum duplum
    c. organum triplum
    d. discant
    e. versus

    Answer: d

11. The center for polyphonic composition in the thirteenth century was __________.
    a. Paris
    b. southwestern France
    c. Italy
    d. Germany
    e. Worcester, England

    Answer: a

12. The most outstanding feature of the Petronian motet is __________.
    a. long sections in free organum
    b. the use of texts that trope the chant source
    c. the use of texts by Petrarch
    d. the similarity of rhythm among all the voices
    e. a faster-moving triplum voice than in previous motet styles

    Answer: e

13. The writer who named two composers of the Notre Dame school was __________.
    a. Pérotin
    b. Anonymous IV
    c. Petrus de Cruce
    d. Franco of Cologne
    e. the same anonymous author who wrote *Musica enchiriadis*

    Answer: b

14. The *Magnus Liber Organi* was __________.
    a. a book of organum begun by Léonin and updated by Anonymous IV
    b. a book of organum begun by Anonymous IV and updated by Pérotin
    c. a book of organum begun by Léonin and updated by Pérotin
    d. a book of organum that accompanied the *Liber Usualis*
    e. a book of instructions on how to make organum

    Answer: c

15. The correct chronological order for sources of organum is __________.
    a. *Magnus Liber Organi, Ad organum faciendum, Musica enchiriadis*
    b. *Musica enchiriadis, Ad organum faciendum, Magnus Liber Organi*
    c. *Ad organum faciendum, Musica enchiriadis, Magnus Liber Organi*
    d. *Musica enchiriadis, Magnus Liber Organi, Ad organum faciendum*
    e. *Ad organum faciendum, Magnus Liber Organi, Musica enchiriadis*

    Answer: b

16. Polyphonic treatment was applied to __________.
    a. solo portions of the Proper and troped parts of the Ordinary of the Mass and Office
    b. solo portions of the Ordinary of the Mass and Office
    c. choral portions of the Proper of the Mass and Office
    d. choral portions of the Ordinary of the Mass and Office
    e. solo and choral portions of both the Ordinary and Proper of the Mass and Office

    Answer: a

17. By the twelfth century, cadences on an octave were typically preceded by __________.
    a. contrary motion from a tenth
    b. contrary motion from a sixth
    c. oblique motion
    d. parallel motion in octaves
    e. contrary motion from a fifth

    Answer: b

18. Which genre could have words in both French and Latin?
    a. organum triplum
    b. motet
    c. conductus
    d. rondellus
    e. cauda

    Answer: b

19. The Worcester fragments are __________.
    a. the earliest source of polyphonic music outside of France
    b. a collection of tropes to be used by solo singers
    c. sources of Latin-texted polyphony from the thirteenth century
    d. sources of English-texted polyphony from the thirteenth century
    e. sources of French-texted polyphony from the thirteenth century

    Answer: c

20. Which of these descriptions best characterizes English music in the thirteenth century?
    a. Strict adherence to early compositional rules allowing only perfect consonances
    b. Slavish imitation of Parisian polyphonic styles of the same era
    c. Improvisational quality, with little written down
    d. Through-composed works with little repetition and sparse textures
    e. Preference for voice-exchange and imperfect consonances

    Answer: e

## SHORT-ESSAY QUESTIONS

1. Explain the ways in which a chant's structure and style dictated the polyphonic treatment it could receive.
2. Compare and contrast the main features of the thirteenth-century motet and the polyphonic conductus.
3. Discuss the relationship between compositional style and developments in notation, naming composers and theorists.
4. Discuss the following example (use **NAWM 21a**) in terms of its compositional style, the texts, its use of modal rhythms (if any), and the treatment of the chant voice. During what time period might this example have been composed?

## TERMS FOR IDENTIFICATION

polyphony
organum
*Musica enchiriadis*
organal voice
principle voice
parallel organum
parallel motion, contrary motion, oblique motion
Winchester Troper
*Ad organum faciendum*
Aquitanian polyphony
versus
florid organum
organum duplum or organum purum
discant
Notre Dame polyphony
modal notation
rhythmic modes
clausula
triplum
quadruplum
conductus
caudae
motet
motetus
tenor (in florid organum, discant, and motet)
cantus firmus
Anonymous IV
Franco of Cologne
Franconian notation
*Ars cantus mensurabilis*
Petronian motet
Worcester fragments
voice-exchange
rondellus
rota

## CHAPTER 6

# French and Italian Music in the Fourteenth Century

I. European Society in the Fourteenth Century
  A. Conditions were more difficult for Europeans than in the thirteenth century.
    1. Cooler weather reduced agricultural production.
    2. Floods caused famines in northwestern Europe.
    3. The Black Death (bubonic and pneumonic plagues) killed a third of Europe's population from 1347–50.
      a. Victims died in agony within days of contracting the plague.
      b. Survivors often fled Europe's cities.
    4. Frequent wars, especially the Hundred Years' War (1337–1453) between France and England, strained the economy.
  B. A division of the Church, with one pope in Rome and one in Avignon (France) for most of the fourteenth century, led to criticism of the church.
    1. King Philip IV (the Fair) of France engineered the election of a French pope, who resided in Avignon rather than Rome.
    2. During the Great Schism of 1378–1417 there were two claimants to the papacy, one in Avignon and one in Rome.
    3. Clergy were often corrupt, which drew criticism.
  C. Science and secularism
    1. Philosophers such as William of Ockham (ca. 1285–1349) and his followers believed that knowledge of nature and of humanity should rest on experience of the senses.
    2. An emphasis on natural explanations rather than supernatural ones led to increasing secularization.
    3. New technologies, such as eyeglasses, mechanical clocks, and the magnetic compass, changed society's perceptions.
  D. The arts
    1. More naturalistic style in art (see **HWM Figure 6.1**)
    2. Increased literacy led to more literature in the vernacular.
      a. Dante Alighieri and Boccacio in Italian
      b. Geoffrey Chaucer in English
    3. In music, there was an increase in attention to secular song, though sacred music continued to be composed.
  E. The *Roman de Fauvel* (Story of Fauvel) captured the spirit of the turn of the century.
    1. Allegorical poem that satirizes corrupt politicians and church officials
    2. Fauvel is the central character.
      a. The name is an anagram for Flattery, Avarice, Villainy ("u" and "v" were interchangeable), Variété (fickleness), Envy, and Lâcheté (cowardice).
      b. Fauvel is a horse that rises to a powerful position, symbolizing a world turned upside down.
      c. He marries and produces offspring who destroy the world.
      d. One manuscript (**HWM Figure 6.2**) contains 169 pieces of music interpolated within the poem, including some of the first examples in the new style, the Ars Nova.

II. The Ars Nova in France
  A. Philippe de Vitry (1291–1361)

1. The term *ars nova* comes from the final words of a treatise attributed to de Vitry, written ca. 1320: "this completes the *Ars nova* of Magister Philippe de Vitry."
2. Poet, composer, church canon, and administrator for a duke, king and bishop
3. Aside from the treatise, he is named in another source as the "inventor of a new art" (Ars Nova).

B. Ars Nova innovations in the notation of rhythm (see **HWM Innovations,** pages 122–23)
1. Both duple and triple division of note values possible for the first time
2. Division of the semibreve into smaller note values called minims
3. Conservative writers (see **HWM Source Reading** on Jacques de Liège, page 121) criticized the new ways, especially "perfection brought low [and] imperfection is exalted," i.e., the use of duple division.
4. Noteshapes retained their value regardless of their context (unlike Franconian notation), making syncopation possible.
5. By the end of the century, mensurations signs indicated divisions of time and prolation.
   a. Time was indicated with a complete or incomplete circle.
   b. Prolation was indicated by the presence or absence of a dot.
   c. Imperfect time with imperfect prolation came down to us as the sign for 4/4 meter.
6. After a few additional modifications in the Renaissance, this system developed into the one we use today.

C. Isorhythm
1. Motets by Philippe de Vitry are among the earliest musical works to employ developments of the Ars Nova, including isorhythm.
2. The tenor is laid out in segments of identical rhythm.
   a. Thirteenth-century motets often employed short repeating patterns in the tenor.
   b. In the fourteenth century, the tenor pattern was longer and more complex.
   c. The slow pace of the tenor makes it less a melody and more of a foundational structure.
   d. The melody is called the color and may repeat, but not necessarily with the rhythm.
   e. The rhythmic pattern is called the talea.
3. **NAWM 24** *In arboris/Tuba sacre fidei/Virgo sum,* attributed to Vitry
   a. The tenor includes two statements of the color (**HWM Example 6.1**).
   b. The color statements include three repetitions of the talea.
   c. Red ink (coloration) marks a change of meter from duple to triple division of the long.
   d. The upper voices are isorhythmic during the duple sections of the tenor (**HWM Example 6.2**).
4. Hocket technique (**HWM Example 6.2**)
   a. Two voices alternating in rapid succession, each resting while the other sounds.
   b. The device was developed in the thirteenth century.
   c. In the fourteenth century, the technique often marks a repetition of the talea in the tenor.
   d. Pieces that use the technique exclusively are called hockets and could be performed by voices or instruments.
5. Harmonic practice
   a. Greater prominence of imperfect consonances
   b. Cadences required perfect consonances, but their resolution could be sustained (e.g., **HWM Example 6.2a,** measures 25–28).
   c. Parallel octaves and fifths continued to be used.

III. Guillaume de Machaut (ca. 1300–1377, see **biography,** page 127, and **HWM Figure 6.6**)

A. Biography
1. The leading composer of the French Ars Nova
2. Born in northeastern France, probably to a middle-class family
3. Educated as a cleric and took Holy Orders
4. Ca. 1323–1340, worked as secretary for John of Luxembourg, King of Bohemia, accompanying the king on his travels
5. Resided in Reims after 1340, with time to write poetry and music despite his position as canon of the cathedral there
6. Royal patrons supported him, including the kings of Navarre and France.
7. First composer to compile his complete works and to discuss his working method
   a. He paid for the preparation of several illuminated manuscripts of his works.
   b. He wrote his poems first, then the music.
   c. He was happiest when the music was sweet and pleasing.
8. He composed many major musical works and numerous narrative poems.

B. Motets
1. Twenty-three motets, most from early in his career
2. Twenty are isorhythmic, three of which use secular songs as tenors
3. Often include hockets
4. Four four-voice motets

C. *Messe de Notre Dame* (Mass of Our Lady)
1. Probably the earliest polyphonic setting of the Mass Ordinary to be composed by a single composer and conceived as a unit
   a. In the fourteenth century, anonymous composers in France, England, and Italy set individual movements polyphonically.
   b. A few cycles were assembled from individual movements.
2. Composed for the cathedral in Reims
   a. Performed at a Mass for the Virgin Mary celebrated every Saturday
   b. After Machaut's death, an oration for Machaut's soul was added to the service.
   c. It continued to be performed there until the fifteenth century.
3. Unifying devices
   a. Recurring motives
   b. Tonal focus on D in the first three movements and on F in the last three
   c. All six movements are for four voices, including a contratenor (against the tenor) that moves in the same range as the tenor.
4. Isorhythmic movements (**NAWM 25** and **HWM Example 6.3**)
   a. Kyrie, Sanctus, Agnus Dei, and Ite, missa est are isorhythmic.
   b. In the opening of the Christe section, the upper two voices are partly isorhythmic.
   c. Rhythmic repetition in the upper voices makes the recurring talea easier to hear.
5. Elements of Machaut's style in the Christe
   a. Sustained notes contrast with lively rhythms.
   b. Repeating figuration generates rhythmic activity (**HWM Example 6.3**).
6. Conductus style movements
   a. The Gloria and Credo are syllabic and largely homorhythmic.
   b. Sustained chords emphasize important words, e.g., *Jesu Christe* and *ex Maria Virgine*.

D. Monophonic songs in the trouvère tradition
1. Lais (similar in form to the sequence)
   a. Fifteen monophonic
   b. Four with polyphony
2. Virelais
   a. One of the three *formes fixes* (fixed forms)
   b. Refrain form with stanzas using new material as well as refrain music
   c. Typical form is A bba A bba A bba A
   d. Three stanzas typical
   e. The number of poetic lines for each section of music varied.
   f. Most of Machaut's virelais are monophonic, but eight are polyphonic.

E. Polyphonic songs (*chansons*, "songs") in the *formes fixes*
1. The *formes fixes* were originally genres for dancing.
   a. Machaut's monophonic virelais could be used for dancing (see **HWM Figure 6.8**).
   b. Refrains were typical of dance genres.
   c. The texts of the stanzas sometimes invested the words of the refrain with new meaning.
2. Treble-dominated songs were a major innovation of the Ars Nova period.
   a. The treble or cantus carries the text
   b. A slower-moving, untexted tenor supports the cantus.
   c. A contratenor may be added.
3. Machaut sometimes wrote a triplum in the same range and style as the cantus.
4. Ballades
   a. Three stanzas, each sung to the same music and ending with the same line of poetry
   b. The musical form of the stanza resembles bar form (AAB)
   c. The ending of the B section sometimes has the same music as the end of the A.
   d. Machaut composed ballades for two, three, and four voices.
   e. Later composers continued to use the form (e.g., Du Fay, **HWM Chapter 8**).
5. Rondeaux
   a. Two musical phrases and a refrain
   b. Form: AbaAabAB
   c. Most are for solo voice with accompanying tenor or tenor and contratenor.
   d. **NAWM 26** *Rose, liz, printemps, verdure* has a fourth voice, probably added later.
6. Typical Machaut characteristics
   a. Varied rhythms, including supple syncopations
   b. Stepwise melody
   c. Long melismas fall on structural points.

F. Machaut's poetry influenced other poets, including Chaucer.

IV. The Ars Subtilior
   A. Composers at the court of the Avignon pope, across southern France, and throughout northern Italy cultivated complex secular music.
   B. Continuation of Ars Nova traditions
      1. Polyphonic songs in the *formes fixes*
      2. Notation of duple and triple meter using coloration
      3. Pieces notated in fanciful shapes, as in **HWM Figure 6.9**
      4. Love songs intended for an elite audience
   C. Rhythmic complexity
      1. Complexity to an extent not known again until the twentieth century
      2. Voices in contrasting meters and conflicting groupings
      3. Harmonies purposely blurred through rhythmic disjunction
   D. *Sus un fontayne* (**NAWM 27, HWM Example 6.5**) by Johannes Ciconia (ca. 1370–1412)
      1. A virelai composed for Ciconia's patron in Padua, Italy.
      2. The top voice (cantus) carries the main melody.
      3. The three voices move in different meters.
      4. Longer melismas than in Machaut's chansons, with a few sustained sonorities as guideposts
      5. Each phrase has a distinctive rhythmic profile.
      6. Modern performance of the tenor and contratenor can be either vocal or instrumental.

V. Italian Trecento Music (from *mille trecento,* Italian for "1300")
   A. Italy was a collection of city-states, not unified as France was.
      1. Several city-states cultivated secular polyphony.
      2. Florence, Bologna, Padua, Modena, Milan, and Perugia were the main centers for secular polyphony.
      3. Church polyphony was mostly improvised, but a few notated works have survived.
      4. Boccacio's *Decameron* describes music in social life (see **HMW Source Reading,** page 135)
   B. Italian notation differed from French Ars Nova notation.
      1. Breves could be divided into two to twelve equal semibreves.
      2. Groupings of semibreves are marked off by dots (akin to the modern bar line).
   C. Squarcialupi Codex (copied about 1410–15)
      1. One of the main sources for Italian secular polyphony from pre-1330
      2. Named for a former owner
      3. 354 pieces, grouped by composer, with a portrait of each composer at the beginning of the section containing his works (see **HWM Figure 6.10**)
   D. Fourteenth-century madrigal (not related to the sixteenth-century madrigal)
      1. Song for two or three voices without instrumental accompaniment
      2. All voices sing the same text.
      3. Subjects: love, satire, pastoral life
      4. Form
         a. Each stanza set to the same music.
         b. Ritornello (Italian for "refrain"), a closing pair of lines, set to different music in a different meter
      5. **NAWM 28,** *Fenice fú* by Jacopo da Bologna (fl. 1340–1386)
         a. The two voices are relatively equal.
         b. The last accented syllable of each poetic line is set with a long, florid melisma.
   E. Caccia (Italian, "hunt")
      1. Similar to the French *chace* (French for "hunt"), a popular-style melody set in strict canon with lively, descriptive words
      2. Popular from 1345–1370
      3. Two voices in canon at the unison with an untexted tenor
      4. Sometimes the text plays on the concept of a hunt, e.g., **NAWM 29,** *Tosto che l'alba* by Ghirardello da Firenze.
         a. Imitations of hunting horns
         b. High-spirited and comic
      5. Other texts concern pastoral settings, battles, or a dialogue.
      6. Some caccias end with a hocket or echo effects between the voices.
   F. Ballata
      1. Popular later than the madrigal and caccia (after 1365)
      2. Influenced by the treble-dominated French chanson
      3. The form is AbbaA, like a single stanza of a French virelai.
         a. The ripresa (refrain) is sung before and after a stanza.
         b. The stanza consists of two piedi (feet) and the volta, the closing line sung to the music of the ripresa.
   G. Francesco Landini (ca. 1325–1397, see **biography,** page 139, and **HWM Figure 6.12**)
      1. Biography
         a. He was blind from boyhood.

b. He played many instruments but was a virtuoso on the small organ (organetto).
c. Worked for a monastery and a church but composed mainly secular ballate
(1) 89 two-part ballate
(2) 42 three-part ballate
(3) Nine surviving in both two- and three-part versions
2. **NAWM 29** *Non avrà ma' pietà*
a. Sonorities containing thirds and sixths are plentiful, though never at the beginning or end of a section.
b. Arching melodies that are smoother than Machaut's melodies despite syncopation
c. Melismas on the first and penultimate syllables of a poetic line (characteristic of the Italian style)
3. Under-third cadence, typical of Trecento music
a. The upper voice descends a step before leaping a third to the octave resolution with the tenor.
b. Called the Landini cadence, though it is common in both Italian and French music
4. French influence overtook the Italian style at the end of the century.

VI. Fourteenth-Century Music in Performance
A. There was no uniform way to perform polyphonic music.
1. Pictorial and literary sources indicate vocal, instrumental, and mixed groups.
2. Purely vocal performance was most common.
3. **HWM Figure 6.13** shows a singer accompanied by an organist.
B. Instruments
1. Haut ("high") instruments were loud, for outdoor entertainment and dancing.
a. Cornetts (wooden instruments with finger holes and brass-type mouthpieces)
b. Trumpets
c. Shawms
2. Bas ("low") instruments were soft in volume.
a. Stringed instruments such as harps, lutes, and vielles
b. Portative organs
c. Transverse flutes and recorders
3. Percussion instruments were common in all kinds of ensembles.
C. Keyboard instruments
1. Portative and positive organs were common in secular music (see **HWM Figure 6.10**).
2. Large organs began to be installed in German churches.
D. Instrumental music
1. Instruments played vocal music.
2. Instrumental dance music was likely memorized or improvised.
3. Fifteen istampitas survive.

VII. Musica Ficta: Chromatic Alterations
A. Raising or lowering a note by a half-step to avoid a tritone
B. Pitches could also be altered to make a smoother melodic line.
C. The resulting pitches lay outside the gamut and were thus false, or *ficta*.
D. Often used at cadences
1. To make the sixth preceding an octave a major sixth rather than minor
2. In three-voice pieces, both upper voices could be raised for a double leading-tone cadence.
E. Singers were trained to recognize situations in which a pitch needed alteration, so the accidentals were rarely notated. (Modern editions put these accidentals above the staff.)

## SUGGESTIONS FOR SUPPLEMENTARY READING/LISTENING/ACTIVITIES

For additional examples of the music discussed in this chapter, see *Polyphonic Music of the Fourteenth Century*, 24 vols, ed. Leo Schrade (Monaco: Éditions de L'Oiseau-Lyre, 1956–1991).

Bring the published facsimile of *Roman de Fauvel* to class. Point out the allegorical depiction of Fauvel, the intermingling of music, poetry, and art, and the presence of both monophonic and polyphonic pieces. Compare the style of notation to examples from Chapter 3, noting the addition of stems and the widening rhythmic gap between the tenor voice and upper voices.

Clemençic Consort's recording of excerpts from *Le Roman de Fauvel* (Harmonia Mundi France 190994, 1992) intersperses poetic recitation and sometimes-raucous performances of musical works. Have students listen to this recording while viewing the facsimile of the charivari scene. Ask how they would stage or perform this work.

Project a color slide or transparency of a tenor voice written in red and black notation. Have the students find the repetitions of the color and talea and the changes of meter.

Give students a melismatic segment of chant and have them generate an isorhythmic tenor voice, using the given segment as the color. They should be able to label both the talea and color using the conventions discussed in this chapter.

The structures of the *formes fixes* and their representation through lower- and upper-case letters can seem daunting to students. Introduce the structure of the poetic texts before dealing with musical forms and ask students to devise ways of setting such texts. Since the musical forms are outgrowths of the poetic structures, they seem far more logical once the literary forms are grasped.

For examples of Machaut's monophonic works, see *Oeuvres completes*, transcribed by Leo Schrade (Monaco: Éditions de L'Oiseau-Lyre, 1977), volumes I, IV, and V.

For additional examples of Machaut's polyphonic works, see *Polyphonic Music of the Fourteenth Century*, vols. II and III, edited by Leo Schrade (Monaco: Éditions L'Oiseau Lyre, 1974). Of particular interest is *Ma fin est ma commencement* ("My end is my beginning"), composed as a palindrome, and the "David" hocket. *Ma fin est ma commencement* has been recorded by the Orlando Consort on "Dreams in the Pleasure Garden" (Archiv 457 618-2, 1998) and by the Hilliard Ensemble on "Messe de Notre Dame" (Hyperion CDA 663581989).

Have students take a melody and turn it into a hocket, then have them sing it as a demonstration of the skill involved in performing Ars Nova polyphony.

Compare Machaut's *Rose, liz* (**NAWM 26**) with Adam de la Halle's *Robins m'aime* (**NAWM 10**). Both are in rondeau form, but Machaut's approach to the form is much more expansive.

Discuss Machaut's interpolated story, *Remede de Fortune*, relating it to the *Roman de Fauvel.* Assign small groups of students to act out and sing small sections and to report on the form of the song they sing. (Both text and music can be found in Wimsatt, Kibler, and Baltzer, eds., *Le jugement du roy de Behaigne and Remede de fortune*; Athens: University of Georgia Press, 1988.) *Remede de Fortune* contains examples of each of the secular genres of Machaut's time. The musical selections have been recorded by Project Ars Nova on "Remede de Fortune" (New Albion D105812, 1994). Excerpts from *Le jugement du Roi de Navarre* have been recorded by the Ensemble Gilles Binchois (Cantus C9626, 1998).

Performances of works by Ciconia in various combinations of voice and instrument can be found on "Johannes Ciconia" (Opus 111 30101, 1994). Examples of other Ars Subtilitor works have been performed by Project Ars Nova on "Ars Magis Subtiliter" (New Albion 21, 1989) and by the Ferrara Ensemble on "Fleurs de vertus: Chansons subtiles à la fin du XIVe Siècle" (Arcana A40, 1996).

Additional examples of music by Jacopo da Bologna and Francesco Landini are available on "Landini: The Second Circle," performed by Anonymous 4 (Harmonia Mundi 907269, 2001) and "Il Solazzo: Music for a Medieval Banquet," performed by the Newberry Consort (Harmonia Mundi France 907038, 1993).

## OBJECTIVE QUESTIONS

1. Which feature of Ars Nova composition was most offensive to conservatives?
   a. isorhythm
   b. duple meter
   c. division of semibreves
   d. fast-moving upper parts
   e. secular texts

   Answer: b

2. Roman de Fauvel was __________.
   a. the composer who wrote the *Ars nova* treatise
   b. an allegorical story interspersed with Ars Nova music
   c. the theorist who objected to the Ars Nova style
   d. a book of rules for how to notate Ars Nova motets
   e. a thirteenth-century writer whose thinking influenced fourteenth-century composers

   Answer: b

3. Which of the following letter schemes best represents the form of the ballade?
   a. AAB
   b. AbbaA
   c. aabC
   d. AbaAabAB
   e. aaaaaa... (strophic)

   Answer: a

4. Which of the following letter schemes best represents the form of the rondeau?
   a. AAB
   b. AbbaA
   c. aabC
   d. AbaAabAB
   e. aaaaaa... (strophic)

   Answer: d

5. In three-voice secular songs by Machaut, __________.
   a. all parts move in roughly equal note values.
   b. the top two parts carry the melody, while the lower voice is slow-moving.
   c. the top part carries the melody, while the lower voices are slow-moving.
   d. isorhythm is used in all parts throughout.
   e. each voice sings a separate poetic text.

   Answer: c

6. Who wrote a famous treatise and composed isorhythmic motets?
   a. Guillaume de Machaut
   b. Philippe de Vitry
   c. Johannes Ciconia
   d. Francesco Landini
   e. Jacopo da Bologna

   Answer: b

7. Who composed isorhythmic motets, polyphonic songs, and a Mass Ordinary setting?
   a. Guillaume de Machaut
   b. Philippe de Vitry
   c. Johannes Ciconia
   d. Francesco Landini
   e. Jacopo da Bologna

   Answer: a

8. Who was the blind composer known for his ballate?
   a. Guillaume de Machaut
   b. Philippe de Vitry
   c. Johannes Ciconia
   d. Francesco Landini
   e. Jacopo da Bologna

   Answer: d

9. In an isorhythmic work, the repeating rhythmic pattern is called the __________.
   a. tempus
   b. diminution
   c. color
   d. prolation
   e. talea

   Answer: e

10. The *Messe de Notre Dame* is notable because __________.
    a. it was composed for the Cathedral of Notre Dame in Paris
    b. it was the first mass composed using isorhythm throughout
    c. it was the first time Ordinary portions of the mass were set in polyphony
    d. it was the first time Proper portions of the mass were set in polyphony
    e. it was the first time the Ordinary of the mass was composed as a cycle

    Answer: e

11. Late in the fourteenth century, composers of the papal court of Avignon and surrounding areas cultivated which type of music?
    a. ars antiqua
    b. Ars Nova
    c. Ars Subtilior
    d. Trecento
    e. rondellus

    Answer: c

12. A cadence in which the upper voice moves down a step before moving up a third to the resolution is called a __________.
    a. perfect cadence
    b. clausula
    c. double leading-tone cadence
    d. Landini cadence
    e. Machaut cadence

    Answer: d

13. Changes between red and black ink __________.
    a. were intended to confuse the singers
    b. indicated new statements of the color
    c. indicated changes between duple and triple meter
    d. indicated that the passages in red should be performed by instruments and the passages in black should be performed by voices
    e. were purely for decorative purposes

    Answer: c

14. Musica ficta is __________.
    a. the use of pitches outside of the gamut
    b. music added by an editor
    c. any accidental
    d. a duple relationship between the breve and the semibreve
    e. notation made into the shape of a circle or other artistic image

    Answer: a

15. The fourteenth-century French system of rhythmic notation was based on __________.
    a. the Italian system of notation
    b. a theory of proportions developed in ancient Greece
    c. Franconian notation
    d. the Papal Schism
    e. rhythmic symbols in chant notation

    Answer: c

16. Musical instruments of the fourteenth century were divided into high and low depending on __________.
    a. pitch
    b. length of tubing or strings
    c. social status of the performer
    d. loudness or softness
    e. whether they were performed in towers or on the ground

    Answer: d

17. Trecento composers used all but which of these genres?
    a. caccia
    b. madrigal
    c. ballata
    d. rondeau
    e. discant clausulae

    Answer: e

18. The Squarcialupi Codex is __________.
    a. a book containing an allegorical and satirical story interspersed with music
    b. one of the main sources of Trecento music
    c. a treatise on Italian notation
    d. a set of rules for writing madrigals
    e. the complete works of Landini, which he compiled himself

    Answer: b

19. The sign for imperfect time and imperfect prolation survives today as the sign for __________.
    a. dal segno repeats
    b. cut time
    c. 4/4 time
    d. treble clef
    e. whole note

    Answer: c

20. The composer whose poetry influenced Chaucer and other famous poets is __________.
    a. Guillaume de Machaut
    b. Philippe de Vitry
    c. Johannes Ciconia
    d. Francesco Landini
    e. Jacopo da Bologna

    Answer: a

## SHORT-ESSAY QUESTIONS

1. Explain the structure of an isorhythmic motet, using **NAWM 24** *In arboris/Tuba sacre fidei/Virgo sum* as an example. Contrast the compositional techniques used in each of the voices.
2. Discuss the ways in which secularization of society impacted the music of the fourteenth century. Cite examples from *NAWM* as appropriate.
3. Describe the ways in which Guillaume de Machaut was unusual for his time.
4. Compare and contrast the musical styles of northern France, Avignon, and Italy. How did each affect the other? How did each remain autonomous?

## TERMS FOR IDENTIFICATION

Avignon
Papal Schism
Ars Nova
Roman de Fauvel
minim
talea
color
coloration
hocket
contratenor
*formes fixes*
lai
virelai
ballade
rondeau
Ars Subtilior
Trecento
Squarcialupi Codex
madrigal
caccia
ballate
ripresa
piedi
volta
Landini cadence
musica ficta
double leading-tone cadence

# CHAPTER 7 The Age of the Renaissance

I. Renaissance in Culture and Art
   A. The Renaissance (French for "rebirth") began at different times for different aspects of culture.
      1. In some aspects it began in the 1300s.
      2. Some areas experienced a renaissance beginning in the 1500s.
      3. The term was coined in 1855 by a French historian.
      4. For the purposes of *HWM,* the period includes the fifteenth and sixteenth centuries.
   B. Developments in music
      1. An international style developed due to composers from northern Europe working in Italy.
      2. New rules for counterpoint controlled dissonance and elevated thirds and sixths in importance.
      3. The predominant textures were imitative counterpoint and homophony.
      4. Printing made notated music available to a wider public, including amateurs.
      5. The Reformation generated changes in music for both Protestant and Catholic churches.

II. Europe in the Renaissance (Refer to Timeline: The Age of the Renaissance)
   A. European expansion
      1. Europeans established colonies around the world.
      2. Columbus's 1492 trip led to Spanish and Portuguese colonies in the Americas, followed by colonies established by other countries.
   B. The European economy stabilized around 1400.
      1. Trade between regions with specialized products brought wealth to towns, cities, and individuals.
      2. The middle class continued to grow in numbers and influence.
      3. Rulers glorified themselves and their principalities.
         a. Impressive palaces and country houses
         b. Decoration with new artwork and artifacts from ancient civilizations
         c. Lavish entertainment
         d. Private chapels staffed by professional musicians
   C. Humanism
      1. Access to Greek writings influenced thinkers.
         a. Byzantine scholars fled to Italy because of Ottoman attacks, taking ancient Greek writings with them.
         b. Italian scholars learned Greek and translated Greek texts into Latin.
         c. The works of Plato and the Greek plays and histories became available to western Europeans for the first time.
      2. Humanism (from the Latin *studia humanitatis,* "the study of the humanities," that is, things pertaining to human knowledge)
         a. Humanists emphasized the study of grammar, rhetoric, poetry, history, and moral philosophy.
         b. They believed that the humanities prepared students for lives of virtue and service.
         c. The Church borrowed from classical sources and supported humanists.

III. Renaissance Sculpture, Painting, and Architecture
   A. Classical models of beauty
      1. Nude statues based on Greek ideals (see **HWM Figure 7.1**) depicted the beauty of the

human figure, as opposed to human shame in medieval art.
   2. Classical Greek and Roman styles were used to portray Christian themes.
   3. Musicians consulted Greek theoretical treatises for ideas on how to create classical beauty in music.
- B. Realistic depictions in painting
   1. Perspective, a method of showing three dimensions on a flat surface by orienting objects on a single point with vanishing lines toward it, made more-realistic images possible.
   2. Chiaroscuro, naturalistic treatment of light and shade
   3. **HWM Figure 7.3** uses perspective and light to create a more-realistic image than the medieval image in **HWM Figure 7.2.**
- C. Clarity and clean lines are the new architectural style, the opposite of the ornate decoration of the Gothic style.
- D. Interest in individuals
   1. Patrons commissioned paintings to memorialize themselves.
   2. Minor figures in paintings were painted in detail.
- E. Musical parallels
   1. Expansion of range, allowing contrast between high and low registers and fuller textures
   2. Clarity of musical structure through frequent cadences and stylistic contrasts
   3. Focusing on a single tonal center was the equivalent of using a single vanishing point in perspective.
   4. Interest in individuals is reflected in unique personal styles and memorial works.

IV. The Musical Renaissance
- A. Renaissance musicians could refer only to treatises from ancient Greece, not to any actual pieces, so musical humanism does not imitate Greek music.
- B. Court chapels (e.g., **HWM Figure 7.5**)
   1. Rulers, aristocrats, and church leaders had their own chapels.
   2. Musicians at the chapels were on salary.
   3. Because they worked for the ruler, not the Church, they could be called upon for secular entertainment as well as sacred functions.
   4. Most musicians had other duties as servants, administrators, clerics, or church officials.
- C. Music education
   1. Choir schools in cathedrals and chapels taught singing, music theory, and academic subjects to boys.
      - a. Most prominent composers of the fifteenth and early sixteenth centuries came from northern Europe, which was home to the most renowned centers for musical training: Cambrai, Bruges, Antwerp, Paris, and Lyons (see **HWM Figure 7.6**).
      - b. In the sixteenth century, Rome and Venice became centers of musical training, and more composers were Italian.
      - c. Noblewomen and women in convents received some musical instruction.
   2. Instrumentalists trained in the apprentice system.
- D. Patronage for music
   1. Competition for the best composers and performers erased regional differences.
   2. Court musicians in Italy came from France, Flanders, and the Netherlands (Franco-Flemish).
   3. English, French, and Italian styles merged into one international style in the fifteenth century (see **HWM Chapter 8**).
   4. Composers were able to compose in regional vernacular song styles because of their travels.
- E. The new counterpoint
   1. Thirds and sixths, now seen as consonances, required new approaches to counterpoint.
   2. Johannes Tinctoris: *Liber de arte contrapuncti* (A Book on the Art of Counterpoint, 1477, **HWM Source Reading,** page 158)
      - a. He references composers active ca. 1430–1477, including many discussed in upcoming chapters of *HWM.*
      - b. Without access to examples from ancient Greece, Tinctoris uses these composers as models for "the arranging of concords," i.e., counterpoint.
      - c. His rules for counterpoint include rules for the treatment of dissonance, including suspensions.
   3. Gioseffo Zarlino's *Le istitutioni harmoniche* (The Harmonic Foundations, 1558) synthesizes the rules for counterpoint as developed after Tinctoris.
- F. New compositional methods and textures
   1. All voices became equal by the second half of the fifteenth century.
   2. Composers stopped basing works on the cantus-tenor relationship and began composing all voices simultaneously (see Pietro Aaron **HMW Source Reading,** page 159).
   3. Two textures emerged: imitative counterpoint and homophony.

4. Imitative counterpoint
   a. Voices echo each other, repeating a motive or phrase.
   b. Repetitions are usually a fourth, fifth, or octave away.
5. Homophony
   a. All voices move together in essentially the same rhythm.
   b. The lower parts accompany the cantus line with consonant sonorities.

G. Tuning and temperament
1. Music using thirds and sixths requires more sophisticated tuning than styles emphasizing perfect consonances.
2. Pythagorean intonation
   a. Based on fourths and fifths and used during the Middle Ages
   b. Created dissonant-sounding thirds and sixths using complex ratios
   c. The ratio for a major third was 81:64, which sounds out of tune compared to the pure major third (5:4 or 80:64)
3. Just intonation
   a. Walter Odington observed that musicians used simpler ratios in practice ca. 1300.
   b. He laid the foundation for tuning based on simple ratios for thirds (5:4) and sixths (6:5).
   c. In 1482 Bartolomé Ramis de Pareia proposed a system now known as just intonation to create perfectly tuned thirds and sixths.
4. Temperaments
   a. Tuning systems designed to create the best-sounding intervals over the range of a keyboard were developed to accommodate works that used pitches outside the gamut.
   b. Singers could sing G-sharp and A-flat at slightly different pitches, but keyboards could not do this.
   c. Mean-tone temperament employs fifths tuned slightly smaller than perfect in order to create consonant thirds and usable black keys.
   d. Temperament was now governed by accommodations to the ear rather than adherence to past authority, in keeping with humanist principles.

H. Reawakened interest in Greek theory
1. Greek writings on music came to the West during the Renaissance.
   a. Aristides Quintilianus
   b. Claudius Ptolemy
   c. Cleonides
   d. Aristotle's *Politics*
   e. Plato's *Republic*
   f. By the end of the fifteenth century, they had been translated into Latin.
2. Franchino Gaffurio (1451–1522)
   a. The most influential treatise writer of his time
   b. Gaffurio incorporated ideas from Greek treatises into his.
   c. Topics influenced by Greek theory included the modes, consonance and dissonance, relationship of music and words, and tuning.
3. Heinrich Glareanus (1488–1563)
   a. Swiss theorist
   b. He added four new modes in his book *Dodekachordon* (The Twelve-String Lyre, 1547).
      (1) Aeolian and Hyperaeolian, with the final on A
      (2) Ionian and Hypoionian with the final on C
   c. By his time, composers frequently used C and A as tonal centers.

I. New applications of Greek ideas
1. Music as a social accomplishment
2. Music as a servant of the words
   a. The structure of the text dictated the structure of the music.
   b. By the end of the sixteenth century, composers were following the rhythm of speech as well.
3. Conveying emotion through music
   a. Inspired by ancient Greek descriptions of the emotional effects of music
   b. By ca. 1500, composers used various compositional devices to convey the feeling of the text.
   c. Greek descriptions of the qualities of the modes inspired composers to connect modes with emotional effects.
4. Chromaticism, inspired by the chromatic genus of ancient Greek music

J. Music printing and distribution (see **HWM Innovations,** pages 164–65)
1. Printing from movable type began around 1450 for text and in the 1450s for chant notation.
2. Printing from a single impression (see **HWM Figure 7.8**)
   a. Pieces of type contained the printed staff, notes, and the text together.

   b. John Rastell in London after ca. 1520
   c. Pierre Attaingnant in Paris (ca. 1494–1551/52)
   d. Staff lines were not continuous, but the method was a commercial success.
3. Printing from three impressions: the printing press created the staff, the notes, and the words in separate passes over the paper.
4. *Harmonice musices odhecaton A*, 1501, published by Ottaviano Petrucci (1466–1539), **HWM Figure 7.7**
   a. The first collection of polyphonic music printed entirely from movable type
   b. One Hundred Polyphonic Songs (actually only ninety-six)
   c. Volumes B and C followed a few years later.
   d. He held a patent on the three-impression process, preventing other publishers from using it.
   e. He printed both vocal and instrumental music.
5. Amateur musicians used partbooks (each book contained one voice or part) for home gatherings, creating a large market for printed books (see **HWM Figure 7.9**).
6. Effect of music printing
   a. Composers' works could be heard throughout Europe and the Americas.
   b. Composers could make more money, either through publication or through the growth of their reputations.
   c. New musical styles evolved to satisfy demands for popular and regional styles.
   d. The music of the Renaissance is available to modern performers and scholars.

V. Music as a Renaissance Art
   A. The humanist focus created a musical style that would appeal to the listener.
      1. Consonance
      2. Natural declamation of the words
      3. Emotional expressivity
   B. Developments in musical language, temperament, and musical aesthetics have persisted to the present.
   C. Renaissance counterpoint continued to be the main style for Catholic church music through the eighteenth century.
   D. In the late nineteenth and early twentieth centuries, scholars began transcribing Renaissance works into modern notation.

## SUGGESTIONS FOR SUPPLEMENTAL READING/LISTENING/ACTIVITIES

To expand on the discussion of humanism in this chapter, see "Renaissance Humanism" and "Humanism in Italy" in *The Dictionary of the History of Ideas* (New York: Scribner, 1973, and online at etext.virginia.edu/DicHist/dict.html).

For a brilliant series of essays on music and humanistic thought, see Claude V. Palisca, *Humanism in Italian Renaissance Musical Thought* (New Haven: Yale University Press, 1985), especially chapters 1 (Introduction: An Italian Renaissance in Music), 2 (The Rediscovery of the Ancient Sources), and 9 (Gaffurio as a Humanist).

Translations of important Renaissance theoretical writings are available in Gary Tomlinson, ed., *Source Readings in Music History*, rev. ed., Vol. 3: The Renaissance (New York: Norton, 1998) or Section III of *Source Readings in Music History* (New York: Norton, 1998).

To stress the revolutionary nature of music printing, bring facsimile reprints of early printed music books to class or make a class trip to the rare books section of the library. Side-by-side comparisons of meticulously hand-copied manuscripts and early printed books will help students develop an idea of the significance of this new technology.

Several of the early printed books mentioned in this chapter are available in reprint editions. See, for example, *Harmonice musices odhecaton A*, edited by Stanley Boorman and Ellen S. Beebe (New York: The Broude Trust, 2001 and Bologna: A. Forni, 2003), with an introduction by Iain Fenlon; and *The Bay Psalm Book, a Facsimile Reprint of the First Edition of 1640* (Chicago: University of Chicago Press, 1956).

For a performance of music from the *Harmonice musices odhecaton* using wind instruments, use examples from "Music from the Odhecaton" by Piffaro (Dorian xCD-90301). The first track, *Alons ferons barbe* by Compère, uses syncopated patterns reminiscent of Machaut's style, and the second, *Latura tu* by Antoine Bruhier, demonstrates imitative counterpoint. This CD includes excellent performances on shawms, recorders, sackbuts, and cornetto.

Silvestro Ganassi's *Opera intitulata Fontegara* (1535) is available in a modern edition (Roma: Societàà italiana del flauto dolce, 1991), part of the *Hortus musicus* series.

For a review and recorded examples of instruments available in the Renaissance, see the CD, "The Instruments of the Middle Ages and Renaissance" (Vanguard Classics, OVC 8093-OVC 8094, 1997), mentioned in Chapter 4.

## OBJECTIVE QUESTIONS

1. The Renaissance period is marked by an interest in __________.
   a. ancient Greek culture
   b. religious conversion
   c. exotic cultures
   d. preserving medieval ideals
   e. equality for all humans, no matter what their economic status

   Answer: a

2. The Renaissance period of music comprises roughly which centuries?
   a. The thirteenth and fourteenth
   b. The fourteenth and fifteenth
   c. The fifteenth and sixteenth
   d. The sixteenth and seventeenth
   e. The fourteenth through the seventeenth

   Answer: c

3. The movement to embrace human knowledge was called __________.
   a. humanism
   b. secularism
   c. secular humanism
   d. medievalism
   e. chiaroscuro

   Answer: a

4. Renaissance painters achieved realistic effects through the use of __________.
   a. more advanced application of medieval techniques
   b. principles they learned in greek treatises
   c. paints with chemical additives imported from North Africa
   d. techniques borrowed from Byzantine style
   e. perspective and treatment of light

   Answer: e

5. Court chapels were significant for music history because __________.
   a. musicians deposited copies of their manuscripts there
   b. contracts for guilds, the predecessors of unions, were signed there
   c. they hired musicians for both sacred and secular music
   d. they settled disputes between musicians and employers
   e. they published the works of important composers

   Answer: c

6. For much of the Renaissance, musicians working in Italy had been trained in __________.
   a. Italy
   b. France, the Netherlands, or Flanders
   c. England
   d. Spain
   e. Byzantium

   Answer: b

7. In Italy, the main patrons for music were __________.
   a. the heads of small city-states and the church
   b. major cathedrals
   c. the king and some of the nobility under him
   d. the middle class
   e. young ladies who played the keyboard as part of their education

   Answer: a

8. The theorist who first described counterpoint that considered thirds and sixths consonances was __________.
   a. Boethius
   b. Tinctoris
   c. Zarlino
   d. Walter Odington
   e. Petrucci

   Answer: b

9. Temperament is __________.
   a. the belief that music should be moderate in order to create good citizens
   b. a method for printing music
   c. a system of voice-leading rules for counterpoint
   d. tuning all pitches of a keyboard instrument to make thirds and sixths sound good
   e. the belief that each mode has its own mood

   Answer: d

10. The idea that music could be a social accomplishment came from __________.
    a. ancient Greece
    b. fifteenth-century Greece
    c. Flanders
    d. England
    e. the Bible

    Answer: a

11. Which of the following statements is true?
    a. Musicians in the Renaissance did not believe in music's power to influence emotion.

b. Renaissance musicians believed the magical properties of Greek music were lost forever.
c. Renaissance musicians believed music had power to influence human emotion, but they were not interested in putting their belief into practice.
d. Renaissance musicians used many devices to try to sway listeners' emotions.
e. The pope forbade Renaissance musicians from attempting to portray emotion in music.

Answer: d

12. Ottavio Petrucci is known for __________.
    a. writing a treatise naming the best composers of his time
    b. developing a realistic style of painting
    c. hiring the first paid, secular choir
    d. translating Greek treatises into Latin
    e. publishing music using a three-impression method

    Answer: e

13. Partbooks were __________.
    a. books of music with all parts on the same page
    b. books of music with the high parts on the right and the low parts on the left
    c. sets of books, one part to a book
    d. pedagogical books with the cantus firmus laid out and blank staves above it for students to fill in the other parts
    e. treatises on counterpoint

    Answer: c

14. In the Renaissance, secular music was __________.
    a. banned by the Church
    b. the predominant type of music
    c. performed but never written down
    d. composed by musicians who also composed church music
    e. composed by specialists who never composed church music

    Answer: d

15. Social factors influencing Renaissance music included __________.
    a. equal rights for women
    b. Europe's economic vitality
    c. the Black Death
    d. church control over secular life
    e. suppression of the middle class

    Answer: b

16. The primary audience for printed music was/were __________.
    a. the Church
    b. missionaries in the new world
    c. collectors who viewed them as works of art
    d. amateur musicians throughout Europe and the Americas
    e. a tiny group of the economic elite

    Answer: d

17. Music and art of the Renaissance shared which of these characteristics?
    a. They aimed to use art to convert more people to Christianity.
    b. an interest in the individual
    c. complex textures that obscured each individual line
    d. an attempt to preserve medieval values
    e. decorative figuration in complex patterns

    Answer: b

18. The main textures for the Renaissance were __________.
    a. monophony and heterophony
    b. heterophony and homophony
    c. homophony and imitative counterpoint
    d. imitative and nonimitative counterpoint
    e. monophony and nonimitative counterpoint

    Answer: c

19. Aeolian and Ionian modes were __________.
    a. added to the modal system by Heinrich Glareanus
    b. discarded from the modal system in the sixteenth century
    c. modes used for secular music only
    d. added to the modal system by the Church
    e. tuning systems used for harps

    Answer: a

20. Which of these statements best describes women's role in Renaissance music-making?
    a. Women were not permitted to perform in public.
    b. Women could perform in public but only in the theater.
    c. Only nuns were permitted to learn to read music.
    d. Noblewomen and women in convents received some instruction.
    e. Women performed extensively and were considered equal with men.

    Answer: d

## SHORT-ESSAY QUESTIONS

1. Describe the ways in which Greek music theory influenced Renaissance music.
2. Discuss the similarities between Renaissance art and Renaissance music in terms of their aesthetic values and reliance on Greek models.
3. Compare and contrast the main features of Renaissance music with those of medieval music.
4. What were the social factors influencing music in the Renaissance and how did they affect the kinds of music produced?

## TERMS FOR IDENTIFICATION

Renaissance
imitative counterpoint
homophony
humanism
perspective
chiaroscuro
chapel
Tinctoris
counterpoint
imitative counterpoint
Pythagorean intonation
just intonation
Walter Odington
Bartolomé Ramis de Pareia
temperament
Franchino Gaffurio
Heinrich Glareanus
Aeolian
Ionian
Ottaviano Petrucci
*Harmonice musices odhecaton A*
partbooks

# CHAPTER 8 England and Burgundy in the Fifteenth Century

I. Influence of English Music on Continental Style
  A. The English presence in France
    1. Kings of England held territory in northwest and southwest France.
    2. Hundred Years' War (1337–1453): England and France fighting for control of France
    3. English rulers brought musicians with them, especially to Belgium and Burgundy.
  B. Contenance angloise ("English guise" or quality)
    1. Tinctoris (**HMW Source Reading,** page 158) cites Du Fay and Binchois as founders of a new art.
    2. Du Fay and Binchois were the main composers influenced by the English style.

II. English Music in the Early Fifteenth Century
  A. Characteristics of English music (review of chapter 5 concepts)
    1. Preference for thirds and sixths, especially in parallel motion
    2. Simple melodies
    3. Few dissonances
    4. Syllabic text setting
    5. Homophonic
  B. Polyphony on Latin texts (e.g., **HWM Example 8.1**, *Credo*)
    1. Characteristics
      a. Composed for service in the Sarum rite (English liturgy)
      b. Chant voice in the middle
      c. Lowest voice a third below
      d. Top voice a parallel fourth above the chant voice
      e. The result is a stream of parallel 6-3 sonorities.
    2. Faburden
      a. Improvised 6-3 sonorities
      b. There are a few notated examples.
      c. The word might derive from "burden" for the lowest voice and "fa" for the need to use B-flat, "fa," in the soft hexachord.
    3. Cantilena
      a. Freely composed piece, not based on chant
      b. Homorhythmic
      c. Streams of sixths alternate with other consonances.
    4. Isorhythmic motets until ca. 1400
    5. Polyphonic settings of Mass Ordinary texts
    6. The Old Hall manuscript (**HWM Figure 8.1**) is the primary source of fifteenth-century English polyphony
      a. The largest number of pieces are settings from the Mass Ordinary.
      b. It also include motets, hymns, and sequences.
    7. The carol in the fifteenth century (**HWM Example 8.2** and **NAWM 31,** *Alleluia: A newë work*)
      a. Religious songs in Latin or English
      b. Favorite topics were Christmas and the Blessed Virgin Mary.
      c. Solo and choral sections alternate.
        (1) Stanzas were all to the same music.
        (2) Refrain was called the "burden."
        **(3) NAWM 31** has two burdens.
      d. Folk-like melodies and triple rhythms
  C. John Dunstable (ca. 1390–1453)
    1. Biography
      a. Sometimes also spelled "Dunstaple"

b. The most highly regarded English composer of the first half of the fifteenth century
c. Served many noble patrons, including the Duke of Bedford, who was Regent of France in 1422
d. Probably spent part of his career in France
e. The English composer most often cited as influencing continental composers
f. His compositions are preserved chiefly in manuscripts copied on the continent.
g. His works include settings of the Mass Ordinary, twelve isorhythmic motets, and over twenty other sacred works in Latin.

2. **HWM Figure 8.1** is an isorhythmic motet by Dunstable (*Veni Sancti Spiritus*)
   a. The tenor voice has the chant melody in isorhythm.
   b. A preference for thirds with fifths and sixths is evident.
3. Three-voice settings of chant (e.g. **HWM Example 8.3,** *Regina caeli laetare*)
   a. The chant melody can be a cantus firmus in the tenor or placed in the top voice.
   b. Rhythmic variety, typical of Dunstable's style
   c. Melodies by stepwise motion or by thirds
   d. When placed in the top voice the melody is paraphrased, with decorative notes added around chant notes.
4. **NAWM 32,** *Quam pulchra es*
   a. Original music using setting of the words of an antiphon
   b. Each of the three voices is equal in importance.
   c. Homorhythmic
   d. A few streams of 6-3 sonorities lead to cadences.

D. Redefining the motet (see **HWM Figure 8.2**)
1. Previous definition: any work with texted upper voices above a cantus-firmus
2. Isorhythmic motet
   a. Old-fashioned by ca. 1400
   b. Disappeared by ca. 1450
3. New definition by 1450: any setting of a chant text, whether the original melody was used or not (e.g., **NAWM 32**)
4. From the sixteenth century on:
   a. Any polyphonic Latin-texted piece
   b. Sometimes also applied to music using texts in other languages

III. Music in the Burgundian Lands

A. Duchy of Burgundy (see **HWM Figure 8.3**)
1. The duke of Burgundy's influence was nearly equal to that of the king of France.
2. From 1419–35 Burgundy was allied with England during the Hundred Years' War.
3. Burgundy held many territories, including today's Holland, Belgium, and northeastern France.
4. Dukes traveled among regional centers rather than maintain a permanent residence.
5. Chapel
   a. Philip the Bold (r. 1363–1404), the first duke of Burgundy, established a chapel in 1384.
   b. By 1445 the chapel had 23 singers under Philip the Good (r. 1419–67).
   c. Most of the musicians came from Flanders and the Low Countries (Belgium and the Netherlands).
6. Band of Minstrels (see **HWM Figure 8.4**)
   a. The musicians were imported from France, Italy, Germany, Portugal
   b. Instruments included trumpets, shawms, vielles, drums, harps, organ, and bagpipes.
7. Charles the Bold (r. 1467–77)
   a. Amateur instrumentalist and composer
   b. He died without a male heir, leaving much of the duchy to be absorbed into France.
8. Visits from foreign musicians helped forge a cosmopolitan style, which influenced music in other regions.

B. Genres and texture
1. Four principal types of polyphonic composition
2. Secular chansons with French texts
   a. Rondeaux the most popular
   b. Ballades for special occasions
3. Motets
4. Magnificats
5. Settings of the Mass Ordinary
6. Three-voice texture
   a. Cantus, spanning a wide range, contained the melody.
   b. Tenor and contratenor within the same range, about a sixth lower
   c. Each line had a distinct role.

C. Binchois and the Burgundian chanson
1. Chanson in the fifteenth century
   a. Any polyphonic setting of a French secular poem
   b. Stylized love poems in the courtly tradition
   c. Rondeau (ABaAabAB) was the most popular form.
2. Binchois (ca. 1400–1460; see **HWM biography,** page 179, and **HWM Figure 8.5**)
   a. Known as Binchois, but his name was Gilles de Bins

b. Before working for the duke of Burgundy, he spent some time in the service of an English earl who was part of the forces occupying France.
c. Worked for Philip the Good at the Burgundian court, 1427–1453
d. His works include mass movements, motets, and secular songs.
e. His works were widely copied and imitated by others.

3. **NAWM 33,** *De plus en plus*
    a. Composed around 1425
    b. Like Dunstable's, in Binchois's compositions there is the rhythmic interest within a 6/8 meter, sometimes also employing hemiola (three quarter-notes against the duple division of the meter).
    c. The cantus declaims the text in a mostly syllabic setting.
    d. The tenor is smooth but slower moving, forming counterpoint against the cantus in thirds and sixths.
    e. The contratenor leaps to fill in the harmony.
4. Cadences
    a. The cantus-tenor relationship moves from a sixth to an octave, sometimes with the additional under-third decorative note.
    b. The contratenor moves from a fifth below the tenor to a fifth above it, giving the modern ear the impression of a dominant-tonic cadence.

IV. Guillaume Du Fay (ca. 1397–1474)

A. The most famous composer of his time (see **HWM biography,** page 181, and **HWM Figure 8.6**)
1. Traveled widely throughout his career, serving as chapel musician in Italy and southwestern France
2. His early training was in Cambrai, which he visited often and where he later settled.
3. His wide travels made it possible for him to absorb many styles and stylistic traits.

B. **NAWM 34,** *Resvellies vous,* 1423
1. Composed while working in Italy to celebrate his patron's wedding
2. Ballade form (aab with refrain)
3. Ars Subtilior characteristics
    a. Rapid notes in various divisions of the beat
    b. Cross-rhythms between the parts (see **HWM Example 8.5**)
    c. Dissonant ornamental notes
    d. Too difficult for an untrained singer
4. Italian elements
    a. Smooth melodies
    b. Melismas on the last accented syllable of each line of text
    c. Meter change for the "B" section

C. **NAWM 36a,** *Se la face ay pale*
1. Ballade, composed ten years after *Resvellies vous*
2. English elements added to the French and Italian traits
    a. The tenor is as tuneful as the cantus.
    b. Phrases are brief.
    c. Consonant harmony, favoring thirds, sixths, and triads (though the term had not yet been coined)
    d. Form is freely composed, not fixed (i.e., not aab).

D. Fauxbourdon
1. A style probably inspired by English faburden
2. Only the cantus and tenor were written out, moving mostly in parallel sixths and cadencing on an octave.
3. An unwritten third voice sang a parallel fourth below the cantus, producing a stream of 6-3 sonorities.
4. Used for settings of simpler office chants, such as hymns, antiphons, psalms, and canticles
5. **NAWM 35,** *Conditor alme siderum*
    a. The chant is paraphrased.
    b. Only the even-numbered stanzas were sung polyphonically; the odd-numbered stanzas were sung as chant.

E. Isorhythmic motets
1. For solemn public occasions, composers continue to use the then-archaic isorhythmic motet.
2. *Nuper rosarum flores*, 1436, was composed for the dedication of the dome of the Cathedral of Santa Maria del Fiore in Florence (see **Figure 8.7**).
    a. Two isorhythmic tenor voices, both based on the same chant, reflect the use of two vaults to support the dome.
    b. Du Fay was in the service of Pope Eugene IV, who officiated at the dedication.
3. *Supremum est mortalibus bonum* (1433)
    a. Commemorated the meeting of Pope Eugene with King Sigismund of Hungary
    b. Alternates sections in the isorhythm, fauxbourdon, and free counterpoint

V. The Polyphonic Mass

A. Until 1420, polyphonic settings of the Ordinary texts were usually composed as separate pieces.
1. Machaut's mass was an exception.
2. Sometimes compilers put movements together into groups.

B. During the fifteenth century, composers began to set the Ordinary as a coherent whole.
   1. Dunstable and English composer Leonel Power (d. 1445) led the development.
   2. At first only two sections would be linked together.
   3. Eventually all five of the main items were composed as a cycle.

C. Plainsong mass
   1. Mass in which each movement is based on an existing chant for that text
   2. Machaut's mass is an example.
   3. Many were written to be sung at a Lady Mass, dedicated to the Virgin Mary.

D. Motto mass
   1. Mass in which each movement begins with the same melodic motive
   2. Called a motto mass when that opening motive (called head-motive) is the primary linking device
   3. Example in chapter 9, Ockeghem's *Missa mi-mi*

E. Cantus-firmus mass (also called tenor mass)
   1. Mass in which the same cantus firmus, usually in the tenor, is the basis for all five movements
      a. The cantus firmus could be a chant or the tenor from a polyphonic secular song.
      b. Sometimes also employs a unifying head-motive
   2. Began in England and became the principal type of mass on the continent by the mid–fifteenth century
   3. Cantus-firmus treatment
      a. When the cantus firmus is sacred the rhythm is usually isorhythmic, as in the isorhythmic motet.
      b. When the cantus firmus is the tenor of a secular song, the original rhythm is used, but not at the original tempo.
      c. When other voices from a polyphonic chanson are also used, the mass is called an imitation mass.
   4. One of the most popular cantus firmus melodies was *L'homme armé* (The Armed Man), **HWM Example 8.7.**
   5. Four-voice texture became standardized by the mid–fifteenth century
      a. A part added below the tenor served as a harmonic foundation.
      b. The lower voice was called contratenor bassus (low contratenor) and later simply bassus, now "bass" in English.
      c. The contratenor above the tenor was called contratenor altus (high contratenor), later simply altus, now "alto" in English.
      d. The top voice was called superius (highest), later "soprano."
   6. Du Fay's *Missa Se la face ay pale* (**NAWM 36b,** Gloria)
      a. The cantus firmus is the tenor of his own earlier ballade (**HWM Example 8.6** and **NAWM 36a**).
      b. The cantus firmus appears three times, but it is only easily recognized in the third appearance because the first two are in longer durations.
      c. At the end of "Amen," the tenor sings the final melisma from the original tenor, and the other voices borrow from the original as well.
      d. Borrowing in multiple voices makes the work a cantus-firmus/imitation mass.
      e. Du Fay creates variety by contrasting textures of two, three, and four voices.
   7. Popularity of the cantus-firmus mass
      a. Settings of the Mass Ordinary were often commissioned for specific occasions.
      b. Specific cantus-firmus melodies linked the Mass to location or event.
      c. *L'homme armé*'s popularity may be connected to the Order of the Golden Fleece, an association of knights at the Burgundian court.
      d. Composers proved their compositional skill in this form.

VI. The Musical Language of the Renaissance
   A. Composers working between the 1420s and the 1450s forged a cosmopolitan musical language.
      1. French concern for structure and rhythmic interest
      2. Italian emphasis on lyrical melodies
      3. English preference for consonant sonorities, especially thirds and sixths
      4. These elements continued to predominate in European music through the nineteenth century.
   B. Tinctoris and Martin Le Franc acknowledged the newness of this musical language.

## SUGGESTIONS FOR SUPPLEMENTAL READING/LISTENING/ACTIVITIES

Several excerpts in Gary Tomlinson, ed., *Source Readings in Music History,* rev. ed., *Vol. 3: The Renaissance* (New York: W. W. Norton, 1998), can expand students' perception of the Burgundian court and its style. For a sense of how the Renaissance interest in Greek writers influenced music, read the dedication to Tinctoris's

*Proportionale musices,* in which he invokes Greek authors in his praise of English compositional style. Du Fay's Letter to Piero and Giovanni de' Medici gives students a sense of how the nobility supported composers. Olivier de la Marche's *Memoir* on the House of Burgundy portrays a court performance.

For additional background for this chapter, see Craig Wright, *Music at the Court of Burgundy, 1354–1419: A Documentary Study* (Henryville, PA, 1979) and Andrew Wathey, "The Peace of 1360–1369 and Anglo-French Musical Relations," *Early Music History* ix (1990), 129.

Additional examples of carols can be found in *Musica Britannica* (London: Stainer & Bell, 1952) Vol. 4, or in a reprint of this volume, titled *Invitation to Medieval Music, Book 6. Medieval Carols* (London: Stainer & Bell) or *The New Oxford Book of Carols,* edited by Hugh Keyte and Andrew Parrott (London: Oxford University Press, 1998).

Dunstable's complete works can be found in *Musica Britannica*, vol. 8 (London: Stainer and Bell, 1953). The isorhythmic motet, *Veni creator spiritus*, Figure 8.1, is MB 32. For a recording of this work, use "Dunstable: Motets" (EMI 61342, 2000). This CD also includes Dunstable's setting of the Marian antiphon *Alma redemptoris mater* and a troped version of *Salve regina.* Marian antiphons are an important subset of Renaissance motet types, and most composers of the Renaissance set the texts of the four most important antiphons, sung at compline: *Alma redemptoris mater*, *Ave regina caelorum, Regina caeli,* and *Salve regina.* (See the *New Grove* article on "Antiphon, §5: Other antiphons in the Gregorian repertory(v) Marian antiphons" for an explanation). Direct comparisons of styles and techniques throughout the period can be facilitated by using examples drawn from this category of motet.

*Regina celi letare* (MB 38) has been released on "Dunstable: Cathedral Sounds Arte Nova" Records 34055, 1998), sung by the Clemencic Consort (Clemencic Edition Vol. 1).

Note that the editor of NAWM 32, *Quam pulchra es,* indicated ficta only for the top voice. Have students look for instances in which the middle voice might also be raised or lowered by a half-step (there are many) before playing the CD. Ask students if they agree with all the performers' decisions.

Respected singers have recorded several works from the Old Hall manuscript, including two mass movements by Leonel Power, on "Old Hall Manuscript" (EMI Records 61393, 2000). Power's *Quam Pulchra es* and other works are available on "Leonel Power" (EMI Records 61345, 2000), performed by the Hilliard Ensemble.

One of Charles the Bold's works is available on a compact disc titled "The Castle of Fair Welcome" (Hyperion 66194, 1993), performed by Gothic Voices. This CD also includes chansons by Robert Morton (of *L'homme armé* fame) and Du Fay.

The compact disc titled "Gilles Binchois: *Mon souverain désir*" (EMI 45285, 2000) by the Ensemble Gilles Binchois contains several secular songs. Binchois' secular works can be found in *Die Chansons von Gilles Binchois (1400–1460)*, ed. Wolfgang Rehm, *Musikalische Denkmäler,* Vol. ii (Mainz: Schott, 1957).

Du Fay's complete works comprise part i, volumes 1–6 of *Corpus mensurabilis musicae,* (1951–1966, and a rev. ed., 1995).

To demonstrate faburden and fauxbourdon, have students sing the examples from *NAWM.* Ask them which is easier, and whether they would need to have the added voice notated if they were fifteenth-century singers.

For a recording of Du Fay's *Nuper rosarum flores,* use Pomerium's "The Virgin and the Temple: Chants & Motets" (Deutsche Grammophon 447773, 1997) or "O gemma lux" (Harmonia Mundi s.a. HMC 901700, 2000), performed by the Huelgas Ensemble. This work's origin as a ceremonial or commemorative piece can help generate a discussion of the role of "old-fashioned" music in civic ceremony. Remind students that although *Nuper rosarum flores* was newly composed, it used a technique that was old-fashioned in its time. Ask students to name pieces that they have heard in ceremonies (examples might include "Happy Birthday," "Pomp and Circumstance No. 5," or the "Bridal March" by Wagner), noting the longevity of functional music compared to "modern" styles. If students have heard newly composed works for ceremonial use, ask them to describe the style. Although some may be "modern," chances are good that these works are at least tonal.

Du Fay's *Supremum est mortalibus bonum* and his *Missa L'homme armé* have been released on a CD aptly titled "DuFay: *Missa L'homme armé; Supremum est mortalibus bonum*" (Naxos 553087, 1995). For an instrumental version of *L'homme armé* that begins with a straightforward performance of the main tune, have students listen to "Music from the Time of Richard III" by the York Waits (Saydisc 364, 1995).

After studying the Gloria from Du Fay's *Missa Se la face ay pale,* have individuals or groups report on Du Fay's treatment of the cantus firmus in other movements of the mass, or in his *Missa L'homme armé*. Have students analyze Du Fay's division of the longer mass texts (Gloria and Credo) and compare these divisions to the chant settings in *NAWM* 3. The entire mass and the chanson have been recorded by David Munrow and The Early Music Consort (EMI 61283, 1996).

## OBJECTIVE QUESTIONS

1. In what way did the Hundred Years' War influence music?
   a. It put a halt to all secular music.
   b. The nobility could no longer afford to support music.
   c. English composers spent time in France.
   d. Composers from different regions became isolated from one another.
   e. It inspired nationalistic genres.

   Answer: c

2. The *contenance angloise* refers to __________.
   a. the English style of polyphony
   b. an anti-English secular song that became very popular in France
   c. a musical instrument that was the forerunner of the English horn
   d. a dance that was popular in England
   e. French disdain for the English style

   Answer: a

3. In England, most composition in the early fifteenth century was __________.
   a. secular monophony
   b. secular polyphony
   c. monophonic tropes and sequences
   d. polyphony on Latin texts
   e. composed for two languages simultaneously, usually English and Latin

   Answer: d

4. Cantilena is best defined as __________.
   a. a compositional style that imitates a bagpipe
   b. an improvised third voice added to a two-voice piece
   c. a freely composed, homorhythmic piece
   d. secular song in the French style
   e. using two cantus firmus tenor voices

   Answer: c

5. The Old Hall manuscript contains __________.
   a. sacred polyphony, including the works of Dunstable
   b. the earliest mass cycles built on secular French songs
   c. secular song from Burgundy
   d. Tinctoris's treatise
   e. Walter Odington's treatise

   Answer: a

6. The form which contains a burden is the __________.
   a. Burgundian chanson
   b. ballade
   c. isorhythmic motet
   d. polyphonic hymn
   e. carol

   Answer: e

7. By the first half of the fifteenth century, the word motet was applied to__________.
   a. any polyphonic composition on a sacred Latin text other than the Ordinary of the Mass
   b. any polyphonic composition in Latin
   c. only polyphonic compositions in which all voices had different texts
   d. any polyphonic composition using isorhythmic techniques
   e. any polyphonic composition using Latin words from the Ordinary of the Mass

   Answer: a

8. Which of these polyphonic genres was **not** one that Dunstable used?
   a. Settings of mass movements
   b. Settings of hymns
   c. Isorhythmic motets
   d. Settings of antiphons
   e. Cantus-firmus masses

   Answer: e

9. Which of these statements is true of the duchy of Burgundy?
   a. Though small, it was very wealthy.
   b. It occupied vast tracts of land and rivaled the kingdom of France in influence.
   c. It was ruled by the king of England.
   d. It was at war with Italy during most of the Hundred Years' War.
   e. The pope spent half of his time there, making it the most important region in Europe.

   Answer: b

10. The duke of Burgundy employed __________.
    a. only singers for his chapel
    b. only singers for his chapel and organists
    c. singers for his chapel, organists, and wind instrument players, but no string instumentalists
    d. singers for his chapel, organists, wind instrument players, and string instrumentalists
    e. no musicians, in contrast to other nobility of his era

    Answer: d

11. The language used for secular song texts composed in the Burgundian style was __________.
    a. Burgundian
    b. French
    c. English
    d. Flemish
    e. Latin

    Answer: b

12. Four-voice texture as developed in the fifteenth century consisted of __________.
    a. quadruplum, triplum, duplum, tenor
    b. motetus, duplum, tenor, contratenor
    c. superius, cantus, tenor, contratenor
    d. cantus, altus, tenor, contratenor
    e. superius, contratenor altus, tenor, contratenor bassus

    Answer: e

13. Du Fay's career was spent __________.
    a. entirely in the service of the duke of Burgundy
    b. entirely in the Church, at a cathedral in Cambrai and one in Paris
    c. divided between secular posts in Italy and a cathedral post in Cambrai
    d. traveling from court to court, including courts in England, France, Italy, and Spain
    e. at the University of Paris, where he taught composition and rhetoric

    Answer: c

14. The Burgundian chanson was usually composed in which form(s)?
    a. rondeau or ballade
    b. virelai or lai
    c. rondeau, ballade, virelai, or lai
    d. rondellus
    e. isorhythm

    Answer: a

15. Fauxbourdon is best defined as __________.
    a. alternation of two- and three-voice textures
    b. an English approach to isorhythm
    c. three-voice works composed in streams of 6-4 chords
    d. two composed voices with an improvised third voice, creating 6-3 chords
    e. a work composed in imitation of a bagpipe, with a single melody composed over a drone in parallel fifths

    Answer: d

16. Which statement is true of the isorhythmic motet in the early fifteenth century?
    a. It was an experimental form on the cutting edge of compositional inventiveness.
    b. It was considered old-fashioned and was only composed in backwards regions.
    c. It was considered old-fashioned but was composed in honor of special occasions.
    d. It had ceased to be composed or performed by ca. 1400.
    e. Although no new isorhythmic motets were being composed, Machaut's motets were rediscovered and then widely performed.

    Answer: c

17. A mass in which each movement is based on a pre-existing chant for that text is called a(n) ________.
    a. motto mass
    b. plainsong mass
    c. imitation mass
    d. cantus-firmus mass
    e. *L'homme armé* mass

    Answer: b

18. A mass that quotes more than one voice of a pre-existing polyphonic work is called a(n) __________.
    a. motto mass
    b. plainsong mass
    c. imitation mass
    d. cantus-firmus mass
    e. *L'homme armé* mass

    Answer: c

19. A mass in which all movements are based on the same pre-existing melody is called a(n) __________.
    a. motto mass
    b. plainsong mass
    c. imitation mass
    d. cantus-firmus mass
    e. *L'homme armé* mass

    Answer: d

20. A mass in which all movements begin with the same motive is called a(n) _________.
    a. motto mass
    b. plainsong mass
    c. imitation mass
    d. cantus-firmus mass
    e. *L'homme armé* mass

    Answer: a

## SHORT-ESSAY QUESTIONS

1. Discuss the development of the motet from the late fourteenth century to the fifteenth century.
2. Discuss the ways that composers tied together the Ordinary movements of the Mass in the early fifteenth century, naming an example from *NAWM.*
3. In what ways did the social and political atmosphere of the early fifteenth century contribute to changes in compositional style? Be specific, naming people and events that influenced music.
4. Compare and contrast secular and sacred genres in the early fifteenth century. In what ways did they influence each other? In what ways did they maintain their sacred or secular character?

## TERMS FOR IDENTIFICATION

contenance angloise
faburden
cantilena
burden
carol
Old Hall manuscript
duchy of Burgundy
Band of Minstrels
fauxbourdon
mass cycle
plainsong mass
motto mass
head-motive
cantus-firmus mass
imitation mass
*L'homme armé*
contratenor bassus
contratenor altus
superius

# CHAPTER 9 Franco-Flemish Composers, 1450–1520

I. Political Change and Consolidation (see map, **HWM Figure 9.1**)
  A. France
    1. Defeated England in the Hundred Years' War
    2. The duchy of Burgundy came under control of the king of France.
    3. By ca. 1525, France was a strong, centralized state.
  B. Spain
    1. The marriage of Queen Isabella of Castile and Léon and Ferdinand of Aragon united north-central and eastern Spain.
    2. Isabella and Ferdinand in 1492
      a. Conquered the Moors, taking over southern Spain
      b. Expelled the Jews from Spain
      c. Sponsored Columbus's journey, beginning the era of European colonization
  C. Hapsburg Empire
    1. United with Spain through marriage in the sixteenth century
    2. Ruled Austria, the Low Countries, southern Italy, Spain, and Spanish America
  D. Italy
    1. Invaded by France in 1494
    2. Continued to be composed of independent city-states and dominated by foreigners until the nineteenth century
    3. Wealthy Italian courts continued to hire musicians trained in the north.

II. Ockeghem and Busnoys
  A. Ockeghem and Busnoys were the most renowned composers of their generation.
  B. Jean de (or Johannes) Ockeghem, ca. 1420–1497 (see **HWM biography,** page 193, and **HWM Figure 9.2**)
    1. Sang in the Antwerp cathedral choir
    2. Served Charles I, duke of Bourbon, for a short time
    3. Served the kings of France from the 1450s to his retirement
      a. Entered the service in 1451
      b. 1454–1465: Held the post of chaplain
      c. 1464: Became a priest
      d. After 1465: Was master of the chapel
    4. Traveled a little, and had contact with Du Fay, Binchois, and Busnoys, but was not as cosmopolitan as Du Fay
    5. Composed relatively few works
      a. Masses, motets, chansons
      b. Developed his own style, synthesizing past, present, and his own style elements
      c. Known for his unique masses
  C. Antoine Busnoys (or Busnois, ca. 1430–1492)
    1. Served the Hapsburg Empire
    2. Known for his chansons
  D. Chansons
    1. Three-voice texture in treble-dominated style
    2. Use the *formes fixes,* especially rondeau
    3. Characteristics from Du Fay's generation are still evident (smooth melodies, preference for thirds and sixths, careful dissonance treatment)
    4. New features
      a. Longer melodies
      b. More imitation
      c. Greater equality between the voices
      d. More frequent use of duple meter

5. **HWM Example 9.1,** *Je ne puis vivre* by Busnoys
   a. Smooth, arching melody employing a wide range
   b. Constantly changing rhythms
   c. The contratenor is more singable than in Du Fay's style.

III. Masses
A. Comparison with Du Fay
1. Ockeghem and Busnoys were influenced by Du Fay.
2. Du Fay quoted from Ockeghem and Busnoys' *Missa L'homme armé* when he composed his mass on the same tenor.
B. Vocal ranges (see **HWM Example 9.2**)
1. Four-voice texture with a wide range
2. Bassus voice goes a fourth lower than in Du Fay's generation.
3. Each voice sings a span of a twelfth or thirteenth.
4. Passages in two- or three-voice texture contrast the dark, full texture resulting from the lower, wider ranges.
C. Phrases are long, with few cadences and elision to smooth them.
D. Cantus-firmus treatment (**NAWM 37** or **HWM Example 9.3**)
1. Both of Busnoys' masses and seven of Ockeghem's are cantus-firmus masses.
2. Ockeghem's *Missa de plus en plus* paraphrases the tenor.
   a. Rhythm not exactly the same as in the song
   b. Adds decorative notes

IV. Ockeghem's masses
A. Several motto masses
B. One plainsong mass
C. Requiem mass (also plainsong)
D. *Missa cuisvis toni* (mass in any mode) can be sung in mode of 1, 3, 5, or 7 using different clef combinations and musica ficta.
E. *Missa prolationum* (Prolation Mass, **HWM Examples 9.4a** and **9.4b**)
1. Technical tour de force
2. Notated in two voices but sung in four
3. Uses all four prolation signs, a different one in each voice
   a. Superius and alto sing the same music but in different meters
   b. Tenor and bass sing another melody, also in different meters
4. Canon (Latin, "rule")
   a. Deriving two or more voices from a single melody
   b. Voices may be delayed, inverted, or retrograde.
   c. Mensuration canon is when the "rule" is meter.
   d. Double canon is when there are two melodies treated according to a rule.
   e. *Missa prolationum* is both a mensuration canon and a double canon.

V. The Next Generation of Franco-Flemish composers
A. Three composers born at about the same time: Jacob Obrecht (1457 or 1458–1505), Henricus Isaac (ca. 1450–1517), and Josquin des Prez (ca. 1450–1521)
1. Born in the Low Countries
2. Trained in the Low Countries
3. Traveled widely
B. General traits
1. Singable parts
2. Each voice equal
3. Bass became the foundation voice.
4. Full triadic sonorities throughout, sometimes using triads at cadences
5. Borrowed melodies are distributed through all the voices.
6. Sacred genres: mass and motet
7. Secular genres no longer limited to *formes fixes*
8. More untexted (presumably instrumental) works
C. Jacob Obrecht (see **HWM Figure 9.3**)
1. Works
   a. Thirty cantus-firmus masses
   b. Twenty-eight motets
   c. Many chansons
   d. Songs in Dutch
   e. Instrumental works
2. Imitation
   a. Used more often than in previous generation
   b. Point of imitation: quick series of imitative entrances (**HWM Example 9.5**)
3. Clarity
   a. Clear tonal center, confirmed by cadences
   b. Clearly audible structure
D. Henricus Isaac
1. Worked for Lorenzo de' Medici in Florence and Emperor Maximilian I in Austria
2. Works
   a. Thirty-five masses
   b. Fifty motets
   c. *Choralis Constantinus,* cycle of settings for the Proper for most of the church year
   d. Secular songs in French, Italian, and German

e. Untexted works (probably instrumental)

3. Homophonic texture
   a. Isaac encountered homophonic song in the carnival tradition of Florence.
   b. His songs in German (Lied, pl. Lieder) include homophonic texture borrowed from Florentine tradition.
   c. Homophonic texture became part of the sixteenth-century style.
4. **NAWM 38** (and **HWM Example 9.6**), *Innsbruck, ich muss dich lassen*
   a. German secular song: Lied (pl. Lieder)
   b. Composed for court or elite circles but in a folk or popular style
   c. Homophonic with melody in the superius
   d. Strophic
   e. Cadences resolve to triads.
   f. Later became a chorale, *O Welt, ich musss dich lassen* (O world, I now must leave thee)

E. Text-setting
1. This generation was concerned with fitting music to the words.
2. In their compositions, phrases of text could be grasped as an uninterrupted thought.
3. Printed and handwritten music now had to be more precise in text underlay.

VI. Josquin Des Prez (ca. 1450–1521)

A. Biography (see **HWM biography,** page 203, and **HWM Figure 9.4**)
1. Most influential composer of his time
2. His given name was Josquin Lebloitte; "des Prez" was a nickname.
3. Probably born in northern France
4. Served in the chapel of the duke of Anjou in the 1470s
5. Ca. 1484–89: singer in the duke's chapel in Milan
6. 1489–95 or later: singer for the Sistine Chapel in Rome
7. 1501–03: worked in France, possibly for King Louis XII
8. 1503: appointed maestro di cappella to Duke Ercole I d'Este in Ferrara for a noble court and earned the highest salary in that court's history
9. 1504: left Ferrara, possibly to escape the plague, then took a position as provost at the church of Notre Dame at Condé-sur-l'Escaut, where he remained until his death.

B. Works
1. Eighteen masses
2. Over fifty motets
3. Sixty-five chansons (ten instrumental)
4. Many other works attributed to him were probably composed by others.

C. Fame (see **HWM Source Readings,** page 204)
1. Martin Luther called him "Master of Notes" in 1538.
2. Glareanus compared him to Homer.
3. Cosimo Bartolo (1567) compared him to Michelangelo.
4. Composers emulated his style.
5. His works were performed for almost a century after his death.
6. Publishers falsely attributed works to him in order to boost sales of their books.

D. Motets (**NAWM 39,** *Ave Maria . . . virgo serena*)
1. Style characteristics consistent with his generation:
   a. Texts drawn from Mass Proper or other sources
   b. Music freely composed, i.e., not based on chant
   c. Clarity in phrasing, form, and total organization
   d. Textures include imitation and homophony and are transparent throughout.
   e. Careful declamation of text
2. Text depiction and expression: Josquin was the first major composer to use music to depict the meaning of the text.
3. *Ave Maria . . . virgo serena* (**NAWM 39**)
   a. One of his earliest motets (1485) and one of his most popular
   b. Texture begins with point of imitation then constantly shifts in number of voices and between imitation and homophony.
   c. The text structure defines the musical sections, with each couplet or strophe given unique treatment.
   d. Rhythmic activity accelerates toward the conclusion of the first section ("drive to the cadence," a technique he probably learned from Ockeghem).
   e. Two meter changes provide contrast.
   f. The final lines, "O mother of God, remember me. Amen," are set in simple harmonies in homophonic texture.
   g. In Josquin's time, this would have been performed by one to a few singers per part, but this motet is often performed by choirs today.

E. Josquin's masses
1. Josquin composed masses using a variety of techniques.
   a. Most use a secular tune as a cantus firmus.
   b. *Missa L'homme armé super voces musicales* transposes the cantus firmus to successive degrees of the hexachord for each movement.

    c. *Missa Hercules dux Ferrariae* uses a *soggetto cavato dalle vocali* ("subject drawn from the vowels" of the hexachord syllables) as the theme.
  2. Imitation mass
    a. Sometimes also called "parody mass"
    b. Josquin's *Missa Malheur me bat* borrows from all voices of the original polyphonic song.
    c. Resemblance to the original is strongest at the beginning and end of the new work.
    d. This technique works best when the source is composed for equal voices, i.e., imitative or homophonic.
    e. Became the most common type of mass after ca. 1520
F. Paraphrase mass: *Missa Pange lingua* (**NAWM 40**)
  1. Based on a plainchant
    a. All four voices sing the source chant at some point.
    b. Phrases from the original generate motives for the new work.
    c. The original chant is paraphrased.
  2. Source chants chosen for their context, e.g., to honor a patron or a saint
  3. Imitation in paired voices, a characteristic of Josquin's style
  4. The *Credo* highlights important words with homophony.
G. Chansons
  1. New style in this generation
    a. Strophic texts, with virtually no use of the *formes fixes*
    b. Four- or five-voice texture, all voices meant to be sung
    c. All parts equal
    d. Employ imitation and homophony
  2. **NAWM 41,** *Mille regretz*
    a. Attributed to Josquin though perhaps not by him
    b. Representative of his style ca. 1520
    c. Each new phrase of text receives its own particular treatment; e.g., **HWM Example 9.8** sets one phrase in paired imitation and the next in four-voice imitation.

## SUGGESTIONS FOR SUPPLEMENTAL READING/LISTENING/ACTIVITIES

Scholars and performers have recently taken an interest in music of Spain and the New World during the Renaissance. The Hilliard Ensemble's two-CD compilation "Spanish and Mexican Renaissance Vocal Music" (EMI Classics CDS 754341 2,1991) contains an excellent introduction by Tess Knighton. The San Antonio Vocal Arts Ensemble's recording "Guadalupe: Virgen de los Indios" (Iago CD210) contains music composed in sixteenth and seventeenth centuries by native Aztec and Nahua composers who had converted to Christianity. Ockeghem's reworking of the Spanish song *Qu'es mi vida preguntays* is available on "Music for the Spanish Kings," recorded by Hesperion XX (Virgin Classics Veritas 61875, 2001) on a CD that also includes several works by Spanish composer Antonio de Cabezón (1510–1566).

Pomerium's performance of *Je ne puis vivre* by Busnoys on "*In hydraulis* and Other Works" (Dorian, DOR-90184, 1993) is an excellent performance that gives an idea of Busnoys' style.

A number of plates of manuscript sources for Ockeghem's masses are reproduced in Dragan Plamenac, ed., *Johannes Ockeghem: Collected Works,* Vol. 2 (New York: American Musicological Society, 1966).

The Clerks Group's recording "Ockeghem: *Missa Fors Seulement*" includes Ockeghem's chanson and three movements of the mass he based on it.

Ockeghem's *Missa L'homme armé* is available on compact disc, performed by the Oxford Camerata (Naxos 554297, 1998) and by The Clerks Group (ASV Gaudeamus 204, 2000), and Busnoys' *Missa L'homme armé* is available on a recording by the Binchois Consort (Hyperion 67319, 2002). Have students listen to the Kyrie of each and raise their hands when they hear the *L'homme armé* theme. Knowing that the theme will be in the tenor and in longer note values will help them hear it. Note that fifteenth-century listeners would have known what to listen for as well.

Ockeghem's *Missa de plus en plus* and the original chanson by Busnoys have been issued on the same compact disc, sung by the Clerks Group (ASV Gaudeamus 153, 1996) and also by the Tallis Scholars (Gimell, 2001). The Orlando Consort's recording of *Missa de plus en plus* includes seven of his chansons as well, but not the Busnoys original (Deutsche Grammophon/Archiv 53 419-2, 2002).

Ockeghem's *Missa mi-mi* is available in a study score (Kalmus/Warner K 06357) and on compact disc, performed by the Clerks Group (ASV Gaudeamus 139, 1994).

Ockeghem's canonic works include a chanson, *Prenez sur moi vostre exemple,* available in *Motets and Chansons* (Collected Works, Vol. 3), edited by Richard Wexler with Dragon Plamenac (Boston: American Musicological

Society, 1992), and on a recording by the Orlando Consort (Archiv 471727, 2002). The recording also includes *Missa de plus en plus* and other chansons.

To help students appreciate how *L'homme armé* and other songs could be recognized within a polyphonic work, ask them to name examples of popular songs of today that "sample" songs by other groups. If they are unfamiliar with current popular music, play a recording of the Beatles' *All You Need Is Love,* which quotes their previous song *She Loves You,* to generate a discussion of quotation and borrowing.

Obrecht's *Missa Fortuna desperata* has not been issued on compact disc, but it was issued on LP, recorded by the Clemencic Consort (Musical Heritage Society MHS 4122, 1978, and Harmonia Mundi 998, 1978).

The Orlando Consort has recorded the Proper for Easter from Isaac's *Choralis Constantinus* on "Passion" (Metronome 1511103, 1997). The first two parts as appeared as volumes 10 and 32 of *Denkmäler der Tonkunst in Österreich* and the third was published as *Choralis Constantinus. Book III* (Ann Arbor: University of Michigan Press, 1950).

Have students analyze other Josquin motets for the ways in which Josquin pays attention to the relationship between words and music. Motets and several of his secular songs can be found on the compact disc "Josquin Des Prez: Motets et Chansons," performed by the Hilliard Ensemble (EMI D112649, 1987 and Virgin Classics 61302, 1997). *Josquin Anthology,* edited by Ross Duffin (New York: Oxford University Press, 1999), includes twelve motets, commentaries on each, and an essay by Paul Hillier on performance practice. "Passion," a CD by the Orlando Consort (Metronome, 1997), includes Josquin's *Victimae Paschali Laudes,* which is in the Duffin edition.

Have groups of students analyze the use of the cantus firmus in other movements of the *Missa Pange Lingua,* available in several editions, including Vol. 4 of his complete works: *Masses Based on Gregorian Chants,* edited by Willem Elders (Utrecht: Koninklijke Vereniging voor Nederlandse Muziekgeschiedenis, 2000).

Assign one mass by Josquin to each student or group of students and have them report on the occasion or meaning of the mass, the source material, Josquin's treatment of the source material (i.e., paraphrase, imitation, etc.), and the ways in which Josquin takes the original material through all the movements.

A famous chanson by Josquin, included on the Hilliard Ensemble CD mentioned above, is *Nymphes des bois/Requiem aeternam* or *Déploration de le mort de Johannes Ockeghem* (Lament on the Death of Johannes Ockeghem). This work demonstrates the fame of Ockeghem, Josquin's admiration of the older composer, and the practice of composing works for specific occasions. The cantus firmus is *Requiem aeternam* from the Mass for the Dead, but the text of the lament is in French.

## OBJECTIVE QUESTIONS

1. Ockeghem spent most of his career in the service of __________.
   a. the nobility of Mantua
   b. Ferdinand and Isabella
   c. the Pope
   d. the kings of France
   e. the duke of Burgundy

   Answer: d

2. Ockeghem's *Missa prolationem* employs which compositional technique?
   a. Cantus-firmus
   b. Canon
   c. Motto
   d. The main motive is based on solfège syllables.
   e. Imitation of all the voices of a motet whose text begins with the word *Prolationem*

   Answer: b

3. The *Missa Cuisvis toni* is special because __________.
   a. it can be sung in any mode
   b. it was composed for the pope's anniversary
   c. it uses all seven notes of the diatonic octave in its theme
   d. the solfège names for the notes spell the name of the person to whom it is dedicated
   e. the composer intended for it to be performed at his tomb after his death

   Answer: a

4. Busnoys favored which form(s) for his chansons?
   a. The *formes fixes*, especially the rondeau
   b. Free compositions with no repetition
   c. Forms incorporating a *burden* section
   d. Paired stanzas with open and closed endings
   e. Cantus-firmus treatments based on chant melodies

   Answer: a

5. Which of the following statements describes the way(s) in which the *bassus* voice of the late fifteenth century differs from that of the masses of Du Fay?
   a. The range is a fourth lower.
   b. The range is a fourth higher.
   c. It sings the cantus-firmus melody instead of the tenor voice.
   d. It is a drone.
   e. There was no *bassus* voice in the late-fifteenth-century mass.

   Answer: a

6. Vocal ranges of the late fifteenth and early sixteenth centuries tended to span __________.
   a. less than an fifth
   b. slightly less than an octave
   c. about an octave
   d. slightly more than an octave
   e. about a twelfth

   Answer: e

7. Composers of the late fifteenth and early sixteenth centuries take what approach to cantus-firmus composition?
   a. They continue using cantus firmus in the way earlier composers did.
   b. They give the chant melody of its own rather than use an isorhythm.
   c. They treat the rhythm freely.
   d. They treat the melody freely, adding notes for decoration.
   e. They drop the use of chant melodies and use only secular songs.

   Answer: d

8. Which of the following is true of musical style in the late fifteenth and early sixteenth centuries?
   a. The top voice became the primary voice.
   b. The top two voices were the primary voices, with other(s) playing supporting role(s).
   c. All voices were nearly equal in rhythmic motion but the bottom voices were less singable.
   d. All voices were nearly equal and all were singable.
   e. The tenor continued to be slower-moving and was most likely played on an instrument.

   Answer: d

9. Cadences of the late fifteenth and early sixteenth centuries were marked by __________.
   a. a return to the Landini cadence
   b. frequent use of the double-leading tone cadence
   c. occasional use of full triads for the closing sonority
   d. almost universal use of full triads for the closing sonority
   e. formulas that reinforced the qualities of the church mode

   Answer: c

10. Obrecht's works include secular songs in which language?
    a. English
    b. Spanish
    c. Dutch
    d. Polish
    e. Greek

    Answer: c

11. Point of imitation is defined as __________.
    a. the second entrance of a theme
    b. a quick succession of imitative entrances
    c. the interval relationship between imitative entrances
    d. the rhythmic relationship between imitative entrances
    e. a change of meter, signaling a new section

    Answer: b

12. Isaac's Lieder can best be described as __________.
    a. secular but in the same highly contrapuntal style as a motet
    b. similar in style to French language chansons
    c. composed for court or elite circles but in a folk or popular style
    d. based on Lutheran chorales
    e. most likely intended for performance by instrumental ensemble

    Answer: c

13. Which of these compositional techniques used by Isaac can be traced to popular music in Italy?
    a. imitation
    b. contrafacta
    c. canon
    d. homophony
    e. paraphrase

    Answer: d

14. Which of the following statements best reflects Josquin's approach to text setting?
    a. He was preoccupied with counterpoint and paid little attention to the text.
    b. Through his use of imitation, the voices often sing different words simultaneously.
    c. He never allowed more than one word to be sung simultaneously.

d. He gave a new melody to each new phrase of text to make it clear.
e. Extended melismas often obscure the meaning of the text.

Answer: d

15. Which of the following statements best describes Josquin's career?
 a. He was largely unknown in his lifetime, and his works were discovered after his death.
 b. He worked for one employer for almost his entire career.
 c. He worked for a series of secular courts.
 d. He worked for a series of religious institutions.
 e. He worked for several employers, both secular and religious.

 Answer: e

16. Imitation in paired voices is a characteristic of __________.
 a. Ockeghem
 b. Busnoys
 c. Isaac
 d. Obrecht
 e. Josquin

 Answer: e

17. Josquin's *Missa Pange lingua* is an example of which mass type?
 a. tenor mass
 b. paraphrase mass
 c. plainsong mass
 d. imitation mass
 e. motto mass

 Answer: b

18. Which of the following statements best describes the style of Josquin's chansons?
 a. They used strophic texts, with virtually no use of the *formes fixes.*
 b. Most were ballades or rondeaux.
 c. Most were in refrain forms devised by Josquin himself for each new poem.
 d. The texts came from epic stories of romance.
 e. Most were contrafacta based on pre-existing motets

 Answer: a

19. Josquin's motets would most likely have been performed by __________.
 a. a solo singer accompanied by lute
 b. an ensemble of solo singers, one voice to a part
 c. a small choir, with a few voices to a part
 d. a large a capella choir of up to 100 singers
 e. a large choir accompanied by organ

 Answer: c

20. Which composer used solfège syllables to create the cantus firmus for two masses?
 a. Ockeghem
 b. Josquin
 c. Busnoys
 d. Obrecht
 e. Isaac

 Answer: b

## SHORT-ESSAY QUESTIONS

1. Discuss the main changes in compositional style in the late fifteenth century, including texture, form, and the use of pre-existing material.
2. Discuss the main characteristics of Josquin's style, comparing it to Du Fay's as a point of reference.
3. Discuss the types of masses composed by Ockeghem and Josquin. In what ways were they innovative? How were they similar to each other?
4. Looking at a motet by Josquin (use **NAWM 39** or another, such as *Ut Phoebi radiis*), discuss the ways in which the composer is sensitive to the text.

## TERMS FOR IDENTIFICATION

Ferdinand and Isabella
Prolation Mass
motto mass
canon
mensuration canon
double canon
Lied
*Choralis Constantinus*
point of imitation
soggetto cavato delle vocali
imitation mass
paraphrase mass

# CHAPTER 10 Sacred Music in the Era of the Reformation

I. Protestant Reformation
   A. Rebellion against the authority of the Catholic Church
      1. Spread throughout most of northern Europe (see map, **HWM Figure 10.1**)
      2. Germany and Scandinavia: Lutheran movement
      3. Switzerland, Low Countries, Britain: Calvinist movement
      4. England: Church of England
   B. Martin Luther (1483–1546, see **HWM Figure 10.2**)
      1. Professor of biblical theology at the University of Wittenberg in Germany
      2. Concluded that salvation came through faith alone, not good works or penance, as preached by the Catholic Church.
      3. Rebelled against nonbiblical practices in the Catholic Church
      4. Ninety-five Theses (points or arguments)
         a. A list of complaints against the Catholic Church, posted on a church door in Wittenberg on October 31, 1517
         b. Widely printed and disseminated, making Martin Luther famous
         c. When he refused to recant the theses, he was excommunicated from the Catholic Church (1520).
      5. New church: New Evangelical, or Lutheran
         a. German princes adopted Lutheranism, freeing them from Roman control.
         b. The vernacular was used for the liturgy, but Luther considered some Latin essential for education.
      6. Music continued to be important because of Luther's belief in its ethical power and his appreciation of composers such as Josquin.

II. Music in the Lutheran Church in Germany
   A. Texts were in the vernacular, but much of the Catholic liturgy was retained.
   B. Churches were free to use music as they wished.
      1. Large churches with trained choirs kept much of the Latin liturgy and polyphony.
      2. Smaller churches used Luther's *Deutsche Messe* (German Mass, 1526)
         a. Followed main outlines of the Roman Mass
         b. Replaced most musical elements with German hymns (chorales)
   C. Lutheran chorale
      1. Metric, rhymed, strophic poetry for unison, unaccompanied performance by the congregation
      2. Most important form of Lutheran church music
      3. Congregations sang several chorales at each service.
      4. Luther wrote many chorales himself.
      5. Four collections were published in 1524.
   D. Sources for chorale melodies
      1. Adaptation of existing Gregorian chant, as in **NAWM 42a** and **42b,** and **HWM Example 10.1**
      2. Existing devotional songs in German, e.g., *Christ is erstanden*, which comes from *Victimae paschali laude*
      3. Secular songs given new words (*contrafacta*, sing. *contrafactum*), e.g. *O Welt ich muss dich lassen*, based on **NAWM 38,** *Innsbruck ich muss das lassen*

4. Newly composed melodies, e.g., **NAWM 42,** *Ein feste Burg*
    a. Luther adapted Psalm 46 for the text.
    b. *Ein feste Burg* became an anthem of the Reformation.
    c. The original rhythm suits the text, but modern versions use a more regular rhythm.

III. Polyphonic Chorale Settings
  A. Purposes
    1. Group singing in home settings
    2. Performance in church by choirs, alternating stanzas with the congregation in unison
    3. Luther wanted "wholesome" music for young people, to "rid them of their love ditties and wanton song."
  B. Techniques
    1. Traditional Lied technique, e.g., **NAWM 42d** and **HWM Example 10.3a**
      a. Chorale in tenor
      b. Three or more free-flowing parts
      c. Johann Walter was Martin Luther's chief musical collaborator.
    2. Chorale motets
      a. Franco-Flemish motet style
      b. Chorale appears as a cantus firmus in long notes in some motets.
      c. Some chorale motets use the source chorale imitatively in all voices, e.g., **HWM Example 10.3,** *Ein feste Burg*
    3. Homophony (cantional style, from the Latin *cantionale,* "songbook")
      a. Popular in the last third of the century
      b. Tune in the highest voice
      c. Accompaniment in block chords
      d. After ca. 1600 the accompaniment was usually played on organ, with the choir singing the melody in unison.

IV. Music in Calvinist Churches
  A. Jean Calvin (1509–1564)
    1. Led the largest Protestant movement outside of Germany and Scandinavia
    2. Rejected papal authority
    3. Embraced the idea of justification through faith alone, but believed that predestination determined a person's salvation or damnation
    4. Believed all aspects of life should fall under God's law
    5. Required his followers to live lives of piety, uprightness, and work
  B. Regional churches
    1. France: Huguenots
    2. Dutch Reformed
    3. England: Presbyterian and Puritans
  C. Calvin and music
    1. Calvin stripped churches and services of possible distractions from worship, including decorations (see **HWM Figure 10.3**), ceremony, and polyphony.
    2. He believed congregational singing united worshipers in faith and praise.
    3. Only biblical texts were permitted (see **HWM Source Reading,** page 213).
  D. Psalms
    1. Psalms rewritten for congregational singing with meter, strophes, and rhymes are known as "metrical" psalms.
    2. Psalters: collections of metrical psalms
      a. Calvin issued several in French in 1539.
      b. The first complete psalter in French was published in 1562.
    3. The French metrical psalms were adapted in other countries.
      a. In Germany, many psalm melodies were used as chorales.
      b. The *Bay Psalm Book* (1640), containing metrical psalms in English, was the first book published in North America.
    4. Catholics and Lutherans also published metrical psalters.
    5. Some tunes are still used today, e.g., **NAWM 43**, **HWM Example 10.4**
      a. Published as Psalm 134 in France
      b. In English psalters the melody was used for Psalm 100.
      c. The tune is now known as "Old Hundredth."
  E. Polyphonic psalm settings
    1. Composed by well-known Dutch composers
    2. Four or five parts, for home or amateur singing
    3. Tune in the tenor or superius
    4. Texture ranges from homophonic to chorale-motet style
    5. Various combinations possible, including voice with lute or organ alone

V. Church Music in England
  A. Background
    1. Henry VIII (r. 1505–47, see **HWM Figure 10.4**) wanted to annul his marriage in order to try to have a male heir with a new wife.
    2. In 1534 he persuaded Parliament to separate from Rome so he could get an annulment, creating the Anglican Church, or Church of England.
    3. Henry VIII's new church retained Catholic doctrine.

4. Under Edward VI (r. 1547–53) the Church adopted Protestant doctrines.
    a. English replaced Latin in the liturgy.
    b. Official prayers were published in the *Book of Common Prayer* in 1549.
5. Catholicism was briefly the official religion during the reign of Mary (r. 1553–58)
6. Under Elizabeth I (r. 1558–1603) the Anglican Church blended elements of Catholic and Protestant theology.
7. The Anglican Church's doctrine has remained the same since.
8. In the United States, the Anglican Church is known today as the Episcopal Church.

B. Music for the Anglican Church
1. Music in Latin
    a. Latin motets and masses continued to be composed under Henry VIII and Mary.
    b. Elizabeth I allowed Latin music in her royal chapel and in some churches.
2. Service
    a. With the anthem, one of the two principal forms of Anglican music
    b. Combines elements of Matins, Mass, and Evensong (Vespers and Compline)
    c. Great Service: sets the text contrapuntally
    d. Short Service: sets the text syllabically and in homophonic texture
3. Anthem
    a. English equivalent of motet
    b. Sung by the choir
    c. Texts come from the Bible or the Book of Common Prayer
    d. Full anthem: unaccompanied, contrapuntal
    e. Verse anthem: for solo voice(s) with organ or viol accompaniment, alternating with passages for full choir doubled by instruments

C. John Taverner (ca. 1490–1545)
1. Leading composer of sacred music in England in the first half of the sixteenth century
2. Composed masses and motets
3. English traits: long melismas, full textures, cantus-firmus structures

D. Thomas Tallis (ca. 1505–1585)
1. Leading composer of the generation following Taverner
2. Composed Latin masses and hymns
3. Also composed English service music
4. His style weds the melody to the natural inflection of speech.

VI. William Byrd (ca. 1540–1623, see **HWM biography,** page 223, and **HWM Figure 10.5**)

A. Biography
1. The most important English composer of the Renaissance
2. Probably studied with Thomas Tallis
3. Catholic, yet served the Church of England as organist and choirmaster
4. Worked in the royal chapel from 1572 to 1623
5. Composed both Anglican service music and Latin music
6. Also composed secular music (see **HWM Chapters 11** and **12**)
7. His style shows the influence of continental imitative techniques.

B. Anglican music
1. Byrd composed in all the Anglican genres.
2. **NAWM 44,** *Sing joyfully unto God*
    a. Anthem for six voices in Ionian mode (with a final on C, transposed to E-flat in **NAWM 44**)
    b. Points of imitation open the work.
    c. Homophonic declamation used sparingly (e.g., at "Blow the trumpet")
    d. Bass motion a fifth down or a fourth up for cadences
    e. Passages in imitation vary the intervals and rhythm.

C. Latin-texted music
1. His best-known compositions were for Catholic worship.
2. By the 1590s he was composing for Catholics worshiping in secret.
3. Three masses, one each for three, four, and five voices
4. *Gradualia* (1605 and 1607)
    a. Two books
    b. Polyphonic settings of the complete Mass Proper for the church year.
    c. Similar in scale to Leonin's *Magnus Liber* and Isaac's *Choralis Constantinus*

VII. Catholic Church Music

A. Composers from Flanders dominated the generation active ca. 1520–1550
1. Adrian Willaert (ca. 1490–1562)
    a. Held positions in Italy
    b. Director of Music at St. Mark's in Venice
    c. Trained many eminent musicians, including Zarlino
2. Nicolas Gombert (ca. 1495–1560)
3. Jacobus Clemens

B. Style features
1. Careful treatment of dissonance

2. Equality of voices
3. Five- or six-voice compositions, using contrasting combinations of voices
4. Clearly defined mode
5. Duple meter with brief contrasting passages in triple
6. Imitative polyphony, but successive entrances vary the motives
7. Imitation mass the most common type, but composers still use paraphrase and cantus-firmus techniques

C. **HWM Example 10.5,** Gombert's motet, *Quem dicunt homines*
1. Six voices
2. Point of imitation, with each slightly varied
3. Each new phrase begins with point of imitation in a different order of entrances.
4. Overlapping phrases, not like Josquin's clarity of structure

D. Mode in polyphony
1. Composers attempted to apply Greek theory to achieve emotional effect.
2. Cadences on the final or reciting tone
3. Superius and tenor ranges define plagal or authentic mode.

E. Willaert and humanism
1. Willaert never allowed a rest to interrupt a word or thought.
2. He insisted that syllables be printed under their notes.

F. Catholic response to the Reformation (Counter-Reformation or Catholic Reformation)
1. Jesuits (Society of Jesus)
   a. Founded by St. Ignatius Loyola (1491–1556) in 1534
   b. Founded schools to teach proper Catholicism
   c. Proselytized, reconverting Poland, southern Germany, and much of France
2. Council of Trent (1545–1563, see **HWM Figure 10.6**)
   a. Series of meetings held in Trent (northern Italy)
   b. Reaffirmed doctrines that Calvin and Luther had attacked
   c. Purged the Church of abuses and laxities
   d. Eliminated tropes and all but four sequences (one sequence that survived is **NAWM 5,** *Victimae paschali laudes*)
   e. Music was a subject for debate, especially the use of secular song in the composition of masses.
   f. The final statement was vague, leaving it to bishops to regulate music.

VIII. Giovanni Pierluigi da Palestrina (1525/1526–1594)

A. Biography (see **HWM biography,** page 228, and **HWM Figure 10.7**)
1. Born in Palestrina, near Rome
2. Educated in Rome, where he was a choirboy
3. 1544–1551: Organist and choirmaster in Palestrina
4. 1551–55 and 1571–1594: Choirmaster of Julian Chapel at St. Peter's
5. 1555: Sang in the pope's official chapel (Capella Sistina) briefly but could not continue because he was married
6. 1555–1560 and 1561–1566: Held two other important posts in Rome
7. Spent his last forty years as choirmaster and teacher at influential churches in Rome
8. Taught music at the new Jesuit seminary
9. Works
   a. 104 masses, more than any other composer
   b. Madrigals, which he later regretted having composed
   c. Over three hundred motets
   d. Other liturgical compositions
   e. Participated in the reformation of chant-books, which were published after his death
10. Credited with saving polyphony from the Council of Trent
    a. According to legend, his *Pope Marcellus Mass* (**NAWM 45**), dedicated to the pope, demonstrated that sacred words could be intelligible in polyphonic music.
    b. Palestrina said the mass was composed "in a new manner," and it does show attention to text-setting for clarity, but the legend exaggerates Palestrina's role.

B. Palestrina's style
1. Mass types
   a. Fifty-one imitation masses
   b. Thirty-four paraphrase masses, most based on chant, with paraphrasing occurring in all voices
   c. Eight cantus-firmus masses, including two on *L'homme armé*
   d. A few canonic masses
   e. Free masses, using the borrowed melodies or canon, including the *Pope Marcellus Mass*
2. Melodies often move stepwise in an arched line, similar to Gregorian chant melodies.
3. His harmonic style includes triadic harmony and very little chromaticism.
4. Counterpoint follows Zarlino's rules (*Le istitutioni harmoniche*) closely.
   a. Dissonances introduced in suspensions and resolved on strong beats

b. Dissonances between beats are allowed if the moving voice is doing so in a stepwise fashion or as a suspension (see **HWM Example 10.6**).
c. Downward leap of a third, from a dissonance to a consonance (later called cambiata), is also allowable.
d. The resulting harmonic style comprises an alternation of consonance and dissonance.

5. Palestrina achieves variety by using different combinations of chord voicings, e.g., **HWM Example 10.7.**
6. Palestrina makes the text intelligible by using syllabic text-setting and homophony in movements with long texts, e.g., **HWM Example 10.6** and **10.8.**
7. Texture within a six-voice context
   a. Each new phrase uses a different combination of voices.
   b. All six voices come together for important words, cadences, and musical climaxes.
   c. Voice combinations sometimes used for text-painting, e.g., three voices to symbolize the Trinity.
8. Rhythm
   a. Each voice has its own natural rhythm, e.g., **HWM Example 10.9,** which rebars **Example 10.6.**
   b. Syncopation sustains momentum and links phrases.

C. Palestrina's style was a model for subsequent generations and is still the ideal in present-day textbooks on counterpoint.

IX. Spain and the New World
A. Spain's monarchy was strongly Catholic.
   1. The Spanish Inquisition of the 1480s sought to root out heresy.
   2. The monarchy's links to the Low Countries and Italy brought the Franco-Flemish central musical style to Spain.
B. Cristóbal de Morales (ca. 1500–1553)
   1. Sang in the papal chapel, 1535–45
   2. Famous in Italy and Spain
   3. Composed masses, quoting Josquin, Gombert, and Spanish songs.
   4. Teacher of Francisco Guerrero (1528–1599), whose diatonic, singable music was widely performed in Spain and the New World.
C. Tomás Luís de Victoria (1548–1611)
   1. Most famous Spanish composer of the sixteenth century.
   2. Influence of Palestrina
      a. Victoria spent two decades in Rome, where he probably knew Palestrina.
      b. He was the first Spanish composer to master Palestrina's style, yet his music departs from that style in many ways.
   3. Style, e.g., **NAWM 46a,** *O magnum mysterium* (motet)
      a. Published in his first book of motets (1572)
      b. Shorter than a Palestrina motet
      c. Melodies are less florid
      d. More chromatic than Palestrina
      e. More contrast of texture
      f. Features similar to Josquin's style include paired imitation and word-painting, e.g., large leaps on the word *magnum* (great or large)
   4. Victoria and the imitation mass, e.g., **NAWM 46b,** *Missa O magnum mysterium*
      a. Based his imitation masses on his own motets
      b. The Kyrie begins with an exact quotation of the motet's imitation, then changes to a dialogue between two themes derived from the original.
      c. Each movement reworks the original in a new way.
D. Spanish music in the New World
   1. After the Spanish conquest of Mexico (1519–21) and Peru (1527–33) missionaries arrived to convert original inhabitants to Christianity.
   2. Aztec and Incan music were often associated with dancing (see **HWM Source Reading,** page 234)
      a. Chieftains had chapels with singers/composers.
      b. Singers rehearsed for important festivals, which lasted all day.
      c. Singers were accompanied by drums.
   3. Catholic music
      a. Missionaries taught European styles to native musicians.
      b. Masses by Morales, Victoria, Palestrina, and Guerrero were performed.
      c. European composers came to the New World and created some works in native languages, including the first polyphonic work composed in the New World (1631), which was in the Quecha language of Peru.

X. Germany and Eastern Europe
A. Areas that remained Catholic included southern Germany, Poland, Austria, and Bohemia.
B. Franco-Flemish music predominated, but there were some local composers.
   1. Wacław of Szamotuł (ca. 1520–ca. 1567) in Poland

2. Jacob Handl (1550–1591) in Bohemia
3. Hans Leo Hassler (1564–1612) in Germany
   a. Studied in Venice
   b. Composed settings of Lutheran chorales as well as Catholic polyphony and secular music

C. Orlando di Lasso (1532–1594)
1. Biography (see **HWM biography,** page 236, and **HWM Figure 10.8**)
   a. Born in Hainaut, the region where Du Fay, Ockeghem, and Josquin were trained
   b. His early career was spent in the service of Italian patrons.
   c. By age twenty-four he had published books of sacred and secular music.
   d. From 1556 to his death, he served the Dukes of Bavaria (Albrecht V and Wilhelm V).
   e. He traveled frequently, which gave him the opportunity to hear others' works.
2. He composed over two thousand pieces.
   a. Fifty-seven masses
   b. Over seven hundred motets
   c. Hundreds of other liturgical compositions
   d. Two hundred Italian madrigals
   e. 150 French chansons
   f. Ninety German Lieder
3. Style, e.g., **NAWM 47** and **HWM Example 10.10,** *Tristis est anima mea* (1565)
   a. He was an advocate of emotional expression and depiction of text through music, especially in motets.
   b. The text is based on Jesus' words before his crucifixion (Matthew 26:38, Mark 14:34).
   c. Suspensions depict sadness (*tristis*) as marked with an "S" in **HWM Example 10.10**—a secular Italian trait (which will be discussed in Chapter 11).
   d. A running subject repeated eleven times depicts the words "you will take flight," which refers to the eleven disciples.
4. Lasso influenced later German composers.

XI. Jewish Music

A. Jewish traditions in Europe were primarily oral, not written.
1. Psalms were sung to recitational formulas.
2. Cantillation was used for reading Hebrew Scripture.
3. Cantillation was notated with the system to mark accents, division of text, and the melodies to be used for improvisation.

B. Local influences on Jewish music
1. The Ashkenazi of Germany were influenced by Gregorian chant and Minnesang.
2. The Sephardic Jews of Spain were influenced by Arab sources.

## SUGGESTIONS FOR SUPPLEMENTARY READING/LISTENING/ACTIVITIES

Translations of Martin Luther's foreword to the *Wittemberg Gesangbuch* and other writings are available in *Source Readings in Music History*, rev. ed., Vol. 3: The Renaissance (New York: W. W. Norton, 1998).

Show students a facsimile of the German Mass, pointing out similarities to the Catholic Mass. A few pages of a copy in the Pitts Theological Library at Emory University are available online at www.pitts.emory.edu/woodcuts/dm/k1526luthr.html. Page C3 recto has a plainly legible Kyrie and C3 verso introduces an example with the Latin word *Exemplum.*

The hymn contrafactum of Isaac's song, *Innsbruck, ich muss dich lassen* (NAWM 38), is available in many modern hymnbooks. The tune is known as "Innsbruck," and the German words of the hymn began *O Welt, ich muss dich lassen*. One English-texted version is "The Duteous Day Now Closeth." Have the students compare the hymn and the original version as a demonstration of how composers adapted complex songs for untrained singers. Several examples in Chapter 11 will feature the same evenly measured chordal homophony, but in secular genres.

Calvin's "Epistle to the Reader" from *The Geneva Psalter* (1542) is available in its entirety in Gary Tomlinson, ed. *Source Readings in Music History,* rev. ed., Vol. 3: The Renaissance (New York: W. W. Norton, 1998).

*The Bay Psalm Book* included words only. Bring a facsimile page to class (several facsimile editions have been published, and the Library of Congress Web site has an image online: www.loc.gov/exhibits/treasures/images/tlc0005.jpg) and ask students how congregations would have sung the music with only the words available and no organ. For background, read *The New Grove Dictionary of Music and Musicians,* "Psalmody: ii, II (North America)." Although most of the psalms could be sung to a few tunes, the lack of printed music and of music literacy in the congregation would lead to a variety of later developments, including "lining out" the melody, singing schools, and shape-note notation.

John Taverner's music comprises several volumes of *Early English Church Music* and many works have been published separately. His *Western Wind* mass, based on a secular song, is available on a CD by the Tallis Scholars (Gimell 27, 2001) and in a performance edition, edited by Anthony G. Petti (Chester Music CH 55433, 1997).

Tallis is best known for his Latin works, especially for an unusual work, *Spem in alium*, composed for forty voices in eight choirs (New York: Oxford University Press, Tudor Church Music 299, 1966). It is available on CD, sung by the Tallis Scholars (Gimell 6, 2001) and "Tallis Scholars Sing Thomas Tallis" (Gimell, 2004), and by the Winchester Cathedral Choir (Hyperion 66400, 1993). Another of his best-known works is his setting of the *Lamentations of Jeremiah,* two five-voice motets for Good Friday (New York: Oxford University Press, Tudor Church Music 47a–b, 1995), which demonstrate English parallelisms combined with imitative texture. These and other Latin motets have been recorded by the Tallis Scholars (Gimell 25, 2002) and by the Hilliard Ensemble (ECM 21341, 1994). "The Sixteen Choir" recording (Chandos 513, 1992) includes both the *Lamentations* and *Spem in alium,* as does "Tallis Scholars Sing Thomas Tallis," mentioned above.

Byrd's introduction to his *Gradualia* is available in Gary Tomlinson, ed., *Source Readings in Music History,* rev. ed., Vol. 3: The Renaissance (New York: W. W. Norton, 1998). Several works from the *Gradualia* have been released on "Byrd: Gradualia: The Marian Masses," performed by the William Byrd Choir (Hyperion 55047, 2002). These masses comprise volume 5 of *The Byrd Edition* (London: Stainer & Bell B 367), edited by Philip Brett.

Gombert's *Quem dicunt homines* (**HWM Example 10.5**) is not available on CD, but other examples can give students an idea of the difficulty of hearing the text compared to Josquin and others. *In te Domine speravi,* a six-voice motet sung by the Huelgas Ensemble on "Nicolas Gombert: Music from the Court of Charles V" (Sony 48249, 1993), begins with a point of imitation and quickly builds up to a thick texture that makes the words virtually inaudible. The score is available in volume 9 of his *Opera Omnia,* edited by Joseph Schmidt-Görg in the *Corpus Mensurabilis Musicae* series (Rome: American Institute of Musicology, 1974).

Have students analyze the approach and departure from dissonances in Palestrina's *Missa Papae Marcelli* in terms of Zarlino's basic rules for counterpoint. This exercise will help prepare students for the Artusi-Monteverdi controversy of Chapter 13.

For more on the myth about Palestrina's *Pope Marcellus Mass,* see Piero Weiss and Richard Taruskin, eds., *Music in the Western World: A History in Documents* (New York: Schirmer, 1984), 140–43.

For more examples of Palestrina's style, have students listen to some of his motets. Lionheart's recording "Palestrina: Soul of Rome" (Koch International Classics 7513, 2001) includes mass movements and motets by Palestrina and Victoria. Have students listen to his early *Ave Maria,* paying special attention to phrase setting and comparing it to Josquin's motet. Ask students to speculate on the economics of motet composition compared to mass composition (more of Palestrina's motets were published in his lifetime than his masses).

For an example of a mass by Morales, use his *Missa Mille regretz,* based on **NAWM 41.** It is available in volume xi of *Monumentos de la música española,* edited by Higini Anglés (Barcelona: Consejo Superior de Investagaciones scientificas, Instituto de musicologia, 1952) and in two performances on CD: by the Hilliard Ensemble (Alma Viva 101, 1995) and Chanticleer (Chanticleer Records 8809, 1993).

*Alma redemptoris mater,* a beautiful motet by Guerrero, opens with a very singable stepwise melody. It is in volume xxvi of *Monumentos de la música española,* edited by I. M. Llorens Cisteró (Barcelona: Consejo Superior de Investagaciones scientificas, Instituto de musicologia, 1978) and is available on CD (Arsis Records 113, 1999 and Astrée 9953, 2001).

To expand on the concept of the imitation mass, have students listen to other movements of Victoria's *Missa O Magnum mysterium* to compare them with the motet. Both the mass and the motet are available on a recording that also pairs his motet *Ascendens Christus in altum* and the mass based on it. (Hyperion CDA66190, 1986).

Some compositions written in the native languages of Latin America have been recorded. "Guadalupe: Virgen de los Indios," performed by the San Antonio Vocal Arts Ensemble (Iago CD210, 1998), includes several songs written in Guatemalan dialects. The ensemble researched instruments and rhythmic patterns of the time to create unique performances—as, for example, on *Y technepa sacramento Dios,* a villancico by Tomás Pascual (c. 1595–1635) of Guatemala. *Hanacpachap cussicuinin,* the first polyphonic work published in the New World, was written in the Quecha language of Peru. A recording is available on Hesperus's "Spain in the New World" (Golden Apple GACD 7552, 1990) and The Boston Camerata, "Nueva España" (Erato 2292-45977-2, 1993). The Hilliard Ensemble's "Spanish and Mexican Renaissance Vocal Music" (EMI Classics 7654512, 1991) includes two Aztec-language works. Hesperus's "Spain in the New World" includes Renaissance and Baroque works from several regions, including Bolivia, Peru, Colombia, Guatemala, and Mexico.

## OBJECTIVE QUESTIONS

1. For which composer did Martin Luther have particular admiration?
   a. Machaut
   b. Du Fay
   c. Josquin
   d. Gombert
   e. Palestrina

   Answer: c

2. What did Martin Luther call his simplified order of service, intended for use by smaller congregations?
   a. imitation mass
   b. the Short Service
   c. the Great Service
   d. the German Mass
   e. the chorale

   Answer: d

3. Who was Luther's principal musical collaborator?
   a. William Byrd
   b. Jean Calvin
   c. Heinrich Isaac
   d. Johann Walter
   e. The Council of Trent

   Answer: d

4. What is a contrafactum?
   a. a type of polyphonic elaboration of a chorale, with the melody in the superius or uppermost voice
   b. a piece in which a new text, usually sacred, is added to preexisting music
   c. a chromatically altered note from outside the system of diatonic modes
   d. a new bass line added below an existing chorale melody
   e. a contrapuntal device closely related to canon

   Answer: b

5. Which of the following statements characterizes Jean Calvin's attitude toward music?
   a. He firmly rejected all music as a component of Calvinist worship.
   b. He forbade the congregation from singing, as God would find their voices offensive.
   c. He allowed only unaccompanied singing of psalms at church services.
   d. He retained all aspects of Catholic music, but priests spoke the biblical readings rather than chant them.
   e. He encouraged the singing of Franco-Flemish polyphony, finding it to be the ideal vehicle for preparing listeners for worship.

   Answer: c

6. What is/are the principal form(s) of Lutheran church music?
   a. service and anthem
   b. mass and motet
   c. madrigal and motet
   d. chorale
   e. metrical psalm

   Answer: d

7. What are the principal form(s) of Calvinist church music?
   a. service and anthem
   b. mass and motet
   c. madrigal and motet
   d. chorale
   e. metrical psalm

   Answer: e

8. What is/are the principal form(s) of Anglican church music?
   a. service and anthem
   b. mass and motet
   c. madrigal and motet
   d. chorale
   e. metrical psalm

   Answer: a

9. Byrd's music for the Mass was published in __________.
   a. *The Bay Psalm Book*
   b. *The Gradualia*
   c. the Council of Trent
   d. the Medicean edition of the Gradual
   e. the *Deutsche Messe*

   Answer: b

10. Who published "wholesome" polyphonic music for young people, to "rid them of their love ditties and wanton song?"
    a. Martin Luther
    b. Jean Calvin
    c. Henry V
    d. William Byrd
    e. The Council of Trent

    Answer: a

11. Catholic compositions of the sixteenth century differed from earlier compositions in that __________.
   a. they showed no evidence of mode
   b. they used the vernacular languages
   c. they eliminated imitative counterpoint
   d. there were five or six voices instead of four
   e. composers were more free to employ dissonance

   Answer: d

12. Adrian Willaert held the post of music director at or for __________.
   a. the Vatican
   b. the Council of Trent
   c. Saint Mark's in Venice
   d. the editorial board of the *Bay Psalm Book*
   e. the bishopric of southern Germany

   Answer: c

13. The Council of Trent __________.
   a. met intermittently in a city in modern Germany
   b. devoted most of its time to discussing complaints about church music
   c. directed local bishops to implement reforms in church music
   d. supervised the revision of the official chantbooks
   e. elected Pope Marcellus, one of the great Renaissance patrons of music and the namesake of Palestrina's *Missa Papae Marcelli*

   Answer: c

14. Which of the following statements best describes the Catholic Church's response to Protestant criticisms of its music?
   a. It ignored them.
   b. It followed all the recommendations of the reformers.
   c. It changed its musical practices only slightly.
   d. It leveled attacks against the reformers' opinions and succeeded in changing their minds.
   e. It required priests to celebrate Mass in the vernacular of their congregations, but allowed monks and nuns to continue to chant in Latin within the confines of their monastic communities.

   Answer: c

15. Palestrina spent most of his career at institutions in __________.
   a. Palestrina
   b. Naples
   c. Venice
   d. Ferrara
   e. Rome

   Answer: e

16. Palestrina's *Pope Marcellus Mass* is an example of which mass type?
   a. tenor mass
   b. motto mass
   c. plainsong mass
   d. imitation mass
   e. free mass

   Answer: e

17. The composer who sang in the papal chapel and quoted Josquin in his masses is __________.
   a. Morales
   b. Victoria
   c. Guerrero
   d. Lasso
   e. Zarlino

   Answer: a

18. The composer who quoted his own motet in his *Missa O Magnum misterium* is __________.
   a. Morales
   b. Victoria
   c. Guerrero
   d. Lasso
   e. Zarlino

   Answer: b

19. Which of the following statements is true of Catholic music in colonial Latin America?
   a. Lacking money for books or instruments, priests sang Mass alone, with no choral sections.
   b. Missionaries brought the Spanish language as well as their religion to Latin America by translating the entire Mass into Spanish.
   c. Gregorian chant was sung for daily devotion in monasteries and missions, but the native inhabitants did not hear any Western music.
   d. The music of Morales and other Spanish composers was sung, as well as some original compositions in native languages.
   e. Missionaries turned native inhabitants' religious songs into Catholic songs through contrafacta and did not use any European music.

   Answer: d

20. Which statement best describes Orlando di Lasso's career?
    a. He spent nearly his entire career in the region where Du Fay was trained.
    b. He spent nearly his entire career in Germany.
    c. He received his training in Hainaut, but spent his career in Italy.
    d. He worked for a time in Italy, but spent most of his later career in Germany.
    e. He spent his entire career in and around Rome, much of it in the service of the pope.

    Answer: d

## SHORT-ESSAY QUESTIONS

1. Discuss the main similarities and differences between the Lutheran, Calvinist, and Anglican approaches to music. Use examples from *NAWM* to illustrate your points.
2. For one composer discussed in this chapter, discuss the ways in which his geographical location(s) affected his training and career.
3. Summarize the Catholic response to the pressures of Protestant reform movements in terms of musical style and philosophy.
4. Using examples from the *Pope Marcellus Mass,* characterize the so-called Palestrina style in terms of melody, harmony, counterpoint, dissonance treatment, texture, rhythm, and text-setting.

## TERMS FOR IDENTIFICATION

Reformation
Martin Luther
German Mass
chorale
contrafactum (-a)
chorale motet
cantionale
Jean Calvin
Calvinism
metrical psalms
psalter
*Bay Psalm Book*
*Old Hundredth*
Henry VIII
Service; Great Service; Short Service
anthem
full anthem
verse anthem
Counter-Reformation (Catholic Reformation)
Jesuits
Council of Trent
free mass

# CHAPTER 11 Madrigal and Secular Song in the Sixteenth Century

I. Amateur music-making inspired a flowering of national styles, in contrast to the fifteenth-century unification of styles.
   A. Amateurs wanted secular music in the vernacular.
   B. Homophonic genres for easy singing were popular in Spain and Italy.
   C. The madrigal was an outlet for an interest in humanism, first in Italy and later in England.
   D. The ability to read and perform music became a social grace in the sixteenth century.
      1. Among the elite nobility first
      2. Eventually also among middle class
      3. Paintings show people reading from published music, usually part-books (e.g., **HWM Figure 11.1**).
      4. Amateurs constituted an eager market for a variety of secular genres.

II. Spain: Villancico
   A. Ferdinand and Isabella encouraged Spanish music, especially the villancico.
   B. The villancico
      1. The name of the genre is derived from the word for peasant (*villano*).
      2. The audience/market was the elite class, but the texts were rustic and popular in style.
      3. The music was short, strophic, syllabic, and mostly homophonic, in reaction to the Franco-Flemish style.
      4. Villancicos were often published for voice with lute.
      5. Form
         a. The form varies, but always includes a refrain (*estribillo*).
         b. Stanzas begin with two statements of a contrasting idea.
         c. Stanzas end with a return to the music of the refrain (*vuelta*).
         d. The last line of the refrain text usually recurs at the end of each stanza.
   C. Juan del Encina (1468–1529)
      1. The first Spanish playwright and a leading composer of villancicos
      2. *Oy comamos y bebemos* (**NAWM 48**) is typical of the genre.
         a. The text uses crude language to exhort listeners to eat, drink, and sing the day before Lent begins.
         b. Melody and harmony are simple.
         c. Rhythms are dance-like, with frequent hemiolas.

III. Italy
   A. The frottola (pl. *frottole*)
      1. Italian counterpart to the villancico
         a. Four-part strophic song set syllabically and homophonically.
         b. Melody in the upper voice
         c. Simple harmony
         d. Marked rhythmic patterns
         e. No fixed form, though several subtypes and specific forms
      2. Composed by Italian composers for the amusement of the courtly elite
         a. Petrucci published thirteen collections between 1504 and 1514.
         b. The songs were mock-popular songs, not authentic folk or popular songs.
      3. Performed by solo voice with lute
      4. Among the best-known composers of frottole was Marco Cara (ca. 1465–1525), who worked at the court of Mantua.

a. *Io non compro più speranza* (**NAWM 49**) appeared in Petrucci's first book of frottole.
b. The rhythm moves in six beats per measure, sometimes divided into three groups of two, other times two groups of three (hemiola effect).
c. The poem consists of a four-line ripresa and a six-line stanza.

B. The Italian madrigal
1. The most important secular genre of the sixteenth century
a. Composers enriched the meaning and impact of the text through musical setting.
b. The genre became an experimental vehicle for dramatic characterization, inspiring new compositional devices.
2. Form
a. Single stanza with no refrains or repeated lines
b. The music is through-composed, with new music for every line of poetry.
3. Poetry
a. Composers often chose texts by major poets.
b. Topics included love songs and pastoral scenes.
c. The final lines of the poem were often epigrammatic, bringing home the point of the poem.
4. Music
a. Composers used a variety of techniques and textures.
b. All voices played an equal role, similar to the motet of the same period.
c. The earliest madrigals (ca. 1520 to 1550) were for four voices.
d. By mid-century, madrigals were composed for five or more voices.
e. Performance could be vocal, or some parts could be played on instruments.

C. Early madrigal composers
1. Philippe Verdelot (ca. 1480–ca. 1545)
a. Franco-Flemish composer, active in Florence and Rome in the 1520s, when the madrigal developed
b. His four-voice madrigals are mostly homophonic.
c. His madrigals for five or more voices are more motetlike.
2. Jacques Arcadelt (ca. 1507–1568)
a. Franco-Flemish composer working in Florence and Rome from the 1520s to 1551.
b. His *Il bianco e dolce cigno* (**NAWM 50**), published in 1538, is one of the most famous of the early madrigals.
c. The text alludes to sexual climax (referred to in the sixteenth century as "the little death") in the words "dying fills me fully with joy and desire."
d. A string of imitative entrances portrays the words "thousand deaths a day" ("*mille mort' il dì*").

D. The Petrarchan movement
1. Cardinal Pietro Bembo (1470–1547), poet and scholar, led the movement to revive the sonnets and canzoni of Petrarch (Francesco Petrarca, 1304–1374).
2. Bembo identified the contrasting qualities of pleasingness (*piacevolezza*) and severity (*gravità*) in the sounds of Petrarch's poems.
3. Composers attempted to reflect these qualities in their music.

E. Adrian Willaert
1. Associated major thirds and sixths with harshness or bitterness, and minor intervals with sweetness or grief
2. *Aspro core e selvaggio,* Petrarch's poem about a "harsh and savage heart," uses major intervals and whole steps for harshness (**HMW Example 11.2a**) and minor intervals to portray the lover's "sweet, humble, angelic face" (**HMW Example 11.2b**).

F. Mid-century madrigalists
1. Cipriano de Rore (1516–1565) (see **HWM Figure 11.3**)
a. The leading madrigal composer at mid-century
b. Flemish, working in Ferrara, Parma, and at St. Mark's in Venice (succeeding Willaert as music director)
c. Profoundly interested in humanism and in ideas from ancient Greek music
d. *De le belle contrade d'oriente* (**NAWM 51** and **HWM Example 11.3**), published posthumously, demonstrates his sensitivity to the text (a sonnet modeled on Bembo).
e. Accented syllables receive longer notes than do unaccented syllables.
f. Grief and sorrow are portrayed by frequent changes of voice combinations, chromaticism, and by a single high voice singing the phrase "sola mi lasci" ("alone you leave me").
2. Chromaticism
a. Direct chromaticism was justified by the chromaticism of ancient Greeks (e.g.,

**HWM Example 11.3,** which includes all twelve notes of chromatic scale).
   b. Nicola Vicentino (1511–ca. 1576), composer and theorist, proposed reviving the chromatic and an harmonica genera of time of Greek music.
3. Women as composers and performers
   a. Madalena Casulana (ca. 1544–ca.1590s), who served the duchess of Bracciano, was the first woman whose music was published and the first to regard herself as a professional composer.
   b. Women performed madrigals with men, and some became professional singers.
   c. The *concerto delle donne* (women's ensemble) was a renowned group of trained singers in the service of Duke Alfonso d'Este, inspiring similar ensembles in rival courts (see **HWM Source Reading,** page 253)

G. Later madrigalists
1. Although many northerners composed madrigals, the leading madrigalists at the end of the century were native Italians.
2. Luca Marenzio, e.g., *Solo e pensoso* (**NAWM 52**)
   a. Marenzio was known for depicting contrasting feelings and visual details.
   b. Based on a sonnet by Petrarch
   c. Marenzio depicts the poet walking alone with slow chromatic ascents, moving a half-step per measure.
   d. Quickly moving figures in close imitation depict the words "flee" and "escape."
   e. Literal depictions of individual words later became known as madrigalisms because they were so common in madrigals.
3. Carlo Gesualdo (ca. 1561–1613)
   a. A rare aristocratic composer who published his music
   b. Infamous for killing his wife and her lover when he discovered them in bed together
   c. His madrigals dramatize the poetry through sharp contrasts, e.g., between diatonic and chromatic pitches, chordal and imitative textures, slow and quick rhythms.
   d. *Io parto* (**NAWM 53** and **HWM Example 11.4**) exemplifies all these types of contrasts used to portray individual words (e.g., *vivo son* portrays a return to life with fast, diatonic, imitative figures).

H. Other secular genres
1. Villanella
   a. Popular in Naples beginning in the 1540s
   b. Lively, strophic, homophonic piece for three voices
   c. Rustic character portrayed with crude harmony, such as parallel fifths
2. Canzonetta (little song) and balletto (little dance) were light genres developed for the end of the century.
   a. Homophonic, with simple harmonies
   b. The balletto (pl. balletti) use dance-like rhythms and "fa-la-la" refrains.
   c. Both genres were imitated by German and English composers.

IV. France
A. A new type of chanson was developed under Francis I (r. 1515–47).
1. Light, fast, strongly rhythmic song for four voices
2. Texts were about pleasant, amorous situations, though there were also some serious texts.
3. Syllabic text-setting
4. Homophonic, with the principal melody in the highest voice and occasional points of imitation
5. Composed for amateurs and published in numerous collections, including over fifty collections published by the first French music printer, Pierre Attaingnant (ca. 1490–1552).
6. Many were arranged for voice and lute or for lute alone.

B. Claudin de Sermisy (ca.1490–1562)
1. His chansons were very popular and even appeared in paintings, such as **HWM Figure 11.4.**
2. *Tant que vivray* (**NAWM 54** and **HWM Example 11.5**)
   a. Similar in style to the frottola and villancico, with the melody in the top voice and simple harmony
   b. The form of the poetry is emphasized by long notes or repeated notes at the end of each line.

C. Clément Janequin
1. Composed many types of chanson
2. His descriptive chansons feature imitations of bird calls, hunting calls, and sounds of war.
3. *La Guerre* (The War) depicts a battle.
4. *Le chant des oiseaux* (The Song of the Birds) uses vocal warbles and chirping.

D. The later Franco-Flemish chanson
1. Composers continued to compose in the Franco-Flemish tradition.
2. Other, newer styles often influenced composers.

E. Musique mesurée (measured music)
   1. An attempt by the members of the Académie de Poésie et de Musique (Academy of Poetry and Music), founded in 1570, to revive the ethical effects of ancient Greek music
   2. Poetry in ancient Greek and Latin meters (*vers mesuré à l'antique*, "measured verse in ancient style")
      a. Jean-Antoine de Baïf wrote strophic French verses in ancient meters.
      b. He assigned French vowels to durations because French lacked the natural accent lengths of other languages.
   3. Claude LeJeune was the leading exponent, e.g., *Revecy venir du printans* (**NAWM 55**)
      a. Each long syllable was twice as long as a short one.
      b. Musical rhythms alternated duple and triple depending on the syllables.
   4. This experiment never took hold, but it introduced irregular rhythms into the *air de cour* (court air), the dominant French song style after about 1580.

V. Germany
   A. Meistersinger (master singers) preserved a tradition of an accompanied solo song, derived from the Minnesinger.
      1. Urban amateur singers who formed guilds
      2. Began in the fourteenth century, peaked in the sixteenth, dissolved in the nineteenth
      3. Poetic competitions challenged members to create new poetry on an existing melody and poetic structure.
      4. Hans Sachs (1494–1576), a shoemaker, was the best-known.
   B. Polyphonic Lied
      1. Continued to be composed, with several approaches to melody
      2. After 1550, Germans developed a taste for Italian secular song.
      3. German Lieder survived if they took on Italianate characteristics, as in Lasso's seven collections of Lieder.

VI. England
   A. Consort song
      1. Henry VIII (r. 1509–1547) and his second wife were musicians and composers.
      2. During their reign, a variety of songs and instrumental pieces in three and four parts were composed.
      3. The consort song was for voice accompanied by a consort (group) of viols.
      4. William Byrd's 1588 collection, *Psalmes, Sonets and Songs,* includes consort songs in imitative counterpoint.
   B. English madrigals
      1. Italian culture was in vogue in sixteenth-century England.
      2. Italian madrigals began to circulate in England in the 1560s.
      3. *Musica Transalpina*, 1588
         a. A collection of Italian madrigals translated into English
         b. Published by Nicholas Yonge, who wrote in his introduction that gentlemen and merchants sang the repertory at his own home.
         c. This and similar collections inspired composers to start writing their own madrigals in English.
   C. Thomas Morley
      1. Composed English language madrigals, canzonets, and balletts.
      2. Wrote a treatise, *A Plaine and Easie Introduction to Practiall Musicke* (1597)
         a. Aimed at unlearned amateurs (see **HWM Figure 11.5** for the treatise's contents)
         b. Covered everything from basic notation to composing in three or more voices
      3. *My bonny lass she smileth* (**NAWM 56**) is based on the Italian balletto form.
         a. Strophic, with each stanza comprising two repeated sections (AABB)
         b. Each section begins homophonically.
         c. Sections end with a "fa-la-la" contrapuntal refrain.
   D. *The Triumphs of Oriana,* 1601
      1. Collection of twenty-five madrigals by twenty-three composers.
      2. The title is in honor of Queen Elizabeth.
      3. Each madrigal ends with the words "long live fair Oriana," referring to Elizabeth.
   E. Thomas Weelkes
      1. His *As Vesta was* (**NAWM 57**) is one of the most famous madrigals in *The Triumphs of Oriana*.
      2. Weelkes wrote his own poetry, giving himself numerous opportunities for musical depiction.
      3. A melodic peak describes "hill" and falling scales describe "descending."
   F. Lute songs (or airs)
      1. Solo song with lute accompaniment was a popular genre in the early 1600s.
      2. Leading composers were John Dowland (1563–1626) and Thomas Campion (1567–1620).

3. More personal genre than the madrigal
4. Less word-painting, with lute always subordinate to the melody
5. Published in score format rather than part books
   a. Some alternate arrangements set the lute part for voices, as shown in **HMW Figure 11.6**
   b. The lute part was written in tablature, a notation telling the player where to place fingers on the strings rather than indicating pitch.
6. Dowland's best-known song is *Flow, my tears* (**NAWM 58**).
   a. Published in 1600 in his *Second Booke of Ayres*
   b. Inspired many variations and arrangements (e.g., **NAWM 61**)
   c. In the form of a pavane, with three repeated strains, the last with the same words for a musical pattern of aabbCC
   d. Repetition minimizes opportunities to depict individual words, but Dowland's music matches the dark mood of the poetry.

VII. The Madrigal and Its Impact
   A. The madrigal and the other vernacular genres inspired by it reflect the growing influence of humanism on music.
   B. Expressive codes developed after Willaert's time led to the development of opera.
   C. The vogue for social singing declined after 1600, but the madrigal in English survived to some extent from its origins to today.

## SUGGESTIONS FOR SUPPLEMENTAL READING/LISTENING/ACTIVITIES

One of Encina's best-known villancicos is *Cucú, cucú, cucucú,* published in *La música en la corte de los Reyes Católicos: Cancionero Musical de Palacio,* ed. Higini Anglès, in *Monumentos de la Música Española,* vol. v (Barcelona: Consejo Superior de Investagaciones scientificas, Instituto de musicologia, 1947), and *Juan de Encina: Poesía lírica y cancionero musical,* edited by R. O. Jones and C. R. Lee (Madrid, 1975). It has been recorded by the King's Singers on their "Madrigal History Tour" CD (EMI Classics 5857132, 2004) and on La Colombina's "Canciones, Romances, Sonetos from Juan Del Encina to Lope De Vega" (Accent Records, ACC 95111 D, 1999). The former contains additional examples for this chapter, and the latter also includes works of Francisco Guerrero.

Another interesting Spanish genre is the *ensalada* (salad), a genre similar to the Latin *quodlibet*, which quotes a variety of pre-existing music. Mateo Flecha's *La Guerra* and *Bomba* are performed on "Canciones y Ensaladas: Chansons et pièces instrumentales du Siècle d'Or" (Harmonia Mundi HMC 901627, 1998) by Ensemble Clément Janequin. The quick changes of style and tempo should alert the students to the beginning of quotations, which the audiences of the time would have recognized.

Verdelot's *Fuggi fuggi cor mio* was published as a four-voice madrigal for voice and also intabulated for lute. Several vocal renditions are available on CD, including "A Renaissance Songbook" (Linn Records 142, 2001) and "English and Italian Renaissance Madrigals" (Virgin Classics 61671, 2000). For a score, see *Madrigals for Four or Five Voices: Philippe Verdelot,* edited by Jessie Ann Owens, volume xxviii of *Sixteenth-Century Madrigals* (Garland Press, 1989).

Pietro Bembo exchanged letters and possibly had a romantic relationship with the infamous Lucrezia Borgia Their letters, some in the form of poems, have been published in *The Prettiest Love Letters in the World: Letters Between Lucrezia Borgia and Pietro Bembo,* translated by Hugh Shankland (Boston: David R. Godine, 1987).

For more information about Maddalena Casulana, see volume I of *Women Composers: Music through the Ages* (New York: G.K. Hall, 1996). The volume also includes her *Se scior si ved' il laccio a cui dranz'io,* edited by Ellen D. Lerner. A different madrigal by Casulana is available on the "English and Italian Renaissance" CD mentioned above.

For a villanella example and an example of a work by Willaert, see *Canzone Villanesche Alla Napolitana and Villotte: Adrian Willaert and His Circle,* edited by Donna G. Cardamone (Madison: A-R Editions, 1978). His *Vecchie letrose* is a lively piece that has been issued on several recordings, including "Vecchie Letrose: Italian Renaissance Music" (Arts Music 47504, 1999) and "Viva Napoli" (Astree 8648, 2000).

For more examples of the Parisian chanson, use Janequin's famous *La Guerre,* which depicts a battle. It is included on "Les Cris de Paris: Chansons de Janequin et Sermisy," performed by the Ensemble Clément Janequin (Harmonia Mundi France 7901072, reissued in 1996). It is also available in a recent edition, *Guerre (La Bataille): For Unaccompanied SATB,* edited by Frank Dobbins (Espoo: Fazer Music, 1994), and in volume 6 of *Clément Janequin: Chansons Polyphoniques,* edited by A. T. Merritt and F. Lesure (Monaco: Editions De L'Oiseau-Lyre, 1983). Have students compare this song to Mateo Flecha's *La Guerra,* reminding them that the "sounds of battle" usually included musical instruments.

In addition to his secular songs in *Musique mesurée* style, Claude LeJeune harmonized metered psalms and used psalm melodies from the *Geneva Psalter* as cantus firmi. See *Recent Researches in Music of the Renaissance,* (Madison: A-R Editions, vols. 74–76, 1989 and vol. 98, 1995). Ask students why the sacred application of this process achieved more lasting success than the secular.

Henry VIII's compositions and those he would have heard at court are available in *Music at the Court of Henry VIII,* transcribed and edited by John Stevens, volume xviii of *Musica Britannica* (London: Stainer & Bell, 1962). His *Pastime with Good Company* is a simple song about friendship. It has been recorded on lute ("The Royal Lewters," Harmonia Mundi HMU 907313, 2003), by recorder ensemble ("Pastyme with Good Companye: Music at the Court of Henry VIII," Chandos CHAN 0709, 2004), and by voice with simple instrumental accompaniment ("All Goodly Sports: [The Complete] Music of Henry VIII" Chandos 621, 1998).

Byrd's 1588 collection, *Psalmes, Sonets, and Songs,* comprises volume xii of *Collected Vocal Works of Byrd,* edited by Edmund H. Fellowes (London: Stainer and Bell, 1948). The volume contains facsimiles from the front page of the contratenor part and Byrd's *Epistle to the Reader,* in which he says the pieces had originally been written for solo voice with instrumental accompaniment.

*Musica Transalpina* has been published in facsimile (New York: Da Capo Press, 1972).

Morley's ideas (plagiarized from Zarlino) on madrigal composition, as published in *Plaine and Easie Introduction to Practicall Musicke,* comprise pages 144–145 of Weiss and Taruskin, *Music in the Western World: A History in Documents* (New York: Schirmer, 1984).

## OBJECTIVE QUESTIONS

1. The main secular vernacular genre of sixteenth-century Spain was __________.
   a. cancionero
   b. cantiga
   c. villancico
   d. madrigal
   e. frottola

   Answer: c

2. The frottola was __________.
   a. a folklike homophonic secular song in Italian
   b. a folklike homophonic secular song in Spanish
   c. a folklike homophonic sacred song in Latin
   d. a highly developed polyphonic secular song in French
   e. a dance type with quick rhythms and triple meter

   Answer: a

3. The poet whose work inspired composers of sixteenth-century Italy was __________.
   a. Shakespeare
   b. Milton
   c. Petrarch
   d. Machaut
   e. Ovid

   Answer: c

4. The sixteenth-century Italian madrigal developed from the __________.
   a. fourteenth-century madrigal
   b. frottola
   c. English madrigal
   d. motet
   e. villancico

   Answer: b

5. By the middle of the sixteenth century, the typical Italian madrigal was written for __________.
   a. four voices
   b. five or more voices
   c. voice plus lute
   d. instrumental ensembles
   e. keyboard instrument

   Answer: b

6. Texts for early madrigals sometimes used metaphor to allude to __________.
   a. biblical stories
   b. sexual matters
   c. the names of famous poets
   d. political topics of the day
   e. the nobleman for whom the poem was written

   Answer: b

7. Willaert and Zarlino believed that minor intervals, such as the minor third or sixth, __________.
   a. were imperfect, and thus should not be used
   b. were to be used in strict progressions that resolved to major intervals
   c. could represent sweetness or grief
   d. should be used only on keyboard instruments of a specific tuning system
   e. represented harshness or strength

   Answer: c

8. The leading madrigal composer in the middle of the sixteenth century was __________.
   a. Pietro Bembo
   b. Juan del Encina
   c. Jacques Arcadelt
   d. Cipriano de Rore
   e. Carlo Gesualdo

   Answer: d

9. Which of the following statements is true of women's participation in madrigal performance and composition?
   a. Women were not permitted to compose, sing, or hear madrigals.
   b. Women were often in the audience when madrigals were performed, but did not perform or compose them.
   c. Women performed madrigals but none had the musical training to compose them.
   d. Women both performed and composed madrigals, though not in equal numbers to men.
   e. Women were the equal of men in the composition and performance of madrigals.

   Answer: d

10. The Concerto delle Donne was __________.
    a. a group of women who played viols and recorders in consorts
    b. a group of women renowned for their singing at noble courts
    c. an academy that met to discuss ways to set poetry to music
    d. an orchestra maintained by the Countess of Donne
    e. a collection of music singable by all-women's groups

    Answer: b

11. Madrigalism can be defined as __________.
    a. a cadence formula used in madrigals
    b. the literal depiction of an individual word or phrase
    c. a poetic device used only in poems destined to become madrigals
    d. a cadential flourish in the top voice as the other voices hold a chord
    e. the theory that only in secular music can man's true spirit be revealed

    Answer: b

12. Gesualdo is known for __________.
    a. writing a treatise on counterpoint based on Willaert's style
    b. composing frottole with interesting rhythmic patterns
    c. being the the only member of the pope's chapel to compose madrigals
    d. spending most of his career as the maestro di capella at San Marco in Venice
    e. killing his wife and her lover when he discovered them together in bed

    Answer: e

13. Which composer is known for his/her songs depicting such things as a battle and birds?
    a. Willaert
    b. Sermisy
    c. Casulana
    d. Janequin
    e. LeJeune

    Answer: d

14. Which composer is known for composing French songs in a style similar to the frottola?
    a. Willaert
    b. Sermisy
    c. Casulana
    d. Janequin
    e. LeJeune

    Answer: b

15. The main feature of *musique mesurée* was __________.
    a. the artificial assignment of long and short values to vowel sounds
    b. an interest in using meter to express emotion
    c. extremely polyphonic textures with each voice using a different meter
    d. the translation of Italian madrigals into the French language
    e. extreme chromaticism, used for expressing emotion

    Answer: a

16. Hans Sachs is known for what achievement?
    a. He translated a collection of Italian madrigals into German.
    b. He published a collection of lieder using moveable type.
    c. He was the best known Meistersinger.
    d. He was the first German to serve in the Mantuan court.
    e. He applied techniques of metrical psalm-setting to secular music.

    Answer: c

17. Which of the following statement best describes the polyphonic Lied of the mid-sixteenth century?
    a. Audiences lost all interest in it, so composers turned to other genres.
    b. Composers incorporated concepts developed in the Academy of Poetry and Music.
    c. English-language airs were translated and passed off as original German compositions.
    d. Although German continued to be the language of the Lied, composers were strongly influenced by the madrigal.
    e. A revivalist movement among Lutherans banned all secular music, but the elite continued to cultivate it behind closed doors.

    Answer: d

18. *Musica Transalpina* was a collection of __________.
    a. music theory treatises translated from the Greek
    b. motets that had been turned into madrigals
    c. German songs that had been translated into English
    d. Italian madrigals that had been translated into English
    e. English madrigals that had been translated into Italian

    Answer: d

19. *The Triumphs of Oriana* was __________.
    a. a collection of madrigals in honor of Queen Elizabeth
    b. a set of madrigals depicting an epic translated from Greek
    c. a treatise by Thomas Morley, in which modern practices are seen as triumphing over old-fashioned ones
    d. a satire that attacks the vogue for all things Italian among the English
    e. a semi-autobiographical account of a woman composer at the King's court

    Answer: a

20. One composer known for his lute songs is __________.
    a. Thomas Morely
    b. Thomas Weelkes
    c. Anna Elizabeth Oriana
    d. William Byrd
    e. John Dowland

    Answer: e

## SHORT-ESSAY QUESTIONS

1. Discuss the techniques that composers of Italian madrigals used to portray the text.
2. Compare and contrast the secular polyphonic songs of Italy, France, and England in the sixteenth century.
3. For a madrigal by Gesualdo (use **NAWM 53** or another, such as *Moro lasso* or *lo pur respiro*), discuss the ways in which the composer is sensitive to the text. Discuss his approach to both the structure and meaning of the text. (Be sure students have the score and a translation at hand. To help them find instances of word painting, underline important words and indicate their literal meanings.)
4. Discuss the role of amateur musicians in the creation and dissemination of secular music during the sixteenth century. Name some famous amateurs and give examples of ways in which amateurs could participate in music-making.

## TERMS FOR IDENTIFICATION

villancico
frottola
madrigal
Petrarchan movement
Cardinal Pietro Bembo
madrigalism
concerto delle donne
Villanella
Canzonetta
Parisian chanson
Pierre Attaingnant
*musique mesurée*
Académie de Poésie et de Musique
Meistersinger
consort song
*Musica Transalpina*
English madrigal
lute song
tablature

# CHAPTER 12 The Rise of Instrumental Music

I. Introduction
  A. After 1450, more instrumental music was written down.
    1. Indicates that music without voices was considered worthy of preserving
    2. Indicates musical literacy of instrumentalists
  B. New instruments and genres developed.
    1. Dance music and instrumental versions of vocal music continued to be composed.
    2. New genres were not dependent on dance or vocal models.
    3. For the first time, instrumental music was as interesting and challenging as vocal music.

II. Instruments
  A. Trends of Renaissance instruments
    1. Books in the vernacular described instruments and offered instruction.
      a. *Musica getutscht und ausgezogen* (Music Explained) by Sebastian Virdung, Germany, 1511, was the first.
      b. Michael Praetorius's (ca. 1571–1621) *Syntagma musicum* (A Systematic Treatise of Music, 1618) includes woodcut illustrations of instruments of the time (**HWM Figure 12.1**).
    2. Haut and bas (high and low) continue as designations for loud and soft.
    3. Consorts
      a. Instrument families were built in sets of different sizes, covering a wide range.
      b. Mixed consorts were also used.
      c. Most musicians played several instruments.
  B. Wind and percussion instruments
    1. Instruments from the Middle Ages: recorders, transverse flutes, shawms, cornetts, trumpets
    2. New instruments: the sackbut (early form of trombone) and crumhorn, an instrument with an enclosed double reed (see **HWM Figures 12.1** and **12.2**)
    3. Percussion instruments were more refined and diverse than in the past, but parts were never written out for them.
  C. String instruments
    1. Plucked
      a. The lute was the most popular household instrument (see **HWM Figures 12.3, 11.2, 11.4**).
      b. Lutes have six courses of strings and a round back.
      c. Vihuela was a guitar-like Spanish instrument with a flat back.
    2. Bowed
      a. The viol (viola da gamba or leg-viol) had frets and was played in consorts.
      b. The violin descended from the medieval fiddle and was developed in Italy for dance music.
  D. Keyboard instruments
    1. Organ
      a. Large church organs, similar to today's, were installed by 1500.
      b. Pedal keyboards were used only in Germany.
      c. Builders added more stops (ranks of pipes).
      d. The portative organ was still popular (see **HWM Figure 12.2**).
    2. Clavichord
      a. Soft-sounding solo instrument for small rooms
      b. Tone is sustained until player releases the key.

c. Player can control volume and can create vibrato.

3. Harpsichord family
   a. Includes harpsichord, virginal (England), clavecin (France), clavicembalo (Italy)
   b. Louder than clavichord but without the nuances of dynamics or vibrato
   c. A second keyboard attached to two sets of strings produced a louder sound for contrast.
   d. Strings are plucked, so the pitch is not sustained.

III. Types of Instrumental Music

A. Dance music

1. Social dancing was important for people of "breeding" (see **HWM Music in Context,** page 271).
2. Instruments at first used vocal models for music.
3. Musicians improvised, as in the Middle Ages, but music in improvisational style was printed in books.
   a. Composed for ensemble, lute, or keyboard
   b. Embellishment of melodic line was a common technique.
   c. Adding one or more contrapuntal lines to a bass line
4. Works for lute or keyboard became stylized, not meant for actual dancing.
5. Each dance has a unique character, defined by meter, tempo, rhythmic pattern, and form.
6. Form usually consisted of repeated sections of four-measure phrases.
7. Basse danse and branle were favorite dances of the late fifteenth and early sixteenth centuries. (**NAWM 59a–b**)
   a. Basse danse (low dance): stately couples dance, gradually raising and lowering the body in five kinds of steps
   b. Branle: one of the basse dance steps, eventually becoming its own genre
   c. **NAWM 59a–b**, published by Attaignant (1547), use hemiola, reflecting the dancers' steps.
8. Dance pairs
   a. Pairs were usually on the same theme but with contrasting tempo and meter.
   b. Pavane and galliard (**HWM Example 12.1**) were a favorite pairing.
   c. Pavane: stately dance in three repeated strains (**HWM Figure 12.6**)
   d. Galliard: livelier dance using the same form and melody (**HWM Figure 12.5**)
   e. Passamezzo and saltarello were popularly paired in Italy.

B. Arrangements of vocal music

1. Some music was labeled "for singing and playing."
2. When performed on instruments, players embellished vocal music.
3. Intabulations: arrangements of music notated in tablature
   a. Used for plucked and keyboard instruments
   b. Because plucked instruments could not sustain pitches, arrangers adapted pieces to compensate.
   c. Luys de Narváez (fl. 1526–1549) published a version of Josquin's *Mille regretz* (**NAWM 60**, based on **NAWM 41**) using figures such as runs and turns to fill in long notes.

C. Settings of existing melodies

1. Chant settings for organ (organ verses or versets) to alternate with choir (**HWM Example 12.2,** based on **NAWM 36** *Kyrie*) as part of an "organ mass"
2. Organ chorales
   a. Published after the 1570s but likely improvised earlier
   b. Use various techniques
3. *In nomine* settings
   a. A popular cantus-firmus theme, derived from the Sanctus of John Tavener's *Missa Gloria tibi trinitas*
   b. Tavener transcribed his mass for instruments.
   c. Hundreds were published, especially for viol consort.

D. Variations

1. Presenting a theme and then continuing with an uninterrupted series of variants on that theme demonstrates the imagination and skill of composers and performers (when improvised).
2. Variations on dance themes
   a. Petrucci published collections as early as 1508.
   b. Forms that used repeating sections would be varied in the repetition.
   c. Variations on repeating bass lines (ostinatos), e.g., passamezzo
3. Sets of variations on standard airs
   a. In Italy, the *Romanesca* and *Ruggiero* were popular.
   b. In Spain, *Guárdame las vacas* was popular (e.g., **NAWM 60b; HWM Example 12.3** shows the melody and bass plus the opening of each variation).

(1) Called *differencias* in Spanish
(2) **NAWM 60a** is the standard air, used for singing poetry.
(3) Narváez states the bass clearly but varies the melody from the start.
(4) Each variation uses its own unique figure throughout.

E. English virginalists (harpsichord composers)
1. *Parthenia* (1613), the first published book for virginal (**HWM Figure 12.7**), contains variations, dances, preludes, and fantasias.
   a. Variations were often based on dances or familiar songs.
   b. The melody can vary.
   c. Each variation uses one type of figuration.
2. Byrd's *Pavana Lachrymae* (**NAWM 61**) from the *Fitzwilliam Virginal Book*
   a. Based on Dowland's *Flow my tears* (**NAWM 58**)
   b. The second of each pair of phrases is more active than the first.

F. Abstract instrumental music
1. Improvisation and vocal models inspired new, purely instrumental genres.
2. Performers and composers used expressive effects (see **HWM Source Reading,** page 278).
3. Introductory and improvisatory pieces
   a. Keyboard and lute players often improvised the introduction to a song.
   b. In the early sixteenth century, collections of freely composed compositions in improvisatory style began to appear in Spain and Italy.
   c. Titles varied: prelude, fantasia, ricercare
   d. Pieces often established the tonality of the following song (e.g., Luis Milán's (ca. 1500–1561) *El Maestro* collection of vihuela music).
4. Toccata was the chief keyboard genre.
   a. Name derives from the Italian *tocare* ("to touch")
   b. Claudio Merulo (1533–1604) composed organ toccatas (e.g., **HWM Example 12.4,** from his *Toccata IV in the Sixth Mode,* 1604).
      (1) Exploits the organ's ability to sustain tones, especially in suspensions
      (2) Uses a variety of textures, figurations, and embellishments
      (3) A contrasting middle section (**HWM Example 12.4b**) uses imitation.
      (4) The third and final section slows the harmonic progression while increasing the liveliness of the figuration, leading to a dramatic climax.
5. Ricercare
   a. Evolved into a motetlike succession of imitative sections
   b. Successive themes, each developed imitatively and overlapping
   c. The earliest are for lute, possibly the origin of the name (to "seek out" the tuning of the instrument).
   d. By 1540, the genre could be composed for keyboard or ensemble as well.
6. Canzona
   a. The earliest were intabulations of imitative French chansons (*canzona* in Italian).
   b. By the midcentury the songs were reworked, much as the sources for imitation masses were.
   c. By 1580 original compositions in this style appeared.
   d. They were light, fast-moving, strongly rhythmic pieces.
   e. The typical opening rhythmic figure was a half-note followed by two quarter notes.

IV. Music in Venice

A. The city of Venice
1. An independent state run by several important families, with an elected leader called the doge ("duke")
2. One of the chief ports of Europe
3. Controlled territories in surrounding areas

B. Patronage of the arts
1. The government spent lavishly on public music and art.
2. Through the arts, the city could maintain the illusion of greatness despite wars and misfortunes that diminished its position in the sixteenth century.

C. Church of St. Mark
1. The private chapel of the doge
2. The location of great civic and religious ceremonies (see **HWM Figure 12.8**)
3. The position of choirmaster was the most coveted musical post in Italy.
   a. Willaert, Rore, and Zarlino held the post in the sixteenth century.
   b. Monteverdi held the post in the seventeenth century.
4. A permanent ensemble was instituted in 1568.
   a. Cornetts and sackbuts were the core.
   b. Violin and bassoon were also included.
   c. For major feast days as many as twenty-four instrumentalists might be added.

5. Giovanni Gabrieli (ca. 1555–1612)
   a. Worked for St. Mark's from 1585 until his death (see **HWM biography,** page 283, and **HWM Figure 12.9**)
   b. Composed for multiple choirs
   c. Composed the earliest substantial collections for large instrumental ensemble
   d. Works include about one hundred motets, over thirty madrigals, and almost eighty instrumental works.
6. Polychoral motets
   a. Works for two or more choirs (up to five in Gabrieli's music)
   b. Divided choirs, *cori spezzati,* had been common
   c. Forces could be placed in the two organ lofts of St. Marks, one on each side of the altar, and another on the floor.
7. Ensemble canzonas (**NAWM 62**)
   a. Instrumental version of divided choirs
   b. Gabrieli's *Sacrae symphoniae* (Sacred Symphonies, 1597) uses two groups of four instruments, with organ accompaniment.
   c. The form is AB CB DB E, with B as a refrain.
   d. The groups alternate stanzas and join together for the final stanza.
   e. Instruments are not specified, but they would probably have been cornetts and sackbuts.
   f. The organ doubles the lowest note in the ensemble (*basso seguente*).

V. Instrumental Music Gains Independence
   A. In the sixteenth century, instrumental music began to be cultivated for its own sake, not for dancing or related to vocal music.
   B. Abstract forms developed in the sixteenth century continued to be used in the Baroque period and even into the nineteenth century.
   C. Although some sixteenth-century music continued to be played in the seventeenth century, it was not until the late nineteenth century that scholars revived it.

## SUGGESTIONS FOR SUPPLEMENTAL READING/LISTENING/ACTIVITIES

Have students report on the discussion of their favorite instrument or an assigned one in Michael Praetorius's *Syntagma musicum. II, De organographia: parts I and II,* translated and edited by David Z. Crookes (Oxford: Clarendon Press, 1986). If the *Syntagma musicum* is not available, have them read the appropriate articles in *The New Grove Dictionary of Music.*

If you have access to Renaissance instruments, bring some to class. If there is a museum collection nearby, make a class visit. Depending on the collection, you may be able to see a presentation by a knowledgeable guide or curator.

The 1997 reissue of "The Instruments of the Middle Ages and Renaissance" by the Musica Reservata (Vanguard Classics OVC 809-4, 1997) demonstrates the sounds of early instruments both singly and in consorts. This 2-CD set also includes representative works in the genres discussed in this chapter. Several excerpts on the Amazon.com track listing are of sufficient length to give students an idea of instrumental timbres.

An online guide created at Iowa State University has photographs of instruments with some links to additional resources and .wav files. The URL is www.s-hamilton.k12.ia.us/antiqua/instrumt.html.

Have students read *Music in Italian Renaissance Painting* by Iain Fenlon in Tess Knighton and David Fallows, eds., *Companion to Medieval and Renaissance Music* (New York: Schirmer, 1992), 189–209, for its discussion of music in courtly society and the allegorical uses of musical instruments in painting.

Arbeau's *Orchesography* has instructions for the branle. Have students learn the steps, using the music for **NAWM 59.** Use the translation by Mary Stewart Evans (New York: Dover Publications, 1967) or by Cyril W. Beaumont (reprint edition, Brooklyn: Dance Horizons, 1965). For additional dances, use the compact disc "Danses Populaires Francaises" by Jeremy Barlow and the Broadside Band (Musique D'Abord 1901152, 2000).

Christopher Tye's *In nomine* settings are performed by a consort of viols on "Laudes Deo" by Hesperion XX (Naive Astrée 9939, 2000). A setting by Orlando Gibbons is available on "Music for Viols" by Fretwork (Virgo VJ 7 59691 2, 1992).

Ask students who have experience in jazz and other improvisational idioms to comment on the descriptions of variation forms for the benefit of their classmates. How are the sources different from "charts" used in jazz? How difficult would it be to develop variations using the concept of one figuration per variation? How would they relate the twelve-bar blues form to the variations forms discussed in chapter 12?

For more examples of music by Claudio Merulo, see *Canzoni d'intavolatura d'organo,* edited by Walker Cunningham and Charles McDermott in volumes 90–91 of *Recent Researches of the Renaissance* (Madison: A-R Editions, 1992).

"Music for San Marco in Venice" (Deutsche Harmonia Mundi, 05472 77531, 2003) contains recordings of additional two canzone by Merulo, performed on brass instruments, and vocal works by Gabrieli.

The *Fitzwilliam Virginal Book* is available in an inexpensive edition published by Dover (1980). Numerous recorded examples are available, including two works on "The Instruments of the Middle Ages and Renaissance," mentioned above.

## OBJECTIVE QUESTIONS

1. A consort is __________.
   a. any combination of voices and instruments in a small group
   b. any combination of instruments in a small group
   c. any combination of instruments in a large ensemble
   d. a group of identical instruments
   e. a group of instruments from the same family, made in different sizes

   Answer: b

2. The Renaissance instrument that is related to the modern trombone is the __________.
   a. recorder
   b. lute
   c. sackbut
   d. viol
   e. clavichord

   Answer: c

3. A plucked string instrument of the Renaissance is the __________.
   a. recorder
   b. lute
   c. sackbut
   d. viol
   e. clavichord

   Answer: b

4. A keyboard instrument of the Renaissance is the __________.
   a. recorder
   b. lute
   c. sackbut
   d. viol
   e. clavichord

   Answer: e

5. In the sixteenth century, percussion instruments were __________.
   a. banned by the Council of Trent but used by the military on the battlefield
   b. limited to bells
   c. limited to the pipe and tabor
   d. diverse and refined, but parts were never written out
   e. specified in scores for the first time

   Answer: d

6. Dance music of the Renaissance typically used which form?
   a. refrain forms borrowed from vocal music, especially the rondeau
   b. repeated sections of four-measure phrases
   c. ABAB CBCB ABAB
   d. two large sections, each repeated, with the first ending on a V and the second ending on the tonic
   e. a long improvisatory section followed by an imitative section

   Answer: b

7. In the Renaissance, music for dancing was composed for __________.
   a. liturgical dramas in which dancing played a role
   b. social dancing for people of aristocratic backgrounds
   c. the earliest ballets
   d. young people in Reformation countries, where music's role was to ensure good citizenship and Christian devotion
   e. refrains between the stanzas of popular songs

   Answer: b

8. Which of the following was not a popular dance type in the sixteenth century?
   a. passamezzo
   b. pavane
   c. galliard
   d. minuet
   e. branle gay

   Answer: d

9. The galliard was often paired with the __________.
   a. passamezzo
   b. pavane
   c. galliard
   d. minuet
   e. branle gay

   Answer: b

10. Intabulation is a notation system used for __________.
    a. consorts
    b. instructional books on dance
    c. rhythmic patterns
    d. plucked and keyboard instruments
    e. San Marco

    Answer: d

11. The first published works in improvisatory style were inspired by instrumentalists' practice of improvising in association with which other genre?
    a. chorale settings
    b. songs
    c. dances
    d. free improvisation, for no other genre
    e. masses

    Answer: b

12. Which of the following was not a type of improvisatory composition?
    a. consort
    b. ricercare
    c. toccata
    d. prelude
    e. fantasia

    Answer: a

13. Music in an improvisatory style was sometimes notated for __________.
    a. sackbut
    b. shawm
    c. lute
    d. voice with lute accompaniment
    e. percussion

    Answer: c

14. *Guárdame las vacas* is an example of __________.
    a. a standard air for variations
    b. a dance in which women stood in the middle of the room while men danced in a circle around them
    c. a canzona
    d. a book of pieces for instrumental ensemble
    e. a song dedicated to Queen Elizabeth

    Answer: a

15. Which of the following techniques became popular among English keyboardists?
    a. imitation
    b. variation
    c. mensuration
    d. text-painting
    e. improvisation

    Answer: b

16. The chief sixteenth-century keyboard genre in improvisatory style was __________.
    a. canzona
    b. differencias
    c. passamezzo
    d. ricercare
    e. toccata

    Answer: e

17. The Italian form derived from French songs is __________.
    a. canzona
    b. differencias
    c. passamezzo
    d. ricercare
    e. toccata

    Answer: a

18. The dance movement usually paired with the saltarello is the __________.
    a. canzona
    b. differencias
    c. passamezzo
    d. ricercare
    e. toccata

    Answer: c

19. Gabrieli's *Sacrae symphoniae* were composed for __________.
    a. consort of viols
    b. lute
    c. mixed consort of strings and woodwinds
    d. two groups of four instruments, with organ accompaniment
    e. vocal ensemble, but were performed on instruments

    Answer: d

20. The definition of basso seguente is __________.
    a. an imitative entrance in the bass voice that comes after a statement by a higher voice
    b. a bass line that doubles the lowest note of an ensemble
    c. an extra bass viol in a viol consort
    d. a system for creating variations
    e. a sympathetic string on lute that doubles the lowest string

    Answer: b

## SHORT-ESSAY QUESTIONS

1. Discuss the ways in which a sixteenth-century composer could create an instrumental work from a vocal work and the genres associated with these techniques.
2. Describe the types of instruments available to a sixteenth-century musician and the ways they could be combined.
3. Describe the impact of improvisation on the composed instrumental music of the sixteenth century.
4. In what ways did dance influence musical style in the sixteenth century? Give examples from *NAWM* when applicable.

## TERMS FOR IDENTIFICATION

*Syntagma musicum*
consort
sackbut
crumhorn
lute
vihuela
viol
viola da gamba
violin
clavichord
harpsichord
virginal
clavicembalo
clavecin
basse danse
branle
pavane
galliard
passamezzo
saltarello
intabulation
organ verse/verset
*In nomine*
variations
*Parthenia*
*Fitzwilliam Virginal Book*
toccata
ricercare
canzona
cori spezzati
*Sacrae symphoniae*
basso seguente

# CHAPTER 13 New Styles in the Seventeenth Century

I. Europe in the Seventeenth Century
  A. Scientific revolution
    1. 1609: Johannes Kepler described the orbits of planets.
    2. Galileo Galilei discovered moons around Jupiter, using a newly designed telescope.
    3. Sir Francis Bacon argued for a pure approach to science (i.e., relying on direct observation rather than appeal to authorities).
    4. René Descartes developed a deductive approach to reason.
    5. Sir Isaac Newton
      a. Laws of gravitation (1660s)
      b. Combined observation with mathematics
      c. Set the framework for the scientific method
  B. Politics, religion, and war
    1. Resolution of conflicts, ca. 1600
      a. Henri IV (France) guaranteed freedom to Protestants.
      b. England and Spain ended years of warring between them.
    2. New conflicts
      a. Germany was devastated by the Thirty Years' War (1618–48) within the Holy Roman Empire.
      b. England's civil war (1642–49) temporarily established a Presbyterian state church until the restoration of the monarchy (1660) also restored Anglican rule.
    3. Authority of the state grew in most of Europe.
  C. Colonialism
    1. Americas and Asia were colonized by the English, French, Dutch, Spanish, and Portuguese.
    2. Imports to Europe included sugar and tobacco, farmed by slaves.
    3. Musical exports to the Americas
      a. Catholic music and villancicos to the Spanish colonies
      b. Metric psalmody to the English colonies
  D. Patronage
    1. Capitalism created an atmosphere conducive to music-making.
      a. Investors financed opera houses.
      b. Increased demand for sheet music, instruments, and lessons
    2. Private patronage
      a. Italian nobles and the church continued to hire the best and most innovative composers.
      b. In France, the king supported music.
    3. Public patronage through tickets and subscriptions
      a. The first of many public opera houses opened in Venice in 1637.
      b. Public concerts began in England in 1672.

II. From Renaissance to Baroque
  A. "Baroque"
    1. Definitions: abnormal, exaggerated, in bad taste
    2. Derives from the Portuguese word for misshapen pearl
    3. Applied as a derisive term by post-Baroque critics because of the overly ornate art of the late Baroque (see **HWM Figure 13.2**)
    4. Now applied to music from ca. 1600–1750 without a derisive connotation

B. Drama in the arts
   1. Famous playwrights of the era include Shakespeare, Racine, and Moliére.
   2. Poetry took on a theatrical quality (see **HMW Source Reading,** page 293)
   3. Sculpture (compare **HWM Figures 13.3** and **13.4**)
      a. Movement away from the Greek ideals that Michelangelo had emulated
      b. More drama and emotion
      c. In **HWM Figure 13.5,** a dramatic sculpture is situated where it will be theatrically lit by a window.
   4. Architecture achieved drama using space and size.

C. The affections (i.e., emotional states of the soul)
   1. People believed that spirits or "humors" in the body harbored emotions.
   2. Music could bring these humors into better balance.
      a. Contrasting sections that depicted different moods helped balance the humors.
      b. Instrumental music portrayed generic emotions.
      c. Vocal music conveyed the emotions of the text, character, or dramatic situation.

D. The second practice (see **HWM Source Reading,** page 298)
   1. The first practice, exemplified by Zarlino
      a. Counterpoint rules could not be violated.
      b. Dissonances had to be carefully controlled and restricted.
   2. Claudio Monteverdi (1567–1643, see **HWM biography,** page 297, and **Figure 13.7**)
      a. Believed counterpoint roles could be broken for dramatic effect
      b. His madrigal *Cruda Amarilli* uses unprepared dissonances to express words such as "cruda" (cruel) and "ahi" (alas).
   3. Debate over Monteverdi's use of dissonance
      a. Giovanni Maria Artusi, a student of Zarlino, criticized *Cruda Amarilli.*
      b. Artusi cited examples of unprepared dissonance without referring to the text.
      c. Monteverdi's brother defended him on the grounds that in this second practice (*seconda pratica*) music had to serve the text.
   4. The first practice of counterpoint continued but was no longer the only method of composition.

III. General Characteristics of Baroque Music

A. Texture
   1. Polarity between the two essential lines, bass and melody
   2. Basso continuo (or thoroughbass) notation, specifying only melody and bass with figures to indicate chords other than root position
   3. Cello, bassoon, or viola da gamba played the bass line.
   4. Keyboard or plucked instruments (such as the theorbo, **HWM Figure 13.8**) played both bass and chords.
   5. Realization, the actual playing
      a. Improvised performance
      b. Written-out suggestions in modern editions, indicated by smaller notes (e.g., **NAWM 64**)
   6. Concertato medium (from Italian *concertare,* "to reach agreement")
      a. Combining voices with instruments
      b. Genres included the concerted madrigal and the sacred concerto.
      c. Later, also applied to a contrast between a solo group and the complete group (i.e., concerto grosso)

B. Tuning and harmony
   1. Incompatible tuning systems were thrown together by the concertato medium.
      a. Singers and violinists used just intonation.
      b. Keyboard instruments used mean-tone temperament and only sounded good in keys with few sharps or flats.
      c. Fretted instruments used equal temperament to guarantee all octaves would be in tune.
      d. Equal temperament started to become more common.
   2. Harmony
      a. Figured bass writing led to thinking in terms of chords instead of intervals.
      b. More types of dissonances were permitted.
      c. Chromaticism expressed only emotions at first, but was later used in harmonic exploration.
      d. Harmony drove counterpoint for the first time.
      e. In 1722, Rameau developed a theory of harmony, which replaced modal theory.

C. Pieces were composed in both free and measured rhythmic style.

D. Performance practice
   1. Continuo players fleshed out figured bass, using embellishments as well as chords.

2. Ornamentation consisted of brief ornaments as well as extended figuration (e.g., **HWM Example 13.3**).
3. The written music was only a guideline.
   a. Singers added cadenzas to arias.
   b. Arias might be added to or deleted from operas.
   c. Organists were free to change the length of pieces to suit the service.

E. Many of the characteristics of Baroque music persisted for hundreds of years.

## SUGGESTIONS FOR SUPPLEMENTARY READING/LISTENING/ACTIVITIES

A readable source for additional background on scientific discovery for this and future chapters is *Science Firsts: From the Creation of Science to the Science of Creation* by Robert E. Adler (New York: John Wiley, 2002).

For an example of drama in Baroque painting and for a comparison of the same subject as portrayed in different periods, use images from the Web Gallery of Art (www.wga.hu), which has an excellent search engine. One subject with dramatic potential is the story of Judith, omitted from the Protestant Bible. Judith, a Jewish prisoner, kills Holofernes, commander-in-chief of the armies of Nebuchadnezzar, with his own sword after he lapses into a drunken stupor. Her handmaid, waiting outside, puts the head into her bag, and they transport it back to the town of Bethulia, which lay under siege. The Jews, emboldened by Holofernes' death, defeat the enemy and save Jerusalem from the Assyrians. Caravaggio's *Judith Beheading Holofernes* (www.wga.hu/art/c/caravagg/03/17judit.jpg and other online sources), ca. 1598, depicts the most grisly and dramatic moment of the story, the actual beheading, with each character portraying a different emotion. In the Renaissance painting by Andrea Mantegna (www.wga.hu/art/m/mantegna/2/judith.jpg), Judith's dispassionate expression and clothing recall Greek and Roman style but without any sense of drama. In Francesco Solimena's painting of 1728–33, *Judith with the Head of Holofernes* (www.wga.hu/art/s/solimena/judith_p. jpg), Judith is almost lost in the crowd as she displays Holofernes' head, exemplifying the excess of detail that inspired the derogatory term "Baroque." After showing students these or similar images, ask them which of the paintings evoked the most emotions for them. If they were to compose a piece of music for each painting, what kind of texture, forces, and harmony would they use?

The full text of the Artusi-Monteverdi controversy is available in *Source Readings in Music History,* rev. ed. (New York: W. W. Norton, 1998), volume 4, *The Baroque Era*, edited by Margaret Murata.

**NAWM 53,** Gesualdo's *Io parto,* follows Zarlino's rules despite its chromaticism and madrigalisms. Ask students to take another look at this work with the Artusi-Monteverdi controversy in mind. What would Monteverdi have thought of this work?

Have students look ahead in *NAWM* for instances where figured bass has been realized by an editor. A good example is **NAWM 69,** Barbara Strozzi's *Lagrime mie,* in which the editor has fleshed out chords not specifically notated with figures. Ask students how the accompanist would have known which chords to play with only the bass and melody as guides, i.e., when a figure is lacking. Students with experience in a traditional music theory curriculum should be able to explain the process, thus demonstrating the continuing validity of a practice developed over four hundred years ago. Jazz musicians may have experience with fake books, which give only the melody and names of chords.

Several books on Baroque performance practice are available for further reference, including *Performance Practice: Music after 1600,* edited by Howard Mayer Brown and Stanley Sadie (New York: W. W. Norton, 1990), which includes a chapter on tuning and intonation, and Robert Donington, *Baroque Music, Style and Performance: A Handbook* (New York: W. W. Norton, 1982). If you have books on performance practice for specific instruments, pass them out to members of the class who play those instruments, asking them if they have had experience with the musical situations described.

## OBJECTIVE QUESTIONS

1. The seventeenth century was an era in which __________.
   a. people deferred to Church teachings on all matters, including science
   b. scientists combined deductive reasoning and direct observation for the first time
   c. scientists used inductive reasoning to justify biblical teaching
   d. the Church incarcerated scientists on charges of heresy
   e. scientific theories from China and Japan were brought to Europe via trading routes

   Answer: b

2. In the seventeenth century, __________.
   a. colonies in the Americas imported villancicos from Spain and metric psalmody from England
   b. colonies in the Americas were still too undeveloped to enjoy European music
   c. native American and African musical styles overtook European styles, as the vogue for "savage" music replaced the madrigal in Europe.
   d. colonies in the Americas imported only secular music from Europe
   e. there was an exchange of musical styles between the European colonists, slaves, and native Americans, resulting in a blended style that would epitomize the Baroque

   Answer: a

3. Patronage of seventeenth-century music consisted of __________.
   a. wealthy patrons who hired musicians for their private chapels
   b. wealthy patrons and churches
   c. wealthy patrons, churches, and public performances of operas and concerts
   d. secular patronage only, with wealthy patrons and public concerts supporting musicians who had formerly been employed by the Church
   e. public patronage only, with public opera houses and public concerts replacing private patronage and Church patronage

   Answer: c

4. The term *Baroque* was first applied to __________.
   a. overly ornate embellishments in architecture
   b. Monteverdi s style of composition
   c. basso continuo
   d. unprepared dissonance
   e. arts based on valued from ancient Greece

   Answer: a

5. The term *Baroque* is now applied to __________.
   a. music from ca. 1550–1700
   b. music from ca. 1600–1750
   c. music from ca. 1650–1800
   d. any artwork with dramatic impact
   e. arts based on values from ancient Greece

   Answer: b

6. Seventeenth-century sculpture sought to __________.
   a. replicate classical aesthetics
   b. bring flat medieval painting styles to three dimensions
   c. break down the barriers between art and science
   d. portray more drama and emotion
   e. balance contrasting aspects

   Answer: d

7. In Baroque music, "affections" can be defined as __________.
   a. the Church's belief that God's love was called forth with the proper performance of vocal music
   b. a theoretical idea set forth in Monteverdi's manifesto, printed by his brother, and distributed on the streets of Venice in a pamphlet war against Artusi
   c. a scientific theory of attraction and repulsion that explained the harmonic pull between tonic and dominant tonalities
   d. the belief that a man could persuade a woman to love him based on his excellent performance of madrigals
   e. the spirits or "humors" believed to harbor emotions, and which could be brought into balance with contrasting moods of music

   Answer: e

8. Monteverdi called his approach to composition __________.
   a. doctrine of affections
   b. nuove musiche
   c. Florentine camerata
   d. seconda pratica
   e. baroque

   Answer: d

9. Artusi criticized Monteverdi's *Cruda Amarilli* because it __________.
   a. violated Zarlino's counterpoint rules
   b. had too many madrigalisms
   c. didn't reflect the meaning of the text
   d. used too many accidentals
   e. mixed voices and instruments

   Answer: a

10. Tonal organization in the Baroque featured __________.
    a. the eight church modes
    b. the twelve church modes
    c. major and minor tonalities
    d. a mixture of major, minor, and church modes within the same work
    e. extreme dissonance, with no tonal focus

    Answer: c

11. The texture of Baroque music is marked by __________.
    a. equality of all voices
    b. a return to the focus on the tenor voice, with the others embellishing it
    c. a polarity between bass and treble lines
    d. chordal settings
    e. unaccompanied solo singing

    Answer: c

12. The instruments of the continuo group usually consist of __________.
    a. two treble instruments plus a keyboard
    b. one bass instrument, such as a viol, plus a keyboard or lute
    c. a consort of viols
    d. one bass instrument and one treble instrument
    e. a mixed grouping of voices and instruments

    Answer: b

13. The concertato medium consisted of __________.
    a. two treble instruments plus a keyboard
    b. one bass instrument, such as a viol, plus a keyboard or lute
    c. a consort of viols
    d. one bass instrument and one treble instrument
    e. a mixed grouping of voices and instruments

    Answer: e

14. Tuning systems in the Baroque era gradually came to favor __________.
    a. equal temperament
    b. chromatic temperament
    c. pure tuning
    d. just intonation
    e. mean-tone

    Answer: a

15. Figured bass is __________.
    a. a bass line notated with embellishments to equal embellishments in the top voice
    b. a bass line notated with numbers to indicate chords above it
    c. a bass viol that has been elaborately carved, usually with references to the patron who commissioned it
    d. one of the standard chord progressions used in the Baroque era
    e. a bass line that takes the solo role

    Answer: b

16. Realization is __________.
    a. the process of making emotions in the music seem more "real" through embellishment
    b. Monteverdi's term for the compositional techniques that Artusi criticized
    c. taking a standard melody and creating a set of variations for it
    d. filling in the chords above a bass line according to the numbers above the line
    e. the return of the tonic after a long chord progression

    Answer: d

17. In modern editions of Baroque music, small notes in a keyboard part indicate __________.
    a. alternate pitches
    b. musica ficta
    c. editorial suggestions to flesh out unnotated parts
    d. embellishments
    e. notes to play with a light touch because they are dissonant against the bass

    Answer: c

18. Which of these statements is true of the role of improvisation in Baroque music?
    a. Everything was written out, with no room for improvisation.
    b. The accompaniment and the melody were written, but performers could embellish the melody.
    c. Accompanists improvised the accompaniment based on improvisation in the melody line.
    d. The melody was written out and followed exactly, but the accompaniment was improvised.
    e. Part of the accompaniment was written out, the rest improvised, and the melody could be embellished.

    Answer: e

19. In 1722, Rameau developed an influential theory of __________.
    a. embellishment
    b. harmony
    c. affections
    d. performance practice
    e. seconda pratica

    Answer: b

20. Which of the following statements best describes the use of chromaticism in the Baroque era?
    a. Chromaticism was used only for expression of strong emotions.
    b. Chromaticism expressed only emotions at first, but later was used in harmonic exploration.
    c. Chromaticism was used sparingly, and only when the text called for strong emotions.
    d. Chromaticism was banned by the Church, and composers respected the ban.
    e. Chromaticism was used only for modulation to new keys.

    Answer: b

## SHORT-ESSAY QUESTIONS

1. Define the term "baroque" in terms of its original meaning and the qualities of art and music now associated with the term.
2. Discuss the role of emotions in the music and art of the early seventeenth century.
3. Summarize the debate between Artusi and Monteverdi in terms of the styles and principles they advocated.
4. Describe the role of the bass line in Baroque music. How is it notated? How does it function? Which instrument(s) could perform this line?

## TERMS FOR IDENTIFICATION

Baroque
affections
first practice (prima pratica)
second practice (seconda pratica)
basso continuo
figured bass
theorbo
realization
concertato medium
equal temperament
ornamentation
cadenza

# CHAPTER 14 The Invention of Opera

I. Forerunners of Opera
  A. Opera (Italian for "work") defined
    1. Union of versified play (Italian *libretto,* "little book"), drama, and music
    2. Continuous or near-continuous singing
    3. Staged, with scenery, costumes, and action
  B. Renaissance antecedents
    1. Pastoral drama
      a. Play in verse, interspersed with incidental music and songs
      b. Stories of idyllic love in rural settings
      c. First staged in 1471: *Favola d'Orfeo* (The Orpheus Legend)
      d. The earliest opera composers borrowed heavily from this genre.
    2. Madrigal
      a. Solo madrigals and madrigal cycles had simple plots and they expressed emotion.
      b. Best-known was *L'Amfiparnaso* (The Slopes of Parnassus, 1594) by Orazio Vecchi (1550–1605).
    3. Intermedio (pl. *intermedii*) was the most direct antecedent.
      a. Musical interludes before, after, and between the acts of plays
      b. There were usually six for each play.
      c. Subjects were pastoral, allegorical, or mythological.
      d. For special occasions they could be very elaborate, including chorus, dance numbers, costumes, and staged effects (see **HWM Figure 14.1**).
      e. Music was embellished in performance (see **HWM Example 14.1**).
      f. For the 1589 wedding of Ferdinand de' Medici and Christine of Lorraine in Florence, composers wrote intermedii on the theme of the power of ancient Greek music.
      g. These composers would later write the earliest operas.
  C. Greek tragedy as the model for drama
    1. Scholars put their theories of music's role into practice.
    2. Andrea Gabrieli set only the choruses for his *Oedipus Rex* (1585), using only homophony.
    3. Giralamo Mei (1589–1594) believed that all the text was sung.
      a. He read ancient treatises in the original Greek.
      b. He concluded that Greek music consisted of a single melody.
      c. The melody could be sung by a soloist or a chorus with or without accompaniment.
      d. He persuaded others to his viewpoint via letters.
    4. The Florentine Camerata
      a. A group of scholars in Florence who discussed literature, science, and the arts.
      b. The host was Count Bardi, the man who had conceived the theme of the 1589 intermedii.
      c. Members included Vincenzo Galilei (ca. 1520–1591), theorist and composer, son of the famous astronomer.
      d. Giulio Caccini (ca. 1550–1618), one of the composers of the 1589 intermedii, was a member.

5. Vincenzo Galilei's *Dialogo della musica antica et della moderna* (Dialogue of Ancient and Modern Music, 1581)
    a. Galilei argued against counterpoint and madrigalisms.
    b. He believed the solo melody was ideal for emotional expression.
    c. Natural speech inflections of a good orator were the model.
    d. The term for accompanied vocal melodies of this era, including the type described by Galilei, is *monody*.
6. Caccini's *Le nuove musice* (1602)
    a. Collection of songs (arias) in monody and solo madrigals
    b. The introduction describes ornaments and their use.
    c. Ornamentation enhances the message of the text.
    d. Example: *Vedrò 'l mio sol* (**NAWM 64** and **HWM Figure 13.9**) premiered in Bardi's Camerata.

II. The First Operas
  A. *Dafne* (1598)
    1. Poetry by Ottavio Rinuccini, music by singer-composer Jacopo Peri
    2. Rinuccini and Peri had contributed to the 1589 intermedii and were members of the Camerata.
    3. Premiered at the palace of Jacopo Corsi (1561–1602), who hosted the Camerata after Bardi moved to Rome
  B. *Rappresentatione di Anima et di Corpo* (Representation of the Soul and Body, 1600)
    1. Music by Emilio de' Cavalieri, who was in charge of theater at the duke's court in Florence.
    2. Longer than any previous staged musical play.

III. *L'Euridice* (1600)
  A. Creation
    1. Music by Peri and libretto by Rinuccini, directed by Cavalieri
    2. Produced for the wedding of Maria de' Medici and King Henry IV of France
    3. Some sections were written by Caccini.
  B. The story demonstrates music's power to move the emotions.
    1. Orfeo (Orpheus) causes denizens of the underworld to weep through his music.
    2. He persuades the underworld to restore his wife, Euridice, to life.
  C. Recitative style (see **HWM Example 14.2** and **NAWM 65c**)
    1. Peri invented a new idiom, recitative, to bridge the Greek ideas of pitch in speech and intervallic (diastematic) pitch in song.
    2. Basso continuo sustains a chord and plays the bass line as the singer moves between pitches that are consonant and dissonant against it.
    3. Consonances occur on all stressed syllables.
    4. Peri's goal was dramatic expression, and he performed the role of Orfeo in the premiere.
  D. Monody types in *L'Euridice* (**NAWM 65 a–c**)
    1. Aria, for singing strophic poetry (**NAWM 65a**)
        a. Same as sixteenth-century song styles
        b. Ritornellos, instrumental refrains, separate the strophes.
    2. Song (**NAWM 65b**)
        a. Dance-song or canzonetta style
        b. Framed by a sinfonia, an abstract instrumental piece used especially in introductions
    3. Recitative (**NAWM 65c**)
        a. Dafne (Euridice's maid) tells Orfeo that Euridice has died from a snake bite.
        b. Orfeo's reaction (**HWM Example 14.3**) portrays grief and shock through suspensions, chromaticism, and rests.

IV. Claudio Monteverdi's Operas
  A. *L'Orfeo* (1607)
    1. Monteverdi's first opera, produced in Mantua on commission
    2. Libretto
        a. Five acts, each ending with a vocal ensemble that comments on the action, like a Greek chorus
        b. The centerpiece of each act is an aria sung by Orfeo.
    3. Monteverdi specified instruments in his score.
        a. Recorders, cornetts, trumpets, trombones, strings, and continuo
        b. A regal, a buzzy-sounding reed organ, portrays the underworld.
    4. Monody styles
        a. Arias are strophic, but strophes are varied to reflect the text (strophic variation).
        b. Recitative style varies depending on the situation in the drama.
    5. Ensembles and choruses provide contrast, with ritornellos as division points.
    6. Structure of Act II (**NAWM 66**)
        a. It begins with a series of cheerful celebrations (e.g., **NAWM 66b,** Orfeo's strophic aria).
        b. The tonality changes to Aeolian (A minor) when a messenger delivers news of Euridice's death from a snake bite.

c. Joy and grief alternate as Orfeo's companions continue celebrating, not having heard the news.
d. The messenger's melody recurs as a refrain throughout the act.

7. Orfeo's lament (**NAWM 66d, HWM Example 14.4**)
   a. It begins with expressions of grief, portrayed by built-up phrases and dissonances.
   b. It ends with Orfeo's resolve to retrieve Euridice from the underworld, portrayed by the descending line.

B. Monteverdi's later works
1. *L'Arianna*
   a. Commissioned by Duke Vincenzo Gonzaga in 1608
   b. Only a fragment survives, *Arianna's Lament.*
   c. Staged in other cities after its premiere (as was *L'Orfeo*)
2. In 1613 he moved to Venice to assume the post of maestro di capella at Saint Mark's, but he continued to compose dramatic works.
3. *Il Combattimento di Tancredi e Clorinda* (The Combat of Tancred and Clorinda, 1624)
   a. Narrative poem with music for singing and mime, accompanied by strings with continuo
   b. Most of the narration is sung by tenor in recitative.
   c. The tenor and soprano mime to their short speeches and the narrative.
   d. Instrumental interludes suggest action (e.g., horses and sword fighting).
   e. Passages in *stile concitato* (excited style), which uses repeated notes to convey agitation (this technique would be widely imitated by others)

C. Operas for public theaters in Venice
1. The first public theater opened in 1637.
2. *Ritorno d'Ulisse* (Return of Ulysses, 1640), based on Homer's *Odyssey*
3. *L'Incoronazione di Poppea* (Coronation of Poppea, 1643)
   a. Based on a historical subject, Roman emperor Nero's second marriage, rather than myth
   b. Often considered Monteverdi's masterpiece because of its expressiveness
   c. **NAWM 67,** a scene in which Poppea pleads with Nero to stay with her, shifts between simple recitative, aria, and a style midway between them, *recitativo arioso,* or *arioso.*

V. Spread of Italian Opera

A. Florence after *L'Euridice*
1. The court preferred ballets and intermedii for celebrations of important events.
2. Francesca Caccini (1587–ca. 1645): *La liberazione di Ruggiero dall'isola d'Alcina* (The Liberation of Ruggiero from the Island of Alcine, 1625)
   a. She was the highest-paid musician employed by the grand duke of Tuscany.
   b. Daughter of Guilio, she sang with her sister and stepmother in a *concerto delle donne* rivaling that of Ferrara (see **HWM Chapter 11**).
   c. This work is now considered an opera, but it was originally billed as a ballet.
   d. Musical elements include an opening sinfonia, recitatives, arias, choruses, instrumental ritornellos, and chorus.
   e. The staging was elaborate (see **HWM Figure 14.5**).

B. Rome became the center for opera development in the 1620s.
1. The range of topics expanded to include epics, saints' lives, and comedy.
2. Stage effects were spectacular (e.g. flames consuming devils).
3. Recitative and aria became more clearly defined.
   a. Recitative became more speech-like.
   b. Arias were melodious and usually strophic.
4. Other musical elements
   a. Vocal ensembles
   b. Extended finales for each act, including choral singing and dancing
5. Two-part instrumental sinfonias introduced the operas.
   a. The first part is a slow chordal section.
   b. The second part is a lively imitative canzona.
   c. This two-part form became standard for the opening movements of seventeenth-century opera.
6. Castrato singers
   a. Men who had been castrated before puberty sang treble parts in church because women were not permitted to sing in church.
   b. In Rome, women were not permitted on stage, so castrati sang the treble roles.
   c. Castrati later sang outside of Italy as well, but only in male roles.

C. Venice
1. The first public theaters

a. 1637: Teatro San Cassiano opened as the first public opera house.
b. By 1678, there were nine stages devoted to opera.
c. Visitors who celebrated carnival season from December 26 to Lent attended operas in public theaters.

2. Librettos
   a. Stories for librettos were chosen for their dramatic content and opportunity for special effects.
   b. Sources for plots included mythology, classic epics, and Roman history.
   c. A three-act structure replaced the earlier five-act convention.
   d. Choruses and dances were limited due to financial constraints.
3. Musical style
   a. Recitative and aria became further delineated.
   b. Arias became very lyrical, with persistent rhythmic motives and simple harmonies.
   c. There were more arias per act.
4. The main composers were Francesco Cavalli (1602–1676) and Antonio Cesti (1623–1669).
5. Singers commanded high fees and had music written especially for them.

D. Italian opera abroad
   1. Italian operas were performed in Paris in the 1640s.
   2. No known performance of Italian opera in England in the seventeenth century, but a copy of a Cavalli opera reached England
   3. Austria became a major center of Italian opera.
      a. Cesti composed operas for the archduke of Tyrol and for the imperial court at Vienna.
      b. 1654: Venetian-style opera house built for the archduke of Tyrol
      c. Cesti's most famous opera, *Il pomo d'oro* (The Golden Apple, 1667), was performed at the emperor's wedding in Vienna.

E. Italian opera at midcentury
   1. Many style features established during this era would remain standard for Italian opera over the next two hundred years.
      a. Concentration on solo singing
      b. Separation of recitative and aria
      c. Use of varied styles
      d. Singers and spectacle replaced drama as the focus of interest.
   2. Cesti's *Orontea*
      a. Composed in 1656 for Innsbruck
      b. Popular throughout Italy and German-speaking lands
      c. The plot concerns love at first sight across social levels, not myth or history.
      d. The libretto interweaves comic and romantic scenes.
   3. Recitative style (**NAWM 68a** and **HWM Example 14.5**)
      a. The definitive style for the next hundred years
      b. Used for most of the action
      c. Many repeated notes, with modulating harmonies
   4. Aria style (**NAWM 68b** and **HWM Example 14.6**)
      a. Strophic with some modification
      b. Smooth, diatonic melody with easy rhythms
      c. Violins accompany the voice throughout.

VI. Tension between Drama and Spectacle
   A. Opera began as an effort to place drama at the center of a staged musical performance, but solo singing and spectacle soon overcame this effort.
   B. Later composers would seek to reform opera, bringing drama to the fore again.
   C. Current theatrical productions face the same tension between drama and spectacle.

## SUGGESTIONS FOR SUPPLEMENTARY READING/LISTENING/ACTIVITIES

For additional background on pastoral drama in Italy, see Chapter III of W. W. Greg, *Pastoral Poetry & Pastoral Drama: A Literary Inquiry, with Special Reference to the Pre-restoration Stage in England* (London: A. H. Bullen, 1906, and several reprint editions. Also available as an e-book through Proquest and Bookrags.com). For a recent book-length treatment that includes information on plays by women, see Lisa Sampson, *Pastoral Drama in Early Modern Italy: The Making of a New Genre* (Oxford: Legenda, 2004).

Information on staging is available in a fascinating article, "Il Corago and the Staging of Early Opera: Four Chapters from an Anonymous Treatise circa 1630" (*Early Music,* Nov. 1989), 494–511. Pages 500–502 discuss singing and acting in the context of performance.

Music for the madrigal cycle *L'Amfiparnaso* is available in a modern edition, edited by Cecil Adkins (Chapel Hill: The University of North Carolina Press, 1977). The volume also includes essays for further background. For a lively recording, use the Ensemble Clément Janequin's compact disc (Harmonia Mundi 1951461, 2002).

For more about the celebrations surrounding the 1589 wedding of Ferdinand de' Medici and Christine of Lorraine, see *The Medici Wedding of 1589: Florentine Festival as Theatrum Mundi* by James M. Saslow (Yale University Press, 1996).

Girolamo Mei 's 1572 letter to Vincenzo Galilei is translated in *Source Readings in Music History,* volume III, *The Renaissance,* edited by Gary Tomlinson (New York: W. W. Norton, 1998).

Many of the significant documents relating to the Florentine Camerata are included in Claude V. Palisca's *The Florentine Camerata: Documentary Studies and Translations* (New Haven: Yale University Press, 1988).

Caccini's *Le nuove musiche* is available in a modern edition, along with a translation of its important preface; see H. Wiley Hitchcock, ed., *Giulio Caccini: Le nuove musiche* (Madison, Wis.: A-R Editions, 1970).

Cavalieri's *Rappresentatione di Anima et di Corpo* has been recorded (Naxos 8.554096-97, 1998). The score is available in facsimile (Farnborough, England: Gregg 1967).

Facsimile editions of Peri and Caccini's *Euridice* have been published by Broude Brothers (New York, 1973) and Forni (Bologna, 1976), respectively. *Euridice* is available on several recent recordings, including those released by Pavane Records (ADW 7372-3, 2000) and Arts Music (47274-2, 1995).

Monteverdi's *L'Orfeo* is available on video (New York: Polygram Video, 1988). The introductory fanfare (toccata), though short, demonstrates Monteverdi's interest in instrumental composition, and the Polygram Video production shows several historical instruments during this section.

Several recordings of *L'Orfeo* are available, including Rene Jacob's "Concerto Vocale" performance (Harmonia Mundi 901553, 1995) and one conducted by John Eliot Gardiner (Archiv 419250, 1990).

Monteverdi's *L'Incoronazione Di Poppea* is available on two video performances. The first was directed by Raymond Leppard and stars Maria Ewing (Kultur VHS 1403, 1984, and DVD, 2004, and VHS Thorn EMI/HBO classic performance, 1984). The second is a production conducted by Nikolaus Harnoncourt (London: Polygram Video 071 506-3, 1991). Both have English subtitles.

The recording of *Poppea* conducted by Raymond Leppard (EMI Classics 73842, 2000) also includes *Lamento d'Arianna* and several madrigals in concertato medium. A recording of duets in concertato medium performed by Il Complesso Barocco (Virgin Veritas 724354529320, 1998) includes examples from Book 7 of Monteverdi's madrigals. The liner notes discuss the performers' approach to instrumentation, pitch, and other matters of performance practice. Have students read these notes (or similar notes) to help them understand the relevance of research for modern performers.

For two works by Francesca Caccini, including an aria from *La liberazione di Ruggier dall' isola d Alcina,* see *Historical Anthology of Music by Women,* ed. James R. Briscoe (Bloomington: Indiana University Press, 1987), 22–38. Eight works are available in *Women Composers: Music through the Ages, Vol. 1: Composers Born before 1599* (New York: G. K. Hall, 1996). This series contains brief articles and a bibliography for each composer represented. Caccini's haunting madrigal *Amarilli Mia Bella* is performed by Cecilia Bartoli on her "Live in Italy " CD (Decca 455981, 1998).

For a contemporary (1620) account of an elaborate court ballet, see Lorenzo Bianconi, translated by David Bryant, in *Music in the Seventeenth Century* (New York: Cambridge University Press, 1987), pages 279–284. The account describes instruments, costuming, and dance, and offers selections from texts and a summary of the plot.

A map of seventeenth-century Venice showing its opera theaters is available in Simon Towneley Worsthorne's *Venetian Opera in the Seventeenth Century* (Oxford: Clarendon Press, 1968, and New York: Da Capo Press, 1984).

Cesti's operas no longer enjoy the popularity that they did in his day, but some of his arias remain in singers' repertoire. One example is *Si mantiene il mio amor,* sung by Dmitri Hvorostovsky on "Arie Antiche," (Polygram Records 56543, 1998) a CD that also contains an example by Giulio Caccini.

Review the distinctions among recitative, aria, and arioso by playing examples from operas discussed in *HWM* or suggested here, and ask students to identify changes among the styles.

## OBJECTIVE QUESTIONS

1. The text for an opera is called a(n) __________.
   a. lyrical poem
   b. libretto
   c. pastoral
   d. ritornello
   e. intermedio

   Answer: b

2. Which of the following statements best describes the Renaissance antecedents of opera?
   a. There was no staged music before opera, but dance songs sometimes included dialogue.
   b. Opera arose directly from the madrigal cycle without other influences.
   c. Opera represents the secularization of mystery plays that depict biblical stories.
   d. There were several genres that included some of the elements of opera.
   e. Opera had been improvised by traveling theatrical groups, and trained musicians adopted their techniques for written compositions.

   Answer: d

3. The earliest opera plots were based on __________.
   a. historical events
   b. mythological characters and events
   c. current events
   d. comedic mishaps
   e. plays by contemporary playwrights

   Answer: b

4. The Florentine Camerata was __________.
   a. a traveling band of musicians and actors who brought music and theater to small-town audiences
   b. members of the count of Florence's private chapel
   c. members of the cathedral in Florence who were frustrated with their limited repertoire
   d. a group of scholars in Florence who discussed literature, science, and the arts
   e. a theater in Florence that produced plays, spectacles, and ballets

   Answer: d

5. Monody is the modern term for __________.
   a. the use of repeated pitches over a sustained chord
   b. plays with sung dialogue
   c. instrumental passages that depict the emotional state of a character
   d. all accompanied solo singing of the early seventeenth century
   e. seemingly plain compositions intended to be embellished

   Answer: d

6. *Le nuove musiche* was __________.
   a. Monteverdi's term for the modern style
   b. a collection of songs in monody by Caccini
   c. a group of musicians who performed experimental music
   d. a treatise criticizing the newer styles
   e. one of the first operas

   Answer: b

Use the following set of possible answers for questions 7 through 10:
   a. Mei
   b. Peri
   c. Bardi
   d. Galilei
   e. Rinuccini

7. The count who hosted gatherings of poets and musicians at his home was __________.

   Answer: c

8. The composer who collaborated on the first operas of the Florentine Camerata was __________.

   Answer: b

9. The poet who wrote the text for some of the first operas was __________.

   Answer: e

10. The scholar whose study of ancient Greek texts led him to believe that all Greek plays had been sung was __________.

    Answer: a

11. Monteverdi developed Stile concitato to depict __________.
    a. scenes of extreme sadness
    b. joyous sentiments
    c. agitation
    d. dialogue
    e. transitions between two emotional states

    Answer: c

12. The center for opera development after its initial development in Florence was __________.
    a. Venice
    b. Rome
    c. Ferrara
    d. Vienna
    e. Paris

    Answer: b

13. The style of monody in which a solo singer sings speechlike dialogue to the accompaniment of simple chords is __________.
    a. aria
    b. arioso
    c. recitative
    d. intermedio
    e. dialogo

    Answer: c

14. Two of Monteverdi's pupils and his successors as composers of Venetian opera were __________.
    a. Cavalli and Cesti
    b. Peri and Caccini
    c. Galilei and Bardi
    d. Francesca Caccini and Mei
    e. Vecchi and Rinuccini

    Answer: a

15. Arioso is best defined as __________.
    a. a compositional style aimed at showing off a singer's virtuosity
    b. an instrumental interlude in the middle of an aria
    c. a series of fast, repeated pitches intended to portray agitation
    d. instrumental imitation of aria style
    e. a singing style midway between aria and recitative

    Answer: e

16. In Rome, roles for high voices were sung by __________.
    a. professional female singers
    b. women who had been trained in the church
    c. boy sopranos
    d. men who had been castrated as boys
    e. men who had naturally high voices

    Answer: d

17. Cesti composed his most famous opera for audiences in which region?
    a. Northern Italy, including Venice
    b. Southern Italy, including Rome
    c. Austria
    d. England
    e. France

    Answer: c

18. The first public opera house opened in 1637 in which city?
    a. Venice
    b. Florence
    c. Mantua
    d. Rome
    e. Vienna

    Answer: a

19. Which of the following is *not* true of mid-seventeenth-century Italian opera style?
    a. There was a concentration on solo singing, with more arias per act.
    b. Recitative and aria became highly separated.
    c. Composers used a variety of styles for aria composition.
    d. Singers and spectacle had replaced drama as the focus of interest.
    e. A two-part orchestral *sinfonia* opened the opera.

    Answer: d

## SHORT-ESSAY QUESTIONS

1. Discuss the forerunners of opera and their impact on the first operas.
2. Discuss the career and works of Monteverdi, paying special attention to his innovations and contributions to the development of opera.
3. Compare and contrast the style and features of the earliest operas and those of the mid-seventeenth century.
4. Discuss the role of instruments in the earliest operas.

## TERMS FOR IDENTIFICATION

opera
libretto
pastoral drama
madrigal cycle
intermedio
Giralamo Mei
Florentine Camerata
Count Bardi
*Dialogo della musica antica et della moderna*
monody
*Le nuove musiche*
aria
recitative
sinfonia
ritornello
*stile concitato*
arioso
castrato
Teatro San Cassiano

# CHAPTER 15 Music for Chamber and Church in the Early Seventeenth Century

I. Style and Function
  A. Theorists recognized different styles for church, chamber, and theater music.
  B. Composers gave increasingly distinctive flavors to genres in both vocal and instrumental music.
  C. Styles and techniques developed for opera continued to influence other genres.

II. Italian Vocal Chamber Music
  A. Secular works in concertato style
    1. For solo voice or small vocal ensemble with basso continuo
    2. Included madrigals, canzonettas, strophic songs, dialogues, and recitatives
    3. Widely published and performed
  B. Monteverdi and concerted madrigals
    1. Madrigals with instrumental accompaniment
    2. Monteverdi's madrigals after 1605 used basso continuo and sometimes additional instruments.
    3. Book 7 (1619), titled *Concerto*
    4. Book 8 (1638), *Madrigali guerrieri et amorosi* (Madrigals of Love and War), his last book of madrigals
      a. Large variety of forces: solo voice, small vocal ensemble, chorus, continuo, instrumental ensemble
      b. Includes dramatic works
      c. Styles range from sixteenth-century madrigal style to *stile concitato* and operatic recitative.
  C. Ostinato basses
    1. *Basso ostinato*
      a. Persistent, or obstinate, bass
      b. Also called ground bass (bass that is the ground, or foundation, for the work)
    2. Common features
      a. Triple or compound meter
      b. Two, four, or six measures long
      c. Often features a descending tetrachord
    3. Became a favorite device in opera (e.g., **NAWM 69** and **79**)
    4. **HWM Example 15.1**
      a. From Monteverdi's *Lamento della ninfa* (Lament of the Nymph) from Book 8 of his madrigals
      b. The bass line establishes the tonal center.
      c. The voice conveys distress via dissonance against the bass (marked with an "x").
    5. **NAWM 60b,** *Guárdame las vacas*
      a. A Spanish pattern similar to the *romanesca* and *ruggiero* of Italy (see **HWM Chapter 11**)
      b. Developed from a long tradition in Spain and Italy of extemporizing on a bass
  D. *Chacona* (Italian *ciaccona*)
    1. Dance song with origins in Latin America
    2. Pattern of chords (for guitar originally) used as a refrain
    3. **HWM Example 15.2** from Monteverdi's *Zefiro torna e di soavi accenti* (1632)
      a. Uses fifty-six repetitions of the pattern
      b. Two tenors sing of happy emotions during the chacona portion.
      c. The ending uses a slow, expressive recitative to portray a lover's lament.
  E. Cantata
    1. Definition
      a. Originally simply "piece to be sung" (from the Italian *cantare*)

b. By mid-seventeenth century, the term was used for a secular composition on a lyrical or dramatic text, usually for solo voice with continuo, containing several sections of recitative and aria.

2. Main composers: Rossi, Cesti, Carissimi, and Barbara Strozzi
3. Barbara Strozzi (1619–1677) (see **HWM biography,** page 333, and **HWM Figure 15.1**)
   a. Venetian singer and composer
   b. Studied with Cavalli
   c. Supported by her father (poet and librettist Giulio Strozzi) and wealthy patrons
   d. Published eight collections of music in the mid-seventeenth century, for a total of over one hundred works
   e. Published more cantatas than any other composer of the time
4. **NAWM 69** and **HWM Example 15.3,** *Lagrime mie* (1659), by Strozzi
   a. Sections in recitative, arioso, and aria styles
   b. Recitative (**HWM Example 15.3**) uses descending line, minor mode, and augmented intervals to portray a weeping lover.
   c. Other sections portray different emotions, using styles appropriate to each.

F. Secular music outside of Italy
1. Italian genres of monody spread to northern Europe, especially England and Germany.
2. In France, the *air de cour* (court air) was popular.
   a. Homophonic, strophic song
   b. The text-setting is syllabic, with long and short syllables dictated by the length of the vowel (similar to musique mesurée).

III. Catholic Sacred Music

A. Stile antico polyphony continued to be used throughout the seventeenth century.
1. Pure stile antico, exemplified by Palestrina's style, carried associations of tradition, reverence, and sanctity.
2. Over time, basso continuo was added and the style was updated.
3. *Gradus ad Parnassum* (Steps to Parnassus, 1725)
   a. Treatise by Johann Joseph Fux
   b. Codified the neo-Palestrina style counterpoint of the time.
   c. Used as a counterpoint textbook for over two hundred years

B. Sacred concerto
1. The Church incorporated dramatic tools from opera to convey its message.
2. Large-scale sacred concertos
   a. For major feast days at large churches
   b. Many voices, sometimes in *chori spezzati* (divided choir)
   c. Settings of Vespers, psalms, and movements from the mass
   d. Orazio Benevoli (1605–72) composed works using three or more choirs and organ for St. Peter's in Rome.

C. Small sacred concerto
1. For solo singer(s) with organ and one or two violins
2. Lodovico Viadana (ca. 1560–1627) composed over one hundred
   a. He published the first book of church music to use basso continuo.
   b. **HWM Example 15.4,** *Exsulate Deo,* uses four-voice imitation in a two-voice piece by having each voice enter twice with the theme.
   c. The continuo fills in the harmony, making it possible to perform the piece even if one of the soloists is absent.
3. **NAWM 70** and **HWM Example 15.5,** *O quam pulcrha es* (1625), blends elements of recitative, solo madrigal, and lyric aria.
   a. By Alessandro Grandi (1586–1630), who worked for Monteverdi at St. Mark's
   b. Grandi composed solo motets using monody.
   c. The sensuous text from Song of Solomon represents God's love for the church.
   d. Grandi's sense of drama parallels that in Bernini's dramatic religious sculptures.

D. Music in convents
1. Nuns sang within convent walls for devotion and reflection, not for public audiences, but some insisted on musical accomplishment equal to that of men.
2. Lucrezia Vizzana (1590–1662) published *Componimenti musicali* (Musical Compositions) in 1623.
   a. Twenty motets, most for one or two soprano voices with basso continuo
   b. Style incorporates theatrical monody and elaborate vocal ornamentation
   c. The music expresses the text with declamatory phrases and expressive use of unresolved dissonance.

E. Oratorio
1. Definition: religious dramatic music incorporating narrative, dialogue, and commentary
   a. The text was in Latin or Italian.

   b. Called "oratorio" because it was similar in function to the prayer hall (oratorio), where people met for nonliturgical worship.
   c. Developed in Rome in the seventeenth century
2. Differences from opera
   a. Almost never staged
   b. Used a narrator (a singing role)
   c. The chorus took on different roles and functions.
3. Giacomo Carissimi (1605–1674) was the leading composer of Latin oratorios.
4. *Jepthe* (ca. 1648), by Carissimi, exemplifies the midcentury oratorio.
   a. Biblically-based libretto (Judges 11:29–40) with paraphrasing and added material
   b. Jepthe promises God that he will sacrifice whatever creature first greets him on his return home if God will help him defeat the Ammonites.
   c. The narrator introduces the story and describes the action in recitative.
   d. *Stile concitato* helps to depict the battle scene.
   e. In **NAWM 71,** Jeptha's daughter laments her impending death, accompanied by two sopranos and a small vocal ensemble, using rhetorical devices such as a descending tetrachord in the bass.

IV. Lutheran Church Music
  A. Both Catholics and Protestants adopted concertato medium and monody.
  B. Sacred concerto
    1. Both large- and small-scale were composed
    2. Johann Hermann Schein (1564–1637)
       a. Published two collections (1618, 1626)
       b. Book 1 features duets in the Italian style but based on Lutheran chorales.
       c. Book 2 has more varied styles than Book 1, with solo instruments that contrast with ensembles and more varied styles.
       d. Schein's style set the precedent for later Lutheran works.
  C. Heinrich Schütz (1585–1672)
    1. Biography (see **HWM biography,** page 339, and **HWM Figure 15.2**)
       a. Studied with G. Gabrieli in Venice
       b. 1612: Returned to his home (Kassel)
       c. 1615 to his death: Was in the service of the elector's court in Dresden
       d. Composed in all genres, including the first German opera (1627), German psalms, Latin motets, sacred concertos, and works based on the life of Christ.
    2. Early works
       a. *Psalmen Davids* (Psalms of David, 1619): German-texted but influenced by Gabrieli
       b. *Cantiones Sacrae* (Sacred Songs, 1625): sacred songs (motets) using madrigal-like word-painting
    3. Effect of the Thirty Years' War (1618–1648; see **HWM Source Reading,** page 340)
       a. The economic hardship of the war reduced the number of musicians at the Dresden chapel.
       b. Schütz delayed publication of his *Kleine geistliche Konzerte* (Small Sacred Concertos, 1636, 1639) because of the war.
    4. **NAWM 72,** *O Lieber Herre Gott* (O Beloved Lord God, 1636)
       a. Schütz used Italian monody to portray the text.
       b. **HWM Example 15.6a–b** use techniques developed by Monteverdi to portray the varied affects of the text (supplication, wakefulness, joy).
    5. **NAWM 73,** *Saul was verfolgst du mich:* Post-war works
       a. From Schütz's post-war book of *Symphoniae sacrae* (1650)
       b. Return to large-scale forces, with two choirs, doubled by instruments, six solo voices, and two violins.
       c. The style merges Gabrieli's polychoral style with Monteverdi's expressiveness.
    6. Musical figures
       a. Counterpoint patterns that had become associated with specific emotions
       b. First developed in Renaissance text-painting and enumerated by Schütz's student Christoph Bernhard (1627–1592)
       c. **HWM Example 15.6a** uses *cadentiae duriusculae* (harsh cadential notes) to portray Jesus' words "Why do you persecute me?"
       d. **HWM Example 15.6b** uses *saltus durius* (harsh leap) to suggest the hard road ahead for Saul.
  D. Schütz's *historiae*
    1. Historia, a musical setting based on a biblical narrative, was a prominent Lutheran genre.
    2. Schütz's *Seven Last Words of Christ* (possibly composed in the 1650s) sets Jesus' words in expressive monody and narration in recitative or chorus with sinfonia.
    3. His Christmas history (1664) sets the narration in recitative and scenes in concertato medium.
    4. *Passions,* settings of the story of Jesus'

crucifixion, were the most common type of historia.
5. Schütz used plainsong and polyphonic motet style for his three passions.

V. Jewish Music
  A. European synagogues mixed tradition with innovation.
  B. Cantillation remained the primary form of Jewish musical worship.
    1. Oral, improvisatory style
    2. Cantors incorporated popular non-Jewish tunes into their improvisations.
  C. Polyphony
    1. Introduced to Ferrara and then to Venice by Leon Modena (1571–1648), rabbi, scholar, and humanist
    2. *Hashirim asher lish 'lomo* (The Songs of Solomon, 1622–23).
      a. The first book of Jewish liturgical polyphonic music
      b. Thirty-three pieces composed by Salamone Rossi (ca. 1570–ca. 1630) of Mantua
      c. Modena also wrote a preface (see **HWM Figure 15.3**).
      d. The contents include psalms, hymns, and synagogue songs (not the Bible's Song of Solomon: the title was a pun on Salamone Rossi's name).
    3. Few other attempts were made to write Jewish liturgical polyphony until the nineteenth century.

VI. Instrumental Music
  A. Abstract genres carried over from the sixteenth century were the main focus, but elements of vocal music styles permeated instrumental composition.
    1. Interest in moving the affections
    2. Focus on the soloist and virtuosic embellishment
    3. Styles such as recitative and arias
    4. Violin music imitated the voice and absorbed many vocal techniques.
  B. Ways of categorizing instrumental music
    1. By performing forces
      a. Solo works (for keyboard, lute, theorbo, guitar, etc.)
      b. Chamber works, for soloist or small group with continuo
      c. Large-ensemble works, with two or more players per part (more important after 1650)
    2. By venue or social function
      a. Church
      b. Chamber
      c. Theater (e.g., movements in ballets and operas)
    3. By nationality
      a. Composers in each region preferred certain stylistic elements.
      b. Composers sometimes borrowed and blended styles from other lands.
    4. Types of works through ca. 1650:
      a. Improvisatory pieces (toccatas, fantasias, or preludes)
      b. Fugal or imitative pieces (ricercares, fantasias, fancys, capriccios, or fugues)
      c. Pieces with contrasting sections, often in imitative counterpoint (canzonas or sonatas)
      d. Settings of existing melodies (e.g., organ verse, chorale prelude)
      e. Variations of a melody (variations, partitas), or bass line (partitas, chaconnes, passacaglias)
      f. Stylized dance movements, alone, paired, or in suites
    5. Types of works after ca. 1650:
      a. For keyboard, the principal types were prelude, toccata, fugue, chorale settings, variations, and suite.
      b. Ensemble music consisted of sonatas, suites, sinfonias, and concertos.
      c. Elements from one type of work often appeared in others, to the delight of audiences who knew the distinctions.
  C. Giralamo Frescobaldi (1583–1643) and the toccata
    1. Biography (see **HWM biography,** page 345, and **HWM Figure 15.4**)
      a. The most important composer of toccatas
      b. Born in Ferrara and trained in organ there
      c. 1608–1628: Organist for St. Peter's in Rome, with extra income from performing and teaching harpsichord to noble patrons
      d. 1628–1634: Organist to the Grand Duke of Tuscany, in Florence
      e. 1634: Returned to Rome under the patronage of a noble family
      f. His keyboard music was renowned in his lifetime, and his compositional style became the model for subsequent generations.
      g. Works include toccatas, fantasias, ricercares, canzonas, and partitas, as well as some vocal music.

   h. His collection of three organ masses, *Fiori musicali* (Musical Flowers, 1635), contained the music an organist would play at Mass.
2. Music in the Organ masses in *Fiori musicali*
   a. Toccatas before Mass and at the Elevation of the Host before Communion
   b. Some extra toccatas in two of the masses
   c. Short, sectional pieces with sustained notes idiomatic for organ music
3. Johann Jacob Froberger (1616–1667) was Frescobaldi's most famous student.
   a. Organist at the imperial court in Vienna
   b. His toccatas alternate improvisatory passages with sections in imitative counterpoint.
   c. Later generations merged toccata and fugue more completely, following his example (e.g. **NAWM 84** by Buxtehude and **NAWM 88** by J. S. Bach)

D. Imitative genres: ricercare and fugue
1. Ricercare
   a. Serious composition for organ or harpsichord, using one subject or theme in continuously developed imitation
   b. **NAWM 75** and **HWM Example 15.7,** from Frescobaldi's *Fiori musicali,* uses constantly shifting harmony, a distinctive subject, and a contrasting countersubject.
2. Fugue
   a. From the Italian *fuga,* "flight"
   b. A term used in Germany for serious pieces that treat one theme in continuous imitation (see **HWM Chapters 16** and **18**)
3. Fantasia
   a. Imitative work on a larger scale than the ricercare
   b. Leading composers were Jan Pieterszoon Sweelinck (Dutch, 1562–1621) and Samuel Scheidt (German, 1587–1654).
   c. Sweelinck's fantasias usually use different countersubjects in a series of sections.
   d. Scheidt's *Tabulatura nova* (New Tablature, 1624) notates the parts for each voice on a separate staff, instead of tablature.
   e. English fantasias (called fancy) were composed for consorts of viols by Alfonso Ferrabosco the Younger (ca. 1575–1628) and John Coprario (ca. 1570–1626).
4. Canzona
   a. Imitative piece in contrasting sections for keyboard or ensemble
   b. Characterized by markedly rhythmic themes and liveliness
   c. Frescobaldi's organ masses included canzonas.
   d. Some canzonas use a different theme in each section.
   e. Variation canzona: uses a single theme in each section (e.g. **HWM Example 15.9** by Giovanni Maria Trabaci [ca. 1575–1647])

E. Sonata
1. Early in the seventeenth century, the term meant any piece for instruments.
2. Later the term was reserved for pieces with specific characteristics.
   a. Scored for one or two melody instruments, usually violin(s), with basso continuo
   b. Idiomatic for instrumental capabilities
   c. Similar to canzona in its use of sections
3. **NAWM 76**, *Sonata IV per il violino per sonar con due corde* by Biagio Marini (1594–1663)
   a. Marini was a violinist, serving under Monteverdi at St. Mark's for part of his career.
   b. Idiomatic violin techniques, including double-stops, large leaps, and sequential figures
   c. Alternation of rhapsodic and metrical sections, similar to Strozzi's cantatas
4. By the mid-seventeenth century, the sonata and canzona had merged, and both were called sonata.

F. Settings of existing melodies
1. Organists composed settings of liturgical music in both Catholic and Lutheran churches.
2. Frescobaldi set Gregorian chants in his organ masses.
3. Settings of chorales became known as chorale preludes.

G. Variations (also known as *partite,* divisions)
1. Three common techniques
   a. Repetition of melody virtually unchanged, with variation in accompanimental parts (sometimes called cantus-firmus variations)
   b. Repetition of melody with different embellishment in each variation and accompanimental parts essentially unchanged
   c. Bass or harmonic progression serves as the foundation, as in the romanesca.
2. Variations over a ground bass
   a. The pattern was usually four measures long.
   b. Meter was typically triple.
   c. Tempo was usually slow.

3. Frescobaldi published *Partite sopra ciaccona* and *Partite sopra passacagli* in 1627 (e.g., **HWM Example 15.9**)

H. Dance music
1. Composed for social dancing, dance movements in theatrical productions, and as stylized chamber music
2. Suites of movements extended the idea of linking dance movements in pairs.
   a. Johann Hermann Schein's *Banchetto musicale* (Musical Banquet, 1617) contains twenty suites for five instruments and continuo.
   b. Schein's suites have a standard sequence: pavane, galliard, courante, allemande, and tripla (triple-meter variation of the allemande).
   c. Movements of suites sometimes use the same melodic idea, but may be only subtly linked.

VII. Impact of Early-Seventeenth-Century Music for Church and Chamber
A. Grew from sixteenth-century traditions, but intensified the idea of distinct music styles for different venues
B. Genres developed or codified in this era remained important genres for the next hundred years.
C. Composers continued to study the music of this era, even after it was no longer being played.

## SUGGESTIONS FOR SUPPLEMENTARY READING/LISTENING/ACTIVITIES

The music for Monteverdi's eighth book of madrigals is available in a reprint edition, edited by Gian Francisco Malipiero and translated by Stanley Applebaum (New York: Dover, 1991). Assign a madrigal to each student and have him/her report on the style of the madrigal, or have groups of students search through the book for madrigals of assigned types.

"Monteverdi—Madrigali guerrieri et amorosi" by The Consort of Musicke (Virgin Classics 61570, 1999) puts the warlike and love songs on separate discs. Have the students listen to some of the *guerrieri* songs and describe the techniques that Monteverdi uses to portray or suggest battle. One good example is *Ardo, ardo, avvampo,* which uses several techniques. *Il Combattimento di Tancredi e Clorinda* is also available on compact disc, including performances by The Concerto Ensemble (Tactus Records 560101, 1998) and by Nikolaus Harnoncourt and the Concentus Musicus Vienna (Teldec, 1984 and 1993).

A more modern example of variations over a descending tetrachord is the song "Dazed and Confused," by Led Zeppelin. Have students listen to this song and decide which of the techniques used by this rock band could have been used in the baroque era.

A recording of Monteverdi's duets in concertato medium performed by Il Complesso Barocco (Virgin Veritas 724354529320, 1998) includes examples from Book 7 of Monteverdi's madrigals and *Zefiro torna*. The accompanying booklet discusses the performers' approach to instrumentation, pitch, and other matters of performance practice. Have students read these comments (or similar notes) to help them understand the relevance of research for modern performers.

Recordings of Barbara Strozzi's *Lagrime mie* have been released with some of her other cantatas (Harmonia Mundi 905249, 2000, and Cascavelle 3035, 2002). Her works have been edited in *The Italian Cantata in the Seventeenth Century* (New York: Garland, 1985–6), volume v, and *Barbara Strozzi, Cantate, ariete a una, due, e tre voci, opus 3,* edited by Gail Archer in *Recent Researches in the Music of the Baroque Era,* 83 (Madison: A-R Editions, 1997). Some of her madrigals have been published in modern editions: *Five Madrigals: For 2–5 Accompanied Voices*, edited by Andrew Kosciesza (Bryn Mawr: Hildegard Music, 1998) and *Five Madrigals for Two or Three Voices From Madrigali A Due, Tre, Quattro E Cinque Voci,* edited by Susan J. Mardinly (Fayetteville: Clarnan Editions, 2003).

For facsimiles of cantata manuscripts and prints, see *The Italian Cantata in the Seventeenth Century*, gen. ed. Carolyn Gianturco (New York: Garland, 1986); for the Italian oratorio, see *The Italian Oratorio: 1650–1800,* ed. Joyce Johnson and Howard Smither (New York: Garland, 1986).

*Gradus ad Parnassum* has been published in a facsimile edition (New York: Broude Brothers, 1966) and in translation under the title *Steps to Parnassus: The Study of Counterpoint,* translated by Alfred Mann (New York: W. W. Norton, 1943, and several later editions under different titles).

The works of Orazio Benevoli are less well-known than those of the other composers in this chapter, but a few have been recorded on "Orazio Benevolo - Sacred Music," performed by Le Concert Spirituel (Naxos 553636, 1996). His complete works have been edited in *Opera Omnia*, edited by Lorenzo Feininger (Trent: Societas Universalis Sanctae Ceciliae, 1966–73), and some were reprinted in *Monumenta liturgiae polychoralis Sanctae Ecclesiae Romanae*.

Some of Alessandro Grandi's motets on standard motet texts have been recorded on "Grandi: Motets and Songs" (Rivo Alto 9922, 2000). Three motets are available in a performing edition (Wolfenbüttel: Moeseler Verlag, Das Chorwerk, No. 40).

For works by Lucrezia Vizzana and additional biographical background, see volume I of *Women Composers: Music through the Ages* (New York,: G.K. Hall, 1996), 264–305. Several of her works are on the compact disc "Songs of Ecstasy and Devotion from a Seventeenth-Century Italian Convent" (Linn Records 71, 1999). For additional information on music in Baroque convents, including a translation of the Council of Trent's prohibition against nuns singing polyphony, see Barbara Garvey Jackson, "Musical Women of the Seventeenth and Eighteenth Centuries" in *Women and Music: A History,* edited by Karin Pendle (Bloomington: Indiana University Press, 1991). This chapter also discusses Barbara Strozzi and Elizabeth-Claude Jaquet de la Guerre, whose music is discussed in *HWM* Chapter 16.

Johann Hermann Schein's sacred concertos from his *Opella Nova* comprise volumes 4 and 5 of *Die Neue Schein-Ausgabe*, edited by Adam Adrio and Siegmund Helms (vol. 4) and Walter Werbeck (vol. 5) (Kassel: Bärenreiter, 1973, 1986). His instrumental works and German-language motets are more frequently performed, but some works from *Opella Nova* have been released on "Israels Brünnlein/Opella Nova II" (Deutsche Harmonia Mundi, 1996).

"Heinrich Schütz: Cantiones Sacrae, Op. 4" (CPO Records 999405, 1996) contains examples of these works. The clips on Amazon.com for "Heinrich Schütz: Cantiones Sacrae and Other Choral Works" (Meridian 84337, 1996), which is out of print, are long enough to give students an idea of his style.

Several recordings of Schütz's *Psalmen Davids* are available. Remind students of the paired verses of psalms in plainsong performance and of the metrical settings of Calvinist psalmody, then have them listen to one of Schütz's settings with these influences in mind.

For more on musical figures as delineated by Christoph Bernhard and others, see *Musica Poetica: Musical-Rhetorical Figures in German Baroque Music*, by Dietrich Bartel (Lincoln: University of Nebraska Press, 1997).

For more on Salamone Rossi, see Don Harrán, *Salamone Rossi: Jewish Musician in Late Renaissance Mantua* (New York: Oxford University Press, 1999). Some of his liturgical music can be found on "Salamone Rossi Hebreo" (Zamir 910, 1998).

Superb introductions to various keyboard genres are found in Alexander Silbiger, ed., *Keyboard Music before 1700* (New York: Schirmer Books, 1995).

Plan a class trip to a working Baroque organ, if one is nearby, or devote some class time to a discussion of the mechanics of the organ. The "Organ" article in the *New Grove Dictionary of Musical Instruments* (New York: Macmillan, 1984), includes several drawings and photographs of baroque organs, including a cross-section diagram showing a tracker organ, complete with an assistant pumping the bellows.

For technically undemanding keyboard pieces suitable for students to learn for class performances, along with commentary on performance practice problems, see the volumes edited by Howard Ferguson, especially *Early German Keyboard Music (including Austria and the Netherlands): An Anthology* (London: Oxford University Press, 1970) and *Early French Keyboard Music: An Anthology* (London: Oxford University Press, 1966).

On the distinction between passacaglia and chacona (ciaccona) in the seventeenth century, see Alexander Silbiger, "Passacaglia and Ciaccona: Genre Pairing and Ambiguity from Frescobaldi to Couperin," *Journal of Seventeenth-Century Music* (www.sscm.harvard.edu/jscm/v2nol.html).

Have students read Christopher Simpson's *The Division Viol, or, the Art of Playing Ex Tempore upon a Ground,* published in facsimile (London: J. Curwen, 1955 and New York: Performers' Facsimiles, 1998) and excerpted in Strunk/Treitler, *Source Readings in Music History IV: The Baroque* (New York: W. W. Norton, 1998) and then compose or improvise a set of variations on a simple ground bass (such as the ground in **HWM Example 15.1**).

Frescobaldi's *Fiore musicali* has been recorded on several different organs. For an introduction to the importance of the individual instrument to the timbre of an organ performance, have students listen to different recordings of the same movement. Later organs have much more diverse tone colors, and these possibilities influenced composers discussed in later chapters. Discussing organ performance at this point will prepare students for later discussions of historical performance of instrumental music. An essential question to ask is whether simply performing on an authentic instrument is sufficient to produce an authentic performance.

Johann Jacob Froberger's works are available in modern scholarly editions, *J. J. Froberger: Oeuvres complètes pour clavecin*, edited by Howard Schott (Paris: Heugel, 1979–92) and *Johann Jacob Froberger: Neue Ausgabe sämtlicher Clavier- und Orgelwerke,* edited by Siegbert Rampe (Kassel: Bärenreiter, 1993). The compact disc "Johann Jacob Froberger: Diverse curiose Partite per Cembalo" (Symphonia 96152, 2000) includes both toccatas and suites.

Scheidt's *Tabulatura nova* is available in several modern editions, including Band VI of his *Werke* (Wiesbaden: Deutscher Verlag F. Musik). *Fantasia Super 'Ut Re Mi Fa Sol La'* on "Samuel Scheidt: Tabulatura Nova, Vol. 1" (MD&G Records, 2003) is easy to follow on first hearing. Note the use of solfège syllables to construct and name a theme.

Frescobaldi's *Partite sopra passacagli* has been recorded on "Chaconne" by Jory Vinikour (Consonance 810007, 1997), which also includes music by composers discussed in upcoming chapters, and "Frescobaldi—Partite & Toccate," performed by Pierre Hantaï (Astree 8585, 1997).

Several suites from Johann Hermann Schein's *Banchetto musicale* are available on compact disc, including the recording of five suites by Jordi Savall's group (EMI Records 61399, 1998) and "A Musical Banquet" (EMI 562028, 2002), performed by Hesperion XX. The score of the complete collection comprises Band 9 of *Neue Ausgabe Sämtliche Werke,* edited by Dieter Krickeberg (Kassel: Bärenreiter).

## OBJECTIVE QUESTIONS

1. Monteverdi's seventh and eighth books of madrigals are best known for __________.
   a. compositions in the *prima pratica* style
   b. being attacked by Artusi because they break counterpoint rules
   c. including madrigals in the concertato medium
   d. experimental use of techniques that would later show up in his operas
   e. using texts that were written in Latin instead of Italian

   Answer: c

2. A repeating bass line used as the basis of variations is called __________.
   a. basso continuo
   b. ostinato bass
   c. basso seguente
   d. partite
   e. basso spezzati

   Answer: b

3. Which of the following statements best defines the cantata in the seventeenth century?
   a. A series of variations on a well-known song
   b. A set of variations on a sacred melody
   c. A succession of arias and recitatives in a brief, unstaged work
   d. A large-scale work for chorus, several soloists, and large orchestra
   e. An opera-like work depicting a biblical story

   Answer: c

Use the following answers for questions 4–8:
a. Lodovico Viadana
b. Barbara Strozzi
c. Lucrezia Vizzana
d. Giacomo Carissimi
e. Salamone Rossi

4. Composed Jewish liturgical polyphonic music

   Answer: e

5. Published the first book of sacred music with basso continuo

   Answer: a

6. Though a nun, she published a collection of her compositions.

   Answer: c

7. Published more cantatas than any other composer of the early seventeenth century

   Answer: b

8. The main composer of Roman oratorios

   Answer: d

9. Which of the following is not characteristic of Roman oratorios?
   a. They were elaborately staged.
   b. They were performed in the oratory portions of Roman churches.
   c. They included recitatives and arias.
   d. They drew their stories from the Bible.
   e. A narrator told parts of the tale in recitative.

   Answer: a

10. The Passion is a __________.
    a. multi-movement work depicting the last days of Christ
    b. secular cantata sung in Italian
    c. genre of Italian court entertainment
    d. French opera genre that included dancing and large choruses
    e. libretto that was used for several French operas

    Answer: a

11. The forces for the small-scale sacred concerto typically consisted of __________.
    a. one solo singer and basso continuo
    b. one or more solo singers with organ and one or two violins
    c. one or more solo singers with organ and brass ensemble
    d. several solo singers with small chorus and organ
    e. several solo singers, small chorus, and string orchestra

    Answer: b

12. Which of the following best describes the Italian secular cantata?
    a. A mini-opera with scenery and costumes
    b. A series of arias for several solo singers with full orchestral accompaniment
    c. Many short, contrasting sections with recitatives and arias for solo voice with continuo
    d. A series of religious songs sung outside of church during Lent and Advent, with orchestral accompaniment and scenery
    e. A biblical story set in operatic style but without staging or costumes

    Answer: c

13. Which of the following statements best describes Schütz's training and career?
    a. He was the first major composer to be trained and employed exclusively in German-speaking lands.
    b. He received his training in Vienna, then worked in Italy and France before returning to Germany for the remainder of his career.
    c. He studied with Gabrieli in Venice, then worked in Kassel and Dresden.
    d. He learned violin, keyboard, and composition from his father, and succeeded his father in the service of the elector of Hanover.
    e. He studied opera composition with Monteverdi, then composed oratorios in Rome before moving to Germany as a cathedral musician.

    Answer: c

14. Which of the following statements is true of the effect of the Thirty Years' War on Schütz's music?
    a. The oratorio replaced opera as the favorite genre.
    b. Schütz was forced to compose for smaller ensembles.
    c. Schütz composed for larger ensembles because they gave the impression of economic well-being.
    d. Nationalistic sentiment forced him to give up Italianate elements of his style.
    e. Old Testament stories of Jewish victories in war were the subjects of operas, oratorios, and cantatas.

    Answer: b

15. Musical figures were __________.
    a. the English version of *agréments*
    b. cadential flourishes that eventually evolved into the cadenza
    c. rhythmic patterns derived from dance steps that were sometimes used in an aria to suggest the moral qualities of the character singing it
    d. bass lines that became well-known variations forms throughout Europe
    e. counterpoint patterns that had become associated with specific emotions

    Answer: e

16. The most important composer of toccatas in the early seventeenth century was __________.
    a. Rossi
    b. Frescobaldi
    c. Schein
    d. Scheidt
    e. Marini

    Answer: b

17. What was the most common instrumentation for the sonata after ca. 1650?
    a. Any instrument or combination of instruments could be used.
    b. Solo harpsichord
    c. Solo treble instrument
    d. One or two treble instruments (usually violin(s)) and harpsichord
    e. Five instruments plus basso continuo

    Answer: d

18. *Divisions* and *partite* are terms for __________.
    a. dance steps that divide or partition the measure
    b. variations movements
    c. tuning systems used for seventeenth-century harpsichords

d. composing for more than one choir
e. multi-movement works of any type

Answer: b

19. *Fiori musicali* was __________.
a. a collection of organ music composed for use in Mass
b. a treatise on composing church music according to revised principles of the *prima pratica*
c. a collection of polyphonic music for use in the Jewish liturgy
d. a treatise on the variation forms
e. a collection of suites using dance movements in a standard sequence

Answer: a

20. The *Banchetto musicale* was __________.
a. a collection of organ music composed for use in Mass
b. a treatise on composing church music according to revised principles of the *prima pratica*
c. a collection of polyphonic music for use in the Jewish liturgy
d. a treatise on the variation forms
e. a collection of suites using dance movements in a standard sequence

Answer: e

## SHORT-ESSAY QUESTIONS

1. Discuss the variation forms of the early seventeenth century and their use in both vocal and instrumental music, giving examples from *NAWM.*
2. Compare and contrast the cantata, oratorio, and sacred concerto of the mid-seventeenth century, giving examples from *NAWM.*
3. Discuss the multisection genres of instrumental music composed in the seventeenth centuries and the compositional techniques used.
4. Discuss the ways in which economic or social factors (such as gender prejudice) affected composers discussed in this chapter, including composers of both sacred and secular music.

## TERMS FOR IDENTIFICATION

basso ostinato
chacona/ciaccona
cantata
*Gradus ad Parnassum*
sacred concerto
chori spezzati
musical figures
oratorio
historia
passion
musical figures
*Hashirim asher lish 'lomo*
*Fiori musicali*
ricercare
fantasia
canzona
sonata
partite
divisions
suite

# CHAPTER 16 France, England, Spain, and the New World in the Seventeenth Century

I. National Styles
  A. National styles become distinct in the middle and late baroque period.
  B. Politics and national style
    1. France had a centralized monarchy.
      a. The king sponsored musical innovation.
      b. The French idiom was more elegant and restrained than the Italian style.
    2. England's public concerts were more influential than its monarch.
    3. Germany's small states followed Italian taste in music.
    4. Spain followed its own path.

II. The French Baroque
  A. Louis XIV (r. 1643–1715), see **HWM Figure 16.1**
    1. France was under the rule of Louis' Austrian mother and her Italian lover, Cardinal Mazarin, until 1661.
    2. Louis used the arts to help consolidate his rule.
      a. To project an image of himself as a powerful leader ("The Sun King"), he identified himself with Apollo in visual arts (see **HWM Figure 16.2**).
      b. He centralized the arts and sciences, establishing royal academies for each, including one for opera (1669).
    3. The palace at Versailles (see **HWM Figures 16.3** and **16.4**) projected his power and kept potential rivals busy with court entertainment for much of the year.
  B. The court ballet
    1. Musical-dramatic work, with several acts, staged with costumes and scenery
    2. Members of the nobility were required to take part alongside professional dancers.
    3. Music included solo songs, choruses, and instrumental dances.
    4. Louis XIV took part, playing roles designed to reinforce his identity as the Sun King.
    5. The hierarchy of court ballet production reinforced obedience to authority.
  C. Music at the court
    1. Louis XIV employed 150 to 200 musicians in three divisions.
    2. Music of the Royal Chapel: singers, organists, and others who performed for religious services
    3. Music of the Chamber: string, harpsichord, and flute players who provided indoor entertainment
    4. Music of the Great Stable: wind, brass, and timpani players who provided military and outdoor music
      a. Jean Hotteterre (ca. 1610–ca. 1692), a member of the Great Stable, experimented with the construction of woodwind instruments.
      b. Players and instrument-makers developed the modern oboe, which replaced the shawm.
    5. *Vingt-quatre Violons du Roi* (Twenty-Four Violins of the King)
      a. The first large ensemble of the violin family
      b. Five-part texture, with violins on the melody, bass violins (tuned a whole tone lower than the modern cello) on the bass, and alto and tenor violins (both tuned like

a modern viola) divided among three inner parts.

c. In 1648, another group, the *Petits Violons* (Small Violin Ensemble) was established for Louis' personal use.

d. The *Vingt-quatre Violons du Roi* and the *Petits Violons* accompanied ballets and other court entertainments.

e. By the 1670s, the term "orchestra" began to be used to describe large ensembles; the term came from the orchestra area in front of the stage in a theater.

D. Jean-Baptiste Lully (1632–1687) and French opera

1. Biography (see **HWM biography,** page 360, and **HWM Figure 16.6**)

a. Born in Florence and came to Paris at age fourteen

b. 1653: Louis XIV appointed him court composer of instrumental music and director of the *Petits Violons*.

c. 1661: Appointed Superintendent of Music for the King's Chamber, a position that included the *Vingt-quatre Violons du Roi*

d. He became a French citizen, and the king and queen attended his wedding.

e. 1672: Granted exclusive right to produce sung drama in France, and established the Académie Royale de Musique

f. After a sexual scandal in 1684, he lost favor with the king.

g. 1687: Hit his foot with his staff while conducting (he did not use a baton) and developed fatal gangrene from the injury

h. As a conductor, he insisted on uniform bowing and coordination of ornaments, and established a long tradition of conductors exercising dictatorial control over orchestras.

i. Works include fifteen operas, fourteen comédie-ballets, twenty-nine ballets, and liturgical music.

2. Influences on French opera

a. Cardinal Mazarin introduced Italian opera to France, but it met with opposition on political and artistic grounds.

b. French audiences could not accept sung dialogue.

c. Lully and playwright Jean-Baptiste Molière collaborated on *comédies-ballets,* which blended ballet and opera.

d. Elements of ballet were incorporated into French opera (see below).

E. *Tragédie en musique* (tragedy in music), later called *tragédie lyrique,* was the French version of opera.

1. New genre established by Lully and playwright Jean-Philippe Quinault (1635–1688) after Lully purchased the royal privilege granting him the exclusive right to produce sung drama in France.

2. Librettos

a. Librettos consisted of five acts.

b. Plots were serious stories drawn from mythology or chivalric tales.

c. Divertissements (diversions) of dancing and choral singing were interspersed throughout.

d. Prologues praised the king, and plots reinforced parallels between his reign and ancient Greece and Rome.

e. Stories included opportunities for spectacles to entertain the audience (see **HWM Figure 16.7**).

3. French overture (French *ouverture,* "opening"), **NAWM 77a**, from *Armide* (1686)

a. The form came from ballet tradition.

b. The first section is slow and stately, with a homophonic texture, and marked by dotted rhythms.

c. The second section is faster, with some fugal imitation.

d. The second section sometimes closes with a return to the tempo and figuration of the first section.

4. Divertissements

a. Unrelated material that appeared at the center or end of every act

b. Colorful and spectacular episodes that included opportunities for ballet and choruses

c. Dances from Lully's ballets were arranged into independent instrumental suites and inspired others to compose suites in similar styles.

5. Recitative (see **NAWM 77b,** from *Armide*)

a. The French language did not lend itself to recitative as Italian did.

b. Lully reportedly listened to celebrated French actors in order to imitate their style of declamation.

c. *Récitatif simple* (simple recitative): recitative that followed the contours of spoken French, shifting meter as necessary (**HWM Example 16.1a**)

d. *Récitatif mesuré* (measured recitative): songlike interruptions to simple recitative (**HWM Example 16.1b**)
e. Air: song with continuo accompaniment, with a rhyming text and regular phrasing, often more similar to a dance than to Italian arias (**HWM Example 16.1c**, which has minuet features)

6. Performance practice
   a. Performers altered the notated rhythms in performance.
   b. Notes inégales: performing a series of eighth notes with a lilt similar to dotted rhythms
   c. Overdotting: performing a dotted note longer than its notated value and shortening the following note
   d. Agréments: brief ornaments to be added to cadences and other important notes
7. Tonal organization
   a. Lully's music uses major and minor keys, not modal concepts.
   b. Predictable harmonic progressions close with a dominant-tonic cadence.
   c. Lully sometimes surprised the listener with evaded cadences.
8. Focus on drama
   a. Lully mixed recitative, air, and orchestral interludes depending on the dramatic content of the libretto.
   b. Unlike Italian opera of the period, French opera limited singers' opportunities for vocal display.
9. Lully's influence
   a. Lully's followers imitated his style and sometimes exaggerated it.
   b. His operas were performed after his death in France and other countries.
   c. His style influenced instrumental as well as vocal music.
   d. The French Overture spread throughout Europe thanks to the popularity of Lully's overtures.

F. Song and cantata
   1. Hundreds of collections of airs were published in Paris.
   2. The *air de cour* gradually gave way to new types that were defined by their topics.
   3. Marc-Antoine Charpentier (1634–1704) combined Italian lyricism with French-style embellishments in his airs.
   4. In the 1680s, Charpentier and others began to compose cantatas suited to French taste.

G. Church music
   1. Motets on Latin texts
      a. *Petit motet* (small motet): sacred concerto for few voices with continuo
      b. *Grand motet* (large motet): multisection works corresponding to the large-scale concertos of Gabrieli and Schütz
      c. The main composers were Lully, Charpentier, and Michel-Richard de Lalande (1657–1726).
   2. Oratorio
      a. Introduced to France by Charpentier
      b. Texts in Latin
      c. Charpentier's oratorios combine Italian and French styles and give prominence to the chorus.
   3. Organ music
      a. Music for church services, including organ masses
      b. Pieces resembling French overtures and recitatives in French style
      c. Composers took an interest in the tonal colors of organ pipes.

H. Lute and keyboard music
   1. Lute music influenced music for other media.
   2. Denis Gaultier (1603–1672)
      a. He was the leading composer of lute music.
      b. He published two instructional collections for amateurs.
   3. Lutenists developed a systematic approach to agréments, creating an aesthetic of refined taste that influenced other types of French music.
      a. Composers sometimes notated agréments despite their origin in improvisation.
      b. **HWM Figure 16.10** shows a table of agréments from D'Anglebert's harpsichord treatise of 1689.
   4. Lute players' habit of breaking up melodies was picked up by harpsichord composers and called style luthé (lute style) or style brisé (broken style) (e.g., **HWM Example 16.2**)

III. Dance music
   A. Stylized dance music formed the core of the lute and keyboard repertory.
   B. Binary form replaced earlier forms.
      1. Two roughly equal sections, each repeated
      2. The first section leads from tonic to dominant (or relative major).
      3. The second section returns to the tonic.
   C. Suites (example: **NAWM 78**, **HWM Example 16.2** by Elizabeth-Claude Jacquet de la Guerre)

1. French composers grouped dance movements into suites.
2. The French order of suite movements differs from the German (see **HWM Chapter 15**).
3. Movements have contrasting tempos, meters, and styles.
4. Titles came from dance origins or were fanciful.
5. Preludes (e.g. **HWM Example 16.2a**)
   a. Unmeasured
   b. In improvisatory style
6. Allemande (French for "German"; **HWM Example 16.2b**)
   a. Moderately fast
   b. 4/4 meter
   c. Begins with an upbeat
   d. Continuous movement in style luthé, with frequent agréments
7. Courante (French for "running" or "flowing"; **HWM Example 16.2c**)
   a. Based on a dignified dance step
   b. Triple or compound meter, or alternation between triple and compound
8. Sarabande (**HWM Example 16.2d**)
   a. Originally a fast dance from Latin America
   b. Brought to France via Spain and Italy
   c. The stylized French version is in a slow tempo.
   d. Triple meter, with an emphasis on the second beat
9. Gigue (French for "gig"; **HWM Example 16.2e**)
   a. Originated in the British Isles
   b. Fast tempo
   c. Compound meter
   d. Movement in continuous triplets
   e. Often begins with a section in fugal or quasi-fugal style
10. Extra dances were often inserted.
    a. Rondeau, a refrain form with contrasting periods paired in couplets
    b. Gavotte, a duple-meter dance starting with a half-measure upbeat
    c. Minuet, a triple-meter couples' dance
11. The French sequence of allemande–courante–sarabande–gigue was adopted by German composers.

D. Influence of French style
1. After the Thirty Years' War, the refinement of French taste in all the arts was admired.
2. Instrumental music styles spread, especially suites and overtures.
3. After the 1660s, the French and Italian styles began to blend.

IV. The English Baroque

A. The English monarchy was more fragile and limited in power than the French
1. 1649: The monarchy is abolished after a seven-year civil war.
2. 1649–1660: Oliver Cromwell (1599–1658) rules England as a commonwealth and a protectorate.
3. 1660: Parliament restores the monarchy.
4. 1660–1689: James II enlarges the scope of the monarch's power.
5. 1689: Parliament controls public funds and the Bill of Rights limits the monarch's power.

B. Music and theater
1. The masque continued to be a favorite genre under Henry VIII.
   a. Long collaborative spectacles similar in scope to French court ballets
   b. More than one composer contributed music to a typical masque.
   c. Aristocrats and schools produced shorter masques.
   d. Under Cromwell's prohibition against stage plays, the addition of masque elements to spoken drama created a mixed genre that was allowable.
2. Dramas with masque elements were the first English "operas."
   a. 1660: The restoration of the monarchy restored staged plays as well.
   b. Masque elements continued to be part of dramatic productions.
   c. *Venus and Adonis* (ca. 1683), by John Blow (1649–1708), was called a masque, but it was sung throughout.

C. Henry Purcell's (1659–1695) dramatic music
1. Biography (see **HWM biography,** page 375, and **HWM Figure 16.12**)
   a. Spent his entire career in service of the English monarchy
   b. Jobs included choirboy, composer, organist, keeper of the king's instruments, and organ maker
   c. Buried in Westminster Abbey
   d. Composed in all genres but focused on vocal music
   e. Known for setting English text in natural-sounding declamation
   f. Incorporated French and Italian elements
2. *Dido and Aeneas* (1689)
   a. French elements: overture, homophonic choruses, and scenes that end with dances.
   b. Italian elements: arias, including three on a

ground bass (e.g., **NAWM 79b**), and using a descending tetrachord for a lament
c. English elements: dramatic action within dance sections, tuneful English airs, and imitation of Locke and Blow's choruses and style of text declamation
d. Recitative incorporates some word-painting (e.g., martial dotted rhythms on "valour" and descending semitones to suggest sighs).
3. Purcell's other music for the stage
a. Semi-opera or dramatic opera: a spoken play with an overture and substantial musical episodes (e.g., *The Fairy Queen* (1692), based on Shakespeare's *A Midsummer Night's Dream*)
b. Incidental music for over fifty plays

D. Other English music
1. Though opera didn't take root in the seventeenth century, England had a lively musical culture.
2. Music for the royal family included Purcell's *Ode for St. Cecilia's Day* (1692) and other large-scale works commissioned for holidays or state occasions.
3. Music for amateur and home performance
a. Vocal music
b. Catch: a round or canon with a humorous, often ribald text, sung at all-male gatherings
4. Anglican church music
a. Anthems and services continued to be the principle genres.
b. Verse anthems for soloists with chorus
c. Coronation ceremonies inspired elaborate works.
d. Purcell set nonliturgical sacred texts for one or more voices with continuo, probably for private devotion.
5. Instrumental music
a. Consort music for viols, played by well-to-do amateurs
b. Locke and Purcell composed viol fantasias and In Nomines for viol consort.
c. Dance music included harpsichord pieces and tunes for country dances, e.g. those collected in *The English Dancing Master* (1651), published by John Playford (see **HWM Figure 16.13**)
d. Public concerts (see **HWM Source Reading,** page 378) began in the 1670s, with the king's musicians making extra money in concerts attended by the middle class.

V. Spain and the New World
A. Spain's power
1. Spain was the richest country in Europe and the most powerful nation on earth.
a. Spain's European possessions included Portugal, half of Italy, and the Netherlands.
b. Outside of Europe, Spain controlled the Philippine Islands and much of the Americas.
2. Spain's colonies created multicultural mixtures of musical styles from European traditions and those of African slaves and native populations.

B. Opera, zarzuela, and song
1. Two operas composed in Spain
a. Pedro Calderón de la Barca, librettist
b. Juan Hidalgo (1614–1685), composer
c. Music for the first was lost.
d. The second, *Celos aun del aire matan*, consists of syllabic strophic airs in Spanish styles and recitative for moments of high drama.
2. The zarzuela was the predominant genre of musical theater in Spain for several centuries.
a. Developed by Juan Hidalgo
b. Light, mythological play in pastoral setting
c. Alternation of sung and spoken portions
d. Uses ensembles and solo song
e. Hidalgo's works appealed both to royalty and to the public.
3. *La púrpura de la rosa* (The Blood of the Rose, **NAWM 80**)
a. The first opera produced in the New World: 1701 in Lima, Peru.
b. Staged at the court of the viceroy of Peru
c. Music by Tomás de Torrejón y Velasco (1644–1728) to a libretto adapted from Hidalgo's first opera
d. Dialogue is in strophic song (see **HWM Example 16.4**).
e. Syncopated rhythms, typical of Spanish style
f. Continuo played by harps, guitars, and viols rather than keyboard or lute
g. Chorus and dance sections close the scene
4. Songs
a. Few Spanish songs were printed because there were no music printers in Spain.
b. Songs from theatrical productions circulated in manuscript.
c. Solo songs included the romance, for one to four voices with guitar or harp, and the tonada, for solo voice.

C. Church music: The villancico (**NAWM 81**)
   1. Vernacular, sacred version of the secular villancico
   2. Scored for choir, choir with soloists, or solo voice with continuo
   3. Especially for Christmas, Easter, and other important feasts
   4. A typical example is *Los coflades de la estleya* (**NAWM 81** and **HWM Example 16.5**), a Christmas villancico by Juan de Araujo (1646–1712)
      a. Syncopations typical of both Spanish and African music
      b. References to poor black boys (meaning Africans and Native Americans) going to Bethlehem to see the infant Jesus.

D. Instrumental music
   1. Organ music
      a. Strong contrasts of color and texture
      b. Tiento, an improvisatory imitative piece similar to the sixteenth-century fantasia
      c. *Tiento de batalla* (Battle Tiento) by Juan Bautista José Cabanilles (1644–1712) imitates trumpet calls resounding from opposite sides of a battlefield.
   2. Harp and guitar music
      a. Harp and guitar were the main chamber instruments.
      b. Compositions were mainly in stylized dance forms.
      c. Most of the rest of Europe knew only these contributions of Spanish composers.

## SUGGESTIONS FOR SUPPLEMENTARY READING/LISTENING/ACTIVITIES

For a brief description of the court ballet under Louis XIV and a discussion of women's entry into ballet, see "Ballet in France: The Sun King" in *Dancing Times*, February 2004, 98–100 (or www.dancing-times.co.uk/dancingtimes200402-3.html).

Jean Hotteterre was part of a family of woodwind players and innovative instrument-makers that included grandson Jacques (1673–1763), author of *Principes de la flûte traversière* (Paris, 1707), the first published method for flute, and composer of some of the first published work for that instrument. This method is available in an English translation as *Principles of the Flute, Recorder, and Oboe,* translated by Paul M Douglas (New York: Dover, 1968 and 1983). If a Baroque flute is available, bring it to class or have students visit a museum to generate a discussion of how the technological innovations of the time—i.e., three separable parts and the addition of a key—may have affected musical composition.

For an idea of the professionalism of seventeenth-century instrumentalists, have students read the revised guild statutes governing the players of the *Vingt-quatre Violons du Roi* and other instrumentalists in France. The translation is available in Margaret Murata, ed., *Source Readings in Music History*, rev. ed., Vol. 5: The Baroque Era (New York: W. W. Norton, 1998). Significantly, the head of the guild, Guillaume Dumanoir, was known as the "King of the Violins."

Assign research papers centering on overdotting and the use of notes inégales in works in French overture style. For bibliography and a balanced treatment of the subject, see Stephen Hefling, *Rhythmic Alteration in Seventeenth- and Eighteenth-Century Music: Notes Inégales and Overdotting* (New York: Schirmer Books, 1993), especially pp. 145–60. Alternately, choose a particular French overture and hold a class debate in which two teams take opposite sides, one advocating overdotting and another advocating performance as written.

Have students read François Raguenet's "Comparison between the French and Italian Music and Operas" and Laurent Le Cerf de la Vieville's "Comparison between Italian and French Music." Have them list the features that the writers see as typical of each of the national styles. These writings are translated in Margaret Murata, ed., *Source Readings in Music History,* rev. ed., Vol. 5: The Baroque Era (New York: W. W. Norton, 1998).

Despite the wide range of his compositional output, Marc-Antoine Charpentier is mainly known today for a trumpet fanfare that opens the second of his four settings of *Te Deum.* The complete work demonstrates the grace of Charpentier's style, and may remind students of the style of later composers, especially Handel. The work is available on several CDs (Glossa 921603, 2001; Elektra 17893, 1999; and Teldec/Elektra 12465, 1996). The opening fanfare has been recorded at many tempos and for many instrumentations. Les Arts Florissant, which specializes in seventeenth-century music, has recorded several of Charpentier's works. including the above-mentioned *Te deum,* oratorios, and incidental music. If you have access to several recordings of the *Te deum* fanfare, ask students to decide which is most appropriate for a church performance, which has the most authentic sound, and which makes the most appropriate use of agréments.

Denis Gaultier (1603–1672) was a leading composer who published two instructional collections for amateur lutenists. Two of Denis Gaultier's suites have been recorded on "Gaultier: La Rethorique Des Dieux" (Astree 7778, 1993); "Pièces de Luth" (Astree 8830, 2002) contains suites that have some movements with fanciful titles.

D'Anglebert's harpsichord treatise was published with his *Pièces De Clavecin,* which is available in facsimile as Volume 30 of *Clavecinistes Français Du Xviiie Siécle* (Geneva: Minkoff, 2001), and in the Performers' Facsimiles series (New York: Performers' Facsimiles, 2002) *Musique Francaise Classique de 1650 a 1800,* No. 126 (Courlay: Fuzeau, 1999).

King Henry VIII was an amateur composer. His complete works comprise vol. 18 of *Musica Britannica* and as an offprint from that series, and they have been recorded on "All Goodly Sports: Music of Henry VIII" (Chandos 621, 1998). They are brief enough for performance in class, some so brief students will find them amusing.

John Blow's *Venus and Adonis* is available on CD (Harmonia Mundi, 2003) and in score (Monaco: Editions de l'Oiseau Lyre, 1949).

The modest length of Purcell's *Dido and Aeneas* and the fact that it was written in English make it an ideal Baroque opera to study in its entirety. Have students collectively prepare a booklet to serve as an introduction to the opera, including a synopsis of the plot and/or a brief summary of the principal stylistic features of each number. For brief introductions to the opera, see Donald Jay Grout, *A Short History of Opera,* 3rd ed. (New York: Columbia University Press, 1988), 140–48; and Joseph Kerman, *Opera as Drama,* rev. ed. (Berkeley and Los Angeles: University of California Press, 1988), 43–47. For a more detailed treatment, see Ellen T. Harris, ed., *Henry Purcell's Dido and Aeneas* (Oxford: Clarendon Press, 1987). The complete libretto is available on the liner notes to the Bach Guild's LP (HM 46 SD). It is available on VHS video (Oley, PA: Bullfrog Films, 1995) and as a ballet accompanied by a Baroque orchestra on DVD (Image Entertainment, 2000).

Purcell's *The Fairy Queen* includes dance movements in the forms discussed in this chapter, and the overture to the fourth act, titled *Symphony,* is a French Overture that begins with an impressive fanfare for brass and timpani. These movements comprise the movements of the *Suite* from this work. The English National Opera's production of *The Fairy Queen* is available on DVD (Image Entertainment, 2000). Good historical performances are available on CD (Harmonia Mundi 901308, 1992; Archiv Produktion 419221, 1990; and others).

Purcell's *Ode for St. Cecilia's Day* has been frequently recorded. One recording, "Ode for St. Cecilia's Day / Te Deum" (Naxos 8.553444, 1996), also includes other religious works by Purcell. The score is widely available (Borough Green Kent: Novello, 1978). Other Anglican church music can be found in *Musica Britannica,* which is still coming out with new volumes.

Locke's chamber music is contained in vols. 31 and 32 of *Musica Britannica* (London: Stainer and Bell, revised in 1975 and 1977 respectively). "Locke: Consort of Fower Parts," a compilation including performances by several groups, contains suites with courantes and sarabandes. Most of the other movements are titled "fant" or "ayre."

*The English Dancing Master* is available in facsimile editions; the fourth edition of 1728 is available online at the Library of Congress's *American Memory* site. Ask students to imagine how the performers would have fleshed out these dance pieces, keeping in mind the instructions to the dancers at the bottom of the page and the title page illustration, which shows two violinists and no accompaniment. "The Elector of Hanover's March," page 160 of the fourth *(American Memory)* edition (http://memory.loc.gov/musdi/233/0172.tif) poses the interesting problem of a four-measure sustained note in the middle of the dance.

For more information on colonial Latin America, see the first two chapters of Gerard Béhague, *Music in Latin America: An Introduction* (Englewood Cliffs, New Jersey: Prentice Hall, 1979).

*La púrpura de la rosa* is an example of the work done by musicologists and early-music performers to bring neglected music to new audiences. Though composed in 1701, it was not transcribed for modern performance until 1973 in *Foundations of New World Opera, with a Transcription of the Earliest Extant American Opera, 1701,* by Robert Stevenson (Lima, Peru: Ediciones Cultura, 1973) and has been issued on CD (BMG International 77355, 2000). An interesting library project would be to assign other works from *NAWM* and have students report on the first publication and the date of a revival performance.

*Tiento de batalla* and other works by Juan Bautista José Cabanilles have been recorded on "Cabanilles: Batalles, Tientos and Passacalles" (Alia Vox AV9801, 1998).

## OBJECTIVE QUESTIONS

1. The main patron(s) of music in the French Baroque was/were __________.
   a. the Cathedral of Notre Dame
   b. middle-class concert audiences
   c. competing members of the nobility who ruled over small regions
   d. Louis XIV
   e. amateur musicians who purchased published music

   Answer: d

2. Louis XIV and other members of the nobility took part in performances of which genre?
   a. the court ballet
   b. masque
   c. opera
   d. zarzuela
   e. mass

   Answer: a

3. Music of the Great Stable was __________.
   a. the first large ensemble of the violin family
   b. music performed in the area in front of the stage in a theater
   c. an ensemble composed of wind, brass, and timpani players who provided military and outdoor music for the French monarchy
   d. a derogatory term describing music performed in overly large music rooms built by dukes and other members of the nobility to impress their peers
   e. music performed on large organs installed in large cathedrals

   Answer: c

4. Jean-Baptiste Lully is best known for his contribution to the development of __________.
   a. opera
   b. oratorio
   c. keyboard music
   d. music theory
   e. organ building

   Answer: a

5. An opera by Lully might also be called a(n) __________.
   a. ouvrage
   b. tragédie en musique or tragédie lyrique
   c. divertissement
   d. air de cour
   e. agrément

   Answer: b

6. Which of the following statements best describes the form of the French overture?
   a. three sections in fast-slow-fast order
   b. a slow opening marked by dotted rhythms, followed by a fast fugal section, with an optional slow closing section
   c. a fast and fugal opening section followed by a slow and homophonic section marked by dotted rhythms, with an optional closing section in a fast tempo
   d. a beginning section that is repeated after a departure into unrelated material in a contrasting key and mood
   e. a series of melodies drawn from the opera

   Answer: b

7. Which scoring is typical of Lully's orchestration?
   a. two violins plus continuo
   b. varied scorings that respond to the meaning of the text
   c. five-part string orchestra without any woodwinds, brass, or keyboard instruments
   d. fivepart string orchestra augmented by woodwinds
   e. twentyfour strings, each with an independent part

   Answer: d

8. The leading composer of church music in France during the late seventeenth century was __________.
   a. Jean-Baptiste Lully
   b. Jean-Philippe Quinault
   c. Denis Gaultier
   d. Cardinal Mazarin
   e. Marc-Antoine Charpentier

   Answer: e

9. Stile brisé, developed by lutenists, was imitated in __________.
   a. opera arias
   b. instrumental movements in French operas
   c. songs for court performances
   d. harpsichord music
   e. ballet movements

   Answer: d

10. Stylized dance music suites in France were most often performed by __________.
    a. lute or harpsichord
    b. the *Vingt-quatre violons du Roi*
    c. the Great Stable
    d. a consort of viols
    e. organ

    Answer: a

11. The tonal organization of a dance movement in binary form (assuming a major key) can best be summarized as __________.
    a. ||: I :|| ||: I :|| ||: I :|| etc.
    b. ||: I–V :|| ||: V–I :||
    c. I–V–I
    d. V–I
    e. I–vi–vi–I

    Answer: b

12. The standard order of movements in seventeenth-century French suites was __________.
    a. allemande, courante, sarabande, gigue
    b. pavane, galliard, courante, allemande
    c. allemande, pavane, courante, gigue
    d. prelude, pavane, galliard, gigue
    e. prelude, gavotte, minuet, gigue

    Answer: a

13. How did Cromwell's prohibition against stage plays affect music performances?
    a. All music was banned from the stage.
    b. Oratorios became the most popular substitution for stage plays.
    c. The addition of music and elements from the masque made stage plays acceptable.
    d. Producers of plays set up an underground venues that attracted composers of experimental genres.
    e. Producers of operas and plays ignored the prohibition and continued as usual.

    Answer: c

14. Henry Purcell is best known for composing in which genres?
    a. English opera, semi-opera, and incidental music for plays
    b. Italian opera and oratorios
    c. liturgical music for the Catholic Church
    d. keyboard music, especially suites in the French style
    e. ballet

    Answer: a

15. Henry Purcell's employer was __________.
    a. the Church of England
    b. the Catholic Church
    c. the English monarchy
    d. a private school for girls
    e. an opera impressario

    Answer: c

16. Public concerts of instrumental music first began in __________.
    a. France
    b. England
    c. Spain
    d. Peru
    e. Mexico

    Answer: b

17. The zarzuela was __________.
    a. an Italian adaptation of French ballet
    b. a dance movement that originated in Latin America and came to Italy via Spain
    c. the predominant genre of musical theater in Spain for several centuries
    d. a six-stringed instrument made popular by Spanish composers of dance music
    e. a type of embellishment reserved for slow arias

    Answer: c

18. *La púrpura de la rosa* was __________.
    a. the first opera produced in the New World
    b. a collection of zarzuelas that helped spread the genre throughout Europe
    c. a treatise on composing church music in concertato medium
    d. an Italian opera that inspired English composers to try their hands at opera
    e. a type of ornamentation added to cadences

    Answer: a

19. The genre cultivated for Christmas and Easter in colonial Latin America was the __________.
    a. carol
    b. hymn
    c. madrigal
    d. zarzuela
    e. villancico

    Answer: e

20. The main chamber instruments in seventeenth-century Spain were __________.
    a. harp and guitar
    b. viols in consorts
    c. harpsichord and clavichord
    d. recorders and shawms
    e. violins in pairs

    Answer: a

## SHORT-ESSAY QUESTIONS

1. Discuss the ways in which having a central monarchy influenced the musical developments of France, England, and Spain.
2. Compare the career and works of Lully and Purcell. In what ways did their circumstances dictate their compositional output?
3. Discuss the ways in which French, English, and Spanish styles differed from the mainstream Italian-based style of the late seventeenth century.
4. Summarize the development of instrumental music in seventeenth-century France.

## TERMS FOR IDENTIFICATION

Louis XIV
Music of the Royal Chapel
Music of the Chamber
Music of the Great Stable
*Vingt-quatre Violons du Roi*
Jean-Philippe Quinault
*tragèdie lyrique*
French overture
divertissement
*récitatif simple*
*récitatif mesuré*
notes inégales
overdotting
agréments
petit motet
grand motet
*style brisé*
allemande
courante
sarabande
gigue
catch
The English Dancing Master
zarzuela
(sacred) villancico
tiento

**CHAPTER 17**

# Italy and Germany in the Late Seventeenth Century

I. Italy and Germany in the Late Seventeenth Century
   A. Both regions continued to be ruled by leaders of small states, rather than a strong central government.
      1. Rulers and cities competed for the best musicians.
      2. Musicians traveled among major centers, bringing innovations with them.
   B. Stylistic changes
      1. In Italy, musical style evolved from existing Italian styles.
      2. In Germany, composers added Italian and French elements to German style.
      3. The international style developed in Germany would become the style of Bach, Handel, and later Haydn and Mozart.

II. Italian Vocal Music
   A. Northern Italy continued to be the center for musical developments.
      1. Venice continued to be an important center for opera because of its public opera houses.
      2. Naples, Florence, and Rome also fostered opera.
   B. Arias became more important as vehicles to display the virtuosity of superstar singers.
      1. The average number of arias per opera increased to around sixty by the 1670s.
      2. Forms included strophic, ground bass, rondo, and ABA (da capo).
      3. The da capo aria became the favorite type because it offered an opportunity for embellishment in the repeat (see below).
      4. The accompaniment often portrayed feelings or moods.
   C. Cantatas became an experimental medium.
      1. They were composed on commission for special occasions and presented to small audiences.
      2. By the 1690s, cantatas lasted about fifteen minutes and consisted of alternating arias and recitatives.
      3. Scoring was usually for one voice with continuo.
      4. The texts were usually love poems.
   D. Alessandro Scarlatti's cantatas (e.g., **NAWM 82,** *Clori vezzosa, e bella*)
      1. Scarlatti composed over six hundred cantatas.
      2. Recitatives use chromaticism and diminished chords (e.g., **NAWM 82a** and **HWM Example 17.1a**) for strong emotions and to reinforce cadences.
      3. Da capo aria (e.g., **NAWM 82b** and **HWM Example 17.1b–c**)
         a. The most common form of aria in Scarlatti's operas and cantatas
         b. The words *da capo* ("from the head") at the end of the second section instruct the performers to repeat the first section, resulting in an ABA form.
         c. A section: small two-part form with two different settings of the same text
         d. Instrumental ritornellos introduce small divisions in the form.
         e. The B section is in a new key and mode to reflect a change of emotion in the text.
   E. Serenata
      1. Semidramatic piece, midway between cantata and opera
      2. Usually composed for a special occasion

3. Composed for small orchestra and several singers
4. Alessandro Stradella (1639–1682) was one of the first composers of serenatas.

F. Church music and oratorio
1. Old and new styles continued to coexist in Italian sacred music.
2. The works of Maurizio Cazzati (1616–1678) are typically diverse.
   a. His works were composed for San Petronio in Bologna.
   b. *Messa a cappella* (Unaccompanied Mass, 1670) is in a slightly modernized *stile antico*.
   c. His *Magnificat a 4* alternates old and new styles.
3. Oratorios became substitutes for operas when theaters were closed for Lent or other seasons.
   a. Texts were usually in Italian rather than Latin, and written in verse.
   b. A division in the middle left time for a sermon or intermission.

III. Italian Instrumental Music

A. Instrumental music for church
1. San Petronio was a center for instrumental music.
   a. Cazzati composed some of the first sonatas for trumpet for San Petronio.
   b. Bolognese composers created restrained and serious instrumental music with little technical display or special effects.
2. Organists in Italy continued to use existing genres (e.g., ricercares and toccatas).

B. Instrumental chamber music
1. Italians were the masters and teachers of instrumental chamber music.
   a. Stradivari (see **HWM Music in Context,** page 392, and **HWM Figure 17.3**) and other violin-makers of the period brought the violin to a pinnacle of perfection.
   b. Sonatas and concertos for strings were the leading genres of instrumental music.
2. Development of the sonata
   a. The earliest sonatas consisted of small sections of contrasting material (see **HWM Chapter 16** and **NAWM 76**).
   b. The contrasting sections eventually evolved to separate movements with different affects, in keeping with the theory of affections (see **HWM Chapter 13**).
3. By ca. 1660, two types of sonata had evolved: sonata da camera (chamber sonata) and sonata da chiesa (church sonata)
4. Sonata da camera: series of stylized dances, often beginning with a prelude.
5. Sonata da chiesa: abstract movements, often including one or more dance movement not titled as such.
6. Both types were played for private concerts, but sonatas da chiesa could also substitute for parts of the liturgy in church.
7. After ca. 1670, the most common instrumentation was the trio sonata: two treble instruments (usually violins) with basso continuo.
8. After ca. 1700, solo sonatas became popular.

IV. Arcangelo Corelli (1653–1713) and the Sonata

A. Biography (see **HWM biography,** page 393, and **HWM Figure 17.4**)
1. Studied in Bologna and began his career there
2. Worked as violinist, teacher, ensemble director, and composer for wealthy patrons in Rome.
3. As a violinist, he established the foundation for violin-playing and exploited the singing qualities of the instrument better than anyone of his generation.
4. All of his surviving works are instrumental: trio sonatas, violin sonatas, and concerto grossos.

B. Trio sonatas (e.g., Opus 3 No. 2, **NAWM 83** and **HWM Example 17.2**)
1. Melodies stress lyricism rather than virtuosity in the violin parts.
2. The two violins are equal in range and musical material.
3. Suspensions (see **HWM Example 17.2**) between the violins drive the harmonic momentum.
4. Walking bass, a bass line in steadily flowing eighth notes, is typical of Corelli's style.

C. Corelli's church sonatas (e.g., Opus 3 No. 2, **NAWM 83** and **HWM Example 17.2**)
1. Four movements usually in slow-fast-slow-fast order.
2. The first slow movement is solemn and contrapuntal.
3. The following allegro is usually fugal, in canzona tradition, with the bass line a full participant (e.g., **HWM Example 17.3**).
4. The second slow movement often resembles an operatic duet in triple meter.
5. The final movement is often in binary form and has a dancelike character (e.g., the gigue of **NAWM 83**).

D. Corelli's chamber sonatas
   1. The opening movement is usually a prelude, sometimes in French overture style.
   2. The bass line is purely accompanimental in fast movements.
   3. Dance movements are in binary form, with the first section ending on the dominant or relative major and the second making its way back to the tonic.

E. Solo sonatas
   1. Composed in both chamber and church sonata styles
   2. More virtuosic than his trio sonatas, with doublestops, runs, arpeggios, and cadenzas
   3. Slow movements were notated as simple pieces, with the expectation that the performer would embellish them.
   4. A version published by Estienne Roger in Amsterdam shows both the plain and embellished version, which he claimed was how Corelli himself had played it (see **HWM Figure 17.5**).

F. Corelli's style
   1. Each movement has a distinct theme that spins out throughout the movement.
   2. He exploits functional tonality, which by the 1680s had replaced modality.
      a. Chord progressions that use circles of fifths in dominant-tonic relationships (e.g., **HWM Example 17.2**)
      b. Sequences and chains of suspensions
      c. Departures from the tonic move most often to the dominant or relative major or minor.

V. The Concerto
   A. By the 1670s, orchestras began to form in Italian cities for performance at special occasions.
      1. Orchestral movements from operas (e.g., Lully's overtures and dance movements)
      2. Chamber sonatas with several players per part instead of one
      3. Instrumental "concerto"
         a. Closely related to the sonata
         b. Played at public events and special gatherings
         c. Sometimes substituted for elements of the Mass
   B. Types of concertos
      1. Orchestral concerto
         a. Several movements
         b. First violin and bass emphasized
         c. Not as popular or important as the other types
      2. Concerto grosso (pl. *concerti grossi*), favored in Rome
         a. Contrasts a small solo group (concertino) against a large group (concerto grosso)
         b. Concertino group was usually two violins with basso continuo.
         c. Similar contrasts in Lully's operas set a precedent.
         d. Corelli's *Concerti grossi* Op. 6 (1680s) were essentially trio sonatas with the larger group punctuating structural divisions.
         e. Corelli's style was imitated by others, including Georg Muffat (1653–1704), who composed works that could be played as either trio sonatas or concerti grossi (see **HWM Source Reading,** page 399)
      3. Solo concerto, usually for solo violin and string orchestra
         a. Composed by Giuseppe Torelli (1658–1709) in Bologna
         b. Torelli wrote trumpet concertos for services in San Petronio.
         c. Torelli's violin concertos of 1692 were the first ever published.
         d. Torelli's concertos consisted of three movements in fast-slow-fast order derived from the Italian opera overture.
         e. Ritornellos often frame sections of Torelli's concertos, creating forms similar to da capo aria forms.
      4. Orchestras usually consisted of first and second violins, violas, cellos, and basso continuo, with bass viol sometimes doubling the cellos.

VI. The Italian Style at the End of the Seventeenth Century
   A. All genres shared some features.
      1. Solo forms highlighted individual performance.
      2. Variety of melodic styles used in both vocal and instrumental music
         a. Lyrical melodies
         b. Arpeggiation derived from trumpet calls
         c. Virtuoso passage work
      3. Forms based on a pattern of establishing a key, then departing from it, then returning to it
      4. Return of opening material at the end of a movement
   B. The Italian style was imitated elsewhere and became the foundation for further developments.

VII. Germany and Austria
   A. Small independent city-states supported music.
      1. Courts of the nobility
         a. Rulers imitated Louis XIV's patronage of music to assert their power and status.

b. Musicians employed at courts had the highest status.

2. Cities employed town musicians, *stadtpfeifers* (German for "town pipers").
   a. Stadtpfeifers held exclusive rights to provide music for the city (e.g. **HWM Figure 17.7,** a New Year's celebration in Nuremberg).
   b. They performed at public ceremonies, weddings, and other festivities.
   c. They supervised the training of apprentices.
3. Tower sonatas (*Turmsonaten*) were played in some cities from the tower of a church or town hall.
4. Amateur music-making
   a. Many towns had a *Collegium musicum,* an association of middle-class amateurs.
   b. Schools had groups that gave public concerts (see **HWM Chapter 19**).

B. Opera and secular vocal music
1. Courts hired Italian composers to compose operas, and German composers began composing Italian operas as well.
2. Opera in German
   a. The first public opera house in Germany opened in 1678 in Hamburg.
   b. Local poets translated Italian librettos and wrote new ones in the same style.
   c. Subjects were biblical in the early years in deference to the Lutheran church.
   d. Recitatives were in Italian style.
   e. Arias could be in Italian, French, or German styles.
   f. The most prolific composer was Reinhard Keiser (1674–1739)
3. Song and cantata
   a. Keiser and other composers composed songs, arias, and cantatas in both Italian and German.
   b. Adam Krieger (1634–1666) of Dresden composed strophic melodies with short five-part orchestral ritornellos.

C. Catholic Church music
1. The southern German-speaking area, including Munich, Vienna, and Salzburg, was largely Catholic.
2. Emperors living in Vienna supported music and were also performers.
3. Liturgical music combined Palestrina-style counterpoint with the concerted style.
4. Orchestras accompanied vocal movements and played preludes and ritornellos.
5. Salzburg's four choir lofts encouraged polychoral music.
6. Heinrich Biber (1644–1704) composed his monumental *Missa salisburgensis,* with one singer and instrumentalist to each part, for Salzburg.

D. Lutheran vocal music
1. After the Thirty Years' War, there were two conflicting viewpoints in Lutheran church music.
   a. The orthodox view was that all available resources should be used.
   b. The Pietists preferred simpler music for personal devotion.
2. New chorales and hymns were composed for use at home, e.g., those in the collection, *Praxis pietatis melica* (Practice of Piety in Song, 1647) by Johann Crüger.
3. Sacred concertos
   a. Often included arias in Italian style set to nonbiblical texts
   b. Chorales for concertos could be in concertato medium or in simple harmonies.
   c. These concertos are usually called "cantatas" today.

E. Dietrich Buxtehude (ca. 1637–1707)
1. Biography (see **HWM biography,** page 406, and **HWM Figure 17.9**)
   a. Played organ at a German church in Denmark and at St. Mary's church in Lübeck, a prestigious post in northern Germany
   b. He held his post in Lübeck almost forty years and influenced other organists, such as Johann Sebastian Bach.
   c. Famed for his public concerts (*Abendmusiken*) of sacred vocal music
   d. His works include sacred vocal music, organ music, harpsichord music, and ensemble sonatas.
2. *Wachet auf* concertato chorale setting (**HWM Example 17.4**)
   a. The melody is paraphrased differently for each stanza.
   b. The result is a series of chorale variations.

VIII. Lutheran Organ Music

A. The period between ca. 1650 and 1750 is a golden age of organ music in the Lutheran areas of Germany.

B. The Baroque organ
1. German organ makers, such as Arp Schnitger (1648–1718) and Gottfried Silbermann (1683–1753), blended technical features of French and Dutch organs.

a. French features: Colorful stops for solos and contrapuntal lines
b. Dutch features: Division of pipes into a main or "great" group (*Hauptwerk*) above the player and other groups, including *Brustwerk* in front of the player and *Oberwerk* above the great organ

2. Even small organs gave performers a range of tone colors.

C. Toccatas and preludes (e.g., **NAWM 84** and **HWM Examples 17.4–5** by Buxtehude)
1. Series of short sections in free style alternating with longer ones in imitative counterpoint
2. Virtuosic for both keyboard and pedals
3. Improvisation is suggested by irregular phrase lengths, inconclusive endings, and abrupt changes of texture, harmony, or melodic direction.
4. Free sections frame the fugal sections.
5. Fugal sections have related themes (see **HWM Example 17.5**).
6. Pieces such as **NAWM 84** could be titled "Toccata" or "Prelude" in the seventeenth century.

C. Fugue
1. By the end of the seventeenth century, "fugue" supplanted other terms for pieces in imitative counterpoint.
2. In the eighteenth century, fugues would be separate pieces rather than sections within preludes.
3. Subjects are livelier and have more sharply drawn melodies than subjects of ricercare.
4. Exposition: a set of entries of the subject
a. Answer: second entrance of the subject, contrasting with the first in a tonic-dominant relationship; sometimes adjusted to fit the new key
b. Other entrances alternate the subject and answer.
c. Cadence to close the exposition
5. Additional sets of statements of the subject alternate with episodes, using different order of entrances or other devices for variety.
6. Episodes: periods of free counterpoint between statements of the subject

E. Chorale settings
1. Organ chorales enhance the melody with harmony and counterpoint.
2. Chorale variations, or partite, were variations on a chorale melody.
3. Chorale fantasia used the chorale melody as a subject.

F. Chorale prelude
1. Short piece presenting the melody just once in recognizable form
2. Probably derived from organists' practice of playing the tune through before the congregation or choir sang the first stanza
3. Techniques used:
a. Each phrase of the melody is set in a point of imitation.
b. The melody appears in the top voice in long notes, with each phrase preceded by imitation in diminution in other voices.
c. The melody appears with Italianate or French-style ornamentation in the top voice, accompanied by freely changing accompaniment (e.g., **HWM Example 17.6a,** *Nun komm, der Heiden Heiland* by Buxtehude)

G. Other instrumental music
1. Froberger adopted the French harpsichord style and helped to establish the standard order (allemande, courante, sarabande, gigue), which would be adopted in Germany.
2. Orchestral suites inspired by French orchestral music were fashionable from ca. 1690 to 1740.
a. Dance movements patterned on those of Lully's ballets, in no standard order
b. Georg Muffat's *Florilegium* (1695 and 1698) is among the earliest collections.
c. *Florilegium* includes an essay on French performance practices.
3. The solo sonata attracted more interest than the trio sonata.
a. Johann Jakob Walther (ca. 1650–1717) published twelve virtuosic violin sonatas under the title *Scherzi.*
b. Biber's *Mystery* (or *Rosary*) Sonatas for violin (ca. 1675) are the most famous German sonatas of the period.
c. Biber's sonatas employed *scordatura*, unusual tunings of the strings.
d. Walther and Biber's sonatas included rhapsodic movements or toccata-like sections.
e. Both composers used theme and variations or passacaglia movements (e.g. Biber's Passacaglia for unaccompanied violin).
f. The first keyboard sonatas are by Johann Kuhnau (1660–1722), *Frische Clavier Früchte* (Fresh Keyboard Fruits, 1696) and "Biblical" sonatas (1700) for amateurs.

IX. Impact of Late-Seventeenth-Century German and Italian Music
   A. As in the past, German composers adopted styles and genres from other countries.
      1. From Italy: opera, da capo aria, trio sonata, solo violin sonata, and concerto
      2. From France: suites for keyboard and orchestra
   B. Works from this period continued to be performed in the early eighteenth century.
      1. Corelli's sonatas
      2. Buxtehude's organ works
      3. Bach was influenced by this generation's style.

## SUGGESTIONS FOR SUPPLEMENTARY READING/LISTENING/ACTIVITIES

Numerous examples of instruments from this period are extant and in museums around the world. The Shrine to Music museum in North Dakota has an online "virtual museum" at www.usd.edu/smm/. Of particular interest in this chapter are the trumpet and violin.

The *New Grove Dictionary of Music and Musicians,* online edition, has illustrations and sound clips for the Baroque trumpet. It also has an interactive 3D model of a violin, pictures of seventeenth-century violinists, and an exploded diagram of the instrument's parts. Note that only a few minor changes have been made to the instrument since the eighteenth century, but playing techniques have changed—e.g., bowing and holding the instrument—while wind instruments have changed considerably, but are played with essentially the same technique.

If instrumentalists with Baroque versions of trumpets and violins are available, have them come to class to demonstrate the main features of the instruments and the differences from modern instruments. In particular, have them demonstrate the features of the instrument that would dictate melodic patterns that students should listen for in examples, e.g., the overtone series of the trumpet and the open strings of the violin. Note that these features lend themselves to the emerging sense of tonic-dominant tonality in Baroque music.

The Corelli Op. 5 sonatas have been recorded with embellishment thanks to renewed interest in historical performance, and each recording sounds different (Harmonia Mundi, 2003; Accent Records 8433, 1999; Hyperion, 1993). To generate a discussion of performance practice, ask students whether they would use the embellishments offered in the Estienne Roger edition, supposedly representing the way Corelli played them, or if they would rather learn the practices of the time and create their own embellished version. Ask whether having the embellishments available to them would be all they needed to know to create an "authentic" performance. Students familiar with jazz performance will have a unique perspective on the question. Ask them if they would rather perform an exact replication of a classic jazz improvisation, such as those of John Coltrane, or perform their own.

A more well-known sonata by Corelli is Op. 5 No. 12, *La Folia,* named for the movement which uses the famous *La Folia* theme. For a recording of several sets of variations by different composers, use "La Folia, 1490–1701" (Alia Vox 9805, 1999). The CD titled simply "Corelli: La Folia" (Hyperion 66226, 1993) contains this movement and examples of all the types of sonatas discussed in this chapter. The prelude and sarabande of *Sonata da Camera in A,* Op. 4, No. 3 demonstrate the subservient role of the basso continuo.

Corelli's Christmas concerto (Opus 6 no. 8) is available on several recordings. The complete Opus 6 performed by the English Concert on period instruments is available: "Concerti Grossi, Op. 6" (Hamburg: Archiv 2894594512, 1988 and 2000). An urtext edition of the score is available (Edition Eulenburg EE 6882, 1997) in study-score size. This work is an excellent example of some of the most salient features of Corelli's style, such as chains of suspensions and walking bass.

For additional source readings on performance practice, see *Georg Muffat on Performance Practice: The Texts from Florilegium primum, Florilegium secundum, and Auserlesene Instrumentalmusik: A New Translation with Commentary,* edited and translated by David K. Wilson (Bloomington: Indiana University Press, 2000).

Torelli's music is well-represented on recordings made by specialists in baroque trumpet music, including "The Art of the Baroque Trumpet, Vol. 1" by Niklas Eklund (Naxos 553531, 1996), which includes Torelli's *Concerto in D Major.*

Reinhard Keiser's *Croesus* is available on CD (Harmonia Mundi 901714, 2000 and Nuova Era 6934, 2001). The overture opens with a boisterous fanfare for trumpet, as does the first chorus, which uses a trumpet fanfare for its ritornello.

Recordings of works by Adam Krieger are rare, but songs have been recorded on "Jews in Germany, 1250–1750" (Raum Klang 9401, 2000) and "Andreas Scholl: German Baroque Songs" (Harmonia Mundi 901505, 1995).

Plan a class trip to a working baroque organ, if one is nearby, or devote some class time to a discussion of the mechanics of the organ. The "Organ" article in the *New Grove Dictionary of Musical Instruments,* 3 vols. (New York: Macmillan, 1984), includes several drawings and photographs of Baroque organs. One is a cross-section diagram showing a tracker organ, complete with an assistant pumping the bellows.

The Web site for the public radio show "Pipedreams" (http://pipedreams.publicradio.org/) has a photo gallery that includes a few baroque organs. Have students identify the *Hauptwerk, Brustwerk,* and *Oberwerk* in organs pictured here or in other sources. Other photos can be found in the liner notes for compact discs of organ music.

For technically undemanding keyboard pieces, suitable for students to learn for class performances, along with commentary on performance-practice problems, see the volumes edited by Howard Ferguson, especially *Early German Keyboard Music (including Austria and the Netherlands): An Anthology* (London: Oxford University Press, 1970); and *Early French Keyboard Music: An Anthology* (London: Oxford University Press, 1966).

*Missa salisburgensis* by Biber is available on CD (Archiv Produktion, 2003). Its use of trumpets and timpani in the opening of the Kyrie will give students a sense of the grandeur of church music in the new style. It was published in volume 7 of Laurence Feininger, *Orazio Benevoli: Opera Omnia* (Rome, 1966–73) due to earlier misattribution.

*Wachet auf* (**HWM Example 17.4;** BuxWV 100) is available in *Dieterich Buxtehude: The Collected Works* (New York, 1987), but only BuxWV 101, a different work based on the same chorale, has been recorded.

*Nun komm, der Heiden Heiland* by Buxtehude is contained on "Buxtehude: Complete Organ Works" (Classico 143, 1996) and "Buxtehude: Organ Works" (Novalis 150048, 1994).

Several of Froberger's suites have been recorded on "Froberger: Suites de Clavecin & Toccatas" (Harmonia Mundi 1951372, 2002), "Froberger: Strasbourg Manuscript" (CPO Records 999750, 2000), and "Keyboard Music in Germany Before Bach" (Pro Gloria Musicae Recordings 101, 1996), which also includes sonatas by Johann Kuhnau. Froberger's works are available in several editions. Have students compare one of his suites to those discussed in chapters 15 and 16. Use these suites as examples for aural identification of the standard movement types.

## OBJECTIVE QUESTIONS

1. Which of the following letter schemes best represents the formal plan of a da capo aria?
   a. AAAAA
   b. ABCA
   c. AAB
   d. ABA
   e. AABB

   Answer: d

2. Which of the following statements best describes Venetian operatic arias in the latter part of the seventeenth century?
   a. The da capo form was the most commonly used form.
   b. Composers used several forms but favored the strophic aria.
   c. The strophic aria was standard.
   d. Composers did not compose arias because they believed arias interrupted the narrative of the story.
   e. Arias were brief diversions within recitatives.

   Answer: a

3. Which of the following statements best describes the Italian secular cantata?
   a. a mini-opera with scenery and costumes
   b. a series of arias for several solo singers with full orchestral accompaniment
   c. many short, contrasting sections with recitatives and arias for solo voice with continuo
   d. a series of religious songs sung outside of church during Lent and Advent, with orchestral accompaniment and scenery
   e. an opera with sections between the acts that have unrelated plots and extended dance scenes

   Answer: c

4. Alessandro Scarlatti is known mainly for works in which genre(s)?
   a. concerto grosso and sonata
   b. secular cantata and opera
   c. Mass and oratorio
   d. music for harpsichord
   e. music for organ

   Answer: b

5. Which genre substituted for opera when public theaters were closed?
   a. oratorio
   b. cantata
   c. serenata

d. aria
e. magnificat

Answer: a

6. San Petronio in Bologna was known for being a center for developments in __________.
   a. church music in the Palestrina style
   b. sacred concerto
   c. instrumental music
   d. organ chorales
   e. scordatura violin-playing

   Answer: c

7. Antonio Stradivari was instrumental in the development of the __________.
   a. organ
   b. violin
   c. flute
   d. harpsichord
   e. guitar

   Answer: b

8. The instrumentation for a trio sonata typically consisted of __________.
   a. two treble instruments and a cello
   b. two bass instruments and a keyboard instrument
   c. two treble instruments, an optional cello or viola da gamba, and harpsichord or organ
   d. a solo organ
   e. two sopranos or two tenors plus a keyboard instrument

   Answer: c

9. Which of the following statements best describes a typical sonata da camera?
   a. It consisted of four movements, usually in slow-fast-slow-fast order.
   b. It consisted of several stylized dances preceded by a prelude.
   c. The term was synonymous with "cantata."
   d. It was composed for groups of musicians occupying several choir lofts.
   e. It was written for large instrumental ensemble.

   Answer: b

10. Which of the following statements best describes a typical sonata da chiesa?
    a. It consisted of four movements, usually in slow-fast-slow-fast order.
    b. It consisted of several stylized dances preceded by a prelude.
    c. The term was synonymous with "cantata."
    d. It was composed for groups of musicians occupying several choir lofts.
    e. It was written for large instrumental ensemble.

    Answer: a

11. In a trio sonata in a major key, a movement not in the tonic key would very likely be in the key of the __________.
    a. parallel minor
    b. subdominant
    c. dominant
    d. mediant
    e. relative minor

    Answer: e

12. The composer known for his performance on the violin was __________.
    a. Stradella
    b. Alessandro Scarlatti
    c. Arcangelo Corelli
    d. Froberger
    e. Buxtehude

    Answer: c

13. The large instrumental ensemble in a concerto grosso is referred to as the __________.
    a. concertino
    b. concertato
    c. collegium musicum
    d. concerto grosso
    e. corelli

    Answer: d

14. The small instrumental ensemble in a concerto grosso is referred to as the __________.
    a. concertino
    b. concertato
    c. collegium musicum
    d. concerto grosso
    e. corelli

    Answer: a

15. The typical movements of a Torelli concerto are __________.
    a. fast-slow-fast
    b. fast-slow-fast-slow
    c. slow-fast-slow-fast
    d. a succession of fugal and nonfugal movements
    e. a series of contrasting sections based on the same theme

    Answer: a

16. Stadtpfeifers were __________.
    a. members of amateur music-making clubs
    b. the set of organ pipes over the organist's head
    c. musicians hired to provide music for the city
    d. separable parts of a baroque trumpet
    e. the trumpets used for official city events

    Answer: c

17. Which of the following statements best describes the state of Lutheran church music after the Thirty Years' War?
    a. Lutherans believed that only the minor mode should be used for the following thirty years.
    b. Lutherans believed all available resources should be used, including choirs and orchestras.
    c. Lutherans believed in simple music for personal devotion only.
    d. Lutherans believed no music should be sung in church in honor of those who had died in the war.
    e. Lutherans were divided in their opinions about the type of music that should be used.

    Answer: e

18. Concerts of sacred music given by Buxtehude were called __________.
    a. Singspiels
    b. Abendmusiken
    c. masques
    d. grand motets
    e. *Praxis pietatis melica*

    Answer: b

19. The form of the typical late-seventeenth-century toccata is __________.
    a. a series of entrances on a theme, followed by improvisatory music
    b. a series of short sections in free style alternating with longer ones in imitative counterpoint
    c. four movements in slow-fast-slow-fast tempos
    d. four movements in fast-slow-fast-slow tempos
    e. a series of variations with increasingly fast rhythmic divisions of a main theme

    Answer: b

20. What instrument was most commonly featured in solo sonatas?
    a. recorder
    b. violin
    c. trumpet
    d. viola da gamba
    e. No instrument was more commonly used than others.

    Answer: b

## SHORT-ESSAY QUESTIONS

1. Discuss the political and social trends common to Italy and Germany. In what ways did these trends affect music in these two regions?
2. Summarize the main features of the music of Arcangelo Corelli. What genres did he favor? What were the characteristics of his compositional style?
3. Describe the main genres of Lutheran church music in Germany in the late seventeenth century, giving names of representative composers and examples from *NAWM*.
4. Describe the instrumental music of the late seventeenth century, comparing genres for small ensembles and those for larger ensembles and giving names of representative composers and examples from *NAWM.*

## TERMS FOR IDENTIFICATION

| | | | |
|---|---|---|---|
| da capo aria | concerto | *Praxis pietatis melica* | fugue |
| serenata | concerto grosso | Abendmusiken | exposition |
| San Petronio | concertino | Hauptwerk | chorale prelude |
| Antonio Stradivari | Stadtpfeifers | Brustwerk | scordatura |
| sonata da camera | Turmsonaten | Oberwerk | *Frische Clavier Früchte* |
| sonata da chiesa | Collegium musicum | | |

# CHAPTER 18

# The Early Eighteenth Century in Italy and France

I. Europe in a Century of Change
  A. Music of the early eighteenth century
    1. The general stylistic features and principal musical genres of the seventeenth century continued.
    2. Historical interest has justifiably centered on the works of Vivaldi, Couperin, Rameau, J. S. Bach, and Handel.
    3. The works of these masters represent the last generation of the Baroque era, which overlaps with the beginning of a new musical age.
  B. Europe's balance of power
    1. France had the largest army, but spent money lavishly.
    2. Britain, with the most powerful navy, expanded its colonial holdings.
    3. Vienna, the seat of the Austro-Hungarian Empire, became the leading music center of Europe.
    4. Prussia emerged as a major military power.
    5. Poland was divided between Prussia, Russia, and Austria.
    6. The American Revolution and French Revolution would bring about dramatic political changes at the end of the century.
  C. The population of Europe expanded rapidly.
    1. Improved agricultural methods produced a greater food supply.
    2. As trade increased, the middle class grew in size and power.
    3. With the growing industrialization and urbanization of Europe, nature was increasingly idealized (see **HWM Figure 18.1**).
  D. Education played a larger role in society.
    1. Many new schools were founded.
    2. With the increase in literacy, daily newspapers appeared in London in 1702.
    3. More books were published and read, including novels.
    4. Intellectuals, such as Voltaire, gathered to discuss a variety of issues, which lead to a movement known as the Enlightenment.
  E. The rise of the middle class created an increasing demand for public music.

II. Music in Italy
  A. Naples
    1. Naples became an independent kingdom in 1734.
    2. The city had four conservatories.
      a. Originally, these were orphanages that specialized in teaching music.
      b. Later, the conservatories took on paying students as well.
      c. Students from the conservatories traveled all over Europe.
      d. Most of the conservatory students were singers, including castrati.
        (1) Castrati were the leading male roles in opera.
        (2) Some became international superstars, such as Carlo Broschi Farinelli (see **HWM Music in Context**, page 420, and **Figure 18.2**).
    3. Naples was a strong center of opera, the dominant type of music in Italy.
      a. Alessandro Scarlatti was the leading composer.

b. New types of comic opera gained popularity.
c. More significantly, a new serious type of opera emerged in the 1720s.
d. Recitatives and da capo arias alternated in serious and comic opera.

B. Rome
1. Opera was less central in Rome's music scene.
2. Patrons supported academies in which cantatas, serenatas, sonatas, and concertos were performed.
3. The city attracted instrumentalists, including Geminiani and Locatelli, who later spread the Italian style of Corelli to other regions.

C. Venice
1. Although declining in political power, Venice remained the most glamorous city in Europe.
2. A wide variety of music could be heard in Venice.
a. Music was performed on the streets and sung by gondoliers.
b. Amateurs made music in the homes.
c. Public festivals were characterized by musical splendor.
d. Church music flourished.
e. The city never had fewer than six opera companies.

III. Antonio Vivaldi (1678–1741)

A. Vivaldi was Italy's best-known composer of the early eighteenth century (see **HWM biography,** page 422, and **Figure 18.3**).
1. He was a virtuoso violinist.
2. He was considered to be a master teacher.
3. He composed opera, cantatas, and sacred music.
4. He is primarily remembered for his violin concertos.

B. Biography
1. He was born in Venice and spent most of his life in this city.
2. He was known as *il prete rosso* (the red-headed priest).
3. Vivaldi's principal position was at the Pio Ospedale della Pietà (1703–1740).
a. This was one of the four "hospitals" in Venice that, like the conservatories of Naples, taught music to orphans.
b. The Pietà was restricted to girls, who were not allowed to become professionals.
c. The musical training made them more desirable for marriage or prepared them for convent life.
d. Performances of the girls also helped earn donations (see **HWM Figure 18.4**).
e. Travelers wrote about these performances with enthusiasm (see **HWM Source Reading,** page 424).
4. Vivaldi served as a teacher, composer, conductor, and superintendent of musical instruments.
a. Vivaldi composed sacred music, including the Gloria in D Major.
b. Most of the works were instrumental.

C. Concertos
1. Vivaldi composed about five hundred concertos.
2. The orchestra
a. Vivaldi's orchestra probably had twenty to twenty-five strings.
b. The strings were usually divided into four parts: violins I, violins II, violas, and cellos/string basses.
c. The continuo was either a harpsichord or organ.
d. Vivaldi sometimes used flutes, oboes, bassoons, and horns.
e. Vivaldi used color effects, such as pizzicato and muted strings.
3. The soloists
a. About 350 concertos are for one solo instrument, usually violin.
b. Solo concertos are also written for bassoon, cello, oboe, flute, viola d'amore, recorder, and mandolin.
c. The concertos with several soloists are written in the style of a solo concerto, not in the style of Corelli's concerti grossi, as the soloists are given equal prominence.
d. Vivaldi composed about sixty orchestral concertos, which do not have soloists.
4. Vivaldi's three-movement structures established a standard for future concerto composers.
a. The first movement is in a fast tempo.
b. The middle movement is slow and in the same or closely related key.
c. The final movement, also fast and in the original key, is often shorter and livelier than the first movement.
5. Fast movements are usually set in a ritornello form.
a. Ritornellos, played by the orchestra, alternate with episodes for the soloist.
b. The ritornello melody contains small melodic units that can be manipulated by the soloists or in other ritornellos.
c. Later statements of the orchestral ritornello may present only part of the original theme.

d. The first and last ritornellos are in the tonic, the second ritornello is usually in the dominant, and the others are in closely related keys.
e. The solo sections often contain virtuosic display.
f. The solo sections may modulate to a new key.
g. The soloist may interrupt or play part of the closing ritornello.

6. Slow movements
   a. Vivaldi is the first composer to treat this movement as equal to the fast movements.
   b. The melodies tend to be long, cantabile, and expressive, like an opera aria.
   c. Some are through-composed; others use a simplified ritornello form or a two-part from.
7. Despite relying on formulas, Vivaldi's concertos reflect a wide variety of expression, forms, and ideas.
8. Vivaldi published nine collections of concertos, often with fanciful titles.
   a. Opus 3 was titled *L'estro armonico* (Harmonic Inspiration, 1711).
   b. Opus 8 was titled *Il cimento dell'armonia e dell'inventione* (The Test of Harmony and Invention, 1725).
9. Opus 8 contains his four most famous concertos, known as *The Four Seasons*.
   a. A sonnet describing a season accompanies each of the concertos.
   b. The music depicts images of each season.

D. Concerto for Violin in A Minor, Opus 3 No. 6 (see **NAWM 85, HWM Figure 18.5** and **Examples 18.1–2**)
1. Opus 3 established Vivaldi's reputation and was the most influential collection of music in the early eighteenth century.
2. The twelve works of the set alternate concertos featuring one, two, and four violin soloists.
3. Opus 3 No. 6 has three movements, with the outer fast movements set in ritornello forms.
4. First movement
   a. The opening ritornello presents three melodic ideas.
   b. The second ritornello is in the minor dominant, and the remaining ritornellos are in the tonic.
   c. These ritornello sections contain varied statements of the three principal melodic ideas.
   d. The episodes (solo sections) either develop the melodic ideas or present new figuration.
5. Second movement
   a. The movement is in D minor, the subdominant of A minor.
   b. The accompaniment is by violins and violas only.
   c. The rhapsodic solo violin melody includes flowing sequences over a chromatic accompaniment.
6. Third movement
   a. The opening ritornello contains more thematic ideas than the first movement.
   b. The subsequent ritornellos are more varied in key areas and content.
   c. One ritornello contains modulation, which is normally reserved for the episodic sections.
   d. The freedom of form in this movement suggests the variety of Vivaldi's treatments of ritornello structures.
   e. The repetitive rhythmic drive of the fast movements, typical of late Baroque music, differs from the rhythmic flexibility of the early Baroque.

IV. Music in France

A. Paris was the only major center of music in France.
1. Paris was the home of the prestigious Concert spirituel, a public concert series founded in 1725.
2. Louis XV supported music, but not to the extent of Louis XIV.

B. The relative merits of Italian and French music were frequently discussed.
1. The latest Italian music was performed in Paris.
2. Some French composers sought to blend Italian and French styles.
   a. Louis Nicolas Clérambault (1676–1749) published cantatas that alternated French and Italian recitatives.
   b. Jean-Marie Leclair (1697–1764) combined Italian and French qualities in his violin sonatas.

C. François Couperin (1668–1733) (see **HWM Figure 18.6**)
1. Couperin's career reflects the growing diffusion of patronage in France.
   a. He was the organist to the king.
   b. He taught harpsichord to members of the aristocracy.

c. He published his own music.
2. Couperin's ordres
   a. The ordres or suites were published between 1713 and 1730.
   b. Each ordre contains a number of miniature works, generally based on dance rhythms and set in a binary form.
   c. Most of the pieces have evocative titles.
3. *Vingt-cinquieme ordre* (Twenty-fifth Order, 1730)
   a. *La visionaire* (The Dreamer) takes on the conventions of the French overture (**NAWM 86a**).
   b. *La misterieuse* (The Mysterious One) is an allemande.
   c. *La Montflambert* is a tender gigue, probably named after the wife of the king's wine merchant.
   d. *La muse victorieuse* (The Victorious Muse) is a passepied.
   e. *Les ombres errants* (The Roving Shadows) contains a syncopated middle voice that shadows the top melody, creating chains of suspensions.
4. *La muse victorieuse* (**NAWM 86b**)
   a. The passepied, in triple meter, is a faster relative of the minuet.
   b. The tempo is marked *Audacieusement* ("audaciously" or "boldly").
   c. The last eleven measures of the first half reappear at the end of the second half in the tonic.
5. Couperin's treatise *L'art de toucher le clavecin* (The Art of Playing the Harpsichord, 1716) contains useful information about French Baroque performance practice.
6. The chamber music of Couperin synthesizes French and Italian styles.
   a. He claimed that the perfect music would be a union of the two national styles (see **HWM Source Reading,** page 431).
   b. He dedicated suites to both Corelli and Lully.
   c. Couperin was the first and foremost French composer of trio sonatas.
   d. *Les nations* (The Nations, 1726) and other works contain characteristics of both French and Italian music

V. Jean-Philippe Rameau (1683–1764)
   A. Biography (see **HWM biography,** page 434, and **Figure 18.7**)
      1. Rameau began as an organist in the provinces of France.
      2. By age forty, he was recognized as a theorist.
      3. He achieved fame as a composer in his fifties.
      4. For an extended period, he served the wealthy patron Jean-Joseph de la Pouplinière, whose gatherings attracted many significant figures.
      5. His music was initially criticized for being radical, but later it was thought to be reactionary.
   B. The theories of Rameau
      1. His principal work, *Traité de l'harmonie* (Treatise on Harmony, 1722), is one of the most influential of all theoretical works.
      2. Rameau based his theory practice on the laws of acoustics.
      3. The triad and the seventh chord were the primal elements of music.
      4. He defined the root of each chord and recognized chord inversions.
      5. The roots in a succession of chords created the fundamental bass (see **HWM Example 18.3**).
      6. Music was propelled by dissonance and rested with consonance.
      7. Using the terms *tonic, dominant,* and *subdominant,* Rameau established these three chords as the pillars of harmony.
      8. Although a piece could change keys through modulation, each work had a central tonic key.
      9. The strongest chord progression is the dominant-seventh to tonic.
      10. Rameau was the first to bring all of these theoretical ideas together.
   C. The operas of Rameau
      1. As a composer, Rameau was best known for his operas, although he also wrote keyboard music, a set of trio sonatas, and some vocal music.
      2. Because of a monopoly by the Académie Royale de Musique, operas could only be produced in Paris.
      3. After eleven years in Paris, Rameau produced his first opera, *Hippolyte et Aricie* (1733), which is based on a drama by Racine.
      4. A number of outstanding works followed.
         a. *Les Indes galantes* (The Gallant Indies, 1735) is an opera-ballet.
         b. *Castor et Pollux* (1737) is considered to be his masterpiece.
         c. *Zoroastre* (1749), a tragic opera, is the most important of his later works.
      5. Rameau's early operas created controversy.
         a. Two camps developed, one favoring Rameau and the other attacking him for subverting the opera traditions of Lully.

   b. During the French and Italian opera controversy of the 1750s, the Lully supporters hailed Rameau as the champion of the French style.
6. Rameau's operas resemble Lully's in numerous ways.
   a. The recitatives have realistic declamation with precise rhythmic notation.
   b. Recitatives mix with more tuneful airs, choruses, and instrumental works.
   c. The differences between recitative and air are minimized.
7. Rameau also introduced a number of significant changes.
   a. The melodies are derived from the harmony.
   b. Rameau uses a richer harmonic palette, including more chromaticism.
   c. Rameau's orchestral writing is exceptional, as seen in his overtures, dances, and descriptive orchestral passages.

D. *Hippolyte et Aricie,* close of Act IV (**NAWM 87**)
1. The passage begins with a divertissement of hunters.
2. The orchestra suggests the sudden storm and presence of a monster.
3. Hippolyte and Aricie sing a dramatic accompanied recitative.
4. Hippolyte is engulfed by flames, which are depicted in the orchestra.
5. The chorus sings a dissonant lament highlighted by appoggiaturas and silence.
6. Hippolyte's stepmother Phèdre laments her role in this tragedy.
   a. She sings a *récitatif simple* with basso continuo.
   b. An accompanied *récitatif mesuré* follows with sounds of thunder, lightening, and earthquake.
   c. An accompanied *récitatif simple* returns at the end.
7. A final comment is heard from the chorus.

## SUGGESTIONS FOR SUPPLEMENTARY READING/LISTENING/ACTIVITIES

For additional background on music and culture during this period, organized by region, see George J. Buelow, ed., *The Late Baroque Era* (Englewood Cliffs, N.J.: Prentice Hall, 1994).

The numbering of Vivaldi's works is more problematic than that of any other composer. Now is a good time to discuss the works of scholars who have identified, numbered, edited, and published the works of the great composers of the Baroque period. Begin by pointing out that few of Vivaldi's works were published during his lifetime, yet most are available today. Ask students how they would find out about the unpublished works of a Baroque composer. Ask how they would figure out who composed a work that has no name, or one with two names. Show them the various catalogues of the works of Vivaldi, noting that there are many different concertos in the same few keys. Follow up this discussion by showing students the catalogue and editions of the works of J. S. Bach.

Vivaldi's *Cimento dell'armonia e dell'inventione* is available on a compact disc performed by Europa Galanta on period instruments (Virgin Classics 45465, 2001). Have students compare this performance with some of the numerous recordings on modern instruments. Have them discuss differences in sound, tempo, and ornamentation. In the Europa Galanta recording, you will find other concertos with programmatic titles, such as No. 5, *La tempesta di mare.* With these works and *The Four Seasons,* discuss how Vivaldi creates programmatic images.

Have some of the violin students listen to the two violin concertos (BWV 1041, 1042) and the Concerto in D Minor (BWV 1043) by Bach and compare aspects of their styles and the technical demands placed on the violinist with those of Vivaldi.

Vivaldi composed significant concertos for flute/piccolo, trumpet, bassoon, cello, and guitar (mandolin/lute). Assign some students with an appropriate background to look up these concertos and listen to available recordings. Ask the students how Vivaldi maintains a ritornello structure with concertos for instruments other than violin.

Vivaldi's opera *Orlando furioso* is available on DVD (Image Entertainment, 2000). Have students compare selected scenes with excerpts from operas by Alessandro Scarlatti and Handel. Let the students debate whether Vivaldi's operas are justifiably neglected.

Images of paintings by Jean-Antoine Watteau provide visual analogies to the musical poise, refinement, and delicacy of Couperin's ordres. Draw students' attention to the use of ornament, attention to detail, use of color, and the refined bearing of the characters. Why would these images have appealed to the French aristocracy?

Have keyboard students read Couperin's *L'Art de toucher le clavecin* and learn a short keyboard composition by the composer, applying the instructions from the treatise. A useful source is Margery Halford's translation (Port

Washington, N.Y.: Alfred Publishing Co., 1974). Facsimiles of *L'Art de toucher le clavecin* are also published by Minkoff (Geneva, 1986) and in *Monuments of Music and Music Literature in Facsimile. 2d ser, Music Literature*, Vol. 23 (New York: Broude Brothers, 1969). Useful passages are excerpted in MacClintock, ed., *Readings in the History of Music in Performance* (Bloomington: Indiana University Press, 1979).

Several compact-disc recordings of Couperin's music have appeared recently. One entitled *L'Apothéose de Lulli* (Harmonia Mundi 1951269, 2001) also contains excerpts from *L'Apothéose de Corelli. Les Nations* is recorded on Chandos 684, 2002.

Rameau's *Les Indes galantes* (available on several recordings) can be used to illustrate several points and to generate a discussion of difficult issues. First, it is an example of an entrée. Second, it includes several instances of descriptive orchestral writing. Third, it demonstrates the exoticism of French music and the European view of the Americas. Have students listen to the Inca sun worship scene and the earthquake portrayed in Act II. Ask students if they can hear any Inca elements in the sun worship scene (they won't) and whether they can hear when the earthquake begins (they will).

For a contrasting view of music in Latin America during the eighteenth century, have students read pages 62–68 of Gerard Béhague's *Music in Latin America: An Introduction* (New York: Prentice-Hall, 1979). These pages describe operas produced in Peru during the early eighteenth century, including Torrejón y Velasco's *La Purpura de la Rose,* which premiered in 1701. This opera is available on compact disc (Deutsche Harmonia Mundi 77355, 2000). Have students contrast Rameau's view of Latin American music with excerpts from this opera.

Rameau's *Pièces de clavecin* has been issued on compact disc, and a modern edition is available (New York: Bärenreiter 3800, 1958). Have students select a movement and report on its form and technique, and how the movements reflect their titles. Some of the movements have standard titles (e.g., Allemande) and others are character pieces, such as *La Joyeuse, L'Indifférente, Les Sauvages,* and *L'Enharmonique*.

After discussing the above examples from Rameau's *Pièces de clavecin,* have the students look at selected excerpts and identify the fundamental bass line.

## OBJECTIVE QUESTIONS

1. Of the following, which statement does *not* describe the changing Western world of the eighteenth century?
   a. The major political powers included France, Britain, and Prussia.
   b. The middle class grew in size and power.
   c. An increase in literacy promoted daily newspapers and novels.
   d. People continued to move away from urban centers to live in rural villages.
   e. Nature was increasingly idolized.

   Answer: d

2. Which city had conservatories that became centers of music training, especially for singers?
   a. Venice
   b. Vienna
   c. Paris
   d. Rome
   e. Naples

   Answer: e

3. Which city attracted instrumental performers, including Geminiani and Locatelli?
   a. Venice
   b. Vienna
   c. Paris
   d. Rome
   e. Naples

   Answer: d

4. In which city did Vivaldi spend most of his career?
   a. Venice
   b. Vienna
   c. Florence
   d. Naples
   e. London

   Answer: a

5. Which instrument did Vivaldi feature as a soloist in most of his concertos?
   a. flute
   b. violin
   c. cello
   d. harpsichord
   e. bassoon

   Answer: b

6. Most of Vivaldi's concertos were first performed by __________.
   a. professional musicians
   b. adult amateurs
   c. male students
   d. female students
   e. traveling orchestras

   Answer: d

7. Which of the following is one of Vivaldi's important contributions to the concerto genre?
   a. preference for three-movement structures
   b. establishment of fugal forms for fast movements
   c. preference for multiple soloists in a concerto
   d. superficial treatment of the slow movement
   e. assigning all of the principal melodies to the soloist

   Answer: a

8. Of the following, what does *not* characterize Vivaldi's typical ritornello form?
   a. The opening and closing ritornellos are in the tonic key.
   b. The ritornello melody is composed of several smaller units.
   c. The solo sections often modulate to related key areas.
   d. The ritornello always recurs in its complete form.
   e. The solo sections often have virtuosic display.

   Answer: d

9. Of the following, which describes Vivaldi's *Four Seasons*?
   a. It was published in *L'estro armonico*.
   b. It contains four works that have programmatic images.
   c. Vivaldi attached sonnets by Metastasio to the works.
   d. The principal soloist is a flute.
   e. Two of the works are orchestral with no soloists

   Answer: b

10. What kind of concert was sponsored by the Concert spirituel?
    a. sacred church concerts
    b. private chamber concerts
    c. public concerts
    d. royal concerts
    e. oratorio concerts

    Answer: c

11. The leading composer of French violin sonatas in the early eighteenth century was __________.
    a. François Couperin
    b. Louis Nicolas Clérambault
    c. Jean-Philippe Rameau
    d. Jean-Marie Leclair
    e. Jean-Jacques Rousseau

    Answer: d

12. What is the subject matter of Couperin's *L'art de toucher le clavecin*?
    a. instructions on playing the harpsichord
    b. instructions on tuning harpsichords
    c. instructions on building harpsichords
    d. instructions on composing for harpsichords
    e. a comparison of harpsichords and organs

    Answer: a

13. Of the following, what does *not* describe the ordres of Couperin?
    a. They comprise a loose collection of miniature pieces for the harpsichord.
    b. Most of the pieces are based on dance rhythms.
    c. Binary forms are prevalent.
    d. Many pieces have evocative titles.
    e. They were intended for professional performances.

    Answer: e

14. Which two composers were honored by Couperin in published suites for two violins and harpsichord?
    a. Vivaldi and Rameau
    b. Corelli and Rameau
    c. Scarlatti and Lully
    d. Scarlatti and Handel
    e. Corelli and Lully

    Answer: e

15. Which patron was instrumental in Rameau's earliest successes as a composer?
    a. Louis XIV
    b. Jean-Baptiste Lully
    c. Pierre Corneille
    d. Jean-Joseph de la Pouplinière
    e. Louis XVI

    Answer: d

16. Which of the following professions was *not* part of Rameau's background?
    a. organ performer
    b. teacher at an orphanage
    c. theorist
    d. composer of opera
    e. composer of instrumental music

    Answer: b

17. For Rameau, the fundamental bass was __________.
    a. the succession of fundamental tones in a series of chords
    b. the succession of lowest pitches in a set of chords
    c. the French equivalent of basso continuo
    d. the lowest set of pipes on a Baroque organ
    e. the cadential formula that defines tonality

    Answer: a

18. Which of the following characterizes Rameau's operatic style?
    a. a mixture of recitative, air, instrumental music, and chorus
    b. a subordinate orchestral role
    c. virtuosic arias
    d. recitative written in the style of Italian recitativo secco
    e. elimination of dance from the productions

    Answer: a

19. Rameau's first major opera in Paris was __________.
    a. *Les Indes galantes*
    b. *Hippolyte et Aricie*
    c. *Castor et Pollux*
    d. *Platée*
    e. *Zoroastre*

    Answer: b

20. In which way do the operas of Rameau differ from those of Lully?
    a. They use accompanied recitative.
    b. They contain a prominent role for the orchestra.
    c. Melodic ideas are often triadic.
    d. The music flows freely from recitative to airs.
    e. They have prominent roles for the chorus.

    Answer: c

## SHORT-ESSAY QUESTIONS

1. Compare musical life in Naples, Rome, and Venice.
2. Describe Vivaldi's contributions to the concerto genre.
3. Describe the synthesis of French and Italian styles by French composers, with a particular emphasis on the works of François Couperin.
4. Compare the operatic styles of Lully and Rameau. Be sure to include the titles of specific works by Rameau.

## TERMS FOR IDENTIFICATION

Carlo Broschi Farinelli
*il preto rosso*
Pio Ospedale della Pietà
ritornello form
*L'estro armonico*
*Il cimento dell'armonia e dell'inventione*
*The Four Seasons*
Concert spirituel
ordres
*L'art de toucher le clavecin*
Jean-Joseph de la Pouplinière
*Traité de l'harmonie*
fundamental bass

# CHAPTER 19 German Composers of the Late Baroque

I. Contexts for Music in Germany and England
   A. In the eighteenth century, German-speaking composers became prominent in Europe for the first time in history.
      1. Among the outstanding composers are Telemann, Handel, the Bach family, Haydn, and Mozart.
      2. These composers created an international style by mixing elements of Italian, French, and German traditions.
   B. German-speaking regions were divided into numerous political entities.
      1. Austria, Saxony, and Brandenburg-Prussia, were among the larger regions.
      2. There were also many smaller independent areas.
      3. Many of the most powerful rulers, such as Frederick II (the Great) of Prussia, employed significant numbers of musicians.
   C. Many German aristocrats actively performed and composed music.
      1. Frederick the Great performed on flute (see **HWM Figure 19.1**).
      2. Anna Amalia, duchess of Saxe-Weimar, was a keyboard player, patron, and composer; her output includes two Singspiels.
   D. In Britain, public concerts helped sustain musicians as aristocratic patronage declined.

II. Georg Philipp Telemann (1681–1767) (see **HWM Figure 19.2**)
   A. Like many German composers, he was exposed to a wide variety of international styles.
   B. Telemann was a prolific composer and wrote over three thousand works.
      1. Almost every contemporary style can be found in his works.
      2. Telemann synthesized German counterpoint with styles from other regions.
      3. His music had wide appeal; he was more highly regarded than J. S. Bach.

III. Johann Sebastian Bach (1685–1750)
   A. The historical view of Bach differs from the contemporary perception.
      1. In his day, Bach was known as an organist and a composer of learned works, but little of his music was published or circulated.
      2. Contemporary critics thought that his music was old-fashioned, but a revival of interest in his works began in the early nineteenth century (see **HWM Source Reading,** page 456).
      3. Today, Bach is seen as one of the greatest of all composers.
      4. Bach wrote in all the major styles, forms, and genres of his time except for opera.
   B. Biography (see **HWM biography,** page 442, and **Figures 19.3** and **4**)
      1. Bach came from a large family of musicians.
      2. He was born in Eisenach and apparently learned violin from his father.
      3. He later lived with and studied organ with his older brother, a student of Pachelbel.
      4. Bach went to school at Lüneburg.
         a. He encountered the organist Georg Böhm.
         b. He had contact with French repertoire and performance style.
      5. Bach married twice.
         a. He married Maria Barbara Bach in 1707, and they had seven children.

   b. Following her death, he married Anna Magdelana in 1721, and they had thirteen children.
6. In his first positions as an organist, Bach primarily composed organ music.
   a. Arnstadt (1703–7), church organist
   b. Mühlhausen (1707–8), church organist
   c. Weimar (1709–14), court organist
7. He became concertmaster at Weimar (1714–17) and wrote sacred cantatas.
8. Bach became court music director at Cöthen (1717–23) and composed solo and ensemble music, as well as pedagogical works.
9. Leipzig (1723–50)
   a. Bach was in charge of four churches and wrote a significant amount of religious music (see **HWM Figure 19.5**).
   b. With his appointment as director of the Leipzig collegium musicum, he wrote concertos and chamber works.
   c. He also composed keyboard music at Leipzig, including pedagogical works.
10. As an employee, Bach faced many restrictions.
   a. The duke of Weimar imprisoned Bach for a month before letting him go to Leipzig.
   b. In Leipzig, he had to promise to lead an exemplary life and not leave town without permission.
   c. Bach had numerous clashes with the Leipzig town council.
11. Duties at Leipzig
   a. He taught Latin and music four hours a day.
   b. He composed, copied, and rehearsed music for church services; in the early years he composed a new cantata every week.
   c. He directed the top choir and oversaw the other three church choirs.
   d. He trained students on instruments and directed the church orchestra.
   e. He was responsible for music at town ceremonies and composed music for weddings, funerals, and other special occasions.
12. Bach's compositional process
   a. He learned composition by copying and arranging works of other composers.
   b. He composed at the keyboard.
   c. With instrumental music, the shaping of the initial theme was critical.
   d. With vocal music, Bach began with the vocal melody, matching the accents and meaning of the words.
   e. The manuscripts show that he revised his music continuously.
   f. He often adapted earlier material into new works.

IV. Organ Music
   A. General
      1. Bach performed at church and wrote in a wide variety of genres and styles.
      2. He was known as an outstanding improviser and often tested new organs.
      3. Influences
         a. Bach was aware of a wide range of organ composers.
         b. He traveled 225 miles to Lübeck to hear Buxtehude.
         c. Bach arranged a number of works by Vivaldi, which affected his style.
   B. Preludes and fugues
      1. Buxtehude had composed works that alternated sections of free fantasia and fugues (see **NAWM 84**).
      2. Bach's Toccata in D Minor (BWV 565) has a central fugue; it begins and ends with toccata sections and has toccata-like interpolations in the fugue.
      3. Prelude and Fugue in A Minor (BWV 543) (**NAWM 88**)
         a. This work was probably composed while Bach was at Weimar.
         b. Typical of Bach's practice, this work has only two main sections, a prelude and a fugue.
         c. The virtuosic prelude begins in the tonic, modulates through various keys, and returns to the tonic.
         d. The prelude has pedal points, pedal solos, and some imitation.
         e. Vivaldi's influence can be seen in the violinistic figuration in the prelude (see **HWM Example 19.1a**) and other general features.
         f. The form resembles the ritornello structure of a concerto, in which the fugue subject functions as the ritornello.
         g. The fugue subject is also violinistic (see **HWM Example 19.1b**).
         h. The episodes have the character of solo sections.
   C. Chorale settings
      1. These works were played before each chorale and were sometimes used to accompany the singing of the congregation (see **HWM Source Reading,** page 451)

2. Bach composed over two hundred works, using all known types.
3. *Orgelbüchlein* (Little Organ Book)
   a. This manuscript collection of chorale preludes was written at Weimar.
   b. The book had a pedagogical aim in addition to providing repertoire.
4. In each prelude of the *Orgelbüchlein,* the chorale tune is heard once in one of the following ways:
   a. In canon
   b. Elaborately ornamented
   c. Unadorned with a variety of accompaniments
5. *Durch Adams Fall* (Through Adam's Fall) (BWV 637) (see **NAWM 89b** and **HWM Example 19.2**)
   a. The chorale tune, in the top line, is heard once with few embellishments.
   b. The chorale melody is in bar form (aab).
   c. Jagged descending leaps in the bass depict Adam's fall from grace.
   d. The chromatic line in the alto suggests the writhing of the serpent.
   e. The downward-sliding tenor suggests the pull of temptation.
6. Later organ chorales use grander proportions and focus more on musical development.

V. Harpsichord Music
  A. Suites
    1. Bach composed three sets, each containing six suites.
       a. *English Suites*
       b. *French Suites*
       c. *Partitas*
    2. The French and English suites contain elements of French and English styles, but follow the standard four dance movements of Germany.
       a. Allemande
       b. Courante
       c. Sarabande
       d. Gigue
    3. Each of the *English Suites* opens with a prelude containing Italian elements.
  B. *Well-Tempered Clavier* (1722 and ca. 1740)
    1. There are two separate publications, each of which has twenty-four preludes and fugues.
    2. The pairs of movements in each collection are set in all of the major and minor keys, in order to demonstrate the possibilities for playing in all keys using an instrument tuned in near-equal temperament.
    3. The works had pedagogical functions as well.
    4. The preludes illustrate different types of keyboard performance conventions.
    5. The fugues are a compendium of fugal writing, ranging from two to five voices.
  C. *Goldberg Variations* (1741)
    1. The theme is set with a sarabande rhythm.
    2. The thirty variations preserve the bass and harmonic structure of the theme.
    3. Every third variation is a canon.
       a. The first is at the interval of a unison.
       b. The second canon is at the interval of a second.
       c. This pattern continues until the last canon, which is at a ninth.
    4. The noncanonic variations are in a variety of forms.
    5. The last variation is a quodlibet, which contains two popular-song melodies in counterpoint above the bass of the theme.
  D. *A Musical Offering* (1747)
    1. This collection has a three- and a six-part ricercare for keyboard and ten canons, based on a theme proposed by Frederick the Great (see **HWM Example 19.3**).
    2. Bach added a trio sonata for flute (Frederick's instrument), violin, and continuo and dedicated the work to the king.
  E. *Art of Fugue* (1741)
    1. This collection systematically demonstrates all types of fugal writing.
    2. It has eighteen canons and fugues based on the same subject (see **HWM Example 19.4**).
    3. The collection is roughly arranged in order of increasing complexity.
    4. The last fugue, unfinished at Bach's death, has four themes, including one that spells out his name, B–A–C–H (in German, those are the pitches B-flat, A, C, and B-natural).

VI. Chamber Music
  A. Bach composed fifteen sonatas for solo instruments and harpsichord.
    1. Six violin sonatas
    2. Six flute sonatas
    3. Three viola da gamba sonatas
  B. Bach composed thirteen works for unaccompanied solo instruments.
    1. Six sonatas and partitas for violin
    2. Six suites for cello
    3. A partita for flute

VII. Orchestra Music
  A. *Brandenburg Concertos*

1. The six works are dedicated to the margrave of Brandenburg.
2. Except for the first work, all of the concertos adopt the three-movement structure, ritornello forms, and style of Italian solo concertos.
3. There are no featured soloists in the third and sixth concertos.
4. Bach introduced ritornello material into episodes and featured dialogue between soloists and orchestra.
5. The Fifth Concerto has an astonishing cadenza for the harpsichord.

B. Bach may have composed his two violin concertos and his Concerto in D Minor for Two Violins for performances with the Leipzig collegium musicum (see **HWM Figure 19.6**).

C. Bach also composed and arranged works as harpsichord concertos, including a work for four harpsichords.

D. Bach composed four orchestral suites that reflect Italian and French influences.

VIII. Cantatas

A. In 1700, Erdmann Neumeister, a theologian and poet, created a new type of sacred work that he called by the Italian term *cantata*.

1. Settings of biblical, liturgical, and chorale texts were common in Lutheran services throughout the seventeenth century.
2. Neumeister added poetic texts that could be set as recitatives, arias, and ariosos.
3. The texts would reinforce the meaning of the day's Gospel reading.
4. These new works combined features of the chorale, solo song, and operatic recitative and aria.
5. Bach preferred this new style.

B. The cantata played an important role in the Lutheran liturgy of Leipzig.

1. The principal services included a motet, a Kyrie, chorales, and a cantata on alternate Sundays (see **HWM Source Reading,** page 451).
2. Bach preferred twelve singers in each of the main choirs.
3. The cantatas also required soloists and an orchestra that included strings, winds, and a continuo.
4. The Leipzig churches required fifty-eight cantatas a year in addition to other music.
5. Bach composed three, possibly four, sets of cantatas cycles for Leipzig between 1723 and 1729.
6. Around two hundred church cantatas have been preserved.
7. Bach also composed about twenty secular cantatas, some of which were rewritten as sacred works (see **HWM Figure 19.7**).

C. *Nun komm, der Heiden Heiland* (BWV 62) (**NAWM 90**)

1. Typical of the second cycle at Leipzig, this cantata incorporates a chorale tune of the same name (see **NAWM 42b**).
2. The opening chorus is based on the chorale melody, and the final chorus is a simple four-part arrangement of the tune.
3. In between the chorale movements, Bach inserts recitatives and arias in an operatic style.
4. The opening chorus mixes a variety of styles and genres.
   a. The movement begins with a Vivaldi-like orchestral ritornello that features the chorale tune in the bass (see **HWM Example 19.5**).
   b. The ritornello recurs three times, as in a concerto.
   c. Between the ritornellos, Bach presents the four phrases of the chorale set in cantus-firmus style.
   d. The first and fourth phrases are preceded by the lower voices in points of imitation based on the chorale tune (see **HWM Example 19.6**).
5. The initial aria for tenor is in da capo form.
   a. The text muses on the mystery of the incarnation.
   b. Bach sets the aria in a minuet style, as if to show Jesus's humanity.
6. The recitative for bass includes word-painting.
7. The bass aria follows the conventions for a heroic or martial aria and is accompanied by a unison string melody.
8. The soprano and alto sing a sweet accompanied recitative that describes the nativity scene.
9. The final chorale praises Father, Son, and Holy Spirit.

IX. Other Sacred Music

A. Passions

1. Two Passions by Bach survive: the *St. John Passion* and the *St. Matthew Passion*.
2. Both use recitatives, arias, choruses, chorales, and orchestral accompaniment.
3. In both, a tenor narrates the biblical story in recitative.

4. Soloists sing the roles of Jesus and other figures.
5. The chorus sings as part of the drama, such as the crowd, and comments like the chorus in a Greek drama.
6. Recent research suggests that Bach performed these works with a small number of singers.

B. Mass in B Minor
1. The Mass in B Minor, Bach's only complete setting of the Catholic Mass Ordinary, was assembled between 1747 and 1749.
2. Bach adapted much of the music from earlier compositions.
3. The work juxtaposes diverse sacred styles.
4. Too long to function in a service, the work can be seen as an anthology of sacred music types.

X. George Frideric Handel (1685–1759)

A. Handel traveled more than Vivaldi, Rameau, and Bach.
1. Born in Halle, he learned organ, harpsichord, and counterpoint in Germany.
2. During four years in Italy (1706–10), he met a number of major Italian composers and assimilated the Italian style.
3. Handel matured as a composer in England (1712–59).
   a. England's strong choral tradition made Handel's oratorios possible.
   b. Handel was enormously popular.
4. Handel created an eclectic style using elements of German, Italian, French, and English music.

B. Patrons (see **HWM biography,** page 458, and **Figure 19.8**)
1. Marquis Francesco Ruspoli was Handel's principal patron in Italy.
   a. Handel worked as a keyboard player and composer in Rome and at the Ruspoli country estate.
   b. Handel composed Latin motets and numerous chamber cantatas.
2. In 1710, Handel became music director for the elector of Hanover, the heir to the British throne.
3. London trips
   a. Handel used the elector of Hanover's position to establish himself in London.
   b. During a trip to London in 1710 and 1711, Handel composed the opera *Rinaldo*.
   c. During a second trip in 1712, he received support from the earl of Burlington.
   d. James Brydges, who became duke of Chandos, also became a patron.
4. Handel's most important patrons were the British monarchs.
   a. Handel received several ceremonial commissions from Queen Anne.
   b. The elector of Hanover became King George I in 1714 and doubled Handel's pension.
   c. Handel received support from later monarchs as well.
5. Despite this support, most of Handel's major compositions were for public performances.

XI. Operas

A. Handel's first opera, *Almira* (1705), written in Hamburg at the age of nineteen, shows his assimilation of international influences.
1. The overture and dance music are based on French models.
2. The arias are in the Italian style and language.
3. The recitatives are sung in German.
4. Handel incorporates German counterpoint and orchestration.

B. Handel assimilated the Italian style more fully during his stay in Italy.
1. He was influenced by the operas and cantatas of Scarlatti.
2. The Italian style is evident in *Agrippina* (Venice, 1709).

C. The early years in London
1. *Rinaldo* (1711), Handel's first Italian opera to be performed in London, was a major success with its brilliant music and elaborate stage effects.
2. Handel composed four more operas in the 1710s.

D. The Royal Academy of Music, devoted to producing Italian opera, was established in 1718–19.
1. Handel was engaged as the music director.
2. Performances were at the King's Theatre in the Haymarket (see **HWM Figure 19.9**).
3. Handel gathered outstanding musicians, including the celebrated castrato Senesino.
4. Handel composed some of his finest operas for this company.
   a. *Radamisto* (1720)
   b. *Ottone* (1723)
   c. *Giulio Cesare* (Julius Caesar, 1724)
   d. *Rodelinda* (1725)
   e. *Admeto* (1727)

E. Characteristics of Handel's operas
1. The plots were based on the lives of Roman heroes or on adventures from the Crusades.

2. Recitatives
   a. Long passages of dialogue and monologue were set in a speechlike fashion accompanied by the basso continuo, which would be called *simple recitative* and *recitativo secco* (dry recitative).
   b. Tense situations used recitative accompanied by the orchestra, called *recitative obbligato* and *accompanied recitative.*
3. Arias
   a. Arias were typically in da capo form.
   b. Each aria represented a single mood or affection.
   c. The number of arias for a singer depended on his or her position in the hierarchy of singers.
   d. The principal female was called the *prima donna* (first lady) and had the most and best arias.
4. Handel wrote in a wide variety of aria styles.
   a. Some contained brilliant displays of ornamentation known as *coloratura.*
   b. Some were expressive songs.
   c. Arias ranged from regal grandeur with counterpoint and concertato accompaniments to simple and folklike melodies.
   d. Pastoral scenes exemplify eighteenth-century nature painting.
   e. Solo instruments often contribute to the mood of the arias.
5. Handel used orchestral interludes and ballets more frequently than Scarlatti, and he used winds in the manner of French operas.
6. Choruses and ensembles larger than duets were rare.

F. *Giulio Cesare* Act II, scenes 1–2 (**NAWM 91**) form a scene complex, in which recitatives, ariosos, arias, and orchestral passages are freely mixed.
   1. The scene opens with simple recitative.
   2. Cleopatra's da capo aria is interwoven with other musical elements.
   3. The aria presents a mixture of national styles (see **HWM Example 19.7).**
      a. The rhythm is based on a French sarabande.
      b. The da capo form is Italian.
      c. The doubling of the voice by instruments is German.
      d. The orchestra is divided like an Italian concerto grosso.

G. Primarily for financial reasons, the Royal Academy dissolved in 1729, and Handel formed a new company.
   1. He had several major successes with Senesino in major roles.
   2. Senesino left in 1733 and joined another company.
   3. The two companies competed, and both nearly went bankrupt.
   4. Handel's later operas could not match the success of his earlier ones.

XII. Oratorios

A. In the 1730s, Handel created a new genre, the English oratorio.
   1. Oratorios were sacred entertainments based on well-known biblical stories.
   2. The English oratorio continued the Italian tradition of setting dialogue in recitative and lyrical verses as arias, which resemble his operatic settings.
   3. Handel also incorporated elements from non-Italian sources.
      a. French classical drama
      b. Ancient Greek tragedy
      c. The German passion
      d. The English masque and full anthem

B. The most important innovation was the prominent use of the chorus.
   1. Handel was familiar with Lutheran choral music and had learned the English choral traditions.
   2. Roles of the chorus
      a. Participate in the action
      b. Narrate the story
      c. Comment on events, like the chorus in Greek drama
   3. His choral style is less contrapuntal than that of Bach.
   4. He alternated sections of fugal texture with block harmonies.

C. *Esther* (1718), Handel's first oratorio, premiered in London in 1732.

D. *Saul,* the closing scene of Act II (1739) (**NAWM 92**)
   1. The passage opens with an accompanied recitative in a martial style (see **HWM Example 19.8**).
   2. Dialogue between Saul and Jonathan is in simple recitative.
   3. A chorus reflects on the morality of the situation.
      a. Each of the three fugues ends with a

homophonic passage (see **HWM Example 19.9**).

b. The falling tritone expresses sorrow in the opening fugue.

c. The rapid repeated notes express rage.

E. *Messiah* premiered in 1741.

1. The libretto, taken from the Bible, does not tell a story, but presents a series of contemplations on Christian ideas.
2. The texts extend from the prophecies of a messiah to the resurrection.
3. The music again reflects a mixture of styles.
   a. French overture
   b. Italian recitatives and da capo arias
   c. Germanic choral fugues
   d. English choral anthem style

F. Performances

1. Handel's oratorios were performed in London during Lent.
2. Handel also played organ works at the performances.
3. The chorus and orchestra each numbered about twenty (see **HWM Figure 19.10**).
4. Oratorios needed no staging or costumes.
5. English singers performed the lead roles rather than the more highly paid Italian opera stars.
6. The oratorios appealed to the middle-class public.

XIII. Instrumental Music

A. Handel composed a significant amount of instrumental music, much of it published in London by John Walsh.

B. Among his instrumental chamber works are two collections of harpsichord suites, twenty solo sonatas, and many trio sonatas.

C. Handel's two suites for orchestra are his most popular instrumental works.

1. *Water Music* (1717), three suites for winds and strings, was performed during a royal procession on the River Thames.
2. *Music for the Royal Fireworks* (1749), originally for winds, accompanied a fireworks display in London celebrating the Peace of Aix-la-Chapelle.

D. Handel's concertos represent a mixture of traditions.

1. The six concerto grossi of Op. 3 feature both woodwind and string soloists.
2. He composed the first organ concertos.
3. His most significant concertos are the Twelve Grand Concertos, Op. 6, which reflect the traditions of Corelli.

XIV. Handel's reputation

A. Handel was regarded in England as a national institution.

B. He was buried with honors in Westminster Abbey (see **HWM Figure 19.11**).

C. The lasting appeal of the oratorios makes them some of the earliest pieces by any composer to have an unbroken tradition of performance up to the present time.

## SUGGESTIONS FOR SUPPLEMENTARY READING/LISTENING/ACTIVITIES

Take students on a tour of the monuments editions collection of your library. Explain what BWV and the other catalog abbreviations mean, and show them the corresponding thematic catalogs and other indexes to composers' works (e.g., *The New Grove Dictionary of Music and Musicians*). The commemorative compact disc set *Bach 2000* (Teldec, 2000) is organized according to BWV number and color-coded according to BWV categories. Have students use library resources to look up and report on the works discussed in *HWM* but not included in *NAWM,* such as the Toccata in D Minor (BWV 565).

Several orchestral works by Frederick the Great, including two flute concertos, are available on compact disc (Capriccio 10064, 1994). A Lied by Anna Amalia along with Lieder by other women composers can be heard on the compact disc entitled *Songs of the Classic Age* (Cedille 49, 1999). For more on women composers from this time see *Women Composers: Music through the Ages,* Vol. 3, Composers Born 1700–1799 (New York: G. K. Hall, 1998).

For a thorough treatment of Bach's life and music, refer the students to Christoph Wolff's *Johann Sebastian Bach: The Learned Musician* (New York: W. W. Norton, 2000).

Bach's duties at Leipzig are enumerated in Weiss and Taruskin's *Music in the Western World: A History in Documents* (New York: Schirmer, 1984), 246–248.

Russell Stinson's "Some Thoughts on Bach's Neumeister Chorals" in *The Journal of Musicology* 11 (1993), 455–477, discusses the recent discovery of previously unknown chorales by Bach.

For analysis of individual cantatas, have students read two critical score editions edited by Gerhard Herz: *Cantata No. 4, Christ lag in Todesbanden* (New York: W. W. Norton, 1967) and *Cantata 140, Wachet auf* (New York: W. W. Norton, 1972).

For an interesting discussion of ways in which Bach's theological ideas influenced his works, see Michael Marissen, *Lutheranism, Anti-Judaism, and Bach's St John Passion,* with an annotated literal translation of the libretto (New York: Oxford University Press, 1998). Marissen argues that Bach was not anti-Semitic and that his musical setting and some of his changes to the libretto soften the anti-Semitic tone of the Gospel according to St. John.

For a discussion of temperament, have students read Mark Lindley's article, "Tuning and Intonation," in Howard Mayer Brown and Stanley Sadie, eds., *Performance Practice: Music after 1600* (New York: W. W. Norton, 1989), 169–185.

Use Bach's first cello suite (BWV 1007) to review the standard movements of the Baroque suite and the binary form. It begins with a prelude and has an added movement, but it is otherwise in the standard sequence. Have a student play excerpts from the fifth suite on a keyboard, viola, or cello and then have a discussion of *scordatura* tuning.

Bach's keyboard works have become part of the standard repertory for pianists, even though the works were composed for harpsichord. Compare performances of a Bach work on both instruments. The *Goldberg Variations,* for example, are recorded on piano (Glenn Gould, Sony 37779, 1990) and harpsichord (Scott Ross, Virgin Classics 61869, 2001). Ask the students who prefer the piano to the harpsichord how they feel about performances of these works on synthesizers with added drum tracks. Wendy Carlos's *Switched-On Bach* is available on compact disc (East Side Digital 81602, 2001). Have them discuss the performer's obligation to the composer's intent.

In a similar vein, recordings of *The Art of Fugue* can be found for organ, piano, string quartet, orchestra, and other combinations using the Naxos library (www.naxos.com). Other comparisons might involve recordings for lute and guitar of the lute suites and viola da gamba and cello for the gamba sonatas. Select appropriate students to listen to these recordings and discuss the relative merits and problems of playing music on the intended instruments.

The performance practice movement began with a focus on the music of Bach. Compare any recordings of Bach on modern and original string or wind instruments in class and discuss the issues faced by present-day performers. Among the contrasting performances of the *Brandenburg Concertos* are those by Martin Pearlman (Telarc 80412, 1996), Neville Mariner (Philips 470934, 2002), Trevor Pinnock (Archiv Produktion 423492, 1989), and Niklaus Harnoncourt (Elektra 77611, 1993).

For additional background on Handel, see *The Cambridge Companion to Handel* (New York: Cambridge University Press, 1997).

Many of Handel's operas are available on compact disc. *Serse* (Kultur, 1988) and *Giulio Cesare* (Kultur, 2004) are also available on DVDs.

*Water Music* and *Music for the Royal Fireworks* have been recorded on period instruments (London: L'Oiseau-Lyre 400 059-2, 1984).

Christopher Hogwood and the Academy of Ancient Music have released a historically informed recording of *Messiah* (London: Éditions de L'Oiseau-Lyre, 411 858-2, 1997). Play examples that demonstrate word-painting. Find a recording by a mass choir or another historically inaccurate recording to generate a discussion of performance practice. In particular, note the various treatments of the dotted-rhythms at the beginning of the overture. The issue of overdotting in performance is still debated.

Many recordings of Telemann's music are available. Several by the Musica Antiqua of Cologne are excellent introductions to the music of this prolific and important composer: *Georg Philipp Telemann: Wassermusik* (Archiv Production 413788, 1990) and *Telemann String Concertos* (Archive Production 463074, 2000).

## OBJECTIVE QUESTIONS

1. Frederick the Great regularly performed on the __________.
   a. harpsichord
   b. violin
   c. flute
   d. oboe
   e. organ

   Answer: c

2. Of the following statements, which describes the music of Telemann?
   a. He produced a limited number of compositions.
   b. His music was more popular than that of J. S. Bach.
   c. He composed only in the Italian styles.
   d. He composed instrumental works only.
   e. His music was little known outside of Leipzig.

   Answer: b

3. In which city did Bach primarily compose ensemble music for courtly entertainment?
   a. Weimar

b. Leipzig
c. Arnstadt
d. Mülhausen
e. Cöthen

Answer: e

4. Bach's duties in Leipzig did *not* include __________.
   a. composing cantatas for the two most important local churches
   b. teaching music and Latin to boys in the St. Thomas School
   c. leading an exemplary Christian life
   d. composing music for court entertainments
   e. playing organ

   Answer: d

5. Bach absorbed elements of the Italian style by __________.
   a. studying with Vivaldi
   b. traveling throughout Italy
   c. teaching at a school for orphaned girls in Venice
   d. copying manuscripts of works by Italian composers
   e. reading textbooks

   Answer: d

6. Bach composed music in all but which of the following genres?
   a. opera
   b. cantata
   c. suite
   d. concerto
   e. sonata

   Answer: a

7. Bach's *Orgelbüchlein* contains what type of works?
   a. preludes and fugues
   b. suites
   c. chorale preludes
   d. variations
   e. toccatas

   Answer: c

8. Which publication contains twenty-four preludes and fugues in all of the major and minor keys?
   a. *Well-Tempered Clavier*
   b. *Goldberg Variations*
   c. *Art of Fugue*
   d. *A Musical Offering*
   e. *English Suites*

   Answer: a

9. Which publication uses a theme by Frederick the Great?
   a. *Well-Tempered Clavier*
   b. *Goldberg Variations*
   c. *Art of Fugue*
   d. *A Musical Offering*
   e. *English Suites*

   Answer: d

10. Which of the following statements best describes the soloists in the *Brandenburg Concertos?*
    a. Each concerto features a single soloist.
    b. All of the concertos feature trio sonata textures as in the concertos of Corelli.
    c. There is a wide variety of soloists, often treated in the style of the solo concerto.
    d. There are no soloists in the six concertos.
    e. The soloists are for violins only.

    Answer: c

11. What did Erdmann Neumeister introduce to Lutheran sacred music?
    a. the use of chorale melodies
    b. the use of solo singers and choir
    c. poetic texts that could be used for recitatives and arias
    d. biblical texts
    e. the use of an orchestra

    Answer: c

12. Bach's cantatas usually end with __________.
    a. a Lutheran chorale in four-part harmony
    b. a fugal chorus with full orchestral accompaniment
    c. a dramatic ensemble number involving all the solo singers
    d. a prayer
    e. an organ prelude

    Answer: a

13. Which of the following is *not* true of Bach's Mass in B Minor?
    a. It contains movements adapted from earlier compositions.
    b. It mixes a variety of sacred musical styles.
    c. Bach never heard the work performed in its entirety.
    d. It was written for liturgical services in Leipzig.
    e. It is Bach's only complete setting of the Catholic Mass Ordinary.

    Answer: d

14. Which of the following statements accurately reflects Bach's reputation after his death?
    a. His compositions were not performed until they were revived in the nineteenth century.
    b. His sons kept his memory alive by continuing to compose in their father's style.
    c. There were annual Bach festivals in Weimar and Leipzig, beginning just after his death.
    d. His publishers promoted his music.
    e. All of Bach's music was published within fifty years of his death.

    Answer: a

15. Handel's first London opera was __________.
    a. *Rodelinda*
    b. *Giulio Cesare*
    c. *Almira*
    d. *Agrippina*
    e. *Rinaldo*

    Answer: e

16. The Royal Academy of Music was established in order to __________.
    a. teach music in the manner of the Paris Conservatory
    b. produce Italian opera
    c. promote ballad operas in English
    d. produce oratorios
    e. test the skills of music students

    Answer: b

17. Of the following statements, which characterizes Handel's operas?
    a. simple recitative
    b. ballets
    c. frequent choral writing inspired by English anthem traditions
    d. simple melodic airs
    e. preference for binary arias

    Answer: a

18. What is the language of the oratorios that Handel composed in London?
    a. English
    b. Latin
    c. Italian
    d. German
    e. French

    Answer: a

19. How do Handel's oratorios differ from Italian oratorios?
    a. lack of scenery and costumes
    b. religious subjects rather than stories from antiquity
    c. use of arias and recitatives
    d. extended use of the chorus
    e. no acting

    Answer: d

20. Which composer influenced Handel's Opus 6?
    a. Telemann
    b. Bach
    c. Corelli
    d. Vivaldi
    e. Scarletti

    Answer: c

## SHORT-ESSAY QUESTIONS

1. Discuss how Bach's employment shaped the types of works that he composed.
2. Bach created several major works that were systematic and comprehensive approaches to a medium or a genre. Briefly describe these works and then discuss two of them in detail.
3. Describe how Handel's music can be seen as a synthesis of international musical styles.
4. Compare the recognition of Bach and Handel during their time and in succeeding generations.

## TERMS FOR IDENTIFICATION

Weimar
Cöthen
Leipzig
St. Thomas's School
prelude
chorale prelude
*Orgelbüchlein*
*Well-Tempered Clavier*
*A Musical Offering*
*Art of Fugue*
*Brandenburg Concertos*
collegium musicum
church cantata
Erdmann Neumeister
Mass in B Minor
Hanover
King George I
Royal Academy of Music
King's Theatre in the Haymarket
simple recitative
accompanied recitative
prima donna
coloratura
English oratorio

# CHAPTER 20 Opera and Vocal Music in the Early Classic Period

I. Europe in the Mid- to Late Eighteenth Century
   A. Aspects of eighteenth-century life
      1. Europe was dominated by a number of strong political powers, most notably France, Great Britain, Prussia, Austria-Hungary, and Russia.
      2. Revolutions in America and France had a strong impact on European politics at the end of the century.
      3. Changes in economic conditions resulted in a rising middle class and a lessening of aristocratic power.
      4. Europe enjoyed a cosmopolitan age, due in part to intermarriages of noble families.
      5. A universal musical style emerged that blended features from all nations (see **HWM Source Reading,** page 474).
   B. The Enlightenment
      1. The Enlightenment was an intellectual movement that applied reason to issues of emotions, social relations, and politics.
      2. Beliefs of the Enlightenment
         a. Individual rights
         b. Naturalness
         c. Universal education
         d. Social equality
      3. Social reformers in France were known as *philosophes*.
      4. Ideas of the Enlightenment were incorporated into the founding documents of the United States.
      4. Interest in the welfare of humankind extended to rulers, who oversaw social reform.
      5. An organization devoted to humanitarian ideas and brotherhood known as *Freemasonry* emerged and spread throughout Europe and North America.
      6. The middle class's increased interest in learning and the arts affected writers and artists.
   C. Social roles for music
      1. Public concerts and private teaching provided musicians with methods to supplement their income (see **HWM Innovations,** page 476, and **Figures 20.1** and **20.2**).
      2. A large repertoire of music was composed for amateur musicians to perform at home (see **HWM Figure 20.3**).
      3. Magazines devoted to music began to appear in midcentury.
      4. The first universal histories of music were written.
         a. Charles Burney, *A General History of Music*
         b. John Hawkins, *A General History of the Science and Practice of Music*
         c. Johann Nicolaus Forkel, *Allgemeine Geschichte der Musik*

II. Musical Taste and Style
   A. Musical styles in the mid- and late eighteenth century
      1. Various musical styles coexisted, including the traditional Baroque style and newer styles.
      2. Contemporary critics developed a number of new values.
         a. Composers should avoid contrapuntal complexity.
         b. Melodies should contain short phrases and have simple accompaniments.

c. The language of music should be international.
d. Music should appeal to all tastes.
e. Music should be natural and immediately pleasing.

B. Terms for styles
1. Galant
a. Galant was a term for everything modern and sophisticated.
b. Melodies built from repeated motives and short phrases were emphasized.
c. Phrases were combined into larger periods.
d. The harmony was simple with frequent cadences.
e. Galant style became the foundation for music of the mid- to late eighteenth century (see **HWM Source Reading,** page 481).
2. Empfindsam style ("sentimental style")
a. Empfindsam style originated in Italy, but it is most closely associated with C. P. E. Bach.
b. It was characterized by surprising turns of harmony, chromaticism, and speechlike melodies.
3. Classical
a. "Classical" music sometimes refers to art music of all ages, and sometimes it specifies the music of the late eighteenth century.
b. The narrowest definition denotes the style associated with the mature music of Haydn and Mozart.
c. The term was applied to music as an analogy to Greek and Roman art.
d. The Classic Period in music is approximately 1730 to 1815.

III. Qualities of the Classical Style
A. Melody
1. Baroque phrasing
a. Baroque melodies were spun out of a single melodic-rhythmic subject.
b. Baroque melodies embodied a single affection.
c. Sequential repetition of phrases with infrequent cadences resulted in integrated movements without sharp contrasts.
2. Periodicity
a. The new melodic style broke up the melodic flow with a succession of short distinct phrases of two to four measures in length.
b. A period, consisting of two or more phrases, formed a complete musical thought.
c. This melodic style is characterized by frequent cadences.
d. Principles of rhetoric and grammar were applied to music, as described by Heinrich Christoph Koch in *Versuch einer Anleitung zur Composition* (see **HWM Example 20.1**).

B. Harmony
1. A hierarchy of cadences developed; the strongest cadences mark the end of a period or of sections and movements.
2. Harmonic movement, such as I–V–I, can be observed as a simple chord progression and as large-scale harmonic schemes.
3. Harmonic movement was slower than in the Baroque era.
4. The *Alberti bass* set chords in repeating patterns to animate harmonies without distracting from melodies (see **HWM Example 20.2**).

C. Distinctions between beginning, middle, and ending gestures allowed composers to communicate location in the musical form.

D. Emotional contrasts
1. In the Baroque era, strong and invariable states of affection were thought to dominate human emotions.
2. Deeper knowledge of blood circulation, the nervous system, and human physiology suggested that emotional states were constantly changing.
3. The music of the classic era began to incorporate contrasting moods rather than projecting a single affection.

IV. Italian Comic Opera
A. Stylistic features of Classic-era music first appeared in Italian opera in the 1720s.
1. Comic opera was most open to the new stylistic trends.
2. Both comic and serious opera emphasized beautiful melodies and used music to show changing emotions.

B. Opera buffa
1. Italian comic opera is known as *opera buffa,* although *dramma giocossa, dramma comico,* and *commedia per musica* were also used at the time.
2. General characteristics
a. A full-length work that was sung throughout
b. Six or more characters
c. Plots caricatured the faults of both aristocrats and commoners.

d. Characters often resembled the stock characters of the *commedia dell'arte*.
e. Dialogue was set in rapidly delivered recitative with continuo.

3. Arias
    a. Short tuneful phrases accompanied by simple harmonies
    b. Da capo forms
    c. Example: *T'aggio mmidea* from *Le zite 'ngalera* (The Spinsters in the Galley) by Leonardo Vinci (see **HWM Example 20.3**)

C. Intermezzo
1. This genre originated as a short, comic, musical interlude between the acts of a serious opera or play (see **HWM Figure 20.4**).
2. Plots were mostly comedies involving ordinary people, sometimes parodying the excesses of serious opera.
3. Most have only two singing roles and incorporate bass voice.
4. The music alternated recitative and arias.
5. *La serva padronna* by Giovanni Battista Pergolesi (1710–1736)
    a. The composer died young from tuberculosis.
    b. There are only three characters, one of whom is mute.
    c. The plot questions the social hierarchy.

D. *La serva padronna*, excerpt (see **NAWM 93** and **HWM Example 20.4**)
1. Recitative section
    a. The opening conversation is set in the standard simple recitative.
    b. As Uberto doubts his actions with Serpina, the orchestra punctuates his thoughts; accompanied recitative is reserved for the most dramatic moments in opera seria.
    c. The harmonies modulate rapidly, suggesting Uberto's changing thoughts.
2. Aria
    a. Da capo form
    b. A ritornello frames the A section.
    c. The A section has two complete statements of poetic text.
    d. The B section has new text, keys, and musical ideas.
    e. The music projects contrasting moods, unlike Baroque arias.

E. Later comic opera
1. Dramatist Carlo Goldoni introduced serious and sentimental elements.
2. *La buona figliuola* (The Good Girl) by Niccolo Piccinni is an example.
3. Italian comic opera introduced ensemble finales in which all the characters are gradually brought on stage.

V. Opera Seria

A. The simple melodic style of opera buffa was assimilated into opera seria—serious Italian opera.

B. The poet Pietro Metastasio (1698–1782) established the form of opera seria.
1. Composers throughout the century set librettos by Metastasio.
2. His librettos were produced in Naples, Rome, Venice, and Vienna.
3. He sought to promote morality through entertainment by portraying heroic characters from ancient Greek or Roman stories.
4. The conventional cast consists of two pairs of lovers and other characters.
5. Stories usually end with a heroic deed or a magnanimous gesture by a principal character.
6. The story is presented in three acts.

C. The music alternates recitatives and arias.
1. Recitatives develop the action through dialogue.
    a. Most of the dialogue is set with simple recitative.
    b. The most dramatic moments use accompanied recitative.
2. Arias are soliloquies in which a principal actor reacts to events.
3. Occasionally there are duets, larger ensembles, and choruses.
4. The role of the orchestra, which was minimal outside of the overture, would expand during the century.

D. Arias were generally in da capo form with variations in detail.
1. Metastasio's two-stanza texts set the standard for the 1720s–1740s.
2. First A section of the da capo aria
    a. The opening ritornello announces the melodic material.
    b. The first vocal statement presents the main idea in the tonic and then modulates to the dominant or related key.
    c. A short ritornello follows.
    d. The second vocal statement, which repeats the first stanza of text, starts in the dominant or related key and ends in the tonic with a florid passage.
3. The B section
    a. Heard only once, this section uses the second stanza of text.

b. Syllabic text-setting is typical, often with light accompaniment.
c. This section may be in a different tempo, meter, or key.

4. The return of the A section
   a. The vocal material of the A section is repeated with embellishments.
   b. The omission of the ritornello, indicated by a sign and the words *dal segno,* could shorten the aria's length.
5. New features in aria forms
   a. The A sections included contrasting moods, often in two keys.
   b. Melodies used four-measure antecedent and consequent phrases, deviating for effect.

E. Johann Adolf Hasse (1699–1783) was the master of opera seria (see **HWM Figure 20.5**).
1. He spent many years in Italy and worked at the court of the elector of Saxony in Dresden.
2. He was the most popular and successful opera composer in Europe in the middle of the century.
3. Most of his operas use Metastasio librettos.
4. *Cleofide* was composed for Hasse's wife, Faustina Bordoni, a professional singer (see **NAWM 94** and **HWM Figure 20.6**).
   a. The da capo aria has contrasting ideas and short phrases.
   b. In the A section, the first vocal statement modulates to the dominant, and the second modulates back to the tonic, E major.
   c. The B section changes to E minor and has a faster triple meter.
   d. An ornamented version of this melody is in **HWM Example 20.5.**

VI. Opera in Other Languages

A. Opera outside of Italy
1. Opera seria maintained its character when performed in other countries.
2. Comic opera reflected local influences.
   a. Set in native language
   b. Music accentuated national musical idioms.
3. Historical significance of comic opera
   a. It was a vehicle for simple, natural singing.
   b. It encouraged the growth of national operatic traditions.

B. France
1. *Querelle des bouffons* (Quarrel of the Comic Actors) was a pamphlet war beginning in 1752 that argued the relative merits of French and Italian opera.
   a. The issue involved nearly every intellectual in France.
   b. The debate was sparked by the presence of an Italian opera troupe in Paris that performed, among other works, Pergolesi's *La serva padronna.*
2. Jean-Jacques Rousseau (1712–1778)
   a. Rousseau praised the emphasis on natural melodies in Italian opera.
   b. He composed an opera, *Le Devin du village* (The Village Soothsayer, 1752), using the melodic style of Italian opera (see **HWM Example 20.6**).
3. Opéra comique
   a. French comic opera, called *opéra comique,* began around 1710 and used simple popular tunes known as *vaudevilles.*
   b. Simple airs, or *ariettes,* inspired by the Italian style, began to appear after 1750.
   c. Opéra comique used spoken dialogue rather than recitative.
   d. By the end of the eighteenth century, serious plots based on social issues were introduced into the operatic genre.
   e. *Richard Coeur-de-Lion* (Richard the Lion-Hearted, 1784) by Grétry sparked a vogue for rescue plots, which influenced Beethoven's *Fidelio.*

C. England
1. *Ballad opera* was the name for the popular opera in England.
   a. Set in English, ballad operas used spoken dialogue.
   b. Initially, the songs were borrowed popular tunes with new words, but later new songs were composed.
   c. Ballad opera peaked in the 1730s and remained influential for decades in Britain and America.
2. *The Beggar's Opera* (1728) by John Gay and Johann Pepusch
   a. The enormous popularity of this ballad opera established the genre.
   b. The play satirizes London society and the conventions of opera seria (see **HWM Figure 20.7**).
   c. The original orchestration includes violins, but the music survives only with basso continuo realization.

D. *The Beggar's Opera*, excerpt from Scene 13 (**NAWM 95**)
1. In this scene, Macheath is fleeing from the law and hiding in Polly's room.

2. Both borrowed melodies are from Henry Playford's *Pills to Purge Melancholy*.
3. *My heart was so free/It roved like a bee* is sung by Macheath.
   a. The song parodies the simile aria of Baroque operas (a predicament is described through comparison).
   b. The words are sung to the melody of *Come fair one be kind,* a courting song.
   c. The tune has a jig character and is in binary form.
4. *Were I laid on Greenland's coast*
   a. This is based on the tune *O'er the hills, and far away*, which is suggested in Polly's text.
   b. The duet is a verse-refrain form of a traditional song.
   c. The tune is modal, in C Dorian.

E. Germany and Austria
1. Serious German opera appeared in the seventeenth and eighteenth centuries.
2. German comic opera, called *Singspiel*, first appeared in Vienna in the 1710s.
   a. Singspiel ("singing play") features spoken dialogue, musical numbers, and a comic plot.
   b. English ballad opera exerted a strong influence.
   c. Its principal composer was Johann Adam Hiller (1728–1804).
   d. In northern Germany, Singspiel merged with more serious opera.
   e. Audiences in Vienna preferred farcical subjects with lively music inspired by Italian comic opera.

VII. Opera Reform
A. Beginnings
1. Some opera composers, librettists, and patrons wanted opera to be more natural.
   a. They wanted more flexibility in recitatives and arias in order to make the action more natural.
   b. They used the orchestra more and reinstated choruses.
   c. They resisted the demands of singers.
   d. Francesco Algarotti articulated these ideals in *An Essay on the Opera* (1755).
2. Opera composers Nicolò Jommelli (1714–1774) and Tommaso Traetta (1727–1779) were important figures in the reform.
   a. Both worked where French tastes were predominant.
   b. Jommelli's works provided models for later opera seria.
   c. Traetta aimed to combine the best of French *tragédie en musique* and Italian opera and borrowed material from Rameau.

B. Christoph Willibald Gluck (1714–1787) (see **HWM Figure 20.8**)
1. Born to Bohemian parents, Gluck traveled throughout Europe.
2. He was influenced by the Italian reform movement and vowed to purge Italian opera of it abuses and excesses.
   a. He did not want singers' wishes or the da capo form to restrict the composer.
   b. He wanted the overture to be an integral part of the opera.
   c. He lessened the contrast between recitative and aria.
   d. His goal was to create music of "a beautiful simplicity."
3. *Orfeo ed Euridice* (1762)
   a. The poet Raniero de Calzabigi supplied the libretto.
   b. As in with *Alceste*, *Orfeo* molds the music to the drama.
4. Gluck believed that the French language could be used successfully in opera.
   a. *Iphigénie en Aulide* (Iphigenia in Aulis, 1774) is based on a French libretto and was a tremendous success in Paris.
   b. Gluck revised *Orfeo* and *Alceste* with French texts and continued to compose other French operas that became models for later composers.

C. *Orfeo ed Euridice*, Act II, Scene I opening (**NAWM 96**)
1. Two orchestras are used, one of which is for plucked strings imitating the sound of Orfeo's lyre.
2. Dissonances and diminished chords create the sense of terror.
3. The ballet of the Furies
   a. The dance quickly modulates to C minor through chromaticism.
   b. The dance is central to the story, unlike the ballets in French opera.
4. Orfeo's song to the Furies
   a. Simple melody, sparse embellishment, and economy of material
   b. The melody has simple phrases.
   c. The Furies periodically respond with "No."
5. The role of Orfeo was originally written for castrato, but is today sung by a male countertenor or a female mezzosoprano.

VIII. Song and Church Music
   A. Reflecting the growth of amateur music, songs were composed in many nations.
      1. Songs tended to be strophic.
      2. Melodies were simple, syllabic, and diatonic.
      3. The accompaniment, usually for keyboard, was easy enough to be played by the singer.
      4. The romance, a common song type in France, featured a simple expressive melody and a sentimental text.
      5. In Britain, ballads were printed with texts only and then sung to a familiar tune.
      6. A fashion for Scottish and Irish folksongs developed at the end of the century.
   B. The Lied (German song) achieved a special artistic importance.
      1. Over 750 collections of Lieder were published in the second half of the century.
      2. Lieder tended to be strophic, easy to sing, and supported by a subordinate accompaniment.
      3. Lieder composition was particularly strong with North German composers, including Telemann, C. P. E. Bach, and Carl Heinrich Graun.
      4. Johann Friedrich Reichardt (1752–1814) incorporated more flexible forms and greater independence for the accompaniment, as seen in *Erlkönig* (The Erl-King, 1794), **HWM Example 20.7.**
   C. Church music maintained traditional styles or adapted prevailing secular styles.
      1. Catholic music
         a. A few composers continued to compose in the *stile antico* of Palestrina and the polychoral style of Benevoli.
         b. The leading composers of sacred music were also opera composers.
         c. Italian oratorios were almost indistinguishable from operas in style.
      2. Lutheran music
         a. Rejecting the elaborate chorale-based compositions, services centered on hymns in the new galant style.
         b. The oratorio was composed in North Germany, such as *Der Tod Jesu* (The Death of Jesus, 1755) by Carl Heinrich Graun.
      3. England
         a. The Baroque style was prevalent in sacred music, largely due to the influence of Handel.
         b. Leading sacred composers included William Boyce, Maurice Green, John Stanley, and Charles Avison.
   D. Sacred music in the New World
      1. Sacred music in European settlements tended to reflect the national styles of the émigrés.
      2. In New England, Calvinists sang metric psalms, some of which were published in the *Bay Psalm Book* (1640).
         a. The first edition had psalms without notated music.
         b. The ninth edition (1698) included thirteen melodies.
      3. In the eighteenth century, singing schools trained amateurs to sing psalms and anthems in parts.
      4. William Billings (1746–1800) wrote over 340 pieces.
         a. Almost all of the works are sacred for unaccompanied four-part choir on newly composed melodies, such as *Chester.*
         b. Most were harmonized hymn tunes called *plain tunes.*
         c. He also wrote about fifty anthems and fifty-one fuging tunes, which use imitation in the middles sections and unconventional voice leading.
         d. Two of his collections are *The New-England Psalm-Singer* (1770) and *The Continental Harmony* (1794).
      5. *Creation* (see **NAWM 97** and **HWM Figure 20.9**)
         a. This is a fuging tune from *The Continental Harmony.*
         b. The first half of the piece is homophonic and syllabic.
         c. The second half, the fuging portion, is imitative.
         d. Homophony returns at the end.
         e. The principal melody is in the tenor line.
         f. Parallel fifths and octaves suggest Billings's lack of training.
      6. Other contributors to Yankee tunebooks include Daniel Read and Andrew Law.
      7. Moravians were German-speaking Protestants from Moravia and Bohemia who settled in Pennsylvania and North Carolina.
         a. They sang concerted arias and motets in their church services and imported music from Europe.
         b. Among the leading Moravian composers are Johannes Herbst, Johann Friedrich Peter, and John Antes.
         c. Moravians collected music libraries and regularly played chamber music and symphonies by European composers.

## SUGGESTIONS FOR SUPPLEMENTARY READING/LISTENING/ACTIVITIES

For translations of numerous primary sources from this period, see Wye Jamison Allanbrook, ed., *Source Readings in Music History,* rev. ed., Vol. 5: The Late Eighteenth Century (New York: W. W. Norton, 1998). Particularly useful as additional reading for this chapter are the excerpts in the section titled "Expression and Sensibility."

For selected readings on eighteenth-century aesthetics with commentary, see Piero Weiss and Richard Taruskin, eds., *Music in the Western World: A History in Documents* (New York: Schirmer Books, 1984), 287–98.

Have students discuss the relative merits of complexity and simplicity in music from the Baroque and early Classic eras and from our own time.

Pergolesi's *La serva padrona* is available on compact disc (Accent Records 96123, 1999) and in a VHS format directed by Sigiswald Kuijken (Allegro Video, 2000).

Piccinni's *La buona figliuola* is available on compact disc (Bongiovanni 2293, 2001), and a score is published by *I Classici Musicali Italiani,* vol. 7 (Verona, 1942). Have students look at the ensemble finales in preparation for their study of the opera buffas by Mozart.

Hasse's *Cleofide* is available on compact disc (Capriccio 10193, 1995).

Have students review and then debate the two positions of the *Querelle des bouffons*.

*Le Devin du village* is available in score edited by Deborah Lemon for *Recent Researches in the Music of the Classical Era,* 50 (Madison, WI: A-R Editions, 1998), and on compact disc (Nuova Era, 7335, 1999).

Have students select an excerpt from *The Beggar's Opera,* perform it, and describe its social significance in terms of Enlightenment ideals. The work is available in score (Jeremy Barlow, ed., *The Music of John Gay's The Beggar's Opera* [New York: Oxford University Press, 1990]) and on compact discs (EMI Silver Doubles, CD-CFPSD 4778, 1995 and London: Hyperion Records, CDA66591-CDA66592, 1991). The performance described in the anthology with Roger Daltry is available on VHS (Kultur Video, 1997).

Gluck's *Orfeo ed Euridice* is available on compact disc (Teldec 4509-98418-2, 1996; and Harmonia Mundi 901742, 2001) and DVD (Kultur, 2004).

Assign a paper comparing and contrasting parallel scenes from Gluck's *Orfeo ed Euridice* and Monteverdi's *Orfeo*. For an analysis of both works, have them read Chapter 2 "Orpheus: The Neoclassic Vision" in Joseph Kerman, *Opera as Drama* (Berkeley: University of California Press, 1988), 18–38.

The full text of the preface to Gluck's *Alceste,* the manifesto for his operatic reforms, is found in Wye Jamison Allenbrook, ed., *Source Readings in Music History,* rev. ed. Vol. 5: The Late Eighteenth Century (New York: W. W. Norton, 1998), 198–200. Have students read this preface and then read Marcello's *Teatro alla moda* in the translation by Reinhard G. Pauly, *Musical Quarterly* 34 (1948): 371–403 and 35 (1949): 80–105, and prepare a list of the abuses that Marcello satirizes. To which of these problems did Gluck object? What were his solutions? *Alceste* is available on compact disc (Naxos 660066, 1999) and DVD (Image Entertainment, 2001). Have students listen to excerpts and compare them to *Orfeo*. How effective is Gluck at putting his theories into practice?

Have a student locate the reproduction of Reichardt's published score to *Erlkönig*, found in *Göthe's Lieder, Oden, Balladen, und Romanzen mit Musik von J. F. Reichardt* (Breitkopf und Härtel, reissued in 1969). Discuss how the structure of the poem remains intact and how Reichardt expressively uses and expands upon the strophic form. Compare this song to the later version by Schubert.

Have the students sing Billing's *Chester*. Listen to a recording of the setting of this tune by William Schuman for wind symphony in *New England Triptych*. How does Schuman retain the sense of colonial times in his arrangement? The complete works of William Billings can be found in many libraries.

Several recordings of Moravian music are available on compact disc, including *Lost Music of Early America* (Telarc 80482, 1998) and *Music for All Seasons* performed by a trombone ensemble (Crystal Records 220, 1995). Have a low-brass student research and report upon the use of trombones by Moravians.

## OBJECTIVE QUESTIONS

1. Which of the following was *not* part of the Enlightenment movement?
   a. a belief that reasoning could be applied to social issues
   b. a belief that religion should govern public morality
   c. a belief that the state should improve the human condition
   d. reverence for nature and naturalness
   e. a belief that individuals had rights

   Answer: b

2. Of the following, which describes concert life in the late eighteenth century?
   a. Courts and churches no longer sponsored performances.
   b. All professional performances were opened up to female musicians.
   c. Technical demands of music relegated the amateur to a mere listener of music.
   d. Public concerts became more important.
   e. Choral music was restricted to churches.

   Answer: d

3. Of the following, which was a prevailing musical value in the late eighteenth century?
   a. Music should have contrapuntal complexity.
   b. Music should emphasize vocally conceived melodies with short phrases.
   c. Music should aim at the tastes of the connoisseur only.
   d. Music should be a vehicle for virtuosity.
   e. Music should reflect only one affect.

   Answer: b

4. Of the following, which describes the galant style?
   a. originated in German Lieder
   b. emphasized spun-out melodies
   c. featured simple harmonies and accompaniments
   d. was considered to be a learned style
   e. featured frequent imitative counterpoint

   Answer: c

5. Which of the following does *not* characterize the classical style?
   a. a single emotional mood projected in each movement
   b. periodic melodies
   c. slow harmonic movement
   d. differentiation of musical material according to its function
   e. frequent cadences

   Answer: a

6. Which of the following characterizes a typical opera buffa?
   a. three acts
   b. characters drawn from Antiquity
   c. tuneful arias with short, periodic phrases
   d. accompanied recitative
   e. a plot that caricatured the faults of commoners only

   Answer: c

7. What is the name of the musical entertainment performed between the acts of a serious opera or play?
   a. dramma comico
   b. commedia per musica
   c. intermezzo
   d. interlude
   e. dramma giocoso

   Answer: c

8. Which of the following was an important contribution of opera buffa?
   a. ensemble finales
   b. expanded role for chorus
   c. virtuosic singing
   d. large orchestral role
   e. mixture of arias and recitative

   Answer: a

Use the following answers for questions 9–12.
   a. Pergolesi
   b. Hasse
   c. Gluck
   d. Metastasio
   e. Goldoni

9. He was the master of opera seria.

   Answer: b

10. This poet's librettos established opera seria traditions.

    Answer: d

11. He composed *La serva padronna.*

    Answer: a

12. He introduced refinements into the comic-opera libretto.

    Answer: e

13. Of the following, which is a characteristic of opera seria?
    a. five acts
    b. comic scenes mixed with serious ones
    c. plots drawn from recent history
    d. frequent duets
    e. frequent da capo arias

    Answer: e

14. The *Querelle des bouffons* was a dispute about ___________.
    a. the relative merits of French and Italian opera
    b. the relative merits of strict counterpoint and the galant style
    c. the relative merits of the operas of Lully and Rameau
    d. the role of comedy in opera
    e. the financial support of opera

    Answer: a

15. Of the following, which characterizes opéra comique?
    a. simple melodies called ariettes
    b. simple recitative
    c. ballet
    d. chorus
    e. three acts

    Answer: a

16. Of the following, which characterizes the operas of Jommelli and Traetta?
    a. limited orchestral role
    b. expanded role for the chorus
    c. spoken dialogue
    d. da capo arias only
    e. avoidance of French characteristics

    Answer: b

17. Of the following, which is *not* a belief of Gluck?
    a. The demands of soloists should not affect opera composition.
    b. The French language could be used effectively in opera.
    c. Recitative and aria should be less distinct.
    d. The overture should be an integral part of the opera.
    e. Music should assimilate learned complexities.

    Answer: e

18. Of the following, who was *not* known as a composer of Lieder?
    a. Telemann
    b. Reichardt
    c. C. P. E. Bach
    d. J. S. Bach
    e. Carl Heinrich Graun

    Answer: d

19. Which of the following religions adapted church music to the style of opera?
    a. Catholic
    b. Lutheran
    c. Anglican
    d. Calvinism
    e. Buddhism

    Answer: a

20. What was the primary type of sacred music in New England during the colonial period?
    a. anthem
    b. psalm-setting
    c. cantata
    d. polyphonic mass
    e. oratorio

    Answer: b

## SHORT-ESSAY QUESTIONS

1. Discuss how the goals and values of the Enlightenment are reflected in the music of the Classic era.
2. Compare the role of affect in the Baroque and the early Classic periods.
3. Compare the comic opera genres of Italy, France, Germany, and England.
4. Describe how the opera reform movement changed the style of opera seria.

## TERMS FOR IDENTIFICATION

Enlightenment
philosophes
Charles Burney
galant style
empfindsam style
classical style
periodicity
Heinrich Christoph Koch
Alberti bass
opera buffa
Leonardo Vinci
intermezzo
Giovanni Battista Pergolesi
Carlo Goldoni
Niccolò Piccinni
opera seria
Pietro Metastasio
da capo aria
Johann Adolf Hasse
Fautina Bordoni
*Querelle des bouffons*
Jean-Jacques Rousseau
opéra comique
ballad opera
Singspiel
Nicolò Jommelli
Tommaso Traetta
Christoph Willibald Gluck
Raniero de Calzabigi
romance
ballad
Lied
*Bay Psalm Book*
*The Continental Harmony*
William Billings
fuging tunes
Moravians

CHAPTER 21

# Instrumental Music: Sonata, Symphony, and Concerto at Midcentury

I. Instruments and Ensembles
  A. Rise of instrumental music
    1. The new musical style in opera was adapted for instrumental works.
    2. Instrumental music became more independent and gained prominence.
    3. Important developments
      a. The piano replaced the harpsichord and clavichord.
      b. The string quartet was developed for social music-making.
      c. The sonata became the leading genre for solo and chamber music.
      d. The concerto and symphony dominated orchestral music.
      e. Sonata form emerged as an important new structure.
  B. Roles of instrumental music
    1. Much music was written for the enjoyment of the players, to be performed either alone or in a social function.
    2. Professional musicians performed at dinners and parties.
    3. Orchestras, both amateur and professional, gave concerts.
    4. Music accompanied social dancing.
  C. The piano
    1. The harpsichord and clavichord continued to be played into the nineteenth century, but the piano was dominant in the late eighteenth century.
    2. Bartolomeo Cristofori invented the piano in Florence in 1700.
      a. In the piano, hammers strike the strings.
      b. This mechanism allows the performer to change dynamics.
    3. Two types of pianos were created: the grand piano, which is shaped like the harpsichord, and the square piano (see **HWM Figures 21.1** and **21.2**).
    4. Eighteenth-century pianos are often called *fortepianos* to distinguish them from later models.
  D. Chamber ensembles
    1. Music for melody instruments and keyboard
      a. Much music was composed for melody instruments and basso continuo.
      b. In music in which the keyboard part is written out, the keyboard part tends to dominate.
      c. Women often performed the keyboard parts.
    2. Music for string ensembles without keyboard
      a. Ensembles for two to five string performers were common.
      b. The string quartet for two violins, viola, and cello became dominant.
      c. Quartets were primarily composed for the enjoyment of the performers and their companions (see **HWM Figure 21.3**).
    3. Wind instruments and ensembles
      a. The clarinet was invented around 1710, joining the flute, oboe, and bassoon as the principal woodwind instruments.
      b. Ensembles of wind instruments were common in France.
      c. By midcentury, the combination of oboes, clarinets, horns, and bassoons was common (see **HWM Figure 21.4**).

d. Amateurs tended not to play wind instruments other than the flute.

E. Orchestra

1. The concert orchestra of the eighteenth century was smaller than today's.
2. Clarinets were added to the orchestra near the end of the century.
3. The basso continuo was gradually abandoned.
4. The leader of the violins tended to be the conductor.
5. Typically, the strings played the essential material in an orchestral piece, but gradually wind instruments became more prominent.

II. Genres and Forms

A. Genres of the Classic era

1. Numerous Baroque genres fell out of fashion, including preludes, toccatas, fugues, fantasias, and keyboard dances.
2. The sonata in three and four movements became a major genre.
3. Chamber ensembles, also with multiple movements, were named according to the number of musicians playing, such as a duet or trio.
4. Orchestral music
   a. The concerto was an extension of the Baroque solo concerto.
   b. The symphony emerged from the Italian opera *sinfonia* or overture.
5. Compositions with three movements tended to be fast–slow–fast.
6. Compositions with four movements added a minuet before or after the slow movement.

B. Sonata form

1. The first movement of a sonata, chamber work, or symphony from the classic period is usually in sonata form (or first-movement form).
2. In the eighteenth century, sonata form was seen as a two-part structure, but nineteenth-century theorists described it in three (see **HWM Figure 21. 5**).
3. In the last volume of *Introductory Essay on Composition* (1793), Koch divides sonata form into two large sections, each of which may be repeated.
   a. The first section is organized into four phrases.
      (1) The first two phrases are in the tonic.
      (2) The third phrase modulates to the dominant or relative major.
      (3) The fourth phrase is in the new key.
   b. The second section has two principal periods.
      (1) The first consists of any number of phrases and moves back to the tonic.
      (2) The second parallels the first section, but the third and fourth phrases remain in the original key.
   c. Koch describes sonata form as a set of principles, not as a rigid mold.
   d. The Koch model is best seen in compositions before 1780.
4. Sonata form by the 1830s
   a. The exposition, which is usually repeated, contains four sections.
      (1) The first theme group in the tonic
      (2) A transition to the dominant or relative major
      (3) A second theme group in the new key
      (4) A closing theme in the new key
   b. The development presents themes from the exposition and modulates to new and sometimes remote keys.
   c. The recapitulation restates material from the exposition in the original order, but in the tonic.
   d. There may be a slow introduction before the exposition and a coda after the recapitulation.
   e. This description is best suited to sonata forms created after 1800.
5. After 1780, composers began to omit the repetition of the second half.

C. Other forms can be observed in sonatas, chamber works, and symphonies.

1. The slow-movement sonata form follows the Koch model, but has no repeats and omits the first period of the second section.
2. Variations form often presents a small binary form theme followed by variants.
3. The minuet and trio form joins two binary-form minuets in an ABA pattern.
4. The rondo form is common for last movements.
   a. The principal theme is a small binary form or a single period.
   b. The principal theme alternates with episodes, which are often in other keys.
   c. Common patterns are ABACA or ABACADA.

III. Keyboard Music

A. Composers created a large number of keyboard works in the middle and late eighteenth century.

1. Sonatas were regarded as the most challenging.
2. Other works include rondos, variations, and minuets.

B. Domenico Scarlatti (1685–1757)
    1. Son of Alessandro Scarlatti (see **HWM Figure 21.6**)
    2. Left Italy in 1719 to work for the king of Portugal
    3. Moved to Madrid in 1729 and served the Spanish court the rest of his life
    4. Scarlatti's sonatas
        a. He composed 555 sonatas, thirty of which were published in 1738 under the title *Essercizi* (Exercises).
        b. Scarlatti used a rounded binary form that bears some similarities to Koch's first-movement form.
        c. Striking features include the harmony and the spinning-out of motives.
    5. Sonata in D Major, K. 119 (**NAWM 98** and **HWM Example 21.1**)
        a. Rounded binary form
        b. After the opening tonic, a new phrase imitates the sound of castanets.
        c. A new theme in the minor dominant follows the modulation.
        d. Scarlatti builds to a climax with trills and growing dissonance that includes chords of five and six notes.
        e. The total effect suggests the sound of a Spanish guitar.
        f. Other typical features include wide leaps and hand-crossing.

C. Carl Philipp Emanuel Bach (1714–88)
    1. The son of J. S. Bach, he studied with his father and became one of the most influential composers of his time (see **HWM Figure 21.7**).
    2. He served in the court of Frederick the Great from 1740 to 1768.
    3. He became music director of the five principal churches in Hamburg.
    4. His most numerous and important works are for keyboard.
    5. He wrote a valuable treatise on performance practice entitled *Essay on the True Art of Playing Keyboard Instruments* (1753–62).
    6. Keyboard sonatas
        a. Bach preferred the clavichord for its delicate dynamic shadings.
        b. He published eight sets of six sonatas and five sets of sonatas with other keyboard works.
        c. The first two sets, called the *Prussian* (1742) and *Würtenberg* sonatas (1744), were influential.
        d. Many of his slow movements exemplify empfindsam style.
    7. The fourth sonata of *Sechs Clavier-Sonaten für Kenner und Liebhaber* (Six Clavier Sonatas for Connoisseurs and Amateurs, composed in 1765 and published in 1779), second movement (**NAWM 99**)
        a. The movement features an expressive melody in short phrases.
        b. The binary form can be described as sonata form without development.
        c. The music projects a restless quality (see **HWM Example 21.2**).
        d. Bach also exploits the element of surprise with unexpected turns.
        e. Passages in dialogue or recitative style add to the emotionality.

IV. Orchestral Music

A. The origin of the symphony was in Italy.
    1. The name comes from *sinfonia,* the Italian opera overture.
    2. The early sinfonia developed a three-movement structure.
        a. The first movement was allegro.
        b. The second movement was a short lyrical andante.
        c. The finale used dance rhythms, such as a minuet or gigue.
    3. There are other influences on the early symphony.
        a. Orchestral concertos of Torelli
        b. Church sonatas in northern Italy
        c. Orchestral suite

B. Giovanni Battista Sammartini (ca. 1700–1775) was the first prominent composer of symphonies (see **HWM Figure 21.8**).
    1. He was active in northern Italy.
    2. Symphony in F Major, No. 32 (ca. 1740), first movement (see **NAWM 100** and **HWM Example 21.3**)
        a. The symphony is scored for four-part strings and probably harpsichord.
        b. It has three movements (fast–slow–fast), each of which is relatively short.
        c. The movement is in binary form and follows Koch's description of symphonic first movements.
        d. Each half is repeated, and the material heard in the dominant in the first half is repeated in the tonic in the second half.

C. Mannheim was one of the most prominent centers of symphonies in Europe.
    1. The Mannheim orchestra was famous for its discipline and technique.

2. Johann Stamitz (1717–1757) was the leader of the orchestra.
   a. Stamitz is the first composer to use consistently the four-movement structure.
   b. He also used a full contrasting theme after the modulation in the first section of an allegro movement.
3. Sinfonia in E-flat Major (mid-1750s, **NAWM 101**)
   a. The work was published in *La melodia germanica* (1758), a collection of symphonies by several composers.
   b. The symphony has four movements.
   c. The work is scored for strings and two oboes and two horns.
   d. The first movement follows the Koch model, but on a large scale.
   e. The transition exploits the famous Mannheim crescendo.
   f. The move to the dominant is highlighted by a lyric and graceful new melody.
   g. Following the development, the recapitulation begins with the second theme.

D. Vienna and Paris were also active centers for symphony composition.
1. Georg Wagenseil (1715–1777) wrote symphonies using contrasting theme groups in Vienna.
2. Paris was an important center of composition and publication.
3. François-Joseph Gossec (1734–1829) was one of the leading composers of symphonies in France.
4. The *symphonie concertante* developed in France around 1770.
   a. The new genre combined orchestral sonorities with virtuoso solos.
   b. The soloists, generally two or more, come from the orchestra.

E. The concerto remained a popular genre throughout the Classic era.
1. Johann Christian Bach (1735–82) was among the first to compose piano concertos.
   a. He was the youngest son of J. S. Bach (see **HWM Figure 21.9**).
   b. He moved to London in 1762 and worked as a composer, performer, teacher, and impresario; he was known as "the London Bach."
   c. His works are largely in the galant style.
   d. He was a major influence on the young Mozart.
2. Concertos continued to be set with three movements.
3. The first movement of the classical concerto combines the ritornello structure of the baroque era with aspects of sonata form.
4. The first movement of J. C. Bach's Concerto for Harpsichord or Piano in E-flat Major (**NAWM 102**) illustrates this fusion (see **HWM Figure 21.10**).
   a. The movement is framed by ritornellos.
   b. The first ritornello presents the principal themes in the tonic key.
   c. The three episodes function as exposition, development, and recapitulation.
5. The soloist traditionally improvises a cadenza in the first movement just before the final orchestral ritornello.
   a. An orchestral 6/4 chord introduces the cadenza.
   b. The soloist signals the end of the cadenza with a trill over a dominant chord.

F. Many orchestral pieces were composed as background music, including the divertimento, cassation, and serenade.

## SUGGESTIONS FOR SUPPLEMENTARY READING/LISTENING/ACTIVITIES

Have students discuss how the social function of music affects a composition. Have them consider how a composer might shape a piece that is enjoyable for amateurs to play, how a concert piece might be conceived in order to appeal to an audience, and how music for background entertainment would differ from either of the other conceptions. Ask them if we have similar distinctions in music today.

Have groups of students report on the technical features of instruments of the eighteenth century, including keyboard instruments (fortepiano, harpsichord, and clavichord), strings (and bows), woodwinds, brass, and percussion. Have each group locate recordings of historic instruments, photographs, and diagrams showing the action of the instrument from Web sites or books.

Have students select one of Scarlatti's sonatas and report on its form and the number of themes presented. As part of the report, have them compare recordings made with a piano and harpsichord. Several recordings with each instrument are available through the Naxos library.

For Charles Burney's description of Frederick the Great as an amateur musician, see Weiss and Taruskin, eds., *Music in the Western World: A History in Documents* (New York: Schirmer, 1984), 304–6.

For a work in the empfindsam style by a woman composer of the eighteenth century, see Marianne von Martinez's Sonata in James R. Briscoe, *Historical Anthology of Music by Women* (Urbana: University of Illinois, 1987), 88–93.

The portion of Carl Philipp Emanuel Bach's treatise on keyboard playing that deals with embellishments is excerpted in Wye Jamison Allanbrook, ed., *Source Readings in Music History,* rev. ed., Vol. 5: *The Late Eighteenth Century* (New York: W. W. Norton, 1998). Have students read this selection, then find quotations showing C. P. E. Bach's modernism and his view of Baroque style.

On the changing conceptions of instrumental music and what constituted an orchestra in the eighteenth century, see Neal Zaslaw, "When Is an Orchestra Not an Orchestra?" *Early Music* 16 (1988): 483–95. Also see the "Introduction" to the classical portion of *Performance Practice: Music after 1600* (New York: W. W. Norton, 1989) by the same author.

Burney's description of the Mannheim Orchestra is available in Ruth Halle Rowen, *Music through Sources and Documents* (Englewood Cliffs, N. J.: Prentice-Hall, 1979), 219–20.

For a comprehensive study of Stamitz and his role in the development of the symphony, see *The Symphonies of Johann Stamitz: A Study in the Formation of the Classical Style* by Eugene K. Wolf (Antwer: Bohn, Scheltema, & Hokema, 1982).

Have students select one of the symphonies from Barry S. Brook and Barbara B. Heyman, *The Symphony 1720–1840* (New York: Garland, 1979), Series B (Austria, Bohemia, Slovakia, and Hungary) or Series C (Germany, including the Mannheim School and C. P. E. Bach) and report on its form and its composer.

A compact-disc recording of chamber music entitled *Music at the Court of Mannheim* by Nikolaus Harnoncourt (Elektra 91002, 1993) includes some quartets by Franz Xaver Richter. Listen to these along with the earliest string quartets of Haydn. Have the students discuss the differences between a composition for string orchestra and one for a string quartet.

Find a recording of some violin concertos by Tartini, such as *Tartini: Violin Concertos* (Hyperion, 2003). Have students listen to the works and compare the structures to that of J. C. Bach. Have them discuss the differences between a concerto for violin and one for keyboard.

## OBJECTIVE QUESTIONS

Use the following answers for questions 1–3.

a. harpsichord
b. clavichord
c. organ
d. fortepiano
e. celesta

1. Which instrument uses hammers to strike strings?

   Answer: d

2. Which instrument uses a mechanism that plucks the strings?

   Answer: a

3. Which instrument uses tangents to strike the strings, which stay in contact until the key is released?

   Answer: b

4. Of the following, which instrument was invented in 1710 and became a standard woodwind member by 1780?
   a. flute
   b. oboe
   c. clarinet
   d. bassoon
   e. saxophone

   Answer: c

5. By the end of the eighteenth century, the role of leading the orchestra fell to __________.
   a. the harpsichord player
   b. the leader of the violins
   c. a specialized conductor who did not play an instrument
   d. the composer
   e. violist

   Answer: b

6. Of the following, which Baroque instrumental genre continued into the Classic era?
   a. fugue
   b. toccata
   c. dance suite
   d. prelude
   e. solo concerto

   Answer: e

7. Of the following, which is *not* a characteristic of sonata form as described by Heinrich Christoph Koch?
   a. It is an expanded version of binary form.
   b. The form is divided into three principal sections.
   c. The first section moves from the tonic to the dominant or relative major.
   d. The first section presents the principal ideas.
   e. The form is not a rigid mold, but a plan or set of principles.

   Answer: b

8. Which of the following would be considered a rondo form?
   a. ABACADA
   b. ABA
   c. rounded binary
   d. A repeated with variations
   e. ABAB

   Answer: a

9. The composer who published some of his keyboard sonatas with the title *Essercizi* was __________.
   a. J. C. Bach
   b. Domenico Alberti
   c. Domenico Scarlatti
   d. C. P. E. Bach
   e. J. S. Bach

   Answer: c

10. Of the following, which does *not* describe the sonatas of C. P. E. Bach?
    a. They helped to establish the three-movement structure.
    b. They sustain the Baroque style well into the Classic era.
    c. They often contain expressive melodies with short phrases.
    d. In them, Bach introduced sections of dialogue and recitative.
    e. They exemplify the empfindsam style.

    Answer: b

11. In which region did the symphony originate?
    a. Italy
    b. France
    c. Austria
    d. England
    e. Germany

    Answer: a

Use the following answers for questions 12–16.
   a. Stamitz
   b. Gossec
   c. Wagenseil
   d. Sammartini
   e. J. C. Bach

12. This Italian was the first important composer of symphonies.

    Answer: d

13. Writing in Vienna, his symphonies featured contrasting themes.

    Answer: c

14. Active in London, he was an important influence on the young Mozart.

    Answer: e

15. He is considered to be one of the leading composers of symphonies in France.

    Answer: b

16. He was the founder of the symphony school in Mannheim.

    Answer: a

17. Which center developed an orchestra, referred to as "an army of generals," that was renowned throughout Europe for its precision and technique?
    a. Milan
    b. Stuttgart
    c. Vienna
    d. Mannheim
    e. Paris

    Answer: d

18. The Classic-era genre that combines characteristics of the symphony and the concerto is called the __________.
    a. divertimento
    b. symphonie concertante
    c. sinfonia
    d. concerto grosso
    e. cassation

    Answer: b

19. Of the following, what characterizes the concerto form of J. C. Bach?
    a. The opening ritornello modulates to the dominant.
    b. There are five principal solo sections.

c. The first solo section contains no thematic material.
d. The ritornellos serve as a frame for a sonata form structure.
e. There are typically four movements.

Answer: d

20. Of the following, what does *not* characterize a concerto cadenza in the Classic era?
a. It was usually improvised.
b. A heavy orchestral 6/4 chord introduced the cadenza.
c. The soloist signaled the end of a cadenza with a trill.
d. The cadenza was placed at the end of the second solo section.
e. The cadenza developed from vocal arias.

Answer: d

## SHORT-ESSAY QUESTIONS

1. Compare the descriptions of sonata form by Koch and by theorists of the early nineteenth century. How does sonata form differ from instrumental forms of the Baroque?
2. Using the model of a sonata form by Koch, analyze the movements in your anthology by Scarlatti (**NAWM 98**), Sammartini (**NAWM 100**), and Stamitz (**NAWM 101**).
3. Describe how elements of empfindsam style are reflected in the sonata movement of C. P. E. Bach (**NAWM 99**). Compare these to the characteristics of the galant style found in the concerto movement of J. C. Bach (**NAWM 101**).
4. Describe how the first movement of the late-eighteenth-century concerto combines the formal traditions of the Baroque concerto with sonata form.

## TERMS FOR IDENTIFICATION

clavichord
fortepiano
string quartet
sonata
exposition
development
recapitulation
coda
slow-movement sonata form
variations form
minuet and trio form
rondo form
*Essercizi*
Frederick the Great
sinfonia
Mannheim
symphonie concertante
concerto first-movement form
cadenza
divertimento

# CHAPTER 22 Classic Music in the Late Eighteenth Century

I. Joseph Haydn (1732–1809)
  A. Historical position
    1. Haydn was the most celebrated composer of his day (see **HWM Figure 22.1**).
    2. He is best remembered for his symphonies and string quartets (see **HWM biography,** page 526).
  B. Early life
    1. Haydn was born near Vienna.
    2. He was a choirboy at St. Stephen's Cathedral in Vienna, where he studied singing, harpsichord, and violin.
    3. Dismissed when his voice changed, he worked freelance in Vienna and studied music.
    4. Around 1757, he became music director for Count Morzin and composed his first symphonies for him.
  C. The Esterházy years
    1. Haydn spent most of his career working for the Esterházys, a wealthy Hungarian noble family.
    2 Prince Paul Anton Esterházy hired Haydn in 1761.
    3. Nikolaus Esterházy succeeded his brother Paul in 1762 and became Haydn's principal patron for nearly thirty years (see **HWM Source Reading,** page 528).
    4. Haydn's duties for the Esterházy family:
      a. Compose music
      b. Conduct performances
      c. Train and supervise musical personnel
      d. Keep the musical instruments in good condition
    5. Esterháza
      a. In 1766, the Esterházy family moved from Eisenstadt in Austria to Esterháza, a remote country estate in Hungary (see **HWM Figure 22.2**).
      b. The estate, which rivaled the splendor of Versailles, had two theaters and two music rooms.
      c. Haydn built an orchestra of about twenty-five performers and gave weekly concerts, occasional opera performances, and daily chamber music sessions.
    6. Nikolaus played a large string instrument with sympathetic strings called a *baryton*, for which Haydn composed numerous works (see **HWM Figure 22.3**).
    7. Although Haydn kept abreast of current musical developments, his isolation at Esterháza and the encouragement of his patron helped him to become original.
    8. A new contract in 1779 allowed Haydn to publish his music in major European centers, which further enhanced his reputation.
    9. Prince Nikolaus died in 1790, and Haydn was given permission to live in Vienna.
  D. The London years
    1. Johann Peter Salomon, a violinist and impresario, persuaded Haydn to come to London for concert tours between 1791 and 1795.
    2. For the London concerts. Haydn composed numerous new works, including his last twelve symphonies.
    3. Haydn and his music were received with great acclaim in London.

II. Haydn's Style
  A. Although his music relied on contemporary conventions, Haydn frequently introduced the unexpected.
  B. Sources of Haydn's style (see **HWM Source Reading,** page 531)
    1. The galant style
    2. The expressiveness of the empfindsam style
    3. Baroque counterpoint
    4. Generic clichés
  C. String Quartet in E-flat Major, Op. 3, No. 2 (*The Joke*), finale (see **NAWM 104** and **HWM Example 22.1**)
    1. The rondo form is ABACA.
    2. The binary opening theme has a playful, unfinished character.
    3. The two episodes do not introduce new material.
    4. Much of the material of the movement is derived from the idea introduced in the first two measures, an indication of Haydn's sense of economy and novelty.
    5. Haydn heightens drama with extensions and delay.
    6. The exaggerated drama is humorous, creating a witty effect.
    7. The quartet derives its name from Haydn's playful final cadence of the movement (see **HWM Example 22.2**).
    8. Haydn's wit is especially endearing to players and connoisseurs, but also appeals to inexperienced listeners.
  D. Haydn's compositional process
    1. He began by improvising at the keyboard.
    2. After settling on an appropriate idea, he worked with the keyboard and on paper, writing the melody and harmony on several staves (see **HWM Figure 22. 4**).
    3. He completed the process by writing a full score.

III. Symphonies
  A. General
    1. Haydn composed approximately 106 symphonies.
    2. Numbers are used to identify Haydn's symphonies, ending with 104.
    3. Many of the symphonies also have nicknames, few of which came from the composer.
    4. His symphonies generally have four movements.
      a. A fast sonata-form movement, often with a slow introduction
      b. A slow movement
      c. A minuet and trio
      d. A fast finale, usually in sonata or rondo form
    5. All of these movements are in the same key, except for the slow movement, which is in a related key.
    6. Haydn's format became standard for later composers.
  B. Early symphonies, 1757–67
    1. Haydn's earliest symphonies were composed for Count Morzin (1757–61).
      a. Typically, they were scored for two oboes, two horns, and strings.
      b. Most of these are in three movements.
      c. The sonata-form movements tend to use themes that could be broken up and recombined.
    2. Haydn composed about thirty symphonies in his early years with the Esterházy family (1761–67).
      a. The ensemble was often augmented with flute, bassoon, and other instruments.
      b. These diverse works are characterized by novelty and variety.
      c. Three symphonies, with common titles, feature solo passages for a variety of orchestral instruments.
        (1) Symphony No. 6, *Le Matin* (Morning)
        (2) Symphony No. 7, *Le Midi* (Noon)
        (3) Symphony No. 8, *Le Soir* (Evening)
  C. Symphonies of 1768–72
    1. Beginning in about 1768, Haydn's symphonies were presented in the mirrored concert room in Esterháza (see **HWM Figure 22.5**).
    2. The twelve symphonies of this period are longer, more rhythmically complex, contrapuntal, and challenging to play.
    3. The character of many of these symphonies has been associated with a literary movement known as *Sturm und Drang*.
      a. Six of the twelve symphonies are in minor keys.
      b. Dynamic extremes, sudden contrasts, crescendos, and sforzatos are used to startling effect.
      c. The harmonies are richer and more varied.
      d. In general, the symphonies project an emotional, agitated character.
  D. Symphonies of 1773–81
    1. Beginning around 1773, Haydn's symphonies mixed popular elements with serious, stirring, and impressive qualities.

2. Symphony No. 56 in C Major (1774)
   a. This festive work encompasses a broad emotional range.
   b. *Sturm und Drang* elements serve as contrasts to arpeggiations, fanfares, and songlike phrases.

E. Symphonies of 1781–1791
1. In the 1780s, Haydn sold his symphonies to patrons and publishers abroad.
2. Standard orchestration: flute, two oboes, two bassoons, two horns, strings, and sometimes trumpets and timpani.
3. The Paris Symphonies (Nos. 82–87,1785–6) were his grandest up to this point.
4. Symphonies Nos. 88–92 were also composed on commission.
5. These works combine popular and learned elements, giving them immediate and lasting appeal.

F. Symphonies of 1791–1794, the London Symphonies
1. The twelve London Symphonies, commissioned by Salomon, are his greatest symphonic achievements.
2. Distinctive qualities
   a. More daring harmonies
   b. Intensified rhythmic drive
   c. Memorable thematic inventions
   d. Expanded orchestra: trumpets and timpani are standard, and clarinets frequently appear
   e. The woodwinds and string bass are more independent.
   f. The effect is spacious and brilliant.
3. Haydn employed novel ideas to outdo competition from a rival concert series featuring Ignaz Pleyel (1757–1831).
   a. A fortissimo crash on a weak beat in the slow movement of Symphony No. 94 gave this work the nickname *Surprise*.
   b. He employed folk-like tunes (see **HWM Example 22.5**).
   c. "Turkish" effects can be heard in the *Military* Symphony, No. 100.
   d. A ticking sound is used in the andante of Symphony No. 101 (the *Clock*).

IV. Symphony, No. 92 in G Major (*Oxford*, **NAWM 103**)

A. Composed in 1789, the work derives its name from a 1791 performance at Oxford when Haydn received an honorary doctorate from that university.

B. The first movement is in a sonata form.
1. The slow introduction makes the following allegro sound energetic.
2. Throughout the movement, the alternation of tonally stable thematic ideas and unstable passages helps us follow the form.
3. Exposition
   a. The first theme group contains three distinct ideas (see **HWM Example 22.3**).
   b. Haydn begins the second thematic group with the opening idea and a countermelody in the winds.
   c. The closing subject is repetitive and cadential.
4. Development
   a. Haydn modulates through several related keys.
   b. The section features sequences, counterpoint, and motivic development.
5. Recapitulation
   a. Haydn playfully begins the recapitulation with the theme in the flute and with new counterpoint.
   b. In the recapitulation, the second and closing themes appear in the tonic, and the transition is extended and intensified.

C. The slow movement is in ABA form.
1. Haydn's slow movements tend to provide a calm and gentle melody in contrast to the dramatic first movements.
2. Other common slow-movement forms are the sonata form without repeats and the theme and variations.
3. The Oxford has a songlike theme, a dramatic middle section in the tonic minor, and an abbreviated reprise.
4. The coda features woodwind instruments and uses chromatic harmonies.

D. Minuet and trio
1. The overall structure is ABA; each of the sections is binary.
2. The trio (the B section) is often in the same key as the minuet, but may change mode or be in a closely related key.
3. In general, the trio has a lighter orchestration.
4. The minuet and trio is shorter and more popular in nature than the other movements of a symphony.
5. In the *Oxford,* Haydn creates humor through unexpected harmonies, syncopations, pauses, and changes of dynamics.

E. The finale is in sonata form.
1. The final movement of a symphony is generally faster and shorter than the first.

2. The first theme of the Oxford finale (see **HWM Example 22.4**) reappears on the dominant to open the second thematic group and at the close of the exposition.
3. The development is dominated by the first theme.
4. After 1770, Haydn finales are often rondos, such as the ABACABA form.
5. Some of Haydn's rondos are sonata-rondos.
   a. The A and B sections resemble a sonata-form exposition.
   b. The C is largely developmental.
   c. The return of B is in the tonic key.

V. Other Instrumental Music
  A. String quartets
    1. Although he was not the first to compose string quartets, he was the first great master of the genre.
    2. Many of his quartets were intended for amateurs.
    3. The quartets have been described as conversations between four instruments.
    4. The first quartets resemble divertimentos, Opp. 1 (1764) and 2 (1766).
    5. The next eighteen quartets, Opp. 9 (ca. 1770), 17 (1771), and 20 (1772), established the four-movement structure.
       a. A number of the Op. 20 quartets are in minor keys and exhibit *Sturm und Drang* qualities.
       b. Three quartets from Op. 20 end with fugues.
       c. These quartets helped establish his international reputation.
    6. Opus 33 was composed in a "quite new and special way."
       a. The works are lighthearted and tuneful (see **HWM Example 22.6**).
       b. The minuets are titled *scherzo* (joke or trick), a title that will be applied to a faster replacement of the minuet and trio.
       c. Haydn uses rondos as finales for the first time in his string quartets.
       d. The works are filled with playful humor (see **HWM Examples 22.1** and **22.2** and **NAWM 103**).
    7. After Op. 33, Haydn composed thirty-four quartets.
       a. The six quartets of Op. 76 incorporate elements of concert hall performance.
       b. Expanded harmonic vocabulary foreshadows Romantic harmony.
       c. Like the late symphonies, serious and popular elements are juxtaposed.
  B. Keyboard sonatas and trios
    1. These were generally written for amateur performers.
    2. Both genres had three movements (fast–slow–fast).
    3. Both genres focused on intimate expression.
    4. The keyboard trio was essentially a keyboard sonata accompanied by strings (see **HWM Figure 22.6**).

VI. Vocal Music
  A. Operas
    1. Haydn held his vocal works in higher regard than his instrumental works, though his present-day reputation places more value on the latter.
    2. Haydn spent much of his time at Esterháza composing and producing operas.
    3. *Armida* (1784), a serious opera, is remarkable for its dramatic accompanied recitatives and grand arias.
    4. Haydn's operas are rarely performed today.
  B. Masses
    1. His last six masses are large-scale festive works, including
       a. *Missa in tempore belli* (Mass in Time of War, 1796)
       b. *Lord Nelson Mass* (1798)
       c. *Theresienmesse* (1799)
       d. *Harmoniemesse* (Windband Mass, 1802)
    2. They are set for four vocal soloists, chorus, and orchestra with trumpets and timpani.
    3. Haydn retains traditional elements, such as fugal writing.
    4. Haydn also incorporates symphonic elements.
  C. Haydn's Oratorios
    1. Haydn heard Handel's oratorios in London and was deeply moved (see **HWM Figure 22.7**).
    2. Major works
       a. *The Creation* (1798), based on the Book of Genesis and Milton's *Paradise Lost*
       b. *The Seasons* (1801)
    3. Both works were published in German and English.
    4. Baron Gottfried van Swieten wrote the German texts.
    5. Haydn's *Depiction of Chaos* at the beginning of *The Creation* is remarkable for its harmonies and drama (see **HWM Example 22.7**).

VII. Wolfgang Amadeus Mozart (1756–1791)
   A. Mozart and Haydn
      1. The two composers were friends and admired each other.
      2. Mozart and Haydn were seen as equals and defined the music of the era.
      3. Fundamental differences between their careers
         a. Mozart achieved international recognition earlier, despite being twenty-four years younger.
         b. Mozart never found a permanent position and worked as a free agent in Vienna (see **HWM biography,** page 546, and **Figure 22.7**).
   B. Early Life
      1. Mozart was a remarkable child prodigy.
      2. Mozart's father was Leopold Mozart (1719–1787) (see **HWM Figure 22.8**)
         a. Leopold was a performer and composer for the archbishop of Salzburg.
         b. He published a highly regarded treatise on violin-playing in 1756.
         c. Leopold sacrificed his own career to promote the musical lives of young Mozart and his talented sister Nannerl (1751–1829).
      3. Mozart toured throughout Europe (1762–1773) (see **HWM Figure 22.9**).
         a. He gave performances on the keyboard and violin in aristocratic homes and in public.
         b. He was seen as a wonder of nature.
         c. He composed minuets at age five, a symphony just before turning nine, his first oratorio at eleven, and his first opera at twelve.
         d. During these travels, Mozart absorbed local musical qualities, which he synthesized into his own works.
      4. Significant influences
         a. Johann Schobert (ca. 1735–1767) was a prominent keyboard composer in Paris (see **HWM Example 22.8**).
         b. Johann Christian Bach, whom Mozart met in London, used songful themes, tasteful appoggiaturas and triplets, harmonic ambiguities, and contrasting themes in sonata forms, qualities that appealed to Mozart.
      5. Between 1769 and 1773, Mozart spent much time in Italy.
         a. In Italy, Mozart studied counterpoint with Padre Martini and composed operas and string quartets.
         b. The influence of Sammartini is evident in the symphonies written between 1770 and 1773.
         c. Mozart's visit to Vienna in 1773 introduced him to current trends, and his six quartets, K. 168–173, reflect Viennese traditions.
   C. The Salzburg years (1774–1781)
      1. In Mozart's time, musicians earned money either with steady employment with a patron or with freelancing.
      2. Mozart held a position with the archbishop of Salzburg for eight years.
         a. Unhappy with the archbishop, Mozart looked for other employment.
         b. He received a commission to compose the opera seria *Idomeneo* (1781).
         c. He soon decided to leave the archbishop's service and go to Vienna.
   D. The Vienna years (1781–1791)
      1. As a freelance musician, Mozart earned an income from several sources.
         a. Mozart's Singspiel *Die Entführung aus dem Serail* (The Abduction from the Harem, 1782) was a great success.
         b. He took piano and composition students.
         c. He earned the reputation as Vienna's finest pianist and performed in private and public concerts.
         d. Acting as an impresario, Mozart organized his own concerts (see **HWM Figure 22.10**).
         e. He composed on commission and for publication.
         f. In 1787, he was appointed chamber-music composer to the emperor.
      2. Due to his declining income and mismanagement of funds, Mozart seems to have had financial problems following 1788.
      3. Later influences
         a. Haydn spent winters in Vienna, and they became friends.
         b. The music of J. S. Bach was brought to Mozart's attention through Baron van Swieten, and Mozart responded with increased contrapuntal textures.
         c. Swieten also introduced Mozart to Handel.

VIII. Instrumental Music
   A. Piano music
      1. Mozart composed sonatas, fantasias, variations, rondos, and piano duets.
      2. These works were intended for his pupils, domestic music-making, and publication.
      3. Mozart's nineteen piano sonatas are among his most popular works.

   a. A set of six sonatas (K. 279–284) was composed in Munich in 1775.
   b. Three sonatas were written in Mannheim and Paris in 1777–78 (K. 309–311).
   c. Three sonatas were published in 1784 (K. 330–332) and reflect his mature Viennese style.
4. Sonata in F Major, K. 332, first movement (**NAWM 105** and **HWM Example 22.9**)
   a. The movement, in sonata form, has repeats for both halves of the structure.
   b. Mozart's themes tend to be songlike, as seen in the opening theme.
   c. Typically, a contrasting idea is introduced gracefully within the first theme.
   d. Mozart effortlessly employs galant, learned, hunting, and *Sturm und Drang* styles within the first thirty measures.
   e. The development begins with a new melody.

B. Chamber music
1. Mozart composed sixteen string quartets in the early 1770s.
2. He returned to the genre with six quartets composed in Vienna (1782–85).
   a. Dedicated to Haydn, these quartets are known as the *Haydn* Quartets.
   b. These works are more developed and contrapuntal.
3. Some of Mozart's finest chamber works are the quintets for two violins, two violas, and cello.
4. Mozart felt that the Quintet for Piano and Winds, K. 452 was his best work.
5. Mozart composed a number of other works for winds and strings.

C. Serenades and divertimentos
1. Mozart composed these works for garden parties and outdoor performances.
2. Although background music, Mozart gave them serious treatment.
3. These works appear in a variety of settings, ranging from duets to six or eight wind instruments.
4. *Eine kleine Nachtmusik* (A Little Night Music, K. 525, 1787) is Mozart's best-known serenade and can be played by a string quintet or a string orchestra.

D. Piano concertos
1. Mozart composed piano concertos in Salzburg in the 1770s, most notably the Piano Concerto in E-flat Major, K. 271 (1777).
2. The seventeen piano concertos composed in Vienna are major works in Mozart's compositional output; each is a masterpiece.
3. Similar to the works of J. C. Bach, Mozart's concertos are in three movements, and the first movements combine elements of ritornello and sonata forms.
4. The first movement of the Piano Concerto in A, K. 499 (1786) (**NAWM 106**)
   a. The three solo sections resemble the exposition, development, and recapitulation of a sonata form.
   b. The opening orchestral ritornello presents the first theme, transition, second theme, and closing themes in the tonic key.
   c. Ritornellos return to mark the end of the first and third solo section.
   d. The orchestra also punctuates the long solo sections.
   e. The cadenza appears in the final ritornello section.
   f. The orchestral transition material serves as a strong contrast to the lyric themes.
   g. A significant new idea is introduced at the beginning of the development.
5. The second movement of a Mozart concerto resembles a lyrical aria.
   a. The key is often in the subdominant and sometimes in the dominant or relative minor.
   b. Typical forms are sonata without development, variations, and rondo.
6. The final movement is usually a rondo or sonata-rondo based on themes of a popular character.
7. Mozart balanced virtuosic display with colorful orchestral material, as evident in the numerous wind solos.

E. Symphonies
1. Mozart composed nearly fifty symphonies prior to moving to Vienna, many of which are in three movements.
2. Mozart wrote only six symphonies in his Vienna years; each a masterpiece.
   a. *Haffner* Symphony, K. 385 (1782)
   b. *Linz* Symphony, K. 425 (1783)
   c. *Prague* Symphony in D Major, K. 504 (1786)
   d. Symphony in E-flat Major, K. 543 (1788)
   e. Symphony in G Minor, K. 550 (17880
   f. *Jupiter* Symphony in C Major, K. 551 (1788)
3. The G-Minor Symphony opens quietly with an undulating melody.
4. The finale to the *Jupiter* Symphony is a contrapuntal masterpiece, in which the coda

links five themes together in a passage of ars combinatoria (the art of musical combination and permutation; see **HWM Example 22.10**).

XI. Operas
   A. Early operas
      1. In 1768, Mozart composed his first operas.
         a. *La finta semplice* (The Pretend Simpleton), an opera buffa
         b. *Bastien und Bastienne,* a Singspiel
      2. He composed two opere serie in the early 1770s for Milan.
      3. Two operas were composed for Munich.
         a. *La finta giardiniera* (1775), an opera buffa
         b. *Idomeneo* (1781), an opera seria that reflects the reformist trends of Gluck.
   B. *Die Entführung aus dem Serail* (1782) established his operatic reputation.
      1. Mozart raised the Singspiel to the level of an artwork.
      2. The "oriental" setting was popular at this time, and Mozart uses Turkish-style music (see **HWM Source Reading,** page 560).
   C. Mozart's next three operas were based on librettos by Lorenzo Da Ponte (1749–1838; see **HWM Figure 22.12**).
      1. All three were Italian comic operas.
         a. *The Marriage of Figaro* (1786)
         b. *Don Giovanni* (Don Juan, 1787)
         c. *Così fan tutte* (Thus Do All Women, 1790)
      2. Da Ponte and Mozart gave greater depth to the characters.
      3. Mozart's ensembles allowed characters to express contrasting emotions at the same time.
      4. Mozart's orchestration, particularly his use of winds, helped define the characters and situations.
   D. *Don Giovanni*
      1. The opera premiered in Prague.
      2. Da Ponte and Mozart took the legendary character of Don Juan seriously as a rebel against authority.
      3. The opera mixes opera seria characters and opera buffa characters.
      4. All character types are combined in the brilliant dance music in the finale of Act I.
      5. The opening scene of *Don Giovanni* (**NAWM 107**)
         a. Leporello complains in an opera-buffa style with an ABCBB' form.
         b. Donna Anna and Don Giovanni sing in a dramatic opera seria style, while Leporello frets in a buffa style; the form is ABB.
         c. The ensuing duel ends in a death, a shocking scene in a comic opera.
         d. A powerful trio in F minor laments the turn of events.
         e. At the end, Don Giovanni and Leporello revert to comic banter.
      6. Donna Elvira's aria *Ah fuggi il traditor* (see **HWM Example 22.11**)
         a. Her aria depicts herself as a tragic character.
         b. The aria is an out-of-date style, making her sound insincere.
   E. *Magic Flute*
      1. This Singspiel was composed in the last year of his life, along with the opera seria *La clemenza di Tito* (The Mercy of Titus).
      2. The story contains symbolism, largely drawn from the teachings and ceremonies of Freemasonry.
      3. Mozart interweaves a wide variety of vocal styles.

X. Church Music
   A. His early sacred music is not considered to be among his major works.
   B. The masses reflect the current symphonic-operatic idiom with standard fugal sections.
   C. *The Requiem,* K. 626
      1. The work was commissioned by Count Walsegg in 1791.
      2. Unfinished at Mozart's death, it was completed by his pupil, Franz Xaver Süssmayr (1766–1803).

## SUGGESTIONS FOR SUPPLEMENTAL READINGS/LISTENING/ACTIVITIES

Daniel Heartz's *Haydn, Mozart, and the Viennese School 1740–1780* (New York: W. W. Norton, 1995) provides a rich contextual background for the earlier works of the composers.

For detailed accounts of Haydn's life and background on nearly all of his works, consult H. C. Robbins Landon's massive *Haydn's Chronicle and Works,* 5 vols. (Bloomington: Indiana University Press, 1976–80).

For a description of the state of keyboard instruments during the late eighteenth century, see Malcolm Bilson's "Keyboards" in *Performance Practice: Music after 1600,* edited by Howard Mayer Brown and Stanley Sadie (New York: W. W. Norton, 1989), 223–38.

For more on the development of the pianoforte, see Michael Cole, *The Pianoforte in the Classical Era* (Oxford: Clarendon Press, 1998). The *NAWM* recordings for Mozart's Piano Sonata in F Major, K. 332, and Piano Concerto in A Major, K. 488, allow for comparisons between period and modern instruments. Play some contrasting performances and have the students focus initially on the advantages of Mozart's piano. With the concerto recording, period orchestral instruments can also be heard.

Haydn's named symphonies have been collected on a ten-disc set performed by the Academy of St. Martin in the Fields (Philips 454 336-2 through 454 345-2, 1982). Have students select one of these symphonies and report on the circumstances of its composition, the reason for its title, and how the title is portrayed by the music.

One of the earliest known classical musicians of African descent is Chevalier de Saint-Georges, who conducted the *Concerts de la Loge Olympique,* for which Haydn composed his Paris Symphonies. For more information, see Samuel A. Floyd, Jr., ed., *International Dictionary of Black Composers* (Chicago: Fitzroy Dearborn Publishers, 1999), Vol. 2, 983–989.

Haydn's duties at Esterháza are enumerated in Weiss and Taruskin, eds., *Music in the Western World: A History in Documents* (New York: Schirmer, 1984), 298–300.

Have students select one string quartet movement from each opus number and report on the roles played by each of the instruments, beginning with the earliest opus numbers and moving to the last. How did the instruments' roles change? How did Haydn's musical style change with the changing roles of the instruments?

For more on Haydn's *Creation,* see N. Temperley, *Haydn: The Creation* (New York: Cambridge: University Press, 1991).

Have students listen to the depiction of chaos at the beginning of the *Creation* and list the devices Haydn uses for this depiction. Have students discuss these devices in terms of the Classical values of rationality, balance, and scientific discovery and the Baroque Doctrine of Affections.

Introduce students to the thematic catalogues by Hoboken and Köchel and the collected editions of Haydn and Mozart. Have them look up the *NAWM* examples in the collected works editions, using the works lists at the end of the *New Grove Dictionary* articles on each composer.

Useful biographies of Mozart include Neal Zaslaw, with William Cowdery, *The Compleat Mozart* (New York: W. W. Norton, 1990), Stanley Sadie, *Mozart: The Early Years, 1756–1781* (New York: W. W. Norton, 2006), and A. Hyatt King, *Mozart* (London: Bingley, 1970). For fascinating recent studies of the composer, see also Wolfgang Hildesheimer, *Mozart,* trans. Marion Faber (New York: Vintage Books, 1983) and Maynard Solomon, *Mozart: A Life* (New York: HarperCollins, 1995).

For a description of the Mozart family on tour, see Weiss and Taruskin, *Music in the Western World: A History in Documents* (New York: Schirmer, 1984), 306–10.

Excerpts from Leopold Mozart's treatise on violin-playing can be found in Wye Jamison Allabrook, ed., *Source Readings in Music History,* rev. ed., Vol. 5: *The Late Eighteenth Century* (New York: W. W. Norton, 1998).

Have the students select quotations from Mozart's correspondence that they believe portray aspects of Mozart's character or his views on music and read them to the class. Use *The Letters of Mozart and His Family,* 2 vols., ed. Emily Anderson (New York: W. W. Norton, 1989) or Robert Spaethling, *Mozart's Letters, Mozart's Life* (New York: W. W. Norton, 2000). The latter also has a map on its flyleaves showing cities where Mozart traveled. For commentary on some of Mozart's letters and other contemporary documents, see Robert L. Marshall, *Mozart Speaks: Views on Music, Musicians, and the World* (New York: Schirmer Books, 1991).

*Eine kleine Nachtmusik* is one of Mozart's most popular works. Have students study the form and style of the first movement, and then ask them what qualities may have inspired such popularity. Why can average listeners relate to this work? Would *NAWM* works enjoy equal popularity if given the same amount of exposure?

Mozart composed chamber music for a variety of wind instruments. Have appropriate wind students report to class on chamber music for their instrument. Of particular interest are the wind serenades and the quintet for piano and winds, K. 452. Ask students to speculate why Mozart might have thought that this was his best work.

Have students write a brief paper on Mozart's *Jupiter* Symphony, tracing the initial theme through all movements and finding the origins of the themes that are combined in the finale. This exercise will prepare students for the cyclical processes of Beethoven.

For information on cadenzas and improvisation, see Robert D. Levin, "Instrumental Ornamentation, Improvisation and Cadenzas" in *Performance Practice: Music after 1600* (New York: W. W. Norton, 1990), which includes a section on Mozart's concertos. Have students bring to class cadenzas from Mozart's concertos, both by Mozart and later composers. Compare them to the generalizations found in the above reading.

See Tim Carter's *W. A. Mozart: The Marriage of Figaro* (Cambridge: Cambridge University Press, 1987) for additional material for class discussion.

Have students discuss how Mozart lifted the popular medium of Singspiel to an artform in *Die Entführung aus dem Searail* and *The Magic Flute*.

Have students select one work from Volume Five of *Women Composers: Music through the Ages* and report on the work and its composer. Have students discuss the ways in which each composer managed to succeed in a field dominated by men. What qualities or advantages made it possible for each woman to develop as a musician?

## OBJECTIVE QUESTIONS

1. Who was Haydn's principal employer throughout his long career?
   a. Emperor Leopold II
   b. the archbishop of Salzburg
   c. Baron Gottfried van Swieten
   d. Prince Nikolaus Esterházy
   e. Johann Peter Salomon

   Answer: d

2. Haydn's patron asked him to compose chamber music for which instrument?
   a. sackbut
   b. baryton
   c. arpeggione
   d. viola d'amore
   e. violone

   Answer: b

3. Who persuaded Haydn to come to London?
   a. Johann Peter Salomon
   b. J. C. Bach
   c. Mozart
   d. Baron Gottfried van Swieten
   e. Prince Nikolaus Esterházy

   Answer: a

4. Of the following, which was the main source of Haydn's idiom?
   a. learned counterpoint
   b. empfindsam style
   c. galant style
   d. *Sturm und Drang*
   e. Italian recitative

   Answer: c

5. Of the following, which does *not* typify a Haydn symphony?
   a. three-movement structures
   b. frequent slow introductions for the first movements
   c. the reappearance of the first theme at the beginning of the second key area
   d. lyric slow movements and stylized minuets for third movements
   e. fast finales that are shorter than the first movements

   Answer: a

6. The heightened expression found in the symphonies of 1768–1772 is associated with which style?
   a. galant style
   b. empfindsam style
   c. *Sturm und Drang*
   d. Baroque style
   e. opera buffa style

   Answer: c

7. Haydn's last symphonies were composed for __________.
   a. audiences in Vienna
   b. the Prince of Ersterháza
   c. London concerts
   d. Paris concerts
   e. Frederick the Great

   Answer: c

8. Which set of Haydn's string quartet has three fugal finales?
   a. Opus 17
   b. Opus 20
   c. Opus 33
   d. Opus 54
   e. Opus 76

   Answer: b

9. Haydn's Opus 33 quartets were composed in what style?
   a. light-hearted and witty
   b. serious and moody
   c. restrained and unemotional
   d. orchestral
   e. theatrical

   Answer: a

10. Which composer inspired Haydn's oratorios?
    a. J. S. Bach
    b. Telemann
    c. Scarlatti
    d. Handel
    e. Mozart

    Answer: d

11. Mozart was a child prodigy on which instrument or instruments?
    a. keyboard
    b. keyboard and violin
    c. keyboard, violin, and flute
    d. 1keyboard, violin, and cello
    e. flute and keyboard

    Answer: b

12. Most of Mozart's masterworks were composed in which city?
    a. Salzburg
    b. Paris
    c. London
    d. Prague
    e. Vienna

    Answer: e

13. Which composer did *not* exert a strong influence on Mozart?
    a. Haydn
    b. J. S. Bach
    c. J. C. Bach
    d. Handel
    e. Vivaldi

    Answer: e

14. Among Mozart's finest chamber works are the string quintets for which combination of instruments?
    a. two violins, viola, two cellos
    b. two violins, viola, cello, string bass
    c. two violins, two violas, cello
    d. violin, two violas, two cellos
    e. piano, violin, viola, cello, string bass

    Answer: c

15. Most of Mozart's piano works were composed for __________.
    a. his own performance
    b. the performance of his patrons only
    c. skilled virtuosos
    d. sketches for orchestral works
    e. pupils, domestic music-making, and publication

    Answer: e

16. Which of the following describes Mozart's first-movement forms in his piano concertos?
    a. They blend elements of ritornello and sonata form, similar to the works of J. C. Bach.
    b. The solo sections are devoted exclusively to virtuosic display.
    c. The two principal themes tend to be identical.
    d. Modulation is limited.
    e. They abandon sonata principals for the sake of ritornello principles.

    Answer: a

17. Of the following, which is *not* a late symphony by Mozart?
    a. *Prague*
    b. *Jupiter*
    c. *Linz*
    d. *Haffner*
    e. *Military*

    Answer: e

18. Which of the following operas is based on a Lorenzo Da Ponte libretto?
    a. *The Marriage of Figaro*
    b. *The Magic Flute*
    c. *Idomeneo*
    d. *Clemenza di Tito*
    e. *La finta semplice*

    Answer: a

19. Which of the following operas is a Singspiel?
    a. *The Marriage of Figaro*
    b. *The Magic Flute*
    c. *Idomeneo*
    d. *Clemenza di Tito*
    e. *Cosi fan tutte*

    Answer: b

20. Mozart's final work, left incomplete at his death, was __________.
    a. *The Magic Flute*
    b. *Clemenza di Tito*
    c. Symphony No. 41
    d. *Requiem Mass*
    e. Clarinet Quintet

    Answer: d

## SHORT-ESSAY QUESTIONS

1. Compare the lives and careers of Haydn and Mozart.
2. Trace the development of Haydn's symphonies.
3. Discuss the interaction of serious and comic elements in Mozart's *Don Giovanni*.
4. Discuss Mozart's concertos in terms of form and style.

## TERMS FOR IDENTIFICATION

Esterházy family
Esterháza
baryton
Count Morzin
*Sturm und Drang*
*Paris* Symphonies
*London* Symphonies
*Surprise* Symphony
Leopold Mozart
Salzburg
Johann Schobert
*Haydn* Quartets
serenade
ars combinatoria
Lorenzo Da Ponte
Freemasonry

# CHAPTER 23 Revolution and Change

I. Revolution and Change
   A. The French Revolution can be seen in three phases.
      1. The first phase (1789–92) sought to reform the monarchy government (see **HWM Figure 23.1**).
      2. The second phase (1792–94), initiated by Austria and Prussia's attack on France, witnessed more radical events, including the execution of the king.
      3. The third phase (1794–99) brought about a more moderate constitution and economic hardships.
   B. Napoleon Bonaparte
      1. A war hero, Napoleon became First Consul of the Republic in 1799.
      2. Napoleon crowned himself emperor in 1804.
      3. He expanded France's political dominance in Europe through military victories.
      4. Napoleon also reformed the French government, making it more efficient.
      5. A failed military campaign in Russia led to Napoleon's defeat and abdication in 1814.
      6. After escaping exile, Napoleon resumed power, only to be defeated at Waterloo.
      7. Despite the failure, Napoleon spread ideas of democracy and nationalism throughout Europe.
   C. The Revolution had a strong impact on music.
      1. Large choral works were composed for public celebrations.
      2. The government supported French opera, but controlled the content; Revolutionary themes were common.
      3. The French government established the Paris Conservatoire in 1795.
         a. The Conservatoire established a standard curriculum for student musicians.
         b. As the first modern conservatory, it became a model for other schools throughout Europe.
   D. The Industrial Revolution
      1. Technology transformed Western economy from agriculture to manufacturing.
      2. The Revolution began in the British textile industry.
      3. Other industries followed, including instrument-making firms.
      4. Men, women, and children worked at factories and coal mines, often in poor working conditions.
      5. The middle class flourished at the expense of the aristocracy and the poor.

II. Ludwig van Beethoven (1770–1827): The First Period (1770–1802)
   A. Beethoven's periods
      1. Beethoven's career is traditionally divided into three periods (see **HWM biography,** page 572, and **HWM Figure 23.2**)
      2. The first period consists of his youth in Bonn and his early years in Vienna.
   B. Bonn (1770–1791)
      1. He studied music with his father and other local musicians.
      2. He entered the service of Maximilian Franz, elector of Cologne.
      3. He attracted attention as a virtuoso pianist and improviser (see **HWM Source Reading,** page 574).

4. Haydn praised Beethoven's music and urged the elector to send him to Vienna.

C. Vienna (1792–1802)
1. He studied with Haydn and took counterpoint lessons with Johann Georg Albrechtsberger.
2. Beethoven established himself as a pianist and composer.
3. He played in public concerts and taught wealthy students.
4. Beethoven earned additional income when he began to publish his compositions.

D. The early pianos sonatas
1. Most of Beethoven's earliest works are for piano.
2. The early sonatas were conceived for amateurs, although the technical demands were increasing.
3. Like Mozart, Beethoven used strong contrasts of style to delineate form and to expand the expressive range.

E. *Sonate pathétique* (Sonata with Pathos), Op. 13 in C Minor (published in 1799)
1. The title suggests suffering and a tragic mode of expression.
2. The sonata has three movements.
   a. The passionate first movement begins with a dramatic slow introduction, which returns twice during the movement.
   b. The serene middle movement is in A-flat major.
   c. The finale returns to the stormy mood and key of the first movement.
3. The third movement (**NAWM 108**)
   a. The pervasive minor mode conveys the sense of pathos.
   b. It is in a sonata-rondo form: ABACAB'A Coda.
   c. The refrain is a simple period.
   d. The refrain and first episode resemble a sonata-form exposition.
   e. The central episode (C), in A-flat major, is contrapuntal and serves as a development section.
   f. The return of the B material in the third episode is in the tonic, as it would in a sonata form.
   g. The refrain theme recalls the second theme of the first movement.
   h. The finale incorporates the key of the middle movement, A-flat major.

F. Op. 18 string quartets
1. Beethoven waited until he was established before composing string quartets and orchestral works.
2. His first quartets, a set of six works, was published as Op. 18 in 1800.
3. Although indebted to Haydn and Mozart, these works bear Beethoven's stamp of individuality.
   a. The tragic final scene of *Romeo and Juliet* may have inspired the dramatic slow movement of quartet No. 1.
   b. Offbeat accents contribute to the humor in the scherzo of No. 6 (see **HWM Example 23.1**).
   c. The rondo finale to No. 6 has a slow introduction labeled "La Malinconia."

G. Beethoven's Symphony No. 1 in C Major premiered in 1800.
1. The work is similar to the late symphonies of Haydn and Mozart.
2. Distinctive features
   a. A slow introduction that avoids a clear tonic cadence
   b. Dynamic shadings
   c. Prominent woodwinds
   d. A scherzo-like third movement
   e. Lengthy codas for the outer movements

III. The Middle Period (1803–1814)

A. Around 1803, Beethoven began to compose in a new style, due in part to support by patrons and publishers.
1. Several patrons joined together to keep Beethoven in Vienna.
2. The Archduke Rudolph was Beethoven's piano and composition student.
3. Publishers competed for Beethoven's music.
4. Beethoven often dodged deadlines, giving him time to revise his works.

B. Beethoven composed with deliberation.
1. His output is significantly less than that of Haydn and Mozart.
2. Beethoven jotted down ideas in notebooks (see **HWM Figure 23.3**).
3. These notebooks allow us to follow the progress of his ideas (see **NAWM 109** commentary).

C. Beethoven realized that he was going deaf in 1802.
1. He considered suicide, but resolved to work for art, as described in his *Heiligenstadt Testament* (see **HWM Source Reading,** page 578).
2. Beethoven appeared less often in public, but kept composing.

D. Many of Beethoven's compositions seem to reflect the struggle of his own life.

1. The themes can be seen as characters in a drama.
2. Instrumental music was no longer just an entertainment or diversion.

E. The music of the middle period builds on the models of Haydn and Mozart.
1. Traditions can be seen in genres, forms, melodic types, phrasing, and textures.
2. Beethoven expanded the forms to unprecedented lengths.
3. Despite the expansions, Beethoven is economical in his material.

F. The *Eroica* Symphony, No. 3 in E-flat Major (1803–4)
1. The *Eroica* is longer than any previous symphony.
2. The title suggests that the symphony is a celebration of a hero.
3. Beethoven originally named the symphony "Bonaparte," but reportedly tore up the title page when Napoleon declared himself emperor (see **HWM Figure 23.4**).
4. The first movement of the *Eroica* can be seen as a story of challenge, struggle, and final victory (**NAWM 109**).
   a. The main motive of the first theme serves as the protagonist, is triadic, and has a surprising C-sharp at the end (see **HWM Example 23.2a**).
   b. This motive undergoes numerous transformations during the movement (see **HWM Example 23.2b–e**).
   c. The principal antagonist theme, which also recurs several times, creates a duple meter with accents on weak beats (see **HWM Example 23.3**).
   d. The antagonist theme leads to a terrifying dissonant climax in the lengthy development section.
   e. Following this climax, a new theme is introduced that is related to the protagonist theme.
   f. The resolution of conflict can be seen in the recapitulation (see **HWM Example 23.4**).
   g. The lengthy coda brings back material from the development and reaffirms the resolution.
   h. Beethoven's sketches provide valuable information about the conception and structure of his music.
5. The slow movement is a funeral march in C minor.
   a. The march is full of tragedy and pathos.
   b. A contrasting section in C major contains fanfares and celebratory lyricism.
   c. The return of the march is varied.
   d. The movement has links to Revolutionary music in France, including a striking parallel to a march by François-Joseph Gossec (see **HWM Example 23.5**).
6. The third movement is a quick scherzo with prominent horn calls in the trio.
7. The finale mixes variations, fugues, development, and marches using a theme from Beethoven's ballet music in *The Creatures of Prometheus.*
8. With this symphony, Beethoven challenged listeners to engage in music deeply and thoughtfully.

G. Dramatic and vocal works
1. Beethoven's only opera, *Fidelio,* is based on a rescue plot.
   a. The opera glorifies heroism and the humanitarian ideas of the Revolution.
   b. Leonore, dressed as a man, rescues her husband from prison.
   c. Beethoven revised the opera several times.
2. Beethoven composed other dramatic music, including incidental music for the play *Egmont,* written by Goethe.
3. In Beethoven's Lieder, the music is as interesting as the poetry.

H. Chamber music
1. Major works include:
   a. Two violin sonatas, including Op. 47 (the *Kreutzer*)
   b. The *Archduke* Piano Trio Op. 97
   c. Five string quartets
2. Beethoven continued to test the technical abilities of amateurs.
3. The three quartets of Opus 59 were dedicated to the Russian ambassador to Vienna, Count Razumovsky.
   a. Beethoven introduced Russian themes into two of the movements.
   b. The first movement of Op. 59 No. 1 is particularly idiosyncratic.

I. Concertos
1. The concertos of the middle period are on a grander scale than earlier works.
2. Beethoven expanded the dimensions and expressive range in the Piano Concerto No. 5 in E-flat Major (the *Emperor*) and in the Violin Concerto in D Major.
3. The soloist opens the Piano Concerto No. 5 with a cadenza.

J. Other symphonies

1. Symphony No. 5 (1807–8)
   a. The work, moving from C minor to C major, symbolizes a struggle for victory.
   b. The first movement is dominated by a famous four-note motive.
   c. This motive is heard in all four movements.
   d. The symphony has a transition between the scherzo and the final movement.
   e. The transition begins softly with the timpani playing the motive.
   f. The entrance of the full orchestra at the beginning of the final movement includes the trombones on a C-major chord.
   g. The finale also adds a piccolo and contrabassoon.
2. Symphony No. 6 (the *Pastoral,* 1808)
   a. This work was premiered on the same program as Symphony No. 5 (see **HWM Figure 23.5**).
   b. Each of the movements has a title describing life in the country.
   c. An extra movement (*Storm*) precedes the finale.
   d. The woodwinds imitate birdcalls in the coda of the second movement (see **HWM Example 23.6**).

IV. The Late Period (1815–1827)
  A. In his later years, Beethoven went further into isolation.
    1. His deafness became increasingly profound.
    2. He became suspicious of friends.
    3. Beethoven also suffered from family problems, ill health, and fear of poverty.
    4. Vienna's postwar depression made it difficult to produce large-scale works.
    5. Vienna suffered from a repressive government instituted by Count Metternich.
    6. Beethoven abandoned the heroic style.
  B. Characteristics of the late style
    1. Beethoven's late quartets were published in score, suggesting that they were to be studied as well as played (see **HWM Figure 23.6**).
    2. The mood became more introspective, and the musical language was more concentrated.
    3. Classical forms remained, but were subject to great upheaval.
    4. Variation structures focused on the substance of a theme.
    5. Beethoven emphasized continuity.
       a. He blurred divisions between phrases.
       b. Successive movements are often played without pause.
       c. The songs of *An die ferne Geliebte* (To the Distant Beloved), which inaugurate the genre of a song cycle, are sung without breaks.
    6. Beethoven explored unusual new sonorities in his late works.
    7. With these works, Beethoven established the tradition that a performer must seek out the composer's vision (see **HWM Source Reading,** page 588).
    8. Works featuring imitative counterpoint, especially fugues, are common.
       a. Fugal finales include:
          (1) Piano Sonatas Opp. 106 and 110
          (2) Symphony No. 9
          (3) *Grosse Fuge* (Great Fugue), originally the finale for the String Quartet in B-flat Major, Op. 130.
       b. Beethoven also used the fugue as the first movement of the String Quartet in C-sharp Minor, Op. 131 (see **NAWM 110a** and **HWM Example 23.7**).
    9. Beethoven often altered the number and arrangement of the movements.
  C. String Quartet in C-sharp Minor, Op. 131
    1. Beethoven thought this was his greatest quartet.
    2. Typical of many late works, this quartet appeals primarily to the connoisseur.
    3. The work has seven movements played without breaks.
       a. Fugue in C-sharp minor
       b. Sonata-rondo in D major
       c. Recitative in B minor
       d. Theme and variations in A major
       e. Scherzo in E major
       f. Introduction in G-sharp minor
       g. Sonata form in C-sharp minor
    4. The finale refers to the fugue subject of the first movement (see **HWM Example 23.8**).
    5. First movement
       a. The slow tempo and fugal form are unusual for a first movement.
       b. The theme begins with a four-note motive ending with a sforzando.
       c. The exposition has four statements of the theme.
       d. The answer form of the theme is on the subdominant.
       e. Later statements of the themes are separated by episodes.
       f. The final entrances are in C-sharp minor and include augmentation.

g. The movement is extremely emotional and uses unusual harmonies.
h. The key areas include E major, G-sharp minor, B major, A major, and D major, all of which are keys of later movements.

6. Second movement
   a. The closing unison C-sharp of the first movement moves up a half step.
   b. The structure is sonata rondo, a form typical of final movements.
   c. The mood is more comic than dramatic.

D. The late period include two major public works.
   1. *Missa solemnis*
      a. Originally intended as a mass for the elevation of Archduke Rudolph to archbishop, the work became too long and elaborate for liturgical use.
      b. The influence of Handel can be seen in the choral writing, but the five movements are unified into a symphonic structure.
      c. The work functions as a concert piece.
   2. Symphony No. 9
      a. This work was first performed in May 1824 (see **HWM Figure 23.7**).
      b. Beethoven did not hear the applause after the scherzo movement.
      c. The first three movements, lasting more than an hour, are on a grand scale.
      d. The most striking innovation of the symphony is the use of voices in the finale, which uses Schiller's poem *Ode to Joy*.
      e. The final movement follows an unorthodox format.

V. Beethoven as a Cultural Hero
   A. His life story defines the Romantic view of the outcast artist.
   B. Many of his works were immediately popular and have remained so.
   C. His late works are now viewed as achieving greatness.
   D. Beethoven's works are central to the performing repertoires of soloists and ensembles.
   E. Beethoven greatly influenced later composers.

## SUGGESTIONS FOR SUPPLEMENTARY READING/LISTENING/ACTIVITIES

Have students select one of the books listed at the end of Chapter 23 in *HWM* and report to the class on the type of book (primary or secondary material), scope, techniques, and bias. Have them discuss the book's usefulness to audience, performer, and scholar. This exercise will acquaint students with the basic sources available on Beethoven as well as the type of work done by musicologists, theorists, and critics.

Bring facsimiles of Beethoven's sketchbooks to class (select examples showing numerous changes) to show how Beethoven struggled to perfect each work. Also bring the comparable passages from performing editions and ask students to discuss how a study of the sketches might influence performers' interpretations. Have them refer to the commentary for **NAWM 109**.

For more on Beethoven's compositional process, see Glenn Stanley, "The Compositional Act: Sketches and Autographs," in *The Cambridge Companion to Beethoven,* edited by Glenn Stanley (New York: Cambridge University Press, 2000).

Discuss the *Pathétique* Sonata in terms of Beethoven's adherence to and departure from Classical norms.

The Op. 18 string quartets can be used to demonstrate Beethoven's approach to form and allows for a good comparison to the works of Haydn. The movements of Op. 18 No. 4 follow Classical structures closely, but they also reflect Beethoven's distinctive new style. Using the third movement of Opus 18 No. 6, have students discuss the meaning of scherzo as a genre and as a mood.

Play the opening of Symphony No. 1 and ask students to think of how audiences might have reacted. Ask them how this opening plays with audiences' expectations and whether it prepares the audience for the coming movement. Compare this opening to Haydn's "Joke " quartet (**NAWM 103**). Use this exercise to prepare for discussions of false recapitulations and other unexpected events in Beethoven's later works.

Have students listen to all four movements of Beethoven's Symphony No. 3. Discuss how the image of a hero is treated in each movement. Have the students discuss whether this work can inspire us as much as it would its original audience. Compare recordings of Symphony No. 3 on period instruments with recordings on modern instruments. In particular, listen to the sound of gut strings in the funeral march and the horn fanfares in the scherzo, which require hand-stopping. Ask how Beethoven takes advantages of these sounds.

For more on *Fidelio,* see Michael C. Tusa, "Beethoven's Essay in Opera: Historical, Text-critical and Interpretative Issues in Fidelio," in *The Cambridge Companion to Beethoven,* edited by Glenn Stanley (New York: Cambridge University Press, 2000), and Paul Robinson, *Ludwig van*

*Beethoven, Fidelio* (New York: Cambridge University Press, 1996). *Fidelio* has been released on DVD (Universal Music and VI, 2003) and is available on compact disc (Testament, 2004).

Have students trace the four-note motive through the Fifth Symphony and write a brief paper describing the techniques Beethoven used to unify the movement and to create variety.

Have students read Berlioz's description of the thunderstorm scene in Beethoven's Sixth Symphony and then listen to the movement. Do they hear the same effects in the same way? How does this scene compare to the programmatic episodes in Haydn's works? Watch the Disney animation from *Fantasia* (1940) and ask them what has been altered to fit the needs of the film.

For a longer yet readable discussion of Beethoven's middle- and late-period works, see the first two chapters of Leon Plantinga, *Romantic Music* (New York: W. W. Norton, 1984).

Have students choose a middle-period work, such as the *Waldstein* piano sonata or a string quartet from Opus 59, and discuss the innovative features. Ask a string player to analyze the fugal finale to Opus 59 No. 1 in terms of both structure and performance difficulties.

Have students select individual movements from Beethoven's late-period works and report on the style features they notice. For each movement, have students identify features consistent with his middle-period style and features that mark the movement as being from his late period.

Have students study the entire string quartet of Opus 131. Discuss how this work deviates from the standard four-movement structure. See if they can perceive an underlying classical structure if some of the movements are considered to be introductions or transitions.

Play the orchestral recitative and the corresponding recitative in the voice from Beethoven's Ninth Symphony, and then play the choral section at the end. Ask students why the audience would have been so enthusiastic at the work's premier. Discuss the integration of voice and orchestra.

## OBJECTIVE QUESTIONS

1. The first modern conservatory of music was founded in __________.
   a. London
   b. Paris
   c. Vienna
   d. Berlin
   e. New York

   Answer: b

2. Beethoven's first music teacher was __________.
   a. his father
   b. Haydn
   c. Mozart
   d. Albrechtsberger
   e. J. C. Bach

   Answer: a

3. Of the following, which was *not* a way that Beethoven earned a living during his first creative period?
   a. performing on the piano
   b. publishing piano music
   c. teaching piano lessons
   d. taking opera commissions
   e. receiving money and accommodations from patrons

   Answer: d

4. Which of the following belongs to Beethoven's first creative period?
   a. *Fidelio*
   b. *Pathétique* Sonata
   c. *Pastoral* Symphony
   d. *Emperor* Concerto
   e. *Missa solemnis*

   Answer: b

5. Of the following, which does *not* describe Beethoven's first string quartets?
   a. They break away completely from the models of Haydn and Mozart.
   b. They show Beethoven's individual personality.
   c. Stark juxtapositions of opposing emotions can be heard.
   d. They call upon and subvert classical traditions.
   e. The slow movement of No. 1 recalls the vault scene of *Romeo and Juliet.*

   Answer: a

6. The slow movement of the *Eroica* Symphony __________.
   a. is in sonata form
   b. is a variation structure
   c. recalls funeral marches from revolutionary France
   d. evokes a pastoral scene by a brook
   e. uses an expanded orchestra

   Answer: c

7. Which of the following can be said of Beethoven's *Fidelio*?
   a. It is a comic opera.
   b. It glorifies the heroism of a woman.
   c. It presents a pacifist plot.
   d. The original production was an immediate success.
   e. It was composed effortlessly.

   Answer: b

Use the following answers for questions 8–12.
   a. *An die ferne Geliebte*
   b. the *Pastoral*
   c. the *Eroica*
   d. the *Grosse Fuge*
   e. the *Emperor*

8. A single-movement work for string quartet from Beethoven's late period.

   Answer: d

9. A song cycle from Beethoven's late period.

   Answer: a

10. The nickname for Beethoven's Piano Concerto No. 5

    Answer: e

11. The nickname for Beethoven's Symphony No. 6.

    Answer: b

12. The nickname for Beethoven's Symphony No. 3.

    Answer: c

13. When Beethoven realized that he was going deaf, he wrote __________.
    a. his last symphony
    b. the *Heiligenstadt Testament*
    c. a suicide note
    d. his autobiography
    e. a string quartet

    Answer: b

14. Of the following, which is *not* a characteristic of Beethoven's late period?
    a. fondness for variation form
    b. unconventional number of movements in works
    c. contemplative quality
    d. imitation of Haydn's more whimsical works
    e. fondness for fugues

    Answer: d

Use the following for questions 15–18.
   a. Napoleon
   b. Rudolph
   c. Lichnowsky
   d. Schiller
   e. Razumovsky

15. Beethoven intended the *Missa solemnis* to be performed when this man became archbishop.

    Answer: b

16. He wrote the words to *Ode to Joy*.

    Answer: d

17. He was a patron who allowed Beethoven to live in one of his houses.

    Answer: c

18. Beethoven dedicated his Opus 59 string quartets to him.

    Answer: e

19. Which composer's works served as models for Beethoven's *Missa solemnis?*
    a. Mozart
    b. J. S. Bach
    c. Handel
    d. Haydn
    e. Palestrina

    Answer: c

20. Of the following, which is unusual about the Ninth Symphony?
    a. the use of chorus
    b. the use of a variation structure
    c. the way movements are played without a break
    d. the four-movement structure
    e. a lively scherzo movement

    Answer: a

## SHORT-ESSAY QUESTIONS

1. Beethoven's life is usually divided into three creative periods. Give the dates and major works of each, and briefly characterize the features of Beethoven's style during each period.
2. Discuss the ways in which events in Beethoven's life affected his music.
3. In what respects was Beethoven's financial situation different from that of Haydn and Mozart? How did his financial circumstances affect his compositional output and style?
4. Name at least five unusual features of Beethoven's Ninth Symphony and describe them briefly.

## TERMS FOR IDENTIFICATION

Napoleon Bonaparte
Paris Conservatoire
Johann Georg Albrechtsberger
Prince Karl von Lichnowsky
*Sonate pathétique*
Op. 18 string quartets
Archduke Rudolf
*Heiligenstadt Testament*
song cycle
Johann von Schiller
*Ode to Joy*

CHAPTER 24

# The Romantic Generation: Song and Piano Music

I. The New Order, 1815–1848
  A. The upheavals of 1789–1815 brought about numerous changes.
    1. Ideas of liberty, equality, and national identity spread across Europe.
    2. The Congress of Vienna (1814–15) redefined national boundaries (see **HWM Figure 24.1**).
    3. Nationalistic feelings became more pronounced.
    4. Composers incorporated national traits in song, opera, and instrumental music.
  B. The Americas
    1. Independence was won in Latin America.
    2. The United States
      a. Expanded west between 1803 and 1848
      b. Began to establish its own cultural identity
    3. French and British provinces in Canada united.
  C. The changing economic order had a strong impact on music.
    1. The decline of the aristocracy
      a. Patronage dwindled as the aristocracy declined.
      b. Merchants and entrepreneurs became economic leaders.
    2. Musicians turned to public performance, teaching, and composing for commissions and publication for money.
    3. Virtuoso performers, such as violinist Nicolò Paganini and pianist Fryderyk Chopin, were among the most prominent musicians.
    4. Music-making became an important outlet for the middle class.
    5. Music was used for social control.
      a. State-sponsored operas carried political messages.
      b. Churches and factories created amateur ensembles for diversion.
      c. Music kept women occupied at home.
  D. The piano became a central part of the home.
    1. Innovations in design allowed for new effects and an expanded range.
    2. Inexpensive pianos found their way to many homes (see **HWM Figure 24.2** and **Innovations,** pages 600–601).
    3. Many women played the piano.
      a. Pianist-composers, like Chopin and Liszt, gave lessons to wealthy women.
      b. A number of professional women pianists appeared in the early nineteenth century, such as Clara Wieck.
      c. Most women used piano-playing for social purposes.
      d. A favorite pastime was playing piano duets at one piano.
  E. The growth in amateur music-making created a boom in music publishing.
    1. The amount of music surviving from the nineteenth century is much greater than from any earlier period.
    2. The public had an unprecedented influence over what music was created.
    3. Arrangements were the only way that many people could hear major concert works.
    4. Musical style catered to amateur tastes.
      a. Tuneful melodies with attractive accompaniments
      b. Little counterpoint

c. Rhythm and level of difficulty was uniform from measure to measure.
d. Extramusical imagery and evocative titles were common.
e. Harmonies mixed conventional and dramatic progressions.
f. Predictable four-measure phrases dominated.
g. Idiomatic writing exploited the sonorities of the modern piano.
h. Novelties often made a work more successful.

5. These characteristics defined a new style known as the early Romantic style.

II. Romanticism

A. The term "romantic" has several meanings.

1. The word derived from the medieval *romance*.
   a. A romance was a poem or tale about heroic events or persons.
   b. The term connoted something distant, legendary, and fantastic.
   c. It suggested something imaginary, far away from reality.
2. In the nineteenth century, the term was applied to literature, music, and art.
   a. The term contrasted with "classic" poetry, which was objectively beautiful.
   b. "Romantic" poetry, not bound by rules and limits, expressed insatiable longing and the richness of nature.
   c. The focus was on the individuality of expression.
   d. Haydn and Mozart were viewed as Classic, and Beethoven was seen as both Classic and Romantic.

B. By the end of the nineteenth century, the Classic and Romantic eras were seen as two periods divided around 1820.

1. The divisions between the two periods have been viewed in a variety of ways.
2. In this text, 1815 will be the starting point for the Romantic period.

C. Romanticism can be seen as a reaction to several trends.

1. In a society driven by technology, Romanticism provided refuge in various ideals:
   a. The past
   b. Myths
   c. Dreams
   d. The supernatural
   e. The irrational
2. With the rise of a national concept, Romanticism viewed common people as the embodiment of the nation.
3. As people moved to urban centers, nature was increasingly valued.
4. As industrialization brought about a mass society, Romantics esteemed solitude and individuality.
5. Romantics pursued novelty and the exotic, while life in general became routine in factories, shops, and homes.
6. In a capitalist society, artists began pursuing their dreams not for money but for art (see **HWM Figure 24.6**).

D. Music was seen as the ideal art.

1. Composers respected conventions, but let their imagination lead them to explore new sounds.
2. Instrumental music was seen as the ideal art because it was free from words and visual images.

E. Distinctions were made between types of instrumental music.

1. *Absolute music* refers to music with no programmatic or descriptive aspects.
2. *Programmatic music* recounts a story, which is often given in an accompanying text.
3. A *character piece* suggests a mood, personality, or scene that is usually suggested in the title.

F. Connections with literature

1. Many composers were also writers or had friends who were writers.
2. Composers sought to draw out the inner meanings of the text in song or opera.
3. Instrumental pieces were often linked to literary works.
4. Literary associations often led to musical innovations that enhanced the appeal of the composition.
5. At times, literary associations and descriptive titles were added after a work was created.

III. Song

A. General trends

1. Songs were predominantly set for voice and piano.
2. Settings varied from simple strophic forms to through-composed miniature dramas.
3. At the end of the century, a line emerged between popular songs and art songs.
4. The German Lied, the most prestigious repertoire of songs in the century, featured:
   a. The fusion of music and poetry
   b. The expression of individual feelings

c. The use of descriptive musical imagery
d. Elements of folk style
5. Also significant was the tradition of the British and American parlor song.

B. The Lied
1. The Romantic Lied was built upon a strong eighteenth-century tradition.
2. The popularity of German Lieder grew after 1800.
3. Poets at the time drew upon elements from classical and folk traditions.
4. Nature was a common theme.
5. The lyric was the chief poetic genre.
a. Lyric poetry was meant to be sung.
b. It was characterized by short strophes, regular meter, and rhyme.
c. The poem was strophic and expressed a feeling about one subject.
d. The models were the lyric poets of antiquity, such as Sappho and Horace.
e. Influential collections
(1) *Volkslieder* (Folk Songs, 1778–79) by Johann Gottfried von Herder
(2) *Des Knaben Wunderhorn* (The Boy's Magic Horn, 1805) by Clemens Brentano and Achim von Arnim

C. The ballad was a new type of Lied from the late eighteenth century.
1. Ballads often alternated narrative and dialogue.
2. The subject was usually a romantic adventure or supernatural incident.
3. The expanded length encouraged composers to vary the musical material.
4. The role of the piano changed from mere accompaniment to equal partner in illustrating the meaning of the poem.

D. Song cycles
1. Songs were often grouped into collections with a unifying characteristic, such as a single poet or a common theme.
2. In these cycles, the songs were to be performed in order, enabling the composer to tell a story.
3. Beethoven's *An die ferne Geliebte* introduced the concept of the song cycle.

IV. Franz Schubert (1797–1828) (see **HWM biography,** page 606, and **Figure 24.7)**

A. Biography
1. Schubert was the first great master of the Romantic Lied.
2. Schubert was born and spent his entire career in Vienna.
3. He composed with astonishing speed and wrote over 140 songs in 1815.
4. Schubert composed over six hundred Lieder.
5. Many of his songs were performed at Schubertiads, home concerts for friends (see **HWM Figure 24.8**).
6. He never secured a patron and lived off of his publications.
7. Schubert died at the age of thirty-one, possibly from syphilis.

B. Song texts
1. Schubert set poetry by many writers, including fifty-nine by Goethe.
2. Schubert attempted to make the music equal to the words.
3. Some of his finest works are his two song cycles on poems by Wilhelm Müller.
a. *Die schöne Müllerin* (The Pretty Miller-Maid, 1823)
b. *Winterreise* (Winter's Journey, 1827)

C. Song forms
1. Strophic
a. Schubert typically uses this form for poems that have a single image or express a single mood.
b. Each stanza is sung to the same music.
c. Examples:
(1) *Heidenröslein* (Little Heath-Rose, 1815)
(2) *Das Wandern* (Wandering) from *Die schöne Müllerin*
2. Modified strophic
a. The music repeats for some strophes but is varied for others.
b. Example: *Der Lindenbaum* (The Linden Tree) from *Winterreise*
3. Ternary form (ABA or ABA'): *Der Atlas* (Atlas) from *Schwanengesang* (Swan Song, 1828)
4. Bar form (AAB): *Ständchen* (Serenade), also from *Schwanengesang*
5. Through-composed
a. Each strophe has new music.
b. This form is typically found in longer narrative songs, such as the ballad *Erlkönig* (The Erl-King, 1815).
c. This form may incorporate declamatory and arioso styles as in an opera scene, like *Der Wanderer* (The Wanderer, 1816).

D. Melody
1. Schubert created beautiful melodies that captured the spirit of the poem (see **HWM Example 24.1**).

2. Many melodies are simple and folk-like.
3. Other melodies suggest sweetness and melancholy.
4. Some melodies are declamatory and dramatic.

E. Accompaniment
1. Accompaniments vary from simple to dramatic (see **HWM Example 24.1**).
2. The accompaniment may reflect an image in the poem.

F. Harmony
1. Schubert uses harmony to reinforce the poetry.
2. *Das Wandern* has only five different chords.
3. *Ständchen* alternates minor and major keys and triads.
4. Complex modulations can be found in some songs, such as *Der Atlas*.
5. Modulations by third rather than by fifth are frequent in Schubert's songs and instrumental works.
6. Schubert uses unusual harmonic relationships as an expressive device.
7. Schubert's harmonic practice greatly influenced later composers.

G. *Gretchen am Spinnrade* (Gretchen at the Spinning Wheel, 1814, **NAWM 111**)
1. The text is taken from Goethe's *Faust.*
2. In the poem, Gretchen is spinning thread and thinking of Faust.
3. The top line of the piano suggests the movement of a spinning wheel (see **HWM Example 24.2**).
4. The left hand of the piano imitates the sound of the wheel's pedal.
5. The sixteenth-notes also represent Gretchen's agitation.
6. Schubert repeats the opening poetic lines to create a refrain and give the song a rondo-like form.
7. The harmony suggests Gretchen's restlessness.
8. The piano stops when Gretchen recalls her beloved's kiss.
9. The spinning begins again as she regains her composure.

H. *Der Lindenbaum* (**NAWM 112**)
1. This song is from *Winterreise,* a cycle of twenty-four songs expressing the regrets of a lover over a failed romance.
2. In *Der Lindenbaum,* the lover passes a linden tree associated with the romance.
3. The prelude suggests summer breezes, but later turns to cold winter wind.
4. The melody is simple and folk-like.
5. The song has a modified strophic form: AA'BA".
6. Major and minor keys denote the contrast between happy memories and the chill of winter.

V. Robert and Clara Schumann (see **HWM biography,** page 612, and **Figure 24.9**)

A. Robert Schumann (1810–1856) was the first important composer of Lieder after Schubert.
1. Biography
   a. Schumann wanted to be a concert pianist but injured his hand.
   b. He turned to composition and criticism, serving as the editor of *Neue Zeitschrift für Musik* (New Journal of Music) from 1834 to 1844.
   c. In his reviews, he opposed empty virtuosity and urged the study of older music.
   d. Schumann's song-writing was inspired both emotionally and financially by an impending marriage.
   e. In 1840, Schumann composed over 120 songs and married Clara Wieck, an outstanding pianist and composer.
   f. Schumann suffered from hallucinations and tried to commit suicide in 1854.
   g. He was confined to an asylum and died in 1856.
2. Characteristics of Schumann's songs
   a. Schumann felt that the music should capture a poem's essence.
   b. He believed that the piano and voice were equal partners and often gave the piano long preludes, interludes, or postludes.
   c. Schumann often used a single figuration to convey a central emotion or idea in a poem.
3. His focus on love songs can be seen in two of his song cycles from 1840.
   a. *Dicterliebe* (A Poet's Love)
   b. *Frauenliebe und -leben* (Woman's Love and Life)
4. *Im wunderschönen Monat Mai* (In the marvelous month of May) from *Dichterliebe* (see **NAWM 113** and **HWM Example 24.3**)
   a. *Dichterliebe* contains sixteen settings of poems from *Lyrical Intermezzo* by Heinrich Heine, one of Germany's foremost poets.
   b. The poems are arranged to suggest the course of a relationship.
   c. *Im wunderschönen Monat Mai,* the first song of the cycle, is strophic.
   d. The opening harmonic ambiguity suggests tentative feelings.

e. Longing and desire are expressed through suspensions and appoggiaturas.
f. The lack of harmonic resolution suggests that the love may remain unrequited.
g. The piano is an equal partner in expressing meaning in this song.

B. Clara Schumann (1819–1896) (see **HWM biography,** page 612, and **Figure 24.9**)
1. After Robert's death, Clara Schumann stopped composing and devoted herself to concertizing and promoting her husband's music.
2. Clara Schumann wrote several collections of Lieder.
3. Clara's approach to song was similar to that of her husband.
a. Her compositions contain long piano preludes and postludes.
b. Similar figuration is used throughout a song.
c. The voice and piano are treated as equals,
4. *Geheimes Flürstern* (Secret Whispers, 1853)
a. This work is from her last song cycle.
b. The poem projects an image of the forest whispering to the poet.
c. Continuous arpeggiation suggests rustling leaves and branches.

VI. British and North American Song
A. A tradition emerged in which songs were primarily intended for home performance.
1. In Great Britain, these songs were called *ballads* or *drawing-room ballads.*
2. In the United States and Canada, they were called *parlor songs.*
3. Such songs were also sung in musical theater productions and public concerts.
4. These songs were popular in nature.
5. Characteristics
a. Usually strophic with piano preludes and postludes based on phrases from the tune
b. The expressivity lies in the melody.
c. The accompaniment contains conventional figurations, as opposed to the more dramatic material found in Lieder.
d. The singers were free to reshape the melody or accompaniment.

B. *Home! Sweet Home!* (1823, **NAWM 114**) by Henry R. Bishop (1786–1855)
1. This is perhaps the best-known song of the nineteenth century.
2. Bishop was England's foremost composer for musical theater in the early nineteenth century.
3. This song was intended for the English-language opera *Clari, or The Maid of Milan* (1823).
4. The text, which extols the joys of home, appealed to a displaced generation.
5. The strophic song is set with a verse-refrain structure.
a. The tune unfolds in regular four-measure phrases: AA'BB'.
b. The refrain has elements of both the A and B phrases.
c. Typical of the genre, it is simple, mostly diatonic and triadic.
d. The tune is charming and expressive, with opportunities for embellishment.
e. Attention is given to declamation.
6. The accompaniment provides several moments of support to the text, such as trills suggesting the sound of birds.

C. James P. Clarke (1807/8–1877) was the most notable song composer in Canada.
1. He was the first to earn a Bachelor of Music degree from a North American university.
2. *Lays of the Maple Leaf* (1853), Clarke's song cycle, was the most substantial work published in Canada at that time.

D. Stephen Foster (1826–1864) was the leading song composer in the United States.
1. Biography
a. He had no formal training and taught himself several instruments.
b. *Oh! Susanna* (1848), a minstrel song, achieved great success.
c. He became the first American to earn a living solely as a composer.
d. Foster turned away from minstrel songs and composed for the parlor and the stage.
2. Foster typically wrote his own texts.
3. Combining elements of a variety of song types, Foster made his works easy to perform and remember.
4. General characteristics
a. Foster's tunes are almost always diatonic or pentatonic.
b. The melodies move stepwise and are set in four-measure phrases.
c. The harmony and accompaniment are simple.
5. *Jeannie with the Light Brown Hair* (1853, see **NAWM 115** and **HWM Example 24.4**)
a. This is one of Foster's best-known songs.
b. The text on sentimental love incorporates images of nature.
c. The strophic song is framed by a prelude and postlude for each verse.
d. The melody has four-measure phrases: AA'BA".

e. The simplicity brings out the subtle dissonances.
f. A brief cadenza provides an operatic touch.

VII. Music for Piano
A. Piano music rivaled songs as the most popular medium of the nineteenth century.
B. Piano music has three overlapping purposes.
1. Teaching
a. Muzio Clementi's *Gradus ad Parnassum* (Steps to Parnassus, 1817–26) contains one hundred exercises of increasing difficulty.
b. Carl Czerny wrote numerous method books and *études* (studies).
2. Amateur enjoyment
a. Dances
b. Lyrical pieces modeled on songs
c. Character pieces
d. Sonatas
3. Public performance: bravura pieces
C. Schubert piano music
1. His dance works include marches and waltzes.
2. Short lyrical pieces
a. Six *Moments musicaux* (Musical Moments, 1823–28)
b. Eight *Impromptus* (1827)
3. The numerous piano duets include the beautiful Fantasy in F Minor (1828).
4. The *Wanderer Fantasy* (1822) for solo piano
a. The virtuosity and unusual form fascinated later composers.
b. Four movements are played without a break.
c. A central variation movement is based on his song *Der Wanderer*.
d. Motives from this song can also be found in other movements.
5. Schubert completed eleven sonatas.
a. These works show an evident conflict between his song-inspired style and the demands of a multimovement sonata.
b. His themes tend to be expansive melodies that do not lend themselves to thematic development.
c. His sonata-form movements use three keys in the exposition.
d. The slow movements tend to be songlike and resemble impromptus.
6. Schubert's last three sonatas: C minor, A major, and B-flat major.
a. An awareness of Beethoven is evident in the stormy first movement of the C-minor sonata.
b. The works are characterized by a pervasive lyricism.
c. The first movement of the B-flat sonata features a long singing melody.
D. Felix Mendelssohn (1809–47) (See **HWM biography,** page 616, and **Figure 24.10**)
1. Biography
a. He was the grandson of Moses Mendelssohn, the leading Jewish philosopher of the German Enlightenment.
b. His father converted the children to Christianity.
c. Mendelssohn was a remarkable child prodigy, whose youthful productivity rivals that of Mozart.
d. He founded the Leipzig Conservatory in 1843.
e. Mendelssohn died at the age of thirty-eight after a series of strokes.
2. He blended characteristics of Bach, Handel, Mozart, and Beethoven with those of his contemporaries.
a. Contrapuntal activity and formal clarity
b. Romantic expression
c. Beautiful melodies
d. Interesting and often unpredictable melodies
e. Fluent technique was emphasized over bravura display.
3. His larger piano works include three sonatas, variations, and fantasias.
4. The *Seven Character Pieces* (1827) introduced the term and helped define the genre.
5. *Lieder ohne Wörte* (Songs without Words)
a. Mendelssohn published forty-eight works in eight books.
b. Mendelssohn believed that music could express feelings that words cannot (see **HWM Source Reading,** page 618).
6. *Lieder ohne Wörte*, Op. 19 No. 1 (see **HWM Example 24.5)**
a. Like a Lied, the music can be divided into three parts: the left-hand bass, the right-hand arpeggiations, and a singer's melody.
b. It is a challenge to play all three parts smoothly.
c. The work projects an engaging melody and an interesting accompaniment.
E. Clara Schumann and Fanny Mendelssohn Hensel (1805–47)
1. Both were highly skilled pianist-composers, but they had contrasting careers.

2. Clara Schumann was an acclaimed pianist at a young age.
   a. By playing only what was written, she focused attention on the composer rather than the performer.
   b. She also performed her own music, as well as that of her husband.
   c. Her works include polonaises, waltzes, variations, preludes and fugues, character pieces, and a sonata in G minor.
3. Fanny Mendelssohn performed primarily in private settings.
   a. She was almost as talented as her brother Felix and married a painter, Wilhelm Hensel.
   b. She performed at her salons, gatherings of friends and guests.
   c. She composed more than four hundred works, including at least 250 songs and 125 piano works.
   d. Most of her works were unpublished because of the objections of her father and brother.
   e. Her masterpiece is *Das Jahr* (The Year, 1841), a series of character pieces on the twelve months of the year.
   f. She died of a stroke less than a year after the publication of her Opus 1, a set of six songs.
   g. Her importance and the quality of her works have only recently been discovered.

F. Robert Schumann
1. Prior to 1840, all of Schumann's published music was for piano.
2. Most of his works were short character pieces.
3. The character pieces are often grouped in sets with colorful names.
   a. *Papillons* (Butterflies)
   b. *Carnaval*
   c. *Fantasiestücke* (Fantasy Pieces)
   d. *Kinderscenen* (Scenes from Chilhood)
   e. *Kreisleriana*
   f. *Album für die Jugend* (Album for the Young) contains pieces for children.
4. Although the titles of the pieces suggest poetic descriptions, Schumann said he composed the works before giving them titles.
5. His own contradictory personality is reflected in the many moods.
6. He personified the various sides of his own personality.
   a. Florestan is the impulsive revolutionary.
   b. Eusebius is the contemplative dreamer.
   c. Meister Raro is the wise and mature master.
   d. These characters were members of the Davidsbund, an imaginary league that campaigned against the Philistines of music.
7. *Fantasiestücke* (1837)
   a. This set was dedicated to the British pianist Anna Robena Laidlaw.
   b. The title, taken from a work by E. T. A. Hoffmann, suggests that the works are original, unusual, evocative, and emotional.
   c. There are eight pieces in the set, including *Aufschwung* and *Warum?*.
8. *Aufschwung* (Soaring, **NAWM 116a**)
   a. The impulsive nature of Florestan can be seen in the diverse themes (see **HWM Example 24.6**).
   b. The piece can be diagrammed: ABA' CDC Trans AB'A"
9. *Warum?* (Why?, **NAWM 116b**)
   a. The fragmentary nature of the work makes it both complete and yet seemingly unresolved.
   b. The harmonic ambiguity and inconclusive ending suggest the endless contemplative nature of Eusebius.

VIII. Fryderyk Chopin (1810–49) (see **HWM biography, page 624, and Figure 24.11)**

A. Biography
1. Chopin was born near Warsaw in Poland.
2. An established performer, he moved to Paris in 1831.
3. Chopin met the leading musicians in Paris, including Liszt.
4. He had a tempestuous nine-year affair with novelist George Sand (the pseudonym of Aurore Dudevant).
5. He died from tuberculosis in 1849.

B. Chopin composed almost exclusively for the piano, including:
1. Around two hundred solo piano pieces
2. Six works for piano and orchestra
3. Around twenty songs
4. Four chamber works

C. His idiomatic writing opened new possibilities for the piano that appealed to both amateurs and connoisseurs.

D. Études
1. Chopin composed twenty-seven études.
   a. Opus 10 (1829–33) has twelve.
   b. Opus 25 (1832–37) has twelve.
   c. Three have no opus number.

2. Each étude addresses a specific skill.
3. Chopin's études were the first with significant artistic content and can be called *concert études*.

E. Preludes
1. Chopin composed twenty-four preludes as Op. 28 (1836–39).
2. Like Bach's *Well-Tempered Clavier*, they are in all the major and minor keys.
3. These brief mood pieces illustrate an astounding inventiveness of figuration (see **HWM Example 24.7**).
4. The rich chromatic harmonies and the varied textures influenced many later composers.

F. Dances
1. Chopin composed waltzes, mazurkas, and polonaises for his students.
2. The dances are idiomatic for the piano and are often only moderately difficult.
3. The waltzes evoke the ballrooms of Vienna.
4. Polonaises
   a. The polonaise is a Polish dance in 3/4 meter.
   b. It often has an eighth note and two sixteenth notes on the first beat.
   c. Some are vigorous and suggest a militaristic national identity.
5. Mazurkas
   a. The mazurka was a Polish folk dance that had become popular in Paris ballrooms.
   b. In triple meter, the mazurka features two eighth notes (or a dotted eighth-sixteenth) on the downbeat followed by two quarter notes.
   c. This rhythmic pattern emphasizes the second beat of the measure.
6. Mazurka in B-flat Major, Op. 7, No. 1 (1832, see **NAWM 117** and **HWM Example 24.8**)
   a. This work exemplifies the typical meter and rhythmic gesture of the mazurka.
   b. The accompaniment is simple, and the melody has four-measure phrases.
   c. The overall form can be diagrammed: AA//:BA://:CA://
   d. The A period begins on the dominant; the B and C periods end on the dominant and link back to A.
   e. The melody, which is instrumental and not vocal, exhibits several Polish characteristics.
   f. The marking *rubato* indicates a departure from the regular pulse either in the right hand only or with both hands together.

G. Nocturnes
1. Nocturnes are short pieces with beautiful, embellished melodies and sonorous accompaniments.
2. Chopin's conception of the nocturne is indebted to the nocturnes of the Irish pianist-composer John Field (1782–1837).
3. The genre, a type of song without words, is similar to the nocturne for voices and is indebted to the embellished singing style of Italian opera.
4. Chopin composed eighteen nocturnes.
5. Nocturne in D-flat Major, Op. 27, No. 2 (1835, **NAWM 118**)
   a. This work features an angular melody with embellishments.
   b. The accompaniment spans two octaves.
   c. The form is songlike and can be seen as modified strophic with three verses: AB trans A'B' trans A"B" trans Coda.
   d. The unpredictable A theme unfolds through constant variation.
   e. The B theme is in a contrasting key, but is more regular than A.
   f. Each transition is different.
   g. The coda features parallel diminished seventh chords, but remains firmly in D-flat.

H. Ballades and scherzos
1. The ballades and scherzos are longer and more demanding than Chopin's other one-movement piano works.
2. Ballades
   a. Chopin was one of the first to use the name for an instrumental work.
   b. The ballades capture the spirit of the Polish narrative ballads and are infused with fresh turns in harmony and form.
3. Scherzos
   a. The scherzos are not playful, but serious and passionate.
   b. The scherzos are also tricky and quirky, particularly in their rhythm and thematic material.

I. Sonatas
1. Chopin composed three piano sonatas, all of which have four movements: sonata form, minuet or scherzo, slow movement, finale.
2. Sonata No. 2 in B-flat Minor, Op. 35, includes Chopin's famous funeral march.

J. Chopin's achievement
1. Incorporation of Polish nationalistic traits
2. Concentration on piano music only
3. Mix of virtuosity with elegant lyricism

4. Originality in melody, harmony, and pianism
5. Appeal to amateurs and connoisseurs
6. Creation of an idiomatic piano sound

IX. Franz Liszt (1811–86) (see **HWM biography,** page 626, and **Figure 24.12**)
 A. Liszt was an astounding piano virtuoso and an important composer.
 B. Early career
  1. Liszt was a child prodigy in Hungary and Vienna.
  2. He came to Paris with his family in 1823, at the age of twelve.
  3. He exploited technological advancements on the piano and developed a new virtuoso style.
  4. At Parisian salons, he met many leading writers, painters, and musicians.
  5. He lived in Switzerland and Italy with Countess Marie d'Agoult.
  6. His impressions of these countries can be found in several publications.
   a. *Album d'un voyageur* (Album of a Traveler, 1837–38)
   b. *Années de pèlerinage* (Years of Pilgrimage)—three books
   c. In these works, Liszt sometimes responded to a specific poem or painting.
  7. Liszt gave over one thousand concerts between 1839 and 1847.
   a. He toured Europe, Turkey, and Russia.
   b. He was the first pianist to give solo concerts in large halls, which he termed *recitals*.
   c. He was also the first to play a range of music, from Bach to his contemporaries, and the first to play from memory.
   d. Liszt was often received like a rock star.
  8. Liszt stopped touring in 1848 in order to focus on composition.
 C. Influences
  1. His Hungarian roots can be heard in works based on Hungarian melodies and rhythms, such as the *Hungarian Rhapsodies* for piano.
  2. He absorbed a number of Chopin's qualities after he moved to Paris in 1831.
  3. Nicolò Paganini was perhaps his most important influence.
   a. A hypnotic performer, Paganini raised violin virtuosity to new heights.
   b. Liszt vowed to accomplish the same feat for the piano.
 D. *Un sospiro* (A Sigh) (see **NAWM 119** and **HWM Example 24.9**)
  1. This is the third of his Three Concert Études (1845–49)
  2. This work addresses the technical problem of projecting a slow-moving melody while playing rapid broken-chord figurations.
  3. The unusual form can be interpreted in several ways:
   a. A series of variations on the opening idea
   b. An extended ABA, with the A sections in the tonic and B in other keys
   c. A modified sonata form, with two themes in different keys recapitulated in the tonic
  4. The étude also illustrates Liszt's use of chromatic harmony.
  5. The harmonic scheme has three principal key areas separated by major thirds.
  6. The chromatic cadenza is an elaborate harmonic and melodic decoration of a dissonant sonority.
  7. The coda features an octatonic scale (alternates whole and half steps) in the bass (measures 66–70).
  8. The final cadence brings back chords representing the three principal key areas.
  9. Such harmonic treatment was influential and led Liszt to abandon traditional harmony in his later works
 E. The Sonata in B Minor (1853) is Liszt's only work in that genre.
  1. The work is in one extended movement, but it is divided into three sections that are analogous to the movements of a Classic sonata.
  2. The work is unified by four main themes that are transformed and combined in a free manner.
 F. Many of Liszt's piano works are arrangements, which are of two types:
  1. Operatic paraphrases (sometimes called *reminiscences*) are free fantasies based on popular operas.
  2. The transcriptions include works based on Schubert songs, Berlioz and Beethoven symphonies, Bach organ fugues, and Wagner operas.
 G. Reputation
  1. As a performer, he established most of the traditions of the modern recital, developed new techniques, and provided a model for other performers.
  2. As a composer, he explored new formal and harmonic possibilities while offering deeply felt music on a wide variety of subjects.

X. Louis Moreau Gottschalk (1829–69)
   A. Gottschalk, the first American composer with an international reputation, was also celebrated for his showmanship.
   B. Biography
      1. He was born in New Orleans and studied piano and organ from age five.
      2. He went to study in Paris in 1841 and toured France, Switzerland, and Spain.
      3. Chopin predicted in 1845 that he would become "the king of pianists."
      4. He published pieces based on melodies and rhythms of his mother's West Indian heritage, and these established his reputation.
      5. His 1853 New York debut received wildly enthusiastic reviews.
      6. He spent most of the rest of his life touring the United States, the Caribbean islands, and South America.
   C. *Souvenir de Porto Rico* (**NAWM 120)**
      1. Gottschalk composed this work during a Caribbean tour in 1857–58.
      2. The subtitle *Marche des Gibaros* refers to the Jibaros, peasants who farmed the lands of Puerto Rico.
      3. The form is variations, and dynamic changes suggest a band of musicians approaching and then marching off in the distance.
      4. Two principal themes are presented with a march rhythm.
         a. The initial theme is derived from a Puerto Rican song performed by strolling musicians during Christmas.
         b. The second is marked *malinconico* (melancholy).
      5. Seven variations follow.
         a. Several variations use Afro-Caribbean rhythms with the A theme.
         b. Figurations from European virtuoso music is used for B theme and some of the A theme variations.
         c. The climactic and complex fifth variation, in the relative major, incorporates four Caribbean rhythms.
         d. The final two variations borrow from earlier ones, creating a type of arch form.

XI. The Romantic Legacy
   A. Home music-making declined in the late nineteenth and early twentieth centuries.
      1. New recreations and technologies replaced family music gatherings.
      2. Lieder, parlor songs, and piano pieces either disappeared, became established as art music, or became old favorites.
      3. Piano music written for the home or for virtuoso display fell out of fashion.
   B. Songs
      1. The Lieder of Schubert and Schumann formed the core of the art song repertoire.
      2. Foster's songs became traditional American favorites.
      3. The works of all three have been sung in an unbroken tradition.
   C. Piano music
      1. Bach's *Well-Tempered Clavier* and the sonatas of Mozart and Beethoven were already considered classic pieces of piano music by the 1820s.
      2. The relatively short works of Mendelssohn, Schumann, Chopin, and Liszt created a new repertoire for pianists.
      3. The sonata and fugue became prestige genres; Schubert, Chopin, Schumann, and Liszt all contributed to this repertoire.
   D. Music by women composers was treated differently.
      1. Attitudes changed only at the end of the twentieth century, as scholars began exploring music by women.
      2. Clara Schumann and Fanny Mendelssohn Hensel emerged as key figures.
      3. Current research is exploring other women composers of the era.
   E. The melody-centered style of song and piano music affected every other genre of the nineteenth century.
   F. Romantic views of music have been influential.
      1. Composers created music to express their own ideas and feelings rather than to suit the tastes of their patrons.
      2. Originality became a requirement for all later composers.
      3. Many of our attitudes about music stem from the Romantic era.

## SUGGESTIONS FOR SUPPLEMENTAL READING/LISTENING/ACTIVITIES

For more on romanticism, see Leon Plantinga, *Romantic Music* (New York: W. W. Norton, 1984) or Rey M. Longyear, *Nineteenth-Century Romanticism in Music,* 3rd. ed. (Englewood Cliffs, N. J.: Prentice Hall, 1988). Carl Dahlhaus's *Nineteenth-Century Music,* trans. J. Bradford Robinson (Berkeley: University of California Press, 1989), is difficult reading for lower-level undergraduates, but with guidance, pages 1–53 and 152–60 will complement the discussion in this chapter.

To help students draw a sharper contrast between Classic and Romantic styles, see Arnold Whittall, *Romantic Music: A Concise History from Schubert to Sibelius* (London: Thames and Hudson, 1987), 16–30 and Léonie Rosentiel, ed., *Schirmer History of Music* (New York: Schirmer Books, 1982), 596–608.

Have students make charts comparing the Classic and Romantic approaches to form, harmonic relationships, thematic development, and programmatic description. Ask students to relate each of these to the ideals of the Enlightenment and Romanticism, respectively.

For supplementary works by women, see *Women Composers: Music through the Ages:* Volume 6, *Composers Born 1800–1899, Keyboard Music* and Volume 5, *Large and Small Instrumental Ensembles* (New York: G. K. Hall, 1999), and the *Historical Anthology of Music by Women*, edited by James R. Briscoe (Bloomington: Indiana University Press, 1986), with accompanying compact discs. Have students read "Music as a Proper Occupation for the British Female" in Weiss and Taruskin, eds., *Music in the Western World: A History in Documents* (New Yorks: Schirmer, 1984), 335–6, as an introduction to amateur music-making, and "P. T. Barnum Brings the Swedish Nightingale to America," 385–88, for a glimpse of professional concertizing by a woman.

For insight on the musicale as a performance venue and information about a woman whose importance has only recently come to light, have students read Meg Freeman Whalen, "Fanny Mendelssohn Hensel's Sunday Musicales," in *Women of Note Quarterly: The Magazine of Historical and Contemporary Women Composers* 2 (1994), 9–20.

Jean Mongrédien's *French Music from the Enlightenment to Romanticism, 1789–1830,* trans. Sylvain Frémain (Portland, Oregon: Amadeus Press, 1996), 205–60, discusses salons and public concert venues in France.

For more background on the German Lied, see Lorraine Gorrell, *The Nineteenth-Century German Lied* (Portland Oregon: Amadeus, 1993).

For more on Schubert, see Maurice J. E. Brown, ed., *The New Grove Schubert* (New York: W. W. Norton, 1980) and Otto Erich Deutsch, ed., *The Schubert Reader: A Life of Franz Schubert in Letters and Documents,* trans. Eric Blom (New York: W. W. Norton, 1947).

Schubert's *Erlkönig* can be used for a variety of demonstrations. This is another good time to compare this setting with Reichardt's as described in the suggestions for *HWM* Chapter 20. One can also use this to compare performances by a tenor (Decca 467901, 2002), baritone (Deutsche Grammophon 457747), and soprano (Schwarzkopf on Emi Classics, 2004). In addition, the work can lead to a discussion of transcriptions. You may want to play the Liszt adaptation for piano (Decca 467801, 2001) or the Franz Heinrich Franz Caprice for violin (Cedilc 41, 1998). Naxos provides a variety of performances in its online library (www.naxos.com).

A good introduction to Schubert's songs is Susan Youens, "Franz Schubert: The Prince of Song," in Rufus Hallmark, ed., *German Lieder in the Nineteenth Century* (New York: Schirmer Books, 1996), 36–45. Have students use this article as the basis for their analysis of a Schubert Lied and report on it to the class.

For a postmodern view of Schubert's songs, see Lawrence Kramer, *Franz Schubert: Sexuality Subjectivity and Song* (Cambridge University Press, 1998), especially pages 69–74, in which Kramer analyzes *Death and the Maiden* from the point of view of the performer and the audience. Have students read these pages than apply the Kramer's ideas to a Lied in *NAWM.*

Recent researchers have examined the sex lives of famous composers. For a discussion of the women in Schubert's life, see Rita Steblin, "Schubert's Relationship with Women: An Historical Account," in *Schubert Studies* (Brookfield, Vt.: Ashgate, 1998), 220–43.

For background on Fanny Mendelssohn Hensel's style, see Marcia J. Citron, "The Lieder of Fanny Mendelssohn Hensel," *Musical Quarterly,* 69 (1983), 570–94.

Renewed interest in Lieder composed by women has resulted in several recordings, among them "Lieder by Women Composers from the Classical Period to Modern Times, Vol. 1: From Maria Walurgis to Clara Schumann" (The Musical Heritage Society, 1989); Clara Schumann, "Lieder" (Arte Nova Classics 74321 43308 2, 1996); and Fanny Mendelssohn Hensel, "Lieder" (Hyperion CDA67110, 2000).

Women's music has been overlooked partly because women were, with few exceptions, excluded from professional music-making and confined to music in the home. Judith Tick's book *American Women Composers Before 1870,* rev. ed. (Rochester, N.Y.: University of Rochester Press, 1995), includes a chapter titled "A Woman Composer's Place Is in the Parlor" that includes a discussion of parlor music and facsimiles of some parlor works.

The minstrel song played a significant role in nineteenth-century American music. Its overt racism has inhibited detailed analyses of the repertoire, but you can assign students to locate original texts and report to the class. The efforts of Stephen Foster to bring refinement to the genre and rid it of, in his words, "trashy and really offensive words" are treated at length by PBS (www.pbs.org/wgbh/amex/foster/sfeature/sf_foster.html).

For studies of American parlor music, direct students to the Historic American Sheet Collection, http://memory.loc.gov/ammem/award97/ncdhtml/hasmhome.html. Here students can find valuable information about songs, piano music, and Tin Pan Alley.

For studies of music from Canada, direct students to Carl Morey, *Music in Canada: A Research and Information Guide* (New York: Garland Publications, 1997).

For more on the development of the piano and piano repertoire, see Robert Winter, "Keyboards," in *Performance Practice: Music after 1600,* edited by Howard Mayer Brown and Stanley Sadie (New York: W. W. Norton, 1989), 346–73 and Gordon Stewart, *A History of Keyboard Literature: Music for the Piano and Its Forerunners* (New York: Schirmer Books, 1996).

Several of the articles in *Nineteenth-Century Piano Music,* edited by R. Larry Todd (New York: Schirmer, 1994), can supplement the material in this chapter.

Schubert's *Wanderer Fantasy* is based on his Lied *Der Wanderer.* Have students listen to the song and discuss its treatment in the variations and whether they can hear aspects of the Lied in other sections. Recordings of both the Lied and *Fantasy* are available in the Naxos library.

Have students locate scores for Mendelssohn's *Lieder ohne Wörte* (Dover has a reprint of the Mendelssohn's complete output) and then listen to Opus 19 No. 1. Recordings of the complete set are available in the Naxos library and on Deutsche Garmmophon 453061, 1997. Discuss the relationship of songs and piano music and have a pianist describe the difficulties in creating a singing quality from the piano.

For additional source reading on the Mendelssohns, see *The Mendelssohn Family 1729–1847 from Letters and Journals,* 2nd rev. ed., trans. Carl Klingemann (New York, Greenwood Press, 1968).

For more on Fanny Mendelssohn, see Françoise Tillard, translated by Camille Naish, *Fanny Mendelssohn* (Portland, Oregon: Amadeus Press, 1996).

Many of Fanny Mendelssohn Hensel's piano works have been recorded. See "Klavierwerke," Vol. 1, *Das Jahr* (CPO 999 013-2, 1986) and Vol. 2, *Sonatas* in C minor, G minor, *Sonatensatz* in E major, and Lieder op. 6, nos. 3–4 (CPO 999015-2, 1987).

Have students select a programmatic piano miniature by Robert Schumann and report on the techniques Schumann uses to portray the movement's title.

For Schumann's writings on music, see *Robert Schumann on Music and Musicians,* trans. Paul Rosenfeld (repr. ed., Berkeley: University of California Press, 1983). Excerpts from Schumann's *Davidsbündlerblätter* are available in Ruth Solie, ed., *Source Readings in Music History,* rev. ed., Vol. 6: *The Nineteenth Century* (New York: W. W. Norton, 1998).

The correspondence between the Schumanns is available in *The Complete Correspondence of Clara and Robert Schumann,* ed. Eva Weissweiler, trans. Hildegard Fritsch and Ronald L. Crawford (New York: P. Lang, 1994).

For more information on Clara Schumann, see Nancy B. Reich, *Clara Schumann, the Artists and the Woman* (Ithaca, N. Y.: Cornell University Press, 1985).

Clara Schumann's piano works are available on compact disc: "Soirées musicales" (Tudor 7007, 1996), "Pièces pour piano" (DCAL 6211, 1996) and "Clara Schumann: Complete Piano Works" (CPO 999758, 2001).

Franz Liszt's description of John Field's nocturnes is available in Ruth Halle Rowen, *Music through the Sources and Documents* (Englewood Cliffs, N. J.: Prentice-Hall, 1979), 262–64.

Fétis's review of Chopin's performance at a soirée is available in Ruth Solie, ed., *Source Readings in Music History,* rev. ed., Vol. 6: The Nineteenth Century (New York: W. W. Norton, 1998). Have students read this excerpt and then discuss Chopin's style in terms of its intended audience and performance venue. This discussion will prepare students to contrast Chopin's style with Liszt's.

For more source readings on Chopin, see *Chopin through His Contemporaries: Friends. Lovers, and Rivals,* ed. Pierre Azoury (Westport, Conn.: Greenwood Press, 1999).

For extensive essays on Chopin's compositional style, see Charles Rosen, *The Romantic Generation* (Harvard University Press, 1995), 279–471.

Have students select a mazurka or a polonaise by Chopin and report on the features that derive from Polish folk music. How does Chopin create an art form from a folk form? In a similar vein, have students select a prelude, perhaps using **HWM Example 24.7** as a guide, and discuss the variety of moods created by Chopin.

For more on the ballade, see James Parakilas, *Ballads without Words: Chopin and the Tradition of the Instrumental Ballade* (Portland, Oregon: Amadeus Press, 1992).

Discuss with students the relative merits of original compositions and transcriptions. Is there an implied hierarchy of artistic value? Lead them to a discussion of the necessity of transcriptions in the time before recordings and to the works of Franz Liszt. You may wish to draw parallels to twentieth-century popular music in the discussion.

## OBJECTIVE QUESTIONS

1. Of the following, which is not a theme of Romanticism?
   a. the supernatural
   b. nationalism
   c. individualism
   d. objective beauty
   e. insatiable longing

   Answer: d

2. Schubert favored which form(s) in setting his Lieder?
   a. strophic and modified strophic
   b. through-composed
   c. ballade form borrowed from medieval music
   d. da capo
   e. ternary form

   Answer: a

3. The piano parts of Schubert's Lieder are notable for their ___________.
   a. pictorial and dramatic roles
   b. restraint and subservient roles
   c. extremely chromatic harmonies set against diatonic vocal melodies
   d. virtuosic demands on the pianist
   e. octave doublings of the voice

   Answer: a

4. *Dichterliebe* is ___________.
   a. a song cycle by Schubert
   b. a song cycle by Schumann
   c. a set of miniatures for piano solo by Schumann
   d. a set of piano pieces by Mendelssohn
   e. an operatic paraphrase by Liszt

   Answer: b

5. *Winterreise* is based on poems by ___________.
   a. Goethe
   b. Heine
   c. Schiller
   d. Müller
   e. E. T. A. Hoffmann

   Answer: d

6. Robert Schumann wrote ___________.
   a. poems for his own and others' Lieder
   b. essays and reviews about music
   c. treatises on piano technique
   d. a book on orchestration
   e. librettos for operas

   Answer: b

7. Fanny Mendelssohn Hensel's masterpiece is ___________.
   a. *Papillons*
   b. *Das Jahr*
   c. six songs of Opus 1
   d. Sonata in G Minor
   e. *Carnaval*

   Answer: b

8. A group of Lieder designed to be performed as a set is called a ___________.
   a. Wiegenlied
   b. Liedersprache
   c. song cycle
   d. ballad
   e. Schwanengesang

   Answer: b

9. *Gradus ad Parnassum* is a set of études composed by ___________.
   a. Franz Schubert
   b. Robert Schumann
   c. Franz Liszt
   d. Muzio Clementi
   e. John Field

   Answer: d

10. Of the following, which was the major piano genre for Schubert?
    a. sonatas
    b. mazurkas
    c. preludes
    d. études
    e. transcriptions

    Answer: a

11. *Lieder ohne Worte* were composed by ___________.
    a. Schubert
    b. Schumann
    c. Chopin
    d. Liszt
    e. Mendelssohn

    Answer: e

12. Chopin composed piano works inspired by the folk music of which country?
    a. France
    b. Germany
    c. Austria
    d. Poland
    e. Hungary

    Answer: d

13. Which of the following genres did *not* find a place in Chopin's output?
    a. polonaise
    b. mazurka
    c. étude
    d. nocturne
    e. Lieder ohne Wörte

    Answer: e

14. The dazzling violin virtuoso who influenced Liszt was ___________.
    a. Vivaldi
    b. Paganini
    c. Viotti
    d. Field
    e. Pope

    Answer: b

15. Of the following, which would be the subject of a ballad?
    a. romantic adventures and supernatural incidents
    b. symbolic fairy tales
    c. tragic love affairs
    d. the conflict between good and evil
    e. stories from antiquity

    Answer: a

16. Which of the following is a major collection of piano pieces by Robert Schumann?
    a. *Das Jahr*
    b. *Annés de pélerinage*
    c. *Gradus ad Parnassum*
    d. *Carnaval*
    e. *Preludes*

    Answer: d

17. Who were Florestan, Eusebius, and Raro?
    a. Robert and Clara Schumann's three oldest children
    b. characters in a play for which Mendelssohn composed incidental music
    c. fictitious characters who represented aspects of Schumann's personality
    d. operatic singers who also excelled in the performance of Lieder
    e. titles of character pieces by Gottschalk

    Answer: c

18. Chopin was influenced by the nocturnes of ___________.
    a. Schubert
    b. Field
    c. Clementi
    d. Liszt
    e. Paganini

    Answer: b

19. The first American composer with an international reputation was ___________.
    a. Stephen Foster
    b. Henry R. Bishop
    c. James P. Clarke
    d. John Field
    e. Louis Moreau Gottschalk

    Answer: e

20. Who created and first used the term *recital*?
    a. Paganini
    b. Chopin
    c. Liszt
    d. Schumann
    e. Field

    Answer: c

## SHORT-ESSAY QUESTIONS

1. Describe the forms and techniques that Schubert used in his Lieder, citing examples from *HWM* and *NAWM*.
2. Describe the impact of middle-class audiences on piano music and song intended for performance in the home and in the concert hall. Include a discussion of Chopin and Liszt and how their music reflects the social changes of the nineteenth century.
3. Name and describe at least three genres of piano composition that originated in the nineteenth century. Cite examples of each and name the composer associated with them.
4. Compare the lives and music of Clara Schumann and Fanny Mendelssohn Hensel. Describe how their roles as women in nineteenth-century society impacted their careers as performers and composers.

## TERMS FOR IDENTIFICATION

Romanticism
absolute music
characteristic music
program music
Lied
lyric poem
ballad
song cycle
Schubertiad
Wilhelm Müller
modified strophic form
Johann Goethe
Heinrich Heine
drawing-room ballads
parlor songs
James P. Clarke
*Gradus ad Parnassum*
Carl Czerny
*Lieder ohne Wörte*
character pieces
*Carnaval*
*Neue Zeitschrift für Musik*
Florestan
Eusebius
Raro
concert étude
mazurka
polonaise
nocturne
John Field
ballades
Nicolò Paganini
operatic paraphrases
transcriptions

CHAPTER 25

# Romanticism in Classic Forms: Orchestral, Chamber, and Choral Music

I. Musical Developments in the Early Nineteenth Century
   A. Growth in public concerts
      1. Amateur orchestras and choral societies gave public performances.
      2. New professional orchestras and touring virtuosos contributed to a vibrant concert life.
      3. Chamber music was now performed as concert music.
   B. Musical classics
      1. Musical classics are works that continue to be performed after the composer's death.
      2. Classical repertories first formed in choral music, beginning with the oratorios of Handel and Haydn.
      3. Orchestral and chamber music began with the symphonies and string quartets of Haydn, Mozart, and Beethoven.
      4. Nineteenth-century composers aspired to have their works considered to be classics.
   C. Music for orchestra, chamber ensemble, and chorus
      1. Since older works for these ensembles were still being performed, historical awareness of them was more acute than it was for piano music and songs.
      2. Composers mixed classic forms and genres with the new musical style.
      3. Tradition was balanced with individuality.

II. Orchestras and Concerts
   A. Orchestras in the nineteenth century
      1. The number of orchestras increased rapidly.
      2. Some orchestras consisted of amateurs only.
      3. Professional orchestras were established as well.
         a. London Philharmonic (founded 1813)
         b. New York Philharmonic (1842)
         c. Vienna Philharmonic (1842)
         d. Most major European and American cities had orchestras by the end of the century.
      4. Orchestras also appeared in opera houses, theaters, cafes, and dance halls.
      5. During the century, the size of the orchestras increased from about forty players to as many as ninety.
   B. Orchestral instruments
      1. Changes were introduced to wind instruments (see **HWM Innovations,** pages 600–601, and **HWM Figures 24.3–24.5**).
         a. Flutes, oboes, clarinets, and bassoons acquired elaborate systems of keys, enabling them to play faster and better in tune.
         b. The piccolo, English horn, bass clarinet, and contrabassoon were used occasionally.
         c. Horns and trumpets added valves, enabling them to reach chromatic notes.
         d. Tubas began to appear in orchestras in the 1830s.
      2. Orchestral music became more colorful.
         a. Winds and brass became equals to the strings.
         b. The bass drum, triangle, and other percussion instruments were used in some works.
         c. The new, fully chromatic pedal harp was also added.
      3. Other than harp players, professional performers were usually men.

C. Conductors
   1. In the eighteenth century, a violin or harpsichord player led the orchestra.
   2. A conductor took over these duties in the nineteenth century.
   3. Using a baton, the conductor beat time and cued entrances.
   4. By the 1840s, conductors like Louis Jullien began to assert themselves as interpreters of music and became stars in their own right (see **HWM Figure 25.1**).

D. Audiences and concerts
   1. Audiences for the new orchestras were primarily middle class, often the same people who were home music enthusiasts.
   2. Many orchestral pieces appeared in piano transcriptions for home playing.
   3. Orchestra music was prestigious, partly due to Beethoven's symphonies.
   4. Programs in the nineteenth century offered a wide variety of works.
      a. The variety of performing forces might include a symphony, choral ensemble, and a chamber group.
      b. Genres could include solo vocal, choral, and orchestral works.
      c. Concerts of music in a single medium, like the recitals of Liszt, did not become the rule until late in the century.

E. The rise of a classical repertoire impacted concerts.
   1. In the 1780s, about 85 percent of the pieces performed by the Leipzig Gewandhaus Orchestra were newly composed.
   2. By 1879, nearly three-quarters of the repertoire was from earlier generations.
   3. Reasons for this change
      a. Some composers, such as Haydn and Beethoven, achieved such popularity during their life that their music continued to be performed.
      b. Earlier music was cheaper to publish and more readily available.
      c. Critics used music of the past to measure contemporary music.
      d. Many performers established themselves as interpreters of past music.
   4. The shadow of Beethoven's orchestral masterpieces touched almost all later composers.

III. Franz Schubert and the New Romantic Style

A. Schubert maintained the outward form of a symphony, but infused it with the new Romantic style.
   1. Tuneful melodies
   2. Adventurous harmonies
   3. Colorful instrumentation
   4. Strong contrasts
   5. Heightened emotions
   6. For the Romantics, the theme was the most important element in form.

B. *Unfinished* Symphony (1822) was Schubert's first large-scale symphony.
   1. Schubert completed only two of the planned four movements.
   2. The two principal melodies are songlike melodies (see **HWM Example 25.1**).
   3. The development and coda sections focus on the introductory subject.

C. Symphony No. 9 in C Major (The *Great,* 1825–28).
   1. Schubert blends Romantic lyricism and Beethovenian drama within an expanded Classic form.
   2. An unaccompanied chorale-like melody played by horns opens the symphony (see **HWM Example 25.2**).
      a. The theme is repeated several times as a set of variations.
      b. The section serves as a slow introduction to a sonata-allegro form.
      c. Portions of the theme will reappear in the exposition.
   3. The sonata form has a three-key exposition: C major, E minor, G major.
   4. The sonata-form themes are easily fragmented, as one would find in works of Haydn and Beethoven.
   5. Robert Schumann praised the C-Major Symphony for its "heavenly length" (see **HWM Source Reading,** page 637).
   6. Like the *Unfinished* Symphony, this work was not performed in Schubert's lifetime.

IV. Hector Berlioz (1803–1869) (see **HWM biography,** page 638, and **Figure 25.2**)

A. Biography
   1. Born in southeastern France, he taught himself harmony and began composing in his teens.
   2. He played flute and guitar, but not piano.
   3. He won the Prix de Rome in 1830 and worked in that city for several years.
   4. Harriet Smithson
      a. Berlioz became infatuated with Harriet Smithson and made her the subject of *Symphonie fantastique*.
      b. They later married and divorced.

5. One of the most literary of composers, he often based his compositions on great works of literature.
6. Berlioz turned to musical criticism as his chief profession.
7. Berlioz produced his own concerts, and later started a career of conducting.

B. *Symphonie fantastique* (1830)
1. This five-movement symphony, inspired by Smithson, deals with the passions aroused by a woman.
2. Berlioz employs a recurring melody, which he called the *idée fixe* (fixed idea) (see **HWM Example 25.3**).
   a. The theme appears in each movement representing the hero's beloved.
   b. The theme is transformed to suit the mood and situation of the story.
   c. It is first heard as the extended first theme of the first movement.
3. Berlioz subtitled the work "Episode in the Life of an Artist" and gave it a program (see **NAWM 121**).
   a. The program functions as the words of a drama that are read, not spoken.
   b. The text of the program is in a passionate prose that reveals several literary influences.
4. The first movement is entitled "Dreams and Passions."
   a. A slow introduction precedes an allegro that resembles sonata form.
   b. The development section is interrupted by the main theme in the dominant.
5. The second movement, a waltz instead of a minuet, reenacts a ball scene.
6. The slow third movement is a pastorale with dialogues between piping shepherds.
7. In the fourth movement, a macabre orchestral tour de force, the hero dreams of his execution.
8. The fifth movement depicts a Witches' Sabbath (**NAWM 121**).
   a. The colorful opening suggests the convergence of ghosts, wizards, and monsters.
   b. A distorted idée fixe in the clarinet represents the debauched beloved.
   c. The E-flat clarinet mockingly plays the entire idée fixe.
   d. Bells sound with fragments of the round dance.
   e. Three phrases of the *Dies irae* are played; each phrase is given three times.
   f. The round dance begins as a fugue.
   g. The round dance and the *Dies irae* are played together.
9. Originality of *Symphonie fantastique*
   a. Using a symphony for a narrative
   b. Unifying a work through a recurring theme and thematic transformation
   c. Use of an astonishing array of instrumental colors
10. Orchestration
   a. Muted strings suggest dreaming.
   b. Harps are heard at the ball.
   c. The English horn and an offstage oboe imitate shepherds' pipes.
   d. A snare drum and cymbals are heard in the march to the scaffold.
   e. Tubular bells represent church bells.
   f. The violins play with the wood of the bow during the witches' dance.

C. *Harold en Italie* (Harold in Italy, 1832)
1. This symphony draws its title from Lord Byron's poem *Childe Harold.*
2. The substance is drawn from Berlioz's recollections of Italy.
3. The work features a solo viola, which is not as prominent as in a concerto.
4. Paganini commissioned the work, but refused to play it.
5. A recurring theme in the viola appears in each movement and is combined contrapuntally with other themes.
6. In the final movement, the earlier themes are summed up, but the mood remains passive, like Byron's antihero.

D. Later symphonies
1. *Romeo et Juliette* (1839, revised ca. 1847) is a dramatic symphony with a chorus and soloists.
2. The *Grande symphonie funèbre et triomphale* (Grand Funeral and Triumphant Symphony, 1840), for military band with optional strings and chorus, is one of the early masterpieces of band music.

E. Berlioz's achievement
1. *Symphonie fantastique* and other works made him the leader of the radicals in the Romantic era.
2. All subsequent composers of program music were indebted to him.
3. He enriched orchestral music with new harmonies, color, expression, and form.
4. The idée fixe inspired other cyclical symphonies in the century.

5. His orchestration initiated an era in which instrumental color rivaled harmony and melody as expressive tools for composers.
6. He wrote the first book on orchestration: *Treatise on Instrumentation and Orchestration* (1843).

V. Felix Mendelssohn and Classical Romanticism
 A. Mendelssohn's works have a more Classic sound than those of Berlioz.
  1. He was trained in Classic forms in his youth, composing thirteen string symphonies with Classical forms and procedures.
  2. His mature symphonies blend Classic models with elements of Romanticism.
 B. Symphonies
  1. The five symphonies are numbered by date of publication.
  2. Symphony No. 5 (*Reformation,* 1830) concludes with a movement based on Luther's chorale *Ein' feste Burg*.
  3. Symphony No. 2, titled *Lobgesang* (Song of Praise, 1840), includes solo voices, chorus, and organ.
  4. Symphony No. 3 (*Scottish,* 1842) was based on impressions from a trip to the British Isles.
  5. Symphony No. 4 (*Italian,* 1833) is based on impressions from a trip to Italy (see **HWM Figure 25.3**).
   a. This work projects the energy of the sunny, vibrant south.
   b. The slow movement suggests a procession of chanting pilgrims.
   c. The finale presents a spirited saltarello, a lively Italian dance.
  6. The first movement of the *Italian* Symphony has three primary themes.
   a. The symphony opens with a theme inspired by Italian opera (see **HWM Example 25.4**).
   b. The second theme is similar in character to the first.
   c. A new theme appears in the development section.
   d. All three themes are recalled in the recapitulation, creating a Classical sense of unity.
 C. Overtures
  1. Several overtures painted musical landscapes.
   a. *The Hebrides* (or *Fingal's Cave,* 1832) is based on his Scottish travels.
   b. *Meerestille und glückliche Fahrt* (Becalmed at Sea and Prosperous Voyage, 1828–1832)
  2. *Midsummer Night's Dream Overture* (1826) is inspired by Shakespeare's comedy.
   a. This masterwork was composed when he was seventeen.
   b. It became the standard for all subsequent concert overtures.
   c. The perpetual motion of the opening suggests dancing fairies.
   d. A clear sonata form underlies an imaginative use of musical figuration and orchestral color.
   e. The overture projects various images, ranging from fairy dust to the braying of a donkey.
   f. Mendelssohn would later write additional music for the play, including the famous *Wedding March*.
 D. Concertos
  1. Mendelssohn emphasized musical content rather than empty virtuosity.
  2. Of the four piano concertos, two were published in his lifetime.
   a. No. 1 in G Minor (1831)
   b. No. 2 in D Minor (1837)
  3. The Violin Concerto in E Minor (1844) was written for his friend, violinist Ferdinand David.
  4. The violin concerto has three movements played without pauses.
   a. A transition leads from the first movement to the lyrical andante.
   b. The transition to the finale alludes to the opening theme of the first movement.
  5. The first movement has several formal innovations.
   a. The movement begins with the violin solo instead of an orchestral statement, creating a sonata-form structure.
   b. The cadenza is placed before the recapitulation rather than in the closing ritornello.
  6. The ABA' middle movement is a romance for violin and orchestra.
  7. The last movement is a sonata-rondo form: ABACAB'A. (**NAWM 122**).
   a. The lightness suggests the character of a scherzo.
   b. The violin and orchestra share equally in the finale.

c. The leading melodies move seamlessly between the soloist and orchestra.
d. The initial return of A is in G major, rather than the tonic.
e. A new lyric theme is introduced in C.
f. At the reprise of A in the tonic, the C theme becomes a countermelody.
g. The coda is based on motives from B.

VI. Robert Schumann
A. Schumann viewed the symphony as a prestigious genre and modeled his works after Schubert's *Great* Symphony and the works of Mendelssohn.
B. Schumann composed four major symphonies.
1. Symphony No. 1 in B-flat Major (*Spring,* 1841) is fresh and spontaneous.
2. Symphony No. 4 in D Minor, from 1842, has strong cyclic qualities.
a. The four movements are played without a break.
b. They are joined by harmonic links and a transitional passage that leads to the finale, as in Beethoven's Symphony No. 5.
c. All movements contain themes derived from the slow introduction.
d. The work appears as an extended symphonic fantasia that encompasses the standard four movements of a symphony.
3. Schumann's symphonic themes typically dwell on one rhythmic figure (see **HWM Example 25.5**).
4. He creates variety by constantly changing the presentation of the theme, reflecting the Romantic generation's interest in creating something new and distinctive in each individual work without abandoning tradition.

VII. Chamber Music
A. Past masterpieces greatly influenced the composition of chamber music.
1. Chamber music was still played at home, but performances were increasingly found in concerts by professional ensembles (see **HWM Figure 25.4**).
2. Genres associated with Haydn, Mozart, and Beethoven, such as the string quartet, violin sonata, and piano trio, were treated seriously.
3. Composers increasingly aspired to match the individuality of Beethoven's middle and late quartets.
B. Schubert
1. Schubert composed several string quartets for home performance in his youth.
2. The *Trout* Quintet (1819) is for piano, violin, viola, cello, and bass.
a. The work has five movements.
b. The fourth movement presents variations on his song *Die Forelle* (The Trout).
3. Schubert's most important chamber music are dramatic concert pieces.
a. String Quartet in A Minor (1824)
b. String Quartet in D Minor (*Death and the Maiden,* 1824)
c. String Quartet in G Major (1826)
d. String Quintet in C Major (1828)
4. String Quintet in C Major (1828)
a. This work is often considered to be his chamber music masterwork.
b. It is written for a string quartet with an additional cello.
c. All five instruments are treated equally, and they are grouped in ever-changing ways.
d. The second theme of the first movement appears in a variety of instrumental combinations (see **HWM Example 25.6**).
e. There are strong contrasts of mood and style between the movements.
C. Mendelssohn
1. His numerous youthful works are modeled after Haydn, Mozart, and Bach.
2. His first recognized masterpiece was the String Octet, Op. 20 (1825).
3. String Quartets in A Minor, Op. 13 (1827) and E-flat Major, Op. 12 (1829)
a. These works show the influence of Beethoven's late string quartets.
b. The movements are integrated through thematic connections, while each maintains a distinctive character.
4. Piano Trios in D Minor, Op. 29, and C Minor, Op. 66
a. His most characteristic works, these trios are tuneful and feature idiomatic writing.
b. Both have a slow movement in the manner of his *Song without Words* and scherzos in pixieish style.
c. In such works, the classic genre and forms serve as vessels for the Romantic material.
D. Schumann
1. Schumann enjoyed a "chamber music year" in 1842–43.
a. He published three quartets as Op. 41.
b. These were followed by a piano quintet and a piano quartet.
2. Schumann felt that a string quartet should resemble a four-way conversation.
3. He also believed that quartet composers should build on the tradition of the Classic masters rather than simply imitate them.

4. His chamber works reveal a strong influence of Haydn, Mozart, and Beethoven.
5. Piano Trios No. 1 in D Minor, Op. 63, and No. 2 in F Major, Op. 80
    a. Schumann incorporated more polyphony in these works due to the influence of Bach.
    b. Although the two works differ in mood, they both balance intellectual rigor with expressivity.
    c. This balance made these his most influential chamber works.

E. Fanny Mendelssohn Hensel
1. Women composers wrote relatively little chamber music.
2. Fanny Mendelssohn Hensel composed several works, but only the Piano Trio Op. 11 was published in her lifetime.
    a. The work exhibits idiomatic writing, expressive themes, and convincing development.
    b. The first movement is a long dramatic sonata-form movement with virtuosic material for the piano.
    c. An expressive andante and a song without words follow.
    d. In the finale, a recitative and a nocturne-like passage for unaccompanied piano precede an impassioned sonata form.
    e. In all movements, the instruments share melodic material.

F. Clara Schumann
1. She regarded the Piano Trio in G Minor (1846) as her best work.
2. The work has four movements, instead of the usual three.
3. The first and last movements, set in sonata form, combine traits from Baroque, Classic, and Romantic models.
    a. Memorable songlike themes
    b. Rich polyphonic treatment
    c. Motivic development
    d. Imitation and fugal treatment
    e. Rousing codas
4. The second movement is in a minuet tempo, but is labeled a scherzo to highlight subtle rhythmic tricks.
5. The slow movement is in G major (**NAWM 123**).
    a. It is in a modified ABA form.
    b. The A sections, like nocturnes, are somewhat melancholy.
    c. The B section, in D minor, is more animated.
    d. The textures are constantly changing (see **HWM Example 25.7**).

VIII. Choral Music

A. Background
1. Amateur choirs became more common than professional ones.
    a. Church choirs were increasingly made up of amateurs.
    b. Outside of the church, most choirs were for the enjoyment of the singers.
    c. Because of the association with amateurs, choral music has been seen as less prestigious than orchestral music and opera.
2. Choral music was one of the first repertoires to be dominated by past music.
3. Newly composed music retained traditional genres and formats, but not necessarily traditional style.
4. Types of choral music in the nineteenth century
    a. Oratorios
    b. Short choral works on secular texts
    c. Liturgical works
5. Choral music was a lucrative field for publishers.
6. Choral societies were amateur choirs in which singers paid dues to pay for the conductor and concert expenses.
7. The Berlin Singakademie
    a. One of the first choral societies, it began as a singing class for wealthy ladies.
    b. Men were accepted in 1791, and the group gave its first concert.
    c. By 1800, it had grown to almost 150 members.
    d. The director at that time, Carl Friedrich Zelter, also added an orchestra.
    e. By his death in 1832, the chorus had over 350 singers.
8. Similar organizations appeared throughout Europe and the United States.
9. All-male choruses, often with working-class men, were popular, especially with German populations.
10. Choral singing was seen to have many social benefits (see **HWM Source Reading,** page 652).
11. Choral festivals
    a. Music festivals allowed amateur choirs from a region to gather and perform.
    b. The first festival, focusing on the works of Handel, appeared in England in 1759, the year of the composer's death.
    c. Festivals spread across Europe and the United States.
    d. Festival choirs grew to enormous sizes (see **HWM Figure 25.5**).

e. Patrick S. Gilmore organized a performance in Boston with an orchestra numbering two thousand and a chorus of twenty thousand.

B. Oratorios and other large works
1. Oratorios by Handel and Haydn were the core of the repertoire for large choruses.
2. The Handel and Haydn Society, founded in Boston in 1815, is the oldest music organization in the United States that is still active.
3. The Bach revival
a. In 1829, Mendelssohn conducted the first performance of the *St. Matthew Passion* since Bach's death.
b. Revivals of Bach's *St. John Passion* and Mass in B Minor followed.
c. Bach's choral music, which was intended for performance by eight to twelve singers and a small orchestra, was transformed into concert works for large chorus and orchestra.

C. Oratorios by Mendelssohn
1. Mendelssohn composed two oratorios that became standards of choral repertoire.
a. *St. Paul* (1836)
b. *Elijah* (1846)
2. Common features
a. Composed for choral festivals
b. Treated biblical subjects
c. Received great acclaim in Europe and North America
3. *Elijah* is rooted in Baroque traditions, but also has new features.
a. Chorales mark structural divisions, as in Bach's *Passions*.
b. Mendelssohn employs a wide variety of styles and textures, like Handel.
c. Unifying motives and links between movements integrate the work into a cohesive whole.
4. The final chorus of *Elijah* (**NAWM 124**) is Handelian in spirit.
a. The work opens with a powerful homorhythmic statement.
b. A vigorous fugue culminates in a chordal statement of the theme.
c. An imitative "Amen" closes the work.
d. Contrasts of minor, major, and chromaticism suggest more recent musical styles.

D. Grand choral works by Berlioz
1. Grandiosity reached a pinnacle in two works by Berlioz.
a. Requiem (*Grande Messe des Morts,* 1837)
b. *Te Deum* (1855)
2. These works are not ecclesiastical, but belong to a patriotic tradition of massive music festivals.
3. Both works are huge in length and number of performers.

E. Partsongs
1. The partsong became the staple of small choirs.
2. Parallel to the Lied or parlor song, partsongs were composed by most major vocal composers.
3. The subjects were patriotic, sentimental, and convivial; nature was a particular favorite.
4. *All Among the Barley* (1849) was one of the most popular English partsongs (see **HWM Example 25.8**).
a. Elizabeth Stirling (1819–1895), the composer, was a renowned organist and composer in London.
b. The music is attractive to amateur singers.
5. The partsong declined after the nineteenth century, and no permanent repertoire of classics developed.

IX. Church Music

A. Catholic
1. Catholic churches tended not to use amateurs, but clerics and choirboys instead; women generally did not perform in church.
2. A number of Catholic composers still created concert liturgical music.
a. Schubert created two exemplary masses, in A-flat and E-flat major.
b. Rossini's *Stabat Mater* (1832, revised 1841) brought current operatic styles into church.
3. A revival of the sixteenth-century choral style of Palestrina began in the second quarter of the century.
a. In the nineteenth century, the term *a cappella* came to mean "unaccompanied."
b. By midcentury, the Church promoted composition in the unaccompanied style of Palestrina.
c. The Cecilian movement, which encouraged a cappella performances of old and new music, centered in German-speaking areas.

B. Protestant
1. Protestant churches also built on their musical heritage.
a. The Berlin Singakaemie performed Bach's *Passions*.

   b. New music was composed using Bach as a model, such as the psalm-settings of Mendelssohn.
   c. Other works from the past were recovered, including the anthems of Samuel Sebastian Wesley.
 2. Women began to sing in churches and serve as professional organists.
 3. The *Oxford Movement,* beginning in 1842, sought to restore all-male choirs and revive sixteenth-century unaccompanied polyphony.

C. Russian Orthodox music
 1. Dmitri Bortnyansky (1751–1825), director of the imperial chapel choir at St. Petersburg, helped create a new style of Russian church music.
 2. The style was inspired by modal chants of the Orthodox liturgy.
 3. It used free rhythm and unaccompanied voices with octave doublings.

D. The United States
 1. African American churches developed their own style of music, which would have enormous influence.
   a. Reverend Richard Allen organized the first congregation of the African Methodist Episcopal Church in the 1790s.
   b. He published a hymnbook designed for his all-black congregation.
 2. In white churches, music was subject to European trends.
 3. Both old and new songs were published in collections, such as the popular *The Sacred Harp* (1844).
 4. Shape-note singing is the tradition of performing this music using a special notation derived in part from the syllables introduced by Guido of Arezzo.
 5. The tune *New Britain* was set with the poetic text of "Amazing Grace" (see **HWM Figure 25.6**).
   a. The setting uses shape-note notation.
   b. The principal tune is in the tenor line.
   c. The harmonization has many open fifths, dissonant fourths over the bass, and parallel fifths and octaves.
 6. Lowell Mason (1792–1872)
   a. Mason became president of the Handel and Haydn Society and helped found the Boston Academy of Music, which provided musical instruction for children.
   b. He introduced music into the regular curriculum of the public schools, setting a model for other cities.
   c. He deplored the crude music of Yankee tunesmiths and championed a modest European style.
   d. He composed some 1,200 original hymn tunes and arranged many others.
 7. *Bethany* (1856) by Lowell is set to the poem "Nearer, My God, to Thee" (see **HWM Example 25.9**).
   a. The melody is largely pentatonic and in a modified AABA form.
   b. The harmony follows the rules of European music of the time.

## SUGGESTIONS FOR SUPPLEMENTAL READING/LISTENING/ACTIVITIES

*The Nineteenth-Century Symphony,* edited by D. Kern Holoman (New York: Schirmer, 1997), includes chapters on each of the orchestral composers addressed in *HWM* Chapter 25.

Readings from a variety of important nineteenth-century sources are translated in Ruth Solie, ed., *Source Readings in Music History,* rev. ed., Vol. 6: The Nineteenth Century (New York: W. W. Norton, 1998). Particularly useful as supplementary readings for this chapter are "Berlioz and His 'Harold Symphony,'" 116–32, "Beethoven's Instrumental Music," 151–55, and "Music in America," 207–15.

See Martin Chusid, ed., *Schubert's Unfinished Symphony* (New York: W. W. Norton, 1971) for more information on this important work.

The complete Schubert symphonies have been recorded on period instruments led by Nikolaus Harnoncourt (Elektra 91184, 1993), and Symphonies Nos. 4, 5, 6, 8, and 9 are recorded by Roger Norrington (Emi Records: A11429, 2003 and Capitol 49949, 1993).

Consult the Norton Critical Scores edition of the *Fantastic Symphony,* edited by Edward T. Cone (New York: W. W. Norton, 1971) for more detailed analyses of the idée fixe.

Several compact discs are available with excerpts from Berlioz's melodrama *Lelio,* such as "Berlioz Symphonie Fantastique, Lelio, Tristia" (Decca 458011, 2001). Have students listen to the excerpts with special attention to the use of the idée fixe. Discuss their reactions to melodrama and then ask them to find parallels in today's film music.

Have students select an instrument and read what Berlioz says about it in his *Treatise on Instrumentation,* translated by Theodore Front (New York: E. F. Kalmus, 1948). Ask them to report to the class on the technological state of the instrument and the instrument's role in the orchestra after consulting with *The New Grove Dictionary of Musical Instruments,* 3 vols. (New York: Macmillan, 1984). Have them look at excerpts from orchestral works by Beethoven, Schubert, Mendelssohn, and Berlioz and compare their treatments. Have a brass student research the ophecleide and report on its history and sound. Listen to its distinctive character in the *March to the Scaffold* recording by Roger Norrington.

Have a student violist from the class report on *Harold in Italy* by Berlioz. Include in the discussion the role of the solo viola and a comparison of this work with a concerto.

For examples of American symphonies, see *Three Centuries of American Music: A Collection of American Sacred and Secular Music,* Vol. 9: *American Orchestra Music, 1800 through 1879,* edited by Sam Dennison.

Have students listen to recordings of Mendelssohn's *Hebrides* and *Midsummer Night's Dream* Overture. Discuss how the images and moods are created in the music and whether these works should be considered as symphonic poems.

Schubert's late string quartets and cello quintet are available in a compact-disc recording by the Emerson String Quartet and Mstislav Rostropovich (Deutsche Grammophon 459151, 1999).

Mendelssohn's Octet for Strings performed on period instruments is available on compact disc: "Mendelssohn/Gade Octets for Strings" (Sony 48307, 1992).

In order to introduce students to the concept of a musical canon and the drawbacks of such a canon in a pluralistic era, have them read Peter Burkholder, "Museum Pieces: The Historicist Mainstream in Music of the Last Hundred Years," *The Journal of Musicology* 2 (1983), 115–34, or Marcia Citron, *Gender and the Musical Canon* (Cambridge: Cambridge University Press, 1993), 22–41. If concert programs of major symphony orchestras are available, have students look through programs from different eras to see if they notice a difference in works performed, and report their findings to the class.

For more on chamber music, see John H. Baron, *Intimate Music: A History of the Idea of Chamber Music* (Stuyvesant, N. Y.: Pendragon Press, 1998) and Stephen E. Hefling, *Nineteenth-Century Chamber Music* (New York: Schirmer Books, 1998).

Shape-note books continue to be printed, including the *Original Sacred Harp 1844–1971* (Cullman, Alabama: Sacred Harp Publishing, 1971). Copy pages from one and have students attempt to sing from the notation. Discuss the advantages of this notation over modern notation.

Have the students sing through *Amazing Grace* and perhaps bring in other versions or improvise on the tune. Then listen to a recording of Berlioz's *Requiem,* such as on the compact disc "Berlioz: Requiem and Te Deum" (Polygram International, 2001). Discuss the contrast between intimate and grandiose in both nineteenth-century music and in religion in general.

## OBJECTIVE QUESTIONS

1. What did Berlioz call the recurring theme used in his *Symphonie fantastique*?
   a. idée fixe
   b. *Dies irae*
   c. *Lelio*
   d. *Childe Harold*
   e. cantus firmus

   Answer: a

Use the following answers for questions 2–5.
   a. *Unfinished* Symphony
   b. *Scottish* Symphony
   c. *Spring* Symphony
   d. *Pastoral* Symphony
   e. *Harold en Italie*

2. Symphony by Berlioz

   Answer: e

3. Symphony by Schubert

   Answer: a

4. Symphony by Schumann

   Answer: c

5. Symphony by Mendelssohn

   Answer: b

6. Which composer used themes from his own Lieder in his chamber music?
   a. Robert Schumann
   b. Mendelssohn
   c. Chopin

d. Clara Schumann
e. Schubert

Answer: e

7. The Cecilian movement was __________.
    a. a cult that worshipped St. Cecilia with special music
    b. a movement that advocated the return to a cappella performances
    c. a group of composers who followed the aesthetic principles of Cecil of Hungary
    d. a movement within the Anglican Church to purge all Catholic elements from its music
    e. a movement that promoted large choral festivals

    Answer: b

8. What was *not* a trend in the early nineteenth century?
    a. The number of public concerts increased.
    b. A Classic repertoire was developed.
    c. Composers and audiences became more aware of historical styles.
    d. Choirs were increasingly made up of professional singers only.
    e. Chamber music was increasingly performed as concert music.

    Answer: d

9. Of the following, which is a characteristic of nineteenth-century orchestras?
    a. The size of the orchestra remained consistent.
    b. Women musicians began playing in most professional orchestras.
    c. Changes to wind instruments gave them wider ranges and greater facility.
    d. Music was predominantly conducted by the leader of the violins.
    e. Strings continued to dominate the orchestrations.

    Answer: c

10. Which work did Robert Schumann praise for its "heavenly length"?
    a. *Great* Symphony
    b. *Symphonie fantastique*
    c. Beethoven's Symphony No. 9
    d. *Italian* Symphony
    e. *Unfinished* Symphony

    Answer: a

11. *Treatise on Instrumentation and Orchestration* was written by __________.
    a. Robert Schumann
    b. Schubert
    c. Mendelssohn
    d. Berlioz
    e. Louis Jullien

    Answer: d

12. Which of the following does *not* describe the Violin Concerto by Mendelssohn?
    a. The cadenza in the first movement is placed just prior to the recapitulation.
    b. The first movement begins with a lengthy ritornello.
    c. The three movements are connected together.
    d. Mendelssohn balances virtuosity and musical content.
    e. The slow movement appears as a romance for violin and orchestra.

    Answer: b

13. Schubert's quintet, the late chamber-music masterpiece, is composed for string quartet and what additional instrument?
    a. viola
    b. clarinet
    c. piano
    d. string bass
    e. cello

    Answer: e

Use the following answers for questions 14–18.

a. *Elijah*
b. Te Deum
c. Stabat Mater
d. *The Sacred Harp*
e. Mass in A-flat

14. A massive choral work by Berlioz

    Answer: b

15. A collection of spiritual songs in shape-note notation

    Answer: d

16. An oratorio by Mendelssohn

    Answer: a

17. One of Schubert's choral masterworks

    Answer: e

18. A sacred work with operatic elements by Rossini

    Answer: c

19. Of the following, which is *not* a contribution of Lowell Mason to American music?
    a. He introduced music into the public school curriculum.
    b. He was president of the Handel and Haydn Society
    c. He championed the work of Yankee tunesmiths and shape-note singers.
    d. He helped found the Boston Academy of Music.
    e. He composed over one thousand hymn tunes.

    Answer: c

20. Who published a hymnbook designed for an all-black congregation?
    a. Reverend Richard Allen
    b. Samuel Sebastian Wesley
    c. Patrick S. Gilmore
    d. Elizabeth Stirling
    e. Carl Friedrich Zelter

    Answer: a

## SHORT-ESSAY QUESTIONS

1. Describe the major changes to orchestras and public concerts that occurred in the nineteenth century.
2. Compare the orchestral output of Berlioz and either Schubert or Mendelssohn.
3. Describe the influence of Beethoven on composers of both orchestral and chamber works.
4. Discuss the reliance on the past and the incorporation of newer styles in choral music of the nineteenth century.

## TERMS FOR IDENTIFICATION

Louis Jullien
idée fixe
choral societies
Berlin Singakademie
partsong
Elizabeth Stirling
Cecilian movement
Oxford movement
Dmitri Bortnyansky
Reverend Richard Allen
*The Sacred Harp*
shape-note singing
Lowell Mason
Haydn and Handel Society

# CHAPTER 26

# Romantic Opera and Musical Theater to Midcentury

I. The Roles of Opera
  A. General trends
    1. Opera played a central role in musical life, especially in Italy and France.
    2. Opera was both an elite entertainment and a popular diversion for all classes.
    3. Composers continued to follow national trends.
      a. Italian composers dominated.
      b. New types of opera were cultivated in France and Germany and became lasting influences.
    4. America
      a. A lively operatic life centered on performances of European opera.
      b. The minstrel show sprang up in the United States and became the first American music to be exported to Europe.
  B. Opera enjoyed a golden age in the first half of the nineteenth century.
    1. New opera houses appeared throughout Europe and the New World.
    2. Most operas were run for profit by an impresario, usually supported by the government or private sources.
    3. Members of the aristocracy and middle class attended opera as a sign of their social status.
    4. Performances of excerpts helped to popularize opera.
      a. Amateurs, singing from piano reductions, performed individual numbers in salons.
      b. Operatic selections were transcribed for solo piano.
      c. Overtures and arias appeared in concerts.
      d. Operas were parodied in popular theater.
      e. Café orchestras and even barrel organs played opera melodies.
    5. Operatic stories varied considerably, but they appealed to the middle class by addressing issues that spoke to them.
    6. As the music became the most important element of opera, the composer increasingly became a dominant force.
    7. By 1850, a permanent repertory of operas began to emerge.

II. Italian Opera
  A. Gioachino Rossini (1792–1868) (see **HWM biography,** page 661, and **Figure 26.1**)
    1. Rossini may have been the most famous composer in Europe in the 1820s.
    2. He is primarily known for his operas.
      a. *Tancredi* and *L'Italiana in Algeria* (The Italian Woman in Algiers), both from 1813, established his international reputation.
      b. In 1815, he became musical director of the Teatro San Carlo in Naples.
      c. *Il Barbieri de Siviglia* (The Barber of Seville, 1816), a comic opera, was his most successful work.
      d. Rossini moved to Paris and became director of the Théatre Italien.
      e. *Guillaume Tell* (William Tell, 1829) is his last major opera.
    3. During the last forty years of his life, he wrote no more operas.
      a. His life was marred by illness, and he ate to excess.
      b. He wrote witty piano pieces and songs that influenced French composers.

4. The popularity of his operas is partially due to his ability to blend aspects of opera buffa and opera seria.
5. The conventions that he helped to create for Italian opera would endure for over fifty years.
6. Rossini helped establish bel canto.
   a. Literally "beautifully singing," the term refers to lyrical lines, effortless vocal technique, and florid delivery.
   b. In bel canto, melody is the most important element.

B. Rossini's operatic style
1. Rossini combines tunefulness with snappy rhythms and clear phrases.
2. The sparse orchestration lightly supports the voice and has occasional solos for individual instruments for color.
3. Harmonic schemes are simple and original; he favored third-related keys.
4. A popular device was the "Rossini crescendo," created by gradually getting louder as a single phrase was repeated.

C. Rossini's scene structure
1. Rossini distributed the action throughout each act by constructing scenes (*scena*) rather than confining the action to recitatives.
2. Scenes have several standard sections (see **HWM Figure 26.2**).
   a. Instrumental introduction
   b. Recitative accompanied by orchestra
   c. Cantabile, the slow and lyrical section of the aria, generally expresses calm moods
   d. In some, an interlude called tempo di mezzo (middle movement) interrupts and changes the mood
   e. Cabaletta, the final and more active part of the aria, is usually repeated in whole or in part with embellishments.
   f. The finale brings together many characters.
3. The cantabile and cabaletta together constitute the aria; some scenes contain nothing else.
4. A duet or ensemble may follow a similar pattern, but it was often preceded by a tempo d'attacco, in which the characters trade melodic phrases.

D. *Una voce poco fa* from *The Barber of Seville* (**NAWM 125**)
1. Rosina sings of her love for the count and her determination to outwit her guardian (see **HWM Example 26.1**).
2. This is an entrance aria, which was known as a cavatina.
3. The orchestral introduction presents ideas that will be heard later.
4. Rosina begins with a cantabile.
   a. The opening resembles recitative, which suggests her tentativeness.
   b. Coloratura, florid figuration, suggests her passion for Lindoro.
   c. She vows to evade her guardian in a comic patter song.
   d. The coloratura music addressing Lindoro returns.
5. The cabaletta follows immediately.
   a. The various emotional sides of Rosina are depicted.
   b. A Rossini crescendo increases the excitement.
   c. The music for the last three lines is repeated.

E. Rossini's serious operas
1. Rossini is best known for his comic operas, but his serious operas were equally significant in his day.
   a. *Otello* (1816)
   b. *Mosè in Egitto* (Moses in Egypt, 1818)
   c. *Guillaume Tell* (William Tell, 1829)
2. *Guillaume Tell*
   a. The opera had five hundred performances in Paris during Rossini's lifetime.
   b. The story dealt with revolution and was subject to censorship.
   c. Rossini includes choruses, ensembles, dances, processions, and atmospheric instrumental interludes in the manner of French grand opera.

F. Rossini's overtures
1. His overtures have found an independent life in the concert hall.
2. Most consist of a slow introduction and a fast sonata form without a development section.
3. The overture to *Guillaume Tell,* his most famous overture, has four sections.
   a. A slow pastoral introduction
   b. A musical depiction of a storm
   c. Another pastoral featuring a *ranz de vaches* (a Swiss cowherd's call) played by an English horn.
   d. A galloping allegro that was used as the theme for *The Lone Ranger*.

G. Vincenzo Bellini (1801–1835)
1. Bellini came into prominence after Rossini retired.
2. He preferred dramas of passion with gripping action.
3. Action was not limited to recitative, but was also built into arias.
4. Bellini composed ten operas, including:

a. *La Sonnambula* (The Sleepwalker, 1831)
b. *Norma* (1831)
c. *I Puritani* (The Puritans, 1835)

5. His style is characterized by long, sweeping, highly embellished, intensely emotional melodies.
6. *Casta diva* (Chaste Goddess) from *Norma* (see **HWM Example 26.2**)
   a. The form of this scene follows the structure established by Rossini.
   b. In each section, the chorus plays an important role in creating a sense of continuous action.

H. Gaetano Donizetti (1797–1848)

1. Donizetti composed over seventy operas, about one hundred songs, several symphonies, and a number of other vocal works.
   a. *Lucia di lammermoor* (1835), a serious opera
   b. *La Filled u regiment* (The Daughter of the Regiment, 1840), an opéra comique
   c. *Don Pasquale* (1843), an opera buffa
2. Donizetti's melodies captured the sense of a character, situation, or feeling.
3. By averting cadences, he avoided applause until a scene was finished.
4. The music often has a seamless continuity.
5. The "mad scene" from *Lucia di Lammermoor* has an unbroken flow of events.
   a. A chorus opens with a commentary on Lucia's appearance after she has killed her husband.
   b. The orchestra then plays foreboding music.
   c. Lucia's recitative with flute ends with a florid cadenza.
   d. The flutes and clarinets recall a previous love theme, a device that is known as a reminiscence motive.
   e. The tempo di mezzo section is a trio.
   f. The cabaletta begins, but the chorus and trio break in.
   g. Lucia ends the scene in a faint.

I. Classics of Italian opera

1. Rossini, Bellini, and Donizetti were performed throughout Europe and America.
2. Many of their arias became popular tunes that were known in large segments of society.
3. Several of their operas became permanent classics of the operatic repertoire.

III. French Opera

A. Opera in the early nineteenth century

1. Opera remained the most prestigious musical genre in France.
2. Napoleon allowed only three theaters to present opera.
   a. The Opéra, which primarily showed tragedies, was the most prestigious.
   b. The Opéra-Comique gave operas with spoken dialogue.
   c. The Théatre Italien presented Italian operas.
3. Other theaters presented a variety of theatrical works often using music.
4. A new building for the Opéra theater was built in 1821 during the Restoration (see **HWM Figure 26.3**).
5. After the "July Revolution" of 1830, the government continued to subsidize opera.

B. Grand opera

1. Grand opera appealed to the middle class.
2. Spectacle was as important as music (see **HWM Figure 26.4**).
   a. Machinery
   b. Ballets
   c. Choruses
   d. Crowd scenes
3. The leaders of grand opera were librettist Eugène Scribe and composer Giacomo Meyerbeer (1791–1864).
4. Meyerbeer, born to a German-Jewish family in Germany, established the genre with two works:
   a. *Robert le diable* (Robert the Devil, 1831)
   b. *Les Huguenots* (1836)
5. *Les Huguenots* typifies grand opera.
   a. Five acts
   b. Large cast
   c. Dramatic scenery and lighting effects
   d. Tragic story set in sixteenth-century France
   e. Combination of entertaining spectacle and glorious singing, as exemplified by the closing scene of Act II
6. Other grand operas
   a. *Guillaume Tell* (1829) by Rossini
   b. *La Juive* (The Jewess, 1835) by Jacques Halévy
   c. *Don Carlos* (1867) by Verdi
   d. *Rienzi* (1842) by Wagner
7. *Les Troyens* (1856–58) by Berlioz has elements of grand opera and the traditions of Lully.
   a. Berlioz created the libretto from Virgil's *Aeneid*.
   b. He condensed the narrative in a series of powerful scene-complexes that incorporate ballets, processions, and other musical numbers.

C. Opéra comique
   1. Differences from grand opera
      a. Opéra comique used spoken dialogue instead of recitative.
      b. It was less pretentious and required fewer singers.
      c. The plots presented comedy or semiserious drama.
   2. In the early nineteenth century, there were two kinds of opéra comique, romantic and comedy.

D. Ballet
   1. Ballet had been popular in France since the seventeenth century.
   2. Marie Taglioni introduced a new style called Romantic ballet (see **HWM Figure 26.5**).
      a. Ballerinas were preeminent and moved with lightness.
      b. They wore translucent skirts and shoes that allowed them to stand *en pointe.*
      c. Taglioni introduced the new ballet to Russia, Europe, and North America.
   3. Composers for Romantic ballet fit the music to the choreography.
   4. *Giselle* (1841) by Adolphe Adam, one of ballet's highlights, uses recurring motives to underscore the progress of the drama.

IV. German Opera

A. General
   1. The interaction between music and literature was strong in German-speaking regions.
   2. Singspiel integrated romantic elements from French opera with the genre's national features.

B. *Der Freischütz* (The Rifleman) by Carl Maria von Weber (1786–1826) (see **HWM Figure 26.6)** established German Romantic opera.
   1. The opera exemplifies German Romantic opera.
      a. Ordinary folk, with their concerns and loves, are placed center stage.
      b. The plots are drawn from medieval history, legends, or fairy tales.
      c. The story involves supernatural beings set against a background of wilderness and mystery.
      d. Scenes of a humble village and country life are interspersed.
      e. Mortal characters represent superhuman forces, both good and evil.
      f. The triumph of good represents a type of religious redemption.
      g. The musical style draws upon traditions of other countries, but also uses simple, folklike melodies, giving it a distinctly German quality.
      h. The chromatic harmonies and orchestral color are also distinctive.
   2. "Wolf's Glen" scene (**NAWM 126**)
      a. The scene is set around midnight at the eerie Wolf's Glen (see **HWM Figure 26.7**).
      b. The scene incorporates elements of melodrama, a genre of musical theater that combines spoken dialogue with background music.
      c. While casting seven magic bullets, various terrifying images appear in the dark forest.
      d. Daring harmonies, a colorful orchestration, and an offstage chorus support the supernatural elements of the plot.

V. Opera and Theater in the United States

A. European influence
   1. Traveling theater companies performed spoken plays, ballad operas, and English versions of foreign-language operas with spoken dialogue.
   2. These companies presented opera as entertainment for all classes.
   3. Foreign-language operas took hold slowly.
      a. In New Orleans, French operas were common; the Théatre d'Orléans produced both French and Italian operas in their original language.
      b. In New York, a European troupe presented a season of Italian operas.
      c. Several attempts were made to establish a permanent Italian opera house, including one in 1833 that involved Lorenzo da Ponte, then a professor at Columbia University.
      d. The Academy of Music (1854) was the first company to last more than a few years.
      e. By the 1850s, operas in Italian and English were established in San Francisco.
   4. Opera achieved a high level of popularity.
      a. Overtures, arias, and other excerpts were freely performed.
      b. Swedish soprano Jenny Lind toured the United States (1850–52), singing before tens of thousands of people.

B. American opera
   1. There was little demand for opera by American composers.
   2. The early attempts were influenced by European models.

C. Minstrel shows
  1. Minstrelsy, a theatrical form in which white performers blackened their faces, was the most popular form of musical theater in the United States.
  2. One of the most successful troupes was Christy's Minstrels (see **HWM Figure 26.8**).
  3. These shows allowed white performers to behave outside accepted norms and hence to comment candidly on social, political, and economic conditions.
  4. Today's audiences would find these shows offensive for their racial stereotyping.
  5. Minstrelsy grew out of solo comic performances that produced some of the first bestseller songs to be a hit overseas.
  6. The songs for minstrel shows remained popular long after the shows went out of fashion.
     a. Dan Emmett from the Virginia Minstrels composed *Dixie* (1860).
     b. Stephen Foster wrote a number of songs for Christy's Minstrels that evoke some qualities of African-American music.
        (1) *Oh! Susanna* (1848)
        (2) *Camptown Races* (1950)
        (3) *Old Folks at Home* (1951)
        (4) *My Old Kentucky Home* (1953)
  7. Minstrelsy was the first in a long succession of entertainment forms that white musicians have borrowed from the music of African Americans.

## SUGGESTIONS FOR SUPPLEMENTARY READING/LISTENING/ACTIVITIES

For a good overview of Rossini's style and contribution to Italian opera, read Julian Budden, *The Operas of Verdi: From Oberto to Rigoletto,* Chapter 1, "Verdi and the World of the Primo Ottocènto" (New York, Praeger Publishers, 1973), 1–41.

A number of DVD recordings of Rossini operas are available, including *Il barbiere di Siviglia* (Naxos, 2003) and *Guillaume Tell* (Image Entertainment, 1998).

Rossini overtures remain popular repertory material for symphony orchestra concerts. Have the students diagram a typical overture structure, such as for *The Barber of Seville.* Make particular note of the placement of the crescendo. Then have them diagram the nontypical but well-known overture to *Guillaume Tell.* Discuss the pictorial images in the latter that have contributed to its use in many different mediums.

Like the *Guillaume Tell* overture, many opera themes are recognized by the general public from their use in film, television, and commercials. Have students explore this extended use of classic music. The Web site www.musicweb.uk.net/film/links/classicslink.htm lists classical themes used in films.

For more information about *Norma,* see *Vincenzo Bellini, Norma* by David R. B. Kimbell (New York: Cambridge University Press, 1998), a Cambridge Opera handbook.

*Norma* is available on VHS (Bel Canto BCS-0698, 1998: Video Artists International, CBC Home Video 69411, 1998, and Kultur 0027, 1991).

For more on the mad scene as a convention in nineteenth-century opera, see Stephen Ace Willier, "Madness, the Gothic, and Bellini's *Il Pirata,*" *The Opera Quarterly* 6 (1989), 7–23.

For more on Donizetti's style and *Lucia* especially, see William Ashbrook, *Donizett and His Operas* (Cambridge: Cambridge University Press, 1982), 375–82.

*Lucia* is available on VHS (Bel Canto / Paramount Home Video, 1983) in a classic performance by Joan Sutherland. The same performance is available on DVD.

For more on Meyerbeer's *Robert le Diable,* see Mark Everist, "The Name of the Rose: Meyerbeer's Opera Comique, *Robert le Diable,*" *Revue de musicology* 80 (1994), 211–50.

*Les Huguenots* is available on compact disc (Portland, OR: Allegro OPD-1217, 2000) and DVD (Kultur, 2002).

For a theory of the unity of *Les Troyens,* see Louise Goldberg, "Aspects of Dramatic and Musical Unity in Berlioz's Les Troyens," *The Journal of Musicological Research* 13 (1993), 99–112.

Adolphe Adam's *Giselle* is available on a DVD featuring Rudolf Nureyev (Kultur, 2004).

Unfortunately, videos of *Der Freischütz* are marred by idiosyncratic and sometimes offensive staging. The best available choice would be the production directed by Nickolau Harnoncourt (Naxos of America, 2004).

For more on Weber's operas, read Stephen C. Meyer, *Carl Maria von Weber and the Search for a German Opera* (Bloomington: Indiana University Press, 2003).

The Jenny Lind phenomenon is one of the more fascinating musical events in nineteenth-century America. Have an opera student review her memoirs, compiled in 1891 and now generally available in facsimile. If you have access to microfilms of newspapers from the 1850s, have students research the public reaction to the visit of the "Swedish Nightingale." Students might also be able to browse through *Dwight's Journal of Music* at that time.

For a detailed description of American theater music in the nineteenth century, see Russell Sanjek, *American Pop Music and Its Business,* vol. 2, *From 1790 to 1909* (New York: Oxford University Press, 1988).

For more information on minstrelsy and the Christy Minstrels see Eileen Southern, *The Music of Black Americans: A History,* 3rd ed. (New York: W. W. Norton, 1997).

## OBJECTIVE QUESTIONS

1. A fast, brilliant, concluding section in an Italian operatic is called a ___________.
   a. cavatina
   b. cantabile
   c. cabaletta
   d. casta diva
   e. canto bravo

   Answer: c

2. The most famous and important opera composer in Europe around 1825 was __________.
   a. Rossini
   b. Bellini
   c. Beethoven
   d. Spontini
   e. Bellini

   Answer: a

3. Which city was the center of opera in the early nineteenth century?
   a. Venice
   b. Dresden
   c. London
   d. Prague
   e. Paris

   Answer: e

4. The typical scene structure of a Rossini opera is __________.
   a. dry recitative plus a da capo aria
   b. introduction–recitative–cantabile–cabaletta
   c. recitative–aria–ensemble–chorus
   d. introduction–aria–cadenza
   e. through-composed

   Answer: b

5. Of the following, which describes the aria style of Rossini?
   a. spare use of the orchestra
   b. thick orchestration that obscures the vocal line
   c. endless melodic lines
   d. a dominant orchestra that portrays the inner drama with recurring motives
   e. richly chromatic harmonies

   Answer: a

6. The main composers of Italian opera in the beginning of the nineteenth century were _________.
   a. Rossini, Bellini, Verdi
   b. Rossini, Donizetti, Meyerbeer
   c. Rossini, Bellini, Donizetti
   d. Bellini, Donizetti, Meyerbeer
   e. Bellini, Meyerbeer, Weber

   Answer: c

Use the following answers for questions 7–11.
   a. Rossini
   b. Meyerbeer
   c. Weber
   d. Donizetti
   e. Bellini

7. This composer created German Romantic opera.

   Answer: c

8. He composed *Guillaume Tell.*

   Answer: a

9. He composed *Norma.*

   Answer: e

10. He composed *Les Huguenots.*

    Answer: b

11. He composed *Lucia di Lammermoor.*

    Answer: d

12. Who was the principal librettist for grand opera?
    a. Romani
    b. Metastasio

c. Scribe
d. Berlioz
e. Wagner

Answer: c

13. Of the following, which does not characterize grand opera?
    a. chorus
    b. machinery
    c. ballet
    d. large cast
    e. three acts

    Answer: e

14. Which opera contains the "Wolf's Glen" scene?
    a. *Lucia di Lammermoor*
    b. *Norma*
    c. *Les Huguenots*
    d. *Der Freischütz*
    e. *Barber of Seville*

    Answer: d

15. Which opera contains a famous "mad scene"?
    a. *Lucia di Lammermoor*
    b. *Norma*
    c. *Les Huguenots*
    d. *Der Freischütz*
    e. *Barber of Seville*

    Answer: a

16. Who composed the Romantic ballet *Giselle*?
    a. Taglione
    b. Berlioz
    c. Meyerbeer
    d. Adam
    e. Tchaikovsky

    Answer: d

17. Of the following, which is a characteristic of German Romantic opera?
    a. characters acting as representatives of superhuman forces
    b. stories based on recent history
    c. predominance of virtuosic singing
    d. standard urban settings
    e. large role for ballet

    Answer: a

18. Operas of which nationality were particularly popular in New Orleans in the mid-nineteenth century?
    a. American
    b. Italian
    c. English
    d. French
    e. Creole

    Answer: d

19. Of the following, which describes the American operatic scene in the nineteenth century?
    a. Opera first began as an elitist entertainment.
    b. American composers were greatly encouraged to write operas.
    c. Operatic excerpts became the popular music of the time.
    d. Most cities preferred opera to be performed in their original language.
    e. Opera did not reach the West Coast until the twentieth century.

    Answer: c

20. Of the following, which does *not* describe American minstrel shows?
    a. They featured white performers who impersonated African Americans.
    b. They were vehicles for candid social commentary.
    c. They had little influence outside of America.
    d. They featured many new songs.
    e. They would seem offensive to many by today's standards.

    Answer: c

## SHORT-ESSAY QUESTIONS

1. Name the three most important composers of Italian opera in the beginning of the nineteenth century and discuss both the similarities and differences among their styles.
2. Describe the principal differences between grand opera and opéra comique, giving examples of each.
3. Describe the blend of nationalistic and international characteristics in the German Romantic operas of Weber.
4. Discuss the distinctively American qualities of the minstrel show and describe their influences on European and American cultures.

## TERMS FOR IDENTIFICATION

bel canto
cantabile
cabaletta
tempo di mezzo
tempo d'attacco
reminiscence motive
grand opera
Eugéne Scribe
opéra comique
Romantic ballet
Marie Taglioni
German Romantic opera
melodrama
minstrelsy
Christy's Minstrels
minstrel songs

# CHAPTER 27 Opera and Musical Theater in the Later Nineteenth Century

I. The Late Nineteenth Century
  A. Industrialization
    1. Europe and the United States became industrial leaders.
    2. Railroads on both continents transported people and goods rapidly.
    3. New technologies, such as the electric lightbulb and telephone, altered daily life and created new industries.
    4. Life expectancy and population numbers rose dramatically.
    5. The modern corporation emerged.
    6. Mass consumption became a driving force for the economy.
  B. Revolutions of 1848
    1. France toppled King Louis Philippe and established the short-lived Second Republic (see **HWM Figure 27.1**).
    2. Revolts also took place in Germany, Italy, and Austro-Hungary.
    3. For the most part, these revolutions changed little.
  C. Political reforms
    1. Greater freedoms were granted to people in Europe and America.
    2. Russia abolished serfdom in 1861; the United States abolished slavery in 1865.
    3. Workers gained new rights, and women demanded equal treatment.
    4. Expanded exploration came at the expense of indigenous populations.
  D. Nationalism
    1. Throughout Europe, people attempted to unify themselves into nations based on a common language, shared culture, and other characteristics.
    2. In France, Britain, and Russia, nationalism supported the status quo.
    3. In Germany and Italy, unification movements were strong.
      a. Germany united under Bismarck between 1864 and 1871.
      b. Italy unified under Victor Emmanuel II in 1859–61.
    4. While a common heritage helped unify Germany and Italy, the variety of ethnic groups worked against political unity in Austria-Hungary.
    5. Music played a role in promoting nationalism, and nationalism had a profound impact on music (see **HWM Music in Context,** page 682, and **Figure 27.2**).
  E. Other themes in the arts
    1. Realism was a strong movement in art and literature.
    2. Exoticism, fantasy, and the distant past provided escapes from modern city life.
    3. Impressionism depicted outdoor scenes.
  F. Opera
    1. Strong national schools continued in Italy, France, and Germany.
    2. Nationalism linked opera to political and cultural currents.
    3. A core repertory of operas developed.
      a. The number of new operas declined as composers took more time to write.
      b. Originality became more important than conventions.

4. Singers had to have more powerful voices as opera houses became larger and orchestras louder.
5. Melodies were more syllabic and less ornamented.
6. Subjects ranged from fantastic to realistic.
7. Electricity made it possible to dim the house lights.
8. It gradually became unacceptable to talk during performances.

II. Giuseppe Verdi (1813–1901) (see **HWM biography,** page 684, and **Figure 27.3**)
  A. Verdi was the dominant opera composer in Italy for fifty years after Donizetti.
  B. Biography
    1. Verdi was born in northern Italy, the son of an innkeeper.
    2. He worked as a church organist at age nine and later became music director in Busseto.
    3. After the death of his first wife, he went to Milan to pursue a career as an opera composer.
    4. Verdi composed twenty-six operas, beginning when he was twenty-six and ending when he was eighty.
    5. Verdi's name became a patriotic rallying cry: "Viva Verdi" was an acronym for "Viva Vittorio Emanuele Re d'Italia" (Long live Victor Emmanuel, king of Italy)
    6. Although he supported the unification movement, nationalism was not an overt element of his operas.
  C. Opera characteristics
    1. He composed memorable melodies that captured the character and feeling of the drama.
    2. Verdi preferred stories that had been successful plays, including works by Shakespeare, Schiller, and Victor Hugo.
    3. Verdi built upon the conventions of Rossini, Bellini, and Donizetti.
    4. Like Donizetti, Verdi often used reminiscence motives.
  D. Early operas
    1. *Nabucco* (1842) was his first triumph and launched his career.
    2. *Luisa Miller* (1849) reveals a keen sense of psychological portrayal.
    3. In the early 1850s, he entered a productive period that includes:
      a. *Rigoletto* (1851)
      b. *Il trovatore* (1853)
      c. *La traviata* (1853)
    4. In *Il trovatore* and *La traviata*, the overture is replaced by a briefer prelude.
    5. *La traviata* is based on a novel by Alexandre Dumas, fils.
      a. Unique among his operas, it is set in the mid-nineteenth century.
      b. The work is realistic in its characters, situations, and emotions.
  E. *La traviata*, Act III, excerpt (**NAWM 127**)
    1. The scene follows Rossini's standard structure for duets.
      a. Scene (recitative)
      b. Tempo d'attacco (opening section)
      c. Slow cantabile
      d. Tempo di mezzo
      e. Fast cabaletta
    2. Verdi focuses on three keys: E major (tempo d'attacco), A-flat major (cantabile), and C major (cabaletta).
    3. Opening scene
      a. The orchestra accompanies the recitative.
      b. The dialogue is set in short phrases above a continuous melodic flow in the orchestra.
    4. Tempo d'attacco (measure 35)
      a. A Rossiniesque crescendo builds to a climax as the lovers embrace.
      b. The ensuing dialogue features tuneful vocal melodies and a simple accompaniment.
    5. Cantabile (measure 75) (see **HWM Example 27.1**)
      a. The form is AABB with coda.
      b. In the A section, Alfredo and Violetta sing a simple and direct melody that resembles a slow waltz.
      c. In the B section, Alfredo sings grandly of the future, and Violetta sings a light chromatic melody of suffering and recovering.
    6. Tempo di mezzo (measure 177)
      a. Hope gives way to despair; Violetta will not recover.
      b. Stark contrasts of style capture the changing moods.
    7. Cabaletta (measure 227)
      a. The form is AABA' with coda.
      b. Violetta voices her desperation, and Alfredo tries to calm her.
      c. The coda builds to a climax of despair.
  F. Middle-period operas
    1. Verdi wrote only six new operas in the next two decades.
      a. The action becomes more continuous.

b. Solos, ensembles, and choruses are freely combined.
c. Harmonies are more daring.
d. The orchestra is treated with great originality.
2. *Les vepres siciliennes* (The Sicilian Vespers, 1855), based on a libretto by Eugene Scribe, is a grand opera inspired by Meyerbeer that blends French and Italian characteristics.
3. *Un ballo in maschera* (A Masked Ball, 1859) introduces comic roles.
4. *Aida* (1871) was commissioned for the Cairo opera.
   a. Verdi chose an Egyptian subject, which allowed him to introduce exotic color and spectacle.
   b. Verdi officially retired after this opera.

G. Late operas
1. Giulio Ricordi persuaded him to compose two more operas, both on librettos by Arrigo Boito (1842–1918).
2. *Otello* (1887)
   a. The flow of the music is unbroken in each of the acts.
   b. The traditional schemes are still present, but they are arranged in larger scene-complexes.
   c. The orchestra develops themes in a more symphonic manner.
3. *Falstaff* (1893) (see **HWM Figure 27.4**)
   a. This pinnacle of opera buffa is based on Shakespeare's *The Merry Wives of Windsor* and *Henry IV*.
   b. The final act ends in a fugue for the entire cast.

III. Later Italian Composers
A. Verismo
1. This operatic movement parallels realism in literature.
   a. It presents everyday people, generally from the lower classes.
   b. The stories often depict brutal or sordid events.
2. Two verismo operas have entered the permanent repertory.
   a. *Cavalleria rusticana* (Rustic Chivalry, 1890) by Pietro Mascagni
   b. *I Pagliacci* (The Clowns, 1892) by Ruggero Leoncavallo

B. Giacomo Puccini (1858–1924)
1. Puccini is the most successful Italian opera composer after Verdi.
2. Puccini blended Verdi's vocal style with Wagner's approach, including the use of leitmotives (see Wagner discussion in section IV below).
3. *Manon Lescaut* (1893), his third opera, brought him international fame.
4. Other major works
   a. *La bohème* (1896)
   b. *Tosca* (1900)
   c. *Madama Butterfly* (1904)
   d. *Turandot* (1926)
5. Puccini's scenes are more fluid than in earlier operas.
6. The blurred distinction between aria and recitative can be seen in an excerpt from *La bohème* (see **HWM Example 27.2**).

IV. Richard Wagner (1813–1883) (see **HWM biography,** page 690, and **Figure 27.5**)
A. Wagner was a crucial figure in nineteenth-century culture and one of the most influential musicians of all times.
1. He brought German Romantic opera to a new height.
2. He created a new genre, the music drama.
3. His rich chromatic idiom influenced later composers.

B. Biography
1. He was born in Leipzig, Germany, the ninth child of a police actuary.
2. Wagner began writing operas in the 1830s and held positions with several regional companies.
3. He worked as a music journalist in Paris from 1839 to 1842.
4. He was appointed second Kapellmeister for the king of Saxony in Dresden in 1843.
5. Wagner supported the 1848–49 insurrection and had to flee.
6. In Switzerland he wrote his most important essays.
7. He received support from a new patron, King Ludwig II of Bavaria, in 1864.
8. Although married to Minna (1836–66), he had relationships with other women, including Mathilde Wesendonck.
9. In 1870, he married Cosima von Bülow, a child of Franz Liszt.

C. Writings (see **HWM Source Reading,** page 692)
1. In a series of essays, Wagner argued that music should serve dramatic expression. His essays include:
   a. *The Artwork of the Future* (1850)
   b. *Opera and Drama* (1851, revised 1868)
2. Beethoven
   a. Wagner felt that Beethoven had exhausted instrumental music.

   b. The Ninth Symphony showed the path to the future with its union of music and words.
   c. He saw himself as the true successor to Beethoven.
3. Gesamtkunstwerk
   a. Wagner felt that poetry, scenic design, staging, action, and music should work together to create a Gesmatkunstwerk (total or collective artwork).
   b. The words related the events and situations, while the orchestra conveyed the inner drama.
4. Anti-Semitism
   a. Wagner wrote about politics and morals in several essays, including the anti-Semitic polemic *Das Judentum in der Musik* (Jewishness in Music).
   b. He attacked both Meyerbeer and Mendelssohn for being Jewish and lacking national roots, although he admired and was influenced by both.

D. Operas
1. *Rienzi* (1842), a five-act grand opera, was his first major success.
2. *Die fliegende Holländer* (The Flying Dutchman, 1843)
   a. A Romantic opera in the tradition of Weber, the work is based on a German legend.
   b. Wagner wrote the libretto.
   c. Themes from one of the vocal ballads appear in the overture and recur throughout the opera, functioning like reminiscence motives.
3. *Tannhäuser* (1845)
   a. The story is also adopted from Germanic legends.
   b. Semi-declamatory vocal writing appears in this work, which would become Wagner's normal type of text-setting.
4. *Lohengrin* (1850)
   a. Medieval legend and German folklore combine in a moralizing and symbolic plot.
   b. The declamatory style is expanded, and recurring themes are more fully developed.

E. *Der Ring des Nibelungen* (The Ring of the Nibelungs)
1. Wagner composed four music dramas based on Teutonic and Nordic legends.
   a. *Das Rheingold* (The Rhine Gold)
   b. *Die Walküre* (The Valkyrie)
   c. *Siegfried*
   d. *Götterdämmerung* (The Twilight of the Gods)
2. Wagner wrote the first two operas and part of *Siegfried* by 1857; he completed the rest in 1874.
3. Wagner built his own theater in Bayreuth, where he gave the first performance of the *Ring* cycle in 1876 (see **HWM Figure 27.6**).

F. Other music dramas
1. *Tristan und Isolde* (1857–59)
   a. Wagner wrote the libretto, basing it on a thirteenth-century romance by Gottfired von Strassburg.
   b. It became one of Wagner's most influential works.
2. *Die Meistersinger von Nürnberg* (The Meistersingers of Nuremberg, 1862–67)
3. *Parsifal* (1882), his last work, uses diatonic and chromatic music to suggest redemption and corruption respectively.

G. The leitmotiv
1. A leitmotiv is a musical theme or motive associated with a person, thing, emotion, or idea in the drama.
2. All of the music dramas are organized around these themes.
3. Use of leitmotives
   a. The meaning of the motive is usually established the first time it is heard.
   b. The leitmotiv recurs whenever its subject appears or when it is mentioned.
   c. A leitmotiv can be transformed and varied as the plot develops.
   d. Similarities among leitmotives may indicate connections between the subjects they portray.
4. Leitmotives differ from reminiscence motives.
   a. Leitmotives are for the most part short and characterize their subjects at various levels, as seen in **Example 27.3d**.
   b. Leitmotives are the basic material of the score and are used constantly.
   c. The musical material surrounding the leitmotives and their developments creates a sense of an "endless melody."

H. *Tristan und Isolde,* Act 1, scene 5 (**NAWM 128**)
1. The scene has a continuous musical flow.
   a. The orchestra maintains the continuity.
   b. The melodies vary from speechlike to soaring and passionate.
2. The passage uses a number of leitmotives (see **HWM Example 27.3**).

a. Tristan's honor is introduced at measure 38 and is developed throughout the section.
b. The melodic idea at measure 64 is associated with the love potion.
c. Measures 66–69 contain the "Tristan chord," which was the first chord in the opera.
d. The rising chromatic motive in measures 69–70 represents longing.

3. A pantomime follows as the potion takes control; the actors move and gesture at specific moments in the music.
4. A climax is reached at measure 102 with a deceptive cadence.
5. A new melody begins in the violas at measure 103, joined by the voices calling to each other.
6. Following interruptions from the sailors and Brangäne, the lovers' dialogue uses many of the above motives.
7. A new leitmotiv appears at measure 160.
8. The music hailing the king begins to penetrate the lovers' consciousness at measure 192.

I. Wagner's influence
1. More has been written about Wagner than any other musician.
2. His view of the total artwork affected all later opera.
3. His emphasis on musical continuity was also important.
4. A master of orchestral color, he influenced many composers.
5. Painters and poets found inspiration in Wagner.
6. Unfortunately, Wagner's anti-Semitic writings also found followers, including the Nazis in Germany.

V. France
A. Although there was no dominant composer there, Paris remained a center for producing new works.
1. Because of state subsidies, many of the works were by French composers, but nationalism was not reflected in their plots.
2. Musical theaters presented a variety of musical entertainments.

B. Grand opera
1. The genre remained prominent through the 1860s.
a. *L'Africaine* (1865) by Meyerbeer
b. *Don Carlos* (1867) by Verdi uses the French form and Italian language.
2. The genre began to fade thereafter and blend with other types of serious opera.

C. Ballet
1. Ballet had long been a part of grand opera, but it became popular as an independent genre (see **HWM Chapter 26**).
2. Leo Delibes (1836–91) was the leading composer for ballet.
a. *Coppélia* (1870)
b. *Sylvia* (1876)

D. Lyric opera
1. A new operatic genre called lyric opera grew out of the romantic type of opéra comique.
2. The genre is named after the Théatre Lyrique, founded in 1851.
3. Like opéra comique, its main appeal is through melody.
4. The subject matter is usually romantic drama or fantasy.
5. The scale is larger than opéra comique, but smaller than grand opera.
6. *Faust* by Charles Gounod (1818–1893)
a. This lyric opera was the most frequently performed opera in Europe and the Americas in the last third of the nineteenth century.
b. It was first performed as an opéra comique, with spoken dialogue, and was later arranged with recitatives.
7. Other popular lyric operas include:
a. *Roméo and Juliette* by Gounod (1867)
b. Works by Jules Massenet (1842–1912)
(1) *Manon* (1884)
(2) *Werther* (1892)
(3) *Thaïs* (1894)

E. *Carmen* by Bizet (1875)
1. The opera was originally an opéra comique with spoken dialogue.
2. The dialogue was later set to recitative.
3. Set in Spain, the opera combines exoticism and realism.
4. The plot is a dark tale of seduction and murder.
5. Carmen, a gypsy, works in a cigarette factory and lives for pleasure (see **HWM Figure 27.7**).
6. Bizet created a Spanish character with his music.
a. He borrowed three Spanish melodies, including the famous habanera.
b. Bizet added other elements of gypsy and Spanish music.
c. The augmented second in the fate motive suggests a gypsy origin (see **HWM Example 27.4**).

7. Carmen seduces Don Jose by singing a seguidilla (**NAWM 129**).
   a. The seguidilla is a type of Spanish song in a fast triple meter.
   b. A recurring refrain frames the song.
   c. The accompaniment imitates the strumming of a guitar.
   d. The melody contains melismas and grace notes.
   e. The harmony suggests the Phrygian mode, a feature of Spanish music.
8. The opera provoked outrage because of Carmen's lack of morality, but it eventually became one of the most beloved of all operas.

F. Opéra bouffe
   1. A new genre called *opéra bouffe* emerged in the 1850s.
   2. The genre emphasized the smart, witty, and satirical elements of comic opera.
   3. Its composers used their freedom from government control to satirize French society.
   4. The founder was Jacques Offenbach (1819–1880).
      a. *Orphée aus enfers* (Orpheus in the Underworld, 1858) introduced a can-can dance for the gods.
      b. Offenbach influenced comic opera in England, Vienna, and the United States.
      c. His music has a deceptively naïve quality that satirizes opera and society.

G. Popular music theaters
   1. Cabarets, such as the Chat Noir (Black Cat, opened 1881)
      a. These nightclubs offered a variety of serious and comic entertainment.
      b. They promoted innovation and brought together artists and the public.
   2. Café-concerts featured food, beverage, and musical entertainment.
   3. Music halls, such as the Folies-Bergère and Moulin Rouge, offered revues, featuring a series of dances, songs, comedies and other acts, usually with some common theme.

VI. Russia

A. Nationalism
   1. A visiting Italian troupe performed the first opera in Russia in 1731.
   2. In the eighteenth century, most of the operas were composed and performed by foreigners.
   3. A permanent national company was established at the Imperial Court in St. Petersburg in 1755, and it gave the first opera in Russian.
   4. The czar used opera as a tool of propaganda for his absolutist government.

B. Mikhail Glinka (1804–1857)
   1. Glinka was the first Russian composer to be recognized internationally.
   2. *A Life for the Tsar* (1836)
      a. This pro-government historical drama established Glinka's reputation.
      b. This is the first Russian opera that is sung throughout.
      c. The recitative and melodic writing has a distinct Russian character.
   3. *Ruslan and Lyudmila* (1842)
      a. Glinka's second opera is based on an Aleksander Pushkin poem.
      b. The music features whole-tone scales, chromaticism, and dissonance.

C. Czar Alexander II freed the serfs in 1861 and sought to modernize Russia.
   1. Russia became split.
      a. Nationalists, or "Slavophiles," idealized Russia's distinctiveness.
      b. Internationalists, or "westernizers," sought to adapt Western technology and education.
   2. The split affected composers, although all were in debt to Western traditions.
   3. The nationalists rejected formal Western training.
   4. Anton Rubinstein (1829–1894), a virtuoso pianist and founder of the St. Petersburg Conservatory (1862), was a leading internationalist.

D. Piotr Il'yich Tchaikovsky (1840–1893) (see **HWM Figure 27.8**)
   1. Tchaikovsky studied at the St. Petersburg Conservatory and taught at the Moscow conservatory.
   2. His patron was a wealthy widow, Nadezhda von Meck.
   3. He sought to reconcile nationalist and internationalist tendencies.
   4. *Eugene Onegin* (1879) is based on a Pushkin story.
      a. A germ motive in the prelude generates numerous themes
      b. The chorus has folklike music, and the soloists sing in a Russian style.
   5. *The Queen of Spades* (1890) is also based on a Pushkin story.
   6. Tchaikovsky's ballets combine hummable melodies with colorful orchestrations, which are well suited to his fairy-tale subjects.
      a. *Swan Lake* (1876)

b. *The Sleeping Beauty* (1889)
c. *The Nutcracker* (1892)

E. The Mighty Handful
1. A group of five composers stood against the professionalism of the conservatories.
a. Mily Balakirev (1837–1910)
b. Aleksander Borodin (1833–1887)
c. César Cui (1835–1918)
d. Modest Musorgsky (1839–1881)
e. Nikolay Rimsky-Korsakov (1844–1908)
2. Only Balakirev had conventional training in music, but they all studied Western music on their own (see **HWM Source Reading,** page 703).
3. They incorporated aspects of Russian folk song, modal and exotic scales, and folk polyphony.
4. Balakirev, the leader of the circle, wrote little for the stage.
5. Cui composed fourteen operas, but none entered the permanent repertory.
6. *Prince Igor* is the major work of Borodin, a professional chemist who had little time to compose.
a. It was completed after his death by Rimsky-Korsakov.
b. Russian characters in the opera are given folk song material.
c. The Polovtsians, from central Asia, have an exotic vocal style with melismas, chromatics, and augmented seconds.
d. The *Polovtsian Dances* from Act II are frequently performed separately.

F. Modest Musorgsky (see **HWM Figure 27.9**)
1. Musorgsky, who studied with Balakirev, was the most original of the Mighty Handful.
2. He worked as a clerk in the civil service.
3. Principal stageworks
a. *Boris Godunov* was based on a Pushkin play.
b. *Khovanshchina* (The Khovansky Affair) was completed by Rimsky-Korsakov.
3. The realism of Russian literature is reflected in *Boris Godunov*.

G. Coronation scene from *Boris Godunov* (see **NAWM 130, HWM Figure 27.10,** and **Example 27.5**)
1. The vocal melody is sometimes speechlike.
a. The text is treated syllabically, and the music follows the natural accents.
b. The melody sometimes recites on one or two notes (measures 40–42 and 94–97).
c. Operatic recitative appears in measures 134–136.
2. Much of the singing is a fluid arioso similar to Russian folk songs.
a. Narrow range
b. Repetition of short motives
c. Tendency to rise at beginnings of phrases and slowly sink to a cadence
3. The opera is built from large blocks of material.
4. The scene opens with alternating dominant seventh chords with roots a tritone apart.
a. Ostinatos in winds and strings overlay the harmonies.
b. The passage is repeated with the pealing of bells (measure 21).
5. After Prince Shuisky's cheer, the people sing one of the few genuine folk melodies ever used by Musorgsky.
6. The tune is developed and contrasted with other material.
7. Musorgsky's treatment of harmony was influential.
a. The music is tonal, but his progressions are novel.
b. The principal key of the scene is C.
c. The chords accompanying Prince Shuisky do not function as a normal harmonic progression.
d. The folk song harmonization (measure 50) is the first functional progression in the scene.

H. Nikolay Rimsky-Korsakov
1. Rimsky-Korsakov studied with Balakirev and other private teachers.
2. He had a career in the Russian Navy, and became a professor at the St. Petersburg Conservatory in 1871.
3. He was an active orchestra conductor and a master of orchestration.
4. As professor and conductor, he championed the works of Glinka and other Russian nationalists.
5. He wrote a harmony treatise and taught some important students, including Glazunov and Stravinsky.
6. He edited two collections of folk songs and incorporated folk tunes into his own compositions.
7. Rimsky-Korsakov completed fifteen operas.
a. *Sadko* (1895–97)
b. *Tsar Saltan* (1899–1900)
c. *The Golden Cockerel* (1906–7) alternates diatonic music for the real world with chromatic music for the supernatural world.

8. Rimsky-Korsakov used both whole-tone and octatonic scale systems (see **HWM Example 27.6**).
   a. Both systems have a limited number of transpositions.
   b. Both lack a strong leading tone, which creates an ethereal quality.
9. The octatonic scale and folklike melody can be seen in the second scene of *Sadko* (see **HWM Example 27.7**).

VII. Opera in Other Nations
A. Bohemia (now Czech Republic; see also **HWM Chapter 29**)
   1. Bohemia was an Austrian crown land, and German was the official language.
   2. Mainstream opera was performed in Prague, including the premiere of Mozart's *Don Giovanni*.
   3. A movement to promote Czech language in the theater began in the 1860s.
   4. Bedrich Smetana (1824–1884)
      a. Smetana composed eight operas in Czech.
      b. Smetana created a Czech national style with folklike tunes and dance rhythms, while avoiding Italian and Germanic operatic conventions.
      c. *The Bartered Bride* (1866) was an international sensation.
   5. Antonín Dvořák (1841–1904)
      a. Dvořák composed twelve operas, some of which are based on Czech legends and Slavic history.
      b. *Dmitrij* (1882, revised 1894) is a historical drama influenced by Meyerbeer and Wagner.
      c. *Rusalka* (1900) is a fairy-tale opera that alternates between a diatonic style for world of humans and a fantastic style for the supernatural.
B. Poland
   1. Poland was ruled by Russia, and opera was part of its national cultural revival.
   2. *Halka* (1848), by Stanislaw Moniuszko (1819–1872), inaugurated the movement.
C. Spain
   1. Although politically independent, Spain adopted the musical styles of France, Italy, and Germany.
   2. Felipe Pedrell (1841–1922) sparked a nationalist revival with editions of sixteenth-century Spanish composers and with his operas, such as *Los Pirineos* (The Pyrenees, 1891).
D. Britain
   1. Britain was dominated by foreign opera, despite numerous nationalist movements.
   2. Ethel Smyth (1858–1944) composed six operas, including *The Wreckers* (1904).
E. The New World
   1. The New York Metropolitan Opera Company opened in 1883 and performed European opera.
   2. Antonio Carlos Gomes (1836–1896)
      a. A Brazilian, he was the first internationally recognized opera composer from the Americas.
      b. His operas in Portuguese were not successful, but his later works in Italian, including his masterwork *Il Guarany* (1870), were highly acclaimed.
F. Operetta
   1. Lighter forms of musical theater flourished in nearly every country.
   2. Operetta was a type of light opera with spoken dialogue.
   3. Modeled after the opéra bouffe of Offenbach, it could be both funny and romantic.
   4. Johann Strauss the Younger (1825–1899) from Vienna created the popular *Die Fledermaus* (The Bat, 1874).
   5. In England, Gilbert (librettist, 1836–1911) and Sullivan (composer, 1842–1900) created a string of popular successes.
      a. *HMS Pinafore* (1848)
      b. *The Pirates of Penzance* (1879)
      c. *The Mikado* (1885)
   6. *When the foeman bares his steel* from *The Pirates of Penzance* (**NAWM 131**) illustrates the satirical humor of Gilbert and Sullivan operettas.
      a. The police, given martial dotted rhythms, pretend their clubs are trumpets, singing "Tarantara!" like boys playing at soldiers.
      b. The melodies of Mabel and the sergeant and many of the later actions and singing mock the traditions of tragic opera.
G. Other types of musical theater
   1. Diverse musical entertainments could be found throughout Europe.
   2. The United States also featured a variety of musical theater.
      a. European opera was heard in several major cities.
      b. Minstrel shows continued, including all-black troupes.
      c. Operettas were imported from Europe, and Americans composed new operettas, such

as *El Capitan* by John Philip Sousa (1854–1932).

d. *The Black Crook* (1866), a pastiche that combined melodrama with a visiting French ballet troupe, was a tremendous success.

e. *Evangeline* (1874) by Edward E. Rice has been described as the first musical comedy.

F. Variety shows became more respectable, and vaudeville, created by Tony Pastor, became a dominant type of theatrical entertainment.

VIII. Music for the Stage and Its Audiences
  A. Standard opera repertory
    1. Verdi and Wagner created works that were never surpassed.
    2. Their operas have achieved a permanent place in opera repertory.
    3. Excerpts from Wagner's operas have also become part of the standard repertory of orchestral concerts.
    4. Puccini is the only Italian after Verdi to maintain an international reputation.
    5. Traditional operas by a number of other composers have entered the permanent repertory.
  B. Nationalism
    1. Wagner obscured his nationalism with his claim to universality.
    2. Composers from "peripheral" countries used nationalism that was effective in their own countries, but generally did not win international recognition.
  C. Audiences began to split between elite and popular musical theater.
    1. Verdi's operas appealed both to the elite and to the general public.
    2. Wagner aimed at only the elite.
    3. Popular genres, such as operetta and vaudeville, became increasingly more important.

## SUGGESTIONS FOR SUPPLEMENTARY READING/LISTENING/ACTIVITIES

The major operas of Verdi are now available on DVD, including *Nabucco* (Kultur, 2004), *Rigoletto* (Universal Music & VI, 2004), *La Traviata* (Universal Studios, 1999), *Aida* (Deutschegrammophon, 2000), *Otello* (Universal Music & VI, 2004), and *Falstaff* (Sony Music Entertainment, 2002).

Have students compare a scene from an early Verdi opera, such as *Rigoletto* or *La Traviata,* with one in *Otello*. They should look for both musical and dramatic changes.

Have a student read a synopsis of Shakespeare's *Othello* and report how Verdi crafted an opera from the original tragedy.

Assign the subject of nineteenth-century realism to a group of students. Have them report on the characteristics of the realistic novel (such as those by Victor Hugo, Charles Dickens), drama (such as the plays by Ibsen), and painting (such as those by Courbet). Compare these characteristics with realistic opera and verismo.

An important excerpt from Wagner's *The Artwork of the Future* is translated in Ruth Solie, ed., *Source Readings in Music History,* Vol. 6: *The Nineteenth Century* (New York: W. W. Norton, 1998) 52–69.

See Edward A. Lippman, ed., *Musical Aesthetics: A Historical Reader,* Vol. 2, *The Nineteenth Century* (New York: Pendragon Press, 1990), for excerpts by Wagner, Schopenhauer, Kierkegaard, and Nietzsche. Undergraduates will not comprehend these excerpts without considerable editing and commentary from the instructor, but many passages cut to the heart of Wagner's aesthetic ideals and help to explain the ideals underlying leitmotives and Gesamtkunstwerk.

Much ink has been spilled over analyses of the Tristan chord. See the analytical essays included in the Norton Critical Score of the *Prelude and the Liebestod* (New York: W. W. Norton, 1985), edited by Robert Bailey.

DVD performances of all of Wagner's romantic operas are available, including *The Flying Dutchman* (Kultur, 2004) and *Lohengrin* (Image Entertainment, 2001).

Oddly, finding a quality video of *Tristan und Isolde* is difficult. Inadequate recording techniques and absurd staging are prevalent. The DVD of the Metropolitan performance in 2001 (Universal Music & VI, 2004) is suitable for class needs.

Performances of Wagner's *Ring,* conducted by Pierre Boulez at Bayreuth, are available on DVD (Uni/Phillips, 2001).

*Parisfal* is available on DVD (Universal Music VI, 2002).

Have a student watch the film *Excalibur* (1981) and report on the music adapted from *Siegfried, Parsifal,* and *Tristan und Isolde*. Discuss with students the fascination the medieval era held in Wagner's time and our own recent return to Romantic themes. Have student suggest ways in which Wagner has influenced film scoring.

Discuss with students Wagner's anti-Semitic views. Do his views mar our historical image of the composer and his works? Is Israel justified in not permitting performances of music by Wagner?

Gounod's *Faust* is available on DVD (Image Entertainment, 2003).

A movie of *Carmen* is available on DVD (Columbia/Tristars Studio, 1999). Discuss with students the relative merits between a video of a staged opera and that of a movie.

Have students discuss the differences between nationalism and exoticism, with a particular emphasis on *Carmen* and Spain. The article "Exoticism" by Ralph P. Locke in *The New Grove Dictionary of Music* is an excellent starting point. Ask if this comparison has any parallels with today's mixture of musical cultures.

Glinka's *Ruslan und Lydmila* is available on DVD (Universal Music & VI, 2003).

Tchaikovsky's ballet *The Nutcracker* is one of the most commonly performed works in this country, despite the inherent confusions in the plot. Have a student research the story and report to the class. Use any of the numerous videos of the work to discuss the variety of dancing in ballet, extending from pantomime to the *grand pas de deux*.

Musorgsky's *Boris Godunov* is available on DVD (Universal Music & VI, 2002).

Rimsky-Korsakov's *Sadko* is available on a compact-disc recording (Opera D'Oro 1246, 2000).

A compact-disc recording of Ethel Smyth's *The Wreckers* has been issued by the BBC Philharmonic (Conifer, 1994). Use both the music and subject of this opera to discuss the changing role of women in society and music at the end of the nineteenth century.

Have students write out all of the possible transpositions of whole-tone and octatonic scales. In class, create melodies and harmonies derived from each scale system. This exercise will help prepare them for studies of Debussy and Stravinsky.

Discuss with the class the effect that language has upon singing. Using Italian as an example of a language that is well suited to the voice, consider German, French, and English qualities that impact singing. What would be the difficulties of singing in Polish, Russian, or Czech?

Gilbert and Sullivan's operettas are available on DVD, for example, *The Mikado* (Bethesda, Maryland: Acorn Media AMP 3464, 1999), *The Pirates of Penzance* (Acorn Media, 2000), and *HMS Pinafore* (Acorn Media, 2004). All three of these works and several more can be purchased in an inexpensive box set (Acorn Media, 2004).

Numerous recordings of Sousa marches are available. Have students select a few and discuss the common structure and the relationship of the march to other nineteenth-century dance types.

For primary-source descriptions of vaudeville, see *From Traveling Show to Vaudeville; Theatrical Spectacle in America, 1830–1910,* ed. Robert M. Lewis (Baltimore: John Hopkins University Press, 2003).

## OBJECTIVE QUESTIONS

1. Jacques Offenbach is associated most closely with which type of opera?
   a. grand opera
   b. lyric opera
   c. opéra bouffe
   d. opera buffa
   e. Romantic opera

   Answer: c

2. Gounod's *Faust* is which type of opera?
   a. grand opera
   b. lyric opera
   c. opéra bouffe
   d. opera buffa
   e. Romantic opera

   Answer: b

3. Bizet's most famous opera was ____________.
   a. *Carmen*
   b. *Mignon*
   c. *Benvenuto Cellini*
   d. *Thaïs*
   e. *Manon*

   Answer: a

4. Verdi's first great success was ____________.
   a. *La traviata*
   b. *Otello*
   c. *Rigoletto*
   d. *Nabucco*
   e. *Aida*

   Answer: d

5. Of the following, which is not a characteristic of Verdi's late operas?
   a. reminiscence motives
   b. continuous flow of music and action
   c. plots adapted from plays by Shakespeare
   d. spoken dialogue for the most intense scenes
   e. librettos created by Boito

   Answer: d

6. "Viva Verdi" was ____________.
   a. a cheer shouted by the audience after the overtures were played
   b. a nationalistic cry referring to the king of Italy
   c. a chorus used at the end of an opera by Bellini
   d. campaign slogan for Verdi's political ambitions
   e. the cheer that greeted Verdi when he visited Paris

   Answer: b

7. Wagner's term for the union of all the arts in a drama is ____________.
   a. Gesamtkunstwerk
   b. Bayreuth
   c. melodrama
   d. leitmotiv
   e. ewigemelodie

   Answer: a

8. Of the following, which characterizes the librettos of Wagner's operas?
   a. They were modeled after the grand opera librettos of Scribe.
   b. They were created by Wagner.
   c. They were generally drawn from recent European history.
   d. They were based on popular stageplays at the time.
   e. They distinguish between recitatives and arias.

   Answer: b

9. Wagner's *Tristan und Isolde* was influential because ____________.
   a. it used ambiguous harmony that stretched the limits of tonality
   b. it was deeply anti-Semitic and inspired other anti-Semitic operas
   c. it was the first true opera in the German language
   d. it relegated the orchestra to a complete subordinate role
   e. it incorporated magical characteristics

   Answer: a

10. *Der Ring des Nibelungen* is ____________.
    a. the circular theater that Wagner had built for his music dramas
    b. an opera by Weber
    c. a romantic opera by Wagner
    d. a set of stories by Tolkien
    e. a cycle of four music dramas by Wagner

    Answer: e

11. The Mighty Handful were ____________.
    a. five Russian composers who studied folk music and exotic scales
    b. five great Russian operas that inspired composers in other nations to use national folk epics for their operas
    c. five students of César Franck who became important composers in France
    d. five tenors who traveled around Russia singing folk music
    e. the five principal centers of opera in Europe

    Answer: a

12. Of the following, which describes Musorgsky's approach to harmony?
    a. He was inspired by Wagner to use functional harmony with chromatic passages.
    b. He was influenced by Tchaikovsky to use conventional harmony.
    c. He used nonfunctional harmony influenced by polyphonic folk singing.
    d. He developed a totally chromatic system.
    e. He developed a unique harmonic system based on pentatonic and whole-tone scales.

    Answer: c

13. Of the following operas, which is not by Puccini?
    a. *Tosca*
    b. *Manon Lescaut*
    c. *La bohème*
    d. *I Pagliacci*
    e. *Madama Butterfly*

    Answer: d

14. Verismo is associated with the operas of which country?
    a. Italy
    b. France
    c. Germany
    d. Spain
    e. Brazil

    Answer: a

15. Of the following, who was the leading ballet composer in nineteenth-century France?
    a. Gounod
    b. Saint-Saëns
    c. Franck
    d. Massenet
    e. Delibes

    Answer: e

Use the following answers for questions 16–20.
- a. England
- b. Brazil
- c. Bohemia
- d. United States
- e. Spain

16. *The Bartered Bride* is perhaps this country's best-known opera.

    Answer: c

17. This country developed an entertainment form called vaudeville.

    Answer: d

18. Felipe Pedrell sparked a national revival in this country with his opera *Los Pirineos.*

    Answer: e

19. Gilbert and Sullivan were natives of this country.

    Answer: a

20. Antonio Carlos Gomes, who became internationally recognized for his opera *Il Guarany,* was originally from this country.

    Answer: b

## SHORT-ESSAY QUESTIONS

1. Describe Verdi's use of Italian opera conventions and the innovations that he brought to the genre, citing specific examples from his operas.
2. Compare Wagner's romantic operas with his music dramas. Discuss trends that run across both genres.
3. Describe the impact of nationalism, realism, and exoticism on opera in the late nineteenth century.
4. Describe the variety of lighter musical theater found in France, England, and the United States.

## TERMS FOR IDENTIFICATION

nationalism
realism
Viva Verdi
Arrigo Boito
verismo
music drama
*Opera and Drama*
Gesamtkunstwerk
leitmotiv
lyric opera
opéra bouffe
cabaret
revue
Mighty Handful
whole-tone scale
octatonic scale
operetta
W. W. Gilbert
vaudeville

# CHAPTER 28 Late Romanticism in Germany and Austria

I. Variety of Music in the Later Nineteenth Century
   A. Old versus new music
      1. Prior to the nineteenth century, most music performed outside of church was composed within living memory.
      2. By 1850, a basic repertory of musical classics had been created.
      3. The new field of musicology formalized the study of music of the past.
         a. Complete works of composers such as Bach, Handel, Mozart, Beethoven, Schubert, and Chopin were published.
         b. Since Germans did much of the scholarly work, composers from Germany became the primary focus.
         c. Little-known works of the Renaissance and Baroque were collected and published in a number of sets and monuments.
      4. As a result, performers and audiences had both old and new works available to them.
   B. Brahms versus Wagner
      1. Brahms sought to create works within the Classical traditions.
      2. Wagner and Liszt saw the legacy of Beethoven pointing toward new genres and musical approaches.
      3. These divergent views polarized around Brahms and Wagner.
      4. Composers debated the relative merits of:
         a. Absolute and program music
         b. Tradition and innovation
         c. Classical genres and forms and new ones
      5. Both sides linked themselves to Beethoven.
      6. The music from both sides was known as classical music, since it was intended for performance alongside the Classical repertory.
   C. Nationalism versus internationalism
      1. The Classical repertory was performed throughout Europe and the Americas.
      2. Many composers turned to nationalism, not to break with traditions but to add a distinctive new flavor.
      3. In nations like Russia and the United States, composers were split between nationalists and internationalists.
   D. Classical versus popular music
      1. A gulf between classical and popular music grew in instrumental music, song, and choral music.
      2. Earlier composers, like Beethoven, could write both serious and light music.
      3. In the late nineteenth century, composers specialized in one or the other.
      4. Johann Strauss the younger, the "Waltz King," was a master of popular dance music (see **HWM Figure 28.1**).
      5. The difference between a serious symphony and a popular song is much greater today than it was in Mozart's time.

II. Johannes Brahms (1833–1897) (see **HWM biography,** page 719, and **Figure 28.2**)
   A. Brahms combined Classicism with Romantic sensibility.
      1. Brahms matured as a composer just as the Classical repertoire became dominant.

2. He composed in Classical traditions but added new elements in order to appeal to contemporary audiences.
3. He studied the music from the Renaissance and Baroque, and incorporated elements from these traditions into his works.
4. He wrote in virtually all of the musical languages of his time.

B. Biography
1. Born in Hamburg, Germany, he studied several musical instruments.
2. He earned money playing at taverns and restaurants, where he became fond of the Hungarian-Gypsy style of music.
3. Brahms performed as a pianist and directed several musical organizations.
4. He edited music by numerous Baroque, Classic, and Romantic composers.
5. Clara Schumann
   a. In 1853, he met Robert and Clara Schumann and violinist Joseph Joachim, who became his strongest supporters.
   b. Brahms helped take care of the Schumann family so that Clara could resume her career.
   c. Brahms loved Clara, but remained a bachelor throughout his life.
   d. He died less than one year after Clara passed away.

III. Brahms's Symphonies

A. Knowing that any symphony would have to match the standards Beethoven set, Brahms wrote his four symphonies after the age of forty.
1. Symphony No. 1 in C Minor, Op. 68 (1876) was completed after twenty years of work.
2. Symphony No. 2 in D Major, Op. 73 (1877)
3. Symphony No. 3 in F Major, Op. 90 (1883)
4. Symphony No. 4 in E Minor, Op. 98 (1885)

B. Symphony No. 1 is indebted to Beethoven, but also departs from past traditions.
1. It has a standard four-movement format, although the third movement is a lyrical intermezzo instead of a scherzo.
2. Like Beethoven's Symphony No. 5, it begins in C minor and ends in a triumphant C major.
3. The overall key scheme often moves through the circle of thirds.
4. The material in the slow introductions of the first and fourth movements is developed in the allegros, recalling Schumann's Symphony No. 4.
5. The hymnlike theme of the finale is similar in mood to Beethoven's Symphony No. 9.
6. Conductor Hans von Bülow called this work "Beethoven's Tenth."

C. Symphony No. 3
1. The opening measures illustrate several typical characteristics of Brahms's music (see **HWM Example 28.1**).
   a. Wide melodic spans
   b. Cross-relations between major and minor
   c. Metric ambiguity between duple and triple meters
2. The second theme of the final movement contains a metric conflict between duple and triple meter (see **HWM Example 28.2**).

D. Symphony No. 4, finale (see **HWM Figure 28.3** and **NAWM 132**)
1. The finale is a chaconne or passacaglia, a Baroque form consisting of variations over a repeating bass in triple meter.
   a. The key of E minor recalls Buxtehude's Ciaccona in E Minor for organ.
   b. The idea of recurring thematic material may be derived from a work by François Couperin that Brahms edited for the Couperin complete works.
   c. He may have adapted the bass from an ostinato in the final chorus of a Bach cantata (see example in **NAWM 132** commentary).
2. Another model may have been Bach's chaconne finale from Partita No. 2 in D Minor for Solo Violin, which Brahms transcribed as a left-hand exercise for piano.
   a. Both works are in minor with a middle section in the parallel major.
   b. In both, variations are often grouped in pairs.
   c. The points of return are marked by the reappearance of the opening idea and texture.
   d. They also share details of figurations.
3. The use of variations as a finale and the treatment of the theme also recall Beethoven's *Eroica* Symphony.
4. The movement has thirty-one variations on an eight-measure theme and ends with a substantial coda.
5. Brahms grouped variations into five large sections, suggesting sonata form.
   a. Variations 1–12 (measures 1–96) serve as an exposition.
   b. Variations 13–16 (measures 97–128) form an interlude in 3/2 meter that moves to the parallel major.

c. Variations 17–23 (measures 129–184), beginning with a variation that recalls the opening, serve as a development section.
d. Variations 24–27 (measures 185–216) serve as the recapitulation, with varied presentations of earlier variations.
e. The coda (measure 253) is in a faster tempo and freely treats the original theme.
6. Throughout, Brahms presents variations that are extensions of something we have heard before; Schoenberg called this technique "developing variation."

IV. Other Works by Brahms
A. Concertos
1. Piano Concerto No. 1 in D Minor (1861) is his first major orchestral work.
2. Piano Concerto No. 2 in B-flat Major, Op. 83 (1881), with four movements, is his most symphonic conception of the genre.
3. Violin Concerto in D Major, Op. 77 (1878) is parallel in seriousness to Beethoven's Concerto in the same key.
B. Chamber music
1. Brahms is the true successor of Beethoven in chamber music.
2. He composed twenty-four chamber works, of which at least six are masterpieces.
3. As in his orchestral works, Brahms incorporates classical traditions within his own personal style.
4. Seven chamber works feature piano and strings, including three piano trios and three piano quartets.
5. The first movement of the Quintet for Piano and Strings in F Minor. Op. 34 (1864), one of his most popular works, illustrates his technique of developing variation (see **HWM Example 28.3**).
C. Piano music
1. Brahms developed a highly individual musical style.
a. Full sonority
b. Broken-chord figuration
c. Frequent doubling of the melody in octaves, thirds, or sixths
d. Multiple chordlike appoggiaturas
e. Frequent use of cross-rhythms
f. Simple ideas developed into innovative textures
2. Brahms composed three piano sonatas as a young man (1852–53).
a. These works are in the tradition of Beethoven.
b. They incorporate the chromatic harmony of Chopin and Liszt and the songlike style of Schumann.
3. In his twenties, Brahms focused on variations.
a. The variations appear as strings of short character pieces based on the formal and harmonic plan of the theme.
b. Variations and Fugue on a Theme of Handel, Op. 24 (1861) includes evocations of Chopin and Mozart, a variety of other musical styles, and a climactic Beethovenian fugue.
c. Variations on a Theme of Paganini, Op. 35 (1863) has etudelike qualities.
4. In his last two decades, Brahms published six collections of intermezzos, rhapsodies, and other short pieces.
a. These may be his greatest piano works.
b. Most are in ABA' forms and have songlike melodies.
D. Songs
1. Schubert was the model for Brahms's songwriting.
a. The voice dominates.
b. The piano supports with figuration.
2. Brahms composed 260 Lieder, many of which are strophic or modified strophic.
3. Some songs incorporate characteristics of folk songs.
4. The texts often suggest emotional restraint or an introspective, elegiac mood.
5. Many of Brahms's qualities can be seen in the first strophe of *Wie Melodien zieht es mir* (1886; see **HWM Example 28.4**).
E. Choral works
1. Brahms wrote his choral works for amateur performers.
2. He arranged German folk songs for chorus and wrote many short unaccompanied songs for women's, men's, or mixed voices.
3. *Ein deutsches Requiem* (A German Requiem, 1868)
a. Written for soprano and baritone soloists, chorus and orchestra, this is his greatest choral work (see **HWM Figure 28.4**).
b. The German text is not from the Latin Mass, but from the Old Testament, Apocrypha, and New Testament.
c. Brahms draws upon the traditions of Schütz and Bach, but presents them in the colors of nineteenth-century harmony and orchestration.

F. Reputation
   1. Brahms has been viewed as conservative, but he was a trailblazer.
   2. He was among the first to draw upon both the music of the past and present, a process that has been repeated by numerous composers of the twentieth century.

V. Franz Liszt
   A. The New German School
      1. The term "New German School" was coined by a music critic in 1859.
         a. He viewed three composers as leaders: Wagner, Liszt, and Berlioz.
         b. Although the latter two were not Germans, Beethoven was their model.
      2. The term helped polarize the division between supporters of Liszt and Wagner and supporters of Brahms, such as the music critic Eduard Hanslick (see **HWM Source Reading,** page 726).
      3. Among the composers who sided with Wagner and Liszt are Bruckner, Wolf, and Richard Strauss.
   B. Liszt retired from his career as a concert pianist in 1848.
      1. He became court music director at Weimar and focused on composition.
      2. His works then went beyond virtuoso display.
      3. Some of his works reveal a shift towards the classical repertory.
   C. Symphonic poems
      1. Liszt composed twelve symphonic poems between 1848 and 1858.
      2. Each is a one-movement programmatic work for orchestra.
      3. The forms are often closely related to traditional Classical structures.
      4. The program content came from a variety of sources:
         a. *Prometheus* is from a myth and a poem by Herder.
         b. *Mazeppa* is taken from a poem by Victor Hugo.
         c. *Orfeo ed Euridice* pays homage to Gluck's opera and an Etruscan vase.
      5. Liszt also composed two programmatic symphonies that function like a series of symphonic poems.
         a. *Faust* Symphony (1854)
         b. *Dante* Symphony (1856)
      6. *Les Préludes* (The Preludes, 1854)
         a. This symphonic poem is linked to Alfonse-Marie de Lamartine's poem of the same title.
         b. Both poem and music follow the same succession of moods.
         c. Liszt unifies the work through thematic transformation (see **HWM Example 28.5**).
      7. Liszt's thematic transformation techniques are also evident in his four-movement Piano Concerto No. 1 in E-flat Major (1855).
   D. Piano Sonata in B Minor (1853)
      1. The work is written as one extended movement with four major themes that are transformed in a number of ways.
      2. The piece can be seen as both a gigantic sonata form and a condensed four-movement structure: fast sonata, slow, fugue, and fast finale.
   E. Choral music
      1. The choral works also reflect the accommodation between past and present.
      2. *St. Elisabeth* (1857–62) and *Christus* (1866–72), his most important choral works, derive thematic material from plainchants.
   F. Liszt's influence
      1. The symphonic poem was adapted by a number of other composers.
      2. His chromatic harmonies helped to form Wagner's style after 1854.
      3. The even divisions of the octave, such as with the augmented triad, had a strong impact on Russian and French composers.
      4. His thematic transformation parallels Wagner's use of leitmotives and Brahms's developing variation.

VI. Anton Bruckner (1824–1896) (see **HWM Figure 28.5**)
   A. Trained in counterpoint, Bruckner served as organist of the cathedral at Linz and as organist in Vienna from 1867 to his death.
   B. He brought Wagner's style and ethos into his symphonies and choral music.
   C. Symphonies
      1. Bruckner composed nine numbered symphonies and two unnumbered ones.
      2. Most underwent extensive revisions.
      3. Influences of Beethoven
         a. All are four movements, and none is explicitly programmatic.
         b. Beethoven's Symphony No. 9 was a model in its procedure and purpose.
      4. Influences of Wagner
         a. Large-scale structures
         b. Extended lengths
         c. Lush harmonies
         d. Sequential repetition of entire passages
         e. Huge orchestra

5. Bruckner's orchestration is influenced by his experiences as an organist.
6. Symphony No. 4, first movement (see **HWM Example 28.6**)
   a. It opens in a similar manner to Beethoven's Ninth Symphony.
   b. The movement can be seen as a sonata form with continuous development of musical ideas.

D. Choral music
1. Bruckner blended modern elements with the influences from the Cecilian movement, which promoted a revival of the sixteenth-century a cappella style.
2. His motets for unaccompanied choir reflect Cecilian ideas, but they can also include bold harmonic treatment.
3. The Mass No. 2 in E Minor (1866) is a neo-medieval work for eight-part chorus and fifteen wind instruments.
4. The sacred works were designed to function in church and on the concert stage.

VII. Hugo Wolf (1860–1903)

A. Works
1. Wolf is best known for adapting Wagner's methods to the German Lied.
2. He also composed music for piano, chamber ensembles, orchestras, and choruses; he wrote one opera.

B. Lieder
1. Wolf composed 250 Lieder, mostly in periods of intense activity between 1887 and 1897.
2. He published five principal collections of songs, each devoted to a single poet or group, thereby stressing an equality of words and music.
3. Like Wagner, he worked toward a fusion of poetry and music and of voice and piano.
4. *Lebe wohl!* from the Mörike songbook reflects Wagner's influences (see **HWM Example 28.7**).
   a. The arioso vocal line has speechlike rhythms.
   b. Continuity is sustained in the piano part.
   c. Chromatic harmonies are inspired by the idiom of *Tristan und Isolde*; all twelve chromatic notes appear in the first phrase.

VIII. Richard Strauss (1864–1949) (see **HWM Figure 28.6**)

A. Biography
1. He was a dominant figure in German musical life.
2. He was a famous conductor and led most of the world's best orchestras.
3. As a composer, he is best remembered for:
   a. Symphonic poems, mostly written before 1900
   b. Operas, mostly written after 1900
   c. Lieder

B. Symphonic poems
1. Strauss's works are modeled after the program music of Berlioz and Liszt.
   a. Colorful orchestration
   b. Thematic transformation
   c. Types of programs, which are often based on literature
2. Strauss derived his programs from a variety of sources, and his programmatic depictions range from representational to philosophical.
3. *Don Juan* was Strauss's first complete mature work and established his reputation.
   a. Events in the life of Don Juan are depicted, including a graphic sexual scene and his death at the end.
   b. Most of the work evokes moods of boldness and romance.
4. *Till Eulenspiegel* is a representational telling of a trickster's exploits.
   a. Two themes for Till are developed like leitmotives.
   b. The work can be heard with an understanding of the story or as a colorful concert work.
   c. Strauss called the form of the work a "rondo," referring to the recurrence of the Till themes.
5. *Also Sprach Zarathustra*
   a. This work is a musical commentary on Nietzsche's long prose-poem.
   b. Nietzche suggests that the Christian ethic should be replaced by the ideal of a superman, who is above good and evil.
   c. Much of the work is philosophical, but there are some moments of direct representation.
   d. The opening, made famous in the movie *2001: A Space Odyssey*, was inspired by Zarathurstra's address to the rising sun in the prologue.

C. *Don Quixote* (see excerpt in **NAWM 133**)
1. Literary background
   a. This symphonic poem dramatizes Miguel de Cervantes's novel of 1605.
   b. It depicts the adventures of the knight Don Quixote, his squire Sancho Panza, and his horse Rosinante (see **HWM Figure 28.7**).

2. Structure
   a. The opening features two themes, representing Don Quizote and Sancho, followed by ten variations and an epilogue.
   b. The variation structure is loose and builds on Liszt's technique of thematic transformation.
3. Themes
   a. Much of the work sounds like chamber music.
   b. Don Quixote is represented by a solo cello, which is joined by a solo violin and English horn.
   c. The bass clarinet and tenor tuba represent Sancho.
   d. Motives in the solo viola suggest Rosinante.
4. Variation 1
   a. The opening depicts a conversation between cello and bass clarinet.
   b. Tilting windmills can be heard in measures 60–78.
   c. The creaking blades are suggested by the orchestration, which includes *col legno* effects in the cellos.
   d. Don Quixote is knocked off his horse (measures 71–72), but picks himself up to seek a new adventure.
5. Variation 2
   a. The strings suggest Don Quixote's attempts to be bold while the winds ridicule with the Sancho theme.
   b. Fluttertonging in the winds depict the army of sheep that they encounter.

## SUGGESTIONS FOR SUPPLEMENTARY READING/LISTENING/ACTIVITIES

This is a good time for students to explore the nature of nineteenth-century editions. Have them choose a work by Bach, Mozart, Beethoven, or any other composer that seems appropriate, and then compare various editions, including the complete works from the nineteenth century, the current complete works, Dover reprints, miniature scores, and any performing edition that students are using. Discuss what the editorial practices of the different centuries suggest about their eras and what should be the obligations of today's performers.

Introduce students to the monuments of music. Either design a specific assignment or let them explore the overall content of *Denkmäler der Tonkunst, Denkmäler deutscher Tonkunst,* and *Denkmäler der Tonkunst in Österreich.* Include in your discussions how to find works published in sets and monuments.

Have a student read and give a report on the Paul Mast's article "Brahms's Study, Octaven u. Quinten u.A., with Schenker's Commentary Translated," *The Music Forum,* vol. 5, ed. Felix Salzar and Carl Schacter (New York: Columbia University Press, 1980), 1–196. This will be amusing for students who have recently learned part-writing rules, and it points up Brahms intense study of older music.

Have students select a movement from one of Brahms's symphonies or divertimentos and report on the degree to which it is Classic or Romantic in spirit and why. Use this exercise to generate a discussion of the characteristics of Romanticism. Why would a composer living at the end of the century be less Romantic than an earlier composer? Can students think of any parallel developments in twentieth-century music?

For more on Brahms's Fourth Symphony, see the Norton Critical Score edition, *Brahms' Symphony No. 4 in E Minor, op. 98: Authoritative Score, Background, Context, Criticism, Analysis,* edited by Kenneth Ross Hull (New York: W. W. Norton, 2000).

For more on the symphony at the end of the nineteenth century, see Carl Dahlhaus, *Nineteenth-Century Music,* trans. J. Bradford Robinson (Berkeley: University of California Press, 1989), 265–76.

As a study of orchestration, have students compare the four-hand piano and the orchestra versions of *Variations on a Theme by Haydn.*

Eric Sams's *The Songs of Johannes Brahms* (New Haven, Conn.: Yale University Press, 2000) discusses each of Brahms's songs. For a good recording of *Wie Melodien zieht es mir,* see *Christa Ludwig—Les Introuvables* (Emi Classics 64074, 1992).

For other compact-disc recordings of Brahms, you may want to use John Eliot Gardiner's *Ein deutsches Requeim* (Philips 432140, 1991) and the Piano Quintet in F Minor (Hyperion 22018, 1997).

Have students listen to one of Liszt's symphonic poems (*Hamlet* works particularly well) and describe the ways he fits the music to the program. When students disagree about passages, ask them whether they think Liszt intended different people to hear these works differently.

In his later years, Liszt became quite religious. Have students research this development and suggest how it is reflected in his compositions. For contrast, direct a violin student to the biography of Paganini and his refusal to take religious rites at his death. The history of his corpse is fascinating.

Have students read a summary of Goethe's *Faust* and Nicholas Vazsonyi's "Liszt, Goethe, and the Faust Symphony," *Journal of the American Liszt Society* 40 (1996), 1–23, then listen to excerpts portraying various elements.

Have a student listen to Beethoven's Symphony No. 9 and Bruckner's Symphony No. 4 and have them report on the similarities between the two works.

Wolf's *Moricke Lieder* is available on compact disc (Hyperion 67311, 2001).

For more on Wolf's style, see Amanda Glauert, *Hugo Wolf and the Wagnerian Inheritance* (New York: Cambridge University Press, 1999), especially pages 32–47 on Wolf's response to the conflict between folksong and Wagner's music dramas as models for lieder.

For more on Richard Strauss, see Michael Kennedy's *Richard Strauss: Man, Musician, Enigma* (New York: Cambridge University Press, 1999), especially the section on the Third Reich years.

For more on the program for *Also sprach Zarathustra,* see Charles Youmans, "The Private Intellectual Context of Richard Strauss' Also sprach Zarathustra," *Nineteenth-Century Music* 22 (1998), 101–26, and Rey M. Longyear "Nietzsche's and Strauss's Zarathustra," *New Journal for Music* 1 (1990), 7–26.

Strauss's major symphonic poems are available on reissues with Strauss himself as conductor: "Richard Strauss conducts Richard Strauss" (Hexham, Northumberland: APR APR 5527, 1999) and "Richard Strauss conducts Richard Strauss: The 1936–42 RRG Recordings" (Berkeley, California: Music & Arts CD-1057, 1999). The latter includes the *Alpensinfonie, Don Juan, Till Eulenspeigel, Also sprach Zarathustra,* and *Tod und Verklärung*. Use these recordings to introduce a discussion on recording technology and recordings as primary sources.

## OBJECTIVE QUESTIONS

1. According to the text, what is the most important fact about music in the late nineteenth century?
   a. the creation of the solo recital
   b. the growth in the size of orchestras
   c. the emergence of the orchestra conductor
   d. the creation of a new scholarly field, musicology
   e. the establishment of a permanent classical repertory

   Answer: e

2. Which composer was known as the "Waltz King?"
   a. Brahms
   b. Liszt
   c. Richard Strauss
   d. Johann Strauss the younger
   e. Tchaikovsky

   Answer: d

3. Of the following, which describes the symphonies of Brahms?
   a. They were composed quickly.
   b. They incorporate elements of Renaissance and Baroque music.
   c. They expand the standard size of the orchestra.
   d. They use five or more movements.
   e. Each is based on a literary program.

   Answer: b

4. How many symphonies did Brahms compose?
   a. four
   b. five
   c. six
   d. nine
   e. eleven

   Answer: a

5. Brahms's Symphony No. 1 is primarily indebted to the music of ____________.
   a. Wagner
   b. Liszt
   c. Schumann
   d. Schubert
   e. Beethoven

   Answer: e

6. What older form does Brahms use in the finale of his Symphony No. 4?
   a. pavane and galliard
   b. passacaglia/chaconne
   c. prelude and fugue
   d. French overture
   e. toccata

   Answer: b

7. Which type of piano music was not composed by Brahms?
   a. intermezzos
   b. sonatas
   c. études
   d. variations
   e. rhapsodies

   Answer: c

8. An orchestral work in one movement with a literary or other program is called ____________.
   a. a program symphony
   b. a cyclic symphony
   c. a symphonic poem
   d. a sinfonia
   e. an overture

   Answer: c

9. Of the following, who would not be considered a member of the New German School?
   a. Wagner
   b. Richard Strauss
   c. Bruckner
   d. Brahms
   e. Liszt

   Answer: d

Use the following answers for questions 10–14.
   a. *Faust* Symphony
   b. *Don Juan*
   c. *Romantic* Symphony
   d. *Ein deutsches Requiem*
   e. Möricke Songbook

10. This was composed by Bruckner.

    Answer: c

11. This was composed by Richard Strauss.

    Answer: b

12. This was composed by Wolf.

    Answer: e

13. This was composed by Liszt.

    Answer: a

14. This was composed by Brahms.

    Answer: d

15. The technique used by Liszt to unify *Les Préludes* is called ____________.
    a. thematic transformation
    b. developing variation
    c. leitmotives
    d. chromatic saturation
    e. Les Fugues

    Answer: a

16. Of the following, which does *not* describe Liszt's Piano Sonata in B Minor?
    a. It is an extended form in one movement.
    b. Its primary intent is to feature virtuoso display.
    c. It develops four principal themes.
    d. The structure can be analyzed as sonata form.
    e. It can be viewed as having four movements.

    Answer: b

17. Bruckner modeled his symphonies on which work by Beethoven?
    a. Symphony No. 3
    b. Symphony No. 5
    c. Symphony No. 6
    d. Symphony No. 9
    e. *Missa solemnis*

    Answer: d

18. Of the following, which describes the Lieder by Wolf?
    a. folklike melodies
    b. dominant vocal line
    c. equality of words and music
    d. simple harmonic support
    e. introspective mood

    Answer: c

19. *Also sprach Zarathustra* by Richard Strauss is based on ____________.
    a. a philosophical prose-poem by Nietzsche
    b. a pastoral poem by Lammartine
    c. a Norse legend
    d. an autobiographical experience
    e. a short story by Clarke

    Answer: a

20. Of the following, which is not associated with Richard Strauss?
    a. operas
    b. songs
    c. conductor
    d. symphonic poems
    e. concert pianist

    Answer: e

## SHORT-ESSAY QUESTIONS

1. Describe the mixture of classical traditions and a contemporary musical idiom in the music of Brahms.
2. Compare the various methods of developing a theme as heard in works by Brahms, Liszt, and Richard Strauss.
3. Discuss the influence of Beethoven on nineteenth-century symphony composers.
4. Describe the variety of sources used for programmatic works by Liszt and Richard Strauss.

## TERMS FOR IDENTIFICATION

musicology
"The Waltz King"
chaconne
developing variation
The New German School
symphonic poem
thematic transformation
Piano Sonata in B Minor
Cecilian movement
Nietzsche

# CHAPTER 29 Diverging Traditions in the Later Nineteenth Century

I. German Traditions and Nationalism
   A. German and Austrian composers in the late nineteenth century drew upon their national heritage, as observed in **HWM Chapter 28.**
   B. In other regions, composers debated how to deal with the Germanic traditions.
      1. French composers argued about whether to assimilate Bach, Beethoven, and Wagner or to create a new idiom.
      2. Nationalist schools in instrumental music appeared in Russia, Bohemia, and Scandinavia (see nationalism discussion in **HWM Chapter 27**).
      3. Composers in Britain and the Americas avoided overt nationalism.

II. France
   A. General trends
      1. Paris was the principal center of both concert music and opera.
      2. Concerts featured symphonic works of the German tradition and works by French composers.
      3. Conductor Edouard Colonne introduced explanatory program notes in a concert series surveying the history of music (see **HWM Figure 29.1**).
      4. Concerts and musical styles were often tied to politics.
      5. A variety of music schools were established, but the Conservatoire was still the most prestigious.
      6. Two principal strands of music composition dominated prior to the emergence of impressionism.
         a. A cosmopolitan tradition transmitted through César Franck
         b. A French tradition, embodied in the music of Gabriel Fauré
   B. César Franck (1822–1890)
      1. Born in Belgium, Franck studied at the Conservatoire and became professor of organ there in 1871.
      2. Musical characteristics
         a. Classical genres, forms, and counterpoint
         b. Thematic transformation and cyclic unity
         c. Wagnerian harmony
      3. Franck's *Prelude, Chorale, and Fugue* (1884) for piano mixes Baroque forms and procedures with the thematic and harmonic methods of Liszt and Wagner.
      4. Organ music
         a. He often combined original melodies in chorale style with richly developed fantasias and full chordal finales, as in *Three Chorales* (1890).
         b. His improvisatory style inaugurated a new type of organ music in France.
         c. The design of the organ in France changed to accommodate this approach.
      5. Franck is considered the founder of modern French chamber music.
      6. All three of his major chamber works are cyclic and incorporate thematic transformation.
         a. Piano Quintet in F Minor (1879)
         b. String Quartet in D Major (1889)
         c. Violin Sonata in A Major (1886)

C. Gabriel Fauré (1845–1924) (see **HWM Figure 29.2**)
   1. The French tradition drew upon the works of composers from Couperin to Gounod.
      a. Music was viewed more as sonorous form than as expression.
      b. Order and restraint are fundamental.
      c. Music is more lyric or dancelike than epic or dramatic.
   2. Biography
      a. Fauré studied under Saint-Saëns and had several posts as organist.
      b. He was a founder of the Société Nationale, which sought to preserve French traditions.
      c. He became a professor of composition at the Paris Conservatoire in 1896 and served as director from 1905 to 1920.
      d. His large works include the *Requiem* (1887) and two operas.
      e. He primarily composed smaller works, including songs, short piano works, and chamber music.
   3. Fauré developed a new style in which melodic lines are fragmented and harmony is less directional.
   4. *Avant que tu ne t'en ailles* (Before you depart) from the song cycle *La bonne chanson* (The Good Song, 1892) (see **HWM Example 29.1**)
      a. Fragmentary melodic phrases
      b. Harmonic treatment dilutes the need for resolution and creates a sense of repose.

III. Russia
   A. Tchaikovsky
      1. Tchaikovsky successfully combined classical forms and nationalism.
      2. Many of his works have joined the classical repertory, including:
         a. Ballets (see **HWM Chapter 27**)
         b. Piano concertos and a violin concerto (1878)
         c. Symphonies, most notably his last three (Nos. 4–6)
      3. Symphony No. 4 in F Minor (1877–78)
         a. Tchaikovsky suggested that the opening horn call represents fate.
         b. The horn call reappears and unifies this cyclic symphony.
         c. The keys in the first movement move within a circle of minor thirds.
         d. The outer movements are dramatic; the second is wistful, and the third is an airy scherzo.
      4. Symphony No. 6 in B Minor, the *Pathétique* (1893)
         a. The scherzo is replaced by a 5/4 waltz.
         b. The dance movement is second, followed by a vivacious rondo.
         c. The symphony ends with a despairing slow movement.
   B. Borodin
      1. Borodin was a devotee of chamber music and an admirer of Mendelssohn.
      2. His melodies reflect the spirit of folk tunes.
      3. Style
         a. Songlike themes
         b. Transparent orchestral texture
         c. Modally tinged harmonies
         d. Spinning out an entire movement from a single idea
      4. Major works
         a. Two string quartets (1874–79 and 1881)
         b. Symphony No. 2 in B Minor (1869–76)
         c. *In Central Asia* (1880), a symphonic sketch
   C. Musorgsky
      1. Major nonoperatic works
         a. *Night on Bald Mountain* (1867), a symphonic fantasy
         b. *Pictures at an Exhibition* for piano (1874, later orchestrated by Ravel)
         c. Song cycles: *The Nursery* (1872), *Sunless* (1874), and *Songs and Dances of Death* (1875)
      2. *Pictures at an Exhibition*
         a. This set of ten pieces was inspired by an exhibition of sketches, paintings, and designs by Viktor Hartmann.
         b. Several of the images are rendered in character pieces that are joined by a theme that represents the viewer walking.
         c. The image of a commemorative gate to be built at Kiev was set as a grand processional hymn with Western and Russian elements (see **HWM Figure 29.3** and **Example 29.2**).
   D. Rimsky-Korsakov
      1. Although he composed a variety of works, he is best known for his programmatic orchestral pieces.
         a. *Capriccio espagnole* (1887)
         b. *Sheherazade* (1888), a symphonic suite
         c. *Russian Easter Overture* (1888)
      2. These works display his genius for orchestration and musical characterization.
      3. The four movements of *Sheherazade* represent four stories as told to the sultan by his wife, who is portrayed with a solo violin.

IV. Bohemia
  A. Smetana
    1. The String Quartet No. 1, *From My Life* (1876) uses a nationalist style.
    2. *Má vlast* (My Country, ca. 1872–79) is a cycle of six symphonic poems.
      a. *The Moldau*, the best-known work of the set, depicts the river that moves through the Czech countryside to Prague.
      b. *Tábor*, the most stirring of the set, employs a traditional chorale as a symbol of Czech resistance to oppression.
  B. Dvořák
    1. Dvořák's nonoperatic works include:
      a. Nine symphonies
      b. Four concertos, including the Cello Concerto in B Minor
      c. Numerous dances for orchestra
      d. Other chamber works, piano pieces, songs, and choral works
    2. Dvořák could write in both international and national styles.
      a. Symphony No. 6 in D Major (1880) is international in style.
      b. Nationalist works include the *Slavonic Dances* and the *Dumky* Piano Trio.
    3. He served as artistic director of the National Conservatory of Music in New York.
      a. Dvořák was hired to help create a national style in the United States.
      b. He looked to the music of American Indians and African Americans for a source of an American style (see **HWM Source Reading,** page 745).
      c. He applied some of these elements to the Symphony No. 9 in E Minor (*From the New World*), his best-known work, and to the String Quartet No. 12 in F Major (*American*).

V. Northern Europe
  A. Edvard Grieg (1843–1907)
    1. Grieg created a distinctive nationalist style in Norway with a series of songs, short piano pieces, and orchestral suites.
    2. Norwegian elements
      a. Modal melodies and harmonies
      b. Dance rhythms
    3. The nationalist style can best be seen in:
      a. Songs on Norwegian texts
      b. *Peer Gynt* Suite (1875)
      c. *Slatter*, a collection of Norwegian peasant dances arranged for piano
    4. His piano style has some similarities to Chopin's, but folk elements predominate.
    5. Some of Grieg's works were international in character, including the popular Piano Concerto in A Minor (1868, revised 1907).
  B. Edward Elgar (1857–1934)
    1. Elgar was the first English composer to gain international recognition in over two hundred years.
    2. He did not adopt a distinctive national style, and he drew upon the styles of both Brahms and Wagner.
    3. *The Dream of Gerontius* (1900), an oratorio, is influenced by Wagner's *Parsifal*.
    4. His orchestral works include the *Enigma Variations* (1899) and two symphonies.

VI. The United States
  A. Diverse musical styles
    1. Ethnic diversity complicated the creation of a national identity.
    2. Immigrants from various regions brought their own musical traditions.
    3. Three principal types of music emerged, although with some overlapping.
      a. Classical, which centered on the composer and required complex notation
      b. Popular, which was notated and sold but centered on the performer
      c. Folk, which was passed on through oral tradition
  B. The classical tradition
    1. A large number of Germans immigrated to the United States in the middle of the nineteenth century.
      a. German musicians had a strong commitment to their national traditions.
      b. German immigrants filled American orchestras and taught music at all levels.
      c. German tastes and style dominated American music in the classical tradition until World War I.
    2. Theodore Thomas (1835–1905)
      a. He came to the U. S. in 1845 and later played violin in several orchestras.
      b. He conducted the Brooklyn Philharmonic and then founded his own orchestra, the Theodore Thomas Orchestra.
      c. His ensemble was one of the best and most successful classical music organizations in this country.
      d. Despite this success, he still needed to perform lighter dance music periodically.

e. He became the first conductor of the Chicago Symphony Orchestra.

C. American composers in the classic tradition
1. John Knowles Paine (1839–1906) became Harvard's first professor of music.
2. George Whitefield Chadwick (1854–1931) studied at the New England Conservatory in Boston and became its director.
3. Horatio Parker (1863–1919), a student of Chadwick, taught at Yale and was the first dean of its School of Music.
4. Edward MacDowell (1860–1908) was the first professor music at Columbia University.
5. All of the above composers studied in Germany, and their styles were deeply rooted in German tradition.
6. They had varying attitudes about nationalism.
   a. Parker wrote in an international style that is reflected in his best-known work, the oratorio *Hora novissima* (1893).
   b. Chadwick employed pentatonic melodies and distinctive rhythms in his Symphony No. 2 in B-flat (1883–85) and *Symphonic Sketches* (1895–1904).
   c. MacDowell opposed overt nationalism, but he nevertheless wrote several nationalist works, including his Second *Indian* Suite (1891–95) based on American Indian melodies.

D. Amy Marcy Beach (1867–1944) (see **HWM Figure 29.4**)
1. Biography
   a. Beach was a child prodigy.
   b. Excluded from the top universities because she was a woman, she studied privately in Boston and taught herself.
   c. She married a wealthy physician and had time to compose.
   d. Beach was internationally recognized and inspired many women in later generations.
2. Beach composed several large-scale works.
   a. Mass in E-flat (1890)
   b. *Gaelic* Symphony (1894–96)
   c. Piano Concerto (1899)
   d. Piano Quintet (1907)
3. She also wrote about 120 songs and other piano and choral works.
4. Style
   a. Some of her music has an ethnic flavor, like the Irish tunes in the *Gaelic* Symphony and the American Indian melodies in the String Quartet (1929).
   b. Most of her works follow German traditions.

E. Beach Piano Quintet
1. Relation to Brahms's Piano Quintet in F Minor
   a. Beach performed the Brahms quintet with the Kneisel Quartet, which inspired her to compose her own quintet.
   b. Beach adapted a theme from Brahms's quintet in each of her three movements.
   c. These three versions of the theme are related through thematic transformation.
   d. The relationship of Beach's theme to Brahms's is most distant in the finale (see example in the commentary to **NAWM 134**).
2. Last movement (**NAWM 134**)
   a. With its rich harmony and brilliant piano writing, the musical style is clearly rooted in the Romanticism of the late nineteenth century.
   b. The movement is in a modified sonata form.
   c. The development features a fugato, stirring climax, and a reprise of a theme from the first movement.
   d. The recapitulation begins with the second theme, and the first theme reappears briefly near the end of the movement.

F. Bands in America
1. The earliest American bands were in the military, but local bands emerged in the nineteenth century.
2. The invention of valves for brass instruments allowed them to play melodies in any register, and brass instruments became the backbone of the band.
3. Bands played a large role during the Civil War, and they continued to proliferate afterwards.
4. Professional bands enjoyed a heyday between the Civil War and World War I.
5. Patrick S. Gilmore (1829–1892)
   a. He founded his own band in 1858.
   b. He led two mammoth festival concerts with performers numbering in the thousands.
   c. He toured the United States and Europe with his band.
6. John Philip Sousa (1854–92)
   a. Sousa was inspired by the success of Gilmore.
   b. He conducted the United States Marine Band.
   c. He also organized his own internationally recognized band in 1892 (see **HWM Figure 29.5**).

G. Band music
  1. Concerts mixed arrangements of classic works with lighter works, such as dances and popular melodies.
  2. The march was the staple of the band repertory (see **HWM Figure 29.6**).
     a. The march generally opens with a brief introduction, usually four measures.
     b. Two strains or periods follow, each repeated.
     c. A trio appears in a contrasting key, usually the subdominant, with an optional introduction and two repeated strains.
     d. A da capo repetition of the march closes the work.
     e. Strains are typically sixteen measures.
     f. The opening of the trio tends to be soft and lyrical.
  3. Sousa's marches
     a. Sousa dropped the da capo repetition in his marches and instead alternated the lyrical trio with a more aggressive break strain.
     b. He often added countermelodies and increased instrumentation with each repeat of the trio.
  4. *The Stars and Stripes Forever* (1897, **NAWM 135**)
     a. The work begins with a four-measure unison introduction in E-flat.
     b. The march has two repeated sixteen-bar strains of a contrasting nature.
     c. The lyrical trio, also thirty-two bars, is set in A-flat, a fourth higher.
     d. Intended for concert performances rather than parades, the work builds to a climactic finish.
     e. The chromatic break strain creates a dramatic contrast.
     f. Countermelodies are added to the repetition of the trio.
     g. Sousa often performed the work with varied settings.

H. Popular song
  1. In the late nineteenth century, the gulf between art songs and popular songs widened.
  2. Composers of popular songs sought to entertain audiences, accommodate amateur performers, and sell as many copies as possible.
  3. Subjects for songs ranged from love to satire.
  4. Songs were also used to convey ideas about politics, religion, and society.
  5. The standard form of the popular song was the verse and refrain.
     a. The piano plays a four- or eight-measure introduction.
     b. The verse is eight, sixteen, or thirty-two measures in length.
     c. The refrain is similar in size to the verse.
  6. The refrain was often sung in harmony, so that the term *chorus* was applied to the refrain.
  7. Both verse and refrain can have internal repetitions.
  8. The key to success was a catchy phrase, sometimes called a *hook*.
  9. *After the Ball* (1892) by Charles K. Harris
     a. The song has a catchy chorus above a waltz dance rhythm (see **HWM Example 29.3**).
     b. *After the Ball* sold over a million copies, making the composer rich.
  10. Tin Pan Alley, a district in New York that specialized in music publishing, developed strategies for selling sheet music.

I. Music of African Americans
  1. Brought to America as slaves, Africans found it difficult to maintain their own ethnic culture.
  2. Slaves were able to preserve a distinct musical style because it was shared among a number of African societies and because music was encouraged by slaveowners.
  3. Characteristics of African music
     a. Call and response, the alternation of short phrases between a leader (*call*) and a group (*response*)
     b. Improvisation, usually on a simple formula
     c. Syncopation
     d. Repetition of short rhythmic or melodic patterns
     e. Multiple layers of rhythm, including strong offbeats
     f. Bending pitches or sliding from one pitch to another
     g. Shouts, moans, and other vocalizations
     h. Instruments like the banjo, based on a West African stringed instrument
  4. These traits are developed later in ragtime, blues, jazz and other musical styles in the African-American tradition.
  5. Spirituals had the greatest impact on nineteenth-century American music.
     a. A spiritual was a religious song of southern slaves.
     b. The texts were based on images or stories from the Bible, sometimes with hidden messages about freedom.
     c. *Go Down Moses* was the first spiritual to be published (1861).

6. Published spirituals were arranged as songs with piano accompaniments.
7. The Fisk Jubilee Singers popularized spirituals in the 1870s through concert tours in the United States and Europe (see **HWM Figure 29.7**).
8. By the end of the century, spirituals were folk music, popular music, and sources for melodic material in classic music.

## SUGGESTIONS FOR SUPPLEMENTARY READING/LISTENING/ACTIVITIES

For more on French nationalism, see Kay Norton, "The Societé Nationale de Musique: A Cradle and Sanctuary of French Art," *Music Research Forum* 4 (1989), 11–23.

For more on French vocal music, see Graham Johnson, *A French Song Companion* (New York: Oxford University Press, 2000).

Franck's violin sonata has been transcribed for several instruments. Compare recordings of the work featuring a violin (Heifetz and Rubinstein are on RCA 63007, 2001), cello (Jacqueline du Pré and Barenboim are on EMI Classics 65966, 1999), and flute (James Galway is on RCA 63441, 1999).

Fauré's *La bonne chanson* is recorded on compact disc, *Fauré Mèlodies* (EMI Classics 64079, 1992).

Have students compare the chamber music of Fauré and Franck in order to illustrate the diverging styles of French music in the late nineteenth century. Compact-disc recordings of these works are readily available, and some of the works are available through the Naxos online library.

A neglected area of French music is its repertoire for organ. The most well-known work of the repertoire is the often-performed *Toccata* from Organ Symphony No. 5 by Charles-Marie Widor. It is available on a compact-disc compilation that includes other works by French composers performed by Marie Claire Alain ("Great Toccatas," Erato 4509-04812-2, 1994). For additional information, see Lawrence Archibald and William J. Peterson, *French Organ Music: From the Revolution to Franck and Widor* (Rochester, N. Y.: University of Rochester Press, 1997).

Before discussing any of the nationalistic works in this chapter, have students create a list of ways in which a composer can portray a nation or an ethnic group in instrumental music. Refer to this list when discussing nationalistic works as well as those that demonstrate exoticism.

For more on Russian nationalistic music, see Richard Taruskin, *Defining Russia Musically: Historical and Hermeneutical Essays* (Princeton, N. J.: Princeton University Press, 1997), and Stuart Campbell, ed., *Russians on Russian Music, 1830–1880: An Anthology* (New York: Cambridge University Press, 1994).

Have students listen and follow the score to Rimsky-Korsakov's *Scheherazade*. This exercise allows for discussion of orchestration, symphonic form, and program symphonies. Compare this work to Berlioz's *Symphonie fantastique* in terms of orchestration, storytelling, and thematic unity.

See Weiss and Taruskin, eds., *Music in the Western World: A History in Documents* (New York: Schirmer, 1984), 390–96, for source readings on Russian nationalism.

Several of Smetana's works are appealing and can be used to discuss nationalism. Have students listen to *The Moldau* and note the composer's portrayal of both landscape and culture.

For more on Dvořák's role in American nationalistic music, see Emanuel Rubin, "Jeannette Meyer Thurber (1850–1946): Music for a Democracy" in *Cultivating Music in America: Women Patrons and Activists Since 1860* (1997), 134–163; and Charles Hamm, "Dvořák, Nationalism, Myth, and Racism in the United States" and Thomas Lawrence Riis, "Dvořák and His Black Students" in *Rethinking Dvořák: Views from Five Countries* (New York: Oxford University Press, 1996), 265–273 and 275–280, respectively. Also see Jean E. Snyder, "A Great and Noble School of Music," on Harry T. Burleigh's influence on Dvořák, in John C. Tibbetts, ed., *Dvořák in America 1892–1895* (Portland, Ore: Amadeus Press, 1993), 123–148.

Have students listen to Dvořák's Symphony No. 9, *From the New World,* or his *American* Quartet. Discuss the mixture of German traditions, European folk music, and American qualities in these works.

Have students listen to Dvořák's Cello Concerto and Grieg's Piano Concerto and report to the class on the mixture of nationalism and classical traditions in these works.

Have a student read a synopsis of Ibsen's *Peer Gynt* and report to the class how the music of Grieg matches the spirit of the play.

A number of compact-disc recordings of Elgar's *Dream of Gerontius* are available, including EMI Classics 73579, 2000.

Discuss with students the German lineage of music history and teaching that has reached this country. Consider the positive impact and the inherent German bias that still lingers in our conception of music history.

John Knowles Paine's *Poseidon and Amphitrite* and Amy Beach's *Gaelic* Symphony are available in *Three Centuries of American Music,* vol. 10: *American Orchestral Music, Late-Nineteenth-Century Boston,* edited by Sam Dennison (New York: G. K. Hall, 1992). The latter has been issued on compact disc (Musical Heritage Society 513475W, 1993).

Have students listen to Edward MacDowell's Second (*Indian*) Orchestra Suite and discuss its American and European features. A compact-disc recording that also includes the Suite No. 1 and two symphonic poems by MacDowell is available (Naxos 8559075, 2001).

Have students look up "After the Ball" online at Historic American Sheet Music: http://scriptorium.lib.duke.edu/sheetmusic/n/n03/n0353/. Have them explore this site and report their discoveries to the class.

Several recordings of Sousa's music conducted by the composer at the turn of the century are available in the four compact-disc series entitled *Sousa Original* (Altissimo Records, 1996–2001). Have students explore the variety of music composed by Sousa and compare recordings of his band with those of contemporary ensembles.

Listen to the music of the Fisk Jubilee Singers (Curb Records 78762, 2003) and consider their influence on twentieth-century popular music styles. Compare their performances with those of contemporary groups. For additional information, read Michael L. Cooper, *Slave Spirituals and the Jubilee Singers* (New York: Clarion Books, 2001), J. B. T. Marsh, *The Jubilee Singers and their Songs* (New York: Dover Publications, 2003), and Eileen Southern, *The Music of Black Americans: A History* (New York: W. W. Norton, 1997).

## OBJECTIVE QUESTIONS

1. Franck inaugurated a new style of music for the ___________.
   a. piano
   b. organ
   c. violin
   d. flute
   e. harp

   Answer: b

2. Gabriel Fauré is usually associated with which movement?
   a. German Romanticism
   b. the French Tradition
   c. the Cosmopolitan Tradition
   d. neo-Classicism
   e. realism

   Answer: b

3. Who is considered to be the founder of modern French chamber music?
   a. Debussy
   b. Ravel
   c. Fauré
   d. Gounod
   e. Franck

   Answer: e

4. What is new in Fauré's songs of *La bonne chanson*?
   a. Harmonic progressions dilute the pull of the tonic and the need for resolution.
   b. The melody is spun-out in lengthy phrases.
   c. Harmonic tension is enhanced by lingering dominant-seventh chords.
   d. The piano is restricted to a subordinate position.
   e. The chromaticism of Fauré's contemporaries is rejected.

   Answer: a

5. Of the following, which are unusual features of Tchaikovsky's Symphony No. 6?
   a. a recurring fate motive and a pizzicato scherzo
   b. a 5/4 scherzo and a finale that uses cannons
   c. a recurring fate motive and the use of a Russian hymn
   d. a 5/4 scherzo and a slow-movement finale
   e. a pizzicato scherzo and a slow-movement finale

   Answer: d

Use the following answers for questions 6–10.
   a. England
   b. Russia
   c. United States
   d. Norway
   e. Bohemia

6. Borodin's country of origin

   Answer: b

7. Grieg's country of origin

   Answer: d

8. Elgar's country of origin

   Answer: a

9. Smetana's country of origin

   Answer: e

10. MacDowell's country of origin

    Answer: c

11. Which country avoided developing a national style in the late nineteenth century?
    a. Russia
    b. France
    c. England
    d. Bohemia
    e. Norway

    Answer: c

12. Which work by Musorgsky was originally written for piano and was later orchestrated by Ravel?
    a. *Pictures at an Exhibition*
    b. *Night on Bald Mountain*
    c. *Sunless*
    d. *The Nursery*
    e. *In Central Asia*

    Answer: a

13. Which of the following works is a four-movement symphonic suite by Rimsky-Korsakov based on stories from *101 Arabian Nights*?
    a. *Capriccio espagnol*
    b. *Russian Easter Overture*
    c. *Pictures at an Exhibition*
    d. *Sheherazade*
    e. *In Central Asia*

    Answer: d

14. Which of the following works is *not* a nationalist composition from Bohemia?
    a. *Má vlast*
    b. *Peer Gynt*
    c. *Dumky* Piano Trio
    d. *Slavonic Dances*
    e. *From My Life*

    Answer: b

15. Immigrants from which country dominated American classic music in the late nineteenth century?
    a. England
    b. Russia
    c. Italy
    d. France
    e. Germany

    Answer: e

16. Of the following, who is *not* a noted nineteenth-century American composer?
    a. George Whitefield Chadwick
    b. Horatio Parker
    c. Theodore Thomas
    d. Amy Beach
    e. John Knowles Paine

    Answer: c

17. The *Gaelic* Symphony was composed by ____________.
    a. Beach
    b. Dvořák
    c. Elgar
    d. MacDowell
    e. Gilmore

    Answer: a

18. Tin Pan Alley is a nickname for ____________.
    a. a traveling percussion ensemble
    b. a group of composers who collected American melodies
    c. a small area in New York that specialized in music publishing
    d. the first recording studio in Boston
    e. the first song to sell one million copies

    Answer: c

19. Of the following, which is not a characteristic of African-American music in the nineteenth century?
    a. syncopation
    b. call and response
    c. bending pitches
    d. piano accompaniment
    e. banjo accompaniment

    Answer: d

20. What type of music did the Fisk Jubilee Singers specialize in performing?
    a. verse–refrain songs
    b. opera excerpts
    c. minstrel songs
    d. sacred motets
    e. spirituals

    Answer: e

## SHORT-ESSAY QUESTIONS

1. Describe the two principal schools of composition in France during the second half of the nineteenth century, prior to impressionism, and cite composers and works associated with each.
2. Compare the musical styles of nationalist and internationalist composers active in two of the following regions: Russia, Bohemia, Scandinavia, England, or the United States.
3. Describe the growth of popular music in the United States in the second half of the nineteenth century. Include a discussion of band music and popular songs.
4. Describe the contributions of Africans to the American music scene of the nineteenth century.

## TERMS FOR IDENTIFICATION

Theodore Thomas
Patrick S. Gilmore
John Philip Sousa
march
verse and refrain
chorus
hook
Tin Pan Alley
call and response
spiritual
Fisk Jubilee Singers

# CHAPTER 30 The Early Twentieth Century

I. Changing Traditions
  A. New currents
    1. American ragtime and jazz won international recognition.
    2. Composers in the classical tradition attempted to balance the past with novel ideas.
    3. Although many continued to use tonality, other wrote post-tonal music.
    4. Some composers took up the banner of the avant-garde.
  B. Modern times, 1898–1918
    1. This era was self-consciously "modern."
    2. Technological developments include:
      a. Electric lighting
      b. Affordable automobiles
      c. Airplanes
      d. Player pianos and phonographs (see **HWM Innovations,** pages 760–61, and **Figures 30.1** and **30.2**)
      e. Motion pictures, with live musical accompaniment
    3. Economies expanded greatly.
      a. People continued to migrate to cities, and nostalgia for nature increased.
      b. Workers organized labor unions to fight for better conditions.
      c. The great powers competed for dominance.
      d. Increasing tensions led to World War I, in which technological advances contributed to the high number of casualties.
    4. The United States
      a. The country emerged as a global power after World War I.
      b. The Progressive movement created reforms to reduce the dominance of large corporations.
      c. Immigrants continued to stream to the country.
      d. African Americans from the south moved to northern cities, where they settled into segregated neighborhoods.
    5. Freud and Pavlov challenged Romantic views of individual self-determination.
    6. Artists did not necessarily seek popular appeal; many searched for new and unusual content or techniques.
      a. Symbolist poets used intense imagery.
      b. Impressionist painters captured impressions of a subject (see **HWM Figure 30.3**).
      c. Cubist artists depicted subjects with geometrical shapes (see **HWM Figure 30.4** and **30.5**).

II. Vernacular Musical Traditions
  A. Popular song
    1. Popular songs were performed in a variety of venues in many regions.
    2. Tin Pan Alley was in its heyday.
  B. Stage music
    1. Revues with popular songs spread from Paris to London to New York.
    2. Operetta was given new life with popular successes.
      a. *The Merry Widow* (1905) by Franz Léhar (1870–1948) in Vienna
      b. *Babes in Toyland* (1903) and *Naughty Marietta* (1910) by Victor Herbert (1859–1924) in the United States

3. Musical comedies, or musicals, featured popular songs and dances in the context of spoken plays with comic or romantic plots.
   a. George Edwardes established the genre in London during the 1890s.
   b. George M. Cohan inaugurated a distinctive American musical with *Little Johnny Jones* (1904), which featured two famous songs: *Give My Regards to Broadway* and *The Yankee Doodle Boy*.

C. Silent films
1. Moving pictures emerged in the 1890s.
2. The first public display was Emile Reynaud's *Pantomimes lumineuses* (Luminous Mime Shows, 1892) in Paris with music by Gaston Paulin.
3. Films were silent until the 1920s.
4. Silent films were usually accompanied by live music.
5. Role of music
   a. Cover noise of projector
   b. Provide continuity to the succession of scenes and shots
   c. Evoke appropriate moods
   d. Mark dramatic events
6. Musical accompaniment
   a. Music was often performed by a pianist or organist, who might improvise.
   b. Larger theaters had music created by the music director for an ensemble.
   c. Musical techniques and excerpts were borrowed from the Classic repertory.
7. Beginning in 1909, studios issued cue sheets to show the sequence of scenes and events in a movie.
8. Music anthologies, such as Giuseppe Becce's *Kinothek* (Berlin, 1919), were published to help the theater music director.
9. Original scores were created for films.
   a. Saint-Saëns inaugurated the tradition with *L'assassinat du duc de Guise* (1908).
   b. Joseph Carl Breil (1870–1926) created an orchestral score for D. W. Griffith's *The Birth of a Nation,* a film with a racist message.
   c. Breil mixed excerpts from classics with new music.

D. Band music
1. The tradition of bands remained strong and extended to colleges and schools.
2. Among the professional bands to emerge was Helen May Butler's Ladies Brass Band, one of several all-female ensembles.
3. Repertory
   a. Few pieces for band were composed in the Classic and Romantic eras.
   b. New serious works were written for band, largely by English composers.
4. African-American musicians were trained in brass bands, and black bands played important social roles through the turn of the century.

E. Ragtime
1. Ragtime, featuring syncopated (or "ragged") rhythms against a regular bass, was a popular style from the 1890s through the 1910s.
2. This syncopation was apparently derived from the clapping *Juba* of American blacks, a survival of African drumming and hand clapping.
3. Ragtime encompassed piano music, ensemble music, and songs.
4. Cakewalks helped introduce syncopation.
   a. A cakewalk was a couples dance derived from slave dances.
   b. It is marked by strutting and acrobatic movements.
   c. The music was published without syncopations until 1897.
5. Will Marion Cook (1869–1944), an African-American composer, introduced the new rhythmic style to Broadway.
6. Many new songs were written with ragtime rhythms.

F. Scott Joplin (1867–1917) was the leading ragtime composer (see **HWM Figure 30.6**).
1. The son of a former slave, he moved to New York in 1907.
2. He completed an opera, *Treemonisha,* in 1910, but it was not staged until 1972.
3. He is best known for his piano rags, which he intended to be classical works, equivalent to Chopin's mazurkas and waltzes.

G. *Maple Leaf Rag* (1899; see **NAWM 136a** and **HWM Example 30.1**)
1. Background
   a. The rag was named after the Maple Leaf Club in Sedalia, Missouri, where he performed regularly.
   b. The work eventually sold over one million copies.
2. The rag is set in 2/4 and follows the form of a march.
   a. Typically a rag has two sixteen-measure strains, each repeated (AABB).
   b. A trio with two more strains follows, usually in a key a fourth higher (CCDD).

3. Unusual features of *Maple Leaf Rag*
   a. No introduction
   b. The first strain returns before the trio, creating this form: AABBACCDD
   c. The original key returns in the last strain; hence the C strain is in the subdominant D-flat major, while the rest is in A-flat major.
4. The left hand keeps a steady pulse while syncopations appear in melodies of the right hand.
5. The harmony is colorful, with chromatic passing tones, lowered sixth chords, and changes of mode.
6. The repetition of short rhythmic ideas can be traced to African traditions.
7. The recordings feature two early performances: a player piano roll created by Joplin and a jazz version by Jelly Roll Morton.

H. Early jazz
1. Jazz, another type of African-American music, began to develop in the 1910s.
2. Jazz appears to have begun as a mixture of ragtime, dance music, and blues.
3. New Orleans has traditionally been viewed as the "cradle of jazz," although recent research has uncovered early jazz in other regions as well.
   a. The French and Spanish background in the city gave the music a distinctive character.
   b. It was the only southern city in which slaves were allowed to gather in public; hence African traditions were maintained more strongly.
   c. The city had close connections to Caribbean rhythms, including Haitian, Cuban, and Creole.
   d. The style was first known as the New Orleans style of ragtime, but when it was transplanted to other urban centers, it was called jazz.
4. Jazz performers improvised on a given work, allowing each performer to develop a distinctive character.
5. Jelly Roll Morton performed Joplin's *Maple Leaf Rag* in a jazz style (**NAWM 136b**).

III. Modern Music in the Classical Tradition

A. The classic canon
1. At the end of the eighteenth century, audiences demanded new music.
2. At the end of the nineteenth century, audiences demanded old music that had become enshrined as classics.
3. Concert halls became museums for musical artworks created over the last two centuries.
4. Living composers found themselves competing with music of the past.
   a. Composers sought to continue tradition while offering something new.
   b. Decisions about what to preserve and what to change varied greatly.
   c. Individuality took precedence over conventionality.
   d. Some composers abandoned tonality; others redefined it.
   e. Many turned to national styles.

B. Gustav Mahler (1860–1911)
1. Mahler was the leading Austro-German composer of symphonies after Brahms and Bruckner and one of the great masters for voice and orchestra.
2. He was famous as a dynamic and precise conductor (see **HWM Figure 30.7**).
   a. He conducted at numerous opera houses, including the Vienna Opera from 1897 to 1907.
   b. He also conducted the Metropolitan opera in New York (1907–10) and the New York Philharmonic (1909–11).
3. Major works
   a. Nine symphonies, and a tenth that was unfinished
   b. Five orchestral song cycles

C. Mahler symphonies
1. Songs played a large role in his symphonies.
   a. Themes from his *Lieder eines fahrenden Gesellen* (Songs of a Wayfarer) appear in his Symphony No. 1.
   b. Voices are in four of his symphonies.
   c. Symphonies Nos. 2, 3, and 4 use themes from Mahler's songs based on texts from *Des Knaben Wunderhorn* (The Boy's Magic Horn).
2. For Mahler, writing a symphony was to "construct a world," which can be seen in the enormous variety of musical styles that he employed.
3. Orchestration
   a. Huge forces, extending up to Symphony No. 8, the "Symphony of a Thousand"
   b. Great imagination in the combination of instruments, often only a few playing at a time
4. A number of his symphonies have programmatic implications.
5. Symphony No. 4
   a. The symphony begins in G major and ends in E major, and each movement differs from the others.

b. The first movement recalls the eighteenth-century style of Haydn, particularly in the treatment of themes (see **HWM Example 30.2**).
c. Later themes and developments in the first movement create the sense that the Enlightenment was displaced by irrational dreams analyzed by Freud.
d. The movement suggests the contradictions in modern life, similar to what is seen in Gustav Klimt's painting, *Music* (see **HWM Figure 30.8**).

D. Mahler song cycles with orchestra
1. *Kindertotenlieder* (Songs on the Death of Children, 1901–4) is based on five poems by Friedrich Rückert.
2. *Das Lied von der Erde* (The Song of the Earth, 1908)
a. Mahler created this work for tenor and alto soloists with orchestra.
b. The poems are translated from Chinese.
c. The texts alternate between frenzied grasping at the dreamlike whirl of life and sad resignation at having to part with all its joys and beauties.
d. The mood alternates between ecstatic pleasure and deadly foreboding.

E. *Nun will die Sonn' so hell aufgehen* from *Kindertotenlieder* (**NAWM 137**)
1. The text contrasts the death of a child at night with the uncaring rise of the sun in the morning.
2. The sparse use of instruments creates the transparency of chamber music.
3. The poem has four couplets, which Mahler sets in an AABA song form.
4. First couplet
a. The initial duet of horn and oboe is stark and empty.
b. The opening line "Now will the sun so brightly rise" is set to a mournful melody that emphasizes descending half-steps.
c. The next line turns to a radiant D major with a rising chromatic line, creating a contrast between the moods of the text and music.
d. An orchestral interlude leads back to minor for the second couplet.
5. Second couplet
a. The music is a variant of the opening section.
b. The text matches the musical moods more closely.
6. Third couplet
a. This is the only couplet not to mention misfortune or the sun.
b. New music develops from earlier motives.
c. The music reaches a height of dissonance, chromaticism, and intensity.
7. Fourth couplet
a. The music of the first couplet returns.
b. The final line is repeated, and the song closes in a poignant D minor.

F. Strauss operas
1. Strauss tuned to opera after establishing himself with symphonic poems.
a. *Guntram* (1893) was an early failure.
b. *Feuersnot* (The Fire Famine, 1901) was a moderate success.
2. *Salome* (1905)
a. Strauss adapted the libretto from a one-act play by Oscar Wilde (see **HWM Figure 30.9**).
b. In this decadent version of the biblical story, Salome performs the Dance of the Seven Veils and entices Herod to sever the head of John the Baptist.
c. Strauss created harmonically complex and dissonant music that greatly influenced later composers (see **HWM Example 30.3**).
d. For its effect, Strauss depended upon the audience hearing the dissonance in relation to an eventual resolution.
3. *Elektra* (1906–8)
a. This is the first of seven operas to librettos by Viennese playwright Hugo von Hofmannsthal.
b. *Elektra* is adapted from a play by Sophocles and dwells on insane hatred and revenge.
c. The dissonance is at times even more extreme than in *Salome*.
4. *Der Rosenkavalier* (The Cavalier of the Rose, 1909–10)
a. The opera depicts a sunny world of elegance, eroticism, and nostalgia.
b. This sentimental comedy features Viennese waltzes.

IV. Claude Debussy (1862–1918) (see **HWM biography,** page 781, and **Figure 30.10**)
A. Biography
1. Debussy was born in a suburb of France to a middle-class family.
2. He began studies at the Paris Conservatoire at the age of ten.

3. He traveled to Russia and worked for Nadezhda von Meck.
4. Winning the Prix de Rome, he spent two years in Italy.
5. He returned to Paris and befriended symbolist poets and painters.
6. He worked as a music critic.

B. Musical influences
1. Debussy admired Wagner's works, but was repulsed by his bombast.
2. He preferred the French tradition of restraint, such as in the works of Emmanuel Chabrier (1841–1894).
3. He found inspiration in Russian composers, medieval music, and music from Asia.

C. Impressionism and symbolism
1. Although his music is generally referred to as impressionistic, it is closer in spirit to the French poetic movement symbolism.
2. With both movements there is a sense of detached observation.
3. As in symbolism, our attention is drawn to individual images that carry the work's structure and meaning.
4. He creates musical images through motives, exotic scales (whole-tone, octatonic, pentatonic), and timbre.
5. Many of the ideas are not developed or resolved, but simply juxtaposed.

D. Piano music
1. These characteristics are exemplified in a passage from a piano work entitled *L'isle joyeuse* (The Joyous Isle, 1903–4) (see **HWM Example 30.4**).
2. In Debussy's music, the urgency to resolve harmony is absent.
3. Pleasure is derived from the moment, not the drive toward resolution.
4. Many of Debussy's piano pieces have evocative titles.
5. The twenty-four Preludes (two books, 1909–10 and 1911–13) are character pieces with picturesque titles.

E. Orchestral music
1. The orchestral works are similar to those for piano but with the added element of instrumental color.
   a. Motives are often associated with a particular instrument.
   b. The works require a large orchestra, but seldom use the full sound of the ensemble.
2. *Prèlude à "L'après-midi d'un faune"* (Prelude to "The Afternoon of a Faun," 1891–94)
   a. A symbolist poem by Mallarmé is the inspiration for this work.
   b. It evokes moods through suggestion rather than expression.
3. *Nocturnes* (1897–99) contains three movements that suggest night scenes.
   a. *Nuages* (Clouds)
   b. *Fetes* (Festivals)
   c. *Sirèns* (the Sirens of Greek mythology), which uses a wordless female chorus
4. *La Mer* (The Sea, 1903–5) captures the movement of the sea.

F. *Nuages* from *Nocturnes* (**NAWM 138**)
1. The juxtaposition of images replaces traditional development.
2. This work is set in a modified ABA' form.
3. The A section (measures 1–63) is the longest.
   a. The lack of harmonic direction at the beginning suggests slowly moving clouds.
   b. Each appearance of the opening material is different.
   c. A recurring English horn motive is never developed.
   d. The horns usually answer the motive with a tritone (see measure 23).
   e. A chordal idea (measures 15–20) and a unison melody (measures 33–42) provide contrast.
4. The B section (measures 64–79) is more exotic.
   a. Debussy had heard a gamelan orchestra in Paris in 1889.
   b. He simulated the gamelan texture with a simple pentatonic tune (flute and harp) and a static accompaniment.
5. The return of the opening material in the A' section (measures 80–102) is fragmented, as if the clouds are scattering.
6. Harmony
   a. Octatonic and whole-tone scales contribute to the vague imagery.
   b. Chords are not used to shape phrases with tension and release.
   c. Chords are conceived as sonorous units within a phrase.
   d. Oscillating chords, parallel triads, ninth chords, and sustained chords serve to characterize musical images.
   e. Debussy still maintains a sense of tonality; the A sections are in B minor, and the B section centers on the D-sharp Dorian scale.

7. Orchestration
    a. The English horn is identified with a single motive.
    b. The horns are used only for brief gestures.
    c. The combination of unison flute and harp creates a bell-like sonority.
    d. Strings are muted and divided.
    e. Delicate timpani rolls are barely audible near the beginning.

G. Songs and stage music
1. Debussy set texts by a number of major French poets.
2. He wrote music for several plays.
3. He completed only one opera, *Pelléas et Mélisande* (1893–1902).
    a. The opera is a musical response to Wagner's *Tristan und Isolde*.
    b. This work is based on a symbolist play by Maurice Maeterlinck.
    c. The allusions of the text are matched by strange, often modal harmonies, subdued colors, and restraint.
    d. Instrumental interludes carry the mysterious inner drama.

H. Influence
1. A seminal composer, Debussy provided a model for later composers in his use of harmony and the orchestra.
2. He influenced many distinguished composers, including American jazz and popular musicians.

V. The First Modern Generation

A. Maurice Ravel (1875–1937)
1. Ravel's distinctive style is characterized by:
    a. Consummate craftsmanship
    b. Traditional forms
    c. Diatonic melodies
    d. Complex harmonies within an essentially tonal language
2. *Jeux d'eau* (Fountains, 1901) (see **HWM Example 30.5**)
    a. Liszt's pianistic techniques and Debussy's color are combined.
    b. Whole-tone and diatonic music are juxtaposed.
    c. Whole-tone sonorities function as dissonances that need to resolve.
    d. Ravel also employed major-seventh chords.
3. Although he is often considered to be an impressionist, Ravel was subject to a variety of influences.
4. Several works can be viewed as impressionistic in their imagery, orchestration, and harmonies.
    a. *Miroirs* (Mirrors, 1904–5), descriptive piano pieces
    b. *Rapsodie espagnole* (Spanish Rhapsody, 1907–8), an orchestral suite
    c. *Daphnis et Chloé* (1909–12), a ballet
5. Some piano works (which were later orchestrated) evoke the stylized dances of the French Baroque.
    a. *Pavane pour une infante défunte* (Pavane for a Dead Princess, 1899)
    b. *Le tombeau de Couperin* (Memorial for Couperin, 1914–17)
6. His songs draw on French art and popular traditions.
7. He incorporates Classic forms in numerous works.
    a. String Quartet in F (1902–3)
    b. Piano Trio (1914)
8. Ravel also incorporates popular traditions from outside of France.
    a. *La valse* (1919–20) is an orchestral poem using Viennese waltz rhythms.
    b. *Tzigane* for violin and piano (1924) evokes a gypsy style.
    c. The Violin Sonata uses blues.
    d. Piano Concerto for the Left Hand (1929–30) incorporates jazz elements.
    e. *Bolero* (1928) features Spanish idioms.

B. Manuel de Falla (1876–1946)
1. Like other Spanish composers, de Falla composed in a national style.
    a. Wanting to go beyond mere exotic sounds, he studied folk music.
    b. The ballet *El amor brujo* (Love, the Sorcerer, 1915) and other early works are imbued with melodic and rhythmic qualities of Spanish popular music.
2. His finest mature works combine national elements with neoclassic elements.
    a. *El retablo de maese Pedro* (Master Pedro's Puppet Show, 1919–23) is based on an episode from *Don Quixote.*
    b. Concerto for Harpsichord with five solo instruments (1923–26) harkens back to the Spanish Baroque.

C. Gustav Holst (1875–1937) (see **HWM Figure 30.11**)
1. The English musical renaissance begun by Elgar took a nationalist turn in the early twentieth century.
    a. Cecil Sharp and Ralph Vaughan Williams collected and published folk songs.
    b. Both used folk songs in their compositions.

2. Holst's *Somerset Rhapsody* uses folk melodies.
3. *Choral Hymns from the Rig Veda* (1908–12) uses Hindu sacred texts.
4. The orchestral suite *The Planets* (1914–16), his best-known work, is non-nationalist.

D. Ralph Vaughan Williams (1872–1958)
1. Biography
   a. He studied with Ravel.
   b. His influences included Debussy, Bach, and Handel.
2. He composed art music and practical music, using elements from each tradition in the other.
   a. Vaughan Williams used folk melodies and English hymnody.
   b. He edited the new English hymnal in 1904–6.
3. *Fantasia on a Theme of Thomas Tallis* (1910)
   a. Composed for a double string orchestra and string quartet, this works is based on a Tallis hymn in the Phrygian mode.
   b. Fragments of the theme are developed in a free fantasy that uses antiphonal sonorities and triads in parallel motion.

E. Leos Janácek (1854–1928)
1. Janácek was the leading Czech nationalist composer of the twentieth century.
2. He worked within the genres of Western art music, but developed a national style based on his study of folk music from Moravia.
3. His music juxtaposes contrasting sonorities and is closer in procedure to the music of Musorgsky or Debussy than to the German tradition.
4. His operas dominated the Czech stage beginning with *Jenufa* (1904), which is based on a Moravian subject.
5. The juxtaposition of contrasting materials heard in his operas is also found in his instrumental works, such as the flashy orchestral *Sinfonietta* (1926).

F. Jean Sibelius (1865–1957)
1. Finland was part of the Russian Empire from 1809 to 1917 and was culturally dominated by Sweden.
2. Sibelius, a Finnish patriot, sought to create a national musical style.
   a. He wrote songs and derived symphonic poems from the Finnish national epic, the *Kalevala*.
   b. He established himself as the leading nationalist composer with a series of symphonic poems, including *The Swan of Tuonola* (1895) and *Finlandia* (1900).
3. Sibelius gained an international reputation, largely based on his Violin Concerto and seven symphonies.
4. His personal style is characterized by:
   a. Modal melodies
   b. Uncomplicated rhythms
   c. Insistent repetition of brief motives, ostinatos, and pedal points
   d. Strong contrasts of timbres and textures
5. Sibelius employs a "rotational form."
   a. He repeatedly cycles through a series of thematic elements that are varied each time.
   b. The rotational form can be seen in the third movement of his Symphony No. 4 (see **HWM Example 30.6**).
6. His reliance on tonality helped build his popularity in Britain and the United States, but it hurt his reputation elsewhere.
7. He had stopped composing by the late 1920s.

G. Sergei Rachmaninov (1873–1943) (see **HWM Figure 30.12**)
1. Rachmaninov and his classmate Scriabin (see below) at the Moscow Conservatory showed no interest in folk music; each developed an individual style.
2. Rachmaninov made his living primarily as a pianist, and his most characteristic works are for piano, including:
   a. Twenty-four preludes in every major and minor key
   b. Two sets of *Etudes-Tableaux*
   c. Four piano concertos
   d. *Rhapsody on a Theme of Paganini* for piano and orchestra (1934)
3. His orchestral works include:
   a. Three symphonies
   b. *The Isle of the Dead* (1907), a symphonic poem
4. Musical style
   a. Rachmaninov is renowned for his passionate, melodious idiom.
   b. He reworked a variety of elements from the Romantic tradition.

H. Prelude in G Minor, Op. 23, No. 5 (1901) (see **NAWM 139** and **HWM Example 30.7**)
1. The work has an ABA Coda form.
2. The A section (measures 1–34) is in aaba song form.
   a. The principal theme is marchlike and builds to a powerful climax.

b. The theme is simple in conception, but the rhythm and figuration make it unique and memorable.
c. Each repetition of this theme is varied.
3. The B section (measures 35–53)
a. The theme is lyrical and passionate with rolling arpeggiations in the accompaniment.
b. The theme has several subtle connections to the first section.
c. A countermelody is added for the repetition of the theme.
4. The work uses traditional harmonies.
a. The music never leaves the key of G minor.
b. Rachmaninov introduces motion through the circle of fifths in the A section to suggest modulation.
c. The B section focuses on the dominant seventh chord.
5. Rachmaninov's rhythms, registration, and development create a unique character that earned his music a place in the permanent repertoire.

I. Alexander Scriabin (1872–1915) (see **HWM Figure 30.13**)
1. Scriabin began by composing piano works in the style of Chopin, but he gradually absorbed other elements:
a. The chromaticism of Liszt and Wagner
b. The octatonic scale and exoticism of Rimsky-Korsakov
c. The juxtapositions of texture, scale, and figuration from Debussy
2. Scriabin developed a complex harmonic vocabulary of his own.
3. In addition to piano music, he composed symphonies and the notable orchestral work *Poem of Ecstasy* (1908).
4. Scriabin's last five piano sonatas (1912–13) dispense with key signatures and tonality; each develops from a complex chord that functions as a kind of tonic.

J. *Vers la flame* (Toward the Flame), Op. 72 (1914) (see **NAWM 140** and **HWM Example 30.8**)
1. This one-movement work is a tone poem for piano.
a. The title suggests a journey toward enlightenment.
b. The activity and dynamics gradually increase until reaching a transcendent climax at the end.
2. Two main ideas define the form.
a. Theme A (measures 1–6) involves two voices moving in counterpoint.
b. Theme B (measures 27–34) is a single melody.
3. The works has four large sections that place the two thematic elements in new contexts (see diagram in **NAWM 140** commentary).
4. The B theme appears in a different transposition each time, but A returns to the original pitch level in sections 3 and 4, creating a sense of stability.
5. The harmony centers on a referential sonority of two tritones, which are derived from the octatonic scale: E–A-sharp–G-sharp–D.
a. These tritones, heard at the beginning, serve as a kind of tonic chord.
b. Variations appear throughout.
c. At the end, D is raised to D-sharp (measure 125), which resolves the remaining tensions.
6. Harmonic relationships by thirds are common in the work.
7. Most chords have four or more notes; the final sonority has six.
8. The dissonances do not require resolution.
9. Scriabin uses the harmonic color to create static blocks of sound.

K. Tonal and post-tonal music
1. The composers in this survey varied in their treatment of tonality, ranging from Scriabin to Rachmaninov.
2. Many composers continued to work with tonality, some bringing out new flavors and possibilities.
3. Other composers created new approaches that either redefined tonality or abandoned the idea.
4. The term *post-tonal* can be applied to all the new ways composers found to organize pitch, from atonality to neotonality.

VI. The Avant-Garde
A. *Avant-garde* is a term that is best reserved for art that seeks to overthrow accepted aesthetics and start fresh.
1. The movement began in the years before World War I.
2. The music is not marked by a shared style, but by a shared attitude—an unrelenting opposition to the status quo.
B. Erik Satie (1866–1925)
1. The music of French composer Erik Satie wittily upends conventions.
2. In the three *Gymnopédies* (1888) for piano, he challenges Romantic notions of expressivity and individuality with music that is plain and unemotional.

3. Satie composed several sets of piano pieces between 1900 and 1915.
   a. He used surrealistic titles such as *Three Pieces in the Form of a Pear* (1903), which actually has seven pieces.
   b. He added directions to the performer that satirized Debussy.
4. Satie did not attempt to write masterworks.
   a. He challenged the basis of Classical tradition.
   b. His larger works sought to fix our attention on the present.
5. His "realistic ballet" *Parade* (1916–17) was a collaborative production with writer Jean Cocteau, choreographer Léonide Massine, and Picasso (see **HWM Figure 30.14**).
   a. Satie incorporated jazz elements, a whistle, a siren, and a typewriter.
   b. The work caused a scandal, as did some of his other large works.
6. Satie's works question the listener's expectations; no two pieces are alike.
7. Satie influenced the younger French generation and a number of American composers.

C. Futurism
1. Italian futurists even rejected traditional musical instruments.
2. Luigi Russolo (1885–1947)
   a. He argued that musical sounds had become stale (see **HWM Source Reading,** page 798).
   b. He divided noises into six families, and he helped build new instruments called *intuonarumori* (noisemakers).
3. The movement anticipated other later developments, including electronic music.

## SUGGESTIONS FOR SUPPLEMENTARY READING/LISTENING/ACTIVITIES

Have a student or a group of students create a PowerPoint presentation on major art movements of the late nineteenth and early twentieth centuries that includes impressionism, postimpressionism, cubism, futurism, and dadism. You may also want to preview expressionism at this point.

Introduce the students to the music of George M. Cohan by listening to some of his songs or to the musical *George M!* (Sony 3200, 1990). James Cagney won an Oscar for his portrayal of Cohan in *Yankee Doodle Dandy* (1942).

Discuss aspects of traditional African music with students. Recordings of African music are readily available on compact discs. Listen to an assortment of music by African-American composers, including Scott Joplin and later jazz performers, and have students describe elements that might be linked to African music.

Film versions of operetta are available (with some liberties), such as *The Merry Widow* (1934) and *Naughty Marietta* (1935). Have some music theater students watch these operettas and compare their style with that of musical comedies.

Saint-Saëns published his music for *L'assassinat du duc de Guise,* the first major film score, as Opus 128. A recording can be heard on Harmonia Mundi 1951472, 2000.

*The Birth of a Nation* with the original music by Joseph Carl Breil is available on DVD (Kino International, 2002). Have a student report on Breil's use of borrowed and new music. Include in the report how music supports the drama and, unfortunately, contributes to racial stereotyping.

If you are in an area that has a history of a municipal band or perhaps even a major college band, have some students research their choice of concert literature dating back as far as possible. This will introduce those students to the techniques of primary research.

Have some students find background material on Scott Joplin's *Treemonisha.* A recording conducted by Gunther Shuller is available on compact disc (Deutsche Grammophon 435709, 1992).

Bring the scores of Mahler's symphonies to class and have students read aloud the orchestration specified for each. Teach students the shorthand used by music publishers to indicate orchestration (e.g., the "Beethoven" orchestra is 2-2-2-2 4-2-3-0 tymp str) and have them notate the orchestral requirements for several *NAWM* examples and for Mahler's symphonies.

Have students listen to Mahler's First Symphony and discuss whether Mahler seems to have been influenced by Beethoven. In particular, have them suggest possible relationships with Beethoven's Symphonies Nos. 5, 6, and 9.

A particularly beautiful example of Mahler's orchestral writing is the Adagietto of the Fifth Symphony, dedicated to his wife, Alma. A holograph of the score, edited by Gilbert E. Kaplan, was published in 1992. Have a student research the background of this movement and have the class discuss the programmatic qualities of this "love letter." This could lead to an expanded discussion of Alma's role in his life, her subsequent marriage to Walter Gropius, and Berg's Violin Concerto.

Mahler's Sixth Symphony demonstrates his masterful use of the orchestra. Its tone sometimes verges on expressionism, and at other times is impressionistic. Have students listen to the first movement to prepare for twentieth-century aesthetic movements. The influence of Wagner is evident in the sweeping melodic lines of the second "theme" of the first movement and in the contrapuntal intermingling of motives.

For a brief explication of Mahler's internal programs in terms of nineteenth-century aesthetics, especially Schopenhauer's theories, see Carl Dahlhaus, *The Idea of Absolute Music,* trans. by Roger Lustig (Chicago: University of Chicago Press, 1989), 138–40.

Mahler's Lieder have been recorded several times. See, for example, "Kindertotenlieder, Five Rückert Lieder, Lieder eines fahrenden Gesellen" (Angel Records 66996, 1999). Have students select one Lied each and report on its text-setting, orchestration, and compositional techniques.

The operas of Richard Strauss are generally available on DVD. Recommended recordings include: *Salome* (Universal Music & VI, 2003), *Elektra* (Image Entertainment, 2001), and *Der Rosenkavalier* (Kultur, 2004).

Have students compare Mallarmé's poem *The Afternoon of a Faun* with Debussy's music. An excellent source is *Prelude to "The Afternoon of a Faun:" An Authoritative Score, Mallarmé's Poem, Backgrounds and Sources, Criticism and Analysis,* ed. William W. Austin (New York: W. W. Norton, 1970), which will give students a good impression of the nature of symbolism.

For an excellent DVD of Debussy's *Pelleas et Melisande,* see the 2002 Universal Music & VI production.

Have some piano students pick out one Debussy prelude each and describe how the work relates to the descriptive title.

Compare the two versions of any of Ravel's piano works that he orchestrated. Some possible choices are *Menuet antique, Pavane pour une infante défunte, Le tombeau de Couperin,* and *Ma mere l'oye.*

For more on music in England, see Ralph Vaughan Williams, "Should Music be National?" in Bryan Simms, ed., *Composers on Modern Musical Culture* (New York: Schirmer Books, 1999), 108–16.

Janácek's *Cunning Little Vixen* is available on DVD (Image Entertainment, 1999).

For more on Sibelius's use of the Kalevala, see William A. Wilson, "Sibelius, the Kalevala, and Karelianism," in *The Sibelius Companion,* ed. Glenda Dawn Goss (Westport, Conn.: Greenwood Press, 1996), 43–60.

Have students discuss ways to establish tonality without using either traditional functional progressions or total dissonance. Ask them to find examples of various techniques in the musical examples for this chapter.

## OBJECTIVE QUESTIONS

1. George M. Cohan inaugurated a distinctive type of American music with ____________.
   a. *Babes in Toyland*
   b. *The Merry Widow*
   c. *Naughty Marietta*
   d. *Little Johnny Jones*
   e. *Cats*

   Answer: d

2. Which composer inaugurated the era of the film score?
   a. Saint-Saëns
   b. Satie
   c. Breil
   d. Becce
   e. Williams

   Answer: a

3. Which composer introduced ragtime rhythms to Broadway and brought the cakewalk and ragtime to Europe?
   a. Scott Joplin
   b. George M. Cohan
   c. Jelly Roll Morton
   d. Ford Dabney
   e. Will Marion Cook

   Answer: e

4. What city is considered to be the cradle of jazz?
   a. Chicago
   b. New York
   c. Memphis
   d. New Orleans
   e. Kansas City

   Answer: d

5. Early jazz seems to have begun as a mixture of what musical types?
   a. ragtime, impressionism, and blues
   b. ragtime, dance music, and blues
   c. cakewalk, Creole music, and impressionism
   d. ragtime, Creole music, and Haitian rhythms
   e. cakewalk, blues, and Haitian rhythms

   Answer: b

6. Which of the following statements characterizes Mahler's orchestration?
   a. He left details of orchestration to the conductor's discretion.
   b. His symphonies require large orchestras, but there are many passages of light orchestration.
   c. He used a very small orchestra made up of unusual instruments.
   d. He used solo voices and large choruses in all of his symphonies.
   e. He maintained the orchestra size of Beethoven but expanded the percussion.

   Answer: b

7. Mahler's *Kindertotenlieder* and *Das Lied von der Erde* are ____________.
   a. Lieder for voice and piano
   b. symphonic poems
   c. Lieder for voice and orchestra
   d. program symphonies from his early years
   e. piano works in the style of Mendelssohn's *Songs without Words*

   Answer: c

8. Which opera relates a decadent biblical story based on a play by Oscar Wilde?
   a. *Der Rosekavalier*
   b. *Elektra*
   c. *Feuersnot*
   d. *Salome*
   e. *The Robe*

   Answer: d

9. Of the following, which was *not* a source of inspiration for Debussy?
   a. symbolist poets
   b. Wagner's *Tristan und Isolde*
   c. music from Asia
   d. medieval music
   e. English folk music

   Answer: e

10. In what way does Debussy's harmonic style differ from that of Wagner?
    a. The urgency to resolve is absent.
    b. Debussy avoids chromaticism.
    c. Debussy's use of dissonance is continuous.
    d. Debussy avoids tonal centers.
    e. Debussy rejects the use of whole-tone scales.

    Answer: a

11. The poem *L'après-midi d'un faune* was written by ____________.
    a. Verlaine
    b. Debussy
    c. Mallarmé
    d. Valéry
    e. George

    Answer: c

Use the following answers for questions 12–16.
   a. *El amor brujo*
   b. *The Planets*
   c. *Le tombeau de Couperin*
   d. *Finlandia*
   e. *Fantasia on a Theme by Thomas Tallis*

12. Ralph Vaughan Williams composed this work.

    Answer: e

13. Maurice Ravel composed this work.

    Answer: c

14. Gustav Holst composed this work.

    Answer: b

15. Manuel de Falla composed this work.

    Answer: a

16. Sibelius composed this work.

    Answer: d

17. How did Rachmaninov primarily make his living?
    a. as a conductor
    b. as a composer
    c. as a teacher
    d. as a pianist
    e. as a critic

    Answer: d

18. Scriabin modeled his first piano pieces on the music of ___________.
    a. Chopin
    b. Paganini
    c. Beethoven
    d. Mendelssohn
    e. Schubert

    Answer: a

19. What characterizes the music of Erik Satie?
    a. strong emotional content
    b. traditional structures and harmonies
    c. wit and defiance of conventional ideas
    d. meeting the listener's expectations
    e. contrasting musical ideas

    Answer: c

20. Which country fostered futurism?
    a. France
    b. Italy
    c. United States
    d. Germany
    e. Spain

    Answer: b

## SHORT-ESSAY QUESTIONS

1. Describe the types of music used for theater events (including moving pictures) in the United States in the early twentieth century.
2. Discuss the ways in which Debussy incorporated ideas from impressionism and symbolism into his music.
3. Using the music of Rachmaninov and Scriabin as extreme examples, describe how composers in the early twentieth century treated the classical traditions.
4. Discuss the main features of the avant-garde movement of the early twentieth century as exemplified in the works of Satie and the futurists.

## TERMS FOR IDENTIFICATION

symbolism
impressionism
cubism
musical
cue sheet
*Kinothek*
Helen May Butler's Ladies Brass Band
ragtime
cakewalk
jazz
Jelly Roll Morton
Hugo von Hofmannsthal
Mallarmé
post-tonal
avant-garde
futurism
intuonarumori

# CHAPTER 31 Modernism and the Classical Tradition

I. Challenge of Modernism
   A. Composers in the early twentieth century faced the challenge of creating works worthy of performance alongside the classics of the past.
      1. The music had to be of high quality in the tradition of serious art music.
      2. The music had to have lasting value that rewarded performers and listeners through multiple hearings and study.
      3. These criteria were broad enough to apply to a large number of composers.
   B. Younger composers wanted a more radical break from the past.
      1. Known as modernists, these composers reassessed inherited conventions.
      2. Modernists did not aim to please listeners on first hearing.
      3. They challenged perceptions and capacities.
      4. Modernists were critical of easily digested art and saw their own work as continuing the classical traditions.

II. Arnold Schoenberg (1874–1951) (see **HWM biography**, page 803, and **Figure 31.1**)
   A. Schoenberg moved the German classical tradition toward atonality.
      1. *Atonality* is a term for music that avoids tonal centers.
      2. He later developed the twelve-tone method for the systematic ordering of the twelve notes of the chromatic scale.
   B. Biography
      1. Early life
         a. Schoenberg was born in Vienna, the son of a Jewish shopkeeper.
         b. In his younger years, he largely taught himself.
         c. Richard Strauss got him a teaching job in Berlin (1901–03).
      2. Vienna years
         a. Upon his return to Vienna in 1904, he began teaching; his two most famous students were Berg and Webern.
         b. He had support from Mahler, but met resistance from others.
         c. He developed friendships with a number of expressionist painters, and he himself painted (see **HWM Figure 31.1**).
         d. He formulated the twelve-tone method in the early 1920s.
      3. After Vienna
         a. He had converted to Lutheranism, but converted back to Judaism and moved to France in 1933.
         b. He came to the United States in 1934 and taught at UCLA.
         c. He retired from teaching in 1944 at the age of seventy and died on July 13, 1951.
   C. Tonal works
      1. Schoenberg's earliest works are tonal in the late Romantic style.
         a. *Verklärte Nacht* (Transfigured Night, 1899), a tone poem for string sextet
         b. *Pelleas und Melisande* (1902–03), a symphonic poem
         c. *Gurrelieder* (Songs of Gurre, 1900–01, orchestration 1911), a cantata
      2. He later turned away from gigantism toward chamber music.

3. He applied the principal of developing variation to his own works, such as the String Quartet No. 1 in D Minor, Op. 7.
   a. The one-movement quartet combines an enlarged sonata form with the standard four movements of a classical work, similar to Liszt's Piano Sonata in B Minor.
   b. This work exemplifies Schoenberg's goal of continuing tradition but with a new voice (see **HWM Source Reading,** page 804).
4. Nonrepetition between and within pieces was Schoenberg's guiding principle.

D. Atonal music
1. Schoenberg began composing atonal music in 1908.
2. He felt that the prolonged dissonances in recent music had weakened the pull of the tonic and exhausted tonality.
3. "The emancipation of the dissonance" was Schoenberg's concept of freeing dissonance from its need to resolve to a consonance.
4. Schoenberg used three methods to create unity without tonality:
   a. Developing variation
   b. Integration of harmony and melody
   c. Chromatic saturation
5. Gestures from tonal music are used to connect with traditions.

E. *Saget mir, auf welchem Pfade* (Tell me on which path) from the *Book of the Hanging Gardens*, Op. 15 (1908–09) (see **HWM Example 31.1**)
1. Based on a poem by symbolist Stefan George, this is one of his first completely atonal works.
2. The sense of floating in harmonic space is well suited to the vague eroticism of the poetry.
3. Links to Germanic tradition
   a. Scoring for piano and voice
   b. Rise and fall of the vocal melody
   c. Divisions into phrases
   d. Use of dynamics to shape phrases
   e. Descending gestures to indicate cadences
   f. Developing variation is apparent in voice and accompaniment.
4. This song can be analyzed in terms of pitch-class sets.
   a. Pitch-class: any note of a chromatic scale and its enharmonic equivalent
   b. Set: a collection of pitches that can be transposed, inverted, and arranged in any order to generate melodies and harmonies
5. The song also exemplifies chromatic saturation, which uses all twelve pitch-classes within a segment of music.

F. Atonal works completed in 1909
1. *Book of the Hanging Gardens*
2. Three Piano Pieces, Op. 11
3. Five Orchestral Pieces, Op. 16
4. *Erwartung* (Expectation), Op. 17
   a. A one-character opera for soprano
   b. Exaggerated gestures and unrelenting dissonance parallel expressionism (see **HWM Music in Context,** pages 808–09, and **Figure 31.2**).
   c. As befitting a nightmare, the work is atonal and has no themes or reference to traditional forms.

G. *Pierrot lunaire* (Moonstruck Pierrot, 1912)
1. Text
   a. This cycle of twenty-one songs is based on German translations of the Belgian Albert Giraud's symbolist poetry.
   b. The first two lines of each poem function as a refrain; they are repeated in lines 7–8, and line 1 appears as line 13.
   c. Schoenberg typically sets the returning lines with a variant of the original music at the same pitch level.
2. Setting
   a. Schoenberg scored the cycle for speaker and a chamber ensemble of five performers who play nine instruments.
   b. The voice declaims the text in Sprechstimme ("speaking voice"), which approximates the written pitches with gliding speech tones.
   c. The combination of instruments is unique for each song.
   d. The music is atonal.
   e. Schoenberg creates coherence through a developing variation method, which continuously draws out new variants of a basic idea presented at the outset.
   f. Many songs evoke old forms, genres, or techniques.

H. *Nacht* (Night, **NAWM 141a**) from *Pierrot lunaire*
1. Pierrot sees giant black moths casting gloom over the world.
2. The basic motive is a rising minor third followed by a descending major third.
3. The motive reappears constantly, often overlapping itself, such as in the beginning.
4. The motive is subject to inversion and retrograde.
5. Schoenberg called this song a *passacaglia,* a set of variations over a three-note pattern.
   a. The ostinato is stated in measures 4–6.
   b. It reappears, varied, over ten more times.

6. At the end, the original complex of overlapping statements repeats at pitch.
7. Despite the atonal treatment, Schoenberg established a strong tonal center.

I. *Enthauptung* (Beheading, **NAWM 141b**) from *Pierrot lunaire*
   1. Pierrot imagines that he is beheaded by a moonbeam for his crimes.
   2. The first five measures depict the sweep of the scimitar and include both whole-tone scales.
   3. The next ten measures suggest the atmosphere of the moonlit night and Pierrot scurrying to avoid the moonbeam.
   4. The initial ideas are varied constantly throughout.
   5. Augmented chords suggest the image of knocking knees (measure 17).
   6. The movement ends with the downward runs from measures 3–4 at the same pitch level, but now in the piano.
   7. An instrumental epilogue recalls the music of song No. 7.

J. Twelve-tone method
   1. In the twelve-tone method, pitches are related to each other, not to a tonic.
   2. The basis of twelve-tone composition is a row or series.
      a. A row contains the twelve pitch-classes arranged in an order.
      b. The pitches of the row may sound successively or simultaneously.
      c. The composer usually states all of the pitches in a row before going to another row.
      d. The original version of the row is called the prime.
      e. The row can also be used in inversion (inverted intervals), retrograde (backward), and retrograde inversion.
   3. With this system he continued to explore the principal methods of atonality.
      a. Integration of harmony and melody
      b. Developing variation
      c. Chromatic saturation
   4. Schoenberg soon applied these techniques to pieces in classical structures and genres.
   5. In composing sonata forms, Schoenberg had to find an analogue to modulation, as exemplified in his Fourth String Quartet (see **HWM Example 31.3**).
      a. The row is designed so that the last six notes (the second hexachord) is an inversion of the first six.
      b. This restriction allows him to establish a harmonic region.
      c. The second theme appears in a region that is a fifth higher.

K. Piano Suite, Op. 25 (1921–23) (see **NAWM 142** and **HWM Example 31.2**)
   1. The prelude of this suite is Schoenberg's first twelve-tone piece.
   2. Each movement uses the same eight forms of a row.
      a. Two versions of the prime row: P–O, P–6.
      b. Two inversions of the row: I–0, I–6
      c. Four retrogrades, one for each of the above.
      d. Each row either begins or ends with an E or B-flat.
      e. Each prime or inverted row features the tritone G–D-flat in notes 3 and 4.
      f. With this limited number of transpositions, Schoenberg creates a sense of staying in a single key, a typical practice of the Baroque suite.
   3. Rows are used both melodically and harmonically.
   4. Schoenberg often breaks the row into groups of four notes, called tetrachords.
      a. The first four notes of R–0 spell B–A–C–H (in German nomenclature, B is B-flat and H is B-natural); this is a salute to the master of Baroque suites.
      b. The beginning of the prelude manipulates tetrachords in a contrapuntal fashion.
   5. The minuet follows a strict dance form and reflects Baroque conventions.
      a. The trio is lighter in texture, featuring an inverted two-part canon that evokes the spirit of a Bach invention.
      b. The beginning of the minuet presents two-measure phrases in antecedent-consequent relationships.
      c. The systematic grouping of the row is analogous to chord progressions in tonal music.
      d. The standard binary form is followed, except for the lack of repeat in the second section.
      e. The return of the opening material in measures 29–31 suggests a rounded binary form.

L. Late tonal works
   1. Some of Schoenberg's works from the 1930s and 1940s are tonal.
   2. He recomposed two works from the eighteenth century, and their treatment is as radical as the twelve-tone music.

M. Schoenberg as modernist
1. His choices in facing the conflict between classic traditions and modernism shaped the course of music in the twentieth century.
2. His music won a central place in the modernist tradition, but was unpopular with most listeners.
3. With his music we arrive at the widest gulf between audiences and connoisseurs in their evaluation of music.
4. Schoenberg and his students Berg and Webern, both natives of Vienna, were known as the Second Viennese School.

III. Alban Berg (1885–1935) (see **HWM Figure 31.3**)
A. General
1. Berg began studying with Schoenberg in 1904 at the age of nineteen.
2. He achieved greater popular success than Schoenberg by infusing the music with expressive gestures in the tradition of Mahler and Strauss.
3. Berg's expressionistic opera *Wozzeck*, which premiered in 1925, was one of the most successful modern operas and by far the most popular atonal opera.

B. *Wozzeck*
1. The story is adapted from a nineteenth-century play by Georg Büchner.
   a. The play is based on a real event in which a man who may have been insane was executed for killing the woman he lived with.
   b. Incomplete at Büchner's death in 1837, the play was finally staged in 1913.
   c. Berg created his own libretto and completed the music in 1922.
2. The music is atonal, not twelve-tone, and includes some Sprechtstimme.
3. Berg employs leitmotives that are identified with the main characters (see **HWM Example 31.4a**).
4. Each of the three acts has five scenes linked by interludes; the music is continuous.
   a. The first act includes a Baroque suite, a rhapsody, a march and lullaby, a passacaglia, and a rondo.
   b. The second act is a symphony in five movements and includes a sonata form, fantasia and fugue, ternary slow movement, scherzo, and rondo.
   c. Act III is a series of inventions: on a theme (seven variations and a fugue), on a note (B), on a rhythm, on a chord, on a key, and on a duration.
   d. The invention on a key is the Mahlerian interlude before the final scene, the longest interlude of the opera.
5. Act III, scene 3 (see **NAWM 143** and **HWM Example 31.4b**)
   a. Wozzeck sits in a tavern, having just murdered Marie.
   b. In this invention on a rhythm, an out-of-tune onstage piano introduces the basic rhythmic pattern.
   c. Throughout the scene, the rhythmic pattern repeats incessantly, sometimes in augmentation or diminution.
   d. By the end, all are singing the scene's main rhythm.
   e. Berg maintains atonality, but makes references to recognizable tonal styles.

C. Twelve-tone works
1. After *Wozzeck*, Berg adopted the twelve-tone system.
2. Berg chose rows that allowed for tonal-sounding chords and progressions.
3. Principal twelve-tone works
   a. *Lyric Suite* for string quartet (1925–26)
   b. Violin Concerto (1935)
   c. *Lulu* (1928–35), his second opera
4. Violin Concerto (see **HWM Example 31.5**)
   a. The row has four interlocking minor and major triads.
   b. The piece begins with evocations of a violin tuning its open strings.
   c. Berg also uses a Viennese waltz style, a folk song, and a Bach chorale, *Es ist genug*.
   d. The chorale, which alludes to the death of Manon Gropius, contains three rising steps, like the end of the row.

IV. Anton Webern (1883–1945) (see **HWM Figure 31.4**)
A. General
1. Webern began studying with Schoenberg in 1904, the same year as Berg.
2. He also studied musicology at the University of Vienna and received a Ph.D. in 1906.
3. His concept of music history influenced his development.
   a. He felt that evolution in art was necessary and that history can only move forward, not revisit events or ideas of the past.
   b. *The Path to the New Music* is a series of lectures in which Webern argued that twelve-tone music was the inevitable result of music's evolution.
   c. His beliefs gave him the confidence to continue composing despite much

opposition; he saw himself as a researcher making new discoveries.
4. Webern's works were widely influential following World War II.

B. Works and styles
1. Webern passed through the stages of late Romantic, chromaticism, atonality, and twelve-tone organization.
2. He began the last phase in 1925 with the songs of Op. 17.
3. He wrote equally for voice and instruments, usually writing for small chamber ensembles.
4. His music is extremely concentrated.
   a. Some of his works are only a few measures long.
   b. His entire mature output takes less than four hours to play.
5. His texture has been described as pointillistic, since it often features only one to four notes in succession on the same instrument.
6. The dynamics seldom rise above forte.
7. Treatment of the row
   a. He avoided using rows with tonal implications.
   b. He frequently employed canons in inversion or retrograde.

C. Symphony, Op. 21, first movement (see **NAWM 144** and **HWM Example 31.6**)
1. The work is scored for a small chamber orchestra.
2. Each of its two movements is in a traditional classical form.
   a. The first movement is a sonata form.
   b. The second movement is a theme with seven variations.
3. The entire first movement also has a double canon in inversion.
4. The row is a palindrome, with the intervals reading the same forward and backward.
5. Webern reconceives the sonata form in new terms.
   a. Rather than two contrasting themes, Webern presents a contrast of character between canon 1 and canon 2.
   b. The development section is a palindrome.
   c. The recapitulation presents the same succession of rows as the exposition, but with new rhythms and registers.
6. He employs a succession of timbres similar to Schoenberg's concept of *Klangfarbenmelodie* (tone-color melody), in which changes of tone color are perceived as parallel to changing pitches in a melody.
7. At times there is just one note per instrument, creating tiny points of sound, which has been described as pointillism.

V. Igor Stravinsky (1882–1971) (see **HWM biography,** page 820, and **Figure 31.5**)

A. Stravinsky created an individual voice by developing several traits, most from Russian traditions.
1. Distinctive qualities
   a. Undermining meter through unpredictable accents and rapid changes of meter
   b. Frequent ostinatos
   c. Static blocks of sound juxtaposed or layered
   d. Discontinuity and interruption
   e. Dissonance based on diatonic, octatonic, and other collections
   f. Dry, antilyrical, but colorful use of instruments
2. Stravinsky forged these traits during his Russian period.
3. He became arguably the most important composer of his time.

B. Biography
1. Stravinsky was born near St. Petersburg to a well-to-do musical family.
2. He studied composition and orchestration privately with Rimsky-Korsakov.
3. Sergei Diaghilev commissioned Stravinsky to compose for the Ballet Russes.
4. Stravinsky moved to Paris in 1911 and remained there after the Russian Revolution.
5. Capitalizing on the notoriety of the *Rite of Spring,* Stravinsky performed tirelessly as a pianist and conductor, which increased his international recognition.
6. He eventually settled in Hollywood, and several of his pieces incorporate American styles.

C. Russian Period (to 1918)
1. *The Firebird* (1910)
   a. The ballet is based on Russian folk tales.
   b. Human characters are portrayed with diatonic music and supernatural creatures with octatonic or chromatic music.
2. *Petrushka* (1910–11)
   a. The opening scene presents blocks of static harmony with repetitive melodic and rhythmic patterns.
   b. Seemingly unrelated musical events interrupt each other, creating an aural equivalent to Picasso's cubism.

c. Stravinsky borrows several Russian folk tunes and simulates folk harmony (see **HWM Example 31.7**).
d. To depict the supernatural, Stravinsky draws upon a biting octatonic sound.
e. The "Petrushka chord" is derived from an octatonic scale (see **HWM Example 31.8**).

3. *The Rite of Spring* (1911–13)
   a. The ballet, set in prehistoric Russia, does not tell a story, but shows a fertility ritual in which an adolescent girl is chosen for sacrifice and dances herself to death.
   b. Nikolay Roerich designed the sets and costumes, and Vaclav Nijinsky was the choreographer.
   c. The scenario, choreography, and music are marked by primitivism, a deliberate representation of the crude and uncultured (see **HWM Figure 31.6**).
   d. The audience at the premiere broke into a riot (see **HWM Source Reading,** page 824).
   e. The music has since become one of Stravinsky's most commonly performed works.

D. *Danse des adolescents* (Dance of the Adolescent Girls) from *The Rite of Spring* (see **NAWM 145a** and **HWM Example 31.9**)
1. The dissonant opening chord uses all seven notes of the A-flat harmonic minor scale.
2. The emphasis on pure pulse contributes to the sense of primitivism.
   a. The metrical hierarchy of beats is negated as each pulse is played with the same strength.
   b. Unpredictable accents destroy any sense of regularity.
3. The entire scene is built from ostinatos that create static blocks of sound.
4. Stravinsky builds up textures by layering two or more strands of music on top of each other.
5. The contrasting blocks of sound share several pitches, which lend a sense of continuity.
6. The movement incorporates a Russian folk tune (measure 43) and two folklike melodies.
7. Stravinsky often links a motive with a specific instrumentation.
8. Stravinsky prefers a dry, rather than lush, timbre in his orchestration.

E. *Danse sacrale* (Sacrificial Dance) from *The Rite of Spring* (see **NAWM 145b**)
1. This is the last dance of the ballet.
2. Stravinsky adopts two additional strategies that reduce meter to pulse.
   a. Rapidly changing meters
   b. Unpredictable alternation of notes with rests
3. The opening, section A
   a. The main idea (measures 2–5) is repeated many times.
   b. Other similar figures alternate with the main idea.
4. Section B begins in measure 34.
   a. The section begins softly with pulsing chords and a chromatic melodic idea.
   b. The section builds to a frightening climax (measures 91–92).
   c. It suddenly returns to the opening dynamic and begins to build again.
5. The A section returns, transposed down a semitone (measure 116).
6. A new section begins at measure 149.
   a. The section features percussion instruments.
   b. A whole-tone scale, introduced by the horns (measure 154), is transformed into a folklike melody (measures 160–171).
7. The opening of section A briefly interrupts (measures 174–80).
8. A bass ostinato is introduced at measure 203, and the material of section A builds to a final climax.

F. *L'histoire du soldat* (The Soldier's Tale, 1918)
1. Wartime economy forced Stravinsky to turn to small musical ensembles.
2. This ballet is scored for six solo instruments and percussion.
3. Using dance movements, such as a tango, waltz, and ragtime, Stravinsky discovered ways to imitate familiar styles within his own musical style.

G. Neoclassicism
1. Neoclassicism denotes a broad movement that took place from the 1910s to the 1950s.
   a. Composers revived, imitated, or evoked styles, genres, and forms of pre-Romantic music, particularly from the eighteenth century.
   b. Neoclassicism rejected the high emotions of Romanticism.
2. Stravinsky used neoclassicism as a new avenue for his own distinctive style.
3. Stravinsky's neoclassic music has an emotional detachment and can be seen as anti-Romantic.

H. Neoclassical period (1919–1951)
1. *Pulcinella* (1919), a ballet commissioned by Diaghilev

a. The work consists of orchestrations of pieces by Pergolesi, an eighteenth-century composer.
b. Through orchestrating Pergolesi's pieces, Stravinsky discovered the past.

2. *Symphonies of Wind Instruments* (1920)
   a. This work features many of the same methods as *The Rite of Spring,* but unlike *The Rite of Spring,* it is an abstract composition.
   b. Along with *Pulcinella,* this work marks the beginning of Stravinsky's neoclassicism.
3. He became the leading composer in the neoclassic style, which culminated in the opera *The Rake's Progress* (1951).

I. *Symphony of Psalms,* first movement (1930; see **NAWM 146** and **HWM Example 31.10)**
   1. *Symphony of Psalms* is a three-movement work for mixed chorus and orchestra that uses psalms from the Latin Vulgate Bible.
   2. Baroque features
      a. Perpetual motion
      b. Frequent ostinatos
      c. Fully developed fugue in the second movement
   3. Stravinsky maintains an objective rather than emotional sound; he omits violins, viola, and clarinets.
   4. Some traits remain from the *Rite*, such as changing meters and unexpected rests.
   5. But the music is less dissonant and has characteristics of earlier music, such as the Gregorian chant style at the entrance of the voices.
   6. The juxtaposition of contrasting blocks of material articulates an abstract form.
   7. The movement alternates two main sections, and there is a contrasting middle section (see diagram in the commentary to **NAWM 146**).
   8. Neotonality
      a. Tonal centers are established through repetition and assertion, not through traditional harmony.
      b. At the beginning, E-minor chords alternate with sixteenth-note arpeggiations.
      c. When the voices enter, E is the main focus.
      d. E is also sustained in the bass.
      e. The A sections are primarily diatonic, using the notes of E Phrygian.
      f. The B sections are largely octatonic.
      g. Stravinsky juxtaposes E and G and also moves from E to G at the close.
   9. Stravinsky and Schoenberg
      a. Partly because of his use of tonal centers, audiences preferred Stravinsky's music to Schoenberg's.
      b. Both composers had supporters who argued about the need for tradition.
      c. The two composers were closer in spirit than might be first perceived.

J. Serial period (1951–1971)
   1. In the 1950s, Schoenberg's twelve-tone techniques were extended to parameters other than pitch, which became known as serialism.
   2. Stravinsky adapted serial techniques, but maintained many of his distinctive characteristics in his late works, including:
      a. *In Memoriam Dylan Thomas* (1954), a song cycle
      b. *Threni* (1957–58), for voices and orchestra, on texts from the Lamentations of Jeremiah
      c. *Movements* (1958–59), for piano and orchestra

K. Influence
   1. Stravinsky's impact on other composers is similar to that of Wagner and Debussy.
   2. Many elements that he created became commonplace.
   3. He popularized neoclassicism.
   4. His support for serialism helped gain him a strong following.
   5. His writings, such as *Poetics of Music*, have been widely read.

VI. Béla Bartók (1881–1945) (see **HWM biography,** page 830, and **Figure 31.8**)
   A. Bartók synthesized elements of Hungarian, Romanian, and Bulgarian peasant music with elements of the German classical tradition.
   B. Biography
      1. Bartók was born in a small Hungarian city (now in Romania).
      2. He began piano lessons at age five and began to compose at age nine.
      3. He studied piano and composition at the Budapest Academy of Music and returned there in 1907 to teach piano.
      4. A virtuoso pianist, he concertized throughout Europe.
      5. He also edited the keyboard music of classic composers.
      6. Bartók as an ethnomusicologist
         a. Bartók collected thousands of folk songs, edited them into collections, and wrote about folk music.
         b. He used audio recording in his field research (see **HWM Figure 31.9**).

   c. He argued that peasant music better represented the nation than urban music.
   d. In 1934 he accepted a position as ethnomusicologist at the Academy of Sciences.
7. Bartók enjoyed a productive compositional period until the threat from Nazi Germany forced him to flee to the United States.
8. He settled in New York, but suffered financially and physically until his death from leukemia in 1945.

C. Musical influences
1. In his early career, he modeled his music on the works of classical masters, such as Bach, Beethoven, and Liszt.
2. He was later inspired by the works of modernists, including Richard Strauss, Debussy, Schoenberg, and Stravinsky.
3. Bartók and folk music
   a. He arranged many peasant tunes.
   b. He created original works by blending rhythmic, melodic, or formal characteristics of peasant music with classical and modern traditions.

D. Major works
1. He created a distinctive style in his early works.
   a. *Bluebeard's Castle* (1911), a one-act opera, mixes Hungarian elements with influences from Debussy.
   b. *Allegro barbaro* (1911) and other piano music treated the instrument in a percussive manner.
2. Following World War I, his works grew more dissonant.
   a. Two Violin Sonatas (1921 and 1922)
   b. The Third and Fourth String Quartets
   c. *The Miraculous Mandarin*, an expressionistic pantomime
3. His later works are his most widely known.
   a. The Fifth and Sixth String Quartets
   b. *Music for Strings, Percussion and Celesta* (1936)
   c. Concerto for Orchestra (1943)
4. *Mikrokosmos* (1929–33)
   a. 153 piano works in six books of graded difficulty
   b. The work is of great pedagogical value.

E. Musical style
1. Bartók maintained a single pitch center, using diatonic and other scales.
2. He built melodies from repeated and varied motives.
3. Bartók retained elaborate contrapuntal procedures from the classical tradition, such as the fugue.
4. He drew upon complex rhythms and meters common in peasant traditions.
5. His harmonies, often dissonant, are frequently built from seconds and fourths.
6. He was fond of symmetry.

F. *Music for Strings, Percussion and Celesta*
1. The work has four movements, similar to a classical symphony.
   a. Slow fugue
   b. Fast sonata form
   c. Slow arch form
   d. Rondo finale
2. The fugue theme appears in each of the other movements.
3. Each movement contains canon and imitation, often in inversion.
4. The outer movements are in A, and the inner movements center on notes a minor third above (C) and below (F-sharp).
5. The work is neotonal.
   a. All of the movements center on tritone relationships.
   b. The slow movement centers on F-sharp with C as a competing pole (see **HWM Example 31.11**).
   c. The themes, created by varying small motives, are often in diatonic modes.
6. Peasant elements
   a. Bulgarian dance meters alternate twos and threes; Bartók adopts a 2–3–3 pattern in the fourth movement.
   b. The Serbo-Croatian song is heavily ornamented, partly chromatic, and speechlike (*parlando-rubato*), which is imitated near the beginning of the third movement (see **HWM Example 31.13**).
   c. Other characteristics include drones, snapped pizzicatos, and percussive dissonant chords.

G. *Music for Strings, Percussion and Celesta*, third movement (**NAWM 147**)
1. The movement is a modified arch form: ABCB'A'.
2. The four phrases of the opening fugue theme separate these sections (measures 19, 34, 60, and 74).
3. Section A (measures 1–18)
   a. The palindromic form of the third movement is foreshadowed in the opening xylophone solo (see **HWM Example 31.12**).

   b. The section also features glissandos on the timpani, low string tremolos, and chromatic figures in the violas and violins.
   c. The pitches center on F-sharp and C, the tonal poles of the movement.
4. Section B (measures 20–33)
   a. Two solo violins and celesta share the B theme.
   b. The eerie background consists of string trills, parallel major sevenths articulated by the piano, violin glissandos, and tremolos.
5. Section C (measures 35–59)
   a. The section opens with glissandos, pentatonic scales in the harp, piano, and celesta, and a twisting theme in tremolos.
   b. This texture is known as Bartók's "night music."
   c. The theme builds to a climax, where a new motive appears (violin I, measures 44–45).
   d. The new motive, sometimes played in retrograde, is related to the third phrase of the fugue theme, which enters at measure 60.
6. Section B' (measures 63–72)
   a. The B theme is in canon at the tritone.
   b. The accompanying texture is similar to the first half of section C.
7. Section A' (measures 75–83) presents an abbreviated version of the opening section.

VII. Charles Ives (1874–1954) (see **HWM biography,** page 836, and **Figure 31.10**)

A. Biography
1. Ives was born in a small Connecticut city, where his father was a bandmaster and music teacher.
2. He became the youngest professional church organist in the state at age fourteen.
3. His father taught him theory and an experimental approach to sound.
4. He studied music with Horatio Parker at Yale.
5. Ives settled in New York, working as an organist.
6. He chose a career in the insurance business and built one of the most successful agencies in the nation.
7. He composed music in the evenings and weekends, but retired from composing in 1918 due to a health crisis.
8. Although he worked in obscurity, he was later recognized as the first American composer to create a distinctly American body of art music.

B. Ives was fluent in four distinct spheres of composition, and he combined elements of each in his mature music.
1. American vernacular music
   a. He grew up surrounded by American vernacular music, including parlor songs, minstrel shows, and marches directed by his father.
   b. He composed numerous marches and parlor songs.
2. Protestant church music
   a. Ives sang and played organ in church for much of his early life.
   b. He learned all of the styles prominent in American Protestantism, which were cultivated in his studies with Parker.
3. European classical music
   a. He played major organ works by composers such as Bach and transcriptions of other classical works.
   b. He studied art music with Parker.
   c. His First Symphony is modeled after Dvořák's *New World* Symphony.
4. Experimental music
   a. He experimented with new sounds, including polytonality (melody in one key and accompaniment in another), in his youth.
   b. *Processional* for chorus and organ is an essay on possible chord structures (see **HWM Example 31.14a**).
   c. Scherzo: *All the Way Around and Back* for chamber ensemble is a palindrome that builds on dissonant ostinatos (see **HWM Example 31.14b**).
   d. *The Unanswered Question* (1908), his best-known experimental work, combines both tonal and atonal layers in one work.

C. Synthesis
1. Ives composed in classical genres after 1902, but mixed in other styles and sounds that he knew.
2. The Second Symphony paraphrased American popular songs, borrowed passages from classic composers, and combined them in a symphonic idiom.

D. Cumulative form
1. American hymn tunes can be found in Ives's Third Symphony, four violin sonatas, and First Piano Sonata.
2. In each, thematic development occurs first and leads to the themes at the end.

3. In this process, Ives asserts the universal value of his country's music (see **HWM Source Reading,** page 840).

E. Many of Ives's later pieces have programs celebrating American life.
   1. *Three Places in New England* presents orchestral pictures of:
      a. The first African-American regiment in the Civil War
      b. A band playing at a Fourth of July picnic
      c. A walk by a river with his wife during their honeymoon
   2. *A Symphony: New England Holidays* captures the spirit of national holidays.
   3. *Concord Mass., 1840–60,* his second piano sonata, pays tribute to the writers in that city at that time: Emerson, Thoreau, Hawthorne, and the Alcotts.
   4. The Fourth Symphony, a philosophical work, poses and seeks to answer the "searching questions of What? and Why?"
   5. Quotations of American tunes are frequent, often layered on top of each other.
   6. Ives frequently mixed styles within a single work.

F. *General William Booth Enters into Heaven* (1914; see **NAWM 148** and **HWM Example 31.15**)
   1. This song is based on a Vachel Lindsay poem that pictures the founder of the Salvation Army leading the poor and downtrodden into heaven.
   2. Although it is an art song, Ives mixes aspects of American vernacular music, church music, and experimental music.
   3. Several hymns and American tunes are paraphrased, and a cumulative form leads to an entire verse of the hymn *There Is a Fountain Filled with Blood.*
   4. Opening section (measures 1–18)
      a. Ives imitates Booth's bass drum with dissonant chords on the piano.
      b. Over the "street beat," the vocal line presents phrases derived from *There Is a Fountain Filled with Blood.*
   5. Second section (measures 19–39)
      a. Ives gives each group of followers a different musical characterization.
      b. He uses ostinatos, parallel dissonant chords, and other modernist sounds.
      c. The hymn tune returns with the refrain.
   6. The "mighty courthouse" (measures 40–81)
      a. A crowd is suggested through a rising and falling whole-tone scale in the voice and ostinatos in the piano.
      b. The piano paraphrases *Oh, Dem Golden Slippers* in measures 52–55 with the suggestion of banjo playing.
      c. Ives adds a bugle call and a hint of the hymn *Onward, Upward* in measures 70–74.
   7. The appearance of Jesus (measures 82–91)
      a. *There Is a Fountain* is heard in the piano.
      b. This is the first mostly diatonic passage in the song.
      c. The slow tempo and soft dynamics suggest the dignity and serenity of Jesus.
   8. Closing section (measures 92–113)
      a. The march beat returns in the piano.
      b. At the climax, the complete verse of *There Is a Fountain* is sung.
      c. The action stops near the end, and the closing refrain is set twice, over soft arpeggiated chords and then in four-part Protestant harmony.
      d. The parade fades away in the distance.

G. Influence
   1. Ives's influence was felt after World War II.
   2. He could justifiably be called the founder of the experimental-music tradition in the United States.

VII. Composer and Audience
   A. Modernism widened the split between popular and classical music.
      1. Modernism targeted those willing to study and listen to a work repeatedly.
      2. Such works became favorites of other composers, but were held in disdain by audiences.
   B. Films have introduced both excerpts from modernist works and modernist techniques to general audiences.
   C. Compositions by all six of the composers mentioned here have found a permanent place in the classical repertory, and interest in their music has tended to increase.

## SUGGESTIONS FOR SUPPLEMENTARY READING/LISTENING/ACTIVITIES

For essays on twentieth-century music by composers, see Elliott Schwartz and Barney Childs, eds., *Contemporary Composers on Contemporary Music* (New York: Holt, Rinehart and Winston, 1967); Robert P. Morgan, ed., *Source Readings in Music History,* rev. ed., vol. 7: *The Twentieth Century* (New York: W. W. Norton, 1998); and Bryan R. Simms, ed., *Composers on Modern Musical*

*Culture: An Anthology of Readings on Twentieth-Century Music* (New York: Schirmer Books, 1999).

For analytical approaches to the music discussed in this and subsequent chapters, see Stefan Kostka, *Materials and Techniques of Twentieth-Century Music* (Englewood Cliffs, N. J.: Prentice-Hall, 1990).

Have students listen to Schoenberg's *Gurrelieder, Verklärte Nacht* or his first string quartet and name the composers and styles that seem to have influenced him.

A compact-disc recording of both *The Book of the Hanging Gardens* and *Pierrot lunaire* is available. (Nonesuch 79237, 1992). Have students listen to the songs of either cycle and report on the composer's approach to the text in each, and which emotions seem to be expressed.

Have students listen to the *Lyric Suite* and describe it in terms of lyricism and expressionism.

DVD performances are available for *Wozzeck* (Image Entertainment, 2001) and *Lulu* (Kultur, 2004).

Berg's Violin Concerto is one of the enduring classics of the twentieth century. Contrast this work's popularity with the less popular Violin Concerto of Schoenberg. Ask students to speculate on why this work is more popular.

Pierre Boulez has recorded the complete works of Anton Webern; his recordings are available on compact disc (Sony 45845, 1991).

Have students trace the rows and canons in the second movement of Webern's Symphony, Opus 21. Discuss with them how Webern achieves the sense of a variation structure.

For additional source readings on Stravinsky's *Rite of Spring,* see Weiss and Taruskin, eds., *Music in the Western World: A History in Documents* (New York: Schirmer Books, 1984), 438–43.

The original choreography of *Petrushka, Les Noces*, and *Prelude à l'aprés-midi d'un Faune* have been recreated in "Paris Dances Diaghilev" (Elektra Entertainment 40159-3, 1992).

Have students analyze Stravinsky's *In Memoriam Dylan Thomas* to see how a five-tone row functions in a work. Discuss how the work still exemplifies the composer's ability to create unity and continuity with divergent blocks of sound.

A visually stunning VHS video is available for Bártok's *Bluebeard's Castle* (Pdg/London Classics, 1992).

Bartók's *Mikrokosmos* is described in the text as a microcosm of the development of European music in the first third of the twentieth century. Assign students various works to play and analyze with this statement in mind.

Have students listen to movements from Ives's Violin Sonata and discuss the procedure of cumulative form.

Have a keyboard student report on the unusual performing techniques required for Ives's *Concord* Sonata.

Play Ives's *Holidays* Symphony ("Fourth of July" is a good movement) and have students identify melodies that they recognize. A good compact-disc recording is Sony 42381 from 1990.

## OBJECTIVE QUESTIONS

1. In what style were the early works of Schoenberg written?
   a. impressionist
   b. atonal
   c. primitivist
   d. late Romantic
   e. neoclassic

   Answer: d

2. Of the following methods, which did Schoenberg use to give coherence to atonal music?
   a. developing variation
   b. cumulative form
   c. discontinuity
   d. parlando-rubato
   e. pointillism

   Answer: a

3. Of the following works, which was created with the twelve-tone technique?
   a. *Pierrot lunaire*
   b. *Verklärte Nacht*
   c. *Erwartung*
   d. Piano Suite
   e. *The Book of the Hanging Garden*

   Answer: d

4. The vocal technique used in *Pierrot lunaire* is called ___________.
   a. Klangfarbenmelodie
   b. Sprechstimme
   c. parlando-rubato
   d. experimental
   e. chromatic saturation

   Answer: b

5. Which composer combined atonality with the expressive gestures of late Romantic music?
   a. Stravinsky
   b. Webern
   c. Ives
   d. Schoenberg
   e. Berg

   Answer: e

6. Webern received a Ph.D. in ___________.
   a. musicology
   b. ethnomusicology
   c. theory
   d. composition
   e. piano performance

   Answer: a

7. *Wozzeck* is an outstanding example of ___________.
   a. impressionism
   b. primitivism
   c. expressionism
   d. neoclassicism
   e. serialism

   Answer: c

8. Which work did Berg compose as a requiem for the daughter of Alma Mahler?
   a. *Lulu*
   b. *Lyric* Suite
   c. Variations for Orchestra
   d. Violin Concerto
   e. *Wozzeck*

   Answer: d

9. Stravinsky was commissioned to compose his first ballet music by ___________.
   a. Diaghilev
   b. Nijinsky
   c. Rimsky-Korsakov
   d. Fokine
   e. Balanchine

   Answer: a

10. Webern's music exerted the greatest influence on composers who worked ___________.
    a. from 1900 to World War I
    b. between World War I and World War II
    c. during World War II
    d. after World War II to the late 1960s
    e. from the 1970s to the present

    Answer: d

11. Which of the following does *not* characterize Webern's Symphony, Op. 21?
    a. double canons
    b. inversions
    c. classical forms
    d. palindromic structures
    e. full symphonic orchestration

    Answer: e

12. Which work marks Stravinsky's turn towards neoclassicism?
    a. *Petrushka*
    b. *Threni*
    c. *Symphony of Psalms*
    d. *Pulcinella*
    e. *The Rake's Progress*

    Answer: d

13. Stravinsky's late works employ ___________.
    a. serialism
    b. primitivism
    c. impressionism
    d. experimental sounds
    e. electronic music

    Answer: a

14. Stravinsky's approach to harmony can be described as ___________.
    a. atonal
    b. neotonal
    c. pantonal
    d. chromatic saturation
    e. modal

    Answer: b

15. In his early years, Bartók made his career as a(n) ___________.
    a. conductor
    b. singer of folk music
    c. virtuoso pianist
    d. violist
    e. opera singer

    Answer: c

16. The music of Bartók mixes the traditions of which sources?
    a. modern, popular, and peasant
    b. classic, popular, and peasant
    c. classic, modern, and popular
    d. popular, modern, and classic
    e. classic, modern, and peasant

    Answer: e

17. Of the following, which was composed early in Bartók's career?
    a. *Allegro barbaro*
    b. Concerto for Orchestra
    c. *The Miraculous Mandarin*
    d. *Mikrokosmos*
    e. *Music for Strings, Percussion and Celesta*

    Answer: a

18. Charles Ives made his living in what business?
    a. stocks
    b. insurance
    c. organ building
    d. politics
    e. publishing

    Answer: b

19. Of the following, which is a strand not found in the music of Ives?
    a. Protestant music
    b. European peasant music
    c. American vernacular music
    d. experimental music
    e. European classical music

    Answer: b

20. At what point did Ives receive recognition for his work?
    a. with his first cantata
    b. with *The Unanswered Question*
    c. with the premiere of the *Concord* Sonata
    d. after he retired from composition
    e. after he died

    Answer: d

## SHORT-ESSAY QUESTIONS

1. Compare the ways in which Schoenberg, Berg, and Webern use the twelve-tone method, citing specific works discussed in the text.
2. Describe characteristics of Stravinsky's music that remain constant through his three major stylistic periods. Mention key works in each.
3. Describe the major influences on the music of Béla Bartók.
4. Discuss the mixture of American vernacular, American Protestant, European classical, and experimental music in the works of Charles Ives.

## TERMS FOR IDENTIFICATION

modernist
atonality
twelve-tone method
emancipation of the dissonance
pitch class
set
developing variation
chromatic saturation
Albert Giraud
Sprechstimme
row
series
prime
inversion
retrograde
retrograde inversion
Second Viennese School
Georg Büchner
*The Path to the New Music*
Klangfarbenmelodie
Diaghilev
primitativism
neoclassicism
neotonality
serial music
ethnomusicology
parlando-rubato
experimental music
polytonal
cumulative form

# CHAPTER 32 Between the World Wars: Jazz and Popular Music

I. Musical Changes
   A. Phonographs, radios, and movies fostered a mass market for popular music.
      1. The varieties of popular music, especially jazz, were lucrative.
      2. Music, both classical and popular, became an integral part of sound films.
      3. Movie musicals were popular.
   B. Classical concert music and opera remained the most prestigious types of music.
      1. Styles of classical music grew more varied.
      2. Composers continued to respond to both modernism and the avant-garde.

II. Between the Wars
   A. World War I left Western society profoundly disillusioned.
      1. New technology had produced staggering losses; over nine million soldiers were killed.
      2. The economies of many countries were ruined.
      3. A worldwide influenza epidemic killed twenty million people in 1918.
      4. Music, especially popular music, provided an escape.
      5. Interest also grew in music composed before 1750.
   B. Changes in European nations
      1. Several of the traditional empires were brought to an end, and a number of European countries gained independence.
      2. Radical Marxist revolutionaries created the Soviet Union in 1917.
      3. Other dictatorships were established in Italy, Spain, and Germany.
      4. Anti-Semitic laws in Germany forced many Jewish writers, composers, and scholars to emigrate.
   C. Economic and social changes
      1. While European countries faced economic hardships, the United States and Canada enjoyed a financial boom.
      2. The stock market of 1929 sparked a worldwide depression.
      3. Germany invaded Poland in 1939, beginning World War II.
      4. Women gained the right to vote in several nations, including the United States, and they had greater access to careers.
   D. The arts
      1. The 1920s saw extensive experimentation in the arts.
         a. Writers explored new literary techniques.
         b. New movements developed in art, such as dadism and surrealism.
         c. Architects explored less decorated forms.
      2. In the 1930s, many artists created more accessible works due to the depression (see **HWM Figure 32.1**).
         a. Composers hoped to catch the imagination of ordinary working people.
         b. Artists often addressed social issues.

III. Technology's Impact on Music
   A. Recordings allowed performances to be preserved and replayed many times.
      1. A new mass market was created that enabled some performers to become international stars.
      2. Songwriters and bandleaders began creating three- to four-minute works that would fit on the side of a record.

3. The introduction of electronic recording in 1925 (replacing acoustic recording) allowed for more sensitive recordings and encouraged a more intimate style of singing, as heard with Bing Crosby and Frank Sinatra.

B. Radio broadcasts provided new opportunities for musicians.
1. By 1924, there were over 1,400 radio stations around North America.
2. Recordings were too poor in quality to be broadcast, so radio stations employed musicians.
   a. Radio stations sponsored orchestras, such as the BBC Symphony Orchestra (founded 1930) in London and the NBC Symphony Orchestra (1937) in New York.
   b. Dance bands, such as Benny Goodman and his band, were given wide exposure on the radio.
3. Recordings and radio provided widespread dissemination of classical and popular music.

IV. American Musical Theater

A. Popular music entered a productive era in the 1920s.
1. A variety of stage shows enjoyed great popularity.
   a. Revues and vaudeville
   b. Operetta and musicals
2. The Golden Age of Tin Pan Alley extended from 1920 to 1955, when rock and roll brought an end to the sheet music industry.
3. In the 1920s, developments of popular song and theater were interlinked.
   a. Publishers increasingly relied on recordings to popularize their works.
   b. Hollywood musicals became another venue for songwriters.

B. Revues
1. Vaudeville shows, with a loose collection of variety acts, remained popular.
2. In larger cities like New York, high-quality productions called revues featured musical numbers and included many performers.
3. The premier series of revues was the Ziegfeld Follies, created by Florenz Ziegfeld.
4. Important song composers, including Irving Berlin, wrote for revues.

C. Musicals
1. Several new operettas were successful in the 1920s, including Sigmund Romberg's *The Student Prince*.
2. The popularity of musicals soon overshadowed operetta.
3. Some musicals were vehicles for star performers and had loose plots.
4. Increasingly, more musicals featured strong dramatic stories.
5. *Show Boat* (1927), with music by Jerome Kern and text and lyrics by Oscar Hammerstein II, was an enormous success (see **HWM Figure 32.2**).
   a. It brought together a number of traditions and musical styles.
   b. The score is operatic in scope with referential themes.
   c. The plot deals with serious social issues, such as racism and miscegenation.

V. Popular Song

A. The Golden Age of Tin Pan Alley
1. By 1910, several types of Tin Pan Alley songs had solidified, including waltz, ragtime, and novelty songs.
2. Most songs had a standard form:
   a. One or more verses
   b. A chorus of thirty-two measures in an AABA, ABAB, or ABAC pattern
3. The focus was on the chorus, which had the most memorable melodic ideas.

B. Irving Berlin (1888–1989)
1. The Russian-born son of a Jewish cantor, Irving Berlin wrote both music and lyrics for his songs.
2. His lengthy career made him one of the most prolific and best-loved popular songwriters.
3. He composed songs for revues, movies, and musicals.
4. Among his best-known songs are:
   a. *God Bless America*
   b. *White Christmas*
   c. *Alexander's Ragtime Band*, which established his reputation as America's chief ragtime composer

C. Cole Porter (1891–1964)
1. Porter also wrote both music and lyrics for his songs.
2. He studied music at Yale, Harvard, and the Schola Cantorum in Paris.
3. Porter wrote exclusively for theater and Hollywood musicals.
4. His lyrics are urbane and sophisticated and revel in innuendo.
5. Among his best-known songs are:
   a. *Let's Do It*
   b. *It's De-lovely*
   c. *You're the Top*

VI. Blues
   A. General
      1. Revues, musicals, and Tin Pan Alley continued traditions that had begun in Europe.
      2. African-American music and musicians played an increasingly larger role in American musical life.
      3. The 1920s, known as "The Jazz Age," produced two related traditions of African-American origin: blues and jazz.
      4. The origin of the blues is obscure.
      5. Lyrics
         a. The words describe disappointments, mistreatment, or other troubles.
         b. A sense of defiance and a will to survive are also conveyed.
         c. Touches of humor are common.
      6. Music
         a. Melodic contours and syncopation express the feelings of the words.
         b. Distinctive vocal or instrumental effects evoke the sound of a person expressing pain, sorrow, or frustration.
         c. Blues often featured flattened or bent notes on the third, fifth, and seventh scale degrees called *blue notes.*
      7. Two types of blues developed: classic blues and Delta blues.
   B. Classic blues
      1. Classic blues were sung primarily by African-American women.
      2. The accompaniment was typically a piano or a small combo.
      3. Mamie Smith's recording of *Crazy Blues* (1920), the first blues recording by an African-American singer, sold 75,000 copies within months.
      4. Her success prompted record companies to market their products to black audiences.
      5. W. C. Handy (1873–1958), known as the "father of the blues," introduced sheet music forms of blues songs as early as 1912.
      6. With his publications, Handy solidified the standard twelve-bar blues form.
   C. *Back Water Blues* (1927) by Bessie Smith illustrates this form (see **NAWM 149** and **HWM Example 32.1**).
      1. Bessie Smith (1894–1937; see **HWM Figure 32.3**)
         a. Smith wrote the lyrics and the music after a Nashville flood in 1926.
         b. The recording, marketed after another flood in Mississippi in 1927, became one of her best-known records.
      2. Each poetic stanza has three lines.
         a. The second stanza typically restates the first.
         b. The third completes the thought with the same or similar rhyme.
      3. Each line of text has four measures of music with a set harmonic pattern.
         a. The first phrase remains in the tonic.
         b. The second phrase begins in the subdominant and ends in the tonic.
         c. The third phrase touches on the dominant, subdominant, and tonic.
      4. Following a brief piano introduction, each of the seven stanzas follows the same form and general melodic outline.
      5. Blue notes and syncopated melodic inflections can be heard in the performance.
      6. The vocal melody cadences in the third measure of each phrase, allowing for a call and response interchange with the pianist, James P. Johnson.
      7. Possible links to African music include:
         a. Improvisations on a simple formula
         b. Syncopation
         c. Repetition of short patterns
         d. Bent pitches
         e. Call and response
   D. Delta blues
      1. Delta blues came form the Mississippi Delta region.
      2. It is primarily associated with male African-American singers and guitarists.
      3. Delta blues was more directly rooted in oral tradition and hence exhibited more variety than the classic blues.
      4. Archivists, such as Alan Lomax, traveled to remote rural areas and recorded blues artists.
         a. These recordings gave blues singers national recognition.
         b. The singing style is rough, rich in timbre and nuance, and rhythmically flexible.
         c. Each section alternates voice and guitar in the style of call and response.
      5. Many Mississippi Delta blues singers moved to Chicago, where they would influence future generations of performers.
      6. The legacy of Robert Johnson (1911–1938) extended into the 1960s, when British rock musicians rediscovered his recordings.

VII. Jazz
   A. Jazz in the 1920s
      1. Jazz was established in the 1910s, and its popularity grew rapidly.

2. Distinctive features of 1920s jazz
   a. Syncopated rhythms
   b. Novel vocal and instrumental sounds
   c. Unbridled spirit that seemingly mocks social and musical properties
   d. Improvisation
3. Jazz was a performer's art; the recording industry and radio fostered growth and dissemination.

B. New Orleans jazz
1. Named after the city where it originated, New Orleans jazz was the dominant jazz type just after World War I.
2. New Orleans jazz style
   a. It improvises on a twelve-bar blues, a sixteen-measure strain from ragtime, or a thirty-two bar popular song form (usually AABA).
   b. The tune is presented initially over a given harmonic progression.
   c. The harmonic progression is repeated with various soloists and combinations of soloists playing over it.
   d. Each repetition is called a *chorus*.
   e. Each chorus features different instruments and new ideas, creating a theme-and-variations form.
   f. The style recalls the call and response and ecstatic outpourings of the African-American gospel tradition
3. Leading musicians include:
   a. Joe "King" Oliver (1885–1938), cornet
   b. Louis Armstrong (1901–1971), trumpet
   c. Jelly Roll Morton (1890–1941), piano

C. King Oliver and Louis Armstrong
1. King Oliver moved to Chicago in 1918 and formed his own band in 1920.
2. In 1922, Armstrong joined King Oliver's Creole Jazz Band.
3. They made some of the most important recordings in jazz history (see **HWM Figure 32.4**).
4. Armstrong later formed his own band called the Hot Five or Hot Seven.

D. *West End Blues* (see **NAWM 150** and **HWM Example 32.2**)
1. *West End Blues,* composed by King Oliver with lyrics by Clarence Williams, is a twelve-bar blues.
2. The published sheet music (**NAWM 150a**) adapts the blues to Tin Pan Alley verse-refrain form.
   a. The brief piano introduction includes a vamp.
   b. The verse presents one statement of a twelve-bar blues progression.
   c. The refrain has two successive statements of the twelve-bar blues.
   d. For each blues statement, Oliver composes a new melody and varies the harmony slightly.
3. Armstrong recorded this song in 1928 with his Hot Five in Chicago.
   a. Melody instruments: trumpet, clarinet, and trombone
   b. Rhythm section: drums, piano, and banjo
4. The recording maintains the blues form (**NAWM 150b**).
   a. Armstrong plays an introduction, which is followed by five choruses.
   b. In the first, Armstrong plays the tune with increasing acrobatics.
   c. The second features the trombone.
   d. In the third, the clarinet alternates in call and response with Armstrong.
   e. Armstrong sings syllables instead of playing, a technique that is known as *scat singing.*
   f. The piano solos on the fourth chorus.
   g. The entire ensemble plays during the fifth chorus.

E. Big bands
1. A fashion for larger bands began in the 1920s, partially due to larger performance spaces.
2. Many African-American and white musicians formed "big bands."
3. The typical big band of the 1930s was divided into brass, reeds, and rhythm sections.
   a. Brasses might include three trumpets and two trombones.
   b. Reeds consisted of clarinets and saxophones.
   c. The rhythm section had piano, drums, guitar, and double bass.
4. The sections interacted as units and alternated as soloists.
5. Although there was still improvisation, much of the material was written by an arranger.
6. Arrangements led to more sophisticated ensemble playing and more complex harmonies.
7. Some arrangers adapted sounds of modern classical music, including seventh chords, added sixth chords, and chromatic harmonies.
8. The typical big band also featured a vocalist.
9. The combination of stylish arrangements with jazz rhythms produced a music that became known as *swing.*

10. The number of swing bands exploded in the 1930s, a time when white bands established themselves more easily than African-American bands.

F. George Gershwin (see **HWM Figure 32.5**)
   1. Gershwin used jazz and blues to add new dimensions to art music.
   2. *Rhapsody in Blue* (1924) was billed as a "jazz concerto."
      a. It premiered at an extravagant concert organized by Paul Whiteman.
      b. It is scored for piano and jazz ensemble.
      c. It incorporates popular song forms, blue notes, and other jazz elements.
      d. The work became very popular.
   3. Gershwin continued in this direction with his Concerto in F (1925), whose second movement is constructed over a twelve-bar blues pattern stretched into a sixteen-measure theme.
   4. *Porgy and Bess* (1935)
      a. Written for an African-American cast, Gershwin called this work a folk opera.
      b. Elements are drawn from both operatic and Broadway traditions.
      c. The music is continuous and features recurring motives, as found in opera.
      d. African-American idioms include spirituals, blues, and jazz.
   5. Gershwin also wrote popular songs for both revues and musicals.
   6. He wrote songs for *Of Thee I Sing* (1931), which was the first musical to win the Pulitzer Prize for drama.
   7. His music helped launch the careers of numerous stars, including Fred Astaire, Ginger Rogers, and Ethel Merman.

G. *I Got Rhythm* by George Gershwin (**NAWM 151**)
   1. The song was composed for the Broadway musical *Girl Crazy* (1930).
      a. The show introduced Ginger Rogers and Ethel Merman, who later recorded this song.
      b. The song became an instant hit and a vehicle for later jazz improvisations.
   2. The song is in the standard Tin Pan Alley form: a verse and a thirty-two–bar chorus
      a. The chorus has phrases in an AABA' pattern.
      b. Typical of the time, there is only one verse, and the chorus is repeated.
      c. The verse begins in G minor and goes to B-flat major.
      d. The chorus begins in B-flat major, goes to D major in the "bridge" section, and then returns to B-flat through the circle of fifths.
   3. The lyrics by Gershwin's brother Ira are fresh, catchy, and full of slang.

H. Jazz in Europe
   1. In the 1920s, jazz spread quickly throughout North America, Latin America, and Europe.
   2. Europeans were exposed to jazz through imported recordings, sheet music, and traveling jazz ensembles.
   3. African-American musician soldiers in Europe during World War I helped to introduce the style.
   4. By the 1930s, a European jazz tradition was well established, and jazz was a frequent subject in European literature and arts (see **HWM Figure 32.6**).
   5. Django Reinhardt (1910–1953)
      a. The gypsy guitarist formed the Quintette du Hot Club de France, one of the most successful and innovative jazz bands in Europe.
      b. Reinhardt blended jazz with the traditions of gypsy music.

I. Duke Ellington (1899–1974) (see **HWM biography,** page 860, and **Figure 32.7**)
   1. Edward Kennedy ("Duke") Ellington is the most important composer of jazz to date.
   2. Biography
      a. Ellington was born in Washington, D. C., the son of a White House butler.
      b. He studied piano, including ragtime, from the age of seven.
      c. In 1923 he went to New York with his band, the Washingtonians, where he played on Broadway and in Harlem at the famous Cotton Club, and made recordings.
      d. Seen as a national treasure, he made several international tours sponsored by the U. S. State Department.
   3. Cotton Club period (1927–31)
      a. In Harlem, the Cotton Club offered alcohol and entertainment by black performers; it catered to white audiences.
      b. Here Ellington developed his individual style and began to gain national recognition.
      c. The stability of this environment allowed Ellington to experiment.
      d. He created longer jazz works, such as *Creole Rhapsody* and *Reminiscing in Tempo*.

   e. Ellington moved the group towards greater reliance on arrangements.
   f. He often crafted his numbers around specific performers.
4. Ellington and his band began touring in 1931.
5. The band grew in size to reach eighteen performers by 1946.
6. Many of Ellington's works were sold as popular songs, such as *Sophisticated Lady* and *Don't Get Around Much Anymore*.
7. Ellington reached a creative peak in the early 1940s, when he added three important new members to his band:
   a. Jimmie Blanton on bass
   b. Ben Webster on tenor saxophone
   c. Billy Strayhorn as second pianist, composer, and arranger; he produced a number of standards such as *Take the A Train* (1941)
8. *Cotton Tail* (1940; see **NAWM 152** and **HWM Example 32.3**)
   a. Ellington composed the work to showcase Blanton and Webster.
   b. It follows the standard jazz form: a tune, given at the beginning, is followed by a series of choruses.
   c. The tune is composed over the harmonic progression of Gershwin's *I Got Rhythm* (**NAWM 151**), a technique that is called *contrafact.*
   d. Ellington's tune is quite distinct from Gershwin's melody.
   e. The first two choruses feature Ben Webster on tenor saxophone accompanied by the rhythm section.
   f. Webster does not vary the tune, but creates new ideas over the given progressions.
   g. The remaining three choruses present various combinations of instruments in a call-and-response fashion.
   h. Ellington's tune returns at the end of the work
9. Ellington considered his music as "beyond category"; jazz was both entertainment and art music.
10. He pushed the time limits of recordings, composed suites, and created jazz versions of classical favorites, such as Tchaikovsky's *Nutcracker*.

VIII. Film Music
   A. Sound film changed the role of music in film.
      1. *The Jazz Singer* (1927), the first "talking picture," included several scenes of Al Jolson singing.
      2. Two categories of music can be heard in film.
         a. Diegetic music, or source music, is music that is heard or performed by the characters themselves.
         b. Nondiegetic music, or underscoring, is background music that conveys a mood or other aspects of a scene or character.
      3. The advent of sound put theater musicians out of work, but by the mid-1930s Hollywood studios employed composers and other musicians.
   B. Both dramas and comedies included musical numbers.
      1. *Der blaue Engel* (The Blue Angel, 1930) featured Marlene Dietrich's signature song, *Falling in Love Again*.
      2. Hollywood began producing numerous musicals.
      3. Romberg, Gershwin, Berlin, Kern, and Porter all wrote musicals during the Golden Age of the Hollywood musical.
      4. Some musicals were enlivened by the spectacular choreography of Busby Berkeley.
      5. Many performers became stars through musicals, such *The Wizard of Oz* (1939), which launched the career of Judy Garland.
   C. Film scores
      1. In Hollywood, film scores were integrated into the dramatic action.
      2. Max Steiner (1888–1971), an immigrant from Vienna, became one of the foremost composers in Hollywood.
         a. He established the model for Hollywood film scoring with his music for *King Kong* (1933; see **HWM Figure 32.8**).
         b. In this film, Steiner uses leitmotives for characters and ideas and coordinates the music with actions onscreen.
         c. Steiner composed into the 1960s, and his scores include *Gone with the Wind* (1939) and *Casablanca* (1943).
      3. Other major film composers in Hollywood
         a. Erich Wolfgang Korngold (1897–1957), from Vienna: *The Adventures of Robin Hood* (1938)
         b. Alfred Newman (1900–1970), the first major American-born film composer: *Wuthering Heights, The Song of Bernadette, How the West Was Won, Airport*
      4. Animations also featured strong musical accompaniments.
         a. Carl Stalling created music for Disney—*Steamboat Willie* (1928) was the first sound cartoon—and later for Warner Brothers (Looney Tunes).

   b. Disney created the first feature-length animation, *Snow White and the Seven Dwarfs* (1937), with a score by Frank Churchill.

IX. New Canons of Classics
   A. American popular music, jazz, and film music reached audiences around the world.
   B. Since the music could now be preserved, new classics were created.
      1. By 1970, classic canons had developed for popular song, blues, jazz, and film music.
      2. These canons parallel those of classical music that developed in the nineteenth century.
      3. Like much of the traditional classical repertory, the new classics were largely created by performers.

## SUGGESTIONS FOR SUPPLEMENTARY READING/LISTENING/ACTIVITIES

The complete recordings of Enrico Caruso from 1902–1920 were released by Naxos in 2004. Have students listen to both the recording quality and to his artistry. Compare this sound with recordings made after 1925, and compare his interpretation with contemporary tenors. Discuss the impact of recordings on music performers.

Compact-disc recordings are available for other turn-of-the-century performers, such as pianist Sergei Rachmaninov (RCA 61265, 1992, Decca 425964, 1990, and RCA 61658, 1994) and violinist Fritz Kreisler (EMI Classics 64701, 1993 and RCA 69488, 1997). In these recordings, they perform some of their own compositions. Have students compare their interpretations with recent performers. Discuss the obligations of a performer to the composer. How much liberty does a current performer have to reinterpret works that have been recorded by their composer? Direct this discussion then to popular music and new performances of classics by the Beatles and others.

Have a radio show class. Assign students to listen and report on recordings of various types of radio shows, including performances by the NBC Symphony Orchestra as directed by Toscanini, which are readily available from RCA, and Benny Goodman Camel Caravan performances (Phontastic 8818, 2000). Other radio shows, such as Orson Welles's *War of the Worlds,* with music by Bernard Herrmann, are also available. Compare the recording quality with those made before 1925 and discuss the cultural impact of performances such as these that would be heard across the nation. Has the advent of television improved America's cultural life?

Obtain a copy of *Hollywood Revue* (1929) and watch portions to get an idea of the types of productions that would be found in New York revues. Some of the better acts include Joan Crawford dancing the Charleston, a color comedy sketch on *Romeo and Juliet,* and an elaborate dance rendition of *Singin' in the Rain.* The Best Picture winner in 1936 was a biography of Florenz Ziegfeld, *The Great Ziegfeld.* The musical highlight was a performance by the legendary Fanny Brice, who was portrayed by Barbara Streisand in the musical *Funny Girl.*

*The Student Prince* was adapted to film in 1954 starring Mario Lanza. Watch a portion of the film and discuss the attributes of operetta and some of its drawbacks when compared with the musical.

There are three filmed versions of *Show Boat,* from 1929, 1936, and 1951. Of these the second is recommended both for its superior quality and its glimpse into the 1930s. The 1951 production is also of good quality, is more readily available, and is in color.

Several compact-disc recordings (e.g. Razor & Tie 82144, 1997) are devoted to the voice of Ethel Merman, who sings songs by Berlin, Porter, Gershwin, and others.

*The Smithsonian Collection of Classic Jazz* (Washington, D. C.: Smithsonian Recordings, several reissues) contains examples of musical styles covered in Chapter 32. The accompanying booklet is a miniature jazz history reader.

This is a good time to introduce students to some of the major research tools in the library for popular music, including the second edition of *The New Grove Dictionary of Jazz,* ed. Barry Kernfeld (London, Macmillan Publishers, 2002), the second edition of *The Encyclopedia of the Musical Theatre,* ed. Kurt Gänzl (New York: Schirmer Books, 2001), and Ken Bloom's *American Song: The Complete Musical Theatre Companion,* second ed. 1877–1995 (New York: Schirmer, 1996) and *American Song: The Complete Companion to Tin Pan Alley Song* (New York: Schirmer, 2001).

Mamie Smith's recording of *Crazy Blues* is available on compact disc (Sony 065712, 2004). For outstanding examples of Delta blues, listen to the complete recordings of Robert Johnson (Sony 46222, 1990).

King Oliver's Creole Jazz Band can be heard on the compact-disc recording Challenge 79008, 1997. Armstrong's Hot Five and Hot Seven recordings can be heard on the compact disc Sony 63527, 2000.

Many recordings of big bands have been released. An overview of Duke Ellington's recordings is available in a box set (Proper Box UK 1025, 2001). Careful selections taken from Francis Ford Coppola's film *The Cotton Club* (1984) can give students a perspective on ambiance of Duke Ellington's early years.

Assign a brief paper contrasting Duke Ellington's incorporation of classical elements in jazz works (for example, *Black, Brown and Beige* or *Harlem*) and George Gershwin's incorporation of jazz elements in a classic idiom (for example *Rhapsody in Blue*, Concerto in F, or *Porgy and Bess*). For a longer paper, have students place both these composers in the context of the Harlem Renaissance.

Django Reinhardt and the Quintette du Hot Club de France can be heard on a number of compact-disc releases, including ASV Living Era 5267, 1998. A realistic depiction of jazz life in Paris, although from later decades, can be seen in the 1986 film *'Round Midnight* featuring Dexter Gordon and Herbie Hancock.

A DVD recording of Gershwin's *Porgy and Bess* is available directed by Trevor Nunn (EMI Distribution, 2001).

For more information on film music, see Roy Prendergast, *Film Music: A Neglected Art*, second ed. (New York: W. W. Norton, 1992); William Darby and Jack Du Bois, *American Film Music: Major Composers, Techniques, Trends, 1915–90* (Jefferson, N. C.: McFarland & Company, 1990); and Roger Hickman, *Reel Music: Exploring 100 Years of Film Music* (New York: W. W. Norton, 2006).

## OBJECTIVE QUESTIONS

1. The man who created the premier series of revues in New York was ____________.
   a. Sigmund Romberg
   b. Florenz Ziegfeld
   c. Busby Berkeley
   d. James P. Johnson
   e. Franz Léhar

   Answer: b

2. Who composed the music for *Show Boat*?
   a. Irving Berlin
   b. George Gershwin
   c. Cole Porter
   d. Jerome Kern
   e. Richard Rodgers

   Answer: d

3. Of the following, which does *not* describe *Show Boat*?
   a. It is operatic in scope.
   b. The plot is a simple romantic comedy.
   c. It employs the styles of ragtime, spirituals, and marches.
   d. It taps into the traditions of operetta, musical comedy, and revues.
   e. It was a tremendous success.

   Answer: b

4. What characterized Tin Pan Alley songs after 1910?
   a. The length of the verse was doubled.
   b. Blues melodies became the dominant song type.
   c. There was a steady decline in the popularity of song due to radio.
   d. Most songs adopted a free form similar to the Delta blues.
   e. The focus was increasingly on the chorus.

   Answer: e

5. Of the following, which is true of Irving Berlin?
   a. He wrote his own lyrics.
   b. He wrote for Tin Pan Alley, but not for Broadway musicals.
   c. He merged popular songs together with classical European traditions.
   d. He refused to write songs for revues.
   e. He wrote waltz tunes but was uncomfortable with ragtime.

   Answer: a

Use the following answers for questions 6–10.
   a. New Orleans jazz
   b. Delta blues
   c. European jazz
   d. classic blues
   e. swing music

6. W. C. Handy is known for his work in this genre.

   Answer: d

7. Benny Goodman is known for his work in this genre.

   Answer: e

8. Django Reinhardt is known for his work in this genre.

   Answer: c

9. Joe "King" Oliver is known for his work in this genre.

   Answer: a

10. Robert Johnson is known for his work in this genre.

    Answer: b

11. Of the following, which does *not* characterize the blues?
    a. flattened or bent notes
    b. touches of humor
    c. texts about disappointments and troubles
    d. straightforward melodic style without syncopations
    e. distinctive vocal and instrumental effects

    Answer: d

12. What form does the classic blues song take?
    a. verse-chorus
    b. AABA'
    c. three four-measure phrases
    d. strophic
    e. through-composed

    Answer: c

13. King Oliver enticed Louis Armstrong to move to which city?
    a. Chicago
    b. New York
    c. Memphis
    d. Los Angeles
    e. Paris

    Answer: a

14. The New Orleans jazz form is similar to what classical structure?
    a. rondo
    b. theme and variation
    c. sonata
    d. ritornello
    e. da capo

    Answer: b

15. Big bands are divided into which three sections?
    a. strings, brass, rhythm
    b. brass, woodwinds, rhythm
    c. strings, brass, reeds
    d. brass, reeds, rhythm
    e. soloists, ensemble players, rhythm

    Answer: d

16. Gershwin's first attempt to combine jazz and classical traditions was ____________.
    a. *Porgy and Bess*
    b. Concerto in F
    c. *American in Paris*
    d. *Girl Crazy*
    e. *Rhapsody in Blue*

    Answer: e

17. In what way does big band music differ from New Orleans jazz?
    a. It has more improvisation.
    b. It works through arrangements.
    c. It is more spontaneous.
    d. It features a rhythm section.
    e. It accommodates a wider variety of instruments.

    Answer: b

18. The Cotton Club, where Duke Ellington got established, is located in ____________.
    a. Chicago
    b. Harlem
    c. New Orleans
    d. Memphis
    e. Broadway

    Answer: b

19. In film, what is diegetic music?
    a. scores with minimal cues
    b. music that functions in the background
    c. music that is heard by the characters themselves
    d. the same as underscoring
    e. recurring themes in film music

    Answer: c

20. Who composed the music for *King Kong*, *Gone with the Wind*, and *Casablanca*?
    a. Erich Korngold
    b. Max Steiner
    c. Alfred Newman
    d. Carl Stahling
    e. Frank Churchill

    Answer: b

## SHORT-ESSAY QUESTIONS

1. Discuss the impact of technology on popular music between the wars.
2. Describe the two basic types of blues, significant blues performers, and the importance of blues to twentieth-century popular music.
3. Compare New Orleans jazz with big band jazz. Mention major performers and recordings in each style.
4. Give an overview of the life and music of Duke Ellington. Suggest why he is considered to be the foremost jazz musician up to this time.

## TERMS FOR IDENTIFICATION

NBC Symphony Orchestra
Ziegfeld Follies
blues
classic blues
twelve-bar blues
Delta blues
Robert Johnson
New Orleans jazz
King Oliver's Creole Jazz Band
Hot Five
rhythm section
chorus
scat singing
big band
arranger
swing
Django Reinhardt
Cotton Club
contrafact
beyond category
diegetic music/source music
nondiegetic music/underscoring

**CHAPTER 33**

# Between the World Wars: The Classical Tradition

I. Music, Politics, and the People
  A. Music became increasingly tied to politics.
    1. In the nineteenth century, some felt that music transcended politics.
    2. Even then, music could not escape its association with the social elite and nationalism.
    3. In the 1930s, the Soviet Union and Germany suppressed modernist music.
  B. Music in the United States
    1. During the Depression, composers were concerned about the gap between modernism and audiences.
      a. They began to compose in more accessible styles.
      b. They wrote music for films, theater, and dance, some of which addressed social issues.
      c. Music in a modern style was written for amateur performers.
    2. Composers in the Americas won international recognition with music that reflected their national heritage.
    3. In the United States, an ultramodernist tradition emerged as well.
  C. Most governments sponsored musical activities.
    1. Public schools increasingly included music in the curriculum.
    2. A teaching method by Zoltán Kodály was adopted in schools across Europe and North America.
    3. Government-controlled radio in Europe employed musicians.
    4. The New Deal in the United States created programs for unemployed musicians.

II. France
  A. Politics and musical life had long been intertwined in France.
  B. After World War I, nationalists argued that French music was classic, as opposed to the Romanticism of Germany.
    1. Neoclassicism became prevalent in France and was characterized by:
      a. Classical genres and forms
      b. Tonal centers, often created through neotonality
      c. Restrained emotions and the rejection of Romantic excess
    2. The definition of "classic" was debated.
      a. Conservatives, like d'Indy, saw it as meaning balance, order, and tradition.
      b. Leftist composers, like Ravel, saw it as encompassing the international and not merely the national.
  C. Les Six
    1. "*Les Six*" (The Six) was a group of six young composers who drew inspiration from Satie (see **HWM Figure 33.1**).
      a. Arthur Honegger (1892–1955)
      b. Darius Milhaud (1892–1974)
      c. Francis Poulenc (1899–1963)
      d. Germaine Tailleferre (1892–1983)
      e. Georges Auric (1899–1983)
      f. Louis Durey (1888–1979)
    2. They adopted neoclassicism but avoided political dichotomies.
    3. The group collaborated in several joint projects, but each went in an individual way.
      a. Durey never fully conformed to the doctrines.

b. Tailleferre, the most neoclassic, drew upon Couperin and Rameau in her Piano Concerto (1923–24) and other works.
c. Auric was the most taken with Satie's avant-garde approach.
d. Honegger, Milhaud, and Poulenc achieved the greatest success.

D. Arthur Honegger
1. Musical style
a. Dramatic action and graphic gesture
b. Short-breathed melodies
c. Strong ostinato rhythms
d. Bold colors
e. Dissonant harmonies
2. *Pacific 231* (1923), a symphonic movement that creates the impression of a speeding locomotive, was hailed as a modernist masterpiece.
3. *King David* (1923), an oratorio, established his international reputation.
a. Honegger combines the tradition of amateur chorus with allusions to Gregorian chant, Baroque polyphony, and jazz.
b. Neoclassicism can be seen in the use of pre-Romantic styles, traditional forms, and the prevailing diatonic language.

E. Darius Milhaud
1. Milhaud was extremely prolific and composed in a wide variety of genres.
2. His works are stylistically diverse.
a. *Le boeuf sur la toit* (The Ox on the Roof, 1919), a ballet, is comic.
b. *Christophe Colomb* (1928), an opera-oratorio, is earnest.
c. *Sacred Service* (1947) reflects Milhaud's Jewish heritage.
3. Milhaud incorporated sounds from the Americas.
a. *La creation du monde* (The Creation of the World, 1923), a ballet, features saxophones, ragtime syncopations, and the blues.
b. *Le boeuf sur la toit* (The Bull on the Roof, 1919) and *Saudades do Brasil* (Souvenirs of Brazil, 1920–21) contain Brazilian folk melodies and rhythms.
4. *Saudades do Brasil* also features polytonality, a technique that he employed in other works as well (see **HWM Example 33.1**).
5. Although he absorbed neoclassicism, his openness to foreign influences ranging from Schoenberg to jazz set him apart from d'Indy and the others.

F. Francis Poulenc
1. Poulenc drew upon the Parisian popular chanson tradition found in cabarets and revues, thereby violating the strictures of d'Indy.
2. His music can be graceful, witty, and satirical.
3. A wide range of styles were employed by Poulenc in his instrumental works, including neoclassicism, song-influenced melodies, and mild dissonance.
4. He excelled in vocal works, including sacred works and songs.
5. *Dialogues of the Carmelites* (1956), a three-act opera, raises political issues in its depiction of the execution of the Carmelite nuns during the French Revolution.

III. Germany

A. During the Weimar Republic (1919–1933), political contentions were echoed in music.

B. Nazis came into power in 1933.
1. Modernist music was attacked for being decadent.
2. People on the political left and Jews were banned from public life.
3. Many leading musicians left the country.

C. New Objectivity emerged in the 1920s.
1. This was a trend against the emotional intensity and complexity of the late Romantics and the expressionism of Schoenberg and Berg.
2. It used familiar elements borrowed from sources such as jazz, Classical, and Baroque music.
3. Followers believed that music should be objective and widely accessible.

D. Ernst Krenek (1900–1991)
1. *Jonny spielt auf* (1927) exemplifies the ideals of New Objectivity.
a. Krenek's opera uses European and African-American jazz traditions.
b. The opera was a success, but was attacked by Nazis for using African-American elements.
2. Krenek later adopted the twelve-tone method and moved to the United States.

E. Kurt Weill (1900–1950)
1. Weill was also an advocate of New Objectivity.
2. An opera composer, he sought to combine social commentary with entertainment for everyday people rather than the intellectual elite.
3. *Die Dreigroschenoper* (The Threepenny Opera, 1928)

   a. Another collaborative effort with Brecht, this opera is based on the libretto of John Gay's *The Beggar's Opera.*
   b. Lotte Lenya, Weill's wife, sang in the production and championed Weill's works after his death (see **HWM Figure 33.2**).
   c. It parodies American songs and juxtaposes eighteenth-century ballad texts, European dance music, and American jazz.
   d. The work was an enormous international hit, but the Nazis banned it in 1933.
4. *Aufstieg und Fall der Stadt Mahagonny* (Rise and Fall of the City of Mahagonny, 1930)
   a. Weill collaborated with Bertolt Brecht on this allegorical opera.
   b. Weill incorporates elements of popular music and jazz, which can be heard in the inclusion of jazz instruments in the pit orchestra.
   c. The story exposed the failures of capitalism.
5. Weill came to the United States and composed Broadway musicals, where he continued to exhibit characteristics of New Objectivity.

F. Music under the Nazis
1. The Reich Chamber of Culture included a Reich Music Chamber, to which all musicians had to belong.
2. Richard Strauss was the first president, but was forced to resign when he continued to collaborate with a Jewish librettist.
3. Nazis stipulated that music should not be dissonant, intellectual, Jewish, or jazz-influenced.
4. Nazis focused on performances of the German tradition, especially the music of Wagner.

G. Carl Orff (1895–1982)
1. Orff established an international reputation, despite remaining in Germany.
2. He was not sympathetic toward the Nazi regime.
3. His best-known work is *Carmina burana* (1936), for chorus and orchestra.
   a. The texts are medieval goliard songs.
   b. Orff employed a simple neomodal idiom.
   c. Drawing from Stravinsky and other sources, Orff created a pseudo-antique style using drones, ostinatos, harmonic stasis, and strophic repetition.
4. Orff also developed methods and materials for teaching music in schools.

IV. Paul Hindemith (1900–1950)

A. Significance
1. Hindemith was one of the most prolific composers of the twentieth century.
2. He was an important teacher and thought of himself as a practicing musician.

B. The Weimar period
1. He began composing in a late Romantic style.
2. He then developed an individual expressionist style.
3. Soon he adopted the aesthetics of New Objectivity.
   a. He composed seven works entitled *Kammermusik* (Chamber Music, 1922–27) that encompass a variety of forms, including neo-Baroque ritornello.
   b. These later works are neotonal.
4. Gebrauchmusik (music for use)
   a. Hindemith was disturbed by the gulf between modern music and audiences.
   b. Gebrauchmusik was intended for young or amateur performers.
   c. The style was modern, the quality good, and the music challenging and rewarding to perform.
5. *Mathis der Maler* (1934–35)
   a. Hindemith's opera questioned the role of politics in the arts.
   b. He forged a symphony from the opera entitled Symphony *Mathis der Maler* (1933–34), his best-known work.
   c. The story is based on the life the artist Matthias Grünewald, who painted the Isenheim alterpiece (see **HWM Figure 33.3**).
   d. Grünewald struggles between his role in a rebellion and his art, perhaps an allegory for Hindemith's own career.
   e. The Nazis banned the opera in 1936.
6. Harmonic fluctuation
   a. Hindemith developed a neo-Romantic style for *Mathis der Maler* that uses harmonic fluctuation.
   b. Harmonic fluctuation is a harmonic method based on growing dissonance and eventual return to consonance (see **HWM Example 33.2**).

C. Hindemith left Germany and settled in the United States; his later works include:
1. Sonatas for almost every orchestral instrument
2. *Ludus tonalis* (Tonal Play, 1942)
   a. This work for piano recalls Bach's *Well-Tempered Clavier*.

b. It has twelve fugues, each centered on a different note in the chromatic scale.

3. *Symphonic Metamorphosis after Themes of Carl Maria von Weber* (1943)
4. Symphony in B-flat for band (1951)

D. *Un cygne* (A Swan, 1939), from *Six Chansons* (**NAWM 153**)

1. *Six Chansons* are settings of poems by Rainier Maria Rilke for a cappella chorus.
   a. Composed in Switzerland, these works are for amateur or school performers.
   b. In the tradition of the chanson, the text is set syllabically and with sensitive declamation.
2. The first section is based on the first two lines of poetry.
   a. The first phrase suggests the gliding of a swan with a gentle melodic phrase over parallel fourth chords.
   b. The next two phrases vary these ideas.
   c. The second line begins with brief imitation (measures 5–7) and warmly supports the image of the loved one.
3. The second section interweaves the two ideas of the first section.
   a. The opening idea returns (measures 11–14).
   b. The music expands with the reference to "our troubled soul."
   c. The final phrase reprises the opening motive and the idea associated with the loved one.
4. The harmony exemplifies the technique of harmonic fluctuation, which moves from relative consonant to dissonance and back to consonance.

V. The Soviet Union

A. The government controlled all aspects of the arts.

1. Theaters, conservatories, concert halls, and other music institutions were nationalized.
2. Concert programming was strictly regulated.

B. During the relatively freer 1920s, two organizations were established.

1. The Association for Contemporary Music sought to continue modernist trends established by Scriabin and others.
2. The Russian Association of Proletarian Musicians, seeing the modernist tradition as being elitist, encouraged simple music with mass appeal.
3. After Stalin came into power in 1929, dissent was quashed, and the two groups were replaced in 1933 by the Union of Soviet Composers.

C. In 1934, a writers' congress promulgated socialist realism as the ideal for Soviet arts.

1. Realism was adopted for literature, drama, and painting.
2. Works needed to portray socialism in a positive light.
3. Music was created with some of these qualities:
   a. A relatively simple and accessible language
   b. Emphasis on melody, often drawn from folk styles
   c. Patriotic and inspirational subject matter
4. "Formalism" was a derogatory term for interest in modernism and music for its own sake.

D. Sergey Prokofiev (1891–1953)

1. Prokofiev made an initial reputation as a radical modernist.
2. He left Russia after the Revolution.
   a. He resided in North America and western Europe for almost two decades.
   b. During this time he composed solo piano works and concertos for his own performance.
   c. Among his commissioned works are the opera *The Love for Three Oranges* (1921), written for Chicago, and ballets for Diaghilev.
3. Prokofiev returned to the Soviet Union in 1936 and fulfilled several Soviet commissions.
   a. *Lieutenant Kijé* (1934), originally for film and later arranged as an orchestral suite
   b. *Romeo and Juliet* (1935–36), a ballet
   c. *Peter and the Wolf* (1936), a narrated fairy tale for orchestra
   d. *Alexander Nevsky* (1938), a cantata drawn from film music
4. When government control relaxed, Prokofiev turned to classical genres.
5. The Piano Sonatas Nos. 6–8 (1939–44) and the Fifth Symphony are largely tonal, but contain some distinctive features of his earlier style.
6. After World War II, Prokofiev was admonished for being a "formalist."

E. Dmitri Shostakovich (1906–1975) (see **HWM Figure 33.4**)

1. Shostakovich was trained within the Soviet system.
2. In the 1920s, he was aligned with the modernist composers.
3. The First Symphony (1926) brought him international recognition.

4. *Lady Macbeth of the Mtsensk District*
   a. The opera premiered in 1934 and was initially a great success.
   b. Stalin, however, was angered by its content and style.
   c. Shostakovich was criticized in the newspaper *Pravda* for his dissonances and lack of melody (see **HWM Source Reading,** page 879).
   d. The production was closed, and Shostakovich may have feared for his life.

F. The Fifth Symphony (1937) received great acclaim.
   1. The symphony can be seen as a response to the criticism of his opera; the work was described as "a Soviet artist's reply to just criticism."
   2. The symphony conforms to social realism with its optimistic, populist outlook and its easily understood tonal language.
   3. Inspired by Mahler, the work encompasses a wide range of styles and moods.
   4. It is a heroic symphony in the vein of Beethoven and Tchaikovsky, with four movements.
      a. The dynamic opening movement, in sonata form, suggests a struggle.
      b. The scherzo-like allegretto adopts the jarring contrasts of a Mahler scherzo.
      c. The sorrowful slow movement evokes traditional Russian funeral music.
      d. The finale is boisterous, but the triumphal character can also be interpreted as false enthusiasm.

G. The Fifth Symphony (1937), second movement (**NAWM 154**)
   1. The movement follows the traditional ABA of the classical scherzo.
   2. Section A is modified binary form.
      a. The material develops from a number of motives.
      b. Shostakovich provides strong contrasts of colors and styles, including a crude waltz and a boisterous military march.
   3. Section B, in a rounded binary form, features an elegant waltz theme played by a solo violin.
   4. The reprise of A alters the orchestration at the beginning, recalling the timbres of Beethoven's Symphony No. 5.
   5. The harmony contains many unexpected turns.
      a. The tonal areas seem to be more often asserted than established.
      b. The work seems to be neotonal music pretending to be tonal.

H. Later works
   1. The Seventh Symphony (Leningrad, 1941), which deals programmatically with the defense of Leningrad against Hitler's armies, won sympathetic audiences in the United States and Britain.
   2. Shostakovich was subject to the same crackdown that affected Prokofiev.
   3. He signed a number of his works with the notes D–E-flat–C–B (in German nomenclature, that is D–Es–C–H for **D**mitri **SCH**ostakovich).

VI. The Americas

A. Several composers from the Americas gained international recognition between the wars.
   1. These composers created distinctive national styles.
   2. Sometimes their nationalism was linked with politics.

B. Canada
   1. Musical life in Canada was similar to musical life in the United States.
   2. Concerts primarily presented the European classical repertoire.
   3. Professional orchestras were founded in major cities during the twentieth century, beginning with Quebec (1903) and Toronto (1906).
   4. Claude Champagne (1891–1965) was the first Canadian composer to achieve an international reputation.
      a. He learned French-Canadian fiddle tunes and dances in his youth.
      b. As a young man, he was deeply influenced by Russian composers.
      c. He studied in Paris (1921–28), where he encountered Renaissance polyphony and the music of Fauré and Debussy.
      d. He developed a distinctive national style in *Suite canadienne* (Canadian Suite, 1927) for chorus and orchestra, using elements from French-Canadian folk music and polyphonic French chansons.
      e. *Dance villageoise* (Village Dance, 1929), his best-known work, evokes both French-Canadian and Irish folk styles.

C. Brazil
   1. Art music had been established in Brazil by the end of the nineteenth century with the operas of Gomes and the works of several others.
   2. Heitor Villa-Lobos (1887–1959) was the most important Brazilian composer.
      a. He blended traditional Brazilian elements with modernism.

   b. Between 1923 and 1930, he spent most of his time in Paris, where he established himself as Latin America's most prominent composer.
   c. Returning to Brazil in 1930, he promoted music in schools through choral singing.
   d. He has been criticized for supporting the Brazilian dictatorship.
3. *Choros* (1920–28), a series of fourteen pieces, is among Villa-Lobos's most characteristic works.
   a. The title is a type of popular ensemble music in the streets of Rio de Janeiro.
   b. The works are for various media from solo guitar or piano to orchestra with chorus.
   c. Each blends a vernacular style of Brazil with modernistic techniques.
4. *Bachianas brasileiras* (1930–45), a set of nine works, pays homage to Bach.
   a. Each is a suite of two to four movements.
   b. These neoclassic works combine elements of Baroque and Brazilian folk music.
   c. Villa-Lobos's most famous work is *Bachianas brasileiras No. 5* (1938–45) for solo soprano and eight cellos.

D. Mexico
1. Beginning in 1921, the Mexican government promoted a new nationalism in the arts that drew on native Indian cultures.
2. Diego Rivera and other artists were commissioned to paint murals in public buildings that illustrated Mexican life (see **HWM Figure 33.5**).
3. Carlos Chávez (1899–1978) was the first composer associated with the new nationalism.
   a. He served as conductor of Mexico's first professional orchestra and director of the national conservatory.
   b. He composed two ballets on Aztec scenarios.
   c. *Sinfonia india* (Indian Symphony, 1935–36) uses Indian melodies in a modernist idiom.
   d. *Sinfonia romantica* (Symphony No. 4, 1953) is not so overtly nationalist.
4. Silvestre Revueltas (1899–1940)
   a. Revueltas studied in Mexico and the United States.
   b. His music combines folklike melodies and popular music with a modernist idiom.

E. *Sensemayá* (1938) by Silvestre Revueltas (**NAWM 155**)
1. This symphonic work is a song without words based on a poem by the Cuban poet Nicolás Guillén.
2. The poem tells of an African-Cuban magical rite in which a snake is symbolically killed.
3. Revueltas set the poem to a melody, and then used the melody (without the words) throughout the work.
4. The work can be seen in four sections (see diagram in the **NAWM 155** commentary).
5. Section 1 (measures 1–87)
   a. Throughout this section, percussion instruments play a pattern of eight eighth notes in 7/8 meter; the pattern suggests the name "sen-se-ma-yá."
   b. The bass clarinet and bassoon play ostinatos that are passed on to other instruments.
   c. The snake theme enters in the tuba (measures 9–20) and is later picked up by other instruments.
   d. The first four stanzas of the melody alternate between the strings and trombones, beginning in measure 46.
   e. An interlude closes the first section and presents a new theme representing man (trumpet, E-flat clarinet, and flute, measures 76–84).
6. Section 2 (measures 88–99)
   a. The dramatic confrontation with the snake is depicted, as suggested by the fifth stanza.
   b. The "sen-se-ma-yá" rhythm is altered, and the trombones play the new rhythmic figure.
7. Section 3 (measures 100–149)
   a. The material, which is similar to that of the first section, is frequently interrupted by a single measure of 7/16 with rapid sixteenth-note figures.
   b. The struggle between snake and man is suggested.
   c. The theme of man reappears (measure 119).
   d. The trombones state the melody for the sixth stanza (measures 133–142).
   e. An interlude pictures violent blows to the snake (measure 142) and the writhing snake's death agony (measure 145).
8. Section 4 (measures 150–172)
   a. The celebratory postlude presents the last stanza of the poem.
   b. Earlier themes return and build to a powerful climax.

VII. The United States
   A. New musical links developed between the United States and Europe.
      1. Many European composers fled to the United States and became teachers.
      2. American composers went to France instead of Germany for study abroad.
      3. Nadia Boulanger (1887–1979) taught classes in Paris for America's leading composers.
   B. Two trends developed among American composers during this time.
      1. An experimental trend focused on new musical resources.
      2. An Americanist trend blended nationalism with a new populism.
      3. Both drew upon European tradition but asserted independence as well.
   C. Edgard Varèse (1883–1965)
      1. Born in France, Varèse studied at the Schola Cantorum and Conservatoire.
      2. He was influenced by Debussy, Schoenberg, and Stravinsky.
      3. He moved to New York in 1915 and there wrote his first major work, *Amériques* (1918–21).
      5. Varèse created a series of works that sought to liberate composition from musical conventions, such as *Intégrales* (1924–25) and *Ionisation* (for percussion only, 1929–31).
      6. He believed that sounds were the essential structural components of music, and he considered all sounds acceptable as raw material.
         a. He imagined music as spatial, akin to an aural ballet.
         b. Sound masses—bodies of sound characterized by a particular timbre, register, rhythm, and melodic gesture—moved through music space.
         c. These sound masses change and interact.
      6. A great variety of percussion instruments are treated as equals to strings and winds.
      7. For Varèse, form is not something you start with but the result of the working out of material.
      8. Seeking new sounds, he turned to electronic sound generation and the tape recorder in two works created in the 1950s:
         a. *Déserts* (1950–54) for winds, percussion, and tape
         b. *Poème electronique* (1957–58) for tape
   D. Henry Cowell (1897–1965)
      1. Raised in California, Cowell had little training in traditional music.
      2. Many of his early pieces are experimental works for piano.
         a. *The Tides of Manaunaun* (ca. 1917) uses tone clusters sometimes created by pressing his fist or forearm on the keys.
         b. *The Aeolian Harp* (1923) has the player strum the piano strings while holding down chords on the keyboard.
         c. *The Banshee* (1925) requires an assistant to hold down the damper pedal while the pianist applies a variety of techniques to the strings.
      3. He summarized his ideas in *New Musical Resources* (1930).
      4. Eclectic in his choices, Cowell incorporated American, Irish, and Asian elements in his works.
      5. Cowell promoted music of others through concerts and the periodical *New Music*.
   E. Ruth Crawford Seeger (1901–1953) (see **HWM Figure 33.6**)
      1. Ruth Crawford was the first woman to win a Guggenheim Fellowship in music.
      2. She was most active as a composer between 1924 and 1933 in Chicago and New York.
      3. She studied with musicologist Charles Seeger, and they married in 1932.
      4. Seeger developed theories about modern techniques that Crawford refined and applied to her music.
      5. While in New York, she experimented with serial techniques, applying them to parameters other than pitch.
      6. She later believed that preserving folk songs was a greater contribution to the nation's musical life than writing more modernist works and began editing American folk songs from field recordings.
      7. The String Quartet (1931) is Crawford's best-known work.
         a. In the first movement, four thematic ideas unfold in dissonant counterpoint.
         b. The second movement develops a short motive through counterpoint and convergence.
         c. The third movement features all four instruments sustaining long tones and taking turns coming to the foreground with crescendos.
   F. String Quartet, finale by Ruth Crawford (see **NAWM 156** and **HWM Example 33.3**)
      1. The entire musical fabric is repeated in retrograde transposed up a semitone (measures 58–59 are the pivot point).

2. Two-part counterpoint pits the first violin against the other instruments.
   a. The first violin begins with a single note and then continues adding one note at a time, always getting softer, until it reaches twenty-one notes.
   b. The other instruments, playing muted, interject phrases of twenty notes and then subtract one note at a time, always getting louder, until they're playing just one note.
   c. The first violin plays a variety of rhythmic values, but the lower strings play only eighth notes.
   d. The pitches of the lower strings are derived from a ten-note series, in which the notes are rotated (see diagram in commentary to **NAWM 156**).

VIII. Aaron Copland (1900–1990) (see **HWM Figure 33.7**)
   A. Biography
      1. Because of his Jewish faith, homosexuality, and leftist politics, he was somewhat of an outsider.
      2. He was one of the first American composers to study with Nadia Boulanger.
      3. He still became the most important central American composer of his generation.
   B. Compositional styles
      1. Jazz and strong dissonance play a part in his early works:
         a. *Music for the Theatre* (1925)
         b. Piano Concerto (1927)
      2. He developed a new style by reducing his modernist technique and combining it with simple textures and diatonic melodies and harmonies.
         a. *El Salón Mexico* (1932–36), an orchestra suite, incorporates Mexican folk songs.
         b. The ballets *Billy the Kid* (1938) and *Rodeo* (1942) use cowboy songs.
         c. He wrote the opera *The Second Hurricane* (1936) for schools.
         d. Film scores, including *Our Town* (1940), represent music "for use."
   C. *Appalachian Spring* (1943–44) (see **NAWM 157** and **HWM Example 33.4**)
      1. The ballet was written for Martha Graham, a leading modern dancer and choreographer.
      2. The story centers on a wedding in rural nineteenth-century Pennsylvania.
      3. The music won the Pulitzer Prize.
      4. Copland originally wrote this work for an ensemble of thirteen instruments, and later arranged it for full orchestra.
      5. Allegro and presto sections
         a. The changing meters, offbeat accents, and sudden changes of texture show the influence of Stravinsky.
         b. The diatonic melodies and harmonies, syncopation, and guitarlike chords give it an American character.
         c. Many passages combine consonant and dissonant notes of the diatonic scale, which has been called *pandiatonicism.*
         d. The rapid figures of the presto suggest country fiddling (measure 18).
         e. Counterpoint and motivic relationships link the work to European traditions.
      6. The Meno mosso (measure 138) produces a characteristic sound that suggests the open spaces and rugged people of frontier America.
         a. Leaps of fourths and fifths
         b. Wide spacing of chords
         c. Diatonic melodies
         d. Lightly dissonant diatonic chords
         e. A recollection of the beginning of the ballet (measure 151) includes superimposed tonic and dominant or tonic and subdominant triads.
      7. Variations on the Shaker hymn *Simple Gifts* (measure 171)
         a. The tune changes little in the successive variations.
         b. Variation one is for clarinet in A-flat major with simple accompaniment.
         c. Variation two (measure 191) is similar, a step lower, with the melody in the oboe and bassoon.
         d. Variation three, given to trombones and violas and later treated canonically, omits the second half of the tune.
         e. Variation four begins with the tune in the trumpet accompanied by the trombone.
         f. The final variation presents the two halves of the tune in reverse order.
      8. Copland's style has been widely imitated and has become the quintessential musical sound of America, heard often in film and television.
   D. Later works by Copland
      1. The Third Symphony (1946) continues to exhibit his American idiom.
      2. He later adopts the twelve-tone method in some of his works.
         a. Piano Quartet (1950)
         b. Piano Fantasy (1957)
         c. *Inscape* (1967)
      3. Through these stylistic changes, Copland maintained an artistic identity.

IX. Other Americanists
  A. William Grant Still (1895–1978) (see **HWM Figure 33.8**)
    1. Still's musical influences were diverse.
      a. Arranger for W. C. Handy
      b. Studies with Chadwick and Varèse
    2. He earned many "firsts" for an African-American musician:
      a. First to conduct a major orchestra in the United States (Los Angeles Philharmonic, 1936)
      b. First to have an opera produced by a major U. S. company (*Troubled Island* at New York's City Center, 1949)
      c. First to have an opera televised over a national network
    3. He composed over 150 compositions in the classical tradition, many of which incorporated American idioms.
  B. *Afro-American Symphony*, first movement (1930; **NAWM 158**)
    1. This was the first symphonic work by an African-American composer to be performed by a major American orchestra.
    2. It has the traditional four movements.
      a. First movement sonata form
      b. Second movement slow
      c. Third movement scherzo
      d. Fourth movement fast
    3. Although not explicitly programmatic, each movement is a character sketch linked to some verses from a poem by Paul Laurence Dunbar.
    4. Originally each movement had a subtitle: *Longings, Sorrows, Humor,* and *Aspirations*.
    5. The symphony incorporates African-American elements.
      a. Call and response
      b. Syncopations
      c. Varied repetition of short melodic or rhythmic ideas
      d. Jazz harmonies
      e. Dialogue between groups of instruments, as in a jazz arrangement
      f. Instrumental timbres common in jazz, such as trumpets and trombones muted with Harmon mutes
    6. The opening movement blends sonata form with an ABCBA form.
      a. A brief introductory melody in the English horn opens the symphony.
      b. The first theme, in the trumpet, has a twelve-bar blues structure in classic AAB form.
      c. The transition (measure 33) develops motives from the first theme.
      d. The second theme (measures 45–67), in G major, suggests a spiritual and is in an ABA' form.
      e. The development (beginning in measure 68) fragments and develops thematic material in a European manner.
      f. The recapitulation brings back the themes in reverse order (measures 104 and 114 respectively).
      g. The second theme returns in A-flat minor, and the first in A-flat major.
      h. A brief coda suggests the introduction.
  C. Virgil Thomson (1896–1989)
    1. Thomson was a composer and a critic for the *New York Herald Tribune*.
    2. He studied with Nadia Boulanger.
    3. He was greatly influenced by Satie.
    4. He rejected modernism's complexities and the obsession with past classical traditions.
    5. Thomson collaborated with Gertrude Stein on the opera *Four Saints in Three Acts* (1927–28)
      a. The libretto, based on the life of St. Teresa of Avila, seems absurdist.
      b. Thomson's music reflects the nature of the text and mixes dance rhythms with familiar musical styles and diatonic chords.
      c. The result is often wild, with surprising juxtapositions.
    6. Thomson's other music is more overtly American.
      a. *Variations on Sunday School Tunes* (1926–27) for organ and the *Symphony on a Hymn Tune* (1928) evoke nineteenth-century hymnody.
      b. *The Mother of Us All* (1947), another operatic collaboration with Stein, is based on the life of women's suffrage leader Susan B. Anthony.
      c. He composed a number of film scores using American elements, and claimed that Copland borrowed the Americanist style from him.

X. Politics and Art Music
  A. Today's audiences have largely forgotten the political circumstances in which music of this chapter was created.
    1. Works such as Poulenc's sonatas, Orff's *Carmina burana,* Shostakovich's Fifth Symphony, and Copland's ballets now stand on their own without regard to politics.

2. In some works from the Soviet Union, the insistence on immediate wide appeal has made these works popular today.

B. The postwar depoliticizing of art music has led historians to focus more on the music and less on the circumstances of its creation.

C. The most important aspect of music between the wars is its great variety, which is evident in the diverse musical styles of composers in the United States.

## SUGGESTIONS FOR SUPPLEMENTARY READING/LISTENING/ACTIVITIES

Source readings associated with the subjects of Chapter 33 can be found in Weiss and Taruskin, eds., *Music in the Western World: A History in Documents* (New York: Schirmer Books, 1984), including Plato's view of music and the state on p. 8, the goals of Les Six on pp. 467–72, views by Weill, Hindemith, and Copland on "Music and the Social Conscience" on pp. 490–95, glimpses into the Soviet restrictions on composers on pp. 495–502, Cowell's discussion of "New Musical Resources" on pp. 483–87, comments by Varèse on "Organized Sound" on pp. 518–22, and several examples of the writings of Virgil Thompson on pp. 475–76 and 502–06.

Have students listen to Honneger's *Pacific 231* (Denon COCO-78831m 1993 or Sony Classical SMK 60695, 1998, or Music & Arts CD-767, 1993). How does this programmatic work differ from earlier program music? What does it say about industrialized society?

Milhaud's *La création du monde, Saudades do Brasil*, and *Le boeuf sur le toit* are available on a compact disc conducted by Leonard Bernstein (EMI Records 47845, 2000). Have students compare Milhaud's use of jazz in the first of these with that of Kurt Weill, Gershwin, and Ellington. Similarly, juxtapose the latter two works with those by South American composers and Copland's *El Salón Mexico*.

For more on the effect of World War II on German composers, see Guy Rickards' *Hindemith, Hartmann and Henze* (London, Phaidon, 1995), 97–118. Also see Erik Levi, *Music in the Third Reich* (New York: St. Martin's Press, 1994), especially pp. 107–77 on Hindemith and the Nazis, pp. 70–73 on the ban against Mendelssohn's music, and the final chapter on the rewriting of musical history. *The Twisted Muse* (New York: Oxford University Press, 1997) discusses the Nazi attitude toward modernity (pp. 177–87) and toward Richard Strauss and Hans Pfitzner (pp. 203–210). Havery Sach's *Music in Fascist Italy* (New York: W. W. Norton, 1987) discusses attitudes toward Mascagni and Puccini.

Krenek's *Jonny spielt auf* is available on compact disc (Vanguard Classics 8048, 1994).

Kurt Weill's opera *Aufstieg und Fall der Stadt Mahagonny* is available on DVD (Kultur, 2001). The singing is excellent, but the staging is idiosyncratic.

There are numerous DVD recordings of Prokofiev's ballet *Romeo and Juliet*. One of the most enduring remains available only on VHS: the Royal Ballet performance from 1966 with Fonteyn and Nureyev (Kultur Video, 1988). Watch excerpts from this work and compare its classical ballet style to that of a modern-dance ballet by Copland, such as Martha Graham's 1961 performance *Appalachian Spring* (DVD: Kultur, 2002).

Have students watch the film *Alexander Nevsky* with music by Prokofiev. Have them report how music was extracted and shaped into a cantata.

Shostakovich's *Lady Macbeth of Mtsensk* is available on DVD (Chatsworth, California: Image Entertainment, 1999).

Recordings of Shostakovich's Symphony No. 5 are good demonstrations in a discussion of the effect of different interpreters. Compare, for example, the recordings conducted by Rostropovich (LSO Live, 2005) with Bernstein's historic recording (Sony 61841, 1999), with special attention to the closing tempo of the last movement. Bernstein takes the tempo twice as fast as indicated in the score, but it is reported that Shostakovich approved of the upbeat ending when Bernstein and the New York Philharmonic performed the work during the first tour of an American orchestra in the Soviet Union. Have students discuss their responses to the divergent moods.

A recording of Claude Champagne's *Dance villageoise* can be heard on compact disc (Analekta, 1995).

For more on music in Latin America, see Gerard Béhague, *Music in Latin America: An Introduction* (Englewood Cliffs, N. J.: Prentice-Hall, 1979) and his update in Leslie Bethell, ed., *A Cultural History of Latin America: Literature, Music, and the Visual Arts in the Nineteenth and Twentieth Centuries* (New York: Cambridge University Press, 1998).

A good selection of works by Heitor Villa-Lobos, including representative work from the two series *Choros* and *Bachinanas brasileiras,* can be heard on a compact disc from EMI Classics (72670, 1998). Ask the students what they hear of Bach in this work. Is this a neoclassic interpretation like Stravinsky's?

The complete symphonies of Carlos Chávez, including the *Sinfonia india*, is available on compact disc (Vox Classical 5061, 1992). Many works by Silvestre Revueltas, including his *Sensemayá*, have also been recorded (Sony 60676, 1999).

Varèse's complete works are available on compact disc (London: 289 460 208-2 through 289 460 210-2, 1998). Have students listen to excerpts from several works in chronological order. How did Varese's approach to timbre change as new sounds became available?

David Nicholls's *American Experimental Music 1890–1940* (New York: Cambridge University Press, 1990) includes an excellent discussion of Henry Cowell's music.

Judith Tick's *Ruth Crawford Seeger: A Composer's Search for American Music* (New York: Oxford University Press, 1997) discusses the political views of Seeger and her political works (pp. 188–200).

For writings by William Grant Still, see *The William Grant Still Reader*, volume 6, issue 2 of *Black Sacred Music* (Fall, 1992), especially "The Music of My Race," (1941), which discusses his use of the blues in the *Afro-American Symphony;* "The Negro Musician in America" (1970), which discusses his ambivalence toward popular music; and "A Vital Factor in America's Racial Problem" (1950), in which he sets out his view of music's role in ameliorating racial prejudice.

Thompson's *Four Saints in Three Acts* (Nonesuch 79035, 1992) and *Mother of Us All* (New World Records 80288, 1992) are available in compact-disc recordings. Have students read Stein's text and listen to the music. Discuss how Thompson's music parallels the text treatment.

## OBJECTIVE QUESTIONS

1. The members of Les Six were inspired by the music of ___________.
   a. Debussy
   b. d'Indy
   c. Ravel
   d. Fauré
   e. Satie

   Answer: e

2. Of the following, who was not a member of Les Six?
   a. Poulenc
   b. Fauré
   c. Auric
   d. Milhaud
   e. Honegger

   Answer: b

3. Which member of Les Six incorporated jazz into the ballet *La création du monde*?
   a. Poulenc
   b. Cui
   c. Auric
   d. Milhaud
   e. Honegger

   Answer: d

4. Of the following, which characterized New Objectivity?
   a. emotional intensity
   b. complex musical techniques
   c. incorporation of familiar elements, such as jazz
   d. expressionistic visions
   e. autonomous music

   Answer: c

5. Of the following, who stayed in Germany during the Nazi regime?
   a. Orff
   b. Krenek
   c. Hindemith
   d. Weill
   e. Kodaly

   Answer: a

6. Who is associated with Gebrauchsmusik?
   a. Orff
   b. Krenek
   c. Hindemith
   d. Weill
   e. Kodaly

   Answer: c

7. For his major operas, Kurt Weill collaborated with ___________.
   a. Jean Cocteau
   b. Gertrude Stein
   c. Bertolt Brecht
   d. Thomas Beckett
   e. Clifford Odet

   Answer: c

8. The texts for *Carmina burana* are drawn from which era?
   a. Antiquity
   b. Middle Ages
   c. Renaissance
   d. Romantic
   e. Modern

   Answer: b

9. Of the following, which work was composed by Prokofiev before he returned to the Soviet Union?
   a. *Peter and the Wolf*
   b. Symphony No. 5
   c. *Romeo and Juliet*
   d. *The Love for Three Oranges*
   e. *Alexander Nevsky*

   Answer: d

10. Shostakovich was attacked in *Pravda* for which work?
    a. *Lady Macbeth of the Mtensk District*
    b. Symphony No. 1
    c. Symphony No. 5
    d. Symphony No. 7
    e. String Quartet No. 8

    Answer: a

Use the following answers for questions 11–15.
   a. Claude Champagne
   b. Carlos Chávez
   c. Heitor Villa-Lobos
   d. Aaron Copland
   e. Silvestre Revueltas

11. He composed *Bachianas brasileiras.*

    Answer: c

12. He composed *El Salón Mexico.*

    Answer: d

13. He composed *Suite canadienne.*

    Answer: a

14. He composed *Sensemayá.*

    Answer: e

15. He composed *Sinfonia india* .

    Answer: b

16. Which composer is known for works employing tone clusters at the piano?
    a. Varèse
    b. Cowell
    c. Crawford
    d. Still
    e. Thomson

    Answer: b

17. In the 1950s, where did Varèse turn for new sounds?
    a. jazz
    b. rock and roll
    c. electronic music
    d. bird calls
    e. percussion instruments

    Answer: c

18. Ruth Crawford Seeger gave up composition for which activity?
    a. married life and motherhood
    b. performing
    c. teaching
    d. writing music criticism
    e. preserving folk songs

    Answer: e

19. With whom did Aaron Copland and other American composers study in Paris?
    a. Boulanger
    b. Debussy
    c. Satie
    d. Milhaud
    e. Ravel

    Answer: a

20. For his major operas, Virgil Thomson collaborated with ____________.
    a. Jean Cocteau
    b. Gertrude Stein
    c. Bertolt Brecht
    d. Thomas Beckett
    e. Clifford Odet

    Answer: b

## SHORT-ESSAY QUESTIONS

1. Describe the goals of Les Six, and discuss how closely the works of Honegger, Milhaud, and Poulenc adhered to those ideals.
2. Describe the impact of totalitarian governments on music in Germany and the Soviet Union.
3. Discuss the major composers of the Americas (excluding the United States) and how their major works incorporated qualities that reflected their national identity.
4. Compare the American styles of Aaron Copland and William Grant Still. Cite specific works to illustrate your points.

## TERMS FOR IDENTIFICATION

Les Six
Jean Cocteau
New Objectivity
Bertolt Brecht
Gebrauchmusik
harmonic fluctuation
socialist realism
formalist
Nadia Boulanger
sound masses
tone clusters
*New Music*
Gertrude Stein

# CHAPTER 34 Postwar Crosscurrents

I. The Cold War and the Splintering Tradition
   A. The process of musical change accelerated after World War II, due to several factors.
      1. The United States and Western Europe enjoyed an economic boom.
      2. Communications continued to improve and get faster.
      3. Younger generations wanted to explore new possibilities.
   B. Music continued to change.
      1. Rock and roll emerged, and jazz explored new styles.
      2. Increasingly complex serial techniques, electronic sounds, indeterminacy, and other radical approaches were explored in concert music.
   C. Musical support
      1. Governments supported music in Europe, largely through radio stations and institutes.
      2. Colleges and universities became major patrons and teaching centers for music in the United States.
   D. The cost of World War II
      1. World War II was the most destructive war the world had seen.
      2. Millions were dead, both soldiers and civilians.
      3. Cities, artworks, and music had been destroyed.
      4. In response to the atomic attack on Japan, several nations developed nuclear weapons.
   E. The Cold War
      1. By 1948, the Soviet Union had installed Communist governments in most Eastern European countries.
      2. The United States formed an alliance with Western Europe called NATO (see **HWM Figure 34.1**).
      3. The division of Germany symbolized the basic conflict.
      4. The newly created United Nations helped, but could not resolve international tensions.
      5. Numerous conflicts, including the Korean War (1950–53) and the Vietnam War (1954–1975), added further tension to the Cold War.
      6. Outer space, the athletic field, and cultural fields were arenas for competition.
   F. Greater access to music
      1. The economic boom paved the way for a tremendous expansion of colleges and universities, which contributed to the growing access to the arts.
      2. Televisions and stereos brought entertainment into the home.
      3. The 78-rpm records (with 78 rotations per minute) of the prewar phonograph were replaced by LP (long-playing) records and 45-rpm "singles," which became the main medium for popular songs.
      4. Transistors led to portable radios that could go anywhere.
      5. Improvements in tape recorders made electronic music and the preservation of sounds possible.
   G. Musical pluralism
      1. Countries in Asia and Africa gained political and economic significance, leading to greater cultural exchanges.
      2. The era saw unprecedented experimentation and diversification in music.

3. Strident debates about music were frequent.

II. Popular Music
  A. Popular music increasingly catered to the tastes of teenagers.
    1. During the postwar years, teenagers had more money and free time.
    2. Record companies, responding to a market in which teenagers had their own radios and purchased records, produced pop music.
    3. Teenagers of the late 1950s and 1960s listened to rock music, creating a "generation gap" with their parents.
    4. A variety of popular styles emerged, and people used music as part of their identity.
    5. The popularity of music was measured in weekly charts, which ranked the sales of 45-rpm singles.
  B. Country music
    1. Country music, or country-and-western, is associated with white southerners.
    2. With roots in folk music, the style grew in popularity after the war.
    3. Country music is a blend of many sources (see **HWM Figure 34.2**).
      a. Hill-country music of the southeast, based on Anglo-American ballads and fiddle tunes
      b. Western cowboy songs popularized by Gene Autry and other cowboy movies stars
      c. Popular songs of the nineteenth and early twentieth centuries
      d. Blues, banjo music, and other African-American traditions
      e. Big-band swing
      f. Gospel songs
    4. The popularity of country music was due to a variety of reasons.
      a. Energy
      b. Sincere sentiments
      c. Witty wordplay
      d. Ability to articulate the experience of working-class America in a rapidly changing world
    5. The music centered on a singer who also played a guitar.
    6. Other singers might join in close harmony, and an accompaniment of fiddles and additional guitars was common.
    7. Distinctive styles developed, including:
      a. Western swing
      b. Honky-tonk
      c. Bluegrass
    8. Two stars earned national acclaim.
      a. Hank Williams (1923–1953)
      b. Johnny Cash (1932–2003)
    9. Nashville became the center of country music, largely due to venues such as the Grand Ol' Opry.
    10. By the 1970s, country music radio stations had been established across the United States.
  C. Rhythm-and-blues
    1. Rhythm-and-blues developed in urban centers just after the war.
    2. Typical ensembles
      a. Vocalist or vocal quartet
      b. Piano or organ
      c. Electric guitar
      d. Bass and drums
    3. They performed mostly new songs built on twelve-bar blues or thirty-two-bar popular song formulas.
    4. Principal differences with blues:
      a. Insistent accents on the back beats, beats two and four of the measure
      b. Whining guitar
      c. Repetitive amplified bass line
    5. The style was initially intended for African-American audiences.
    6. Interests among whites
      a. White teenagers were attracted by the sexual themes of the lyrics, the strong rhythms, and the intensity of the performances.
      b. Producers began having white singers perform songs already successful by black singers.
      c. *Hound Dog,* a twelve-bar blues, was a minor hit for Willie Mae "Big Mama" Thornton in 1952, but a recording by Elvis Presley sold millions in 1956.
  D. Rock and roll
    1. Rock and roll combined the unrelenting beat of rhythm-and-blues with the guitar background of country music.
    2. Instrumentation
      a. Electric guitars for rhythm and melody
      b. Electric bass and drums
      c. Sometimes other instruments augmented the ensemble
    3. Song forms were derived from Tin Pan Alley and the blues.
    4. Vocal styles ranged from boogie-woogie to country.
    5. The words, often addressing love and sex, spoke to the concerns of teens.
    6. Rock and roll became a national sensation with the appearance of the hit song *Rock*

*Around the Clock,* by Bill Haley and the Comets, in the 1955 film *Blackboard Jungle*.
7. Elvis Presley (1935–1977) was the first megastar.
8. By 1960, rock and roll, or simply rock, was heard around the world.

E. The Beatles
1. From Liverpool, England, the Beatles featured four creative musicians.
   a. John Lennon (1940–1980), singer-songwriter and guitarist
   b. Paul McCartney (b. 1942), singer-songwriter and guitarist
   c. George Harrison (1943–2001), guitarist and songwriter
   d. Ringo Starr (b. 1940), drummer
2. The Beatles brought "Beatlemania" to the United States in a 1964 tour (see **HWM Figure 34.3**).
3. Devoting their energy to studio recordings, the Beatles later experimented with sounds and styles that could not be duplicated live.
4. Albums, such as *Sgt. Pepper's Lonely Hearts Club Band* (1967), embraced a wide variety of styles.

F. Other rock music of the sixties
1. The Beatles' American tour began the "British Invasion," which featured a number of other groups, such as the Rolling Stones.
2. Some blues-based groups were influenced by earlier figures such as Robert Johnson.
3. Virtuosos on the electric guitar created an enormous sensation.
   a. Jimi Hendrix (1942–1970)
   b. Eric Clapton (b. 1945) from the band Cream
4. A wide variety of sounds emerged, including:
   a. California style—The Beach Boys
   b. Heavy metal—Steppenwolf
   c. Hard rock—Led Zeppelin and Aerosmith
   d. Acid rock—Jefferson Airplane
   e. Avant-garde rock—Frank Zappa
5. The youth-oriented lyrics often expressed disillusionment with society.

G. Folk and protest music
1. A new style of popular music arose with ties to folk traditions; it became generally known as folk music.
2. Groups often performed new songs in folk style along with genuine folk songs.
3. Folk music was deliberately simple, featuring one or more singers with guitar.
4. Audiences were encouraged to join in the singing.
5. Folk songs were written to support social causes, such as *We Shall Overcome* for the Civil Rights Movement.
6. Prominent writers and singers from the 1940s include:
   a. Woody Guthrie (1912–1967)
   b. Pete Seeger (b. 1919), the stepson of Ruth Crawford Seeger
7. New voices emerged in the 1960s struggles for civil rights and against the Vietnam War, including Joan Baez (b. 1941).
8. Bob Dylan (b. 1941)
   a. He voiced protests through songs such as *Blowin' in the Wind* (1962).
   b. He combined folk styles with simple guitar harmonies, a rough voice, blues harmonica, and sharp-witted poetry.
   c. By the mid-sixties, Dylan used an electric guitar, bringing together folk and rock traditions.

H. Soul
1. Soul was the leading African-American tradition in the 1960s.
2. It applied the intense expression, melismas, and ecstatic vocalizations of gospel singing to songs on love, sex, and other secular subjects.
3. Soul was closely associated with the struggle for African-American equality.
4. The leading performers included:
   a. Ray Charles (1930–2004) (see **HWM Figure 34.4**)
   b. James Brown (b. 1928), the "King of Soul"
   c. Otis Redding (1941–1967)
   d. Aretha Franklin (b. 1942)

I. Motown
1. Motown was a Detroit-based record company (the *Mo*-tor City).
2. The sounds of Motown dominated the soul charts of the 1960s.
3. Motown was intended to appeal to both black and white audiences.
4. Motown produced a steady flow of well-groomed groups, including the Supremes and the Temptations.
5. Motown also gave a start to figures such as Stevie Wonder (b. 1950) and Michael Jackson (b. 1958).

J. Latino Americans produced styles using traditions of Central or Latin America.
1. Tex-Mex, emanating from Texas and the southwestern United States, combined Mexican mariachi music with American country music.

2. Salsa emerged in the 1960s, a product of New York City and Puerto Rico.
3. Salsa mixes Cuban dance styles with jazz, rock, and Puerto Rican elements.
    a. A typical ensemble includes ten to fourteen members on vocals, piano, Cuban percussion, bass, and brass.
    b. Each instrument plays a distinctive rhythm, forming a driving dance beat.
4. Tito Puente (1923–2000) was a leading figure of salsa.

III. Broadway and Film Music

A. Musicals

1. Musicals continued established traditions, avoiding many of the newer trends in popular music.
2. Most shows were collaborations, including:
    a. Composer Richard Rodgers (1902–1979) with lyricists Lorenz Hart (1895–1943) and Oscar Hammerstein II (1895–1960)
    b. Composer Frederick Loewe (1904–1988) with lyricist Alan Jay Lerner (1918–1986)
3. Some of Broadway's greatest composers from before the war continued to be productive.
    a. Irving Berlin: *Annie Get Your Gun* (1946) and *Call Me Madam* (1950)
    b. Cole Porter: *Kiss Me Kate* (1948)
4. Rodgers and Hammerstein produced some of the most successful shows of the era.
    a. *Oklahoma!* (1943)
    b. *Carousel* (1945)
    c. *South Pacific* (1949)
    d. *The King and I* (1951)
    e. *The Sound of Music* (1959)
5. *Oklahoma!* not only enjoyed a record-breaking run, but established a new highpoint in drama, music, and dance (see **HWM Figure 34.5**).
6. Leonard Bernstein had a large impact on Broadway.
    a. He was initially known as a classical composer and performer, and as the principal conductor of the New York Philharmonic.
    b. His Broadway career began with *On the Town* (1944).
    c. His sensational *West Side Story* (1957) is a retelling of Shakespeare's *Romeo and Juliet*.
    d. In *West Side Story*, Bernstein employs a variety of styles, including Afro-Caribbean dances, jazz, and Tin Pan Alley melodies in AABA format.
7. Later Broadway musicals adapted new styles.
    a. *Fiddler on the Roof* (1964), by Jerry Bock, evoked Jewish folk music.
    b. *Hair* (1967), by Galt MacDermot, mixes rock styles with Broadway.

B. Film music

1. Film music styles diversified in the postwar years.
2. Miklós Rósza (1907–1995) explored musical styles ranging from film noir to mock-ancient for historical epics like *Ben Hur* (1959).
3. Alex North (1910–1991) used jazz in *A Streetcar Named Desire* (1951).
4. Leonard Bernstein used a dissonant style in *On the Waterfront* (1954).
5. Bernard Herrmann (1911–1975) collaborated with Alfred Hitchcock and used a consistently dissonant style in *Psycho* (1960).
6. Italian composer Ennio Morricone (b. 1928) created a new pop-oriented Western sound for scores such as *The Good, the Bad and the Ugly* (1967).
7. Ethnic sounds from other countries were used in films, such as *Zorba the Greek* (1964), with music by Mikis Theodorakis.
8. Electronic music was also used in film scores.
9. Popular music was a strong element in postwar movies.
    a. David Raksin (1912–2004) made a great sensation with his jazz-inspired score to *Laura* (1944).
    b. Rock music made a strong impact beginning in the late 1950s.
    c. The Beatles' *A Hard Day's Night* (1964) was a successful movie and a successful soundtrack, setting a model for future films.

IV. Jazz

A. Postwar developments

1. New styles emerged, and older styles continued to be performed.
2. There developed growing consciousness of jazz history and a desire to preserve it.
    a. By 1970, jazz had developed its own classical repertoire.
    b. Beginning in the 1950s, jazz ensembles were formed in schools.
3. Jazz was increasingly regarded as music that demanded concentrated listening.
4. Most jazz performers were still African American, but many were white, and the audiences were predominantly white.

5. Big bands declined and were replaced by smaller ensembles called combos.

B. Bebop
1. A new style of jazz called *bebop* or *bop* emerged in the early 1940s.
2. Bebop was built around virtuosic soloists featured in combos.
3. The style originated in New York, where big band soloists would meet in clubs after leaving their regular engagements and pit their skills against each other.
4. Characteristics
   a. It was rooted in standards of the swing era.
   b. It added extreme virtuosity and harmonic and rhythmic complexities.
   c. The focus was on soloists and improvisation.
5. Typical combo
   a. Rhythm section: piano, drums, bass
   b. One or more melody instruments: trumpet, sax, or trombone
6. Prominent bebop musicians include:
   a. Charlie "Bird" Parker (1920–1955), saxophone
   b. Dizzy Gillespie (1917–1993), trumpet
   c. Miles Davis (1926–1991), trumpet
   d. John Coltrane (1926–1967), saxophone
   e. Thelonious Monk (1917–1982), piano

C. *Anthropology* (**NAWM 159**)
1. Composers: Parker and Gillespie (see **HWM Figure 34.6**)
2. *Anthropology* is a contrafact.
   a. A new melody is composed over the chord progression from Gershwin's *I Got Rhythm.*
   b. Contrafacts were major sources for new bebop compositions.
3. The *NAWM* recording is from a live broadcast.
4. Performers improvise from an abbreviated score called a lead sheet.
5. The performance is characterized by short, rapid bursts of notes creating an unpredictable melody.
6. Form
   a. The lead melody, called the *head,* is AABA and is played in unison at the beginning and end of the song.
   b. After the head, Parker plays three choruses (statements of the AABA harmonic progression).
   c. Gillespie then solos for three choruses.
   d. Powell on piano plays two additional choruses.
   e. Parker and Gillespie alternate with the drums for two choruses.
   f. The piece ends with a final statement of the head.

D. After bebop
1. New jazz styles were explored in the 1950s.
2. Cool jazz
   a. Miles Davis developed a more relaxed jazz style.
   b. The Modern Jazz Quartet and Dave Brubeck (b. 1920) took up the style.
   c. Cool jazz returned the composer-arranger to a prominent role.
3. Hard bop, dominated by drummers, focused on the percussive side of jazz.
   a. Kenny Clarke
   b. Max Roach
   c. Art Blakey
4. Modal jazz
   a. It featured slowly unfolding melodies over stable modal harmonies.
   b. Miles Davis explored this style as well.
5. Free jazz
   a. Ornette Coleman (b. 1930) and his quartet introduced this radical new jazz language.
   b. He moved away from jazz standards and familiar tunes.
   c. The style is built on melodic and harmonic gestures, new sounds, atonality, and improvisations on free forms.
6. Avant-garde jazz
   a. The style is based on very fast playing, motivic development, new sonorities, and greater dissonance and density of sound.
   b. John Coltrane developed this style.

V. The Classical Tradition

A. Postwar developments
1. The performance and study of classic music became even more pronounced.
2. Some composers attempted to preserve some aspect of tradition.
3. Other composers focused on creating something new.

B. The university as patron
1. Many composers were employed as teachers at colleges and universities.
2. At these institutions, composers had ready access to performers and venues.
3. Academic freedom allowed a vast range of styles, from traditional to experimental.
4. The safety of the ivory tower allowed some composers to isolate themselves from the public.

5. A number of refugee composers taught at universities, including:
   a. Schoenberg at the University of California, Los Angeles
   b. Milhaud at Mills College in Oakland, California
   c. Paul Hindemith at Yale
6. Walter Piston, student of Boulanger, encouraged a neoclassic style at Harvard.
7. Roger Sessions and Milton Babbitt at Princeton focused on the styles of Schoenberg and Webern.

VI. Composers Using Traditional Media
  A. Olivier Messiaen (1908–1992) (see **HWM Figure 34.7**)
    1. Messiaen is the most important French composer born in the twentieth century.
    2. An organist, he became professor of harmony at the Conservatoire in 1941.
    3. His students after the war include:
       a. Pierre Boulez
       b. Karlheinz Stockhausen (b. 1928)
       c. Luigi Nono (b. 1924)
    4. Works
       a. Messiaen composed works on religious subjects.
       b. Several are for organ.
    5. Messiaen notated birdsongs and used them in his compositions.
    6. Harmony
       a. He used scales that have limited transpositions, such as whole-tone and octatonic.
       b. Such scales do not create a strong desire for resolution.
    7. Rhythm and meter
       a. Rhythms create a sense of duration, not meter (see **HWM Example 34.1**).
       b. Messiaen used added values, the addition of small durational value to produce units of irregular length.
       c. He also used nonretrogradable rhythms, which are the same forward and backward.
  B. *Quatuor pour la fin du temps* (Quartet for the End of Time, 1941), first movement of *Liturgie de cristal* (Crystal Liturgy; see **NAWM 160** and **HWM Example 34.1**)
    1. Background
       a. Messiaen was interned at a prisoner-of-war camp in Silesia.
       b. The work is set for violin, clarinet, cello, and piano, instruments played by fellow prisoners (he played piano).
       c. The work was performed for their fellow prisoners.
    2. Meaning
       a. The title refers to the Apocalypse, which will bring about the end of time and the beginning of eternity.
       b. The work is religious, even though there is no text.
       c. Messiaen sought to create a sense of ecstatic contemplation in *Liturgie de cristal.*
    3. Messiaen preferred beautiful timbres, as heard in the high harmonics of the cello augmented by gentle birdcalls in the violin and clarinet and set over soft dissonances in the piano.
    4. The clarinet and violin play stylized birdcalls that change in unpredictable ways but do not develop.
    5. The cello constantly repeats a five-note sequence in high harmonics.
       a. These pitches are presented three times in a rhythmic pattern of fifteen durations.
       b. The pattern repeats every five and a half measures (measures 8, 13).
       c. The pattern combines two nonretrogradable rhythms; the first three durations and the remaining twelve are both palindromes.
       d. The rhythms are the same forward and backward, hence suggesting the unchangeable, the divine, and the eternal.
    6. Messiaen avoids movement towards resolution by repeating harmonies to create a sense of stasis or meditation.
       a. The piano has twenty-nine chords; the second chord cycle begins at the end of measure eight.
       b. The rhythmic pattern has seventeen durations; the second rhythmic cycle begins in measure six and repeats every thirteen beats thereafter.
  C. Benjamin Britten (1913–1976)
    1. One of England's foremost composers, Britten studied at the Royal College of Music.
    2. Like Copland, he tempered modernism with simplicity and created a widely appealing idiom.
    3. He was deeply influenced by humanitarian concerns, which is reflected in his later music.
    4. Most of Britten's choral works were created for amateur ensembles.
    5. Britten was homosexual, and his life partner was the tenor Peter Pears (1910–1986) (see **HWM Figure 34.8**).

a. Britten wrote most of his tenor roles for Pears.
b. Several of his operas have themes that relate to homosexuality, including *Billy Budd* (1950–51) and *Death in Venice* (1971–74).

6. *War Requiem* (1961–62)
a. Britten expressed his pacifism in this choral masterpiece.
b. The work interweaves traditional Latin texts with poems by Wilfred Owen.
c. The Latin texts are set for soprano soloist, chorus, boys' choir, and full orchestra, while the poems are for tenor and baritone soloists with chamber orchestra.
d. The English poems comment upon the Latin text.

D. *Peter Grimes* (1944–45), final scene by Britten (**NAWM 161**)
1. This opera established Britten's reputation and became the first English opera since Purcell to achieve international recognition.
2. The story of a fisherman who is driven to suicide by mobs can be seen as an allegory for the condition of homosexuals.
3. The opening of the final scene
a. The chorus of townspeople repeatedly calls out Peter's name.
b. Peter answers in a meandering recitative that includes a motive from an earlier scene.
c. The only accompaniment is a foghorn pitched at E-flat.
4. Ellen appears, and Peter sings a brief reprise of his love song in Act I.
5. There is no music as Balstrode helps Peter put the boat out to sea.
6. At the end, the indifference to Peter's fate is conveyed through bitonality.
a. Music representing the sea, including a haunting flute melody, is in C major.
b. In A major, the townspeople reprise a hymnlike song about their daily routines heard at the opening of Act I.
c. The report of a sinking boat is dismissed as a rumor.

E. Samuel Barber (1910–1981)
1. One of many composers who remained committed to tonality
2. The *Adagio for Strings*, originally written for string quartet in 1936, expresses his tonal romanticism.
3. He does incorporate modernist resources, such as the twelve-tone rows within a tonal framework in his Piano Sonata (1949).
4. He was renowned for his vocal works.

F. *The Monk and His Cat* from *Hermit Songs* by Barber (1952–53) (see **NAWM 162** and **HWM Example 34.2**)
1. Text
a. The song cycle is based on texts of Irish monks and hermits.
b. W. H. Auden translated the texts into English.
c. The poem describes the contented lives of the scholar and cat, each focusing on his own work—theology and mouse control.
d. Each of the five lines is punctuated in the middle like a psalm verse.
e. The first sentence is repeated at the end.
f. Barber treats the two halves of each sentence in a variety of ways (see the diagram in the commentary to **NAWM 162**).
2. Music
a. Open fifths in the bass create a medieval atmosphere and suggest the monk.
b. Dissonant augmented unisons suggest the cat, either walking on the piano keys or pouncing on a mouse.
c. This song is solidly in F major, although it features almost no consonant harmonies.
d. Barber freely alters the meter to follow the accents of the text.
e. The vocal melody often contradicts the implied meter in the piano.
f. The vocal line is a decorated paraphrase of the piano's chantlike melody.

G. Alberto Ginastera (1916–1983)
1. From Argentina, Ginastera is the most popular Latin American composer after Villa-Lobos.
2. His career can be divided into three phases.
a. "Objective nationalism" (to 1947): tonal music infused with traditional Argentine folk elements
b. "Subjective nationalism" (1947–57): synthesis of native and international elements
c. "Neo-expressionism" (after 1957): earlier traits combined with twelve-tone and avant-garde techniques
3. His turn from nationalism towards more abstract music is typical of the era.

H. Gunther Schuller (b. 1925)
1. Some American composers who were versed in both jazz and classical music sought to merge the two in the 1950s and 1960s.
2. Schuller, one of the most successful, called the combination "third stream."

3. *Transformation* (1957) transforms a pointillistic twelve-tone context into a full-blown modern jazz piece.

I. Michael Tippett (1905–1998)
   1. English composer Tipett synthesized historical, ethnic, and non-Western styles.
   2. His use of rhythmic and metric independence is derived in part from Renaissance music.
   3. Javanese influences can be seen in several works.
      a. Piano Concerto (1953–55)
      b. Triple Concerto for violin, viola, and cello (1979)

VII. Serialism
   A. Many composers adopted twelve-tone methods after the war.
      1. Established composers, such as Stravinsky, Copland, and Ginastera, took up serialism.
      2. The system had its biggest impact on younger composers.
      3. In Germany, some composers adopted the system as a political rejection of Nazi and communist ideologies.
      4. The West German government encouraged these developments and sponsored courses in new music at Darmstadt.
         a. The ideas fostered at Darmstadt inspired musical experiments.
         b. Boulez and Stockhausen became the two principal composers.
      5. In the United States, university composers, free from the need to appeal to audiences, embraced serialism.
      6. Milton Babbitt became the leading serial composer and theorist in the United States (see **HWM Source Reading,** page 916).
      7. Total serialism began to be explored in the late 1940s.
         a. Composers applied the principles of Schoenberg's tone rows to parameters other than pitch, such as durations, intensities, and timbres.
         b. Other new serial techniques were explored as well.
   B. Milton Babbitt (b. 1916) (see **HWM Figure 34.11**)
      1. *Three Compositions for Piano* (1947) is the first piece to apply serial principles to duration.
      2. The complexity of his approach can be seen in the opening measures of his Third String Quartet (1970; see **HWM Example 34.3**).
         a. There are eight layers, with each instrument having two (one arco, one pizzicato).
         b. At the beginning, each layer has its own row.
         c. The rhythm is serialized as well, which is articulated with dynamics (see **HWM Example 34.3b**).
   C. Pierre Boulez (b. 1925)
      1. Independent from Babbitt, Messiaen created several complex systems.
      2. Inspired, Boulez wrote the first European work of total serialism, *Structures* for two pianos (1952).
      3. *Le marteau sans maitre* (The Hammer without a Master, 1954, revised 1957)
         a. The work fuses the pointillist style and serial method with a sensitive musical rendition of the text.
         b. The work has nine movements centering on verses by the surrealist poet René Char.
         c. Each number has a different combination of instruments, as in Schoenberg's *Pierrot lunaire*.
         d. The ensemble comprises alto flute, xylorimba, vibraphone, guitar, viola, and percussion instruments.
         e. The translucent sound suggests Balinese gamelan music.
         f. The contralto vocal line has wide leaps, glissandos, and some Sprechstimme.
         g. Despite the logic, the audience's perception is of randomness.

VIII. Nonserial Complexity and Virtuosity
   A. A new generation of performers responded to musical complexities.
      1. Championing new music, they were capable of playing subtle nuances with accuracy and technical virtuosity.
      2. Their abilities inspired composers to use complex systems other than serialism.
   B. Luciano Berio (1925–2003)
      1. Italian composer Berio created a series of works titled *Sequenza*, each for an unaccompanied solo instrument from flute to accordion.
      2. Each work was composed for a specific performer.
      3. *Sequenza IV* for piano (1965–66) (see **HWM Example 34.4**)
         a. The rapid gestures and sudden changes are typical of the work.
         b. The atonality, figurations, and textures resemble those of his earlier serial music.

c. The sustain pedal allows open strings to continue sounding and to catch harmonics from other notes.

C. Elliot Carter (b. 1908)
1. American composer Carter also wrote for virtuoso performers.
2. He used a complex, nonserial style with innovative rhythms and forms.
3. Carter developed a technique known as metric modulation.
a. Transitions from one tempo and meter to another are through intermediary stages that share aspects of both.
b. The results are precise proportional changes in the value of a durational unit.
c. Cello Sonata (1948) is Carter's first work with this procedure.
4. The String Quartet No. 2 (1959; see **HWM Example 34.5**).
a. Each instrumental part has a distinct personality.
b. The instruments are differentiated by their most prominent intervals.
c. They are also distinguished by rhythms.
d. The first violin effects the metric modulation.
e. The result is a counterpoint of sharply differentiated lines.

IX. New Sounds and Textures
A. In the postwar years, the search for new musical resources intensified, and composers turned to four avenues of exploration.
1. Use of new instruments, sounds, and scales
2. Incorporation of non-Western sounds and instruments
3. Electronic music
4. Music of texture and process

B. John Cage (1912–1992)
1. Cage's long and influential career was characterized by a continuous effort to bring to music sounds that had been traditionally excluded.
2. In the 1930s and 1940s, he wrote numerous works for percussion ensemble that included instruments such as tin cans and an electric buzzer.
3. He invented the prepared piano.
a. Various objects, such as pennies, screws, and plastic, are inserted between the strings of a piano.
b. When the keyboard plays, a variety of percussive sounds are projected.
4. *Sonatas and Interludes* (1946–48)
a. The work contains twenty-six sonatas and four interludes.
b. The sonatas are single movements in two repeated parts, as in Scarlatti sonatas, but without thematic returns.
c. The pianist follows detailed instructions in preparing the piano in advance.
d. Each movement explores a different set of timbres and figurations.

C. Harry Partch (1901–1974)
1. Partch sought out a wholly new system inspired by Chinese, Native American, Jewish, Christian, African, and rural American music.
2. He developed a new scale with forty-three notes to the octave.
3. He built new instruments that could play in this scale, including a gourd tree (see **HWM Figure 34.9**).
4. He created a number of multimedia works in which these instruments accompany speaking and chanting voices and dancing.

D. George Crumb (b. 1929)
1. Crumb has masterfully created new sounds out of ordinary instruments and objects.
2. *Ancient Voices of Children* (1970)
a. This cycle has four songs on poems of Federico Garcia Lorca with two instrumental interludes.
b. Unusual sound sources include toy piano, musical saw, harmonica, mandolin, Tibetan prayer stones, Japanese temple bells, and electric piano.
c. Special effects are also obtained from the traditional instruments.

E. *Black Angels* (1970) by Crumb (**NAWM 163**)
1. The work was written as a protest to the horror of the Vietnam War.
2. The image of a black angel represents a fallen angel; the work is divided into three parts.
a. Fall from grace
b. Spiritual annihilation
c. Redemption
3. Numerology plays a significant role, with an emphasis on the numbers seven and thirteen.
4. A surrealistic character is created through the imaginative use of color.
a. The string quartet is amplified electronically.
b. Innovative string techniques are explored.
c. Quartet members play a variety of percussion instruments and make vocal sounds, including ritualistic counting in several different languages.

5. Images 4 and 5 are linked together.
   a. They are played without a break.
   b. They depict the dance of death based on the image of the devil playing the violin.
   c. Both quote phrases of *Dies irae*.
6. Image 4: *Devil-Music*
   a. The first violin plays an intense cadenza.
   b. The musical material emphasizes a chord that includes the tritone.
   c. *Dies irae* is played with pedal tones accompanied by a tam-tam.
7. Image 5: *Danse macabre*
   a. The second violin and viola create unusual colors.
   b. A motive from Saint-Saëns's *Danse macabre* is quoted several times.
   c. The first violin and cello play *Dies irae* with unusual timbres that includes whistling.

X. Asian Influences
  A. Instruments, sounds, and textures from Asia fascinated Western composers.
    1. Canadian composer Colin McPhee (1900–1964)
       a. He transcribed gamelan music for Western instruments.
       b. *Tabuhtabuhan* (1936) for orchestra draws upon Balinese materials.
    2. Henry Cowell
       a. His travels to Iran, India, and Japan led to works blending Asian and Western elements.
       b. His works include two concertos for the Japanese koto.
    3. Lou Harrison (1917–2003)
       a. He combined Asian and Western instruments.
       b. Harrison also wrote numerous works for traditional Javanese gamelan.
  B. Asian composers, such as Toru Takemitsu (1930–1996) from Japan, also linked Western and Asian traditions.
    1. In his early works, Takemitsu wrote for traditional Western instruments and within Western genres.
    2. In the 1960s, he began to combine the two traditions.
    3. *November Steps* (1967) is like a double concerto, combining a shakuhachi and biwa with a Western orchestra.
    4. Takemitsu used similar combinations in his film scores.

XI. Electronic Music
  A. Musique concrète
    1. Musique concrète works with recorded sound.
       a. The entire world of sound is potential material for music.
       b. The chosen sounds are manipulated and assembled into collages.
    2. Tape recorders, which had recently been developed, made it possible to record, amplify, transform, and arrange sounds.
    3. Pierre Schaeffer (1910–1995)
       a. He created the first major work using this technique, *Symphonie pour un homme seul* (Symphony for One Man).
       b. Schaeffer premiered the work in a 1950 radio broadcast.
  B. Electronic sounds
    1. Most electronic sounds are created by oscillators, invented in 1915.
    2. Early electronic instruments
       a. The Theremin was invented around 1920 by Lev Termen.
       b. The Ondes Martenot was invented in 1928 by Maurice Martenot.
       c. Both instruments produced one pitch at a time and projected voicelike sounds capable of glissandos.
       d. They were featured in some orchestral works and film scores.
  C. Electronic studios
    1. Between 1951 and 1953, a number of major electronic studios were created.
       a. Columbia University in New York
       b. Cologne, Germany
       c. Milan, Italy
       d. Tokyo, Japan
    2. Most composers at these studios focused on producing sounds electronically and manipulating them through electronic devices and on tape.
    3. *Gesang der Junglinge* (Song of the Youths, 1955–56) by Stockhausen
       a. This work combines electronic sounds with a boy's voice.
       b. It is the first major electronic piece to use multiple tracks.
       c. In concert, the various tracks were projected with loudspeakers placed around the audience.
    4. *Poème electronique* (Electronic Poem, 1957–58) by Varèse
       a. *Poème electronique* also combines electronic and recorded sounds.

   b. This eight-minute piece was composed for the 1958 Brussels Exposition.
   c. The music was played through 425 loudspeakers in a pavilion designed by Le Corbusier (see **HWM Figure 34.10**).
   d. Fifteen thousand people a day experienced this multimedia piece over a six-month period.

D. Synthesizers
   1. Electronic sound synthesizers enabled composers to call on pitches from a music keyboard.
   2. Composers could control harmonics, waveform, resonance, and the location of sound sources with switches and knobs.
   3. The RCA Mark II Synthesizer was developed at the joint Columbia-Princeton Electronic Music Center in the late 1950s (see **HWM Figure 34.11**).
   4. Robert Moog and Donald Buchla each developed simpler and more-compact synthesizers in the mid-1960s.
   5. After becoming commercially available in 1966, they were adopted by studios and composers around the world.
   6. *Silver Apples of the Moon* (1967) by Morton Subotnick (b. 1933)
      a. Created with the Buchla synthesizer, this work was the first electronic piece to be commissioned by a record company.
      b. It was designed to fill two sides of an LP.
   7. The Beatles and other pop musicians adopted the new synthesizers.

E. Electronic music and performance
   1. The electronic medium gave composers total control of the music, bypassing human performers.
   2. The absence of performers hindered audiences' acceptance of the medium.
   3. A number of works were created that combined prerecorded tape with live performers.

F. *Philomel* (1964) by Milton Babbitt (**NAWM 164**)
   1. This work combines live performance with prerecorded tape and synthesized sounds.
      a. The tape alters recorded fragments of the singer and uses electronic sounds.
      b. The taped voice often answers the soloist by distorting her line or commenting like a Greek chorus.
      c. The voice sometimes employs Sprechstimme.
   2. The text is derived from an Ovid fable taken from *Metamorphoses*.
      a. Philomel is the sister of Procne, the queen of Thrace.
      b. Tereus, Procne's husband and king of Thrace, rapes Philomel and cuts out her tongue so that she cannot tell what happened.
      c. Philomel weaves the story in a tapestry, and Procne gets revenge by feeding Tereus the butchered corpse of their son.
      d. Tereus pursues the two sisters, but the gods transform them into birds.
      e. Philomel, transformed into a nightingale, regains her voice just as this work begins.
   3. The composition is in three sections.
      a. Section 1: Philomel screams as she recalls the pain of her violation and runs through the forest in fear and confusion (this portion is **NAWM 164**).
      b. Section 2: Philomel seeks answers about her predicament.
      c. Section 3: Philomel sings a strophic lament joined in refrains by her taped voice.
   4. Interludes for tape and synthesized sounds alternate with the voice.
   5. Everything is worked out with serial procedures.
      a. The pitch-class E is central to the construction.
      b. The rows are manipulated in a way that allows E to become successively the first, second, third, fourth, and fifth pitch-class in the row.
   6. Word painting and imagery
      a. The opening pitch E matches the vowel that is being sung.
      b. Synthesized trills support the word "trilled."
      c. Recorded birdsongs are added.

XII. Music of Texture and Process
   A. Varèse's concept of sound masses moving through musical space influenced several composers.
      1. The emphasis was on sound itself.
      2. Electronic sounds stimulated the invention of new sounds from conventional instruments and voices.
      3. Works contained striking sound combinations that created novel textures.
   B. Iannis Xenakis (1922–2001)
      1. Xenakis was a Greek composer who spent most of his life in France.
      2. An engineer and architect, he saw mathematics as fundamental to music.

3. *Metastaseis* for orchestra (1953–54)
   a. Each string player has a unique part.
   b. At times, each has a glissando, moving slowly or quickly.
   c. Xenakis plotted the glissandos on a graph and transferred the lines to music notation (see **HWM Figure 34.12**).

C. Krzysztof Penderecki (b. 1933), *Threnody: To the Victims of Hiroshima* (1960; **NAWM 165**)
   1. Polish composer Penderecki originally wrote this as an abstract work, but his added title and dedication helped make this his most famous piece.
   2. *Threnody* is scored for fifty-two string instruments.
      a. Each instrument has a unique part and is required to use unusual performance techniques.
      b. The unusual timbres delineate five sections.
   3. Section 1 has each instrument playing as high as possible.
   4. Section 2 (beginning in measure 6) features a variety of unusual sounds played as quickly as possible.
   5. Section 3 (beginning in measure 10) introduces sustained tones and quarter-tone clusters linked by glissandos (see **HWM Example 34.6**).
   6. Section 4 (beginning in measure 26) presents isolated pitches and various sound effects in canon.
   7. Section 5 (beginning in measure 56) reintroduces earlier sound effects and clusters that lead to a climactic fifty-two-note chord.
   8. Penderecki used similar sounds in other works.
      a. *St. Luke Passion* (1963–66)
      b. *The Devils of London* (1968), an opera
   9. In the mid-1970s Penderecki turned toward neoromanticism.

D. György Ligeti (b. 1923)
   1. This Polish composer achieved international fame when three of his compositions were used in Stanley Kubrick's film *2001: A Space Odyssey*.
   2. The music for all three works is in constant motion, but static harmonically and melodically, as heard in *Atmosphères* (1961).
      a. *Atmosphères* begins with fifty-six muted strings and a variety of wind instruments playing all the chromatic notes through a five-octave range.
      b. Instruments gradually drop out, leaving only the violas and cellos.
      c. Later, clusters of instruments are pitted against each other.
      d. At times he creates the effect of slowly moving masses of sound.

E. In the wide spectrum of choices that composers have made, listeners are required to forego traditional expectations and engage each work as an experience of sound.

XIII. The Avant-Garde

A. The previously discussed composers are not strictly avant-garde.
   1. These composers intended for their works to be placed in the classic repertoire.
   2. They often drew upon the art music tradition, but with a new and distinctive personality.
   3. They continued the goals of modernism.
   4. Avant-garde composers, like Satie, challenged the concept of permanent classics and wrote music only for the present.
   5. This distinction lies in the purpose of the music, not the technique.

B. John Cage
   1. Cage was the leading avant-garde composer of the postwar years (see **HWM Figure 34.13**).
   2. He argued against the museumlike preservation of music from the past.
   3. He did not seek to write works that expressed emotions, developed material, or had a logical unfolding of events.
   4. Influenced by Zen Buddhism, he created opportunities for experiencing sounds as themselves, not as vehicles for the composer's intentions (see **HWM Source Reading,** page 934).
   5. Three strategies to achieve this goal:
      a. Chance
      b. Indeterminacy
      c. Blurring boundaries between music, art, and life

C. Chance music
   1. Some of the decisions normally made by a composer are left to chance.
      a. Such pieces do not convey the composer's intentions.
      b. His approach varied from work to work.
   2. *Music of Changes* for piano (1951; Book I in **NAWM 166**)
      a. The title is taken from the ancient Chinese book of prophecy *I-Ching* (Book of Changes), which offers a method of divination by tossing coins.

 b. Cage devised charts for possible sounds, dynamics, durations, and tempos.
 c. The methods described in *I-Ching* were used to select the sounds of a given performance.
 d. As a result, sounds occur randomly.

D. Indeterminacy
 1. Certain aspects of the music are unspecified.
  a. He drew the idea in part from a work by his friend Morton Feldman.
  b. The exact sound for *Concert* for piano and orchestra (1957–58) will vary from performance to performance.
  c. *4′33″* (Four Minutes Thirty-Three Seconds, 1952) has the performers sit in silence for this amount of time, thereby allowing the environmental noises to constitute the music.
 2. In both of the above techniques, the listener is invited to hear sounds as sounds.
 3. Value judgments are irrelevant, and there can be no mistakes.
 4. *Variations IV* (1963) uses both indeterminacy and chance and can be combined with other activities, including activities of daily life.
 5. *Musicircus* (1967) has any number of musicians performing different music all at once, while the audience wanders freely.

E. Other composers adopted indeterminacy.
 1. Earle Brown (b. 1926) in *Available Forms I* (1961) and *II* (1962)
 2. Stockhausen in *Klavierstücke XI* (Piano Piece No. 11, 1956)
 3. Penderecki in *Threnody*

F. Witold Lutoslawski (1913–1994)
 1. This Polish composer used indeterminacy selectively while maintaining ties to modernism.
 2. String Quartet (1964) specifies pitches and rhythms, but not the coordination of the parts.
 3. Symphony No. 3 (1983) applies this method with great subtlety.

G. Consequences of indeterminacy
 1. New kinds of notation were developed.
 2. No two performances were exactly alike.
 3. It opened the door to the awareness that earlier music was not a rigidly defined, unchanging work.

H. Performance art
 1. Performing an action as a work of art in a public place is called *performance art.*
 2. It appeared in the 1960s, spearheaded by Fluxus, a loose group of avant-garde artists in Europe and the United States.
 3. *Composition 1960 No. 2* by La Monte Young instructs the performer to build a fire.
 4. Yoko Ono (b. 1933)
  a. *Grapefruit* (1964) is a collection of pieces aimed at the performer and observer.
  b. In *Earth Piece* (1963), the performer is asked to listen to the sound of the earth turning.
  c. She brought her approach to rock music, collaborating with John Lennon after their marriage in 1969.
 5. Korean-born Nam June Paik (b. 1932) created exhibits with multiple television sets that blended music, video, performance art, and sculpture.

XIV. Quotation and Collage
 A. A number of composers quoted existing music, sometimes even creating a collage of multiple quotations.
  1. Modernist composers like Schoenberg and Stravinsky borrowed previously composed material.
  2. Postwar composers used older music to carry meanings that were not available by other means.
 B. Peter Maxwell Davies (b. 1934)
  1. This British composer borrowed from chant and English Renaissance music.
  2. By distorting the source material, he emphasized the gulf between modern times and the distant past.
  3. *Taverner* (1962–70), an opera on the life of the Renaissance composer, reworks the latter's *In Nomine*.
 C. George Rochberg (b. 1918)
  1. American composer Rochberg had written mostly serial music.
  2. After the death of his son in 1964, he turned to writing works based on borrowed material.
  3. *Nach Bach* (After Bach, 1966) for harpsichord is a "commentary" on Bach's Keyboard Partita No. 6 in E Minor, BWV 830.
 D. Lukas Foss (b. 1922) transforms music by Handel, Domenico Scarlatti, and Bach in his *Baroque Variations* (1967).
 E. George Crumb quotes the chant *Dies irae* and Schubert's *Death and the Maiden* Quartet in *Black Angels*.
 F. Stockhausen borrowed music in several works, including *Gesang der Jünglinge* and *Hymen* (1967).
  1. *Hymen* incorporates many different national anthems in a setting for electronic sounds, voices, and instruments.

2. The intention was not to interpret, but to present the familiar.
3. Opus 1970, written for the Beethoven bicentenary, includes recognizable fragments of Beethoven's works.

G. Luciano Berio's *Sinfonia* (Symphony, 1968–69) contains a rich collection of borrowed music.
1. The scherzo incorporates most of Mahler's scherzo to his Symphony No. 2.
2. Superimposed on the Mahler are verbal and musical commentaries.
3. Berio adds quotations from over one hundred other works.

XV. Band and Wind Ensemble Music

A. A large repertoire of serious works was created for band in the postwar era.

B. The wind band grew in popularity throughout the twentieth century.
1. After Sousa, the most famous bandmaster was Edwin Franko Goldman (1878–1956).
2. Along with his son, Richard Franko Goldman (1910–1980), he continued the tradition of outdoor concerts with nationally broadcast performances in New York's Central Park.
3. Bands became especially important in schools across the country.
4. Band associations promoted the concert band for performing serious concert music.
5. Goldman and others commissioned new band works that matched the seriousness of orchestral music.
6. Several prominent composers wrote for concert band, including Schoenberg, Milhaud, and Hindemith.

C. Wind ensemble
1. In 1952, Frederick Fennell (1914–2005) founded the Eastman Wind Ensemble.
2. A wind ensemble was a group dedicated solely to serious music.
3. In a wind ensemble, each instrumental part became essential.
4. A number of composers wrote serious works for the wind ensemble, including Persichetti, William Schuman, Copland, Penderecki, and Joseph Schwantner.

D. *Music for Prague 1968*, introduction and fanfare by Karel Husa (**NAWM 167**)
1. Husa was born in Prague and came to the United States after Communists assumed power in his native country.
2. *Music for Prague 1968* was inspired by the Soviet Union's overthrow of Czechoslovakia's liberal government.
3. Originally composed for wind symphony and later arranged for orchestra, this work has four movements.
   a. Introduction and fanfare
   b. Aria
   c. Interlude for percussion only
   d. Toccata and chorale
4. The central thematic idea is the first phrase of a fifteenth-century Czech chorale tune, *You Who Are God's Warriors.*
   a. Smetana used the tune in two tone poems from *Má Vlast*.
   b. The chorale was a song of the Hussites, followers of religious reformer Jan Hus, who symbolized resistance to outside oppression.
   c. Employing cumulative form, fragments of the tune are developed before it is heard fully at the end.
   d. In the first movement, the first two measures of the tune appear in the brass (measures 74–76), but the tune remains incomplete as the movement ends.
5. In the adagio, the timpani presents fragments of the chorale, with some distortion.
6. At the fanfare (measure 35), the trumpets take notes from the timpani to create a four-note idea: D–E-flat–D-flat–C.
   a. This motive becomes the main material of the movement.
   b. Development of this motive leads to the climactic arrival of the first two measures of the chorale.
   c. The motive is transposed, and its retrograde becomes part of a twelve-tone row in the second movement.
7. The material of the piccolo and flute solos at the beginning is drawn from the chorale or fanfare figure.
8. A three-note motive (measures 3–4), also related to the fanfare, appears later in the movement.
9. Other modernist methods
   a. Instruments sometimes have contradictory dynamics, allowing for chords to change as they sound.
   b. Dynamics sometimes become a virtual melody.
   c. Brass use a variety of mutes to create different colors.
   d. Alto saxophones play quartertones (measures 33–34).
   e. Indeterminate notation is used at the climax (measures 81–87).

10. This work represents a number of trends from this chapter.
    a. The composer is a university composer; Husa taught at Cornell.
    b. A college ensemble commissioned the work.
    c. The work was composed in response to a political event—the occupation of Czechoslovakia by the Soviet Union.
    d. It employs borrowed material, a Czech hymn.
    e. Abstract procedures include twelve-tone methods, indeterminacy, and an all-percussion movement.

XVI. New Classics
  A. The pop world has now established a classical repertoire.
    1. Music from the 1950s and 1960s are "golden oldies" on the radio.
    2. Broadway musicals are continuously revived.
    3. Jazz has been preserved on recordings, and classics are learned in school ensembles.
    4. Film music has begun to receive attention as well.
  B. Postwar art music has not fared as well.
    1. Some works have been established in the permanent repertoire.
    2. Other works are well known by the musical elite.
    3. For the most part, the musical experimentation of the era found no audience.
    4. Still, the techniques that were developed have opened up new doors.

## SUGGESTIONS FOR SUPPLEMENTARY READING/LISTENING/ACTIVITIES

Compact-disc recordings of classic jazz, country music, rhythm-and-blues, rock and roll, and the varieties of rock styles and performers are readily available. Have students listen to the recordings of *Hound Dog* by "Big Mama" Thornton and Elvis Presley. Discuss the differences between the two styles, which your students prefer, and why the Presley rendition was a bigger commercial success. The complete recordings of Thornton are available on compact disc (Vanguard Records, 70175, 2000).

Using Internet sources or the series of reference books by Joel Whitburn, have students research the history of *Billboard* magazine charts. In particular, have them note the changes of music styles in the Top 40 lists in the mid-1950s.

Eric Clapton pays homage to Robert Johnson in the compact disc *Me and Mr. Johnson* (Warner Brothers: B0001HAHXW, 2004).

Assign students to listen to different songs by the Beatles. Have them chart the various instrumentation and describe any unusual features, such as the 7/4 meter in *All You Need Is Love*.

*Woodstock, Three Days of Peace and Music,* the Oscar-winning documentary, is available on DVD (Warner Studios, 1997). This version of the 1969 rock extravaganza extends over three and a half hours and illuminates the spirit and music of the 1960s. Among the many highlights are performances by Jefferson Airplane, Santana, Hendrix, and Joan Baez.

Most of the major musicals of the postwar years were made into movies, and many are available on DVDs. Among the finest are *Oklahoma!* (1955) and three Best Picture winners: *West Side Story* (1961), *My Fair Lady* (1964), and *The Sound of Music* (1965).

DVD recordings of the bebop generation are generally available. Particularly fascinating are the taped performances of Thelonious Monk (BMG Special Products, 2000).

For essays on twentieth-century music by composers themselves, see Elliott Schwartz and Barney Childs, eds., *Contemporary Composers on Contemporary Music* (New York: Holt, Rinehart and Winston, 1967); Robert P. Morgan, ed. *Source Readings in Music History,* rev. ed., Vol. 7: *The Twentieth Century* (New York: W. W. Norton, 1998); and Bryan R. Simms, ed., *Composers on Modern Musical Culture: An Anthology of Readings on Twentieth-Century Music* (New York: Schirmer Books, 1999).

Elliott Carter's *Collected Essays and Lectures, 1937–1995* (Rochester, N.Y.: Rochester University Press, 1997) includes commentary on his own and others' works. Especially interesting is his reminiscence of study with Nadia Boulanger, pp. 281–292.

*Quatuor pour la fin du temps* is available on many recordings. Have students listen to a movement and discuss the unusual combination of instruments. This work is the most extreme example of chamber music instrumentation being determined by circumstances, but many other works in the twentieth century also have unusual instrumentation. Ask students to find other examples of chamber works that use unusual combinations of instruments and voice and report their findings to the class. Have the class vote on which combination is the most bizarre and discuss the advantages and disadvantages of each combination.

An excellent performance of Britten's *Peter Grimes* is available on DVD (Kultur, 2003).

A new performance of *Le marteau sans maitre* conducted by Boulez has recently been released (Deutsche Grammophon, 2005).

John Cage's *Sonatas and Interludes* for prepared piano has been recorded by Boris Berman (Naxos 559042, 1999). With the assistance (permission) of the school's piano technician, experiment with prepared piano sounds in class. Have students compare this sound to that of a gamelan orchestra.

Crumb's *Ancient Voices of Children* and *Black Angels* have been released on several compact-disc recordings. Have students listen to two performances of the same movement and discuss the differences and similarities they hear. Discuss these works in the context of social and political events of the time.

Listen to Takemitsu's *Requiem* and *November Steps,* which are available on a compact-disc recording (Denon Records 79441, 1994). Talk about the mixture of Western and non-Western musical sounds. Compare this fusion to that of Gershwin with classical and jazz styles discussed earlier in the chapter.

The historic first major work of musique concrète, *Symphonie pour un homme seul,* is available on a compact disc entitled *French Music from Early Times to Present Day* (Ades Records 141712, 1995). Listen to this work and compare it to other electronic classics, such as Stockhausen's *Gesang der Jünglinge* and Varèse's *Poème electronique*. For the latter, you might prepare a series of PowerPoint images of the Le Corbusier pavilion built for the Brussels Exposition. These images are readily found on the Internet.

Have several students research the history of the synthesizer and demonstrate the various capabilities of the instrument in class.

*Threnody: To the Victims of Hiroshima* is available on several compact discs. Have students compare passages from this work with selections from Britten's *War Requiem* (Decca 414383 from 1990 features the voices of Britten's life partner Peter Pears and a young Fischer-Dieskau). Discuss the impact World War II had on composers both during and after the war. Have students place these works in the context of earlier movements, such as impressionism, expressionism, and Romanticism, and discuss the ways in which composers responded to war musically.

Ligeti's *Atmosphères* and *Lontano* have been issued together on a compact disc ("Wien Modern," Deutsche Grammophon 429 260-2, 1988).

Lutoslawski's Third Symphony and other works are available on compact disc ("The Essential Lutoslawski," Philips 289 464 043-2, 1999).

Have students or applied faculty demonstrate twentieth-century techniques for strings and woodwinds, and present samples showing how these techniques are notated.

Most college libraries have a good collection of music from the 1950s and 1960s using nontraditional notation. Have students search for examples and bring them to class for discussion.

Have one or more students perform *4'33"* for the class. At the end, have students describe the sounds that they heard during the work. Ask them whether they would have been aware of those sounds in a typical concert. Have them debate the merit of the exercise, encouraging them to think about what music is and is not, and then ask them what they think John Cage would have added to the debate.

Have students listen to the scherzo from Berio's *Sinfonia* and identify as many quotations as they can. A compact-disc recording with Boulez conducting is available (Elektra 45228, 1992).

Discuss with students the differences between a band, concert band, and wind ensemble. Have students bring in a variety of works and present a discussion on the overall style of each.

## OBJECTIVE QUESTIONS

1. Country music centers on a singer playing a __________.
   a. fiddle
   b. banjo
   c. guitar
   d. piano
   e. bass

   Answer: c

2. How does rhythm-and-blues differ from traditional blues?
   a. rhythmic emphasis on beats two and four
   b. revised harmonic underpinning
   c. adapting tunes into four four-measure phrases
   d. more improvisation
   e. happier subjects

   Answer: a

3. Which song launched rock and roll nationally?
   a. *Roll Over, Beethoven*
   b. *Respect*
   c. *Hound Dog*
   d. *Jailhouse Rock*
   e. *Rock Around the Clock*

   Answer: e

4. Which group is associated with acid rock?
   a. Rolling Stones
   b. Beach Boys
   c. Led Zeppelin
   d. Jefferson Airplane
   e. Animals

   Answer: d

5. Of the following, who was a prominent folk singer from the 1940s and 1950s?
   a. Bob Dylan
   b. Joan Baez
   c. Woody Guthrie
   d. Weavers
   e. Peter, Paul, and Mary

   Answer: c

6. Motown is associated with which city?
   a. New York
   b. Chicago
   c. Los Angeles
   d. Detroit
   e. Memphis

   Answer: d

7. Of the following musicals, which features music by Leonard Bernstein?
   a. *On the Town*
   b. *Oklahoma!*
   c. *Kiss Me Kate*
   d. *Hair*
   e. *Carousel*

   Answer: a

8. Of the following, which characterizes bebop jazz?
   a. extreme virtuosity
   b. large bands
   c. orchestrated charts
   d. emphasis on backbeats of the measure
   e. extreme dissonance

   Answer: a

9. Of the following, who is associated with cool jazz?
   a. Ornette Coleman
   b. Kenny Clarke
   c. Modern Jazz Quartet
   d. Thelonious Monk
   e. John Coltrane

   Answer: c

10. Of the following, which was the leading patron of composers in the United States after World War II?
    a. radio stations
    b. federal government grants
    c. professional orchestras
    d. recording companies
    e. universities

    Answer: e

Use the following answers for questions 11–15.
   a. metric modulation
   b. third stream
   c. total serialism
   d. musique concrète
   e. indeterminacy

11. Which is associated with Milton Babbitt?

    Answer: c

12. Which is associated with John Cage?

    Answer: e

13. Which is associated with Gunther Schuller?

    Answer: b

14. Which is associated with Elliott Carter?

    Answer: a

15. Which is associated with Varèse?

    Answer: d

16. Which composer is most closely associated with tonal Romanticism?
    a. Crumb
    b. Ligeti
    c. Penderecki
    d. Partch
    e. Barber

    Answer: e

17. Of the following works, which mixes Western and Asian musical sounds?
    a. *Black Angels*
    b. *Atmosphères*
    c. *I-Ching*
    d. *November Steps*
    e. *Sequenza*

    Answer: d

18. Witold Lutoslawski made use of which technique?
    a. indeterminacy
    b. total serialism
    c. metric modulation
    d. chance
    e. quotation

    Answer: a

19. Of the following, which best describes Berio's *Sinfonia*?
    a. an electronic work created with a synthesizer
    b. a work that is largely based on borrowed material
    c. major sections are given over to indeterminacy
    d. incorporates the sounds of jazz
    e. a complex system of serialism is applied throughout

    Answer: b

20. Frederick Fennell founded which type of performing group?
    a. concert band
    b. national symphony orchestra
    c. performance art ensemble
    d. wind symphony
    e. new music ensemble

    Answer: d

## SHORT-ESSAY QUESTIONS

1. Trace the developments of rock music from its roots in rhythm-and-blues and country music through the 1960s.
2. Discuss the use of serialism and other complex systems during the postwar years.
3. Describe the explorations of new sounds following World War II. Include a discussion of electronic music and its impact on music of this era.
4. Compare the variety of approaches to avant-garde music. Include a description of avant-garde rock and avant-garde jazz.

## TERMS FOR IDENTIFICATION

pop music
country music
Grand Ol' Opry
rhythm-and-blues
rock and roll
British Invasion
heavy metal
hard rock
acid rock
avant-garde rock
folk music
soul
Motown
Tex-Mex
salsa
combos
bebop
cool jazz
hard bop
modal jazz
avant-garde jazz
free jazz
modes of limited transposition
third stream
Darmstadt
total serialism
metric modulation
prepared piano
musique concrète
Theremin
Ondes Martenot
synthesizer
Robert Moog
Donald Buchla
chance
indeterminacy
performance art
Fluxus
*Sinfonia*
concert band
Edwin Franko Goldman
wind ensemble
Frederick Fennell

# CHAPTER 35 The End of the Millennium

I. Developments since 1970
  A. Musical changes during the last few decades
    1. The broadening conception of music as art
    2. The influence of digital technologies
    3. The increasing importance of mixed media
  B. Four trends are especially prominent.
    1. The fragmentation of popular music
    2. Minimalism and its offshoots
    3. Composers in the classical tradition wrote more accessible music.
    4. The influence of non-Western music
  C. Historical developments
    1. The late 1960s and 1970s saw numerous political and economic shocks, including assassinations, riots, and a presidential resignation.
    2. Cold War tensions decreased, and Communism eventually collapsed in Eastern Europe in the 1990s.
    3. New conflicts and threats emerged, most notably in the attacks on September 11, 2001.
    4. Global economies became more interdependent.
    5. Communication technology produced cable television, personal computers, fax machines, and cell phones.
    6. The arts appealed to a growing international audience.
      a. In this multinational world, people are exposed to a great variety of music on a daily basis.
      b. Characteristics of various musical types have crossed over and blended with other musical traditions.

II. Broadening the Meaning of "Art Music"
  A. Jazz
    1. Each style of jazz continues to be performed and to attract listeners.
    2. All styles of jazz are available on recordings; historical recordings have been transferred to compact discs (see **HWM Music in Context,** page 947).
    3. New institutions preserve the classics of jazz, as jazz is now regarded as art music with its own classic canon.
  B. Rock
    1. The history of rock music is now taught at colleges.
    2. The Rock and Roll Hall of Fame preserves the rock legacy (see **HWM Figure 35.1**).
    3. Continuing sales of recordings of rock music from the 1950s and the number of "golden oldies" radio stations give evidence of a tradition of classics.
  C. Country music
    1. Country music has also developed a classic repertory.
    2. The Country Music Hall of Fame and Museum in Nashville opened in 2001.
  D. Musicals
    1. Classic musicals have been revived on Broadway and around the world.
    2. New musicals often aspire to a high art level.
    3. Stephen Sondheim (b. 1930), the dominant figure in American musicals, uses a mixture of art song and popular styles.
    4. Sondheim's subjects would not have been done earlier.

a. *Company* (1970) is a plotless social commentary.
b. *Sweeney Todd* (1979) deals with a murderous barber.
c. *Sunday in the Park with George* (1984) is based on a painting.
d. *Assassins* (1991) features assassins of American presidents.

5. Andrew Lloyd Webber (b. 1948), the leading English composer of musicals, draws on a wide range of styles, while retaining the focus on melody.
   a. *Jesus Christ Superstar* (1970–71) is a rock music retelling of the life of Jesus.
   b. *Evita* (1976–78) is about Eva Peron, the wife of the Argentinean dictator.
   c. *Cats* (1981) is based on poetry by T. S. Eliot.
   d. *The Phantom of the Opera* (1986) is based on the classic book and film.
6. Claude-Michel Schönberg, a French composer, has created a number of successful musicals.
   a. *Les Misérables* (1980) is based on Victor Hugo's novel.
   b. *Miss Saigon* (1989) retells *Madama Butterfly* in the context of the Vietnam War.
7. *Rent* (1996) by Jonathan Larson adapts the plot of *La Bohéme* to a story of New York in the era of AIDS.
8. Asian classic traditions have also received international recognition.

III. New Technologies
   A. Digital synthesis, recording, and reproduction have had a major impact on the creators and listeners of music (see **HWM Music in Context,** page 947, and **Figure 35.2**).
   B. Sampling
      1. This new process allows one to create a new composition by patching together digital portions of previously recorded music.
      2. Sampling has been used extensively in rap, other forms of popular music, avant-garde, and classical concert music.
   C. Composers have explored advancements in computers.
      1. Charles Dodge (b. 1942)
         a. *Speech Songs* (1972) features computer-synthesized vocal sounds.
         b. Manipulations of lifelike imitations of speech create a word-based music.
      2. Paul Lansky (b. 1944) developed his own software to create music.
         a. *Smalltalk* (1988) manipulates speech, and *Night Traffic* (1990) manipulates traffic noises, transforming them beyond immediate recognition.
         b. He also draws upon pop traditions, including tonal harmonies and a regular meter.
      3. Jean-Claude Risset (b. 1938) served as director of the Institute for Acoustic and Musical Research and Coordination in Paris.
         a. *Inharmonique* (1977) uses a computer to mediate between live musical sounds and synthesized sounds.
         b. He continues to design new sounds through the interaction of sound waves, harmonics, timbre, and other elements of sound.

IV. Mixed Media
   A. Stage shows and music videos
      1. By the 1980s, stage shows for popular music concerts involved elaborate sets, costumes, intricate choreography, and visual effects.
      2. Music videos
         a. Short films accompanying the performance of popular songs came of age in the early 1980s.
         b. The cable channel MTV promoted music videos.
         c. Videos were elaborate productions, with sets, costumes, dancing, and quick editing.
   B. Laurie Anderson (b. 1947) is one of the leading performance artists (see **HWM Figure 35.3**).
      1. Anderson employs a wide range of media, including singing and violin-playing.
      2. *O Superman* (1981), featuring her synthesizer-processed voice in a simple song, became a pop hit.
      3. *United States I–IV* (1983) is a seven-hour stage show that uses all the tools of modern media.
   C. Spectacle works
      1. *STOMP* (1991), created by Luke Cresswell and Steve McNicholase, has no dialogue and consists of performers using everyday objects to produce elaborate percussion music with stunning choreography (see **HWM Figure 35.4**)
      2. *Blast!* (2001) by Jim Mason brought the routines of marching-band halftime shows to Broadway.
   D. Film music
      1. In some recent films, music has become a central part of the total artwork.
      2. *American Graffiti* (1973) set a pattern by using pop music of the 1950s and 60s.

3. Full symphonic scores with leitmotives, such as heard in the music by John Williams (b. 1932) for the *Star Wars* movies, has reemerged in film scoring.
4. Symphonic soundtracks have become popular recordings, outpacing other orchestral music.

V. The Splintering of Popular Music
  A. Disco
    1. This style began as a type of dance music in New York during the 1970s.
    2. The music catered to African Americans, Latinos, and gay men before becoming an international craze.
    3. Slick production and lush orchestrations characterized these uniform, 4/4 meter dance works.
    4. Disco reached a height with the film *Saturday Night Fever* (1977), featuring music by the Bee Gees.
  B. Other rock types
    1. Punk featured a hard-driving style and voiced teenager alienation.
      a. The Sex Pistols popularized edgy fashions and preached nihilism.
      b. Most punk musicians were untutored and used raw, unskilled sounds.
    2. New Wave groups, such as Talking Heads, maintained the nihilism of punk but incorporated trained musical skills.
    3. Grunge
      a. This is one type of alternative rock, a general term for rock music that is separate from the mainstream.
      b. Grunge, centering in Seattle in the early 1990s, combined nihilism and the electric-guitar sound of heavy metal with intimate lyrics and dressed-down fashions.
      c. Nirvana's *Smells Like Teen Spirit* (1991) brought grunge to national attention.
  C. Rap
    1. Rap began in the 1970s as part of the African-American urban youth culture.
    2. The style featured rhymed lyrics over repeated dance beats.
    3. From its New York beginnings, it has branched out into multiple types.
      a. Gangsta rap celebrates lawlessness.
      b. Conscious rap voices the woes of inequality and racism.
    4. Public Enemy led the ranks of conscious rap with songs like *Fight the Power* (see **HWM Figure 35.5**).
    5. Rap soon appealed to white suburban teenagers and to international audiences.
  D. Music subcultures
    1. Women's music is often in a folk style and reflects a feminist perspective.
    2. Christian rock uses current popular styles to convey evangelical Christian themes.

VI. Minimalism
  A. Minimalism is considered to be the leading musical style of the late twentieth century.
    1. Materials are reduced to a minimum and procedures are simplified.
    2. The content of the music should be readily apparent.
    3. Minimalism began as an avant-garde style but became a popular and expressive technique.
    4. Influences for minimalism came from numerous sources:
      a. Rock music
      b. African music
      c. Asian music
      d. Tonality
      e. Romanticism
  B. Minimalism in art
    1. The term, first coined by an art critic in 1965, was applied to art that reduced materials and form to fundamentals.
    2. The works were not intended to express feelings or states of mind.
    3. Minimalist works often feature repetition of simple elements (see **HWM Figure 35.6**).
  C. Early minimalism in music
    1. Musicians in New York and California created a parallel movement.
    2. La Monte Young (b. 1935), one of the pioneers, used improvisation over a fundamental drone on synthesizer in *The Tortoise: His Dreams and Journeys* (1964).
  D. Terry Riley (b. 1935)
    1. Riley was a member of La Monte Young's ensemble.
    2. He experimented with tape loops that played the same material repeatedly.
    3. *In C* (1964) applied similar procedures with live instruments.
      a. Any number of instruments can play; each plays the same series of brief repeated figures over a pulsing octave C.
      b. The number of repetitions in each part and the coordination of parts are left to the performers in the tradition of indeterminacy.

c. These elements create a steady pulse with a slow change from consonance to dissonance and back.

E. Steve Reich (b. 1936)
1. Reich, along with Glass and Adams, brought minimalist procedures into art music with the intent of appealing to a wide audience.
2. He developed a quasi-canonic procedure in which musicians play the same material out of phase with each other.
3. *Piano Phase* (1967), for two pianos (see **HWM Example 31.1**)
   a. The same figure is repeated several times.
   b. One pianist then pulls ahead slightly, creating new harmonic combinations,
4. Reich founded his own ensemble, and wrote percussive music in the 1970s.
5. He attracted a wide range of listeners from the classical and pop worlds.
6. Reich used minimalist techniques to create large-scale works with significant emotional content in the 1980s, such as *Tehillim* (1981), a setting of psalm texts in Hebrew.

F. Philip Glass (b. 1937)
1. Glass studied at Juilliard with Nadia Boulanger.
2. In Paris he met and worked with Indian sitarist Ravi Shankar.
3. In the mid-1960s, he composed music that combined the rhythmic organization of Indian music with simple harmonic progressions and the amplification of rock music.
4. *Einstein on the Beach* (1976) is a one act, four-hour opera.
   a. There is no text other than solfege syllables, and the staging is nonsensical.
   b. The music consists primarily of repeated arpeggiations.
   c. The orchestra includes electronic keyboard instruments, woodwinds, and a solo violinist.
5. Other operas followed, including *The Voyage* (1992).

G. John Adams (b. 1947; see **HWM Figure 35.7**)
1. *Phrygian Gates* for piano (1977–78) represents minimalism in its early transitional phase.
2. Adams later combined minimalism with other techniques and styles.
3. *Harmonielehre* (1985), a symphonic poem, recalls Mahler or Berg.
4. *Nixon in China* (1987) is an opera dealing with Nixon's visit to China.
   a. Minimalist techniques are combined with formal Baroque opera.
   b. Short, driving ideas constantly evolve.
5. Later works rely less on minimalism and more on traditional harmonic and contrapuntal means.

H. *Phrygian Gates* by Adams (see **NAWM 168** and **HWM Example 35.2**)
1. This twenty-four-minute piano work relies predominantly on rapid repetitive figuration or alternating chords.
2. The pitch content goes through a number of changes, what Adams calls "gates."
   a. He explores seven tonal centers moving through the circle of fifths: A, E, B, F-sharp, C-sharp, G-sharp, and D-sharp.
   b. Each key center begins with the pitch content of the Lydian mode and then changes to that of the Phrygian mode.
   c. The pitches of the seven tonal centers correspond to the notes of the A Lydian mode, the first set of pitches in the work.
3. In the A Lydian section, pitches are added one at a time, beginning with E and ending with A.
4. The arrival of A Phrygian (measure 114) coincides with the first forte dynamics.
5. The E Lydian area (measure 137) begins with a dynamic drop and builds to a *fff* at the arrival of E Phrygian (measure 236).
6. Adams alters rhythm, register, and chords to provide contrasts and emotional surges.

VII. The New Accessibility

A. Audiences and the classic tradition
1. Composers in the classical tradition faced a new reality in the late twentieth century.
2. Despite the support of universities, they found it difficult to get their works performed after the premieres.
3. Few compositions entered the classical repertory.
4. Some composers sought to appeal to a wider audience through minimalism and other techniques.

B. Accessible modernism
1. Some composers have used modernist ideas and procedures that are simple and easy to grasp.
2. Ellen Taaffe Zwilich (b. 1939; see **HWM Figure 35.8**)
   a. Zwilich combines continuous variation with older formal devices.
   b. Her use of developing variation is similar to the procedure used by Schoenberg, but the idea is much simpler and more readily understood.

C. Symphony No. 1 (1982) by Zwilich (**NAWM 169**)
   1. This work earned Zwilich a Pulitzer Prize in Music, the first ever given to a woman.
   2. Familiar harmonic materials
      a. Tonal centers
      b. Prominent thirds and fifths
      c. Occasional triads
      d. The E-major triad and passionate melody at measure 13 recall Mahler.
   3. Developing variation
      a. All of the melodic material evolves through variation from the first fifteen measures.
      b. The opening threefold rising third serves as a motto and establishes A as the tonal center.
      c. This motive and an answering rising fifth create the central material for the movement.
      d. Several melodies are derived from this material.
      e. Recurring melodies are subject to further variation.
   4. The movement builds in tempo, dynamics, and density to a central allegro and then slows and thins to a quiet close.

D. Radical simplification
   1. Some composers embraced a radical simplification of materials.
   2. One such type is minimalism, but other musical techniques also reflect this trend.
   3. Arvo Pärt (b. 1935)
      a. This Estonian composer began with neoclassical and serial works and juxtaposed modernist and Baroque styles.
      b. He later studied Gregorian chant and early polyphony.
      c. Seeking greater international opportunities, Pärt settled in Germany in 1980.
   4. Tintinnabuli
      a. The term is derived from the bell-like sonorities that it can produce.
      b. It features counterpoint between a mostly stepwise diatonic melody and voices sounding notes of the tonic triad determined by a preset system.
      c. Pärt developed this method in the 1970s

E. *Seven Magnificat Antiphons* by Pärt (1988, rev. 1991) (**NAWM 170**)
   1. These choral works are based on antiphon texts from the week prior to Christmas.
   2. The traditional Latin has been translated into German, and these are Pärt's first works using the language of his adopted country.
   3. *O Weisheit* (**NAWM 170a**)
      a. The text is set syllabically and homophonically.
      b. Measure lines indicate lengths of individual words and do not suggest meter.
      c. The principal melody in the tenors moves by steps within a range of a third.
      d. The pitches from the other voices are from the A-major triad.
      e. The basses and sopranos sing E and A only.
      f. The altos sing the pitches from the triad that are closest to the notes of the tenor melody.
   4. *O König aller Völker* (see **NAWM 170b** and **HWM Example 35.3)**
      a. The second tenor has a modal tune centered on A.
      b. The second soprano forms an augmentation canon with the tenor.
      c. The altos recite the text on D.
      d. The other parts sound notes of the D-minor triad.
      e. The texture alternates between consonance and diatonic dissonance.

F. Quotation and polystylism
   1. Quotation and collage included past and present styles.
   2. This style is similar to postmodernism, which considers all epochs and cultures equally for source material (see **HWM Figure 35.9**).
   3. Alfred Schnittke (1934–1998)
      a. Schnittke worked in the Soviet Union primarily as a film composer and moved to Germany in 1990.
      b. As the Soviet government relaxed its cultural controls in the 1960s, he explored several modernist techniques.
      c. Schnittke later turned to polystylism, a combination of new and old styles.
      d. Symphony No. 1 (1969–72) incorporates passages from works by numerous classical composers that present conflicting styles and historical periods.
      e. His later works, including eight more symphonies, focus more on a small number of ideas borrowed from or modeled on earlier music.

4. John Corigliano (b. 1938)
   a. This American composer often draws upon styles from the Baroque and Classic to avant-garde.
   b. The opera *The Ghosts of Versailles* (1987) uses serial and other modern techniques to portray the ghosts, while the play is set in a Mozart opera style.
   c. Symphony No. 1 (1989) is a memorial to friends who died of AIDS and incorporates quotations of some of their favorite pieces.
5. Peter Schickele (b. 1935)
   a. His early works are mostly tonal and draw upon a variety of styles.
   b. He is best known for creating music under the guise of P. D. Q. Bach, the fictitious youngest and least of J. S. Bach's sons.
   c. With this persona, Schickele spoofed classic traditions, performers, and musicologists.
   d. Example: the cantata *Iphigenia in Brooklyn* (1964)

G. Neo-Romanticism
1. Some composers adopted the familiar tonal idiom of nineteenth-century Romanticism, a trend known as neo-Romanticism.
2. Penderecki
   a. Following his earlier works, Penderecki turned to a style that focused on melody and drew upon neo-Romantic features.
   b. *Polish Requiem* (1980–84) combines neo-Romanticism with elements from Renaissance and Baroque styles and his textures from the 1960s.
3. George Rochberg
   a. After working in serialism and quotation, Rochberg embraced neo-Romanticism in the 1970s.
   b. In String Quartet No. 5 (1978), three of five movements are neo-Romantic; the styles and forms evoke a wide range of composers and periods.
   c. The mixture of styles challenged the notion of stylistic uniformity.
4. David Del Tredici (b. 1937)
   a. His early works are serial and atonal.
   b. He changed styles when he set excerpts from Lewis Carroll's stories for children.
5. *Final Alice* (1975; see **HWM Example 35.4**)
   a. Del Tredici based this work on the text from the final chapters of *Alice's Adventures in Wonderland.*
   b. It is scored for amplified soprano, who narrates and sings several arias, and orchestra, including banjo, mandolin, accordion, and two soprano saxophones.
   c. A rising major sixth is the central motive of "The Accusation," sung by the White Rabbit.
   d. Most of the music is tonal, ranging from folklike to the style of Richard Strauss.
   e. The "strange occurrence" is set with atonal music and the sounds of the Theremin.
   f. Del Tredici renounced the modernist idea of progress (see **HWM Source Reading,** page 962).

H. Extramusical imagery and meanings
1. Composers using various styles sometimes invoked extramusical meanings, such as spirituality, to give unusual sounds clear meanings.
2. Sofia Gubaidulina (b. 1931)
   a. She gave many of her works a spiritual dimension, despite the official atheism of her native Soviet Union.
   b. *Rejoice!* (1981) is a five-movement sonata for violin and cello inspired by devotional texts.
   c. Quotations from the Ukrainian philosopher Grigory Skovoroda appear at the beginning of each movement.
   d. The sonata expresses the transcendence from ordinary reality to joy.
   e. The passage from a fundamental note to its harmonics represents this journey.
3. *Rejoice!*, fifth movement by Gubaidulina (**NAWM 171**)
   a. The fifth movement, *Listen to the still small voice within*, is a study in chromatics, tremolos, and harmonics.
   b. The violin introduces a sequence of four gestures.
   c. Three variations on the same series of ideas follow (measures 33, 70, and 122).
   d. The cello slowly and chromatically descends two octaves during the movement.
   e. The movement ends as both instruments play high natural harmonics.
4. John Tavener (b. 1944)
   a. Stravinsky influenced the early works of this English composer.
   b. He began to incorporate elements of music for the Orthodox Church in works such as *Liturgy of St. John Chrysostom* (1977) for unaccompanied choir.
   c. He developed a harmonically simple, chant-derived idiom and applied it to a

series of instrumental works on religious subjects.

d. *The Protecting Veil* for cello and string orchestra (1987) is the best-known of these works.

5. R. Murray Schafer (b. 1933) is the leading Canadian composer of this era.
   a. He has worked in a variety of styles.
   b. Several orchestral works reflect the culture of the Inuits, natives of Canada.
   c. He developed environmental music, which moves musical performance out of the concert hall.
6. *Wilderness Lake* by Schafer (1979)
   a. This work is to be performed at sunrise and sunset at a lake away from human settlements.
   b. Twelve trombonists, positioned around the shores, play meditative melodies cued by a conductor in a raft.
   c. Animal sounds are also added.
7. Joan Tower (b. 1938)
   a. Many works by this American composer are based on images.
   b. *Silver Ladders* (1986), for orchestra, has rising lines representing ladders and other imagery.

VIII. Interactions with Non-Western Music
- A. Minimalism is inspired in part by music from Asia and Africa.
- B. Some composers draw on Asian and African music more directly.
  1. Bright Sheng (b. 1955)
     a. Born and trained in China, he moved to New York in 1982.
     b. His music integrates elements of Asian and Western music.
  2. *Seven Tunes Heard in China*, No. 1, *Spring* (1999; **NAWM 172**)
     a. This suite for solo cello can be linked to the cello suites of Bach.
     b. Sheng calls upon the style of Chinese music and imitates the sound of Chinese string, wind, and percussion instruments.
     c. The predominantly pentatonic Chinese tune is fragmented and spun out using both Baroque and modernist techniques.
     d. The key area centers on the tritone of A and E-flat.
  3. South African Kevin Volans (b. 1949) has brought about a similar union of Western and African traditions.
  4. Peter Schulthorpe (b. 1929), from Australia, uses Aboriginal melodies.
- C. World Beat
  1. African popular music, called World Beat, reached international audiences.
  2. Musicians like Nigerian Fela Kuti (1938–1997) merged popular styles from the United States with local traditions.
  3. World Beat was assimilated by some Western artists, such as Paul Simon on his album *Graceland* (1986).
  4. All of these works are quintessentially Western, representing the centuries-old capacity of European music to absorb regional and foreign elements.

IX. The New Millennium
- A. Trends change too quickly to complete an overview of recent music.
- B. All music seems to be searching for both a niche of committed listeners and for a wide audience.
- C. The instant success of figures such as Beethoven, Verdi, Duke Ellington, and the Beatles no longer seems to be possible in such a divided world.
- D. Music of the past and of the entire world is more available than ever, allowing us to focus on variety, not just a handful of individual composers.
- E. With technology, the untrained can now make music; we may be returning to a time when every singer sings his or her own song.

## SUGGESTIONS FOR SUPPLEMENTARY READING/LISTENING/ACTIVITIES

Discuss with students the terms *art music, classic,* and *popular* as they relate to traditional European music, jazz, rock, and other popular musical styles. Are all types of music equal? What aesthetics should we use to evaluate works in each style and to compare the relative merits of styles such as disco, rap, and minimalism.

Play excerpts from current musicals and compare them to their counterparts from the 1940s and 50s. What are the major differences? Since the new works seek to achieve an art level, can we consider them to be a popular form of opera? DVD recordings are available for numerous recent musicals, including *Sweeney Todd* (Warner Home Video, 2004), *Phantom of the Opera* (Warner Home Video, 2005), and *Les Misérables* in concert (Columbia/Tristar Studios, 1998).

Have students research and report on the digital revolution and the use of samplings. A number of interesting works by Paul Lansky are available on compact disc.

Have percussion students obtain a video of *STOMP* (Warner Home Video, 2004) and band students a video of *Blast!* (PBS Home Video, 2001). Have them report back to class about these performance spectacles.

For more on Young, Reich, Glass, and Adams, see Keith Potter, *Four Musical Minimalists* (New York: Cambridge University Press, 2000)

John Schaeffer's *New Sounds: A Listener's Guide to New Music* (New York: Harper, 1987) includes a chapter on minimalism. Schaeffer hosted a radio show in New York in the 1980s, and his guests included a diverse array of musicians and composers, including New Age musicians, traditional musicians from Asia and elsewhere, and the minimalists. His book gives the reader a flavor of the eclecticism that inspired New York composers during the 1980s.

Terry Riley's *In C* has been recorded several times. Have students listen to two performances and compare them. Or, have groups of students play through a few segments of *In C* in class, putting one student at either end of a piano and one in the middle. After several groups have played it, have students describe the differences and similarities in the performances. Play the first couple of segments and then play part of Babbitt's *Philomel*. Ask students whether they would describe a work entitled *In C* as revolutionary, counterrevolutionary, retrospective, or retrogressive.

For more on Philip Glass, see *Writings on Glass*, ed. Richard Kostelanetz (New York: Schirmer, 1997).

Philip Glass has written numerous film scores. Discuss the impact of minimalism on films such as the experimental documentary *Koyaanisqatsi* (MGM, 2002) and the feature narrative film *The Hours* (Paramount Home Video, 2003).

An appealing work by John Adams is "The Chairman Dances" from *Nixon in China*, which is frequently performed.

Alfred Schnittke's Symphony No. 1 is available on compact disc (Bis 577, 1994). Have students listen to the work and identify the composers and styles that are drawn upon.

John Corigliano won an Oscar for his score to *The Red Violin* (1999), which follows events surrounding a violin from its creation to its appearance in an auction in the late twentieth century. Have a student watch the film and report how his diverse style was well suited to this film. How did his ability to compose in different historical styles contribute to the plot? A concert version of this music has been published, and a comparison with the film score would be an excellent project.

Ask students to listen and report on one of P. D. Q. Bach's compositions. Have them describe the work and suggest who and what is being spoofed.

The String Quartet No. 5 by George Rochberg is available on compact disc (New World Records 80551, 1999). Listen to the various movements and the styles that are evoked. Discuss the reactions of your students to post-Romanticism.

## OBJECTIVE QUESTIONS

1. Of the following musicals, which was composed by Claude-Michel Schönberg?
   a. *Phantom of the Opera*
   b. *Les Misérables*
   c. *Sweeney Todd*
   d. *Cats*
   e. *Evita*

   Answer: b

2. Of the following, which composer is associated with sampling?
   a. La Monte Young
   b. Avro Pärt
   c. Alfred Schnittke
   d. David Del Tredici
   e. Paul Lansky

   Answer: e

3. Which mixed-media event incorporates marching band routines?
   a. *Blast!*
   b. *O Superman*
   c. *STOMP*
   d. *United States I–IV*
   e. March Madness

   Answer: a

Use the following answers for questions 4–9.
   a. rap
   b. disco
   c. grunge
   d. New Wave
   e. punk

4. The Sex Pistols are associated with this genre.

   Answer: e

5. Nirvana is associated with this genre.

   Answer: c

6. Public Enemy is associated with this genre.

   Answer: a

7. The Bee Gees are associated with this genre.

   Answer: b

8. Talking Heads are associated with this genre.

   Answer: d

9. Of the following, which describes Terry Riley's *In C*?
   a. It is composed for a symphonic orchestra only.
   b. The pitch content is drawn from the C octatonic scale.
   c. The modernistic qualities make the work difficult for audiences.
   d. Instruments play the same series of brief repeated figures over a pulsing octave C.
   e. The lack of a pulse suggests gamelan music.

   Answer: d

10. Of the following, which describes *Einstein on the Beach*?
    a. There is no text, just solfege syllables.
    b. The orchestration is for strings only.
    c. The plot is a theoretical narrative about Einstein's encounter with relatives.
    d. The work evokes Baroque opera traditions.
    e. Mozart operas are suggested in the subject matter and use of ensembles.

    Answer: a

11. *Nixon in China* was written by ____________.
    a. Reich
    b. Glass
    c. Adams
    d. Young
    e. Riley

    Answer: c

12. Tintinnabuli is associated with ____________.
    a. Schnittke
    b. Pärt
    c. Zwillich
    d. Corigliano
    e. Del Tredici

    Answer: b

13. Of the following, who composed *Iphigenia in Brooklyn*?
    a. Corigliano
    b. Del Tredici
    c. Schnittke
    d. Schickele/P. D. Q. Bach
    e. Zwillich

    Answer: d

14. Rochberg's String Quartet No. 5 illustrates which trend?
    a. neo-Romanticism
    b. serialism
    c. minimalism
    d. stylism
    e. quotation

    Answer: a

15. Who is associated with environmental music?
    a. John Corigliano
    b. R. Murray Schafer
    c. John Tavener
    d. Joan Tower
    e. Sofia Gubaidulina

    Answer: b

16. Bright Sheng combined elements from the musical traditions of Europe and ____________.
    a. Japan
    b. South Africa
    c. Nigeria
    d. Australia
    e. China

    Answer: e

17. World Beat refers to popular music from which region?
    a. Africa
    b. Indochina
    c. Caribbean
    d. Japan
    e. South America

    Answer: a

18. Who was the first woman to win a Pulitzer Prize in music?
    a. Joan Tower
    b. Ruth Crawford
    c. Ellen Taaffe Zwilich
    d. Sofia Gubaidulina
    e. Laurie Anderson

    Answer: c

19. Alfred Schnittke's Symphony No. 1 is an example of ____________.
    a. synthesized orchestration
    b. tintinnabuli
    c. minimalism
    d. polystylism
    e. environmental music

    Answer: d

20. Of the following statements, which characterizes postmodernism?
    a. Popular Western music is the dominant musical style.
    b. Each work should be unique in its method of creation.
    c. Modern techniques should be totally rejected in favor of a return to Romanticism.
    d. All musical styles are equal and can be employed as a composer sees fit.
    e. Music should be reduced to its simplest elements.

    Answer: d

## SHORT-ESSAY QUESTIONS

1. Discuss technological changes since 1970 and their impact on music.
2. Trace the development of minimalism from its avant-garde beginnings to its popular acceptance. Include the names of important composers and works.
3. Define neo-Romanticism and discuss the major composers and works influenced by this movement.
4. Describe the interaction of Western and non-Western music in the last three decades of the twentieth century.

## TERMS FOR IDENTIFICATION

digital recording
sampling
Institut de Recherche et Coordination Acoustique/Musique
mixed media
music videos
MTV
*STOMP*
*Blast!*
disco
punk
New Wave
alternative rock
grunge
rap
gangsta rap
conscious rap
women's music
Christian rock
minimalism
phasing
tintinnabuli
postmodernism
polystylism
P. D. Q. Bach
neo-Romanticism
environmental music
World Beat